Hawaii For Dum
5th Edition

W9-CHR-020
Sheet

Waikiki

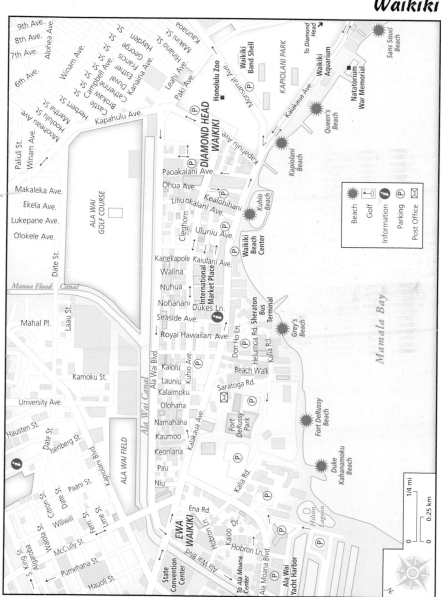

To Diamond Head

Sans Souci Beach

Waikiki Band Shell

KAPIOLANI PARK

Waikiki Aquarium

Natatorium War Memorial

Honolulu Zoo

DIAMOND HEAD WAIKIKI

Queen's Beach

Kapiolani Beach

9th Ave.
8th Ave.
7th Ave.
6th Ave.
Alohea Ave.
Winam Ave.
Martha St.
Hoolulu St.
Herbert St.
Kapahulu Ave.
Moorheau Ave.
Paliuli St.
Winam Ave.

Kaneloa
Kauenoa
Makini St.
Hinano St.
Hayden St.
George St.
Francis St.
Esther St.
Duval Ave.
Campbell Ave.
Catherine St.
Brokaw St.
Castle St.
Kanaina Ave.
Leahi Ave.
Paki Ave.
Monsarrat Ave.
Kalakaua Ave.

Kapahulu Ave.

Makaleka Ave.
Ekela Ave.
Lukepane Ave.
Olokele Ave.

ALA WAI GOLF COURSE

Paoakalani Ave.
Ohua Ave.
Kealohihani
Liliuokalani Ave.
Cleghorn
Uluniu Ave.

Kuhio Beach

Waikiki Beach Center

Date St.

Manoa Flood Canal

Kanekapole
Walina
Nuhua
Nohanani
Seaside Ave.
Royal Hawaiian Ave.

Kaiulani Ave.
International Market Place
Dukes Ln.

Mahal Pl.
Laau St.

Kamoku St.

University Ave.

Hausten St.
Isenberg St.
Date St.

Ala Wai Canal
Ala Wai Blvd.
Kaiolu
Launiu
Kalaimoku
Olohana
Namahana
Kaumoo
Keoniana
Pau
Niu

Kuhio Ave.

Beach Walk
Saratoga Rd.

Don Ho Ln.
Helumoa Rd.
Kalia Rd.

Sheraton Bus Terminal

Grey's Beach

Mamala Bay

Fort DeRussy Park

Kalakaua Ave.

Fort DeRussy Beach

Duke Kahanamoku Beach

ALA WAI FIELD

Kapiolani Blvd.

Citron St.
Date St.
Paani St.
Fern St.
Lime St.

Wiliwili
S. King St.
Algaroba
Walola St.
McCully St.
Pumehana St.
Hauoli St.

Ena Rd.
Hobron Ln.
Kaioo Dr.
Ala Wai Blvd.
Hobron Ln.
Ala Moana Blvd.

EWA WAIKIKI

State Convention Center

To Ala Moana Center

Hilton Lagoon

Ala Wai Yacht Harbor

Beach	Information
Golf	Parking
	Post Office

1/4 mi
0.25 km

N

Honolulu

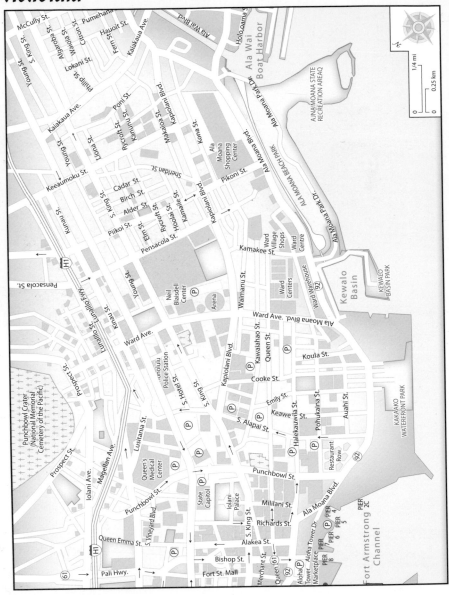

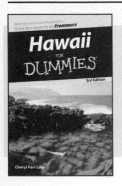
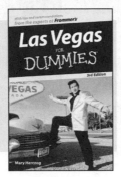
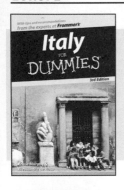

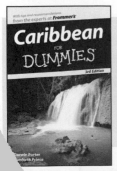
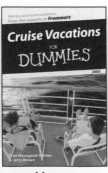

Hawaii
FOR
DUMMIES®
5TH EDITION

by Cheryl Farr Leas

WILEY

Wiley Publishing, Inc.

Hawaii For Dummies,® 5th Edition

Published by
Wiley Publishing, Inc.
111 River St.
Hoboken, NJ 07030-5774
www.wiley.com

Copyright © 2009 by Wiley Publishing, Inc., Indianapolis, Indiana

Published simultaneously in Canada

For general information on our other products and services, please contact our Customer Care Department within the U.S. at 800-762-2974, outside the U.S. at 317-572-3993, or fax 317-572-4002.

For technical support, please visit www.wiley.com/techsupport.

Wiley also publishes its books in a variety of electronic formats. Some content that appears in print may not be available in electronic books.

Library of Congress Control Number available by request from the publisher.

ISBN: 978-0-470-39307-9

Manufactured in the United States of America

10 9 8 7 6 5 4 3 2 1

WILEY

About the Author

Cheryl Farr Leas may live on the mainland, but she's a Hawaii girl at heart. She fell in love with Diamond Head, aloha wear, and mai tais in 1994 and has had trouble staying away ever since. Whenever she's not in the islands, she and her husband, Rob, make their home in Phoenix, Arizona, where they love to hike the desert mountains with their German Shepherd, Caleb.

Before embarking on a writing career, Cheryl served as senior editor at Macmillan Travel (now Wiley), where she edited the Frommer's Hawaii travel guides for the better part of the 1990s. Now happy to be a globetrotting author and branding consultant, Cheryl also writes *Maui For Dummies*.

Dedication

This book is for Rob, for loving Hawaii as much as I do.

Author's Acknowledgments

Thanks to Lisa Renaud for her encouragement and assistance throughout the years, and to Tiffany Ewing for her diligent assistance with this edition. Also, thanks to the many Hawaii-based partners who made this book possible with their kind assistance, generous support, and genuine warmth.

Publisher's Acknowledgments

We're proud of this book; please send us your comments through our Dummies online registration form located at www.dummies.com/register/.

Some of the people who helped bring this book to market include the following:

Editorial

Editors: Christine Ryan,
Jana M. Stefanciosa

Copy Editor: Doreen Russo

Cartographer: Guy Ruggiero

Editorial Assistant: Jennifer Polland

Senior Photo Editor: Richard Fox

Cover Photos: Kayaking in Kaneohe Bay, Oahu

Cartoons: Rich Tennant
(www.the5thwave.com)

Composition Services

Project Coordinator:
Patrick Redmond

Layout and Graphics: Carl Byers,
Sarah Philippart,
Christine Williams

Proofreaders: Debbye Butler,
John Greenough

Indexer: Silvoskey Indexing Services

Publishing and Editorial for Consumer Dummies

Diane Graves Steele, Vice President and Publisher, Consumer Dummies

Kristin Ferguson-Wagstaff, Product Development Director, Consumer Dummies

Kelly Regan, Editorial Director, Travel

Publishing for Technology Dummies

Andy Cummings, Vice President and Publisher, Dummies Technology/General User

Composition Services

Gerry Fahey, Vice President of Production Services

Debbie Stailey, Director of Composition Services

Contents at a Glance

Maps at a Glance

Table of Contents

Introduction

I'm here to spread the good news: Hawaii really does live up to its heady promise. These lovely tropical islands offer all the ingredients of a carefree beach vacation.

Hawaii has an undeniable appeal — whether you're 6 or 60, single or the head of a growing family, the *Survivor* type or a newly minted millionaire. Enjoyment is just a matter of knowing what you want from your island vacation — and how to make it happen.

Planning a Hawaiian escape is easy — too easy, in fact. Far too many people head off to Hawaii blindly without exerting just a bit of effort to tailor a mass-market vacation to their own needs, tastes, and desires. So just knowing that you want to look before you leap puts you well ahead of the pack.

And picking up this guidebook shows that you have the right instincts about your vacation planning.

About This Book

An island vacation is supposed to be easy and fun. *Hawaii For Dummies,* 5th Edition, will make the planning process easy and fun, too.

I've done all the legwork for you, and I'm not afraid to share my honest opinions. I'll help you decide what to include in your island vacation — and, even more important, what *not* to include. You've worked hard to set aside a few precious weeks for relaxation, and I don't want you to waste any time or money.

This book gives you the tools you need — *just* what you need, not too much — so that you can make smart decisions about what works for you and what doesn't. Building your Hawaii vacation is like putting together a jigsaw puzzle. This book helps you assemble the right puzzle pieces so that they interlock smoothly. The finished product will reflect the picture *you* want, not somebody else's image of what your island paradise should be.

Conventions Used in This Book

The structure of this book is nonlinear: You can dig in anywhere to get information on a specific issue without any hassles.

Hotels and restaurants are listed alphabetically with actual prices and frank evaluations. I use the following abbreviations for commonly accepted credit cards:

AE: American Express

DC: Diners Club

DISC: Discover

MC: MasterCard

V: Visa

I include some general pricing information to help you as you decide where to unpack your bags or where to dine. A system of dollar signs shows a range of costs for one night in a double room in each hotel or a typical meal at a restaurant (including appetizer, main course, dessert, one drink, tax, and tip — per person). Check out the following table to decipher the dollar signs:

Cost	Hotel	Restaurant
$	Less than $150	Less than $20
$$	$150–$225	$20–$35
$$$	$225–$325	$35–$50
$$$$	$325–$450	$50–$75
$$$$$	$450 or more	$75 or more

Finally, for those hotels, restaurants, and attractions that are plotted on a map, a page reference is provided in the listing information. If a hotel, a restaurant, or an attraction is outside the city limits or in an out-of-the-way area, it may not be mapped.

Foolish Assumptions

As I wrote this book, I made some assumptions about you and your needs as a traveler:

✓ You may be an experienced traveler who hasn't had much time to explore Hawaii and wants expert advice when you finally do get a chance to enjoy some time in the sun.

✓ You may be an inexperienced traveler looking for guidance when determining whether to take a trip to Hawaii and how to plan for it.

✓ You're not looking for a book that overwhelms you with all the information available about the Hawaiian islands. You don't have time to wade through a gigantic list of every single hotel, restaurant, or attraction out there. Instead, you want to zero in on the places that offer the very best experiences in Hawaii.

If you fit any of these criteria, then *Hawaii For Dummies,* 5th Edition, is the book you've been waiting for!

How This Book Is Organized

Hawaii For Dummies, 5th Edition, contains seven parts. You can read each chapter or part without reading the one that came before it — no need to study up on Kauai if you're heading only to Maui, for example.

Part I: Introducing Hawaii

This first part gives you an overview of what Hawaii is like so that you can start getting excited about all the fun that lies ahead. I provide an easy-to-scan list of the very best of the best — my personal picks of Hawaii's top hotels, restaurants, beaches, golf courses, and more. I also give you a quick overview of Hawaiian history and culture and an introduction to each of the Hawaiian islands to help you decide which islands suit your fancy. I finish up this part with time-tested advice on how to divide your time between the islands you want to visit and the scoop on the best time to go.

Part II: Planning Your Trip to Hawaii

In this part, I get down to the serious trip preparation, starting with telling you how much you can expect your trip to cost and how to find great deals. I offer the pros and cons of planning your trip on your own, using a travel agent, and buying an all-inclusive package deal. I give you all the ins and outs of flying to Hawaii, and how to travel between the islands after you're there. Finally, I give advice to folks with special needs or interests, such as families, seniors, travelers with disabilities, and gay and lesbian travelers. I even provide a how-to guide for couples who want to tie the knot in the Aloha State.

Parts III through VI: Being There — the Islands

These parts form the bulk of the book and cover each destination in detail. Each part is dedicated to one of the major Hawaiian islands — Oahu (Part III), Maui (Part IV), the Big Island (Part V), and Kauai (Part VI) — and offers all the specific advice and recommendations you need while you're there, including finding your way around, choosing the best places to stay and eat within your budget, and how to enjoy the islands best.

Part VII: The Part of Tens

Every *For Dummies* book has a Part of Tens. If Parts III through VI are the main course, think of these fun top-ten-list chapters as dessert. Chapter 18 tells you how to ditch the tourist look and act like a local, and Chapter 19 focuses on one of everybody's favorite topics: food! Chapter 20 advises lovebirds on how to indulge in the islands' romantic charms.

In the back of this book, your Quick Concierge contains lots of handy information, with phone numbers and addresses of hospitals and pharmacies, lists of local newspapers and magazines, and more. Check out this appendix when searching for answers to the little logistical questions that may come up as you travel. You can find the Quick Concierge easily because it's printed on yellow paper.

Icons Used in This Book

Think of the following icons as signposts. I use them to highlight especially useful advice and things that you won't want to miss.

 Keep an eye out for the Bargain Alert icon as you seek out money-saving tips and/or great deals.

 The Best of the Best icon highlights Hawaii's most extraordinary hotels, restaurants, attractions, activities, shopping, and nightlife.

 Watch for the Heads Up icon to identify annoying or potentially dangerous situations such as tourist traps, unsafe neighborhoods, and rip-offs.

 The Kid Friendly icon highlights attractions, hotels, restaurants, and activities that are particularly hospitable to children or people traveling with kids.

 The Local Know How icon indicates well-guarded *kamaaina* (local) advice that will give you the edge over *malihini* (newcomers) who don't know better.

 Find out useful advice on things to do and ways to schedule your time when you see the Tip icon.

Where to Go from Here

As you read through this book and start to assemble your vacation, remember: The planning really *is* half the fun. Choosing your island destinations and solidifying the details don't have to be a chore. Think of it as just the first step on a voyage of discovery. I guarantee that a little planning will produce an experience that's that much more rewarding and relaxing — *really.* So let's get started!

Part I
Introducing Hawaii

The 5th Wave   By Rich Tennant

HAWAII'S ESCALATOR FALLS

In this part . . .

This part of the book introduces you to the wonders of Hawaii. You discover why so many people are drawn to these islands of aloha, and you begin to shape the basic outlines of your trip. I preview each island one by one and offer tips of planning an itinerary. Then I help you figure out when to go, with information on Hawaii's climate, the least crowded (and least expensive) seasons, and a full calendar of special events.

Chapter 1

Discovering the Best of Hawaii

In This Chapter

▶ Scoping out Hawaii's top accommodations

▶ Uncovering the top dining establishments and luaus

▶ Exploring the best beaches and attractions

*H*awaii is such a breathtakingly beautiful place and exudes such a generous spirit of genuine aloha that just about every island experience offers something special. Hawaii is at its best when you experience its simple pleasures in their purest form. Here, everybody can feel like royalty: A simple beach apartment can be your castle, a fresh papaya and a cup of robust Kona joe can be your princely breakfast, and a joyous aloha shirt can be your royal robe.

But if you're looking for more worldly luxuries, that's great, too — these islands are flush with pampering experiences, and you'll run out of time before you exhaust all the possible ways to indulge yourself.

Whether you prefer the simple pleasures of life or are in the market for island luxury at its finest, you'll find it in Hawaii. This chapter is designed as an at-a-glance reference to the absolute best — the Best of the Best — that Hawaii has to offer.

The Best Luxury Resorts

Are you in the market for a little luxury — or a lot of it? Hawaii's your place. These islands are home to some of the world's finest resorts. The following are the best of the best:

✔ **Halekulani** (Oahu): The finest hotel on Waikiki Beach is the epitome of graciousness and elegant aloha. The white-on-white rooms are gorgeous, the service is impeccable, SpaHalekulani is a pampering oasis, and the restaurants are the best on the beach. See Chapter 10.

✔ **Kahala Hotel & Resort** (Oahu): Oahu's only AAA five-diamond resort is a ten-minute drive from Waikiki — and a world away. The Kahala combines big, beautiful rooms (including some of the best bathrooms in the islands), premier service and dining, first-rate amenities, and a virtually private crescent beach for a glorious resort experience. A must for relaxation-seeking grown-ups who want to be within easy reach of urban excitement. See Chapter 10.

✔ **Fairmont Kea Lani Maui** (Maui): This fanciful Moorish palace on the sand not only is one of the finest, most romantic, and most relaxing hotels in the islands, but also gives you so much more for your money than Maui's other luxury resorts. For the same price as a standard hotel room at other places — and sometimes less — here you'll enjoy a large one-bedroom suite with a luxurious living room, a complete entertainment system (including stereo and DVD), and a huge marble bathroom. See Chapter 12.

✔ **Grand Wailea Resort & Spa** (Maui): Many tout the reserved understatement of the neighboring Four Seasons, but I'm underwhelmed. Instead, I prefer this grand beach palace, with its exclusive tropical theme park vibe and over-the-top treat at every turn. Hawaii's best pool complex awaits your (very lucky) kids, and you can indulge in the island's finest spa. The ultra-deluxe Napua Tower offers such extra amenities as personalized concierge service. See Chapter 12.

✔ **Hotel Hana-Maui** (Maui): After years in the doldrums, this breathtaking resort at the end of the "heavenly" Hana Highway has been reborn as a luxurious haven of genuine Hawaiiana thanks to the folks behind Big Sur's Post Ranch Inn. This easygoing yet elegant hideaway on 62 expansive oceanfront acres is reason enough to cruise to the remotest end of the island. The intimate Honua Spa only adds to the ecstasy. See Chapter 12.

✔ **The Fairmont Orchid, Hawaii** (Big Island): This elegant, attractive beach resort is the Big Island's most intimate and understated luxury resort. Fairmont has done an admirable job infusing this elegant property with authentic aloha; as a result, expect a full slate of enticing cultural and outdoor activities. Dining is excellent and service is imbued with warmth. Not quite as fabulous as the Four Seasons or Kona Village (below), it's also not quite so expensive, either. See Chapter 14.

✔ **Four Seasons Resort Hualalai** (Big Island): You'll want for nothing at this elegantly understated resort, Hawaii's best. Ask for a room with an open-air lava-rock shower for the ultimate in natural-style luxury. A stunning oceanfront pool with a graceful wooden deck stands center stage, and a second comes stocked with friendly stingrays. Service is impeccable, the restaurants are among the island's finest, and the superb Jack Nicklaus–designed golf course is for guests only. See Chapter 14.

✔ **Kona Village Resort** (Big Island): Hawaii's only all-inclusive resort is the polar opposite of its sophisticated neighbor, the Four

Seasons Resort Hualalai (see preceding entry). Whereas that resort offers every cutting-edge luxury, this South Seas paradise of tropical cottages offers something else really special: Blissful escape, *Gilligan's Island*–style, where your "Do Not Disturb" sign is painted on a coconut and in-room entertainment is your glorious ocean view. However long you plan to stay, stay longer — it still won't be long enough. See Chapter 14.

✔ **Grand Hyatt Kauai Resort & Spa** (Kauai): From start to finish, this crown-jewel Hyatt is one of Hawaii's most satisfying resorts. Situated on Kauai's sunny south coast, the resort boasts a genuine tropical vibe with big, beautiful rooms; a terrific pool complex that pleases both kids and adults alike; a brilliant spa with open-air treatment rooms; and service that exudes the most genuine aloha. I'd move in if I could afford it. See Chapter 16.

✔ **Princeville Resort Kauai** (Kauai): If it weren't for the fact that guest rooms lack open-air lanais, this stunning North Shore resort would be perfect; as it is, it comes *very* close. Situated on the Garden Isle's most breathtaking coast, the resort offers spectacular views in every direction, and just out the back door is one of the island's finest beaches for snorkeling and sunbathing. The views alone are reason to come — but you won't be disappointed with elegant appointments and attentive service, either. See Chapter 16.

The Best Accommodations Values

Don't have limitless cash? No worries. Get the most for your accommodations dollar by booking into one of these fine establishments:

✔ **The Breakers** (Oahu): This vintage, low-rise charmer remains a breath of fresh air in increasingly expensive Waikiki. Everything is budget-basic but spotlessly kept. Units are set around a sparkling pool and garden blooming with tropical hibiscus, creating an oasis in this increasingly chic corner of Waikiki. Not for everybody, but an excellent choice for budget travelers who want to experience a genuine slice of Old Waikiki aloha. See Chapter 10.

✔ **Embassy Suites — Waikiki Beach Walk** (Oahu): Certainly, the rack rates aren't the lowest. But the all-suite accommodations (including pull-out sofas to accommodate the kids), the generous buffet breakfast with cooked-to-order omelet station, *and* the justifiably popular nightly manager's reception with drinks, pupus, and live entertainment, all included in the rate, make this brand-new heart-of-Waikiki hotel a terrific value. See Chapter 10.

✔ **The Wyland Waikiki** (Oahu): Hawaii's first artist-themed hotel is a boon for modern-minded travelers who crave something stylishly different for a middle-of-the-road price. A confidently relaxed oasis in the heart of Waikiki, this attractive boutique-style hotel evokes the ocean world at every turn in its sleek, contemporary yet comfortable design — and the Outrigger chain runs things wonderfully from behind the scenes. See Chapter 10.

✔ **Kaanapali Beach Hotel** (Maui): This charming, older beachfront hotel is the last hotel left in Hawaii that gives you a real resort experience at a moderate price. The resort brims with genuine aloha spirit and good value — and the on-the-beach location can't be beat. See Chapter 12.

✔ **Napili Bay** (Maui): These petite studios on the sand are one of Hawaii's best beachfront bargains — especially considering their prime location on in-demand Maui. The beach is gorgeous, the snorkeling is prime, the units are thoughtfully outfitted, and the value is even better. The all-studio configuration makes this a terrific option for budget-minded honeymooners. See Chapter 12.

✔ **Noelani Condominium Resort** (Maui): This top-notch oceanfront condo complex is an excellent value and a really enjoyable place to stay. Every unit — from the value-minded studios for two to the family-friendly two- and three-bedroom apartments — boasts an ocean view and all the comforts of home. See Chapter 12.

✔ **Waikoloa Beach Marriott Resort & Spa** (Big Island): Want a beachfront resort with all the perks, but without the hefty price tag? Try this pleasing — and pleasantly affordable — resort, situated on one of the sunny Kohala coast's finest beaches. A prime location, a genuine tropical feel, and activities galore, all for a fraction of the rates at its ritzier neighbors. Not cheap, but a relative bargain. See Chapter 14.

✔ **Nihi Kai Villas** and **Waikomo Stream Villas** (Kauai): These wonderful condo complexes on Kauai's sunny south shore, both managed by the Parrish Collection, offer the best accommodations values on the Garden Isle. Waikomo Stream's one- and two-bedroom apartments are ideal for families who want all the comforts of home at bargain-basement prices. Nihi Kai's one-, two-, and three-bedroom apartments are closer to the beach and a bit more upscale, but offer equally excellent value. See Chapter 16.

The Best Restaurants

Whether you're looking to celebrate a special occasion or mapping out a culinary calendar for the length of your stay, don't overlook these fabulous restaurants:

✔ **Roy's Restaurants** (all islands): Star chef Roy Yamaguchi is the Babe Ruth of Hawaii Regional Cuisine. His chain of Roy's restaurants has brought island-style fine dining to cities across the world, but his best successes remain those closest to home. Roy's restaurants are special occasion–oriented without feeling formal or imposing. My favorite way to dine here is family-style from the tapas-style appetizer menu, which offers the best variety of Roy's signature taste sensations. See Chapters 10, 12, 14, and 16.

✔ **Sansei Restaurant & Sushi Bar** (Oahu/Maui/Big Island): Chef D.K. Kodama's superstar sushi bars offer some of the finest dining in the islands. Choose from an adventurous sushi menu, or opt for family-style dining on a slate of D.K.'s palate-stimulating Euro-Asian signature creations. Best of all, the restaurants are casually comfortable, service is always a delight, and it's easy to keep the bill within reason. I'm pleased to see this Maui favorite expanded to Waikiki and the Big Island's Kohala Coast, where first-rate dining tends to be in short supply. See Chapters 10, 12, and 14.

✔ **Alan Wong's Restaurant** (Oahu): If there is one master of Hawaii Regional Cuisine above all others, it is Alan Wong. His warmly contemporary and tropical Honolulu dining room is the ideal showcase for his fine-dining twists on the local culinary tradition.

✔ **Nobu Waikiki** (Oahu): The first Pacific island venture from internationally acclaimed Japanese chef Nobu Matsuhisa bursts with innovative spirit. Unusual textures, impulsive combinations, and surprising flavors — all served in a setting that sets a new standard for high drama — add up to a first-rate dining adventure that you won't soon forget. A real joy for adventure-seeking gourmands. See Chapter 10.

✔ **Lahaina Grill** (Maui): This Lahaina mainstay still shines as one of Hawaii's most glorious dining experiences. Lahaina Grill gets it all just right, from the pretty sophistication of the dining room to the beautifully prepared dishes to the first-rate service that fuses personal warmth and professionalism perfectly. Special-occasion restaurants hardly come finer than this. See Chapter 12.

✔ **Haiilimaile General Store** (Maui): Star chef Bev Gannon, the queen of Hawaii Regional Cuisine, continues to deliver one of Hawaii's finest all-around dining experiences — top-quality island-style cooking joyfully presented in a refreshingly casual and pretension-free setting. A delight from start to finish — well worth the drive Upcountry. See Chapter 12.

✔ **Mama's Fish House** (Maui): The increasingly sophisticated Valley Isle is coming perilously close to surpassing Oahu as the fine-dining island of choice for vacationing gourmands. My absolute favorite in this well-stocked sea is this delightful seafooder, which offers a magical combination of food, ambience, and service. Sure, prices are high, but the Tiki-room setting is an archetype of timeless Hawaii cool, and fresh island fish simply doesn't get any better than this. See Chapter 12.

✔ **The Hualalai Grille by Alan Wong** (Big Island): The Hualalai Grille strikes all of the same exquisite, inspiring notes that Oahu's original Alan Wong's does, but adds the appeal of a gorgeous, casually sophisticated resort setting for a marriage made in culinary heaven. Service is thoughtful, attentive, and unpretentious, and every course is as it should be. Don't miss it. See Chapter 14.

✔ **Beach House Restaurant** (Kauai): A winning combination of creative island cuisine, cool tropical cocktails, and one of the most romantic oceanfront settings in the islands make this Kauai's finest restaurant, hands down. Just ask *Honolulu* magazine, which once again selected the Beach House as its Kauai favorite in 2008. Come for sunset for the ultimate swoon. See Chapter 16.

The Best Beaches

The world's finest surf and sands fringe the shores of Hawaii's islands. The finest are these breathtakingly beautiful beaches:

✔ **Waikiki Beach** (Oahu): This beach is the most famous one on the planet for a perfectly good reason: It lives up to its reputation in every way. The world's biggest and best beach party actually inhabits a string of stunning beaches fringing crystal clear, turquoise blue waters. There's something for everybody, whether you want to learn to surf, play in the waves, or just bask in the glory of it all. See Chapter 11.

✔ **Hanauma Bay** (Oahu): Without exception, this sunken volcanic crater on Oahu's sunny southeast coast is Hawaii's premier snorkel spot for beginners and experts alike. The bay is preserved as a marine life conservation district, and the fish seem to know it — they'll practically come up and stare into your mask. Even non-swimmers can wade in, look down, and see a whole new kaleidoscopic side of Hawaii. See Chapter 11.

✔ **Waimea Beach Park** (Oahu): This legendary surf spot is my favorite place to watch big-wave riders in action in the winter months. It's a nonstop rollicking beach party when the surf's up and the daredevils are in the water. The rolling waves leave a placid pool behind in summer; that's when everybody can jump in to frolic in the surf. See Chapter 11.

✔ **Kaanapali Beach** (Maui): This fabulous, crescent-shaped beach is reminiscent of the Waikiki of yesteryear, before the entire world made it their destination of choice. There's something for everyone here: crystal-clear snorkeling, thrilling wave jumping, golden sands inviting hours of sunbathing, even beachfront bars for enjoying that perfect middle-of-the-day mai tai. See Chapter 13.

✔ **Hookipa Beach Park** (Maui): Come to watch the world's best windsurfers pirouette over white-capped waves at this glorious north shore beach. Surfers have eminent domain in the mornings, and the colorful windsurfers take over in the afternoons. The action is equally breathtaking at any time of day, especially when the winter waves are in top form. See Chapter 13.

✔ **Hapuna Beach** (Big Island): Don't let anybody tell you that the volcanic Big Island doesn't have any good beaches. Copiously endowed with delicate white sands and gorgeous turquoise waves, this beauty isn't just the star of the Big Island — it just may be the most beautiful beach in all of Hawaii. Great facilities are the icing on the cake. See Chapter 15.

✔ **Kahaluu Beach Park** (Big Island): This roadside salt-and-pepper beach isn't much to look at, but its shallow, protected waters offer some of the finest snorkeling in the islands. See Chapter 15.

✔ **Anini Beach** (Kauai): This North Shore beach is one of the most beautiful — and one of the safest — swimming beaches on Kauai. The golden sands and shallow waters are protected by an offshore reef even when rough winter waves pound other North Shore beaches, making this an ideal snorkel spot. An always-peaceful feeling at this beach makes it ideal for quiet contemplation, too. See Chapter 17.

✔ **Poipu Beach Park** (Kauai): This south shore beach is Kauai's favorite family playground. There's something for everybody here: white sands for sunbathing, grassy lawns for picnicking, shallow pools for little ones to play in, reefs for good snorkeling, and waves for boogie boarders. Lots of great facilities round out the perfect beach day. See Chapter 17.

The Best Activities and Attractions

If all you want is an oceanfront hammock and a mai tai, Hawaii's your paradise. But part of the beauty of Hawaii is that it has a bounteous menu of rich experiences to offer if you're motivated to do more. These activities and attractions are Hawaii's finest:

✔ **Touring the USS *Arizona* Memorial** (Oahu): There's hardly a more moving site than this stark memorial to the nearly 1,200 who lost their lives in the Japanese air raid on Pearl Harbor on December 7, 1941, which launched the United States into World War II. Arrive early for the best experience and pair your visit with a tour of the **Battleship *Missouri* Memorial**, also in Pearl Harbor, for a tragedy-to-triumph view of World War II. See Chapter 11.

✔ **Visiting the Bishop Museum** (Oahu): If you're intrigued by Hawaii's vibrant culture, the best place to get a little background is at this captivating museum, rich with the treasures of Hawaii's past. Pair a visit with a trip to **Iolani Palace,** the official royal residence of Hawaii's last monarchs, for a surprisingly riveting history lesson. See Chapter 11.

✔ **Whale-watching with the Pacific Whale Foundation** (Maui): Whale-watching is a premier activity in the islands from mid-December until mid-March. Boats are available to take you whale-watching from every island, but I love the Pacific Whale Foundation for its excellent naturalist guides and its nonprofit commitment to protecting whales in Hawaii. See Chapter 13.

✔ **Diving Molokini** (Maui): This sunken volcanic crater is one of Hawaii's top dive spots thanks to calm, clear, protected waters; an abundance of marine life, from reef dwellers to manta rays; and exciting viewing opportunities for every level of diver — even first-timers. You don't dive? No worries — Molokini offers excellent viewing for snorkelers, too. Molokini is reachable only by boat, so see Chapter 13 for recommended outfitters.

✔ **Exploring otherworldly Haleakala on horseback** (Maui): A desolate, otherworldly canyon painted in hues of blue and green and red, Haleakala National Park will reshape your idea of breathtaking natural beauty. The best way to experience it is to delve deep into the crater with **Pony Express Tours,** which leads excellent and informative trail rides along Sliding Sands Trail into the heart of the volcano. See Chapter 13.

✔ **Driving the "Heavenly" Road to Hana** (Maui): Hawaii's most spectacular drive is well worth a day of your vacation. For 52 winding miles, this blissful highway takes you past flowering gardens, spectacular waterfalls, and magnificent ocean vistas. Start early and keep in mind that it's all about the drive, not about getting to the end of the road. Rent a convertible for maximum effect. See Chapter 13.

✔ **Snorkeling Kealakekua Bay** (Big Island): This magical marine life preserve, reachable only by watercraft, is my absolute favorite snorkel spot in Hawaii. The coral is the most beautiful I've ever seen, and the calm, clear waters teem with a kaleidoscope of colorful reef fish, octopuses, and sea turtles, plus playful spinner dolphins who often swing by to see what all the fuss is about. My favorite way to get there is with **Fair Wind Snorkel Cruises & Orca Raft Adventures,** although experienced kayakers can rent and paddle their way in. See Chapter 15.

✔ **Exploring the Big Island with Hawaii Forest & Trail** (Big Island): Nobody shows you Hawaii's natural wonders like this terrific nature guide company. You may have seen owner Rob Pacheco on the Travel Channel; Rob and his troupe of well-trained guides take you into the remote valleys of the rain forest, as well as help you scale the star-studded crest of Mauna Kea, and burrow through hidden lava tunnels. You can see a side of Hawaii that few others do — don't miss it! See Chapter 15.

✔ **Visiting Hawaii Volcanoes National Park** (Big Island): In my book, if you do one nonbeach-related activity in Hawaii, this should be it. Hawaii Volcanoes National Park is the only national park that's home to a live, lava-pumping volcano. Witness the yin/yang magic of the oozing red stuff as it leaves destruction in its landscape — and shapes new virgin land. Hikers shouldn't miss the otherworldly Kilauea Iki trail, which traverses four sensational miles of steaming lava beds. See Chapter 15.

✔ **Stepping back in time at Puuhonua O Honaunau National Historical Park** (Big Island): This ancient "city of refuge," the most compelling historic attraction in the islands, is guarded by fierce ancient totems just like it was back in the day. The archaeological excavations and restorations are fascinating, and the ancient sanctuary city is downright fun to explore. See Chapter 15.

✔ **Touring Kauai's Na Pali Coast State Park** (Kauai): Hawaii's most majestic coastline is a 22-mile stretch of green-velvet fluted cliffs that wrap around the northwest shore of Kauai. It's all but inaccessible to people, who can only reach it by sailing by, flying over, or hiking in — and there are outfits to take you there by any route you choose. The effort is well worth it. See Chapter 17 for details on all options.

✔ **Exploring the Allerton & McBryde Gardens** (Kauai): These sister National Tropical Botanical Gardens highlight the breathtaking botanical beauty of the Garden Isle. Even those who don't think they have a passion for horticulture marvel at the natural majesty of these two slices of paradise. I recommend starting with the more manicured Allerton Garden, a turn-of-the 20th-century private estate, and then returning to tour the McBryde Garden if you want more. Check the schedules in advance and plan accordingly. See Chapter 17.

✔ **Learning to surf** (Oahu, Maui, and Kauai): Believe it or not, surfing is easier than it looks — and there's hardly a feeling finer than conquering a wave. A number of good surfing schools guarantee that you'll be hanging-ten in a single two-hour lesson. My favorites are **Hawaiian Fire Surf School** on Oahu, where you'll learn at the hands of moonlighting Honolulu firefighters; the **Nancy Emerson School of Surfing** on Maui; and Kauai's **Margo Oberg Surf School.** See Chapters 11, 13, and 17.

✔ **Hitting the links** (Oahu, Maui, Big Island, and Kauai): All the islands boast championship courses designed to make 18-hole memories, but you'll find the most spectacular challenges on the neighboring islands; others may argue, but I think the Big Island boasts the most breathtaking selection of courses. Book before you leave home to guarantee tee times. See Chapters 11, 13, 15, and 17.

✔ **Getting a bird's-eye view of the islands of Aloha** (Maui, Big Island, and Kauai): Touring Hawaii by helicopter gives you a perspective that others simply can't enjoy — a bird's-eye view of desolate mountain peaks or the heart of a bubbling volcano. These tours give you access to each island's otherwise inaccessible heartland, where nature has been unspoiled by modern man. Expensive, but worth it. See Chapters 13, 15, and 17.

✔ **Saying "aahh . . ." at the spa** (Maui, Big Island, and Kauai): What's the icing on the cake of any vacation? A pampering spa day, of course. The neighbor islands' spas, in particular, have raised the art of relaxation and healing to a new level, showcasing Hawaiian products and traditional treatments. On Maui, nobody does it bigger and better than **Spa Grande,** a temple to the good life whose hydrotherapy circuit is reason enough to come. For something different, try the petite but magical **Maui Spa Retreat,** a hidden Upcountry gem that made me finally understand the magic of aromatherapy. My Big Island favorite is the **Mauna Lani Spa,** a simply glorious open-air retreat. On Kauai, don't miss the **Anara Spa,** which set the standard for alfresco island-style pampering and is still going strong. See Chapters 13, 15, and 17.

The Best Luaus

The best luaus are in high demand, so book your spots before you leave home to ensure access:

✔ **Old Lahaina Luau** (Maui): Hawaii's most authentic and acclaimed luau is justifiably celebrated — it doesn't get better than this. Come early to watch craftspeople at work in the lovely oceanfront setting; you can also watch as the luau pig is unearthed from its underground oven, where it's been slow-cooking all day. The live hula show is dazzling. See Chapter 12.

✔ **The Feast at Lele** (Maui): The folks behind the Old Lahaina Luau (see the preceding entry) also operate this interesting twist on a traditional luau — perfect for romance-seeking couples, or anyone who would prefer a luau with a more upscale demeanor, a more intimate setting, and/or a fine-dining twist. The multicourse meal and thrilling performance troupe reach beyond the Hawaii tradition to celebrate the food and culture of the South Seas as well, and the beachfront setting can't be beat. See Chapter 12.

✔ **Kona Village Luau** (Big Island): The Big Island's best luau is offered on Wednesdays and Fridays only, so plan accordingly. The luau grounds aren't oceanfront, but the South Seas–style setting of grass-roofed huts and swaying palms offers ambience in excess. The food is excellently prepared, and the stage show is a real delight. See Chapter 14.

✔ **Luau Kalamaku** (Kauai): This newcomer is one of the most theatrical and satisfying luau productions in the islands, telling an in-depth story of Hawaii's heritage in an artful, original showcase. The party is held on the lovely grounds of a historic 1930s plantation house at Kauai's lush heart. A traditional *imu* ceremony gives way to a bountiful and delicious luau spread, and a full open bar means real cocktails, not mass-produced mai tais. Tuesday and Friday only, so plan ahead. See Chapter 16.

Chapter 2

Digging Deeper into Hawaii

• •

In This Chapter
▶ Discovering the fascinating story of Hawaii's past
▶ Appreciating Hawaii's local architecture and design
▶ Experiencing the joys of island-style dining

• •

*J*ust thinking about a Hawaii vacation warms the soul, doesn't it? Turquoise waves, white sand, toasty sun. Palm trees swaying in the breeze as emerald-green cliffs rise up to meet a sweet blue sky. The fragrance of orchids filling the air as the music of a slack-key guitar carries you into tropical reverie. . . .

Vacation has long been the ultimate antidote to the stresses and strains of daily life — and no destination is more relaxing and restorative than the exquisite Hawaiian Islands. Renewal calls for total escape to this idyllic tropical paradise, where days of soaking up the island sun are interwoven with easygoing adventuring and plenty of friendly aloha (an all-purpose greeting meaning hello, welcome, or goodbye).

History 101: The Main Events

Hawaii's historic tapestry is far richer than what can be re-created in these few pages. If you're interested in the whole story, pick up *Shoal of Time: A History of the Hawaiian Islands* (University of Hawaii Press) by Gavan Daws. Both definitive and delightful to read, *Shoal of Time* is the ideal one-volume history of Hawaii. From the geological formation of the islands through statehood, the Hawaii story is so well told that it reads like a novel. So rich with detail, the characters who shaped Hawaiian history come alive in its pages.

A.D. 700: The first Hawaiians arrive

The first Hawaiians arrived by canoe from Tahiti and the Marquesas Islands, some 2,500 miles to the south, as part of a greater Polynesian migration. They likely arrived at the southernmost Big Island first; what they found was a pristine and blessedly empty island, roiling with fire from the volcanoes at its heart. An entire Hawaiian culture grew from these first settlers. As islanders migrated throughout the chain, each island became its own distinct kingdom. The inhabitants built temples, fishponds, and aqueducts to irrigate taro plantations. Sailors became farmers and fishermen. The *alii* (high-ranking chiefs) created a caste system and established taboos. Ritual human sacrifices were common. Life was both vicious and blissful — just like the islands' breathtaking landscapes.

1778: The "modern" world arrives

For 1,000 years, no Hawaiian ever imagined that an outsider would appear in these remote "floating islands." But in 1778, Captain James Cook sailed into Waimea Bay on Kauai on his ship the *Resolution* and was welcomed as the Hawaiian god Lono.

Cook stumbled upon the Hawaiian Islands quite by chance. He named them the Sandwich Islands, for the Earl of Sandwich, a great friend and first lord of the British admiralty, who had bankrolled the expedition. The Big Island would ultimately be the death of the world-famous explorer — but not before stone-age Hawaii entered the age of iron, and the West forged a permanent foothold. Gifts were presented and objects traded: nails for fresh water, pigs, and the affections of Hawaiian women. The sailors brought syphilis, measles, and other diseases to which the Hawaiians had no natural immunity.

The islands were united as one kingdom by Kamehameha I in 1810; he used guns seized from a British ship to establish his iron-fisted rule. The door was open, and the new Hawaiian monarchy welcomed the West with open arms. In April 1820, the first missionaries arrived from New England. Victorian mores overtook island style, and eventually subsumed it; hula was abolished in favor of reading and writing, and neck-to-toe dress became the norm. At the same time, missionaries also played a key role in preserving island culture. They created the 13-character Hawaiian alphabet, and began recording the islands' history. Until this time, history was only passed down from generation to generation orally, in memorized chants.

The children of the missionaries became the islands' business and political leaders. They married Hawaiians and stayed on in the islands, causing one astute observer to remark that the missionaries "came to do good and stayed to do well." More than 80 percent of all private land was owned by nonnatives within two generations. Sugar cane became big business, and planters imported immigrants by the thousands to work the fields as contract laborers. The first Chinese came in 1852, followed by Japanese in 1885, and Portuguese in 1888. These immigrants would have a lasting and influential impact on island culture that persists in the present day. King David Kalakaua — known as the "Merrie Monarch" for the elaborate parties he threw — ascended to the throne in 1874, marking the beginning of the end of the short-lived Hawaiian monarchy. He performed a few acts of note, however: He built Iolani Palace in 1882, lifted the prohibitions on the hula and other native arts, and gave Pearl

Harbor to the United States. In 1891, King Kalakaua visited chilly San Francisco, where he caught a cold and died. His sister, Queen Liliuokalani, assumed the throne.

1893: Paving the way for tourism and statehood

On January 17, 1893, a group of American sugar planters and missionary descendants, with the support of U.S. Marines, imprisoned Queen Liliuokalani in her palace, where she penned "Aloha Oe," the famous song of farewell. The monarchy was dead. Hawaii was now an American territory ruled by the powerful sugar-cane planter Sanford Dole. He and his cohorts — known as the Big Five — controlled the entire economic, social, and political life of the islands. Sugar was king, and the native Hawaiians became a landless minority.

The first tourists to the islands were hard-core adventure travelers who came to the Big Island in the late 1800s to see the roiling Kilauea volcano. Among the adventurers was Mark Twain — who lauded Hawaii as "the loveliest fleet of islands that lies anchored in any ocean." But the new industry didn't stick until transportation improved, and the sugar industry became too expensive to support. In 1901, W. C. Peacock built the elegant Moana Hotel (now the Moana Surfrider) on Waikiki Beach. After a concentrated marketing effort in San Francisco, 2,000 tourists came to Waikiki in its first big tourism year, 1903. Tourism came by steamship; the sailing took almost five days. By 1936, visitors could fly to Honolulu from San Francisco on the *Hawaii Clipper,* a seven-passenger Pan American plane; the flight took 21 hours, 33 minutes. Modern tourism was born and was doing brisk business — until the Japanese arrived, that is.

On December 7, 1941, a Japanese air raid wreaked havoc on the American warships parked at Pearl Harbor, drawing the United States into World War II.

1959: Setting the stage for today's Hawaii

The harsh realities of war gave way to the lighthearted culture of *Blue Hawaii,* Trader Vic's, and Arthur Godfrey. Hotels sprouted along curvaceous Waikiki beach. In 1959, this blossoming paradise became the 50th state of the United States. That year also saw the arrival of the first jet airliners. Postwar Americans had disposable cash, and now Hawaii was an easy flight away. Visitors began to arrive in droves — and tourism as we know it was off the ground, surpassing sugar as the premier industry of the islands.

Tired of the plastic aloha that had supplanted genuine island culture, Hawaiian elders started making a concerted effort to integrate traditional hula, chant, visual arts, and values into the vast array of visitor experiences. Tourism and hospitality employees are now educated in Hawaiian history, culture, and genuine aloha spirit. The culture that was once clipped at the root has now come back in full bloom — and, thankfully, it's stronger than ever.

Building Blocks: Local Architecture and Design

Thanks to blessedly mild weather that includes cooling year-round trade winds and temperatures that don't vary by more than 15 degrees Fahrenheit from January to July, Hawaii thrives on open-air living. A seamless blend of indoors and out is the prevailing architectural style. Why put up a wall when you don't have a reason to keep out the weather — or the dazzling view?

The local architectural style is called *kama'aina,* or native born. *Kama'aina* is a style rich in beautiful simplicity and island tradition. True *kama'aina* architecture is generally open plan, in keeping with the importance of multigenerational family living and the strength of the community spirit — and to capitalize on those gentle ocean breezes. Decoration is simple but beautiful, generally focused on the shapes, materials, and hues of nature. My favorite example of a *kama'aina* house is the open-air, native wood **Holualoa Inn,** nestled in the Big Island's Kona coffee country (see Chapter 14).

The finest homes are fitted with natural woods, such as ohia floors and gleaming koa furnishings. Koa is a gorgeous hardwood that has been a favorite of local artisans for centuries thanks to its deep palette and rich grain. Crafts and furnishings made from the wood are increasingly expensive, simply because koa is a slow-growth wood that takes decades to replenish. If you can afford a piece to take home — perhaps a jewelry box or a hand-turned calabash — you'll likely treasure it as a family keepsake for generations to come, as island families do.

Not all native materials are expensive, however. Some of the most beautiful and tropically evocative home furnishings are crafted of simple, light materials like bamboo and rattan. Most floor coverings are woven mats, soft and cool on the bare feet. The finest are tightly woven lauhala, crafted from pandanus leaves by talented artisans. The best place to find lauhala in the islands is just down the road from the Holualoa Inn at **Kimura's Lauhala Shop** (see Chapter 15).

The beautiful shapes and hues of Hawaii's bold fauna have woven their way into the island's favorite fabrics, too. Boldly hued tropical barkcloths — nubby cotton fabrics that wear well and say "old Hawaii" with their large-leafed tropical and storytelling patterns — are famously suited to the furnishings of the islands. Vintage fabrics can often be found at two delightful Kauai shops, **Bambulei** and **Yellowfish Trading Company;** if you want newly woven fabrics on the bolt, you'll find a sea of possibilities at **Vicky's** and **Kapa'a Stitchery,** also on Kauai (see Chapter 17); other fabric shops throughout the islands can be located at www.thestateofhawaii.com/fabric.

Fabric designer **Sig Zane** (www.sigzane.com) has taken on the mantle of master of the new Hawaiian style. His strong, simple duo-tone patterns evoke island nature and culture with a strong sense of stewardship and an unparalleled evocative ability. Sig Zane prints are beautifully simple works of art, the ultimate badge of in-the-know fashion among Hawaiianistas. His shirts, dresses, handbags, and accessories can be purchased at his signature store on the Big Island (see Chapter 15).

Despite its glitz and glamour as a tourist destination, Hawaii is fundamentally a farming and fishing community — and the story is abundant in its streetscapes. Simple plantation cottages were built to house the workers brought in from all over the world to farm the islands' abundant sugar, pineapple, and taro fields; now, plantation style is the most pervasive architectural style in the islands, especially on the still-rural neighbor islands. With their single-story style, bright facades, and sloping roofs (many still crafted of corrugated aluminum), plantation cottages embody the simple beauty of island life. A more elaborate, multistoried style originated as the plantation manager's home.

Ranch life predominates in the cool Upcountry of the Big Island and Maui, where plantation life gives way to *paniolo* (cowboy) style. *Paniolo* style is built for somewhat cooler weather; as a result, you're likely to find it to be a bit more familiar. Expect ranch-style homes with island touches such as brightly painted exteriors and broad porches. Grander buildings take on Victorian details and the aura of the Old West. The bayfront storefronts along the city of **Hilo's Kamehameha Drive,** on the Big Island's lush east coast, and the city's charmingly Victorian **Shipman House Bed & Breakfast Inn** (see Chapter 14) are excellent examples. Experience *paniolo* style in its full glory by visiting **Parker Ranch,** one of America's largest working cattle ranches, located in the Big Island's misty Upcountry (see Chapter 15).

The Victorian influence on Hawaii even hit the beach. One of the most excellent examples of the adaptation of European architecture to island living is the **Westin Moana Surfrider,** Waikiki's very first hotel (see Chapter 10). This genteel clapboarded gray lady looks like it could have been displaced from Nantucket from the street side — but stroll through the structure to the ocean-facing veranda, and the style is all Hawaii.

Hawaii is roughly halfway between Asia and the mainland United States, so the Asian influence is pervasive in island architecture and design. Pagoda-style influences are evident in residential and commercial architecture throughout the islands, especially in areas that absorbed the wealth of Chinese and Japanese immigrants who came to work in the fields generations ago and stayed. Oahu's **Chinatown** offers the most concentrated examples.

A Taste of Hawaii: Local Cuisine

Hawaii has lured some of the world's finest chefs to its kitchens. About a dozen or so years ago, Hawaii Regional Cuisine was born. Local chefs were tired of turning out a stodgy menu of Continental fare that was unsuited to Hawaii living. So they began to celebrate the bounty of the islands, emphasizing the use of fresh, locally grown (often organic) produce, tropical fruits, the freshest seafood, and island-raised beef. Their light, creative combinations often feature Asian accents as a nod to Hawaii's multicultural heritage.

This type of cuisine is often disguised under other names — Euro-Asian, Pacific Rim, Indo-Pacific, Pacific Edge, Euro-Pacific, Island Fusion, and so on — but it all falls under the jurisdiction of Hawaii Regional Cuisine. Although there are variations, you can expect the following keynotes: lots of fresh island fish; Asian flavorings (ginger, soy, wasabi, seaweed, and so on) and cooking styles (searing, grilling, panko crust, wok preparations) galore; and fresh tropical fruit sauces (mango, papaya, and the like).

Thanks to Hawaii's proximity to the Pacific Rim and its large Asian population, the islands boast a wealth of fabulous Chinese, Thai, Vietnamese, and Japanese restaurants. And if Asian fare isn't your thing, you'll find plenty of other options, from the French classics to good ol' ranch-raised, fire-grilled steaks. Hawaii's cooks have even managed to put their own spin on some of the world's most revered foods — pizzas, burgers, and burritos — with rousing success.

Seafood lovers, rejoice: Hawaii offers you an astounding array of fresh-caught fish. In fact, you may find yourself puzzling over lists of unfamiliar fish on island menus. See Chapter 19 for a handy list of definitions that will help you decide what to try.

Lest all this unfamiliar food talk make you think otherwise, remember that the majority of Hawaii islanders are red-blooded, flag-waving Americans — and they love a good burger just as much as your average mainlander. Real local food is generally starchy and high in calories, so the Atkins crowd will want to skip the traditional plate lunch, which usually consists of a main dish (anything from fried fish to teriyaki beef), "two scoops rice," an ice-cream-scoop serving of macaroni salad, and brown gravy, all served on a paper plate. Plate lunches are cheap and available at casual restaurants and beachside stands throughout the islands.

Chapter 3

Deciding Where and When to Go

*H*awaii isn't just one place — it's an entire chain consisting of eight major islands and 124 islets. Together, they form a 1,500-mile crescent that slices a lush, volcanic swath through the sparkling Pacific waters just above the equator (in the North Pacific Ocean, not the South Pacific, as many believe).

The Hawaiian Islands are just a hair's breadth larger, in total landmass, than the state of Connecticut — but oh, what glorious square miles they are. The islands are actually summits of underwater volcanoes that have grown tall enough, in geologic time, to peek above the waves. (All the volcanoes are dormant except for two on the Big Island: Mauna Loa, which is not currently erupting at this writing, and erupting Kilauea, which is part of Hawaii Volcanoes National Park. See Chapter 15 for more information.) A volcanic core gives each island a breathtakingly rugged mountainous heart.

Most of the island development is at sea level, along the sunny coastal fringe of each island. Thanks to Hawaii's proximity to the equator, those coastal areas experience near-perfect weather year-round: temperatures in the high 70s or low 80s, clear skies, and gentle trade winds.

Introducing the Hawaiian Islands

The eight main islands are Oahu (oh-*wa*-hoo), the hub of the Hawaii island chain, and the "neighbor" islands: Maui (*mow*-ee); Hawaii, which is more commonly called the Big Island; Kauai (ka-*wah*-ee); Molokai (mo-lo-k-*eye*); Lanai (la-*nah*-ee); Niihau (nee-*ee*-how); and Kahoolawe (ka-ho-ho-*la*-vay). These islands make up more than 99 percent of the state's landmass. Of these, the first six are prime tourist destinations, each with its own personality, attractions, and tropical appeal. (Niihau is a privately owned island with a tiny population that can be visited on occasional tours from Kauai. Kahoolawe is an unpopulated island that was formerly a U.S. military bombing target; it is now slowly recovering in the loving hands of the Hawaiian people.)

Of the six islands that are open to tourists, four are ideal choices: Oahu, Maui, the Big Island, and Kauai. Molokai and Lanai are much less developed and offer fewer places to stay; they're worth visiting, but I generally recommend that you explore the four major islands first.

See the map on the inside front cover for locations of each of the Hawaiian islands.

The Gathering Place: Oahu

Oahu is the most developed of the Hawaiian Islands and its greatest population center — about 75 percent of Hawaii's residents (about 875,000 people) live on this gateway island. About three-quarters of Oahuans reside in Honolulu, the only real big city in the state. Hawaii's most famous district is the area of Honolulu called Waikiki, an urban beach resort that stretches along the south coast of the island to the landmark crater known as Diamond Head. A compact city of concrete and high-rises, Waikiki is the most densely built of Hawaii's beach resorts.

Oahu is a wonderful destination. It's home to some of Hawaii's best sightseeing, including the **USS *Arizona* Memorial** in **Pearl Harbor,** the most moving tribute to World War II in existence; the best little museum in the Pacific, the **Bishop Museum;** the world's best cultural theme park, the **Polynesian Cultural Center;** and much more. Oahu also boasts the state's finest restaurants and shopping, as well as (believe it or not) some of Hawaii's finest off-the-beaten-path adventures.

And **Waikiki Beach** really is fabulous, which is why travelers from around the world regularly converge on this sunny little haven. In the last few years, formerly kitschy Waikiki has been reinvented along more sophisticated lines. It's an extremely popular destination for Japanese honeymooners, who love to shop along the main drag, **Kalakaua Avenue,** at the couture boutiques (hello, Prada!). A multimillion-dollar beachfront beautification project has been a big success. And recent commercial gentrification in the form of the new Waikiki Beach Walk development has successfully transformed Waikiki's formerly seedy west end, injecting it with a fresh, exciting vibe and a feeling of quality, cohesion, and pedestrian-friendliness that it never had before. What's more, world-class dining has taken Waikiki by storm in recent years, which has improved its quality as a destination considerably. However, this is still Hawaii's most densely populated and touristy destination, so be prepared.

Waikiki maintains some of Hawaii's best moderately priced hotels; you're even likely to score some of the best luxury-hotel rates here, too. In addition, a comprehensive, easy-to-use public transportation system makes Oahu the only choice for those who don't want to rent a car.

Leave Waikiki off your itinerary if your singular goal is to get away from it all. But if you're up for endless diversion and don't mind a few crowds with your aloha — if you're the type who revels in the glitz and energy of it all — this justifiably world-famous beach party is the place for you.

Many newcomers who visit *only* Waikiki leave with the wrong idea about Hawaii — that it's more crowded, overbuilt, and urbanized than a real tropical paradise should be. So if you want to go home without feeling like you missed out on the magic, I also highly recommend that you dedicate a day or more to exploring the island beyond Honolulu. Oahu's Windward Coast and its North Shore (the epicenter of Hawaii's surf culture) offer some of the most gorgeous territory in the state — so gorgeous that you might consider staying in one of these areas. Here are some of Oahu's pros and cons:

- ✔ Yes, Waikiki beach is overbuilt and crowded — but it's still pure magic. If you want some alone time, idyllic Windward Coast beaches like Lanikai and Kailua are just a short drive away.

- ✔ If you want to kick back and do nothing, why hassle with Honolulu? Opt for a neighbor island instead — or head straight to the North Shore or Windward Coast. However, you should be the type who prefers a do-it-yourself vacation if you opt for the latter, because accommodations beyond Waikiki tend toward self-serve vacation rentals.

- ✔ Budget seekers should know that Waikiki now has the cheapest average room rate in Hawaii (about $167 a night) and boasts a surprising number of reasonably priced hotels right on — or a stone's throw from — the sand.

- ✔ Oahu is home to Hawaii's most famous snorkel spot, Hanauma Bay. Sure, it gets crowded — but a whole new world awaits you underwater here. Waikiki is a great place to learn to surf or boogie board, and the windward beaches are great for wannabe windsurfers. Another reason to keep Oahu on your agenda: The magical dolphin-watching cruises offered by Dolphin Excursions.

- ✔ This island is the birthplace, and still the epitome, of surf culture. If you want to learn to surf, you already know how, or you just like to watch, this is the island for you — no question.

- ✔ Oahu boasts a multitude of family-friendly attractions and parks, such as Sea Life Park, the Honolulu Zoo, the Waikiki Aquarium, and Hawaiian Waters Adventure Park, to name a few. Waikiki Beach itself is the perfect kiddie playland.

✔ Honolulu is the destination for serious shoppers, boasting the finest collection of alfresco malls in the country. You can find high-end boutiques, first-rate department stores, and shops carrying top-quality aloha shirts, surf gear, island-accented wares, and more.

✔ Attention, foodies: Dining doesn't get any better in these islands, either. Hawaii's finest fine-dining restaurants have congregated on Oahu; the best of the bunch is Alan Wong's, where the master of Hawaii Regional Cuisine flexes his wok with island-style aplomb. And thanks to a robust multicultural population that has imported culinary traditions from around the globe, it's the best island for eating ethnically and (relatively) affordably, too.

✔ Oahu boasts a nice selection of bars, nightclubs, and live entertainment venues. The Halekulani's House Without a Key is the best place for sunset hula and cocktails in the islands, hands down.

The Valley Isle: Maui

When people think Hawaiian paradise, they usually think Maui. Almost everyone who comes here falls in love with this island, and for good reason: It offers the ideal mix of unspoiled natural beauty, tropical sophistication, action-packed fun, and laid-back island style. In fact, the readers of *Condé Nast Traveler* have voted Maui "Best Island in the World" for 13 out of the past 14 years. That same poll even crowned Maui as the "World's Best Travel Destination" in 2005.

The Valley Isle is more like the mainland than any other place in Hawaii (yes, even Honolulu). The highways and L.A.–style traffic jams and mini-malls will look comfortingly familiar, or annoyingly so — it all depends on your perspective. (Because Maui generally has only one main road going in each direction, traffic can be worse at times in the Valley Isle's prime resort areas than it is on Oahu.) Although hotels have a bit more breathing room on Maui than they do in Waikiki, the shoulder-to-shoulder resort development is far more dense than what you find on the Big Island or Kauai. Also, Maui has the most high-profile population of relocated mainlanders. A quicker pace of living prevails, which can make Maui feel more like Southern California than Hawaii, especially in the resort areas.

Despite the mainland-style development, Maui really is a tropical paradise, with golden beaches, misty tropical cliffs, and countless waterfalls, especially along the **Heavenly Road to Hana,** one of America's most spectacular drives. Offshore are two of Hawaii's finest snorkel and dive spots. Onshore, at the summit of one of the island's two great mountains, is **Haleakala National Park,** a wild, otherworldly place that's hugely popular with hikers, bicyclers, and sunrise-watchers. Hawaii's finest luau, an excellent theater, and an energetic party vibe in Lahaina make Maui the best choice for those who enjoy after-dark activities. Furthermore, Maui is a close second to Oahu as a fine-dining destination.

Maui's attractions are no secret — so expect to battle a few crowds and pay for the privilege of visiting. I've heard an increasing number of complaints about overdevelopment and crowds in the last couple of years. And thanks to the rules of supply and demand, Maui tends to be more expensive than other islands across the board; booked-to-capacity hotels can be less than willing to reduce rates, high demand for car rentals often push rates north of what you'll find in the other islands, restaurants are pricey even at the casual end of the spectrum, and the high cost of all those available activities doesn't help matters. What's more, the tacky heart of Hawaii now beats in the old whaling town of Lahaina (which has superceded newly refined Waikiki as a cheesy tourist center), and Kihei's dominant architectural style is high strip mall. Still, nothing can dull the sheen on Maui, which oozes sex appeal. There's enough excitement and activity to keep even the most go-go-go travelers constantly on their toes.

Here are some of Maui's pros and cons:

✔ The Valley Isle scores for abundant, wide, breathtaking beaches.

✔ Maui is a winner for the sheer variety of great snorkel, dive, and learn-to-surf spots. One caveat: Molokini, a sunken offshore crater that's world famous for snorkeling and diving, has lost a great deal of its appeal because of shoulder-to-shoulder snorkel boats and a worn-down reef. The Big Island's Kealakekua is a much better snorkel-cruise destination.

✔ Despite its popularity and high resort rates, Maui has a decent number of beachfront bargains. If you don't want to go condo, which is probably your best value-for-dollar bet, try the Kaanapali Beach Hotel, one of my midpriced faves. Still, you're likely to pay more for accommodations here than you do on other islands.

✔ Maui has enough world-class golf courses to keep club-wielders happy for a good, long time.

✔ The windsurfers at Maui's Hookipa Beach are a blast to watch.

✔ Maui is the humpback's favorite place to hang offshore. If you show up during prime whale season (Jan–Mar), you're bound to see them, even if you don't head out to sea.

✔ This action-packed island wins for its wealth of kid-friendly condos and beaches, plus family activities galore. Your kids will wonder why you haven't come here before.

✔ Outdoor fun is the name of the game here. There's something new to do around every corner, from riding a bike down a volcano to taking a snorkel cruise.

✔ If you have a yen to frolic among waterfalls, do not pass go, do not collect $200 — head straight to Maui. The drive to Hana is chock-full of fabulous falls, and at the end of the road is the granddaddy of 'em all, Oheo Gulch.

✔ Maui boasts an innovative dining scene, from casual to chic — and with a wealth of beautifully situated oceanfront restaurants to boot.

✔ Attention, shoppers: Maui has an increasingly excellent specialty boutique and gallery scene, especially in Paia and Upcountry.

✔ Maui has surpassed Oahu as the nightlife capital of Hawaii. A party mood characterizes Lahaina town; the resorts offer lots of after-dark fun; and the Old Lahaina Luau is Hawaii's absolute best. This island even boasts the state's best live theater in the form of the Cirque du Soleil–goes-to-the-islands show '*Ulalena,* plus a couple of excellent ongoing magic revues.

✔ Traffic can be a bear on occasion, especially in the prime resort areas — but the other neighbor islands are catching up quickly, so it's becoming increasingly difficult to single out Maui on this front.

The Big Island: Hawaii

Salt-and-pepper beaches, primal rain forests, stark lava fields as far as the eye can see — this otherworldly island simply may not be your idea of a tropical paradise. But travelers with a passion for adventure, an eye for the unusual, or a taste for luxury will think that they've found heaven on earth.

The island that gave the entire island chain its name is the largest in the bunch — twice the size of all the others combined — and a real study in contradictions: Don't be surprised if you spot snow atop the nearly 14,000-foot peaks while you're deep-sea fishing off the legendary **Kona Coast** — considered the Sportfishing Capital of the World — or snorkeling in some of the warmest waters in the Pacific. North of Mauna Kea is vast ranchland, complete with herds of beef cattle and its own *paniolo* (cowboy) culture.

The left (Kona-Kohala) side is hot, dry, and studded with expansive, ultradeluxe beach resorts that add up to the finest collection of luxury resorts in all of Hawaii. The **Kona-Kohala coast** is one of the finest watersports playgrounds on earth for divers, snorkelers, and kayakers, whereas sun worshippers love white-sand **Hapuna Beach,** one of Hawaii's finest.

The right (Hilo-Volcano) side is lush, wet, green, and fragrant with tropical flowers. The misty city of **Hilo** is retro-charming, while postage stamp–size **Volcano Village** puts you right in the heart of a tropical rain forest.

In between are two of the tallest mountain peaks in the Pacific, **Mauna Kea** and **Mauna Loa;** the summit of Mauna Kea offers some of the world's finest stargazing. At the heart of the island is **Kilauea volcano,** the world's largest active volcano, currently in the midst of recorded history's longest-ever uninterrupted volcanic eruption. Most people think of volcanic activity as solely destructive, but Kilauea's eruptions have actually been productive, adding more than 201 hectares of new land (and counting) to the Big Island since January 1983. Needless to say, **Hawaii Volcanoes National Park** is one of the coolest — excuse me, hottest — places you'll ever have a chance to visit in your lifetime. If you like weird places, you won't want to miss it.

The Big Island can, however, dash expectations. It's jaw-droppingly spectacular — force me to choose, and I'll name it as my favorite of the islands — but it falls short of some people's tropical-island fantasies. Rugged chocolate-brown lava fields in every direction greet visitors flying into Kona Airport. Sure, you can lounge on a picture-perfect white-sand beach as wide as a football field, or revel in the scent of wild orchids in flowering rain forests, but you may have to go out of your way to find them. Also, much of the island is rural, so nightlife is scarce.

There's an increasing concentration of tacky development in the town of Kona itself, and on my last visit, I was dismayed by the regular traffic jams along the main roads. But still, the Big Island has a more laid-back, quieter vibe than what you find on Oahu or Maui — and, much of the time, you can also find relatively lower prices at all but the ultraluxury resorts. A nice selection of affordable, family-friendly condos is on hand (although most of them are not directly situated on beaches — budget travelers may have to resign themselves to doing a bit of driving to reach a great beach). And B&B lovers will discover the islands' best collection of inns, most offering an excellent base for visitors looking for a personalized experience. Just remember that the sheer size of this extra-large island makes for longer driving times; either plan on spending a week or limit yourself to one coast only.

Here are some of the Big Island's pros and cons:

- You can find some unusual beaches here, including a number of striking black-sand options, as well as some drop-dead-gorgeous classics like Hapuna Beach State Park, the crown jewel of island sands.

- The Big Island is the place to park yourself in style. You can find a string of terrific megaresorts along the Kona-Kohala coast, where there's plenty of room to spread out on a gorgeous stretch of sand.

- These spectacular championship resort golf courses, each an oasis of manicured green surrounded by a sea of black lava, are simply wild.

- You can find lots of activities here to keep you busy, including visiting the phenomenal Hawaii Volcanoes National Park — but plan on extended driving time getting around if you want to see it all.

- Kealakekua Bay is the best snorkeling and dolphin-watching spot in all Hawaii, and the whole coast is tops for sea turtle spotting. It offers great offshore diving too. And the icing on the cake? The Big Island is a sportfisher's mecca.

✔ Big Island's WOW! factor is a real draw for families, from fantasy megaresorts to that amazing volcano. You can also find some affordable family condos here.

✔ The fabulous resorts make great wedding locations. On the other side of the island, lush rain forests and romantic B&Bs make great places to hide away from the rest of the world.

✔ Also known as the "Orchid Isle," the Big Island earns deserved points for beautiful rain-forest lushness around Hilo and Volcano Village — but the dry, arid Kona-Kohala coast is the antithesis of some folks' island dreams.

✔ The Big Island offers a very respectable slate of restaurants in both the moderate and expensive price ranges, but the driving distance between them can put a strain on your nightly choices.

✔ An abundance of natural resources makes this island tops for quality shopping of island arts and crafts. Expect to go on the hunt for the best galleries, though.

✔ The Big Island is much quieter than Oahu and Maui. There's a concentration of waterfront bars in the town of Kailua-Kona (some of them a little too party-hearty and mass-market for my taste) and some chic cocktail spots at the resorts — but if Kilauea's spouting red-hot lava, there's no better after-dark show around.

✔ Traffic is an increasing problem in the Kailua-Kona area, so it's worth planning your accommodations to generally avoid town if you won't enjoy its touristy vibe.

✔ In recent months, the hazy fog known as "vog" has proven to be quite an issue around the island thanks to the recent volcanic activity, causing scratchy throats and persistent coughs in select regions of the island for days on end (not necessarily ones near the volcano; it all depends on the winds). If you have any respiratory issues that may cause you to worry, check current conditions with your accommodations host.

The Garden Isle: Kauai

Of all the Hawaiian Islands, Kauai is the one that comes closest to embodying the Hawaiian ideal — it's the ultimate in tropical romance and beauty. Even Hollywood thinks so, which is why Kauai has had starring roles in movies ranging from *Blue Hawaii* and *South Pacific* to *Jurassic Park.* The island landscape doesn't get any more spectacular than what you can find on Kauai. Every time I visit, I'm newly wowed by how exquisite it is. Kauai boasts the kind of natural beauty that cameras can't really capture, and that even mere memory can't conjure up. No wonder that Kauai captured the number-two spot on *Condé Nast Traveler*'s "Best Island in the World" list in 2006 and 2007.

Kauai is the perfect place to leave the modern world behind. Although it's beginning to sprout a few traffic jams, gardenlike Kauai is still quieter and less developed than its sister islands; in fact, you can count the number of full-fledged resorts on one hand. (This lack of choice makes it important to book well in advance if you plan on staying at one of the resorts.) Don't come expecting Cancún-style nightlife or St. Thomas–worthy shopping. Discover instead an unspoiled setting of wind-carved cliffs, fertile valleys rich with taro, powder-fine white-sand beaches, and gorgeous vistas in every direction. It's an ideal setting for some well-deserved relaxation time: The North Shore is the most tranquil and beautiful shoreline in all Hawaii, and the South Shore's **Poipu** (poy-*ee*-poo) **Beach** is a fabulous, family-friendly playground that's the ideal place to kick back and paddle around in the waves for days on end.

Kauai is great for adventurous souls too. The island boasts two remote natural wonders: the jagged emerald cliffs of the **Na Pali Coast,** and **Waimea Canyon,** called the "Grand Canyon of the Pacific" for its remarkable resemblance to the multicolored Arizona crater. The otherwise inaccessible Na Pali Coast, in particular, is a tropical dream-come-true for hikers, but you can also see these magical cliffs on a day cruise along the coastline or on an eye-popping helicopter tour.

It takes a lot of rain to keep Kauai so lush, fertile, and flower-fragrant; consequently, the weather here is a little less reliable than on the other islands. Kauai is the one island where a week of rain can quash your fun-in-the-sun plans. This is most likely to happen in winter, but it's happened to me even in May. (Conversely, I've enjoyed a rain-free March on the Garden Isle, and I've enjoyed sunny Kauai when it was raining everywhere else in the islands, so the weather is always anybody's guess.) Kauai's **Mt. Waialeale** is actually the wettest spot on earth, commanding an average annual rainfall of 444 inches; luckily, the coasts stay substantially drier. Still, stick to the South Shore if you have your heart set on a string of sunny days. The superlush North Shore is best for summer vacations, when the wild winter surf has calmed down and the days tend toward dry and sunny. (See "Revealing the Secret of the Seasons," later in this chapter, for more information on Hawaii's weather.)

Here are some of Kauai's pros and cons:

- ✔ It's home to the powdery-white, palm-lined, postcard-perfect beaches you fantasize about — and you're likely to have them virtually all to yourself as soon as you get here.

- ✔ Robert Trent Jones, Jr., called Kauai "the best island for golf there is."

- ✔ It has great snorkeling and spectacular underwater sightseeing, with a kaleidoscopic collection of marine life (although snorkeling is not safe in winter).

- ✔ Although this island is mostly for the relaxation minded, Kauai does have family-friendly condos, and Poipu Beach is fun for kids.

- ✔ Kauai is the undisputed winner in the romance category.

✔ Kauai is the best island for catching up on relaxation time — but you have lots to do if you want it, from movie tours to world-class golf to ocean activities galore.

✔ The Garden Isle is the closest you can come to the realization of the tropical dream — it's simply stunning. Don't miss the North Shore, even if you drive up for only a day.

✔ Kauai has less dining variety than the other islands. However, Poipu is home to my favorite branch of Roy's, the temple of Hawaii Regional Cuisine.

✔ The shopping is minimal in terms of quantity, but excellent for quality, especially if you like retro looks and island styles.

✔ Only one road circles the island. Traffic is becoming an increasing problem on the island's eastern coast (also known as the Coconut Coast), which connects north shore to south. Increased density is also bringing more mainland attitude and beginning to threaten Kauai's appealingly backwater way of life and slow pace.

The most Hawaiian isle: Molokai

Sleepy Molokai is a rural island that's largely untouched by modern development (although, as residents like to boast, they do have a KFC restaurant now). This lean, funky, scruffy little place is often called the most Hawaiian island because it's the birthplace of the hula, and it has a larger native Hawaiian population than any other in the chain. Although it offers some lovely, secluded beaches, the island's most famous site is **Kalaupapa National Historical Park,** a world-famous 19th-century leper colony that can only be reached by mule, prop plane, or helicopter.

I don't really cover Molokai in this book because I don't necessarily recommend making it part of your first visit to Hawaii. It's worth seeing eventually for its unsullied beauty and true Hawaiian spirit, but you should fully explore the other islands before you devote a significant amount of time to Molokai. And now that the Molokai Ranch has shut down, taking the island's best hotel and best restaurant with it, facilities for visitors are minimal. If you're interested in checking it out, however, check out *Maui For Dummies, Frommer's Hawaii, Frommer's Maui,* or *Pauline Frommer's Hawaii,* all of which include complete coverage of the island. Or contact the **Molokai Visitors Association** (☎ **800-800-6367** or 808-553-3876; www.molokai-hawaii.com). The **Maui Visitors Bureau** (www.visitmaui.com) can also provide you with island information because Molokai is part of Maui County. See the Quick Concierge in the appendix for complete contact info.

The private island: Lanai

This tiny island (pop. 3,500) is featured on a few packages, but I don't recommend spending time here until you conquer the other islands. Staying on Lanai is less a Hawaiian experience and more a generic park-yourself-at-a-resort vacation, which you can do with more local flavor elsewhere in the islands. For this reason, I don't cover Lanai in detail in this book.

If you're committed to visiting Lanai, you don't need this book, anyway — this island is where you go to *really* get away from it all. Formerly dedicated to pineapple production, Lanai is not particularly beautiful, nor does it offer much in the personality department. There's little or nothing to do here, which is the entire idea of this getaway island. Just about everything that *is* here is completely handled through the two megaexpensive resorts that have taken over this humble place: the English manor house–style **Four Seasons Resort Lanai, The Lodge at Koele,** and the beachfront **Four Seasons Resort Lanai at Manele Bay,** both of which are operated with élan by the ultraposh Four Seasons chain. If you visit Lanai, plan on eating every meal at the two sister resorts, and otherwise being entirely at their mercy. For the latest details on the hotel upgrades, call Four Seasons at ☎ **800-819-5053** or visit www.fourseasons.com.

I like visiting Lanai for a day of beachgoing, snorkeling, and sightseeing on one of Trilogy Excursions' day and overnight cruises from Maui; I tell you how to sign up in Chapter 13. Golfers may also consider flying or ferrying over from Maui for the day to hit the links, which is what many locals do.

If you really want to make Lanai a more substantial part of your vacation, check out *Maui For Dummies, Frommer's Hawaii, Frommer's Maui,* or *Pauline Frommer's Hawaii,* all of which include complete coverage of the island. Or contact **Destination Lanai** at ☎ **800-947-4774** or www.visit lanai.net. You can also contact the **Maui Visitors Bureau** (www.visit maui.com) because Lanai is part of Maui County. See the Quick Concierge in the appendix for more contact information.

Visiting More Than One Island

Most Hawaii vacationers visit more than one island, which I highly recommend you do. But don't try to cram too much in. About a week per island is a good general rule — or you'll end up spending too much time in the airport, at the car-rental counter, and checking in and out of hotels. Trust me on this one.

As you plan your itinerary, keep the following tips in mind:

✔ **Try to fly directly from the mainland to the island of your choice.** Doing so can save you a two-hour layover in Honolulu and another plane ride on an interisland carrier — a process that can add four or five hours to your total travel time. Oahu, the Big Island, Maui, and Kauai all receive multiple direct flights from the mainland. However, be sure to compare prices if money matters.

✔ **Remember the one-week, one-island rule.** It's smart to allot a week per island. For a two-week vacation, three islands is max — and that's only if you're the kind of traveler who can't handle more than three days amid the hustle and bustle of Waikiki.

✔ **If you have two weeks and your heart is set on seeing three islands, consider the following:** Arrive in Honolulu and spend three days seeing the highlights. Then head to Kauai to kick back on the beach for four or five days and recover from the time you spent running around Honolulu. After that, head to the Big Island, which easily has a week's worth of activities to keep you busy.

✔ **Pass on seeing a third island if you're committed to visiting both Oahu and Maui in two weeks.** Believe me, these two powerhouse islands have more than enough to offer to keep you busy for two months, much less two weeks.

✔ **Never budget fewer than five days on the Big Island.** The Big Island is the size of Connecticut, and just about everything is located on the island's coastline; therefore, you're going to be spending plenty of time in the car if you really want to see everything.

✔ **Don't overplan your itinerary or try to do everything.** If relaxing is number one on your agenda, work plenty of do-nothing time into your travel plans. A Hawaii vacation is less about seeing everything and more about going with the island flow.

✔ **Leave at least one day per island to chance.** Leave at least one day on each island for whatever strikes your fancy, whether it be sightseeing or shopping or just sitting on your condo's oceanfront lanai, soaking up a novel and the laid-back vibe.

✔ **If you're dividing your day between land and sea activities, make mornings your ocean time.** Beaches tend to be less crowded, and the surf and winds tend to be calmer in the morning hours — especially in winter. Always take the first snorkel and dive cruise of the day, when conditions are calmest and clearest; there's a reason why outfitters offer discounts on their afternoon sails.

✔ **Keep an eye on the weather and plan accordingly.** Don't be a slave to your schedule — watch the local weather reports and keep your plans flexible enough to make the most of great weather.

✔ **Book extra-special activities before you leave home so that you won't miss out.** Many of Hawaii's best activities can book up weeks in advance, so read this book and call ahead to reserve a few select adventures before you leave home. After all, it's not every day you get to Hawaii — and I wouldn't want you to miss out on the best luau in the islands or the ecotour of a lifetime. For tips on activities you may want to book before you arrive, see Chapter 9.

Revealing the Secret of the Seasons

Situated in the North Pacific just 1,470 miles above the equator, the Hawaiian Islands enjoy fabulous weather all year-round. Winter is virtually nonexistent. Severe storms are a rarity. Even those times considered the "off season" — spring and fall — are gorgeous, which means that those of you on a budget can save a bundle if you choose the right dates.

Hawaii's high season is during the winter months, from the second half of December through mid-April, when people flee the cold, snow, and gray skies of home for the warm sun of Hawaii. During this winter high season, prices go up and resorts can be booked to capacity. This scenario is especially true during the holiday season; book far in advance for a trip during this period and expect to pay sky-high prices. Although not nearly as bad as Christmastime, Easter week can also be crowded, as West Coast families flock to the islands for a few days of sunshine over spring break.

Summer (mid-June through Aug) is a secondary high season in Hawaii. Because so many families travel over the summer break, you won't find the bargains of spring and fall — but you may still do better on accommodations, airfare, and packages than you would in the winter months.

Hawaii's slowest seasons have traditionally been spring (from mid-Apr to mid-June) and fall (from Labor Day to mid-Dec) — which, paradoxically, also happen to be the best seasons in Hawaii in terms of reliably great weather. Herein lies the secret of the seasons: In spring and fall, hotel rates typically drop, package deals abound, airfares are often at their lowest rates of the year, and you can expect consistently warm, clear days after you arrive.

Because the weather is relatively constant year-round, it's a good bet that you can arrive at any time of year and enjoy prime conditions. It really boils down to how much you want to spend, how important it is to escape a harsh winter back home, how willing you are to deal with crowds, and what's available.

Understanding Hawaii's climate

Hawaii lies at the edge of the tropics, so it really has only two seasons: warm (winter) and warmer (summer). Temperatures generally don't vary much more than 15 degrees or so from season to season, depending on where you are. The average daytime summer temperature at sea level is 85°F, and the average daytime winter temperature is 78°F.

Temperatures stay even steadier when you consider the coastal areas alone: At Waikiki, the average high is 89°F at the height of summer, and the average winter high is 80°F at its coldest — not much difference. Nighttime temps drop about 15 degrees — less in summer, a little more in winter. August and September are usually the warmest months of the year; January and February are the coolest months. Almost-constant trade winds bring a cooling breeze even in the hottest weather.

Each of the islands has a leeward side (the west and south shores), which tends to be hot and dry, and a windward side (the east and north shores), which is generally cooler and wetter. For sun-baked, desertlike weather, visit the leeward side of an island. When you want lush, jungle-like conditions, go windward.

Locals like to say that if you don't like the weather, just get in the car and drive — you're bound to find something different. That's because each island also has many microclimates (highly localized weather patterns based on a region's unique position and topography). On the Big Island, for example, Hilo gets 180 inches of rainfall annually, which makes it the wettest city in the nation — yet only 60 miles away is desertlike Puako, which gets less than 6 inches of rain per year. So if it's raining on your parade, head somewhere else — you'll likely reach a sunny spot in no time. (The south and west coasts are usually your best bet.)

Generally speaking, each island has a mountain (or mountains) at its center. The higher you go in elevation, the cooler it gets. Thus, if you travel inland and upward, the weather can change from summer to winter in a matter of hours. If you visit Maui's Haleakala National Park, for example, you climb from sea level to 10,000 feet in just 37 miles — and it's not uncommon for the temperature to be 30 to 35 degrees cooler at the summit than it is at the beach.

In general, October to March marks Hawaii's rainy season; rainfall averages between 2 and 3 inches during these months. Summer, when average rainfall generally drops below an inch per month, is considered the dry season. The weather can get gray during this season, but, fortunately, it seldom rains for more than three days in a row. Winter isn't a bad time to go to Hawaii; the sun's just a little less reliable, that's all.

If you want assured sunshine year-round — or, at least as close as you can get to a sure bet — base yourself in one or more of the following regions:

- ✔ Waikiki, on Oahu

- ✔ Maui's south coast (Kihei and Wailea)

- ✔ The Big Island's Kona-Kohala coast

- ✔ The south and southwest coasts of Kauai (Poipu Beach and Waimea)

Charting sea changes

Hawaii's ocean waters stay warm year-round. The average water temperature in Waikiki is a warm 76°F even in winter, and reaches a jump-right-in 80°F or so in summer.

Wave action, though, varies greatly between winter and summer, and from coast to coast. All Hawaii's beaches tend to be as placid as lakes in the summer and autumn months. In winter, the islands' north-facing beaches are hit with swells, and the surf goes wild, especially in places like Oahu's North Shore, where daredevil surfers with a death wish hang-ten on monster curls that can reach 50 feet. South-facing beaches like Waikiki generally remain calm and friendly to swimmers and snorkelers of all ages and abilities throughout winter, although spring and early summer bring south swells right about the time North Shore waves flatten out.

If the waves are too powerful for you, seek calmer conditions by taking a short drive to another beach that's more sheltered — there are plenty of dependably calm coves. In the island sections in this book (Parts III through VI), I recommend the best local beaches, including the safest for inexperienced swimmers. When in doubt, ask one of the staff at your hotel or call the local tourist office for recommendations — and watch for warning flags and posted beach conditions at the beach.

 A few important words about ocean safety: Never turn your back on the ocean when you're at the beach. A big wave can come out of nowhere before you can say "aloha." Always watch the surf, even if you're just taking a casual stroll along the shoreline. Also, ocean conditions can change dramatically in a matter of hours — surf that was safe for swimming one day can develop a dangerous undertow the next. Get out of the water when the big swells come.

Avoiding the crowds

 Yes, there are times when coming to Hawaii is a bad idea if you're allergic to crowds. At the very least, you should know what you're getting into.

The entire nation of Japan basically shuts down during Golden Week, which falls annually in late April or early May and encompasses three Japanese holidays. Japanese tourism to Hawaii has generally slipped in the last five years or so, but you'd never know it during Golden Week — especially in Waikiki, the favored destination among Japanese travelers. Be sure to book hotels, interisland air reservations, and car rentals well in advance.

The Big Island's Kona-Kohala coast fills up during Ironman week (which leads up to the Sat closest to the full moon in Oct). Hotels book to capacity, rental cars sell out, and you pay top dollar for everything. People flock to Hilo during the Merrie Monarch Hula Festival, the week after Easter; plan well in advance if you're coming for these events.

On Maui, Halloween in Lahaina is a major event; up to 20,000 people come for the festivities. Booking your Lahaina hotel room a year or more in advance isn't too early. You shouldn't have a problem elsewhere on the island, though.

Additionally, more than 30,000 runners descend on Oahu for the week before the Honolulu Marathon (usually the second Sun in Dec).

And keep in mind that the islands are at maximum capacity during the Christmas holidays; spring break and Easter week can also be crowded. Stay at home during these seasons if you don't want to fight crowds or pay premium prices.

Perusing a Calendar of Events

Here's a rundown of the top events that take place annually throughout the Hawaiian Islands. This list is merely a drop in the bucket, of course; for a complete rundown, as well as the latest event information, visit www.calendar.gohawaii.com. For details on the events on a given island, your best bet is to contact the local visitors bureau directly. See the Quick Concierge at the back of this book for contact information.

Many of the following events absolutely require significant planning before you leave home. Calling ahead before any event is always best because tickets may be required, details may have changed, and so on.

✔ **January and February:** 'Tis the season for world-championship golf in paradise. The season kicks off with the first PGA event of the year, the **Mercedes Championships** at Maui's Kapalua Resort (☎ 877-527-2582; www.kapalua.com/hawaii-golf/pga-tournament), followed almost immediately by the **Sony Open** at Oahu's Waialae Country Club (☎ 808-734-2151; www.sonyopeninhawaii.com). On the senior tour, there's the **MasterCard Championship** at the Big Island's Four Seasons Hualalai (☎ 800-417-2770), and the **Wendy's Champions Skins Game** at either Kaanapali or Wailea, Maui, depending on the year and the deal struck. Expect top-ranked talent at every event. Check www.pgatour.com for complete details on each event, including how to purchase tickets.

✔ **January through April:** These months are Hawaii's prime **whale-watching season,** when humpback whales — the world's largest mammals — make their way from frigid Alaska to the balmy waters of Hawaii. Because whales prefer water depths of less than 600 feet, these endangered gentle giants come in relatively close to shore. You can see them regularly from the beach in prime season. They often prefer the west, or leeward, sides of the islands.

Maui is particularly terrific for whale-watching because the giants love to frolic in the channel separating the Valley Isle from Molokai and Lanai. The best onshore vantage is West Maui's MacGregor Point, a large pullout on the ocean side of Highway 30, halfway between Maalaea and Lanai. The nonprofit Pacific Whale Foundation operates a **Whale Information Station** there that's staffed by friendly naturalists daily (Dec–Apr). Just stop by — they even have high-powered binoculars you can use — or call ☎ 800-942-5311 or 808-249-8811 for more details.

If you happen to be in the islands during whale season, you won't want to miss seeing these remarkable behemoths. For the best views, take a whale-watching cruise. These are offered from each island; I recommend the best ones in Chapters 11, 13, 15, and 17.

✔ **Mid-January or early February:** The annual **Hula Bowl All-Star Football Classic** features America's top college players competing at Oahu's Aloha Stadium. Tickets are available through Ticketmaster; call Hula Bowl headquarters at ☎ **800-971-1232** or visit www.hulabowlhawaii.com for more details.

✔ **Late January through early February:** Help ring in the **Chinese New Year** in Honolulu's historic Chinatown, on the island of Oahu. New Year's events include a pageant, lion dances through the streets of Chinatown, a narcissus and bonsai exhibition, cooking demonstrations, live entertainment, and a festival bazaar. Check www.chinatownhi.com for this year's schedule and dates.

Always ready for any excuse to party, Maui's Lahaina is another excellent place to celebrate the Chinese New Year; events include a traditional lion dance in front of the historic Wo Hing Temple, plus food, music, fireworks, martial arts, Chinese crafts, and much more. Call ☎ **888-310-1117** or 808-667-9175 or go online to www.visit lahaina.com.

January 26, 2009, ushers in the year of the ox; February 10, 2010, inaugurates the year of the tiger.

✔ **Early February:** The National Football League's best pro players get it on in the **NFL Pro Bowl.** This annual all-star game takes place at Oahu's Aloha Stadium the week after the Super Bowl. Call ☎ **808-233-4635** or visit www.nfl.com/probowl well in advance for ticket information. A week's worth of gridiron-oriented fun usually precedes the big event.

✔ **Early February:** Honolulu's most prestigious private school hosts the **Punahou School Carnival,** and it's well worth seeking out. This huge two-day fun fair features everything from high-speed thrill rides to art shows by island artists to traditional Hawaiian food booths. Excellent island-style fun! Call ☎ **808-944-5711** or visit www.punahou.edu for this year's schedule of events.

✔ **Mid-February:** The Pacific Whale Foundation honors the majestic humpback whale with the **Great Maui Whale Festival,** a full winter-long calendar of events that culminates in mid-February with a parade, a regatta, whale-watching events, the annual Whale Day Celebration (usually held on the third Sat of the month), and much more. Call the foundation at ☎ **800-942-5311** or 808-244-8390 or visit www.greatmauiwhalefestival.org for details.

✔ **Mid-March:** The second humpback-themed celebration of the season rules Maui during the **Ocean Arts Festival,** Lahaina's own two-day series of special events honoring the island's most high-profile visitors, including whale-watching, an arts festival, games, and a touch-pool exhibit for kids. Call ☎ 888-310-1117 or 808-667-9175 or check www.visitlahaina.com for details.

✔ **Easter Weekend:** Maui's annual **Ritz-Carlton Kapalua Celebration of the Arts** is the premier interactive Hawaii arts and culture festival. Well-known artists give free lessons in hula, chant, lei making, primitive clay firing, and more. Events include a traditional luau and live entertainment of the highest order. Call ☎ 800-262-8440 or 808-669-6200 or visit www.celebrationofthearts.org for details.

✔ **Easter Sunday:** Since 1902, people from near and far have been gathering for the **Easter Morning Sunrise Services** at Honolulu's National Cemetery of the Pacific, in Punchbowl Crater. Service usually begins at 6:15 a.m. Call ☎ 808-532-3720.

✔ **Week following Easter:** Hawaii's biggest annual cultural event is the **Merrie Monarch Hula Festival,** which sweeps the misty city of Hilo on the Big Island for a full week in spring (usually the week following Easter Sun). The islands' largest and most prestigious hula festival features four nights of modern and ancient dance in honor of King David Kalakaua, the "merrie monarch" who revived the dance, which had been all but forgotten with the coming of Western ways to the islands. Tickets go on sale at the end of December and sell out by late January, so reserve early; some events are free, however, and a limited number of returned tickets may be available at the last minute. Competitions wind down with a festive parade on the final Saturday of the event. Call ☎ 808-935-9168 or visit www.merrie monarchfestival.org for details — and plan to avoid booked-solid Hilo during festival week if you don't plan to participate.

✔ **May 1:** May Day is **Lei Day** in Hawaii — and cause for big-time rejoicing. At Oahu's Kapiolani Park, Hawaii's most colorful and fragrant holiday is celebrated all day with lei-making contests and exhibits, arts-and-crafts fairs, food booths, and more; you can even meet this year's Lei Queen. The crowning event is the big **Lei Day Concert by the Brothers Cazimero,** kings of the Hawaiian music scene, at the Waikiki Band Shell; it's a magical, aloha-filled event well worth planning your trip around. Tickets usually go on sale through Ticketmaster in early April. Call ☎ 808-768-3041 or visit www.honoluluparks.com for details on Kapiolani Park's Lei Day events and ☎ 808-597-1888 for concert information.

✔ **Mid-May:** Oahu's Polynesian Cultural Center hosts the weeklong **World Fireknife Dance Competition,** literally the world's hottest competition, in which fire dancers of all ages gather from around the globe to compete for the title of world-champion fire-knife dancer. It's all part of the annual **Samoa Festival,** which is celebrated with authentic Samoan food and festivities. Contact the Polynesian Cultural Center at ☎ 800-367-7060 or 808-293-3333 for this year's details or go online to www.polynesia.com.

✔ **Memorial Day:** There's no better place to honor past war heroes than at the **USS *Arizona* Memorial,** in Honolulu's Pearl Harbor. Call ☎ **808-422-2771,** or check www.nps.gov/usar for the program of events. At 9 a.m., the armed forces also hold a ceremony recognizing the brave men and women who died for their country at the **National Cemetery of the Pacific** at Punchbowl Crater, the final resting place of 35,224 victims of three American wars fought in Asia and the Pacific; call ☎ **808-532-3720** for further details.

✔ **Mid-June:** The **Maui Film Festival at Wailea** is Hawaii's very own version of Sundance, with five days and nights of premiere screenings, parties, and celebrity appearances; Hawaiian cultural events add island flavor. Call ☎ **808-579-9244** or 808-572-FILM [3456] or visit www.mauifilmfestival.com for details.

✔ **June 11 (or nearest weekend):** In honor of the great chief who united the Hawaiian Islands, **King Kamehameha Day** is celebrated as a statewide holiday, with massive floral parades, slack-key guitar concerts, Hawaiian crafts shows, and lots of partying. Probably the best event is the celebratory parade through Maui's old Lahaina town, which concludes with a food and craft fair, demonstrations of ancient warrior skills, and other entertainment; call ☎ **888-310-1117** or 808-667-9175 or check www.visitlahaina.com for details. Contact the individual island visitor centers (see the Quick Concierge in the appendix) for the full calendar of local celebrations.

✔ **Late June or early July:** See demonstrations of traditional Hawaii arts-and-crafts making, sample traditional island foods, watch living-history reenactments of the Hawaiian royal court, and even learn to shake your hips to the hula at the two-day **Establishment Day Annual Hawaiian Cultural Festival,** which takes place at Puuhonua o Honaunau National Historical Park on the Big Island's South Kona Coast. Call ☎ **808-328-2288** or visit www.nps.gov/puho.

✔ **Late June or early July:** World-famous winemakers and chefs gather (along with appreciative gourmands) on Maui annually for the highly acclaimed — and appropriately grand — **Kapalua Wine & Food Festival,** a bounteous four-day series of wine tastings, cooking demonstrations, and gourmet meals prepared by celebrity chefs. Make your arrangements well in advance. Call ☎ **866-669-2440** or 808-665-9160 or visit www.kapalua.com for details.

✔ **July 4:** Each island celebrates **Independence Day** with a variety of star-spangled accompaniments. But the best event of all is **Turtle Independence Day** at the Big Island's Mauna Lani Resort, in which scores of 3- and 4-year-old endangered green sea turtles, all raised in the shelter of the resort's historic fishponds, are released from captivity. Watching their race to the sea is a sight to behold. Call the Mauna Lani at ☎ **808-881-7911** or visit www.maunalani.com for this year's details.

✔ **July 4:** Discover Hawaii's buckin' bronco side at the **Parker Ranch Rodeo and Horse Races,** a full day of cowboy-themed fun in Waimea, heart of the Big Island's cattle country. Barbecue and foot-stompin' entertainment accompany the traditional rodeo events. Call ☎ 877-885-7999 or 808-885-7655 or go to www.parkerranch.com.

✔ **Third weekend in July:** The one-day **Prince Lot Hula Festival,** held annually at Honolulu's Moanalua Gardens, features authentic performances of ancient and modern hula, plus craft demonstrations, traditional island games, live music, and food vendors. This festival is a wonderful way to discover Hawaii's unique and fascinating culture — and it's absolutely free. Call ☎ 808-839-5334 or visit www.mgf-hawaii.org and click on "Hula Festival" for the exact date and other details.

✔ **Late July or early August:** Hawaii's most prestigious fishing tournament, the **Hawaiian International Billfish Tournament,** takes place in the sportfishing capital of the Pacific: Kailua-Kona, on the Big Island. Call ☎ 808-836-3422 or visit www.hibtfishing.com for this year's schedule.

✔ **Third Friday in August:** Hawaii became the 50th state on August 21, 1959, which is now celebrated as **Admissions Day** on the third Friday in August; all state-related facilities are closed.

✔ **Mid-September:** Running exactly 26.2 miles from Kahului to Kaanapali, the **Maui Marathon** is regularly named one of the ten most scenic marathons in North America. A half-marathon and a 5K are also offered for runners working their way up to the big kahuna. Upcoming dates are Sunday, September 20, 2009, and Sunday, September 19, 2010 (the marathon's 40th anniversary). Visit www.mauimarathon.com for entry details.

✔ **Mid-September:** 'Tis the season in Hawaii for statewide **Aloha Festivals.** Each week from mid-September through October is Aloha Week on a different island, with events running the gamut from parades and royal balls to ethnic days and street festivals. This is serious celebration time. My favorite is always Waikiki's street party, usually the first on the annual calendar. Most events are free with the purchase of an "Aloha Festivals" ribbon (usually around $10); call ☎ 808-589-1771 or go to www.alohafestivals.com for a complete schedule.

✔ **Mid-September: Taste of Lahaina and the Best of Island Music** is Maui's biggest foodie event. Some 30,000 people flock to Lahaina Recreation Park II to sample the signature dishes of Maui's top restaurants. This weekend festival also includes cooking demonstrations, wine tastings, and nonstop live entertainment. The weekend before the main event features Maui Chefs Present, an elegant $100-a-plate dinner and cocktail party featuring about a dozen of the island's best chefs. Call ☎ 888-310-1117 or 808-667-9175, or visit www.visitlahaina.com for details.

✔ **Mid-September:** The **Sam Choy Poke Festival,** a three-day event held at the Big Island's Hapuna Beach Prince Hotel, is my favorite of all Hawaii's culinary events. Top chefs from across Hawaii and the U.S. mainland as well as local amateurs compete in making Hawaiian poke (po-*kay*), chopped raw fish mixed with seaweed and spices. A Hawaiian craft fair is also part of the fun. Call ☎ **808-880-1111** or visit `www.pokecontest.com` for details.

✔ **Late September or early October:** The **Maui County Fair** is Hawaii's oldest and largest county fair, held at the Wailuku War Memorial Complex for four fun-filled days. Expect a parade, rides, games, exhibits, and entertainment — all with an island twist. Call ☎ **808-242-2721** or visit `www.mauicountyfair.com` for info.

✔ **Mid-October:** The world's finest athletes converge on the Big Island's Kona-Kohala coast every October to run (26.2 miles), swim (2.4 miles), and bike (112 miles) in one of the most prestigious events in all of sports, the punishing **Ironman Triathlon World Championship.** I'm not necessarily suggesting that you join in; participate instead by cheering on the contestants along the route. The best place to see the 7 a.m. start is along the seawall on Alii Drive in Kailua-Kona; get there before 5:30 a.m. for a prime spot. Alii Drive is also the best vantage for watching the bike and run portions; park on a side street and walk down to Alii because it's closed to traffic. To watch the finishers come in, line up along Alii Drive from Holualoa Street to the finish at Palani Road and Alii Drive; the winner can come as early as 2:30 p.m., and the course closes at midnight. The Ironman is usually held on the Saturday nearest the full moon; call ☎ **808-329-0063** or visit `www.ironman.com/worldchampionship` for this year's date and details. If you're not interested, you may want to avoid the Kona-Kohala coast while Ironman is in swing.

✔ **Mid-October:** The only statewide film festival in the United States, the **Louis Vuitton Hawaii International Film Festival** specializes in films from Asia, the Pacific Islands, and North America. Most screenings and related events take place on Oahu, but the final weekend finds events on all the islands. Call ☎ **808-528-3456** or visit `www.hiff.org` for more information.

✔ **October 31:** Some 30,000 people show up to celebrate **Halloween** in Lahaina, Maui, an event so festive and popular that some call it the "Mardi Gras of the Pacific." Front Street is closed off from 3 p.m. to midnight for the costumed revelers and accompanying festivities; a children's parade launches the day. The Great Halloween Costume Contest takes place in Banyan Tree Park at 7 p.m. Lahaina is so gung-ho on Halloween, in fact, that the party starts the week prior to October 31 with haunted houses and myriad events about town. Call ☎ **888-310-1117** or 808-667-9175 or visit `www.visitlahaina.com` for this year's program of events.

✔ **Early November:** The **Aloha Classic World Windsurfing Championships,** the final event in the Pro Boardsailing World Tour, is held at Maui's Hookipa Beach, universally considered to be the best windsurfing beach on the planet. Spectating is absolutely free. Check www.alohaclassicwindsurfing.com for this year's dates.

✔ **Early November:** Celebrate the mighty bean with the **Kona Coffee Cultural Festival,** Hawaii's oldest food festival, held in Kailua-Kona on the Big Island. The weeklong series of events includes a bean-picking contest, lei contests, art exhibits, music, a parade, the Miss Kona Coffee pageant, and more. Call ☎ **808-326-7820** or visit www.konacoffeefest.com for this year's schedule.

✔ **November through February:** Surf season arrives! The **Vans Triple Crown of Surfing Series** is the World Series of professional big-wave surfing, the final stop on the ASP (Association of Surfing Professionals) World Tour. These daredevils put on a world-class thrill show, guaranteed, so don't miss the opportunity to watch. Events are held on the North Shore beaches of Oahu in November or December; the wave action determines the schedules. Call ☎ **808-596-SURF [7873]** or visit www.triplecrownofsurfing.com for the latest information on these and other surfing events throughout the islands, including the **Roxy Pro Hawaii,** the **O'Neill World Cup of Surfing,** and the **Quicksilver Big Wave Invitational in Memory of Eddie Aikau** (Dec–Feb), which only runs once wave faces reach a minimum of 40 feet — wow!

✔ **Mid-December:** More than 25,000 runners converge for the **Honolulu Marathon,** one of the largest marathons in the world — and definitely one of its most scenic. Whether you're a potential participant or merely a spectator, call ☎ **808-734-7200** or go to www.honolulumarathon.com for all the details. If you're not coming to Honolulu specifically to run in or watch the marathon, you may want to avoid Oahu entirely while it's on — hotels are booked to capacity, and the island is overrun with out-of-towners.

✔ **Throughout December:** It's a holly, jolly **Christmas,** island-style. The mayor of Honolulu says "Mele Kalikimaka" by throwing the switch to light up the 40-foot-tall Norfolk pine and other trees in front of Honolulu Hale, followed by the Electric Light Parade. On Maui, Santa arrives for the annual lighting of Lahaina's historic banyan tree, followed by Christmas caroling in Hawaiian. Schedules vary, so call ☎ **808-524-0722** for Oahu events, or **800-525-6284** or 888-310-1117 for Maui events. Every island is bedecked in holiday finery throughout the month.

Chapter 4

Managing Your Money

● ●

In This Chapter

▶ Thinking about your major expenses

▶ Using AAA and American Express memberships to your advantage

▶ Zeroing in on cost-cutting tips

● ●

"So, how much is this trip to Hawaii going to cost me, anyway?"

It's a reasonable question, no matter what your income. A vacation is always a big-ticket endeavor, with costs that can add up before you know it — and, as destinations go, Hawaii is a relatively pricey one. So you'll want to plan ahead to keep your budget on track. In this chapter, I tell you what to expect and offer tips that can save you big bucks on major expenses.

Planning Your Budget

The good news is that you can easily structure a Hawaii trip to suit any budget. Airfare and hotels will probably end up being your largest cash outlays. Other things, like rental cars, are relatively affordable on most of the Hawaiian islands.

Your choice of activities also determines how much you spend: Relaxing on the beach or taking in Hawaii's natural beauty generally doesn't cost a dime. But guided tours and organized activities — like snorkel trips, helicopter rides, and luau — can carry surprisingly hefty price tags (see Table 4-1).

Transportation

The cost of your flight to Hawaii will be one of your top two expenses (right up there with hotels). Airfares are almost impossible to predict and can change at the drop of a hat, especially as oil prices continue to rise. Still, here's a rough idea of what to expect: If you're going to Hawaii in the off season — say, May or maybe October — you may be able to snag a round-trip ticket for as little as $500 from San Francisco or Los Angeles or $800 to $900 from the East Coast. If you're traveling in the high season (late Dec to Apr, or in summer), you'll pay more — probably in the $500 to $800 range from the West Coast and between $700 and $1,400 from back east.

Expect to pay more if you're departing from a city that's not a major airline hub. If you're traveling to Hawaii over the Christmas holidays, expect to pay full fare.

 You can score any number of money-saving deals, especially if you consider an all-inclusive package. (See Chapter 5 for more details on travel packages. I also tell you how to save on airfares in that chapter.)

Interisland flights

If you plan to visit more than one island at any time during your stay, you'll need to take an interisland flight. Fares for one-way trips between the islands, which are run through Hawaiian Airlines and recent market entry go! Airlines, average about $160 in the high season. But there's good news: You may not need to pay full fare. Numerous sales and special Internet-only fares are frequently available; one-way fares were available for around $109 at press time, and went as low as $53 per flight in the last off season. See Chapter 6 for details.

Car rentals

Rental cars are relatively affordable in the islands, especially if you're not traveling in the holiday season. Weekly rates almost always save you a bundle. You can often get a compact for as little as $35 to $45 a day, sometimes even less if you book a weekly rental. If you need a family-size car, expect to pay more on the order of $45 to $65 per day, depending on where you're staying and the time of year you're booking. Of course, everybody wants a convertible in the islands, so expect to pay upwards of $75 or more a day in season for one, although you could score a weekly rental for as little as $400, if the stars align. You can sometimes wheel and deal for one at the rental counter in the low season, when business is slower.

 Do yourself a favor and book a rental car with unlimited mileage. You'll be doing plenty of driving no matter which island you're on, and you don't — want to end up paying for your rental on a per-mile basis. Trust me — you'll end up on the short end of this stick. Most of the major car-rental companies rent on an unlimited-miles basis, but be sure to confirm this policy when you book.

And because you'll probably cover a good deal of ground, don't forget to factor in gas, which is typically more expensive in Hawaii than on the mainland, and even higher on the neighbor islands than it is on Oahu. At press time, the gap between mainland and Hawaii prices was about 40 cents per gallon, but Hawaii prices have been known to be as much as a dollar more per gallon.

Also remember to account for any additional insurance costs, which generally run an extra $15 to $25 a day, depending on the coverage you select. Parking, thankfully, is generally free, although most Waikiki hotels and many luxury resort hotels throughout the islands charge a daily fee for parking; be sure to check when you book.

You'll seldom save by waiting to rent your car; generally, prices only go up as your pickup date approaches — especially in the busy travel seasons. Book as far in advance as possible for the best rate. Also see "Cutting Costs — but Not the Fun," later in this chapter, for additional money-saving tips.

You may not have to worry about shopping around or wangling a lower rate on a car rental. Often, rental cars and interisland flights are part and parcel of a package deal. In many hotel and airline packages, they're thrown in for a nominal fee or for free. See Chapter 6 for more details.

Lodging

Hawaii has a wealth of luxury hotels and resorts, but it also offers plenty of affordable choices — especially on the condo market. Still, although you can find decent hotel rooms or budget condo rentals for $125 or so a night, you really shouldn't expect to pay much less than that. After you start adding on amenities — kitchenettes, room service, ocean views — expect room rates to climb from there.

The good news is that you can score reasonable rates on a per-person basis if you're traveling in a group or with your family. Hawaii boasts lots of apartment-style condos that sleep four or more at moderate prices — between $125 and $225 per night on the bottom end, and $250 or more for more luxurious digs. Of course, if you stay at a condo, you'll likely miss out on resort-style amenities and services — concierge, room service, kids' programs, and the like. But it may be worth it to you if you want to have more room to spread out, enjoy the convenience of having a kitchen, and keep costs down, because dining is quite expensive in Hawaii — especially once you start feeding a family.

I've taken care to recommend a range of lodging choices on each island to give you plenty of choices, no matter what your needs or budget. And remember: Although I've listed standard "rack rates" for every hotel, these tend to be the maximum. You rarely have to pay full price — and you can find numerous ways to save. (For one thing, booking a package deal can be a huge money saver when it comes to hotels; for more information on packages, see Chapter 5.) For additional cost-cutting measures, see "Cutting Costs — but Not the Fun," later in this chapter.

Be sure to budget for the 11.42 percent in taxes that will be added to your final hotel bill.

Dining

Hawaii has become something of a culinary mecca. Each island boasts its own slate of top-quality restaurants — often charging top-dollar prices. So think about your bottom line. Many of you, no doubt, look forward to sampling the finest restaurants and won't mind paying for the privilege. But if you'd rather spend your vacation dollars on other activities, the islands offer plenty of opportunities to dine on the cheap: You can spend as little as $5 to $10 for breakfast (a continental breakfast may even be included in your hotel deal), grab a quick-and-easy lunch for $10 to $15, and enjoy a casual dinner for $15 to $30. Still, thanks to the high cost of transpacific transport, island real estate, and labor, you're likely to pay more for even casual food here than you do at home. And, of course, extra niceties like wine or cocktails will drive up dinner costs quickly.

Restaurant bills can add up fast, so if you want to save in this category, I strongly suggest booking a room or condo with kitchen facilities. By preparing a few daytime meals yourself (breakfast, in particular, can be a big money saver, and it's often convenient to pack sandwiches to take to the beach), you'll be in a better position to splurge on a great dinner. Kitchen facilities are a virtual must if you're traveling with kids.

Sightseeing and activities

Here's where the bills can really start to pile up, especially if you're traveling with the family — but it ultimately depends on what you want to do. If you're coming to Hawaii to simply kick back on the sands, you won't have to budget much in this category. Going to the beach is free, and even snorkel gear rentals are cheap.

But if you're planning to schedule some organized activities and tours — which I strongly suggest you do, especially if it's your first visit to Hawaii — plan ahead to see what your budget can handle because they can get surprisingly pricey. Expect to pay $70 to $95 per person for your average snorkel cruise, and even more for your average luau. The best helicopter rides can easily run more than $175 a head. Budget-minded golfers may want to think twice before they tee up — fees commonly run close to $200. (However, wallet watchers can often take advantage of twilight rates, which generally hover around $100.)

This book lists exact prices for activities, entertainment, tee times, admission fees, and the like in the following chapters so that you can budget your money realistically. If there's a way to snag a bargain, I include that information too.

Shopping and nightlife

These two areas are the most flexible parts of your budget. Shopping is a huge temptation in Hawaii. But if money is an issue, do yourself a favor and bypass the souvenirs.

Oahu and Maui are the liveliest destinations in terms of after-dark diversions, but in general, the islands aren't overloaded with nightlife options. You can easily avoid racking up the bills in these categories if shopping and/or evening entertainment isn't a high priority for you.

Table 4-1	What Things Cost in Hawaii
Item/Activity	*Price*
An average cup of coffee	$1.50
A grande mocha latte at Starbucks	$4.00
Compact rental car on Oahu (per day)	$39.00
Convertible rental car on Maui (per day)	$78.00
All-day ticket aboard the Waikiki Trolley	$27.00
Admission to the Bishop Museum (Oahu)	$16.00
Helicopter tour	$179.00–$300.00
Fair Wind snorkel cruise to Kealakekua Bay (Big Island)	$69.00–$119.00
A day at the beach	Free!
Luxury room for two at Princeville Resort Kauai	$600.00–$875.00
Moderate room for two at the Kaanapali Beach Hotel (Maui)	$199.00–$355.00
Romantic cottage for two or four at Volcano Village Lodge, breakfast included (Big Island)	$175.00–$275.00
Budget oceanfront condo for two or four at Wailua Bay View (Kauai)	$155.00–$175.00
Gourmet dinner for two at Alan Wong's (Oahu)	$180.00
Oceanfront dinner for two at Hula Grill (Maui)	$120.00
Casual dinner for two at Cafe Pesto (Big Island)	$45.00
Burgers for two at Duane's Ono Char Burger (Kauai)	$15.00

A Note on Taxes: Hawaii does not have a sales tax, per se. However, the state charges businesses an excise tax on revenue. Therefore, most restaurants and shops pass this on to the consumer as a tax of roughly 4 percent. The percentage may vary slightly depending on the county you're in, and may be embedded in the total purchase price or shown as an independent line item on your bill. Taxes of 11.42 percent are added to hotel bills.

Cutting Costs — but Not the Fun

I don't care how much money you have — nobody wants to spend more than they have to. In this section, I give you some tips on how to avoid spending more of your hard-earned cash than is necessary.

Getting the best airfares

Getting the best fares on both transpacific and interisland air travel is such a huge topic that I've dedicated the better part of a chapter to it. Before you even start scanning for fares, see Chapter 5. That chapter also discusses how to find money-saving package deals.

Getting a break on your room rate

There's often a huge gap between hotels' official "published" rates (also called full-price, or rack rates) and what you actually pay, so don't be scared off at first glance. What's more, savvy travelers can find ways to further widen the margin.

More often than not, the best way to score a cheap hotel room is to buy an all-inclusive travel package that includes airfare, hotel, and car, and sometimes other extras, in one low price; for details on scoring a good-value package, see Chapter 5.

The second-best way to avoid paying the full rack rate when booking your hotel is stunningly simple: Just ask the reservation agent for a cheaper or discounted rate. You may be pleasantly surprised — I have been, many times. But you have to take the initiative and ask because no one is going to *volunteer* to save you money.

Here are a few more potentially money-saving tips:

- ✔ **Rates are generally lowest in spring and fall.** The time of year you plan to visit may affect your bargaining power more than anything else. During the peak seasons — basically mid-December through mid-April and summer — when a hotel is booked up, management is less likely to offer discounts. In the slower seasons — generally mid-April through mid-June and September through mid-December — when capacity is down, they're often willing to negotiate; in fact, many places drop rates by 10 to 30 percent automatically in the less busy times of year. If you haven't decided when you want to visit Hawaii yet, see Chapter 3.

- ✔ **Membership in AAA, AARP, or frequent flier/traveler programs often qualifies you for discounted rates.** (For details on joining AAA, see "The AAA advantage" sidebar, later in this chapter.) You may also qualify for corporate or student discounts. Attention, seniors: You may qualify for discounts even if you're not an AARP member (although I highly recommend joining; see Chapter 8 for details). Members of the military or those with government jobs may also qualify for price breaks.

- ✔ **Inquire about the hotel's own package deals.** Even if you're not traveling on an all-inclusive package (see Chapter 5), you may be able to take advantage of packages offered by hotels, resorts, and condos directly. They often include such value-added extras as a free rental car, champagne and in-room breakfast for honeymooners, free dinners, discounted tee times or spa treatments, a room upgrade, an extra night thrown in free (sometimes the fifth, sometimes the seventh), or some other freebie. I note what kinds of discounts are typically available in my hotel reviews. Properties usually list these deals on their Web sites, but not always, so it never hurts to ask additional questions about available specials.

✔ **If you're booking a hotel that belongs to a chain, call the hotel directly in addition to going through central reservations.** See which one gives you the better deal. Sometimes, the local reservationist knows about packages or special rates, but the hotel may neglect to tell the central booking line.

✔ **Surf the Web to save.** A surprising number of hotels advertise great packages via their Web sites, and some even offer Internet-only special rates.

In addition to surfing the hotel's own sites, you may want to try using a general travel booking site like **Expedia.com**, **Travelocity.com**, **Hotels.com**, or **Orbitz.com** to book your hotel or a pay-one-price package that also includes airfare. Acting much like airline consolidators, these sites can sometimes offer big discounts on rooms as well. See Chapter 7 for a more complete discussion of how to use the Web to find a great hotel bargain.

✔ **Ask innkeepers for a break.** Bed-and-breakfasts are generally non-negotiable on price. Sometimes, however, you can negotiate a discount for longer stays, such as a week or more. You may also be able to score a price break if you're visiting off season. And some do offer AAA and senior discounts. Remember that it never hurts to ask, politely.

✔ **Look for price breaks and value-added extras when booking condos.** Condos are usually pretty flexible on rates. They tend to offer discounts on multinight stays, and many throw in a free rental car to sweeten the deal. Some condo properties have units handled by multiple management companies; if that's the case, call both companies and see which one offers you the better deal. You may also want to check with **Hawaii Condo Exchange** (☎ **800-442-0404** or 323-436-0300; www.hawaiicondoexchange.com), which acts as a consolidator for condo properties throughout the islands.

Cutting other costs

Here are a few more useful money-saving tips:

✔ **Consult a reliable travel agent.** A travel agent can sometimes negotiate a better price with certain hotels and assemble a better–value travel package than you can get on your own. In fact, in a recent *Condé Nast Traveler* investigation, travel agents could always price out Hawaii resort vacations more cheaply than any other outlet (including airline packagers). Even if you book your own airfare, you may want to contact a travel agent to price out your hotel.

On the other hand, hotels, condos, and even B&Bs are sometimes willing to discount your rate as much as 30 percent — the amount they'd otherwise pay an agent in commissions — if you book direct.

So it may make sense to base your decision about using a travel agent on time rather than money — think of a travel agent as a convenience. If you do use a travel agent, it makes sense to be an informed consumer, going into the process with a general idea of what things cost so that you know whether you're getting a bargain. A good first step is consulting this book so that you know which hotels appeal to you and their approximate costs.

And *don't* let an agent steer you to a hotel that's not right for you just because he or she may be getting a better commission. If you sense that your agent isn't working hard to line up a trip that really suits your desires, move on and find someone else.

✔ **Surf the Web to save on your rental car too.** In addition to surfing rental-car agencies' own sites, you might try comparing rates through a general travel booking site like **Expedia.com**, **Travelocity.com**, **Orbitz.com**, **Kayak.com**, or **Priceline.com**. This one-stop-shopping method can save you more than money — it can save you time too.

✔ **Don't rent a gas guzzler.** Renting a smaller car is cheaper, and you save on gas to boot (an especially important point, because gas prices are always higher in Hawaii than on the mainland). Unless you're traveling with a large group, don't go beyond the economy size.

See Chapter 6 for more money-saving tips to keep in mind while booking your island wheels.

✔ **Reserve a hotel room with a kitchenette, or a condo with a full kitchen, and do your own cooking.** You may miss the pampering that room service provides, but you can save lots of money, because restaurant prices are high in Hawaii even for casual eats. Even if you prepare only breakfast and an occasional picnic lunch in the kitchen, you'll save significantly in the long run. Plus, if the beach is right outside your door, you won't ever have to leave it to go on restaurant runs.

✔ **Skip the ocean views, or stay away from the ocean altogether.** Being steps away from the surf is wonderful, but you'll pay through the nose for the privilege: Oceanview rooms are the most expensive rooms in any hotel, especially those on the upper floors. Mountain or garden views are usually much cheaper — and they make sense if you don't plan on hanging out in your room much, anyway. A stay in a hotel that's located a few blocks from the beach, especially in Waikiki, can be even cheaper. For more on this subject, see Chapter 7.

✔ **Ask whether the kids can stay in your room.** Or, better yet, book a condo with a sleeper sofa in the living room or a separate bedroom. A room with two double beds usually doesn't cost any more than one with a king-size bed, and most hotels don't charge an extra-person rate if the additional person is a kid.

If that's a bit too much togetherness for you, book one of the many one-, two-, or three-bedroom condos that are available throughout the islands. These full apartments are often no more expensive than your standard hotel room — and they're always cheaper than having to book two or more hotel rooms. What's more, they solve the expensive eating-out-at-every-meal problem, too.

The AAA advantage

If you aren't already a member, consider taking a few minutes to join the American Automobile Association (AAA) before heading to Hawaii. In addition to providing you with a wealth of trip-planning services, membership can save you big bucks on hotel rates, car rentals, interisland airfares, and even admission to attractions in Hawaii.

The AAA Travel Agency can help you book air, hotel, and car arrangements as well as all-inclusive tour packages to Hawaii. Membership in AAA can also qualify you for hotel discounts of 10 percent or more. Discounts and benefits at 3,000 attractions and restaurants and 44,000 retail locations nationwide are available through AAA's Show Your Card and Save program. And don't forget the free maps — they're comprehensive, indispensable, and absolutely free to members.

Whether it's a discount at an Outrigger hotel or a stress-relieving flat-tire fix, membership will pay itself back before you know it. Annual membership fees vary slightly depending on your home region, but you can expect to spend around $45 per individual (primary member) and $23 to $26 for each additional family member. There is also a one-time $20 enrollment fee, which covers all who join in the family. Note that costs to join vary depending on the home state or region where you join.

To find the AAA office nearest you, look in the phone book under "AAA" or log on to www.aaa.com, where you can link up to your regional club's home page after you enter your home zip code. You can even get instant membership by calling the national 24-hour emergency roadside service number (☎ 800-AAA-HELP), which can connect you to any regional membership department during expanded business hours (only roadside assistance operates 24 hours a day). If you're a resident of Canada, similar services (plus reciprocal benefits with AAA) are offered by the Canadian Automobile Association (www.caa.ca).

After you arrive in Hawaii, the local office is in Honolulu at 1130 Nimitz Hwy., Ste. A-170 (☎ 800-736-2886 or 808-593-2221; www.aaa-hawaii.com). The office is open Monday through Friday from 9 a.m. to 5 p.m., and Saturday from 9 a.m. to 2 p.m. Roadside assistance is available on Oahu, Maui, the Big Island, and Kauai.

✔ **Remember that it doesn't take much luxury to make Hawaii feel like paradise.** To find true Hawaii happiness, the rule is always this: The simpler, the better. You don't need a 27-inch TV, 24-hour butler service, or a telephone in the bathroom to be happy here. So when reserving your accommodations, don't overdo it by booking a place that taxes your budget too much. Save that extra dough for having fun!

✔ **Skip the souvenirs.** I've heard it more than once: "That whale print that looked so right in the art gallery was all wrong back in my living room in Cincinnati." Spend your money on memories, not tchotchkes.

✔ **Look out for the Bargain Alert icon as you read this book.** This icon alerts you to money-saving opportunities and especially good values as you travel throughout Hawaii.

Handling Money

You're the best judge of how much cash you feel comfortable carrying or what alternative form of currency is your favorite. That's not going to change much on your vacation. True, you'll probably be moving around more and incurring more expenses than you generally do, and you may let your mind slip into vacation gear and not be as vigilant about your safety as when you're in work mode. But, those factors aside, the only type of payment that won't be quite as available to you away from home is your personal checkbook.

Using ATMs and carrying cash

The easiest and best way to get cash away from home is from an ATM (automated teller machine). The **MasterCard, Maestro,** or **Cirrus** (☎ 800-424-7787; www.mastercard.com) networks and **Visa PLUS** (☎ 800-843-7587; www.visa.com) network span the globe; look at the back of your bank card to see which network you're on and then call or check online for ATM locations at your destination. Make sure that you know your personal identification number (PIN) before you leave home and find out your daily withdrawal limit before you depart.

Also keep in mind that many banks impose a fee every time your card is used at a different bank's ATM. On top of this, the bank from which you withdraw cash may charge its own fee. (To compare banks' ATM fees within the U.S., use www.bankrate.com.) To beat these fees (and to avoid wasting precious vacation time running errands), it makes sense to withdraw larger sums rather than relying on lots of smaller withdrawals.

Charging ahead with credit cards

Credit cards are a safe way to carry money: They also provide a convenient record of all your expenses, and for foreign visitors, they generally offer relatively good exchange rates.

You can also withdraw cash advances from your credit cards at banks or ATMs, provided you know your PIN. If you've forgotten yours, or didn't even know you had one, call the number on the back of your credit card and ask the bank to send it to you. It usually takes five to seven business days, though some banks will provide the number over the phone if you tell them your mother's maiden name or some other personal information. But keep in mind that cash advances are a bad idea, only to be used in case of emergency. Your issuing bank will start charging interest from the day you make the withdrawal, usually at significantly higher rates than you're charged on regular purchases.

 Some credit card companies recommend that you notify them of any impending trip so that they don't become suspicious when the card is used numerous times in a new destination and block your charges. Even if you don't call your credit card company in advance, you can always call the card's toll-free emergency number if a charge is refused — another good reason to carry the phone number with you.

It's a good idea to carry more than one card with you on your trip; a card might not work for any number of reasons, so having a backup is the smart way to go.

Toting traveler's checks

These days, it's so easy to find a 24 hour ATM that traveler's checks are becoming obsolete. Furthermore, the popularity of credit cards means that businesses are less and less interested in accepting them. Still, if you like the security of traveler's checks, and you don't mind locating a bank and/or showing identification every time you want to cash one, you may prefer to stick with the tried-and-true.

You can get traveler's checks at almost any bank. **American Express** offers denominations of $20, $50, $100, $500, and (for cardholders only) $1,000. You pay a service charge ranging from 1 to 4 percent (which negates any money you might have saved by avoiding ATM fees while you're on the road). You can also get American Express traveler's checks over the phone by calling ☎ **800-221-7282;** Amex gold and platinum cardholders who use this number are exempt from the fee. Traveler's checks can also be ordered online at www.americanexpress.com.

Visa offers traveler's checks at Citibank locations nationwide, as well as at several other banks. The service charge ranges between 1.5 and 2 percent; checks come in denominations of $20, $50, $100, $500, and $1,000. Call ☎ **800-732-1322** for information. **AAA** members can obtain Visa checks without a fee at most AAA offices or by calling ☎ **866-339-3378.** **MasterCard** also offers traveler's checks. Call ☎ **800-223-9920** for a location near you.

 If you choose to carry traveler's checks, keep a record of their serial numbers separate from your checks in the event that they're stolen or lost. You'll get a refund faster if you know the numbers.

Dealing with a lost or stolen wallet

Be sure to contact all of your credit card companies the minute you discover that your wallet has been lost or stolen and file a report at the nearest police precinct. Your credit card company or insurer may require a police report number or record of the loss. Most credit card companies have an emergency toll-free number to call if your card is lost or stolen; they may be able to wire you a cash advance immediately or deliver an emergency credit card in a day or two. Call the following emergency numbers in the United States:

- ✔ **American Express:** ☎ **800-268-9824** or 800-528-4800 (for cardholders) and ☎ **800-221-7282** (for traveler's check holders)

- ✔ **MasterCard:** ☎ **800-307-7309** or 800-627-8372

- ✔ **Visa:** ☎ **800-847-2911** or 410-581-9994

For other credit cards, call the toll-free number directory at ☎ **800-555-1212.**

If you need emergency cash over the weekend when all banks and American Express offices are closed, you can have money wired to you via **Western Union** (☎ **800-325-6000;** www.westernunion.com).

Identity theft and fraud are potential complications of losing your wallet, especially if you've lost your driver's license along with your cash and credit cards. Notify the major credit-reporting bureaus immediately; placing a fraud alert on your records may protect you against liability for criminal activity. The three major U.S. credit-reporting agencies are **Equifax** (☎ **800-685-1111;** www.equifax.com), **Experian** (☎ **888-397-3742;** www.experian.com), and **TransUnion** (☎ **800-680-7289;** www.transunion.com).

Finally, if you've lost all forms of photo ID, call your airline and explain the situation; you may be allowed to board the plane if you have a copy of your passport or birth certificate and a copy of the police report you've filed.

Part II
Planning Your Trip to Hawaii

"Since we lost the dolphins, business hasn't been quite the same.

In this part . . .

The following chapters make the fine details of planning your trip to Hawaii pleasurable rather than painful. I show you how to get a handle on your expenses, help you weigh the pros and cons of buying a package deal, and walk you through booking your hotel and rental car. One chapter even offers savvy advice for travelers with special needs, whether you have a disability, you're traveling with little ones, or you're trying to plan a memorable Hawaiian wedding. Before this part ends, I also help you gather all the loose ends together into one organized bunch.

Chapter 5

Getting to Hawaii

. . . .

In This Chapter

▶ Finding the best airfares

▶ Considering a tour

▶ Taking advantage of package deals

. . . .

*G*etting there may not *really* be half the fun, but it's a necessary step — and a big part of the planning process. How can you beat the high cost of transpacific airfares? Should you reserve a package deal or book the elements of your vacation separately?

In this chapter, I give you all the information you need to make the decision that's right for you.

Flying to Hawaii

These days, nearly as many transpacific flights arrive at Maui's Kahului Airport as arrive at Oahu's Honolulu International Airport. Flights direct from the mainland now land on a daily basis on the Big Island and Kauai as well, which allows you to fly directly to and from the islands you want to visit with a minimum of hassle.

The following major airlines fly between mainland North America and one or more of Hawaii's major airports:

- ✔ **Air Canada** (☎ 888-247-2262; www.aircanada.com).

- ✔ **Alaska Airlines** (☎ 800-252-7522; www.alaskaair.com).

- ✔ **American Airlines** (☎ 800-433-7300; www.aa.com).

- ✔ **Continental Airlines** (☎ 800-523-3273; www.continental.com), which offers nonstop flights from New York (actually Newark) to Honolulu, among many other options.

- ✔ **Delta Airlines** (☎ 800-221-1212; www.delta.com).

- ✔ **Hawaiian Airlines** (☎ 800-367-5320; www.hawaiianair.com), which offers interisland flights in addition to transpacific service from the mainland and other international destinations.

✓ **Northwest Airlines** (☎ 800-225-2525; www.nwa.com), which has a codesharing agreement with Hawaiian Airlines for interisland flights.

✓ **United Airlines** (☎ 800-864-8331; www.united.com).

✓ **US Airways** (☎ 800-428-4322; www.usairways.com).

✓ **WestJet** (☎ 888-937-8538; www.westjet.com), which offers direct flights from Vancouver, Canada.

These days, an increasing number of airlines are charging all travelers except their elite customers an additional $25 per bag to check more than one piece of luggage per traveler. At this writing, United Airlines and US Airways had instituted this policy, and American Airlines has started charging $15 for *every* bag checked, even the first. I expect other carriers to follow suit. Therefore, I recommend contacting your airline and figuring out their checked baggage policy in advance so you can prepare accordingly.

No matter where you're coming from, it's bound to be a long haul to Hawaii. **SeatGuru** (www.seatguru.com) can help you choose the best seat available. The Web site features cabin diagrams for just about every carrier, with individual seat ratings, details on ergonomics, entertainment options, power outlet accessibility, and more.

Getting the best airfare

Competition among the major U.S. airlines is unlike that of any other industry. Every airline offers virtually the same product, yet prices can vary by hundreds of dollars.

Business travelers who need to purchase their tickets at the last minute, might change their itinerary at a moment's notice, or want to get home before the weekend pay the premium rate, known as the *full fare*. Passengers whose travel agendas are more flexible — who can book their tickets far in advance, who don't mind staying Saturday night, or who are willing to travel on a Tuesday, Wednesday, or Thursday — pay the least, usually a fraction of the full fare. On most flights to Hawaii, even the shortest hops, the full fare is more than $1,000, but you might be able to score an advance-purchase ticket from the West Coast for as low as $400. Obviously, I can't guarantee what the fares will be when you book — especially as oil prices continue to reach record highs and competition tightened after two transpacific carriers (Aloha Airlines and ATA) folded their wings for good in early 2008 — but you can almost always save big by planning ahead.

Keep your eye out in the newspaper, on the Internet, and on TV for airfare sales. Sale fares carry advance-purchase requirements and date-of-travel restrictions, but the price is usually worth the restrictions. The sales tend to take place in seasons of lower travel volume (usually spring and fall). You'll almost never see a sale around the peak summer vacation months or in the winter high season.

Here are a few tips that can help you save on airfares:

✔ **Travel on off days of the week.** Airfares vary depending on the day of the week. Everybody wants to travel on the weekend; if you can travel on a Tuesday, Wednesday, or Thursday, you may find cheaper flights to Hawaii. When you inquire about airfares, check to see whether you can get a cheaper rate by flying on a different day. Remember, too, that staying over on a Saturday night may cut your airfare.

✔ **Reserve your flight well in advance.** Take advantage of advance-purchase fares. Sometimes you can snag a last-minute bargain, but I wouldn't count on it. Airfares only get higher as the planes fill up. More often than not, the farther ahead you book, the lower your airfare is likely to be.

✔ **Fly direct to the island of your choice to save on interisland airfares.** The Big Island, Maui, and Kauai all receive direct flights from the mainland. (See the list of carriers in the section "Flying to Hawaii," earlier in this chapter.) While it all depends on the transpacific carrier you choose and your origination point, it's increasingly easy to fly across the Pacific Ocean to or from the neighbor island of your choice, and doing so can save you a few hours, not to mention the additional cost of an interisland flight (see Chapter 6).

✔ **Book online.** In an effort to encourage you to book on their Web sites, most of the major air carriers will charge you a fee — anywhere from $5 to $20 per ticket — to buy your tickets over the phone or in person at ticket offices. Therefore, booking your ticket online at the airline's Web site is usually going to be the cheapest way to buy direct.

Booking your flight online

The big one-stop online travel agencies — **Expedia** (www.expedia.com), **Travelocity** (www.travelocity.com), **Orbitz** (www.orbitz.com), **Hotwire** (www.hotwire.com), and **Yahoo Travel** (www.travel.yahoo.com) are excellent sources for one-stop price comparing across all of the major airlines. (Canadian travelers should try www.expedia.ca and www.travelocity.ca; U.K. residents can go for expedia.co.uk, www.travelocity.co.uk, and opodo.co.uk.) Each has different business deals with the airlines and may offer different fares on the same flights, so shopping around is wise. Expedia and Travelocity will also send you an **e-mail notification** when a cheap fare becomes available to your favorite destination. All of these online travel agencies also purport to save you money with pay-one-price packaging, although I suggest comparing the prices of each piece before you assume that you're saving.

Kayak.com (www.kayak.com) is also gaining popularity and uses a sophisticated search engine developed at MIT to search probably the widest breadth of online resources available to find the best available fare. Kayak is a search engine, not an online travel agency, so once you identify the best fare, they will link you directly to the source to book it. They also have a "fare alerts" tool that will allow you to track fare prices through an e-mail notification system. **SideStep** (www.sidestep.com) works in a similar fashion, and receives good reviews from users.

Newest on the scene is **Farecast** (www.farecast.com), an online travel agency designed to help you buy your tickets with confidence, knowing that you're getting the best deal available. Farecast's airfare prediction tool tracks whether fares are rising or dropping; based on these predictions, the site will let you know whether to buy now or wait. They'll also compare their prices to those available on such sites as Expedia and Hotwire. With these valuable features, it's no wonder that *Time* magazine named Farecast one of its "50 Coolest Sites."

Attention, spontaneous travelers: You can sometimes find great last-minute deals through **Smarter Travel** (www.smartertravel.com), which compiles a comprehensive list of bargain-basement fares available from the airlines and the online agencies looking to fill those final empty seats.

Of course, some of the best fares are available through **Priceline** (www.priceline.com), especially if you're willing to play their "Name Your Own Price" game in which you "bid" for a rock-bottom price — and it's yours if an airline accepts it. You won't know who the carrier is until after you buy, and you may have an out-of-the-way connection (or two). Still, the inconveniences can be minimal compared to the savings. The mystery airlines are all major, well-known carriers, and the possibility of being sent from Phoenix to Honolulu via Tampa is remote. Priceline now offers standard online airfare shopping services as well.

Also remember to check the airlines' own Web sites. Even if you find a good fare from one of the services listed above, you can often shave off a few bucks by booking directly through the airline, which won't have to pay an intermediary for your business. Many airlines have special Internet-only fares that their phone agents don't even know about.

Attention **UPromise** members: Those of you who use this online rewards service to save for your kids' college education (or to pay your own bills) can earn cash-back rewards (usually 1 to 2 percent of the purchase price) by booking airfares and other travel reservations via Expedia, Travelocity, and a wealth of other travel partners when accessed through the UPromise portal (www.upromise.com). If you're not a member but there's someone in your life paying for college, visit the site to sign up.

Consolidators, also known as bucket shops, can be a good place to find low fares, sometimes below even the airlines' discounted rates. Basically, these companies are just big travel agents that get discounts for buying in bulk and pass some of the savings on to you. These days, however, it's a rare day to get a fare through a consolidator that you can't get through mainstream sources like Expedia — or even the airlines themselves — so be sure to price compare. Bucket shop tickets are usually nonrefundable or rigged with stiff cancellation penalties, and some put you on charter airlines you've never heard of — so be sure you know all of the ins and outs before you buy.

Some of the most reliable consolidators include the following:

- ✔ **Cheap Tickets** (☎ **800-504-3249;** www.cheaptickets.com). I usually do better by calling than I do by pricing out fares on its Web site.

- ✔ **STA Travel** (☎ **800-781-4040;** www.statravel.com), the world's leader in student travel, offers good fares for travelers of all ages.

Joining an Escorted Tour

Hawaii is such a foolproof place to visit — and its magic is so dependent on relaxing leisure time — that I strongly recommend traveling on your own. If you really prefer to be led around, however, or if you're not able to drive yourself, you may want to consider an escorted tour.

If you decide to go with an escorted tour, buying travel insurance is a good idea, especially if the tour operator asks to you pay upfront (most do). But don't buy your coverage from the tour operator! If the tour operator doesn't fulfill its obligation to provide you with the vacation you paid for, there's no reason to think that it'll fulfill its insurance obligations either. Get travel insurance through an independent agency. (See Chapter 9 for the details on travel insurance.)

Always ask a few simple questions before you buy:

- ✔ **What is the cancellation policy?** Can the tour operator cancel the trip if it doesn't get enough people? How late can you cancel if you're unable to go? Do you get a refund if you cancel? What if the operator cancels?

- ✔ **How jampacked is the schedule?** Does the tour schedule give you ample time to relax by the pool or shop? If getting up at 7 a.m. every day and not returning to your hotel until 6 or 7 p.m. sounds like a grind, certain escorted tours may not be for you.

- ✔ **How large is the group?** The smaller the group, the less time you spend waiting for people to get on and off the bus.

- ✔ **What exactly is included?** Don't assume anything. You may have to pay to get yourself to and from the airport. A box lunch may be included in an excursion, but drinks may be extra.

- ✔ **How much flexibility do you have?** Can you opt out of certain activities, or does the bus leave once a day, with no exceptions? Are all your meals planned in advance?

The escorted trips offered by **Tauck Tours** (☎ **800-788-7885;** www. tauck.com) are far more luxurious and less structured than your average escorted tour; they're pricey, but worth it if you'd rather put someone else in charge of the itinerary. If you're looking for more afford-able options, try sister companies **Globus** (☎ 866-755-8581; www. globusjourneys.com) and **Cosmos** (☎ 800-276-1241; www.cosmos vacations.com). Globus offers more luxurious vacations, including a combination cruise/tour option, whereas Cosmos is more bargain ori-ented. Both are excellent companies. **Perillo Tours** (☎ 800-431-1515; www.perillotours.com) also offers midpriced multi-island tours.

Cruising to Hawaii

Cruising to and around Hawaii isn't my favorite way to explore and enjoy the islands, but many cruise fans disagree. If you're interested in the cruising options, check with **Carnival** (☎ 800-CARNIVAL [227-6482]; www.carnival.com); **Celebrity Cruises** (☎ 877-202-4345; www. celebritycruises.com); **Royal Caribbean** (☎ 866-562-7625; www. royalcaribbean.com); **Norwegian Cruise Line** (☎ 866-234-7350; www.ncl.com); **Princess Cruises** (☎ 800-PRINCESS [774-6237]; www. princess.com); and **Holland America Line** (☎ 877-932-4259; www. hollandamerica.com). All offer cruises to the Hawaiian Islands.

Choosing a Pay-One-Price Package

Comprehensive, pay-one-price travel packages can be a smart way to go when booking your Hawaii vacation. Besides the convenience of having all your travel needs taken care of at once, a package can often save you lots of money. In many cases, a package that includes airfare, hotel, and transportation to and from the airport costs less than the hotel alone if you book it yourself.

One reason for this savings is that components of the packages are sold in bulk to tour operators, travel agents, and resellers, who bundle and sell them to the public. Even after the packager takes its cut, you may still realize substantial savings.

Package trips can vary widely. Some offer a better class of hotels than others; others provide the same hotels for lower prices. Some book flights on scheduled airlines; others sell charters.

Every destination, including Hawaii, usually has a few packagers that are better than the rest because they buy in even bigger bulk. The time you spend shopping around is likely to be well rewarded.

Finding a package deal

The Internet is probably your best source for package deals. Check out **Expedia** (www.expedia.com), **Travelocity** (www.travelocity.com), **Yahoo Travel** (www.travel.yahoo.com), **Hotwire** (www.hotwire.com), and **Orbitz** (www.orbitz.com), which have become some of the most sophisticated and easy-to-access pay-one-price packagers in the market.

Liberty Travel (call ☎ 888-271-1584; www.libertytravel.com) is one of the biggest packagers in the Northeast. Liberty frequently offers excellent-value packages, with or without air, to all the Hawaiian islands — and its agents are willing to help you construct a multi-island trip. Calling the toll-free number immediately connects you to the Liberty Travel store nearest your home.

Pleasant Holidays (☎ 800-742-9244; www.pleasantholidays.com), the biggest and most comprehensive packager to Hawaii, has more than 40 years of experience and offers tons of package options. Pleasant can arrange just about any kind of vacation you want, including fly/drive packages and land-only deals. And because it buys airfares and hotel-room blocks in such bulk, its deals are often excellent (although it offers better bargains on some properties than others). Another plus is that Pleasant maintains service desks on all the major islands; its employees can help you book activities and answer any questions you may have. These guys can even finance your vacation for you — but be sure to check the interest rates.

If you want to work with a travel agency that specializes in booking packaged Hawaii vacations, offers a more personalized shopping experience, books at all price levels, and really knows its stuff, contact Melissa McCoy's Maui-based **Aloha Destinations Vacations** (☎ 800-256-4280 or 213-784-6143; www.alohadestinations.com).

Be aware that some travel packagers — including Pleasant Hawaiian Holidays— are likely to book you on their own charter flights rather than on commercial flights on major airlines. It doesn't really make a difference, unless you have a particular allegiance to a specific airline (or to collecting miles in a frequent-flier program). Be sure that you know which airline you're flying when you book. And if you really do want to fly with a specific airline, that doesn't rule out a packager. In fact, Pleasant has established relationships with such major carriers as Delta, United, and Hawaiian — and just about any packager will be happy to book you a land-only vacation that lets you arrange your own airfare (even the airline packagers will do this; see the upcoming list).

Uncovering an airline package

Many major airlines also offer travel packages to Hawaii, either directly or through a trusted package partner. I always recommend comparison shopping, but you may want to choose the airline that has frequent service to your hometown or the one on which you accumulate frequent-flier miles; you may even be able to pay for your entire package using accumulated miles. The following airlines offer travel packages to Hawaii as part of their services:

- ✔ **Air Canada Vacations** (☎ 866-529-2079; www.aircanada vacations.com)

- ✔ **American Airlines Vacations** (☎ 800-321-2121; www.aa vacations.com)

- ✔ **Continental Airlines Vacations** (☎ 800-301-3800; www.co vacations.com)

- ✔ **Delta Vacations** (☎ 800-654-6559; www.deltavacations.com)

- ✔ **Hawaiian Airlines** (☎ 800-236-5451 or 808-356-8040; www. hawaiianair.com, click on "Vacation Packages")

- ✔ **Northwest WorldVacations** (☎ 800-800-1504; www.nwaworld vacations.com)

- ✔ **United Vacations** (☎ 888-854-3899; www.unitedvacations.com)

- ✔ **US Airways Vacations** (☎ 888-455-0123; www.usairways vacations.com)

Choosing between a travel agent and a packager isn't an either/or proposition; in fact, your travel agent can be your best source in sorting through the various deals that are available. If you're an AmEx customer, you may consider going through **American Express Travel Service,** which can book a full variety of travel packages for you. To locate the office (or official travel-agent representative) nearest you, call ☎ 800-335-3342 or go online to www.americanexpress.com and select "Travel"; you can also book your vacation completely online, and even pay with Membership Rewards.

Ditto for members of the American Automobile Association, who have access to the **AAA Travel Agency,** which can also book good-value package deals. Visit www.aaa.com or call ☎ 877-934-6222 to book your reservations or to find the regional office nearest you.

Weighing your options

With the multitude of packages on the market, you may need some help weighing the various merits of each one. Follow these tips as you sift your way through the options:

- ✔ **Read up on Hawaii.** Read through the hotel listings in this book and select the places that sound interesting. Compare the rates that I list with the packagers' prices to gauge which operators are really offering a good deal and which have simply gussied up the rack rates to make their full-fare offer sound like a smart buy. Remember, most packagers can offer bigger savings on some properties than on others. For example, Liberty Travel may give you a much better rate on Waikiki's Royal Hawaiian, say, than Pleasant Holidays can, but Pleasant may offer you a substantial savings on the Maui condo that you want.

✔ **Compare apples to apples.** When comparing packages, make sure that you know *exactly* what's included in the quoted price, and what's not. Don't assume anything: Some packagers include everything — including value-added extras like lei greetings, free continental breakfast, and dining discounts — and others don't even include airfare. Additionally, when considering package prices, be sure to factor in add-on costs if you're flying from somewhere other than Los Angeles or San Francisco — some operators price packages directly from your hometown, and some require additional premiums for airfares from your hometown to their Los Angeles or San Francisco gateway.

✔ **Before you commit to a package, make sure that you know how much flexibility you have.** Some packagers require ironclad commitments, but others charge only minimal fees for changes or cancellations. Consider the possibility that your travel plans may change and select a packager with the degree of flexibility that suits your needs. And if you pay upfront for a complete vacation package that carries stiff cancellation penalties, consider buying travel insurance that will reimburse you in case an unforeseen emergency prevents you from traveling. (See Chapter 9 for more on this topic.)

✔ **Don't believe in fairy tales.** Unfortunately, shady dealers and fly-by-night operations are out there. If a package appears too good to be true, it probably is. Any knowledgeable travel agent should be able to help you determine whether a specific packager is on the level.

Chapter 6

Getting Around Hawaii

• •

In This Chapter
▶ Traveling from island to island on interisland carriers
▶ Renting a car — and considering a convertible

• •

*T*he island chapters later in this book explain the specifics of navigating your way around individual islands, but in this chapter I give you the lowdown on traveling between them and also on how to book and save money on car rentals — and you'll almost certainly want to have a car during your trip.

Flying between the Hawaiian Islands

The primary way to travel from island to island is by airplane.

An interisland high-speed catamaran ferry service called **Hawaii Superferry** (☎ 877-443-3779; www.hawaiisuperferry.com) was introduced in 2007. In theory, the service is a great idea, allowing locals and visitors alike to ferry between the islands with their cars and luggage. However, service has been intermittent at best since launching, and was temporarily suspended at this writing. Even when it resumes, only one ferry a day each way between Oahu and Maui was slated. For now, until service can get on a steady track, I recommend sticking with the airlines.

Despite the fact that it's a short and easy shuttle hop between islands — even the longest island-to-island flight clocks in around 45 minutes — it's vital to book in advance. The airlines request that you show up at least 90 minutes before your flight to allow for security inspections, and I've found that to be good advice.

Three interisland carriers serve the islands: Hawaiian Airlines and go!, the upstart carrier operated by Mesa Airlines, carry the bulk of travelers between the islands, while Island Air offers supplemental service, usually between Hawaii's smaller airports. (Aloha Airlines filed for Chapter 11 bankruptcy and halted all service in early 2008, citing skyrocketing fuel and predatory pricing by go! as the pressures that forced Aloha's hand.) Both Hawaiian and go! offer similar schedules — flights between the major islands every hour or so — at competitive prices.

Hawaiian Airlines (☎ 800-367-5320; www.hawaiianair.com) offers interisland jet service aboard Boeing 717-200s; the entire fleet was replaced with brand-new aircraft in 2001, making this the youngest fleet in the Pacific.

 Hawaiian is mileage partners with American Airlines, US Airways, Continental, Delta, Northwest, and Virgin Atlantic airlines, which gives you plenty of mileage-earning potential. They don't make it easy to enter another airline's frequent flier number online, however, so you may need to call to get the appropriate credit.

Island Air (☎ 800-652-6541 or 808-484-2222; www.islandair.com), operates deHavilland DASH-8 and DASH-6 aircraft and serves Hawaii's smaller interisland airports on Maui (Kapalua Airport), Molokai, and Lanai, as well as both Hilo and Kona on the Big Island. You may find yourself on a codeshare flight operated by Island Air if you head to Molokai or Lanai, even if you buy through Hawaiian.

At press time, the full interisland fare was about $109 per one-way segment, depending on the dates and routes you want to fly. (At this writing, experts were forecasting price increases in the wake of lightened competition resulting from Aloha's disappearance, so don't be surprised if you see higher fares.) Booking more than 14 days in advance gives you the best shot at a bargain fare. I recommend price comparing for the best deal.

If you're traveling on a package, you probably don't have to worry about any of this — your interisland flights are most likely included in your package deal, on whichever interisland carrier the packager is affiliated with. For more on all-inclusive travel packages, see Chapter 5.

Arranging for Rental Cars

In order to maximize your time on each of the islands, you need to rent a car. The only island where you can go without a car is Oahu, but you'll be stuck in Waikiki and will be dependent on public transportation.

 Unfortunately, traffic has become an increasing problem on all of the neighbor islands, especially in the prime resort areas. Throughout this book I guide you past traffic hot spots whenever possible.

All the big companies — Alamo, Avis, Budget, Dollar, Enterprise, Hertz, National, and Thrifty — rent cars on all the major Hawaiian Islands. See the Quick Concierge at the back of this book for phone numbers and Web sites.

 Be sure to book your rental cars well ahead. Rental cars are almost always at a premium on Kauai, Molokai, and Lanai and may be sold out on all of the neighbor islands on holiday weekends.

For tips on renting hand-controlled cars or vans equipped with wheel-chair lifts, see Chapter 8.

Getting the best deal

Rental cars are quite affordable in Hawaii, although rates do vary from island to island and from season to season. Of course, I can't guarantee what you'll pay when you book, but you can often get an economy or compact car for between $125 and $250 a week. If you want a family-size car — or a convertible — expect to pay anywhere from $225 to $450 a week, which is still pretty reasonable, especially if you can score a deal. Book ahead for the best rates, as cars tend to only get more expensive as bookings increase.

Car-rental rates vary even more than airline fares. The price depends on the size of the car, the length of time you keep it, where and when you pick it up and drop it off, where you take it, and a host of other factors. Asking a few key questions may save you hundreds of dollars:

✔ **Mention membership in AAA, AARP, and frequent-flier programs when booking.** These memberships may qualify you for discounts ranging from 5 to 30 percent.

✔ **Ask the reservations agency that books your hotel or your inter-island air travel if it also books rental cars.** Many hotels, condo rental agents, and even B&B owners can book rental cars at seri-ously discounted rates; ditto for the interisland air carriers. (See the section "Flying between the Hawaiian Islands," earlier in this chapter.) Often, you can save as much as 30 percent off the stan-dard rate. And many Hawaii hotels and condos offer excellent-value room-and-car packages that make your rental essentially free!

✔ **Shop online.** As with other aspects of planning your trip, using the Internet can make comparison shopping for a car rental much easier. You can check rates at most of the major agencies' Web sites. Plus, all the major travel sites — **Travelocity.com**, **Expedia.com**, **Orbitz.com**, **Priceline.com**, **Hotwire.com**, **Kayak.com**, and **Yahoo Travel** (www.travel.yahoo.com), for example — have search engines that can dig up discounted car-rental rates for you.

✔ **If you see an advertised special, ask for that specific rate when booking.** The car-rental company may not offer this information voluntarily. Make sure to remind them; otherwise, you may be charged the standard (higher) rate.

✔ **Get some friendly help from the locals. AAA Aloha Cars-R-Us** (☎ **800-655-7989;** www.hawaiicarrental.com) is a Hawaii-based travel agency that specializes exclusively in car rentals on all of the islands. These folks are dedicated to the task of getting you the cheapest rate from the major car-rental firms — and making it easy to boot. They combine custom Internet searches utilizing any avail-able discounts you may be eligible for (including association and program memberships) with their exclusive wholesale contract rates to find you the best rate possible. Best of all, there's no fee for using their service.

✔ **Consider booking your car as part of a complete travel package.** Package deals save you dollars not only on airfare and accommodations but also on your rental cars. This one-stop shopping can help streamline the trip-planning process. For more on package deals, see Chapter 5.

✔ **Scrutinize your rental agreement when you pick up your car.** And check your receipt carefully when you return the vehicle. Make sure you get the rate you were originally quoted — and straighten out any discrepancy on the spot.

✔ **Don't forget to ask about frequent-flier mileage.** Most car rentals are worth at least 500 miles on your frequent-flier account. Be sure to find out which airlines the rental-car company is affiliated with so that you can earn mileage. Bring your card with you, and make sure that your account is credited at pickup time.

✔ **Join the rental company's preferred customer program.** Most companies offer such promotions. You may be able to snag a bargain rate or have a better shot at an upgrade if you're a member. Some companies make the process of picking up your car more hassle-free for members, too. And membership can work just like the airlines' frequent-flier plans: Renting from the same company several times can land you a free day or other perks.

✔ **Make sure that you're getting free unlimited mileage.** Thankfully, most of the major car-rental companies rent on an unlimited-miles basis, but you should confirm this policy when you book. Even on an island, the miles you drive can really add up.

✔ **Find out whether age is an issue.** Many car-rental companies add on a fee for drivers under 25, whereas some don't rent to them at all.

 Some companies assess a drop-off charge of around $50 if you don't return the car to the location where you rented it; others (such as National) don't. (However, that extra charge may be embedded in a higher rate — so check closely.) This fee may be an issue on the Big Island, where you might want to fly into Kona Airport, on one side of the island, and leave from Hilo, on the other side (or vice versa), so ask when you book.

In addition to the standard rental prices, other optional charges apply to most car rentals (and some not-so-optional charges, such as taxes). The *Collision Damage Waiver* (CDW), which requires you to pay for damage to the car in a collision, is automatically covered by many credit card companies. Check with your credit card company before you leave home so that you can avoid paying this hefty fee (as much as $20 to $25 a day). In any event, make sure that you're covered (see the section "Following the rules of the road," later in this chapter; Hawaii is a no-fault state, which has important insurance implications).

The car-rental companies also offer additional *liability insurance* (if you harm others in an accident), *personal accident insurance* (if you harm yourself or your passengers), and *personal effects insurance* (if your luggage is stolen from your car). Your car insurance policy back home probably covers most of these unlikely occurrences. However, don't just assume it will — be sure to check before you leave home, and carry your insurance card with you.

If your own insurance doesn't cover you for rentals or if you don't have auto insurance, definitely consider the additional coverage (ask your car-rental agent for more information). See the Quick Concierge at the back of this book for phone numbers and Web sites. You can probably skip the personal effects insurance, but driving around without liability coverage is never a good idea. Note that credit cards will not cover you for liability, even if they cover you for collision.

Some companies also offer *refueling packages,* in which you pay for your initial full tank of gas upfront and can return the car with an empty gas tank. The prices can be competitive with local gas prices, but you don't get credit for any gas remaining in the tank. If you reject this option, you pay only for the gas you use, but you have to return the car with a full tank or face charges of $6 or more per gallon for any shortfall. If you usually run late and a fueling stop may make you miss your plane, you're a perfect candidate for the fuel-purchase option, but for most people, it's not much of a hardship to top off your tank on the way to the airport.

Hawaii how-to: Renting convertibles

Renting a convertible is a lot like booking an oceanview room. It's a great idea if you can afford it, but not worth it if it's going to put a strain on your budget. The cost of going topless can be double or more what you'd pay for a regular car. Expect to pay between $50 and $90 a day for a convertible, compared with $30 or $40 a day for a better equipped mid-size car (with such extras as power windows and power locks that don't usually come with convertibles).

If you really want to rent a convertible for your island driving but you're worried about cost, consider renting a convertible for just part of your trip or just one island if you're going to be visiting two or three of them. Think about Maui, where cruising the road to Hana with the top down really is the ultimate Hawaii vacation dream. Going topless on Oahu is pretty great, too, especially if you're planning to cruise to the North Shore.

If you've rented a regular car, ask about an upgrade when you pick up your car. This may prove especially beneficial if you're visiting in the off season. Sometimes, if a rental-car branch has a few idle convertibles sitting around, you may be offered an on-the-spot upgrade for just $10 or $15 more a day.

Following the rules of the road

Know these driving rules and common practices before you get behind the wheel in Hawaii:

- ✔ **Hawaii is a no-fault insurance state.** If you drive without collision-damage insurance, you're required to pay for all damages before you leave the state, regardless of who is at fault. Your personal auto policy may provide rental-car coverage; read your policy or check with your insurer before you leave home, and be sure to bring your insurance ID card if you decline the rental-car company's optional insurance. Some credit card companies also provide collision damage insurance; check with yours.

- ✔ **Seatbelts are mandatory for everyone in the car, all the time.** The law is strictly enforced, so be sure to buckle up. Hawaii's Child Passenger Restraint Law requires children under 4 years old to ride in a child safety seat.

- ✔ **You can turn right on red unless a posted sign specifies otherwise.** Make sure that you make a full stop first — no rolling.

- ✔ **Pedestrians always have the right of way.** This is true even if they're not on a crosswalk.

- ✔ **Use your horn judiciously.** Honking your horn to express your anger at another driver is considered the height of rudeness in Hawaii. Don't do it unless you're alerting someone to immediate danger. Horns are used to greet friends in Hawaii.

Do *not* use your rental car as a safe in which to store valuables. Don't leave anything that you don't want to lose in the car or trunk, not even for a short time. Be especially careful when you park at beaches, where thieves know that you're going to leave your car for a while (and you're likely to leave goodies in the glove compartment).

The islands are very easy to negotiate, and all the rental-car companies hand out very good map booklets on each island. If all you have is what National or Hertz gives you, you'll do just fine.

Chapter 7

Booking Your Accommodations

*H*awaii's resort hotels are notoriously expensive. Hotels won't hesitate to charge $350 a night for a partial-oceanview room with little more than a queen-size bed in it. To make matters worse, Hawaii is currently experiencing a popularity boom, and hotel rates have responded accordingly. So prepare yourself for the fact that accommodations may take up a large portion of your total travel budget.

That said, the islands boast plenty of excellent values for every budget if you just know where to look — and I include lots of reasonably priced options in the chapters that follow. For general tips on how to save, check out Chapter 4.

Getting to Know Your Options

Before you book your accommodations, you need to figure out what kind of place you want. You can find five types of accommodations in the islands: resorts, hotels, condos, bed-and-breakfasts, and vacation rentals. Table 7-1 gives you an idea of what you can expect to pay in each price category.

Table 7-1	Key to Hotel Dollar Signs*	
Dollar Sign(s)	*Price Range*	*What to Expect*
$	Less than $150 per night	Cheap — a basic hotel room a distance from the beach
$$	$150–$225	Still affordable — midpriced hotel room or condo, possibly near the beach

Dollar Sign(s)	Price Range	What to Expect
$$$	$225–$325	Moderate — a good-quality hotel room or condo on or near the beach, or a luxury bed-and-breakfast
$$$$	$325–$450	Expensive but not ridiculous — a high-quality room in a full-service hotel, or a multibedroom condo, on or near the beach
$$$$$	More than $450 per night	Ultraluxurious — the ultimate in deluxe resort living, generally on the beach

*Each range of dollar signs, from one ($) to five ($$$$$), represents the median rack-rate price range for a double room per night. This system applies to each resort, hotel, condo, or B&B.

Relaxing at a resort

Most resorts (or resort hotels) are multiacre, multibuilding complexes located directly on the beach. Some are sophisticated, ultraluxury affairs geared to well-off adults; others are theme park–like spreads that cater largely to families with kids. More than a few resorts fall somewhere in between the two extremes.

A resort (or resort hotel) offers everything that your average hotel offers — plus much more. Each one is different, of course, but you can expect such amenities as direct beach access, with beach cabanas and chairs, and often beach-toy rentals and ocean activities as well; pools (often more than one), often with poolside bar service; an activities desk; a fitness center and perhaps a full-service spa; a variety of restaurants, bars, and lounges; a 24-hour front desk; concierge, valet, and bell services; twice-daily maid service (which can come in handy after you've dragged sand into your room and used all your towels by 4 p.m.); room service; tennis and golf; a business center; extensive children's programs; and more comforts.

Rooms may be in high-rise towers, but they're often scattered throughout the property in low-rise buildings or clustered cottages. They tend to be done in the same safe, mass-market style throughout the resort — generally, room 101 is going to look exactly like room 1901. As travelers increasingly demand more, however, many newer properties (and savvy new renovations) feature smart, high-style concepts that are intended to heighten the resort's unique setting, concept, or personality. Standards tend to be high, and rooms are usually outfitted with top-quality furnishings and linens. Many luxury resorts also boast an increasing slate of in-room extras, such as flatscreen TVs with Nintendo or other gaming systems, iPod docking units for in-suite music, and DVD players. Internet access is usually present throughout the property, but often you'll find wireless only in the public areas; expect to pay a charge more often than not.

Being the best outfitted, and usually the best located, of Hawaii's accommodations options, resorts are also the priciest choices on the market, although the islands do boast a few midrange resorts. That said, you can sometimes score attractive rates, even at some of the islands' most luxurious resorts. You may hit pay dirt by booking through a packager (see Chapter 5), or just by hitting the reservations line or online booking engine at the right time. Most resorts also offer specials and package deals on their own Web sites.

Hanging at a hotel

Hotels tend to be smaller and have fewer facilities than resorts — you may get a swimming pool, but don't expect a golf course, more than one or two restaurants and/or bars, or the myriad amenities that come with a full-fledged resort. You'll find the greatest number of nonresort hotels in Waikiki, where the shoulder-to-shoulder urban setting simply hasn't allowed for much full-fledged resort development.

Hotels are often a short walk from the beach rather than beachfront (although some, like the Westin Moana Surfrider in Waikiki, are right on the sand). Generally, a hotel offers daily maid service and has a restaurant and/or coffee shop, a bar or lounge, on-site laundry facilities, a swimming pool, and a sundries or convenience-type shop (rather than designer shopping arcades). Top hotels also have activities desks, concierge and valet services, limited room service, a business center, and in-room Internet access (more often than not for a daily charge).

"Boutique" hotels are smaller — maybe 40 or 50 rooms rather than 200 or more — and more intimate than your average Doubletree or Hilton. The rooms are often more stylish and less cookie-cutter and usually have more amenities. They tend to cater to adults rather than families. Again, Hawaii's boutique-hotel boom is centered in Waikiki.

Hotels run the gamut from very expensive to downright cheap. But even the priciest ones tend to be less expensive than fully outfitted resorts.

Enjoying the comforts of a B&B

Staying in a bed-and-breakfast allows you to discover Hawaii's genuine aloha spirit. More often than not, B&Bs offer a more intimate, and often more romantic, setting than your average resort, as well as a host who's more than happy to help you get to know Hawaii as it really is. If you want to experience a real slice of island life, B&Bs are the way to go.

B&Bs vary widely in size, style, and services. Generally speaking, they're composed of several bedrooms in a home or several cottages or suites scattered about a property, each of which may or may not have a private bathroom. (*Note:* All the B&Bs that I recommend in the accommodations chapters that follow have units with private bathrooms.) Most offer Internet access to laptop-toters, but I've found that their networks are not as reliable as those at the big hotels, so book with a name brand if you *must* be online.

I recommend contacting one or more of the following agencies if you're considering a stay at a B&B:

✔ Tops in the state is **Hawaii's Best Bed & Breakfasts** (☎ 800-262-9912 or 808-263-3100; www.bestbnb.com). The owners and staff are committed to representing only quality B&Bs, inns, and vacation rentals, and they're not afraid to say "no" to any property that doesn't meet their standards. They represent only accommodations with private bathrooms, and all are nonsmoking. Some of their units are free-standing cottages that resemble vacation homes more than B&Bs; they even represent a few really nice condos. Note that their bed-and-breakfasts generally have a three-night minimum stay, and vacation rentals tend to require a seven-night minimum stay.

✔ **Bed & Breakfast Hawaii** (☎ 800-733-1632 or 808-822-7771; www.bandb-hawaii.com) can also book you into a range of vacation homes and B&Bs throughout the islands, with prices starting at $65 a night.

✔ You don't get the same personal service from the Web, but you can find lots of useful resources there. **InnSite** (www.innsite.com) features B&B listings in all 50 U.S. states, including Hawaii, and around the globe. Find an inn on the island of your choice, see pictures of the rooms, and check prices and availability; text is included only when the proprietor submits it. (It's free to have an inn listed.) The innkeepers write the descriptions, and many listings link to the inn's own Web sites. What's more, you may be able to score an additional discount by booking your reservation through InnSite.

✔ Other sites that are worth surfing for Hawaii B&Bs are **BedandBreakfast.com** (www.bedandbreakfast.com) and **Bed & Breakfast Inns Online** (www.bbonline.com).

Rooming in a vacation rental

"Vacation rental" usually means that you have a full cottage or house all to yourself. You may never even see an owner, agent, or manager after you pick up the keys. This option is great for families or people who like their space and privacy or don't want to eat every meal out at a restaurant.

The rental may be a studio cottage in a residential neighborhood, a condo, or a huge beachfront multibedroom house — or anything in between. Vacation rentals usually have some sort of kitchen facilities (ask when booking), laundry facilities, at least one TV, and at least one phone. Because vacation rentals are often privately owned homes, they also may come with such extras as TV, DVD player, and stereo (never assume; always ask, if it matters to you). Like condos, many come outfitted with the basics, such as sheets or towels.

Vacation rentals vary greatly in price depending on their size, location, and amenities. They tend to be much better values than similarly priced resort or hotel accommodations, especially if you're trying to accommodate a group or plan a long stay (a week or more). Just make sure that you get a 24-hour contact person for those times when the toilet won't flush or you can't turn on the air-conditioning.

Hawaii's Best Bed & Breakfasts (see "Enjoying the comforts of a B&B" earlier in this chapter) is useful for statewide vacation rentals. A statewide source that's also worth checking out is **Hawaii Beachfront Vacation Homes** (☎ **808-247-3637;** www.hibeach.com).

Hawaii Condo Exchange (☎ **800-442-0404** or 323-436-0300; www.hawaii condoexchange.com) is a Southern California–based agency that acts as a consolidator for condo properties throughout the islands. The agency works to match you up with the place that's right for you and tries to get you a good deal in the bargain.

You can cut out the middle man and rent directly from the owner at a number of quality condo resorts throughout the islands by visiting **Aloha Condos Hawaii** (www.alohacondos.com), an online cooperative of owner-managed units.

You'll also find that most companies that offer all-inclusive travel packages to the islands can book you into any number of island condos, as can your travel agent.

Finding the Best Room Rate

The **rack rate** is the maximum rate a hotel charges for a room. It's the rate you get if you walk in off the street and ask for a room for the night. You sometimes see these rates printed on the fire/emergency exit diagrams posted on the back of your door.

Hotels are happy to charge you the rack rate, but you can almost always do better. Perhaps the best way to avoid paying the rack rate is simple: Just ask for a cheaper or discounted rate. You may be pleasantly surprised. But you have to take the initiative and *ask,* because many hotels bank on the fact that you'll just accept the first rate you're quoted. You should also chat with the reservations agent about which rooms are the best and which units match your needs. You never know what kind of insider advice or upgrade can be won by just asking a question and turning on the charm.

In all but the smallest accommodations, the rate you pay for a room depends on many factors — chief among them being how you make your reservation. A travel agent may be able to negotiate a better price with certain hotels than you can get by yourself. That's because the hotel may give the agent a discount in exchange for steering his or her business toward that hotel. However, these days, you can usually do just as well yourself as long as you're willing to spend some time online and investigate your options.

Reserving a room through the hotel's toll-free number or Web site may also result in a lower rate than calling the hotel directly. On the other hand, the central reservations number may not know about discount rates at specific locations. Your best bet is to call both the local number and the toll-free number and see which one gives you a better deal, and then check it against the rate available online.

Room rates (even rack rates) change with the season, as occupancy rates rise and fall. But even within a given season, room prices are subject to change without notice, so the rates quoted in this book may be different from the actual rate you receive when you make your reservation.

Don't automatically shy away from a hotel if its rack rates seem out of your range at first glance. A hotel's official "published" (full-price, or rack) rates usually represent the upper end of what they charge when they're full to capacity, but most hotels routinely offer better prices. And special deals abound in Hawaii, so in each hotel listing throughout this book, I note what kind of bargains you can typically snag.

Often the best way to get a great deal on a hotel room is to book it as part of an all-inclusive travel package that includes airfare, hotel, and car, and sometimes other extras, in one low price; for details on how to find the best package deals, see Chapter 5.

Check out Chapter 4 for a long list of money-saving strategies. But here are a few reminders:

- ✔ **Rates are generally lowest in the slower seasons.** During peak season — basically winter and summer, and especially around Christmas — demand is high, and you're not going to have much luck fishing for a bargain rate. But in May and September through November, hotels aren't usually full. Not only will you find great deals, but if business is really slow, they'll be willing to negotiate; you might even land a room upgrade.

- ✔ **Start by investigating the hotel's own special deals.** Hawaii's hotels regularly offer a dizzying array of special offers. You might get a free rental car, champagne, and in-room breakfast for honeymooners, free dinners, discounted tee times or spa treatments, a room upgrade, an extra night thrown in for free (sometimes the fifth, sometimes the seventh), or some other freebie. Check out the Web site first, but even if you don't find anything on the Internet, ask about any specials when you call.

- ✔ **Membership in AAA, AARP, or frequent-flier programs often qualifies you for discounted rates.** Be sure to mention membership in these organizations and in any corporate rewards programs you can think of — or your Uncle Joe's Elks lodge in which you're an honorary inductee, for that matter — when you call to book. Even membership to a wholesale club, such as Costco, has been known to pay off. You never know when an affiliation may be worth a few dollars off your room rate.

✔ **Ask innkeepers for a break.** Bed-and-breakfasts are generally non-negotiable on price. Sometimes, however, you can negotiate a discount for longer stays, such as a week or more. You may also be able to score a price break if you're visiting off season. And some do offer AAA and senior discounts. It never hurts to ask.

✔ **Look for price breaks and value-added extras when booking condos.** Condo complexes often feature discounts on multinight stays, and many throw in a free rental car to sweeten the deal. Some condo properties have units handled by multiple management companies; if that's the case, price through both companies and see where you get the better deal. You may also want to check with **Hawaii Condo Exchange** (☎ **800-442-0404** or 323-436-0300; www.hawaiicondoexchange.com), which acts as a consolidator for condo properties throughout the islands.

Surfing the Web for Hotel Deals

Shopping online for hotels is generally done one of two ways: by booking through the hotel's own Web site or through an independent booking agency.

Expedia.com offers a long list of special deals, as well as "virtual tours" or photos of available rooms so that you can see what you're paying for. **Travelocity.com** posts unvarnished customer reviews and ranks its properties according to the AAA rating system. Also reliable are **Hotels.com** (a division of Expedia, so they often offer the same deals), **Orbitz.com**, **Yahoo! Travel** (www.travel.yahoo.com), and **Quikbook.com**.

Keep in mind that hotels at the top of a site's listing are usually there for no other reason than that they paid money to get the placement.

You might also want to check out **TripAdvisor.com** when you're considering your options. TripAdvisor isn't a booking site, per se (although it does offer links to sites that allow you to make bookings), but it does offer untainted, straight-from-the-customer's-keyboard reviews of hotels. Now, I don't recommend putting too much stock in a single review — most of us have unrealistic expectations, or just plain-old bad-luck experiences, now and again — but trends in positive or negative experiences can become apparent. Also, I love the candid travelers' photos, which show you what the hotel rooms *really* look like (and, often, how small they really are).

An excellent free program, **Travelaxe** (www.travelaxe.com), can help you search multiple hotel sites at once, even ones you may never have heard of — and conveniently lists the total price of the room, including the taxes and service charges.

 It's always important to **get a confirmation number** and **make a print-out** of any online booking transaction to avoid any potential issues when you arrive at the hotel.

 In the bidding-site Web site category, **Priceline** (www.priceline.com) and **Hotwire** (www.hotwire.com) are even better for hotels than for air-fares; with both, you're allowed to pick the neighborhood and quality level of your hotel before offering up your money. On the downside, many hotels stick Priceline and Hotwire guests in their least desirable rooms. Be sure to go to the **BiddingForTravel** Web site (www.biddingfortravel.com) before bidding on a hotel room on Priceline; it features a fairly up-to-date list of hotels that Priceline uses in major cities. For both Priceline and Hotwire, you pay upfront, and the fee is nonrefundable. *Note:* Some hotels don't provide loyalty program credits or points or other frequent-stay amenities when you book a room through opaque online services.

Reserving the Best Room

 After you make your reservation, asking one or two more pointed ques-tions can go a long way toward making sure that you get the best room in the house. Most Hawaii hoteliers are very friendly and willing to take the time with you, so don't be shy — try to find out which units are the nicest. If the reservations agent doesn't have any specific recommenda-tions, try asking for a corner room. In some (but not all) cases, they may be larger and quieter, with more windows and light than standard rooms, and they don't always cost more.

Also ask whether the hotel is renovating, or if any construction is taking place nearby; this is especially important in Hawaii, where rampant reno-vation has taken hotels by storm in recent years (and continues to do so for a few more). If it is, request a room away from the renovation work. Inquire, too, about traffic and the location of the restaurants, bars, and discos in the hotel — all sources of annoying noise.

And if you aren't happy with your room when you arrive, talk to the front desk firmly but *nicely*. (Don't get emotional — your mom's old saying about attracting more flies with honey than with vinegar really was good advice.) If they have another room, they should be happy to accommodate you, within reason.

Chapter 8

Catering to Special Travel Needs or Interests

In This Chapter

▶ Taking the kids along

▶ Discovering a world of senior discounts

▶ Getting around the islands of aloha with disabilities

▶ Traveling tips for gays and lesbians

▶ Tying the knot in Hawaii

*T*ravelers don't come in a standard package, of course — they come in all ages, sizes, and configurations. You may want to know: How welcoming will Hawaii be to . . . (pick one or more) (a) my kids? (b) my senior status? (c) my disability? (d) my same-sex partner? If so, you're in the right chapter.

Plus, if you're looking to plan a dreamy tropical wedding, I tell you the ins and outs of tying the knot in the romantic islands of Hawaii.

Traveling with the Brood: Advice for Families

Hawaii is the perfect *ohana* (family) vacation destination. You and the *keiki* (kids) will love the beaches and the wealth of kid-friendly activities. Lots of families flock to the islands every summer and also at holiday time and during the spring-break season.

Most hotels and condo complexes, from luxury to budget, welcome the entire family. Virtually all the larger hotels and resorts have great supervised programs for kids 12 and under — which means that you, Mom and Dad, can have plenty of relaxation time to yourselves as well as playtime with the kids. Most hotels can also refer you to reliable baby sitters if you want a night on the town sans the youngsters.

By Hawaii state law, hotels can accept children only between the ages of 5 and 12 into their supervised activity programs.

Condos are particularly suitable for families who want lots of living space in which to spread out. Parents also appreciate having a kitchen where they can prepare meals for fussy young eaters — and save significantly on dining costs. One drawback of condo complexes is that they typically don't have the extensive facilities (like kids' activities programs) you'd get in a big resort.

If you don't want to cart your own kid stuff across the ocean, **Baby's Away** (www.babysaway.com) rents car seats, cribs, strollers (including jogging strollers), highchairs, playpens, room monitors, and even toys. It serves Oahu (☎ **800-496-6386** or 808-685-4299), Maui (☎ **800-942-9030** or 808-875-9030), and the Big Island (☎ **800-996-9030** or 808-987-9236). Give the company a call, and it'll deliver whatever you need to wherever you're staying and pick it up when you're done. I suggest arranging your rentals before you leave home to ensure availability. Unfortunately, there is no location on Kauai.

You can find good family-oriented vacation advice on the Internet from sites like the **Family Travel Forum** (www.familytravelforum.com), a comprehensive site that offers customized trip planning; **Family Travel Network** (www.familytravelnetwork.com), an award-winning site that offers travel features, deals, and tips; **TravelWithYourKids** (www.travelwithyourkids.com), a comprehensive site that offers customized trip planning; and **FamilyTravelFiles.com** (www.thefamilytravel files.com), which offers an online magazine and a directory of off-the-beaten-path tours and tour operators for families. **BabyCenter** (www.babycenter.com/travel) has terrific recommendations for planning baby's first trip, and even tips on traveling while pregnant.

Here are a few tips for family travel planning:

- ✔ **Don't try to do too much.** I can't say this too strongly. You'll all consider it the trip from you-know-where if you spend too much time in the car or on interisland flights.

- ✔ **Take it slow at the start.** Give the entire family time to adjust to a new time zone, unfamiliar surroundings, and just being on the road. The best way to make this adjustment is to budget a few days in your initial destination without strict itineraries.

- ✔ **Look for the Kid Friendly icon as you flip through this book.** I use it to highlight hotels, restaurants, and attractions that are particularly welcoming to families traveling with kids. Zeroing in on these listings can help you plan your trip more efficiently.

- ✔ **Book some private time for Mom and Dad.** Most, if not all, hotels are prepared to hook you up with a reliable baby sitter who can entertain your kids while you enjoy a romantic dinner for two or another adults-only activity. To avoid disappointment, ask about baby sitting when you reserve. Local visitor centers can also usually recommend baby-sitting services in their areas; see the Quick Concierge in the appendix for contact info.

Making Age Work for You: Tips for Seniors

One of the many benefits of getting older is that travel often costs less. Many hotels and package-tour operators offer deals for seniors. Discounts for seniors are also available at almost all of Hawaii's major attractions, and occasionally at restaurants and luau. So when you're making reservations or buying tickets, it's always worthwhile to ask about senior discounts. Keep in mind, though, that the minimum age requirement can vary between 50 and 65 (it's usually between 55 and 65). Always carry an ID card with you.

The statewide **Outrigger** (☎ **800-OUTRIGGER** or 800-688-7444; www. outrigger.com) and **Ohana** (☎ **800-462-6262;** www.ohanahotels.com) hotel chains offer discounts to all travelers over age 50.

Members of **AARP,** 601 E St. NW, Washington, DC 20049 (☎ **888-687-2277** or 202-434-2277; www.aarp.org), get discounts on hotels, airfares, and car rentals. AARP offers members a wide range of benefits, including *AARP The Magazine* and a monthly newsletter. Anyone over 50 can join.

YMT Vacations (☎ **800-922-9000;** www.ymtvacations.com) and **Grand Circle Travel** (☎ **800-959-0405;** www.gct.com) are just two of the hundreds of travel agencies that specialize in vacations for seniors, including trips to Hawaii. But beware: Many of these outfits are of the tour-bus variety, with free trips thrown in for those who organize groups of 20 or more. If you're the independent type, a regular travel agent may be better for you.

Elderhostel (☎ **800-454-5768;** www.elderhostel.org), a nonprofit group that offers travel and study programs around the world, offers excellent low-cost trips to Hawaii for travelers ages 55 and older (plus a spouse or companion of any age). Trips usually include moderately priced accommodations and meals in one low-cost package.

U.S. citizens or permanent residents age 62 or older who want to visit Hawaii's national parks — including Hawaii Volcanoes National Park and Puuhonua o Honaunau National Historical Park on the Big Island, and Haleakala National Park on Maui — can save sightseeing dollars by picking up an **America the Beautiful National Parks and Federal Recreational Lands Pass** for Seniors from any national park, recreation area, or monument. This lifetime pass has a one-time fee of $10 and provides free admission to all the parks in the National Parks system, plus 50 percent savings on camping and recreation fees, for the cardholder and all passengers (no more than four adults total). You can get one at any park entrance as long as you have a proof-of-age ID on hand. For details, visit www.nps.gov/fees_passes.htm.

Recommended publications offering travel resources and discounts for seniors include the quarterly magazine *Travel 50 & Beyond* (www. travel50andbeyond.com); *Travel with a Challenge* online magazine (www.travelwithachallenge.com); *Travel Unlimited: Uncommon Adventures for the Mature Traveler* (Avalon); and *Unbelievably Good Deals and Great Adventures That You Absolutely Can't Get Unless You're Over 50* (McGraw-Hill), by Joann Rattner Heilman.

Accessing Hawaii: Advice for Travelers with Disabilities

A disability shouldn't stop anyone from traveling. The Americans with Disabilities Act requires that all public buildings be wheelchair accessible and have accessible restrooms.

Hawaii is very friendly to travelers with disabilities. The city of Honolulu alone has more than 2,000 ramped curbs, and most hotels throughout the islands are on the newer side and boast wheelchair ramps, extra-wide doorways and halls, and dedicated disabled-accessible rooms with extra-large bathrooms, low-set fixtures, and/or fire alarm systems adapted for deaf travelers.

Your best bet is to contact the local visitor center for the island you're interested in visiting. Its staff can provide you with all the specifics on accessibility in their locale; see the Quick Concierge at the back of this book for contact info.

Also try the following excellent resources:

✔ An excellent source for trip-planning assistance is **Access Aloha Travel** (☎ 800-480-1143 or 808-545-1143; www.accessalohatravel.com). This Hawaii-based travel agency has been planning accessible trips for travelers with disabilities for decades — and it donates half its profits to the disabled community. Inquire with these folks about renting an accessible van during your stay.

✔ Both **MossRehab ResourceNet** (☎ 800-CALL-MOSS, 215-456-9900 or 215-663-6000; www.mossresourcenet.org) and **Access-Able Travel Source** (☎ 303-232-2979; www.access-able.com) are comprehensive resources for travelers with disabilities. Both sites feature links to travel agents who specialize in planning accessible trips to Hawaii. Access-Able's user-friendly site also features relay and voice numbers for hotels, airlines, and car-rental companies, plus links to accessible accommodations, attractions, transportation, tours, and local medical resources and equipment repairers throughout Hawaii.

✔ You can join the **Society for Accessible Travel & Hospitality** (SATH; ☎ 212-447-7284 or 561-361-0017; www.sath.org) for $49 a year ($29 for seniors and students) to gain access to their vast network of travel connections. The group provides information sheets on destinations and referrals to tour operators that specialize in accessible travel. Its quarterly magazine, *Open World,* is full of good information and resources.

✔ Vision-impaired travelers who use a Seeing Eye dog can usually bypass Hawaii's animal quarantine rules. You can arrange for your guide or service dog to be inspected in the terminal at Honolulu International Airport (saving the owners a trip to the Airport Animal Quarantine Holding Facility) if you notify **Animal Quarantine** (☎ 808-483-7151) at least 24 hours in advance. Call or visit www. hawaii.gov/hdoa for specifics on rules and fees. Contact the **American Foundation for the Blind** (☎ 800-232-5463; www.afb. org) for more travel information.

Gammie HomeCare (☎ 888-540-4032 or 808-877-4032 on Maui, 808-632-2333 on Kauai; www.gammie.com) rents a wide variety of mobility aids, bath safety items, and wheelchairs — including beach wheelchairs that can navigate on sand. They will deliver to any hotel on Maui or Kauai.

Hawaii's **Disability and Communication Access Board** has a roundup of travel tips, with information on arriving, air travel, and where to find local support services. Visit their Web site at www.state.hi.us/health/dcab/home, and click on "Community Resources" in the scroll bar at left. Before you book any hotel room, always ask lots of questions based on your needs. After you arrive, call restaurants, attractions, and theaters to make sure that they're fully accessible.

Consider the following sources for getting around, either on your own or with assistance:

✔ **Avis Rent a Car** has an "Avis Access" program that offers such services as a dedicated 24-hour toll-free number (☎ 888-331-2323; www.avis.com) for customers who are hearing impaired. Special car features such as swivel seats, spinner knobs, and hand controls and accessible bus service are available; call their main customer service number (☎ 800-352-7900) for details. Many of the big car-rental companies — including Avis, **Hertz** (☎ 800-654-3131 or 800-654-2280 for hearing-impaired travelers; www.hertz.com), and **National** (☎ 800-227-7368, 800-328-6323 for hearing-impaired travelers, 888-273-5262 for travelers with medical-related requests; www.nationalcar.com) — rent hand-controlled cars for drivers with disabilities at Hawaii's major airports. At least 48 to 72 hours' advance notice is a must, but do yourself a favor and book further in advance to guarantee availability.

✔ **HandiWheelchair Transportation** (☎ 808-946-6666) offers door-to-door taxi services around Honolulu and the rest of Oahu for wheelchair-bound travelers. Its air-conditioned vehicles are specially equipped with ramps and wheelchair lock-downs. Airport service is also available.

Following the Rainbow: Resources for Gay and Lesbian Travelers

Hawaii is extremely popular with same-sex couples due to its long-standing reputation for welcoming all groups.

The **International Gay and Lesbian Travel Association** (IGLTA; ☎ 954-630-1637; www.iglta.org) is the trade association for the gay and lesbian travel industry, and offers an online directory of gay- and lesbian-friendly travel businesses, gay-friendly structured trips, and occasional travel specials, including special discount codes for National and Alamo rental cars at press time.

The staff at **Pacific Ocean Holidays** (☎ 800-735-6600 or 808-545-5252; www.gayhawaiivacations.com) specializes in crafting Hawaii vacation packages for gay men and women. They can help you arrange a good-value trip that features either gay-friendly hotels serving the general public or those that serve a predominately gay clientele (your choice); you can even book your entire vacation online. Even if you don't want help planning your trip, the Web site is an invaluable resource. Its online island-by-island guide is a terrific community resource directory and guide to gay-owned and gay-friendly businesses throughout Hawaii.

Gay.com Travel (www.gay.com/travel) is an excellent online successor to the popular *Out & About* magazine. Their OutTraveler page provides regularly updated information about gay-owned and gay-friendly lodging, dining, nightlife, and shopping in every major destination worldwide (including popular and emerging "gayborhoods" in cities worldwide), plus valuable trip-planning information.

Purple Roofs (www.purpleroofs.com) is a comprehensive online guide to gay-friendly bed-and-breakfasts, guesthouses, vacation rentals, travel agents, and tour operators worldwide, including extensive listings in Hawaii.

The **Gay and Lesbian Community Center,** 614 South St., Ste. #105, in Honolulu (☎ 808-545-2848), offers referrals for nearly every kind of service that you might need. Also check out the **Gay Community Services Directory,** which you can find online at www.hawaiiscene.com/gsene/comsvc.htm.

Planning a Hawaiian Wedding

No question about it: Hawaii is the perfect place to get married — which is why so many couples from around the country, and the world, tie the knot here every year. What better way to start your life together?

For a rundown of the legalities, visit www.hawaii.gov/doh and click "Getting a Marriage License," where you'll find all the details, including a downloadable license application. You can also call ☎ 808-586-4545 for license information.

Using a wedding planner or coordinator

Wedding planning is a thriving industry in Hawaii. Whether you've got your heart set on a huge formal affair at a luxury resort or an informal beachside ceremony, you won't have any trouble finding assistance.

Many wedding planners are also marriage-license agents. They can take care of the legalities for you with only minimal effort on your part and then arrange everything else too — from providing an officiant to ordering flowers. A wedding planner can cost $500 or more, depending on how involved you want him or her to be and what kind of wedding you want.

Your best bet for finding a reputable wedding planner is to choose one endorsed by the **Hawaii Visitors and Convention Bureau,** whose Web site features a complete list of wedding planners to suit any budget; go to www.gohawaii.com and click "Plan a Wedding or Honeymoon." You can also call its staff for recommendations at ☎ 800-GO-HAWAII, or — even better — contact the individual island bureaus for local recommendations; see the Quick Concierge at the back of this book for contact information. On Kauai, an even better wedding resource than the visitor center is the **Kauai Chamber of Commerce (☎ 808-245-7363;** www. kauaichamber.org), which sells an extensive wedding guide for $25 at their online chamber store.

In addition, virtually all the big resorts employ full-time wedding coordinators. Arranging your nuptials directly through a resort may be pricey, but it's a relatively worry-free option. The hotel coordinators are experts, they'll take all the pesky little details off your hands, and they'll usually offer the whole event to you as a pay-one-price wedding package, including accommodations. What's more, the hotels generally offer prime locations for both the ceremony and the reception.

Great choices include:

- The Halekulani, the Royal Hawaiian, and the Westin Moana Surfrider on Oahu (see Chapter 10)
- The Four Seasons Resort Maui, the Grand Wailea, the Fairmont Kea Lani, and the Ritz-Carlton on Maui (see Chapter 12)
- The Four Seasons Resort Hualalai, Kona Village, the Mauna Lani, and the Fairmont Orchid at Mauna Lani on the Big Island (see Chapter 14)
- The Grand Hyatt Kauai Resort & Spa and the Princeville Resort on Kauai (see Chapter 16)

Keep in mind that more affordable hotels and condos, even some B&Bs, can often recommend wedding coordinators that have a proven track record with them. Maui's Kaanapali Beach Hotel, for example, makes a great affordable option (see Chapter 12). The setting is magical, the hotel works with a very reliable local planner, and the on-site food-and-beverage director can arrange a pleasing reception. Don't hesitate to contact any property that strikes your fancy; most have wedding experience or can offer recommendations.

Do-it-yourself planning

Once you arrive in Hawaii, you and your intended must appear together to a **marriage license agent** (basically, a local official who helps you wrap up the legalities) when applying for the license. A marriage license costs $60 (payable in cash) and is good for 30 days from the date of issue. Both parties must be at least 18 years of age (16- and 17-year-olds must have written consent of both parents, legal guardian, or family court) and can't be more closely related than first cousins. You'll need a photo ID, such as a driver's license; a birth certificate is necessary only if you're 18 or under. No blood tests, citizenship, or residency minimum is required.

In **Honolulu,** go to the **Honolulu Marriage License Office,** State Department of Health Building, 1250 Punchbowl St. (at Beretania Street; ☎ **808-586-4545** or 808-586-4544), weekdays between 8 a.m. and 4 p.m. If you would like to locate a marriage license agent in other areas of **Oahu,** call ☎ 808-586-4544; on **Maui,** call ☎ 808-984-8210; on the **Big Island,** call ☎ 808-974-6008; on **Kauai,** call ☎ 808-241-3498; on **Molokai,** call ☎ 808-553-3663; or on **Lanai,** call ☎ 808-565-6411.

Local marriage-license agents are usually friendly, helpful people who can steer you to someone who's licensed by the state of Hawaii to perform the ceremony. These marriage performers are great sources of information; they usually know picturesque places to have the ceremony for free or a nominal fee.

 Some marriage-license agents are state employees, and, under law, they cannot recommend anyone with a religious affiliation; they can only give you phone numbers for local judges to perform the ceremony. Ask first what their limitations are if it matters to you. If you're interested in arranging a church ceremony, inquire with the visitor center to locate an appropriate venue.

 You can have a ceremony at any state or county beach or park for free, but keep in mind that you'll be sharing the site with the general public. Here are some romantic spots you may want to consider:

  ✔ **Oahu:** Waikiki's **Kapiolani Park,** on Kalakaua Avenue, is ideal at sunset. You can take gorgeous wedding photos with Waikiki Beach in the background and then turn around and take another photo with Diamond Head as your backdrop. I also adore **Lanikai Beach,**

on the lush and gorgeous windward side. Tucked away in a residential neighborhood, it's usually quiet and crowd-free. (Weekdays are best if you want the sand to yourself.)

✔ **Maui:** For a genuine Hawaiian experience, get married at **Keawalai Congregational Church** (☎ 808-879-5557; www.keawalai.org), a vintage 1831 oceanfront coral-block church in picturesque Makena. The gorgeous grounds — with palm trees, ti leaves, and exotic tropical flowers — make a perfect backdrop for your wedding photo. Another great site is **D.T. Fleming Beach Park,** just north of Kapalua in West Maui. This crescent-shaped beach is generally empty on weekdays, so you can enjoy a quiet wedding on the beautiful beach as sailboats skim along offshore.

✔ **Big Island:** If you picture yourself getting married on a long, white-sand beach with gorgeous, emerald-green waves rolling in, **Hapuna Beach State Park** is the spot for you. On the mistier side of the island, along bayfront Banyan Drive in romantic Hilo, is **Liluokalani Gardens,** the largest formal Japanese garden this side of Tokyo. This postcard-pretty park has a dozen different areas that are ideal for a tropical ceremony, and the half-moon bridge is a great spot for wedding photos.

✔ **Kauai:** One of the most dramatic spots in all Hawaii is the North Shore's **Hanalei Beach,** with gorgeous, green Bali Hai–like cliffs in the background. (Remember *South Pacific?* Filmed here!) If you're set on a church wedding, consider **Waioli Hui'ia** ("Singing Waters") **Church** (☎ 808-826-6253; www.hanaleichurch.org), built in 1912 as a mission hall and the oldest surviving church building on Kauai. It sits in an open field in the heart of the charming Hanalei town under the spectacular Bali Hai cliffs for an ultraromantic setting. For those who don't mind spending a little money for a bit more privacy, on the South Shore is the extraordinary **Allerton Garden,** one of five National Tropical Botanical Gardens (☎ 808-742-2623; www.ntbg.org), home to some prime examples of formal landscape gardening that would have made William Randolph Hearst turn green with envy. It's perfect for a wedding of any scope.

Chapter 9

Taking Care of the Remaining Details

● ●

● ●

*T*his chapter helps you shore up the final details — from getting travel insurance to planning for activities.

Playing It Safe with Travel and Medical Insurance

Three kinds of travel insurance are available: trip-cancellation insurance, medical insurance, and lost-luggage insurance. Check your existing homeowner's and auto insurance policies and your credit-card coverage before buying any additional insurance. You may already be covered.

The cost of travel insurance varies widely, depending on the cost and length of your trip, your age and health, and the type of trip you're taking, but expect to pay between 5 and 8 percent of the cost of the vacation itself. You can get estimates from various providers through **InsureMyTrip.com**, which compares more than a dozen companies.

✔ **Trip-cancellation insurance** may make sense if you're paying for your vacation upfront, say, by purchasing a cruise, a package deal, or an escorted tour. Coverage will help you get your money back if you have to back out of a trip, if you have to go home early, or if your travel supplier goes bankrupt. Allowed reasons for cancellation can range from sickness to natural disasters to the State Department declaring your destination unsafe for travel. (Insurers usually won't cover vague fears, though, as many travelers discovered when they tried to cancel their trips in October 2001 because they were wary of flying.)

A good resource is **"Travel Guard Alerts,"** a list of companies considered high-risk by Travel Guard International (www.travelguard. com; click on "Customer Service" to find the alerts, which featured a fair number of in-trouble airlines in 2008). Protect yourself further by paying for the insurance with a credit card — by law, consumers can get their money back on goods and services not received if they report the loss within 60 days after the charge is listed on their credit-card statement.

Note: Many tour operators include insurance in the cost of the trip or can arrange insurance policies through a partnering provider, a convenient and often cost-effective way for travelers to obtain insurance. Make sure that the tour company is a reputable one, however: Some experts suggest that you avoid buying insurance from the tour or cruise company you're traveling with, saying that it's safer to buy from a third-party insurer than to put all your money in one place.

✔ For domestic travel, buying **medical insurance** for your trip doesn't make sense for most travelers. Most existing health policies cover you if you get sick away from home — but check before you go, particularly if you're insured by an HMO.

✔ **Lost-luggage insurance** is also not necessary for most travelers. On domestic flights, checked baggage is covered up to $2,500 per ticketed passenger. On international flights (including U.S. portions of international trips), baggage coverage is limited to approximately $9.07 per pound, up to approximately $635 per checked bag. If you plan to check items more valuable than the standard liability, see whether your valuables are covered by your homeowner's policy, get baggage insurance as part of your comprehensive travel-insurance package, or buy Travel Guard's "BagTrak" product. Don't buy insurance at the airport, because it's usually overpriced. Be sure to take any valuables or irreplaceable items with you in your carry-on luggage, because many valuables (including books, money, and electronics) aren't covered by airline policies.

If your luggage is lost, immediately file a lost-luggage claim at the airport, detailing the contents. For most airlines, you must report delayed, damaged, or lost baggage within four hours of arrival. The airlines are required to deliver luggage, after it's found, directly to your house or destination free of charge.

For more information, contact one of the following recommended insurers: **Access America** (☎ 800-284-8300; www.accessamerica.com); **AIG Travel Guard** (☎ 800-826-4919; www.travelguard.com); **Travel Insured International** (☎ 800-243-3174; www.travelinsured.com); and **Travelex Insurance Services** (☎ 888-457-4602; www.travelex-insurance.com).

Staying Healthy When You Travel

Getting sick will ruin your vacation, so I *strongly* advise against it. (Of course, last time I checked, germs weren't listening to me any more than they probably listen to you.)

Talk to your doctor before leaving on a trip if you have a serious and/or chronic illness. For conditions such as epilepsy, diabetes, or heart problems, wear a **MedicAlert identification tag** (☎ 888-633-4298; www.medic alert.org), which immediately alerts doctors to your condition and gives them access to your records through MedicAlert's 24-hour hot line.

In the unlikely event that you do get sick in Hawaii, keep the following in mind:

- By law, all employers in Hawaii must provide health insurance for their employees, and almost all islanders have insurance. As a result, some doctors simply won't see patients who aren't insured. If you don't have insurance (or you don't have insurance that travels with you) and you need to see a doctor while you're in Hawaii, be sure to inform him or her when you call to make an appointment. Check the "Fast Facts" sections in Chapter 10 (Oahu), Chapter 12 (Maui), Chapter 14 (the Big Island), and Chapter 16 (Kauai) to find a doctor or medical-care clinic that regularly caters to visitors.

- **Longs Drugs,** which has branches throughout the islands, accepts most national prescription cards, such as PCS — so if you have a card, bring it with you. If you get sick and need to fill a prescription during your trip, chances are good that you'll have to pay only a copayment, just like back home, instead of the full price for prescribed medicines. To find a Longs near you, call ☎ 800-865-6647 or visit www.longsdrugs.com.

Avoiding "economy-class syndrome"

Deep vein thrombosis, or as it's mislabeled in the world of flying, "economy-class syndrome," is a blood clot that develops in a deep vein. Over time, it can travel to your lungs and cause a pulmonary embolism, blocking blood flow to your heart. It's a very rare but potentially deadly condition that can be caused by sitting in cramped conditions — such as an airplane cabin — for too long. During a long-haul flight, get up, walk around, and stretch your legs every 60 to 90 minutes to keep your blood flowing. Other preventive measures include frequent flexing of the legs while sitting, drinking lots of water, and avoiding alcohol and sleeping pills. If you have a history of deep vein thrombosis, heart disease, or any other condition that puts you at high risk, some experts recommend wearing compression stockings or taking anticoagulants when you fly; always ask your physician about the best course for you. Symptoms include leg pain or swelling, or shortness of breath and sharp pains in your lungs.

Staying Connected by Cellphone or E-mail

Most major cellphone networks have great coverage in Hawaii. However, don't just assume that because your **cellphone** works at home that it will work in the islands. Take a look at your wireless company's coverage map on its Web site before getting on the plane. You should also check your cellphone contract, because coverage varies depending on the particular package you've purchased. If you need to stay in touch at a destination where you know your phone won't work, **rent** a phone that does from **InTouch USA** (☎ **800-872-7626;** www.intouchglobal.com).

If you're not from the United States, you'll be appalled at the poor reach of our **GSM (Global System for Mobiles) wireless network,** which is used by much of the rest of the world. Your phone will probably work in most major U.S. cities, but rural coverage tends to be haphazard; the good news is that Hawaii is well covered. (To see where GSM phones work in the United States, check out www.wireless.att.com/coverageviewer.) You may or may not be able to send text messages home. Assume nothing — call your wireless provider and get the full scoop. In a worst-case scenario, you can always rent a phone; InTouch USA delivers to hotels.

Travelers **accessing the Internet** away from home have any number of options. Of course, using your own laptop — or even a PDA, pocket PC, or Web-compatible cellphone — gives you the most flexibility. But even if you don't have a computer, you can still access your e-mail and even your office computer from cybercafes and other hotel business centers. It's hard these days to find a destination that *doesn't* have a few cybercafes. Although there's no definitive directory for locations, two places to start looking are at www.cybercaptive.com and www.cybercafe.com.

Almost all but the most budget-basic **hotels** offer wireless or wired Internet access that you can plug right into; the price of access can range from complimentary to $15 or $20 a day. Even most (but not all) B&Bs offer Internet access these days. Check with your hotel in advance to see what your options are.

Most major airports now have **Internet kiosks** scattered throughout their gates, as well as wireless Internet access for laptop toters. Some airports charge, while others provide free service. Kiosks give you basic Web access for a per-minute fee that's usually higher than cybercafe prices. Most Hawaii airports offer limited access for a cost through **Boingo.com.**

To retrieve your e-mail, check with your **Internet service provider (ISP)** to see if it offers a Web-based interface tied to your existing e-mail account. Virtually all do these days. If your ISP doesn't have such an interface, you can use the free **mail2web** service (www.mail2web.com) to view and reply to your home e-mail. Or open a free, Web-based e-mail account with **Yahoo! Mail** (mail.yahoo.com). Microsoft's **Windows Live,** formerly known as Hotmail (mail.live.com) is another popular option.

If you need to access files on your office computer, look into a service called **GoToMyPC** (www.gotomypc.com). The service provides a Web-based interface for you to access and manipulate a distant PC from anywhere — even a cybercafe — provided your "target" PC is on and has an always-on connection to the Internet (such as with Road Runner cable). The service offers top-quality security, but if you're worried about hackers, use your own laptop rather than a cybercafe computer to access the GoToMyPC system.

Wherever you go, don't forget to bring a **connection kit** of the right power and phone adapters.

Keeping Up with Airline Security Measures

Even after the federalization of airport security, security procedures at U.S. airports tend to be uneven. But generally you'll be fine if you arrive at the airport 1½ **hours** before a domestic or interisland flight and **two hours** before an international flight. Be sure to allow extra time if you're traveling on a high-volume holiday getaway day, or if the terrorism alert level has been raised.

Bring a **current, government-issued photo ID** such as a driver's license or passport. Keep your ID at the ready to show at check-in, the security checkpoint, and sometimes even the gate. (Children under 18 don't need government-issued photo IDs for domestic flights, but they do for international flights to most countries.)

E-tickets have made paper tickets nearly obsolete. Passengers with e-tickets can beat the ticket-counter lines by using airport **electronic kiosks** or even **online check-in** from their home computer. Online check-in involves logging on to your airline's Web site, accessing your reservation, and printing your boarding pass; this is usually allowable 24 hours in advance of flight time. If you're using a kiosk at the airport, bring the credit card you used to book the ticket or your frequent-flier card. If you're checking bags or looking to snag an exit-row seat, you'll be able to do so using most airline kiosks. **Curbside check-in** is also a good way to avoid lines, although it's not universally available.

Security checkpoint lines have become more efficient as the TSA has staffed up and streamlined the process, but some doozies remain. If you have trouble standing for long periods of time, tell an airline employee; the airline will provide a wheelchair. Speed up security by **not wearing metal objects** such as big belt buckles. If you've got metallic body parts, a note from your doctor can prevent a long chat with the security screeners. Keep in mind that only **ticketed passengers** are allowed past security, except for folks escorting passengers with disabilities or children.

Federalization has stabilized **what you can carry on** and **what you can't.** Food and beverages are not allowed in containers larger than 3 ounces. Liquids or gels — that is, most toiletries — must be 3 ounces or smaller, and all of them must be placed in one clear quart-sized plastic, zip-top bag and screened separately from your other luggage. All other toiletries must be transported to your destination in your checked luggage.

Travelers in the United States are allowed one carry-on bag, plus a "personal item" such as a purse, briefcase, or laptop bag. Carry-on hoarders can stuff all sorts of things into a laptop bag; as long as it has a laptop in it, it's still considered a personal item. The **Transportation Security Administration (TSA)** has issued a list of restricted items; check its Web site (www.tsa.gov) for details.

Airport screeners may decide that your checked luggage needs to be searched by hand. You can now purchase luggage locks that allow screeners to open and relock a checked bag if hand-searching is necessary. Look for Travel Sentry–certified locks at luggage or travel shops and Brookstone stores (you can buy them online at www.brookstone.com). These locks, approved by the TSA, can be opened by luggage inspectors with a special code or key. For more information on the locks, visit www.travelsentry.org. If you use something other than TSA-approved locks, your lock will be cut off your suitcase if a TSA agent needs to hand-search your luggage.

Making Reservations before You Leave Home

In addition to buying your airfare, booking your accommodations, and reserving a rental car, you may want to make a few plans before you leave home.

You don't have to call ahead to reserve most activities until you arrive in Hawaii. Most snorkel cruises, guided tours, and the like can be reserved a day or two in advance. Even high-profile restaurants can usually get you in within a few days of the day you call.

Still, planning is never a bad idea — especially if you're traveling during a busy time, such as spring break or the holidays. I recommend booking anything you absolutely do not want to miss before you leave home to ensure that you're not disappointed. And it's an absolute necessity for certain special events and activities, including the following:

✔ **Luau:** Maui's **Old Lahaina Luau** is the best in the islands — and it always sells out at least a week in advance, often more, as does its sister luau, **The Feast at Lele.** It's never too early to reserve your seats; see Chapter 12 for contact information. Second-best is the Big Island's **Kona Village Luau,** which is offered only on Friday nights; see Chapter 14. Oahu's top choice, the romantic **Royal Luau at the Royal Hawaiian,** lights up Waikiki Beach on one or two nights a week (call for the current schedule), so plan accordingly; see Chapter 10.

✔ **Snorkel cruises:** Maui's finest snorkel-cruise operator is **Trilogy Excursions.** They're hugely popular, so you may want to book before you leave home (see Chapter 13). Ditto for the Big Island's **Fair Wind Cruises,** the only catamaran operator with rights to take you to the finest snorkel spot in all the Hawaiian Islands, Kealakekua Bay (see Chapter 15). And if you don't want to miss the spectacular dolphin-watching tours off Oahu's leeward coast by **Dolphin Excursions** — I wouldn't! — be sure to secure your spots before you leave home. See Chapter 11.

✔ **Special guided tours:** I especially recommend making advance bookings with **Hawaii Forest & Trail** on the Big Island (see Chapter 15) if you don't want to miss out on its special offerings. Maui's excellent **Pony Express** horseback rides into Haleakala National Park's crater also require before-you-leave-home booking to guard against disappointment (see Chapter 13). The same goes for the terrific garden tour at the **National Tropical Botanical Garden** on Kauai (see Chapter 17), which often sells out a week or two in advance.

✔ **Special events:** Certain special events require planning or arrangements, such as the **Merrie Monarch Hula Festival,** the **Hawaii International Jazz Festival,** the Brothers Cazimero **Lei Day Concert** at the Waikiki Band Shell, and the **Kapalua Wine & Food Festival.** Check Chapter 3 to see what will be on while you're in town, and whether it requires planning. You may also want to check with the individual island visitor centers; see the Quick Concierge at the back of the book for contact information.

✔ **Special-occasion or holiday meals:** You should always make advance reservations to avoid disappointment. I indicate reservations policies in all restaurant reviews. This is especially true on holidays, when the nicer restaurants are overrun with locals and visitors alike. Take it from me on this one — I couldn't get a same-day table at a decent restaurant in Honolulu on Mother's Day to save my life. And if you'd like to dine at **Alan Wong's** on Oahu at any time of year, call at least a week in advance to score a decent dining time.

✔ **Scuba classes:** First-time scuba divers may want to look into the various resort courses that are available, because they differ from outfitter to outfitter. See Chapters 11, 13, 15, and 17 for reputable local dive instructors on each of the main islands.

Consider taking scuba certification classes before you leave home; that way, you don't waste time learning in some resort swimming pool and can dive right in as soon as you get to Hawaii. A great way to find a local scuba instructor is via the **Professional Association of Diving Instructors (PADI)** Web site; go online to www.padi.com.

Planning a few of your activities before you leave home is often the best way to guarantee that you won't miss out on an event or a restaurant that you've been counting on — that way, if a group suddenly decides that it's going to take over a snorkel boat for a full day, or a restaurant is planning to close down for a week to install a new stove in the kitchen, you have the opportunity to amend your plans accordingly. Besides, you don't want to spend your valuable Hawaii time on the phone in your hotel room, do you?

Part III
Honolulu and the Rest of Oahu

In this part . . .

Busier and more developed than the other islands, Oahu is known as "the Gathering Place." It's home to Hawaii's biggest and busiest metropolis, Honolulu, which embodies city life in the islands — a strength or weakness of this vibrant island, depending on your point of view. The two chapters in this part help you plan your trip to this gorgeous, surprisingly diversified island and offer reviews of Oahu's best accommodations, restaurants, adventures, and attractions.

Chapter 10

Settling into Oahu

. . . .

In This Chapter

▶ Getting from Honolulu Airport to your hotel

▶ Finding your way around Waikiki, Honolulu, and the rest of Oahu

▶ Choosing among the island's top accommodations

▶ Discovering Oahu's best restaurants

▶ Arranging for a luau

. . . .

*O*ahu is the busiest and most complex island in the Hawaiian chain, but it's still relatively easy to learn your way around. Because it has a reliable public transportation system, this is the one island where it's possible to get by without a rental car. Still, I recommend that you book your own wheels for freedom of movement.

Whether you're traveling from the mainland or a neighboring island, you'll arrive at Honolulu International Airport. That's where this chapter picks up. I'll tell you everything you need to know to get situated in this beautiful spot.

Arriving at Honolulu International Airport

Honolulu International Airport (☎ **888-697-7813,** 808-836-6411, or 808-836-6413; www.state.hi.us/dot/airports/oahu/index.htm or www.honoluluairport.com) is located on the South Shore of Oahu near Pearl Harbor, west of downtown Honolulu and Waikiki. It's 9 miles, or about a 20- to 30-minute drive, away from Waikiki.

Honolulu International is a large but easily navigable airport. All mainland flights arrive in the **Main Overseas Terminal;** the Baggage Claim area is on the ground level. After collecting your bags, exit to the palm-lined street, where you can pick up taxis, Waikiki shuttles, and rental-car vans. If you're catching a neighbor-island flight, walk to the large **Interisland Terminal** (which takes 10–15 min.) or hop on the **Wiki-Wiki Bus,** a free airport shuttle that links the terminals (*wiki wiki* means "quick" in Hawaiian).

Oahu Orientation

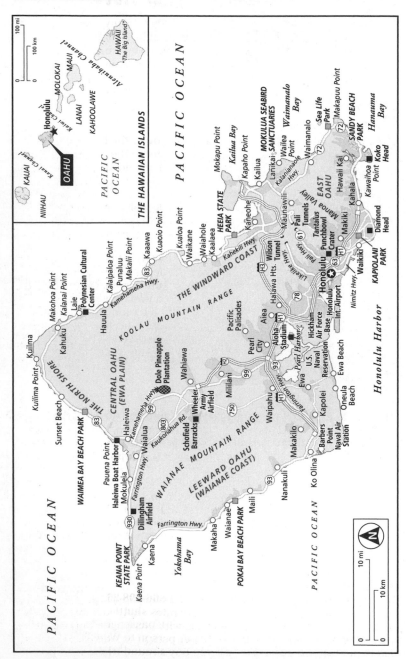

Getting from the Airport to Your Hotel

A rental car isn't a strict necessity on Oahu, but it's my preferred method for getting around. Even if you use public transportation in Waikiki, you'll probably want a car for venturing farther afield. Luckily, rental cars are usually rather inexpensive on Oahu, and all the big companies have cars available at the airport. You'll get the best rate if you book before you arrive, though; see Chapter 6 for more details.

Driving yourself

A van from your car-rental agency will take you to the lot where you can pick up your car. From baggage claim, head out to the well-marked curbside waiting area. The appropriate rental van should swing by within a few minutes.

All the rental-car agencies offer map booklets, which are invaluable for getting around the island. Some car-rental agents can even give you computer-generated, detailed directions from the airport to your hotel.

To get to Waikiki, simply turn right out of the airport (signs are clear) onto Nimitz Highway (Highway 92), which runs directly under the H-1 (one of Oahu's three freeways) for a few minutes. In about ten minutes, Nimitz Highway deposits you onto Ala Moana Boulevard, which takes you past downtown Honolulu (on your left) and Aloha Tower Marketplace (on your right), and then, a few minutes later, the huge Ala Moana Shopping Center (on your left) and grassy Ala Moana Beach Park (on your right). Moments later, you reach Kalakaua (ka-la-*cow*-ah) Avenue, Waikiki's main thoroughfare.

Taking a taxi

The taxi stand is located just outside the automated doors in the Baggage Claim area. You should have no trouble getting a taxi, but if you need help, an attendant is on hand to assist you. **AMPCO Express** (☎ **808-861-8294**) manages the taxi-stand service at the airport. Taxi fare to Waikiki is about $25 to $35, plus tip.

Star Taxi (☎ **800-671-2999** or 808-942-7827; www.startaxihawaii.com) can offer prearranged airport pickups to Waikiki for $22 (plus tip); use the toll-free number to arrange your pickup before you leave home. Be sure to have your airline, flight number, and arrival time on hand when you call.

Catching a shuttle ride

The **Airport Waikiki Express Shuttle** (☎ **1-866-898-2519;** www.robertshawaii.com/hat.htm) operates shuttles between the airport and Waikiki hotels round-the-clock, with passenger vans departing every 20 to 30 minutes. The fare is $8 per person to Waikiki, $15 round-trip (round-trip fare applies only if you buy a round-trip ticket upon

Honolulu and Waikiki Orientation

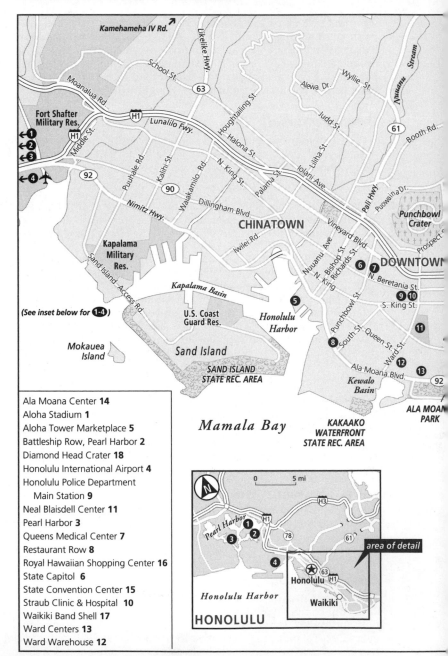

Ala Moana Center **14**
Aloha Stadium **1**
Aloha Tower Marketplace **5**
Battleship Row, Pearl Harbor **2**
Diamond Head Crater **18**
Honolulu International Airport **4**
Honolulu Police Department
  Main Station **9**
Neal Blaisdell Center **11**
Pearl Harbor **3**
Queens Medical Center **7**
Restaurant Row **8**
Royal Hawaiian Shopping Center **16**
State Capitol **6**
State Convention Center **15**
Straub Clinic & Hospital **10**
Waikiki Band Shell **17**
Ward Centers **13**
Ward Warehouse **12**

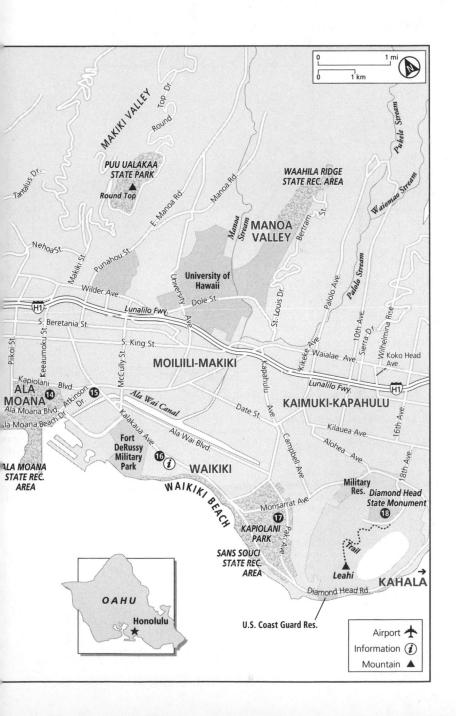

TheBus

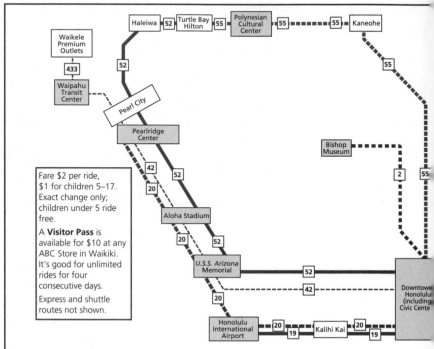

Fare $2 per ride, $1 for children 5–17. Exact change only; children under 5 ride free.

A **Visitor Pass** is available for $10 at any ABC Store in Waikiki. It's good for unlimited rides for four consecutive days.

Express and shuttle routes not shown.

Common Bus Routes:

Ala Moana Shopping Center: Take bus #19 & #20 AIRPORT. Return via #19 WAIKIKI, or cross Ala Moana Blvd. for #20. Other options to/from Waikiki: #8, #23, & #42.

Bishop Museum: Take #2 SCHOOL STREET. Get off at Kapalama St., cross School St., walk down Bernice St. Return to School St. and take #2 WAIKIKI.

Circle Island: Take a bus to ALA MOANA CENTER (TRF) to #52 WAHIAWA CIRCLE ISLAND or #55 KANEOHE CIRCLE ISLAND. This is a 4-hour bus ride.

Chinatown or Downtown: Take any #2 bus going out of Waikiki to Hotel St. Return, take #2 WAIKIKI on Hotel St., or #19 or #20 on King St. Other Chinatown options: #13 & #42.

The Contemporary Museum & Punchbowl (National Cemetery of the Pacific): Take #2 bus (TRF) at Alapai St. to #15 MAKIKI-PACIFIC HGTS. Return, take #15 and get off at King St., area (TRF) #2 WAIKIKI.

Diamond Head Crater: Take #22 HAWAII KAI-SEA LIFE PARK to the crater. Take a flashlight. Return to the same area and take #22 WAIKIKI.

Dole Plantation: Take bus to ALA MOANA CENTER (TRF) to #52 WAHIAWA CIRCLE ISLAND.

Foster Botanic Gardens: Take #2 bus to Hotel-Riviera St. Walk to Vineyard Blvd. Return to Hotel St. Take #2 WAIKIKI, or take #4 NUUANU and get off at Nuuanu-Vineyard. Cross Nuuanu Ave. and walk one block to the gardens.

Aloha Tower Marketplace & Hawaii Maritime Center: Take #19-#20 AIRPORT and get off at Alakea–Ala Moana. Cross the street to the Aloha Tower.

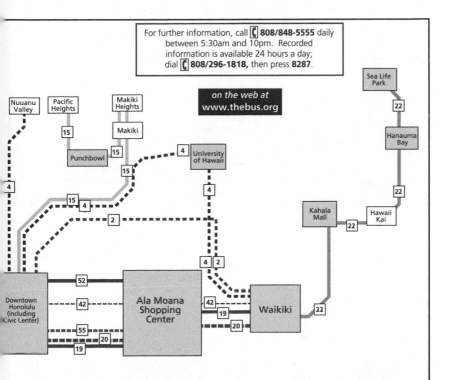

For further information, call [C 808/848-5555 daily between 5:30am and 10pm. Recorded information is available 24 hours a day; dial [C 808/296-1818, then press 8287.

on the web at
www.thebus.org

Honolulu Zoo, Kapionani Park or Waikiki Band Shell: Take any bus on Kuhio Ave. going #4, #8, #19, #20, #22, #23, #42 or "B" City Express. DIAMOND HEAD direction to Kapahulu Ave.

Iolani Palace (also **State Capitol, Honolulu Hale, Kawaihao Church, Mission Houses Museum, Queen's Hospital, King Kamehameha Statue, State Judiciary Bldg.**) Take any #2 bus and get off at Punchbowl and Beretania St. Walk to King St. Return #2 WAIKIKI on King St.

Kahala Mall: Take #22 HAWAII KAI–SEA LIFE PARK to Kilauea Ave. Return, #22 WAIKIKI.

Pearl Harbor (*Arizona* **Memorial):** Take #20 AIRPORT. Get off across from Memorial, or take a bus to ALA MOANA CENTER (TRF) to #52.

Polynesian Cultural Center: Take a bus to ALA MOANA CENTER (TRF) to #55 KANEOHE CIRCLE ISLAND. Bus ride takes 2 hours one-way.

Queen Emma's Summer Home: Take #4 NUUANU, or board a bus to ALA MOANA CENTER (TRF) to #55 KANEOHE.

Sea Life Park: Take #22 HAWAII KAI-SEA LIFE PARK or #23. Bus #22 will stop at Hanauma Bay en route to the park.

University of Hawaii: Take #4 NUUANU. The bus will go to the University en route to Nuuanu.

Waikele Premium Outlets: Take bus #42 from Waikiki to Wapahu Transit Center, then bus #433 to Waikele.

arrival at the airport); children 3 and under ride free. Each passenger is allowed two bags; you'll pay a few dollars extra for additional or oversize baggage. No reservation is necessary. You can buy your tickets at the Roberts Hawaii desk near Baggage Claim turnstile H.

No reservation is necessary to take the shuttle from the airport to your hotel, but be sure to book a hotel pickup for your departing flight at least 24 hours in advance by calling ☎ 808-566-7333. Allow 45 minutes to an hour to get to the airport.

Shuttle service between Waikiki and the airport is offered 24 hours a day from **V.I.P. Trans.** (☎ 866-836-0317 or 808-836-0317; www.viptrans.com). The fare is $11 per person ($20 round-trip), and they'll even meet you at the baggage carousel; the only caveat is that you're restricted to two pieces of luggage per person. Add on a lei greeting for $16 per person.

The island's descriptively named bus system, **TheBus** (☎ 808-848-5555; www.thebus.org), does travel between the airport and Waikiki, and the one-way fare is just $2 ($1 for kids under age 19, or free for a child under age 6 who sits on your lap). Bus nos. 19 and 20 (Waikiki Beach and Hotels) run to downtown Honolulu and Waikiki. The hitch is that you're not allowed to board with any substantive luggage. You can bring on a carry-on or small suitcase as long as it fits under the seat and doesn't disrupt other passengers; otherwise, you have to take a shuttle or taxi. What's more, the ride to Waikiki will take more than an hour, as opposed to 20 minutes or a half-hour if you take a taxi or shuttle.

If you're not going to rent a car, I suggest taking a taxi or shuttle from the airport and then using TheBus to get around town after you've settled in. For more information on TheBus, see the section "Letting somebody else do the driving," later in this chapter.

Choosing Your Location

Oahu's greatest asset is its diversity. This is an island with a destination for everyone, whether you want to be where the action is, prefer to live like a local, or are looking to discover your inner beach bum.

It used to be that visitors came to Oahu to stay in Waikiki, period. Most still do, and for good reason: Waikiki is the Pacific's party central, a laidback, high-rise beach party bustling with energy and easygoing fun. Dining and nightlife options abound. And transportation is a snap; you don't need a rental car to get to the beach, because it's right there, and most of Oahu's major attractions, like Pearl Harbor for sightseeing and Hanauma Bay for prime snorkeling, are a bus ride away.

However, Waikiki isn't for everyone, particularly travelers with a penchant for quieter or more natural settings, or those who prefer off-the-beaten-path experiences. If this sounds like you, Oahu still holds promise: The island's gorgeous, residential Windward Coast and the rural, funky North Shore have begun to welcome visitors in significant numbers, too. These destinations tend to cater to travel do-it-yourselfers who prefer vacation rentals or home-style bed-and-breakfasts over full-service hotels (although the North Shore does boast one excellent full-service resort). Both areas move at a much slower pace than high-energy Waikiki; however, they both tend to receive more rain, on average, than Waikiki's sunny south shore. Also, you will need a rental car to enjoy them, and you should expect to do a decent amount of driving to reach many of the island's main attractions — but you will find plenty of fabulous beaches within shouting distance.

Waikiki

Although all of Waikiki qualifies as a beach party, each of its three neighborhoods, connected along Kalakaua Avenue, Waikiki's main drag, has its own personality.

Mid-Waikiki

Mid-Waikiki is the life of the party. This is Waikiki at its most densely built, but also Waikiki at its most convenient. Restaurants, shopping, and — most important — the city's most popular and celebrated stretch of sand are all within walking distance.

Although it retains some vestiges of cheese, mid-Waikiki has become more sophisticated of late, with respectable restaurants and both midrange and couture boutiques outnumbering the T-shirt shops and tacky souvenir posts. The midsection of the beach has been transformed into a wonderful public playground, with winding flagstone paths, blooming tropical foliage, and grassy knolls. Fortunately, affordable hotels remain; the neighborhood has simply improved around them.

Ewa Waikiki

Ewa (*ee*-va) Waikiki is the western end of the neighborhood, on the way to downtown Honolulu. (Oahuans say "Ewa" to indicate a westerly direction, meaning toward the town called Ewa on the west side of Oahu.) This western end of Waikiki, beyond Saratoga Road (on the other side of Fort DeRussy Park from mid-Waikiki), is a tad removed but plenty convenient. The beach is quieter at this more residential end (mostly high-rise apartments), but you may find yourself getting in the car (or hopping the Waikiki Trolley) to mid-Waikiki destinations.

 Waikiki has received a major update in the form of **Waikiki Beach Walk,** Waikiki's largest development project in 30 years. Developers have entirely reinvented about 8 acres of prime Ewa Waikiki real estate (around Lewers Street and Beach Walk, between Kalakaua Avenue and the ocean) as an exciting, pedestrian-friendly, mixed-use master-plan destination, with 100,000 square feet of new retail space in the form of dining, lodging, shopping, and entertainment. Highlights of the plan include a brand-new **Embassy Suites** hotel; new timeshare units; new restaurants, including the first Waikiki outpost of the famed **Roy's** Hawaiian fusion restaurants and the first Hawaii outlet of world-famous Japanese fusion mecca, **Nobu;** and plenty of good-quality shopping, as well as an outdoor entertainment plaza. With the exception of a luxe new Trump hotel and residence tower, which isn't slated to be complete until early 2010, and an adjacent retail and dining complex that will be the new home to the Hard Rock Cafe, the construction is generally complete. I found the area to be a wonderful place to stay in mid-2008, and it will only get better. For the latest information, including a webcam and a full list of the accommodations, shops, and restaurants that populate the walkable area, visit www.waikikibeachwalk.com.

Diamond Head Waikiki

For those who want both relative quiet and convenience, this eastern-most section of Waikiki is the place to stay. Many (including me) call Diamond Head Waikiki their favorite section of town, thanks to its pretty setting, easygoing vibe, great beach, and prime panoramic views of the rest of Waikiki. A handful of small hotels and condo buildings sits at the foot of Diamond Head crater, separated from the rest of the neighborhood by well-manicured **Kapiolani Park.** The beach here, called Sans Souci Beach, is the locals' favorite stretch, thanks to its beauty (Diamond Head makes a gorgeous backdrop) and intimate, low-key vibe. Waikiki's bustle is still within easy walking distance.

East Oahu: Kahala

This exclusive residential neighborhood on the other side of Diamond Head, just a ten-minute drive east of prime Waikiki, is the perfect compromise for those who want an away-from-it-all vibe and a freeway-convenient location. Expect to dig deep, though — the only hotel in these parts is the **Kahala Resort,** one of Honolulu's finest.

The Windward Coast

This is the Oahu of *Lost* — lush, misty, and almost impossibly green. You can reach this dense but gorgeous residential area via two freeway tunnels that have been bored through the Koolau Mountains, creating easy traffic flow between urban Honolulu and the prime Windward Coast communities of **Kailua, Lanikai Beach,** and **Kaneohe.** Although these communities are far quieter than high-energy Honolulu, don't expect wide-open spaces; most vacation rentals and B&Bs are in attractive but populous suburban or beach neighborhoods. If you don't require a full-service resort, the Windward Coast is your best chance of having it all on Oahu. The beaches are gorgeous, the vibe is laid-back, and the city's restaurants and attractions are an easy drive. However, this lush coast tends more toward rain than Waikiki's sunny south shore (although I've enjoyed plenty of perfect beach days on this side of the island). Also, the Windward Coast is best for morning types, because the sun hides behind the misty Koolau range come late afternoon.

The North Shore

Oahu's rural North Shore is the heart of Hawaii's surf culture. The charming town of **Haleiwa** (ha-lay-*ee*-va), surfdom's unofficial capital, really comes alive in winter, when the monster waves arrive, drawing serious surfers from around the world — and the people who love to watch them in action.

The North Shore is significantly more rural and more spread out than the Windward Coast, but it's not as convenient to town; expect about an hour's drive to Honolulu, which tends to preclude hopping in the car for an easy jaunt. The area quiets down in summer, when it becomes an ideal water playland for couples and families who want a rural, out-of-the-way getaway. The beaches are gorgeous and glassy in the warm months, and the vibe is peaceful and carefree. Surf excitement reigns in winter, when big-wave bad boys and girls show up to ride the big blue crush. However, normal folks will have to drive to the Windward Coast or south shore to find a welcoming beach during these months. Save for one lovely ocean-front hotel, the **Turtle Bay Resort,** accommodations are almost entirely vacation rentals.

Leeward Oahu: The Ko Olina Resort

Past Pearl Harbor, about 40 minutes west of Waikiki via the H-1 freeway, is the carefully manicured **Ko Olina Resort,** the only full-fledged resort development on the arid leeward coast of Oahu. The **JW Marriott Ihilani Resort and Spa** is a refuge for golfers and spa-goers who want to see Oahu's attractions without staying in an urban setting. The downside? Expect to spend a good portion of your island visit in the car and a good deal of money on resort dining because all the island's sights and restaurants are at least a half-hour's drive away. Best for Marriott fans or those who want a quiet, out-of-the-way destination without sacrificing sun or the comforts of a full-service resort hotel.

Getting Around Oahu

Getting around Waikiki and Honolulu is a tad complicated, simply because so many streets are one-way. But with a good map in hand, you won't have a problem. After you get past the city, basically one road circles the island, so you'd have to work hard to lose your bearings.

Navigating your way around Honolulu

A big, bustling city, Honolulu is approximately 12 miles wide and 26 miles long, running east–west roughly between Diamond Head crater and Pearl Harbor. It folds over seven hills laced by seven streams and runs down to the sea.

Honolulu's most famous neighborhood, **Waikiki,** runs along Honolulu's central stretch of coast all the way to grassy Kapiolani Park and

Diamond Head crater to the east. This well-developed strip of land is about 3 miles long, but it extends from the coast inland only a few blocks to the man-made Ala Wai Canal.

Waikiki's primary thoroughfares run east to west. Kalakaua Avenue runs 1 block away from and parallel to the coast in an easterly direction, toward Diamond Head. Ala Wai Boulevard runs along Waikiki's inland (northern) edge one-way toward downtown. Sandwiched in between — 1 block north of Kalakaua, 1 block south of Ala Wai — is Kuhio Avenue, which handles two-way traffic.

West of Waikiki is the Ala Moana section of Honolulu, so named for the **Ala Moana Center,** Honolulu's retail and transportation hub. (You can pick up almost every major bus route here; see the section "Boarding TheBus," later in this chapter.) Drive west on Ala Moana, and you pass more shopping stops — Ward Centre, the Ward Warehouse, a mall of dining options called Restaurant Row, and the historic harbor front Aloha Tower Marketplace shopping and restaurant complex — before reaching downtown Honolulu.

Situated in the blocks inland from the Aloha Tower Marketplace — basically between Nuuanu Avenue and Punchbowl Street — **downtown Honolulu** comprises a tiny cluster of high-rises that serves as the financial, business, and government center of Hawaii. Also here are the **Chinatown Historic District,** the oldest Chinatown in America, and some of Hawaii's most important historic landmarks, most notably **Iolani** (ee-oh-*lan*-ee) **Palace,** the only royal palace on American soil.

Inland from here, and north of the Ala Wai Canal above Waikiki, residential neighborhoods make their way up the hills, creating an urban backdrop unlike any other in a major American city. Running through these neighborhoods is the freeway known as H-1, which leads to the east end of Oahu.

To avoid frustration when driving around Waikiki and downtown Honolulu, always have a map nearby that features directional arrows on the city's many one-way streets. The map on the color tear-out Cheat Sheet at the front of this book — which features Waikiki on one side and Honolulu on the other — should do the trick. Just think of the Waikiki side as the easterly portion and the Honolulu side as the westerly portion; if you were to photocopy them and put them side by side, they'd (roughly) align to cover, in large part, the area where you'll be spending most of your time in the city.

If you stop a local and ask for directions, you're likely to hear a few unfamiliar terms. That's because islanders tend to give directions a bit differently than what mainlanders are used to, particularly in Honolulu:

> ✔ Seldom will anyone direct you north or south; instead, they'll send you either *makai* (ma-*kai*), meaning toward the sea, or *mauka* (*mow*-kah), toward the mountains.

✔ Instead of east and west, locals will tell you to go Diamond Head
when they mean east (in the direction of the world-famous
Diamond Head crater), and Ewa (*ee*-va) when they mean west (in
the direction of the town called Ewa, beyond Pearl Harbor).

So if you ask a local for directions, this is what you're likely to hear:
"Drive 2 blocks *makai* [toward the sea] and then turn Diamond Head
[east] at the stoplight. Go 1 block and turn *mauka* [toward the moun-
tains]. It's on the Ewa [western] side of the street."

Exploring the rest of Oahu

After you move beyond the city, Oahu is simple to navigate. That's
because just a few roads work in concert to form a rough circle.

The "Circle Island" route starts in Honolulu; travels up the middle of the
island to the North Shore; curves around the island's top knob; proceeds
down the eastern, or windward, coast; and curves around the island's
eastern knob back to Waikiki and Honolulu. (Thanks to a few highway
tunnels drilled through the Koolau Mountains, you can also drive directly
between Honolulu and the Windward Coast without having to go all the
way around the east end of the island.)

Driving to the North Shore

The North Shore is the epicenter of Hawaii's surf culture. Small communities and collections of simple houses serve as scant interruption for the
string of fabulous beaches that line this rural coast, where the schizophrenic surf is flat as a pancake in summer and kicks up to monster proportions in winter. The surf town of Haleiwa (ha-lay-*ee*-vah) is the North
Shore's main community. Still small and charming, Haleiwa is nevertheless on a significant growth curve, with an expanding shopping and
restaurant scene — and corresponding traffic — as interest in Hawaii
surf culture continues to explode.

I highly recommend coming here to explore, either to watch the world's
most outrageous daredevil surfers in action in winter, or just to experience the laid-back vibe and play in the baby waves in summer. I discuss
the beaches and other North Shore highlights in Chapter 11.

Haleiwa sits about an hour's drive north of Waikiki, at the junction of
highways 99 and 83, both called Kamehameha Highway. The easiest way
to get there is to cruise north through Oahu's broad and fertile central
valley, past Pearl Harbor, Schofield Barracks, and pineapple and sugar
cane fields until the sea reappears.

From Waikiki, pick up the H-1 freeway heading west. Your best bet is
probably to take Ala Wai Boulevard to McCully Street north to H-1, but it
all depends on where your hotel is; ask at the front desk for the most
direct route.

After you're on H-1, stay to the right, because the freeway divides abruptly. Follow the signs for H-1 and then H-1/H-2. When the two roads divide, follow the H-2 up the middle of the island, heading north toward the town of Wahiawa (wa-hee-*ah*-va). That's what the sign will say — not North Shore or Haleiwa, but Wahiawa.

The H-2 runs out and becomes a two-lane road about 18 miles out of downtown Honolulu, near Schofield Barracks. It then turns into Kamehameha Highway (first Highway 99, then Highway 83) at Wahiawa. Kam Highway, as the islanders call it, is your road for the rest of the trip to Haleiwa.

You can also meander your way to the North Shore by driving along the lush Windward Coast and around Oahu's peak. In fact, I highly recommend driving the full circle and making a day of it. If you're in a hurry to get to the North Shore, take the central route and follow the Windward Coast back south. If you'd rather enjoy one or two of the windward side's magnificent beaches on the way north (see Chapter 11), do that in the morning and come back to Waikiki via the less scenic central route. For windward driving directions, see "Cruising along the scenic Windward Coast," later in this chapter.

Heading to East Oahu

At some point, you're likely to find yourself heading beyond Diamond Head, either bound for Hanauma Bay, one of Hawaii's finest snorkel spots (the best for first-timers), or Sea Life Park, or just to take in some extremely groovy desert-meets-the-sea scenery. You can reach East Oahu simply by heading east on the H-1, which dumps you onto the Kalanianaole (ka-lan-ee-an-*ow*-lay) Highway (Highway 72), the main thoroughfare that takes you around the elbow of Oahu.

Cruising along the scenic Windward Coast

Stand in the heart of Waikiki with your back to the ocean. To your right, you'll see a mountain range called the Koolaus (koo-*oo*-laus); on the other side of them is the east coast of Oahu. This windward-facing coast is the island's wettest side and, therefore, is its most lush and gorgeous. Lined with suburban beach communities and some breathtakingly beautiful beaches, it's well worth seeing.

Three highways will get you from the city to the Windward Coast in about 20 minutes or so: the Pali Highway (Highway 61), the Likelike (lee-kay-*lee*-kay) Highway (Highway 63), and the H-3 freeway, all of which cut right through the mountains. Your best bet from Waikiki is to take the H-1 to the Pali Highway. After you go through the tunnel, turn left on Kamehameha Highway (Highway 83); this coastal highway will be your roadway for the rest of the trip, whether you choose to follow it all the way to Haleiwa (about 1½ hours without stops), whether you're heading to the Polynesian Cultural Center (the South Pacific cultural theme park about an hour from Waikiki), or whether you're simply enjoying the ultralush scenery and some of best beaches in the islands. (See Chapter 11 for specific suggestions.)

Dominating the west side of Oahu is the island's second mountain range, the Waianae (wah-ee-*an*-eh) Mountains. Beyond this ridge is the hot, dry leeward side of the island. There's not much to see there, and locals prefer to keep this one area of heavily touristed Oahu to themselves. Unless you're heading to the area's one master-planned resort community, Ko Olina, up to Waianae to meet a scheduled cruise with **Dolphin Excursions** (see Chapter 11), or for some other prearranged reason, I suggest honoring their wishes and concentrating your efforts on exploring the other parts of the island.

Letting somebody else do the driving

Oahu is the one island that's easy to visit if you can't — or won't — drive yourself. Oahu's islandwide public transportation system, **TheBus** (www. thebus.org), is extremely user-friendly. The **Waikiki Trolley** (www. waikikitrolley.com) is also available for getting around town.

 Although TheBus can take you anywhere you want to go on Oahu, I don't recommend using it to reach areas beyond the city. Not only will you spend a total of 3½ to 4½ hours on the bus getting there and back, but the waits can be extremely long at lonely North Shore bus stops. If you don't want to rent a car for the entire duration of your stay, I strongly encourage you to rent one at least for your day of North Shore and Windward Coast exploring. If, for some reason, you can't rent a car but still want to explore, use one of the tour companies I mention in Chapter 11 to take you around the island.

Boarding TheBus

TheBus is an excellent transit deal. The service is good, the buses are clean, and the cost is low. The one-way fare to ride is $2 per adult and $1 for school-age children, seniors, or riders with disabilities. That low price can get you anywhere you want to go on the island. Service begins daily at 3:30 a.m. and runs until 1:30 a.m. Buses run about every 5 to 15 minutes during the day and every 30 minutes in the evening.

If you plan to use TheBus on multiple occasions, consider purchasing the $20 **4-Day Pass,** which entitles you to unlimited rides over a consecutive four-day period; these passes are sold at ABC Stores and certain 7-Eleven stores. If you're going to be in town for a longer stay, you can buy a **Monthly Pass** for $40 ($20 for kids, seniors, and people with disabilities). These are sold at most 7-Eleven stores, as well as at Foodland, Star, and Times supermarkets. Or you can go directly to TheBus Pass Office at Kalihi Traffic Center, 811 Middle St. (between King Street and Kamehameha Highway) in downtown Honolulu (☎ **808-848-4444**); to get there, take the 1, 2, A, or B lines.

TheBus operates dozens of bus lines, but you'll need to concern yourself only with the handful that pass through Waikiki. Two-way Kuhio Avenue is the main thoroughfare for bus routes through Waikiki.

Virtually all the city's major bus routes converge at the Ala Moana Shopping Center, just west of Waikiki. TheBus makes three stops at the mammoth mall: two on the ocean side of the mall on Ala Moana Boulevard, and one on the mountain side, on Kona Street. Read the posted sign at the stop to make sure that the line you want is going where you want to go.

If you want help with planning a specific route, or if you have other questions pertaining to TheBus system, call ☎ **808-848-5555;** information specialists are available daily between 5:30 a.m. and 10 p.m. Have your departure and destination points handy when you call, as well as the time of day you want to travel.

I highly recommend visiting TheBus's excellent Web site at www.thebus. org to familiarize yourself with the system before you leave home. It offers timetables and maps for all routes, plus directions to many local attractions and a list of upcoming events. (Taking TheBus is sometimes easier than parking.)

Also, don't hesitate to ask the front desk or concierge at your hotel for assistance in navigating TheBus system. And don't be shy about asking the bus drivers for help. In general, they're very friendly and helpful, and they'll be glad to point you in the right direction.

If you plan on using TheBus system a lot and want to get to know it well, pick up one of the handy system reference guides available at any convenience store for just a few dollars.

A few etiquette tips for using TheBus:

✔ When the bus you want approaches, wave to the driver to indicate that you want to board the bus. Back away from the stop if you don't want that particular bus.

✔ You must have the exact fare when you board the bus because the drivers don't make change. You can use either dollar bills or coins.

✔ To transfer to another line, ask the driver of the first bus you board for a free transfer when you board. You can't use a transfer to pick up the same line going in the same direction, nor can you use a transfer to go back to where you came from.

✔ To open the rear door of the bus, push on the door or step on the first step when the green light is lit. Be sure to hold the door open as you get off the bus so that your fellow riders don't get hit by the slamming door.

Taking the Waikiki Trolley

The **Waikiki Trolley** (☎ **800-824-8804** or 808-593-2822; www.waikiki trolley.com), operated by E Noa Tours, is an open-air, motorized trolley similar to a San Francisco cable car. I like using the trolley; it's a fun way to do some sightseeing. The trolley runs along three lines:

✔ The **Honolulu City (Red) Line** runs daily from 10 a.m. to 6:55 p.m. It makes a loop around Waikiki and downtown Honolulu every 45 minutes, stopping at key attractions such as the Duke Kahanamoku statue, the Honolulu Academy of Arts, Aloha Tower Marketplace, the Bishop Museum, Hilo Hattie's, Ward Centre, Ala Moana Center, and other prime stops.

✔ The **Ala Moana Shopping Shuttle (Pink) Line** runs every eight minutes daily from 9:30 a.m. to 9:45 p.m. (7:30 p.m. on Sun), stopping at the DFS Galleria Waikiki, King Kalakaua Plaza, Ala Moana Center, Ward Centre, and other stops.

✔ The **Ocean Coast (Blue) Line** makes its rounds every 45 minutes daily from 9 a.m. to 7 p.m., connecting Waikiki with East Oahu sites, including the Honolulu Zoo, Waikiki Aquarium, Diamond Head, Hanauma Bay, and Sea Life Park. In the morning, there are express buses running directly from Waikiki to Diamond Head.

✔ The **Honolulu Shopping (Yellow) Line** makes its rounds every 45 minutes daily from 10 a.m. to 9:30 p.m. (7 p.m. on Sun), connecting Ala Moana Center with a variety of locals' favorite shopping stops, including the Ward Centre, which is also rich with dining options.

✔ The **Waikele Shuttle (Green) Line** takes shoppers out to suburban Oahu's premium outlet mall; call for the pickup schedule.

Due to some arcane state rule, trolley passengers are allowed to disembark at Hanauma Bay only for a quick photo op; you aren't allowed to use this option to get to and from the marine preserve for a day of snorkeling. If you want to use the trolley to reach Hanauma Bay, disembark at Koko Marina Center, where you can either walk the mile to the park or catch a taxi.

A **one-day jump-on, jump-off pass** costs $27 for adults, $19 for seniors over age 62, $16 for military personnel, $13 for kids ages 4 to 11, and $11 for kids riding with military personnel. This pass allows you to hop on and off all three lines all day long, as much as you want.

A **four-day jump-on, jump-off pass** gives you unlimited trolley privileges for four consecutive days for $48 for adults, $28 for seniors, $26 for military personnel, $20 for kids 4 to 11, and $15 for kids riding with military personnel. The four-day pass is a good deal, but you're probably better off using TheBus to get around for that many days because the trolley routes are simply too limited.

Check the Waikiki Trolley Web site, which often offers online purchase specials. At press time, a four-day pass cost just $39.

You have to purchase your trolley tickets before you board the trolley. The main customer service kiosk is at the **DFS Galleria Waikiki,** in the heart of Waikiki, at the corner of Kalakaua and Royal Hawaiian avenues, open Monday through Saturday from 8 a.m. to 10 p.m., Sunday from 8:30 a.m. to 9 p.m. There's another ticket and information kiosk with more limited hours located at the **Hilton Hawaiian Village,** at Kalia Road and Ala Moana Boulevard, and at **Ala Moana Center,** on the ocean side of the mall. You can also prebook your tickets online (where you might snag a special discount) or through the toll-free number listed earlier in this section.

Staying in Style

Frankly, if you're planning a trip to the liveliest island in the Pacific, you may as well revel in the energy of it and stay in Waikiki. That said, if you do want peace and quiet, you can find it on Oahu, too. A number of the hotels listed in this chapter are located on the quieter fringe of Waikiki, in less densely developed or residential neighborhoods. And in case you'd prefer to stay beyond the city and get away from it all, I'll point you to a couple of luxury resorts well beyond the reach of Waikiki and also show you how to book the B&B or vacation rental of your dreams on the residential Windward Coast or the funky North Shore.

Oahu's best accommodations

In the following listings, each resort, hotel, or condo name is followed by a number of dollar signs, ranging from one ($) to five ($$$$$). Each represents the median rack-rate price range for a double room per night, as follows:

$	Cheap — less than $150 per night
$$	Still affordable — $150–$225
$$$	Moderate — $225–$325
$$$$	Expensive but not ridiculous — $325–$450
$$$$$	Ultraluxurious — more than $450 per night

You almost never need to pay the asking price for a hotel room. Check out Chapter 7 for details on how to avoid paying full price. Also see Chapter 5 for advice on how to score an all-inclusive package that can save you big bucks on both accommodations and airfare, and sometimes car rentals and activities too.

Also, don't forget that the state adds 11.42 percent in taxes to your hotel bill.

A number of Waikiki's inexpensive and midpriced hotels feature rooms whose bathrooms have showers only, no tubs. If you need a full tub, be sure to check that one will be available when booking.

Aqua Palms & Spa
$–$$ Ewa Waikiki

This budget boutique hotel across the street from the much pricier Hilton Hawaiian Village is a prime choice for wallet-watching travelers in pricey Waikiki. A charming, freshly decorated lobby leads to studios that are petite (averaging 325 sq. ft.) but pleasingly outfitted. Every studio, from moderate to deluxe, boasts a comfortable king-size or queen-size bed and a microwave, minifridge, coffeemaker, dining utensils, and TV with built-in DVD. Some units have sleeper sofas and/or private balconies with Diamond Head and ocean views. Expect a petite bathroom. Value-added perks include free continental breakfast delivered daily to your guest room in a Lauhala basket, and free wireless Internet access in the lobby. Service is consistently courteous and professional, and the on-site AquaSPA offers pampering at reasonable prices. A pool and fitness center round out the amenities, but, really, who needs 'em when you're just 2 blocks from a premier stretch of Waikiki beach (the same one that pricier Hilton enjoys)? Next door is an appealingly old-school 24-hour diner. The location, at the far end of Waikiki, is a bit removed; plan on a short walk to the heart of the action. A few tips to maximize your Aqua Palms experience: Rooms on the Ala Moana side can experience street noise, so ask for a room away from the boulevard if you're sensitive. Also ask for a room away from the elevators, which can be noisy; rooms are not soundproof. And reserve a small car; the parking spaces are tight.

See map p. 120. 1850 Ala Moana Blvd. (between Hobron Lane and Ewa Road). ☎ *866-406-2782 or 808-947-7256. Fax: 808-947-7002.* www.aquapalms.com *or* www.aquaresorts.com. *Parking: $18. Rack rates: $140–$230 double, $220–$390 suite. Check for sometimes-terrific Internet rates (as low as $94 at press time), plus spa and romance packages. Discounts available for AAA members, seniors, and government and military personnel. AE, DISC, MC, V.*

Aqua Resorts

Aqua Hotels & Resorts (☎ **866-406-2782;** www.aquaresorts.com) has taken Waikiki by storm in recent years, bringing a range of affordable, well-located hotels paired with good service and a dash of style to wallet-conscious travelers. While Hotel Renew (below) is their "elite" flagship, the rest of their hotels fall into two more affordable groups. The six Aqua Boutique hotels ($–$$) have a boutique feel, good service, and nice perks like high-speed Internet access and free continental breakfast (at most). My favorite of these is Aqua Palms & Spa (above). Also worth checking out is the Aqua Coconut Waikiki, which was under dramatic renovation at this writing (complete by the time you arrive). The five Aqua Lite hotels ($) are designed with budget travelers in mind. These are decidedly smaller, simpler, and a little rougher around the edges in terms of decor, but they're clean and well serviced. Many of the Aqua hotels were undergoing renovation at the time of this writing, or slated for it; I highly recommend opting for a renovated one, especially if your budget is at the Lite level.

Waikiki Accommodations

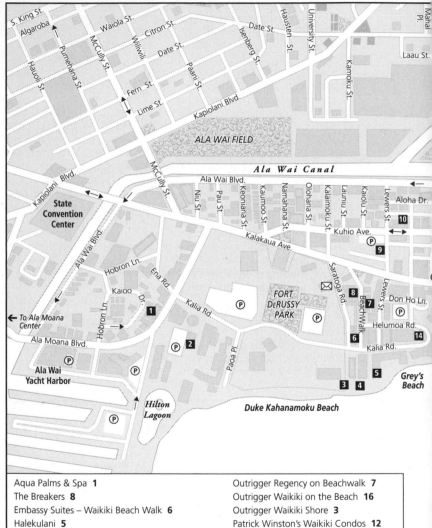

Aqua Palms & Spa **1**
The Breakers **8**
Embassy Suites – Waikiki Beach Walk **6**
Halekulani **5**
Hilton Hawaiian Village Beach Resort & Spa **2**
Hotel Renew **20**
Ilima Hotel **11**
Kahala Hotel & Resort **22**
Moana Surfrider, A Westin Resort **17**
New Otani Kaimana Beach Hotel **21**
Ohana Waikiki Beachcomber **13**
Outrigger Reef on the Beach **4**

Outrigger Regency on Beachwalk **7**
Outrigger Waikiki on the Beach **16**
Outrigger Waikiki Shore **3**
Patrick Winston's Waikiki Condos **12**
ResortQuest Waikiki Beach Hotel **19**
ResortQuest Waikiki Joy Hotel **9**
Royal Hawaiian **15**
Waikiki Beach Marriott Resort & Spa **18**
Waikiki Parc **14**
The Wyland Waikiki **10**

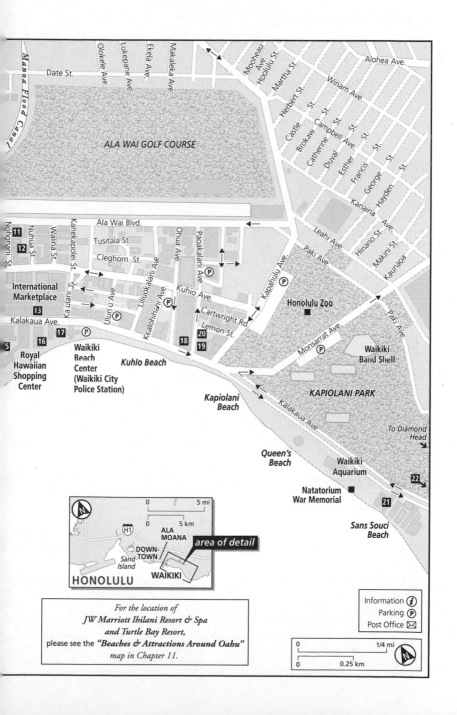

Manoa Flood Canal

Date St.

Olokele Ave.
Lukepane Ave.
Ekela Ave.
Makaleka Ave.

Mooheau Ave.
Hoolulu St.
Martha St.

Alohea Ave.

Winam Ave.

Herbet St.
Castle St.
Brokaw St.
Campbell Ave.
Catherine St.
Duval St.
Esther St.
Francis St.
George St.
Hayden St.

ALA WAI GOLF COURSE

Kanaina Ave.
Hinano St.
Makini St.
Kaunoa

Nohonani St.

Ala Wai Blvd.

Kanekapolei St.

Nuhua St.
Walina St.

11
12

Tusitala St.

Ohua Ave.
Paoakalani Ave.

Cleghorn St.

Leahi Ave.
Paki Ave.

Kapahulu Ave.

International Marketplace

13

Kalakaua Ave.

Iliuokalani Ave.
Kealohilani Ave.

Kaiulani Ave.
Uluniu Ave.

Kuhio Ave.

Cartwright Rd.

Lemon St.

Honolulu Zoo ■

Paki Ave.

5
16
17

Royal Hawaiian Shopping Center

Waikiki Beach Center (Waikiki City Police Station)

Kuhio Beach

18
20
19

Monsarrat Ave.

Waikiki Band Shell

Kapiolani Beach

Kalakaua Ave.

KAPIOLANI PARK

To Diamond Head

Queen's Beach

Waikiki Aquarium

Natatorium War Memorial ■

22

21

Sans Souci Beach

0   5 mi
0   5 km

HONOLULU

H1

ALA MOANA

DOWN-TOWN
Sand Island

area of detail

WAIKIKI

*For the location of
JW Marriott Ihilani Resort & Spa
and Turtle Bay Resort,
please see the "Beaches & Attractions Around Oahu"
map in Chapter 11.*

Information ⓘ
Parking ⓟ
Post Office ✉

0   1/4 mi
0   0.25 km

The Breakers
$ Mid-Waikiki

This vintage low-rise charmer in the midst of prime high-rise Waikiki is a wonderful option for budget-minded travelers who don't want to succumb to chain-hotel conformity. This lovely two-story '50s-style garden motel boasts a friendly staff, a loyal following, a fab location just a two-minute walk from the beach, and a warmly nostalgic Old Waikiki vibe. Units are set around an attractive pool and tropical garden blooming with brilliant hibiscus; wooden jalousies and Japanese-style shoji doors add to the ambience. The spacious rooms are older — updating is in order — but nicely maintained, and they boast dated electric-range kitchenettes and lanais overlooking the pool. The poolside cafe serves up affordable Japanese food and great mai tais in an attractive outdoor setting. Everything is well kept, and the hoteliers have managed to maintain an aura of oasis in their corner of Waikiki. Service is personal and friendly. The Breakers caters to visitors from all walks of life, including families. A coin-op laundry is on-site.

See map p. 120. 250 Beach Walk (between Kalakaua Avenue and Helumoa Road). ☎ **808-923-3181.** *Fax: 808-923-7174.* www.breakers-hawaii.com. *Limited free parking; the hotel will direct you to a nearby paid lot if hotel parking is full. Rack rates: $120–$135 studio, $165–$235 garden suite. AE, DC, MC, V.*

Embassy Suites — Waikiki Beach Walk
$$$–$$$$ Mid-Waikiki

Run impeccably by the locally based Outrigger hotel company, this new all-suite hotel is a wonderful addition to the Waikiki hotel scene. It is located just a block from the beach in the heart of the freshly revitalized Beach Walk entertainment and shopping zone, now the nicest area of Waikiki. It's the first real resort hotel in the Embassy Suites brand, and a benchmark example of what the brand can be. All of the well-outfitted rooms are one- and two-bedroom suites, which makes for significantly more comfortable living than a standard hotel room does — and makes this hotel a great choice for families. The living room features a sleeper sofa, a wet bar with minifridge, and a 26-inch flat-panel TV, while bedrooms feature a king or two double beds and another TV. The island-style decor is fresh and pretty. The fourth-floor pool is larger and much more appealing than most non-beachfront pools in Waikiki, and the whole atmosphere of the hotel is pleasantly energetic (but probably not the best choice for away-from-it-all honeymooners).

Rates include a generous free breakfast buffet, complete with cooked-to-order omelet station, and a well-attended nightly manager's reception with free drinks, pupus, and live entertainment. Other more-for-your-money freebies include free Internet access and free (yes, free) local and long-distance calls within the U.S. and Canada (30-min. limit). The only downside is that the new ultraluxe Trump hotel is under construction next door until January 2010; however, even though my room faced the construction, I barely noticed it during my recent stay.

See map p. 120. 201 Beach Walk (at Kalia Road). ☎ *800-EMBASSY [362-2779] or 808-921-2345. Fax: 808-921-2343.* www.embassysuiteswaikiki.com. *Valet parking: $25. Rack rates: $399–$469 1-bedroom suite, $549–$649 2-bedroom suite. Rates include full breakfast and afternoon manager's reception with free drinks and pupus. Special deals and value-add packages are regularly on offer; Internet specials as low as $269 at press time. AE, DC, DISC, MC, V.*

Halekulani
$$$$$ **Mid-Waikiki**

The finest hotel in Waikiki is the epitome of gracious and elegant aloha; the perfect choice for vacationers who only want the best. This open, low-rise beachfront hotel exudes understated luxury (although some may consider it a tad formal for a beach hotel). The rooms are uniformly oversize and done in a classy but supremely comfortable natural-on-white style. Each one features a sitting area, a large furnished lanai, a sumptuous bathroom with a deep soaking tub and separate oversize shower, and all the extras you'd expect from a hotel of this caliber, including in-room check-in, twice-daily maid service, a DVD player, a bedside control panel, and wireless Internet access. About 90 percent of the rooms have some sort of ocean view. For the ultimate in understated luxury, book the Vera Wang Suite, outfitted by the designer herself.

Service is among the best I've ever experienced. The concierge can arrange everything from flowers and leis to limousine service, and often has complimentary tickets for such cultural institutions as the Bishop Museum, the Honolulu Academy of Arts, the Honolulu Symphony, and Iolani Palace on hand. The two elegant oceanfront restaurants are first-rate, the alfresco lounge is Oahu's most romantic spot for sunset cocktails and hula, and the pool is magnificent. The tranquil, sumptuous SpaHalekulani offers a full range of pampering treatments drawn from Asian, Hawaiian, and South Pacific healing traditions. Only one niggling complaint: The beach is small, and the hotel offers only pool service. So if you want to sit in a chair rather than on a towel, you're stuck behind a hedge — and if you want to recline, forget about an ocean view.

See map p. 120. 2199 Kalia Rd. (at the beach end of Lewers Street). ☎ *800-367-2343 or 808-923-2311. Fax: 808-926-8004.* www.halekulani.com. *Valet parking: $22. Rack rates: $450–$$760 double; call for suite rates. Spa, golf, family, romance, and other packages usually available (many with a 3-night minimum). AE, DC, MC, V.*

Hilton Hawaiian Village Beach Resort & Spa
$$$–$$$$ **Ewa Waikiki**

Spread out over 22 tropical acres featuring exotic wildlife — including flamingos, peacocks, and even tropical penguins — and fronting a gorgeous stretch of beach that feels private even though it's not, Waikiki's biggest resort is my favorite choice for families. It feels like a tropical theme park, with its own lagoon (with Atlantis submarine rides), four pools, a wealth of restaurants (including the very good Golden Dragon for

Chinese, the ultraromantic Bali by the Sea, and Benihana for fun slice-and-dice *teppanyaki* dining), enough shopping to stock a midsize mall, a full slate of bars and lounges, and more — even its own post office. It's a blast to stay here. Rooms are housed in multiple towers and range from comfortable to first-class depending on what you want to spend, but all are large, well outfitted, and laden with amenities.

I do have two complaints, however: This place feels as massive as it is, and the casual dining throughout the hotel is mediocre for a resort charging such high rack rates. The plush Mandara Spa (www.mandaraspa.com), on the other hand, is Waikiki's largest spa, and a real draw. Among the other pleasing extras is a wonderful program for kids, so your little ones will be entertained.

See map p. 120. 2005 Kalia Rd. (at Ala Moana Boulevard). ☎ *800-HILTONS or 808-949-4321. Fax: 808-947-7898.* www.hawaiianvillage.hilton.com. *Parking: $22 self-parking, $28 valet. Rack rates: $299–$850 double, suites from $429. Several packages and special offers are almost always available, including romance packages, discounts on multinight stays, free giveaways for kids, and much more. Best available rates from $219 and packages including full breakfast from $249 at press time. Also ask for AAA, AARP, corporate, military, and other discounts. AE, DISC, MC, V.*

Hotel Renew
$$$ Diamond Head Waikiki

This chic boutique hotel, the flagship of the up-and-coming Aqua Hotels and Resorts group, brings affordable style and great service to Waikiki. This small hotel is an oasis of Zen-like cool in bustling Waikiki; you can feel the mood shift as soon as you walk through the doors. The guest rooms are small, but the hotel compensates with a wealth of special features, including lovely contemporary decor, furnishings, and artwork; plush pillowtop bedding and bathrobes; bedside lighting controls; 32-inch flat-panel TVs (with 80-inch projection TVs in some rooms); appealing modern baths (showers only in some); and free wireless Internet access. My only complaint is that the hallways are rather dour. No pool or bar (a chic bar was in the works at press time), but there are plenty of restaurants out the door, and the beach is just a half-block away, across the street. Best for singles and couples who prize style over space.

See map p. 120. 129 Paoakalani Ave. (between Kalakaua and Kuhio avenues). ☎ *866-687-7700 or 808-687-7700. Fax: 808-687-7701.* www.hotelrenew.com *or* www.aquaresorts.com. *Valet parking: $20. Rack rates: $240–$335 double. Internet rates as low as $170 at press time. Also check for packages and specials (seventh night free at press time). AE, DISC, MC, V.*

Ilima Hotel
$$ Mid-Waikiki

This highly recommended local-style condo hotel is a bargain for families or anybody who wants accommodations that go above and beyond what an average hotel can offer. The roomy studios and one-, two-, and three-bedroom apartments are recently renovated and boast full modern kitchens with microwave and coffeemaker, new bathrooms, sofa beds in the living room, and a lanai; one-bedrooms have Jacuzzi tubs too. Extras include daily maid service (not a given in condo units), free local calls, high-speed Internet access (in deluxe units), a small heated pool with adjacent dry sauna, a rooftop sun deck, an exercise room, and laundry facilities. The service is friendly, and the heart-of-Waikiki location is central to shopping and dining. The beach is a ten-minute walk away, but at these prices, you'll happily put on your walkin' shoes. A great choice for bargain travelers of all stripes.

See map p. 120. 445 Nohonani St. (between Kuhio Avenue and Ala Wai Boulevard). ☎ *800-801-9366 or 808-923-1877. Fax: 808-924-2617.* www.ilima.com. *Parking: Limited free parking (usually available). Rack rates: $178–$268 studio, $245–$309 1-bedroom, $356–$406 2-bedroom, $560–$600 3-bedroom penthouse. Heavily discounted senior (50+), corporate, AAA, government, and military rates. Internet specials from $100 per night offered at press time. AE, DC, DISC, MC, V.*

JW Marriott Ihilani Resort & Spa
$$$$ Leeward Oahu

It's got a lot going for it, but I'm not a huge fan of this resort. It's a beautifully designed property nestled in a lovely manicured resort with a quartet of white-sand coves that are forever calm for even your littlest ones. Rooms are extra-large, averaging 660 square feet, and each has a large lanai and a massive marble bathroom with double vanities, a huge soaking tub, and a separate shower. Some 85 percent of the rooms boast ocean views. The excellent 35,000-square-foot Ihilani Spa (with rooftop tennis courts) has been voted one of the best spas in the world by readers of *Condé Nast Traveler.* The food service is terrific throughout the hotel. For the kids, the Keiki Beachcomber Club offers numerous activities (including outdoor adventures and a computer center), and for the adults, the Ko Olina Golf Club boasts 18 challenging holes of Ted Robinson–designed golf.

So what's my problem? Even with all these amenities, Marriott doesn't seem capable of offering a high-quality luxury resort experience — not here, anyway. Although you do have an ocean view, you may also have an industrial plant in your line of vision. And I'm still annoyed that I was assigned a room with a dirty carpet and then told I couldn't be moved because no more rooms were available in my rate class (pricier accommodations were available) — not exactly what I'd call top-notch service. Whether you'll like the way-out-of-town location is up to you, but be prepared for at least a half-hour drive to get just about anywhere. (The hotel does supply transportation to Waikiki and Ala Moana Shopping Center.) Best for Marriott fans and points earners.

See map p. 162. At the Ko Olina Resort, Kapolei (off Highway 93, 17 miles west of Honolulu International Airport). ☎ *800-626-4446, 888-236-2427, or 808-679-0079. Fax: 808-679-0080.* www.ihilani.com *or* www.marriott.com. *Valet or self-parking: $29. Rack rates: $369–$750 double, suites from $850. Inquire about promotional and* value-added package rates (from $299 at press time). AAA, senior (62+), corporate, government, and military discounts available. AE, DC, MC, V.

Kahala Hotel & Resort
$$$$$ **Kahala**

If you want easy access to Honolulu's sights but Waikiki sounds too bustling for you, the Kahala is the perfect compromise. Oahu's only AAA five-diamond resort stands just a ten-minute drive east of Waikiki, staked out on its own perfect crescent beach in one of Honolulu's most upscale neighborhoods. (The hotel provides shuttle service to Waikiki and major shopping centers.) In fact, the tranquil Kahala is ideal for anybody who likes first-rate service and an ambience that blends T-shirts–and–flip-flops comfort with gracious elegance. The big, beautiful rooms come with CD players, high-speed Internet access, goose-down duvets, and high-quality amenities — including the best bathrooms in the business, with soaking tubs, separate showers, and his-and-her sinks and dressing areas. Hoku's, one of Honolulu's most celebrated restaurants, is named for the most charming of the bottlenose dolphins that live on the premises; ask for a room with a lanai that overlooks the dolphin lagoon and sea, and the world is yours. Even if you end up in a mountainview room, take heart: The vistas are almost as fine. The Kahala offers an outstanding spa, a complete fitness center with personal trainers and classes, free use of bicycles, and complimentary surfing lessons. The poolside desk has books, magazines, CD players, and hand-held TVs ready for your use, and "beach butlers" pamper you with towels and a cooling mist while you lounge on the sands. Romance-seeking couples will love the candlelit Veranda at the music-and-cocktails hour. The dolphin-encounter program and year-round kids' club make the Kahala great for families too.

See map p. 120. 5000 Kahala Ave. (east of Diamond Head, next to the Waialae Country Club). ☎ ***800-367-2525*** *or 808-739-8888. Fax: 808-739-8800.* www.kahalaresort. com. *Valet and self-parking: $25. Rack rates: $395–$895 double (most $515–$620), from $1,600 suite. AAA, government, military, and package rates sometimes available; from $315 at press time. Ask about AAA discounts. AE, DC, DISC, MC, V.*

Moana Surfrider, A Westin Resort
$$$$–$$$$$ **Mid-Waikiki**

Even with a '60s extension and a modern tower, this elegant white-clapboard Victorian — Waikiki's first hotel, built in 1901 — overflows with beachy nostalgia. It's more understated and intimate than Waikiki's other historic hotel, the Royal Hawaiian, and now it's more luxurious, too. In 2007, Starwood made a great decision to upgrade the "First Lady of Waikiki" from a Sheraton to a Westin, with all of the attendant style and luxury upgrades, including the addition of Heavenly Beds to all rooms as well as Waikiki's first beachfront spa. The transformation should be complete by the time you arrive.

The original U-shaped building embraces a 100-year-old banyan tree and the ocean beyond. It exudes a magical back-in-time feel that all guests share in, even if your room has a stucco ceiling. I recommend the Banyan rooms, which are small but have high ceilings and loads of historical charm; for the ultimate old Hawaii vibe, book one with a grand lanai overlooking the Banyan Courtyard and the turquoise surf beyond. If space or ocean views win out over retro ambience for you, book in one of the newer wings, where you'll get more space and a lanai.

Both the service and the facilities are great, especially now that a state-of-the-art workout facility has been added. The Banyan Courtyard is the best place to lounge poolside in Waikiki, period, and I love any excuse — breakfast, high tea, Sunday brunch — to snag a seat on the oceanfront veranda, where live music and mai tais set the right island mood every evening. Another fresh highlight is the addition of the terrific Beachhouse, a stylish oceanfront steakhouse serving Amish-raised and Kobe-style beef. Other winning features include a guests-only beach area with full cocktail service on one of Waikiki's finest stretches of sand.

See map p. 120. 2365 Kalakaua Ave. (on the beach, across from Kaiulani Street). ☎ *866-716-8109 or 808-922-3111. Fax: 808-924-4799.* www.moana-surfrider.com. *Valet parking: $25; self-parking: $20. Rack rates: $430–$740 double, from $1,300 suite. Promotional rates and/or package deals are almost always available, so ask for these, as well as AAA and senior discounts. Internet specials as low as $265 at press time. AE, DC, DISC, MC, V.*

New Otani Kaimana Beach Hotel
$$ Diamond Head Waikiki

Located at the quietest, prettiest end of Waikiki, this boutique hotel is the neighborhood's best beachfront bargain. It sits right on the locals' favorite stretch of Waikiki Beach, Sans Souci, with leafy Kapiolani Park and Diamond Head at its back door, which means that the views are pleasing in almost any direction. The park's jogging path and tennis courts are right at hand. An inviting open-air lobby leads to contemporary rooms that are more Holiday Inn than stylish, but are perfectly comfortable. The most basic rooms are tiny, so spring for a superior one if you can. The junior suites are large enough for families, and corner rooms boast Waikiki's finest views. The airy lobby opens onto the Hau Tree Lanai, a wonderfully romantic restaurant that sits right on the sand; great breakfasts make it the right place to start the day even if you're not staying here. Amenities include VCRs, minifridges, and a coin-op laundry. Many regular visitors who can afford it camp out in the well-priced suites, almost all of which are sizable and offer lovely views. Units in the Diamond Head wing are ideal for longer stays because they add a microwave and coffeemaker to the mix. This is one of my favorite midpriced hotels — an excellent value on all fronts.

See map p. 120. 2863 Kalakaua Ave. (across the street from Kapiolani Park). ☎ *800-356-8264 or 808-923-1555. Fax: 808-922-9404.* www.kaimana.com. *Valet parking: $18. Rack rates: $160–$395 double, $320–$1,280 suite. Ask about package rates (including wedding packages, free-car deals, and fourth-night-free rates), and check for Internet specials. AE, DC, DISC, MC, V.*

Ohana Hotels & Resorts

In addition to Ohana Waikiki Beachcomber, **Ohana Hotels & Resorts** ($$), owned and operated by the excellent island-based Outrigger Hotels & Resorts, features value-minded hotels throughout Honolulu. They are all highly recommendable and within walking distance of Waikiki Beach. If you're looking for affordable sleeps, it's hard to go wrong with Ohana. These hotels are a bit less sexy than budget upstart Aqua Hotels & Resorts (recommended earlier in this chapter), but Ohana has a history of proven reliability for wallet-watching travelers. Most of these properties regularly offer excellent Internet specials, discounts, an assortment of packages, and nice value-added perks like free Internet access. For more information, call ☎ **800-462-6262** or surf your way to www.ohanahotels.com.

Ohana Waikiki Beachcomber
$$$ Mid-Waikiki

First-rate package deals and online discounts make this attractive, beautifully maintained, and well-located hotel — just 297 steps from the beach — an excellent value. It lies in the heart of Waikiki's gentrified main drag, across the street from the Royal Hawaiian Shopping Center. The lovely, open Hawaii-style lobby is located on the second floor, which keeps it blissfully free of bustle from the street; tropical floral arrangements add a splash of elegance. Rooms are freshly renovated with a pretty tropical motif, alder and cherrywood furnishings, 32-inch flat-screen TVs, minifridges, completely updated bathrooms with granite countertops, private lanais, and a nice island-style feeling. One- and two-bedroom suites are a great choice for families. Housekeeping is impeccable. The Moana side of the building scores you gorgeous partial ocean views. Also on-site are a nice pool and Jacuzzi, a cafe, and a coin-op laundry. Complimentary high-speed Internet access is a perk for laptop-toters. A top-notch midrange choice. As if you needed another selling point, Jimmy Buffet's at the Beachcomber, a new restaurant from the Margaritaville man himself, is slated to be open and rockin' by the time you read this. This is also home of illusionist John Horikawa's Magic of Polynesia show (see Chapter 11).

See map p. 120. 2300 Kalakaua Ave. (at Duke's Lane). ☎ *800-462-6262 or 808-922-4646. Fax: 808-923-4889.* www.ohanahotels.com. *Parking: $18. Rack rates: $299–$369 double, $489–$1,700 1- or 2-bedroom suite. Good-value packages often available. Discounts for seniors (50+), AAA members, and government and military personnel. Internet specials offered from $129 per night at press time. AE, DC, MC, V.*

Outrigger Reef on the Beach
$$$$ Mid-Waikiki

This beautifully located hotel is steps from the revitalized Beach Walk development and situated on a lovely stretch of Waikiki beach that feels almost private. And now that a fabulous new renovation has beautified the public spaces and transformed the guest rooms into some of the most beautiful in Waikiki, the substantially upgraded Reef has become one of my favorite choices in Waikiki.

This is a big hotel, with three towers connected by the lobby, but its generous open-air lobby maximizes the ocean breeze and its warm, personalized service belies its mega size. A restored hundred-year-old canoe hangs at the entrance, announcing the cultural infusion the hotel has received. Across from the new sit-down check-in desk — where staff wears beautifully understated uniforms by Hawaii's top aloha wear designer, Sig Zane — Polynesian artifacts are on display. The island-appropriate tone is carried into the elegant guest rooms, which feature elegant Polynesian tapa-patterned fabrics, textured walls and carpets, vibrant underwater photography on the walls, and gorgeous dark wood furnishings with a pineapple motif that represents the spirit of hospitality that pervades the hotel. Amenities include beautiful bathrooms with granite counters, stylish sleeper sofas, and 32-inch flat-panel TVs, plus such perks as free Internet access and free local and long-distance calls to the U.S. and Canada. Ask for a suite with a tub for two if romance is your aim.

On-site is a big freshwater pool, three spas, a pleasing three-meal restaurant on the sand, Starbucks and Jamba Juice outlets in the lobby, and the full-service Serenity Spa Hawaii (www.serenityhawaii.com) for pampering and healing spa treatments. One guest tower was complete at press time, and the public spaces were close to done; all renovations should be complete by early 2009.

See map p. 120. 2169 Kalia Rd. (on the ocean, at the end of Beach Walk). ☎ *800-688-7444 or 808-923-3111. Fax: 808-924-4957.* www.outrigger.com. *Valet parking: $25. Rack rates: $349–$729 double, $769–$3,399 1- to 4-bedroom suite. Better-than-average discounts for AAA and AARP members and seniors (50+), plus corporate, government, and military discounts. 1st-night-free, bed-and-breakfast, room-and-car, and other packages regularly on offer. Internet specials as low as $229 at press time. AE, DC, DISC, MC, V.*

Outrigger Regency on Beachwalk
$$$$ Mid-Waikiki

Hidden behind an unassuming facade in the heart of the revitalized Beach Walk development lies one of Waikiki's most stylish gems. This boutique condo hotel has the feel of an upscale private residence. The elevator will whisk you up to your private apartment, where you'll find chic but comfortable contemporary decor warmed up with the use of zesty accent colors, and plenty of space for wholly satisfying Waikiki living. The one-bedroom apartments are around 600 square feet; two-bedrooms are closer to 800 square feet. Each apartment features a loft-style main room with chocolate-wood floors and cabinetry, a smart sectional sleeper sofa, a flat-panel TV, floor-to-ceiling windows leading out to the lanai, a tiled open kitchen complete with stainless steel appliances (full-size fridge, cook top, microwave, dishwasher), a dining table for four, and all of the accouterments you'll need to serve a full meal. The bedrooms are on the petite side but smartly and comfortably outfitted. Ditto for the white marble and wood bathrooms, which feature gorgeous vessel sinks. Even though these are apartments, they are serviced like a hotel. Perks include free Internet access and use of the pool at the nearby Outrigger Reef. Great for small families or couples looking for an intersection of form and function that few hotels offer. The only downsides of note: Beds are queens only (kings wouldn't fit), bathrooms feature showers only (no tubs), and views are minimal, so I don't advise spending the extra money on a partial ocean view.

See map p. 120. 255 Beach Walk (between Kalakaua Avenue and Kalia Road). ☎ *800-688-7444 or 808-922-3871. Fax: 808-922-3887.* www.outrigger.com. *Valet parking: $25. Rack rates: $349–$399 1-bedroom suite, $449–$499 2-bedroom suite. Better-than-average discounts for AAA and AARP members and seniors (50+), plus corporate, government, and military discounts. Internet rates as low as $209 at press time. AE, DC, DISC, MC, V.*

Outrigger Waikiki on the Beach
$$$$ Mid-Waikiki

I'll make no bones about it — I prefer the gorgeously renovated Outrigger Reef, just down the beach. Still, I like this 16-story oceanfront hotel, too, because of the prime location and the discounted rates and value-added package deals frequently on offer. This Outrigger sits in the center square, right in the heart of the party on Waikiki's absolute best stretch of beach. The guest rooms are attractive, with lovely bathrooms. (Fifteen special oceanfront rooms have oceanfront bathtubs for the ultimate relaxing soak!) Even the standard units are large and comfortable, with big closets, good amenities (fridge, hair dryer, and coffeemaker), and spacious lanais. The lobby and public areas honor Hawaiian history while maintaining a fresh tropical look. Facilities include a fitness center, an oceanfront pool and Jacuzzi, a round-the-clock self-serve business center, and plenty of shops and restaurants — including one of my Waikiki faves, Duke's Canoe Club. There's also a Seattle's Best Coffee, plus the Hula Grill Waikiki (another one of my favorites), boasting sunset views over the ocean. Service is consistently satisfying. Be on the lookout for an upcoming renovation.

See map p. 120. 2335 Kalakaua Ave. (on the ocean, between the Royal Hawaiian Shopping Center and the Moana Surfrider). ☎ *800-688-7444 or 808-923-0711. Fax: 808-921-9749.* www.outrigger.com. *Valet parking: $25. Rack rates: $369–$759 double, $999–$1,200 suite. Better-than-average discounts for AAA and AARP members and seniors (50+), plus corporate, government, and military discounts. 1st-night-free, bed-and-breakfast, room-and-car, and other packages regularly on offer. Internet rates as low as $205 at press time. AE, DC, DISC, MC, V.*

Outrigger Waikiki Shore
$$$–$$$$ Mid-Waikiki

Operated by Hawaii's homegrown Outrigger hotel chain, Waikiki's only beachfront condo option is a wonderful choice for families looking for at-home comforts in an on-the-sand location. The individually decorated one- and two-bedroom condos feature full kitchens with microwave and dishwasher (studios have kitchenettes), air-conditioning and ceiling fans, washer/dryers, and big lanais. Both one- and two-bedroom units come with either one or two bathrooms; ask for your preference. Daily maid service makes it feel like a real vacation. Because full-time residents live here, the complex tends to be quiet, and security is tight. Outrigger guests have access to the concierge, pool, 24-hour self-serve business center, fitness room, Starbucks, and full-service Serenity Spa Hawaii (www.serenity hawaii.com) at the adjacent Outrigger Reef, where you'll check in and check out. Reservations are hard to get — book way in advance.

See map p. 120. 2161 Kalia Rd. (on the ocean at Saratoga Road). ☎ ***800-688-7444*** *or 808-922-3871. Fax: 808-922-3887.* www.outrigger.com. *Parking: $25. Rack rates: $305 studio double, $355–$485 1-bedroom suite (sleeps up to 4), $505–$695 2-bedroom (sleeps up to 6). Better-than-average discounts for AAA and AARP members and seniors (50+), plus corporate, government, and military discounts. Excellent Internet specials regularly on offer. AE, DC, DISC, MC, V.*

Patrick Winston's Waikiki Condos
$–$$ Mid-Waikiki

Pat Winston deals in budget apartments, so you won't get the condo equivalent of the Ritz, but you will find great value for your dollars here. This friendly man manages two dozen clean, comfortable suites in a well-kept, five-story, garden-apartment building with attractive landscaping. It's located on a quiet, central-to-everything street just 2 blocks from the beach. Each of the individually decorated units has a sofa bed, a furnished lanai overlooking the kitschy-cute tropical courtyard and pool, air-conditioning and ceiling fans, a full kitchen with microwave, and a private bathroom (with shower only). Most condos have washer/dryers (coin-op facilities are also on-site). Pat does all the renovation, maintenance, and cleaning himself, and he does a great job. Bursting with aloha spirit, Pat goes the extra mile to do what he can — book activities, make restaurant recommendations, and so on — to make sure that you go home happy. Book well in advance.

See map p. 120. In the Hawaiian King, 417 Nohonani St. (between Kuhio Avenue and Ala Wai Boulevard). ☎ ***800-545-1948****, 808-924-3332, or 808-922-3894 (front desk). Fax: 808-924-3332.* www.winstonswaikikicondos.com. *Parking: $14. Rack rates: $125–$185 1-bedroom suite double. 7-night minimum; extra guests $10 each. A 1-time cleaning fee of $60–$75 is charged, depending on length of stay. Business and government rates available; monthly rates as low as $69 nightly. AE, DC, DISC, MC, V.*

ResortQuest Waikiki Beach Hotel
$$$ Mid-Waikiki

This hotel has won kudos from *Travel + Leisure* magazine as one of the best affordable beach resorts in the world. That's a bit of an overstatement, but it's still a good choice when the deals are flowing in your direction. The hotel is a monster, with 644 rooms; but 85 percent of them offer ocean views, and the location can hardly be better — my favorite stretch of Waikiki Beach is just across the street. The style is Hawaiian nostalgia with a modern flair; it's fun and funky, but the Day-Glo colors may be a bit much for some. Also, rooms are tiny — just 225 square feet, with junior suites running 300 square feet — and maintenance can be less than impeccable. The furnishings are tropical and fun, if a little less practical than I would like. For example, the closets have a beaded hula dancer curtain that sways when the trade winds blow through your room; however, the beads can be a hassle when you're trying to get to your clothes. Still, the hotel's prime location and money-saving deals can make up for a lot if you're pinching pennies. And on-site dining options are good: Tiki's Bar & Grill is an oceanview gem for cocktails, pupus, and live music; Wolfgang Puck Express gives you instant affordable access to the master's creative California fare; and Cold Stone Creamery is the ice-cream star of the Waikiki strip. Practical perks include an on-site coin-operated laundry, complimentary continental breakfast complete with cooler totes so you can take yours to the beach, and a small but appealing pool.

See map p. 120. 2570 Kalakaua Ave. (at Paoakalani Avenue). ☎ *877-997-6667, 800-877-7666 (property direct), or 808-822-2511. Fax: 808-923-3656.* www.resortquest. com. *Valet parking: $13. Rack rates: $295–$425 double, $475 suite. Internet-only eSpecial rates as low as $152 at press time. Ask for AAA, senior (50+), kids, and corporate discounts, and other special packages. Every 3rd night free deals offered at press time, with oceanview rooms starting at $169. AE, DC, DISC, MC, V.*

ResortQuest Waikiki Joy Hotel
$$ Mid-Waikiki

This dated but pleasing hotel features a Jacuzzi tub and a Bose entertainment system in every room — otherwise unheard of for these prices. The open-air lobby sets the scene for bright, clean-lined, comfortable guest rooms, each with a marble entryway, a fridge, a coffeemaker, and a lanai that's wide enough for you to sit and enjoy the views while you listen to your stereo; some suites have wet bars, and others have full kitchens. A cafe, laundry, and a furnished deck with heated pool and sauna are on-site, plus a karaoke studio if you're in the mood. In the negative column, the beach is a good 4 blocks away — but cheer up, the free breakfast makes a good deal even better.

See map p. 120. 320 Lewers St. (between Kalakaua and Kuhio avenues). ☎ *877-997-6667 or 808-923-2300. Fax: 808-924-4010.* www.resortquest.com. *Valet parking: $10. Rack rates: $185–$225 double, $235–$279 suite. Rates include continental breakfast. Online-only eSpecial rates offered from $120 at press time. Also ask for AAA, senior (50+), and corporate discounts, and other special rate programs. AE, DC, DISC, MC, V.*

Royal Hawaiian
$$$$$ Mid-Waikiki

This shocking-pink oasis hidden among blooming gardens in the heart of Waikiki has been the symbol of Hawaiian luxury since 1927. Now managed by Starwood, it still exudes glamour and elegance, recalling a time when travelers arrived by Matson Line ships rather than jumbo jet, with steamer trunks instead of nylon totes in tow. The hotel sits right in the heart of the action on Waikiki's most exciting stretch of sand. You couldn't dream up a better location. Overall, I prefer the Moana Surfrider (listed earlier in this chapter), but the Royal brims with nostalgic appeal, as its legions of loyal fans will tell you.

Every guest room is lovely, and I have a real soft spot for the Historic wing. You'll likely end up in a modern room if you want an ocean view, but the period vibe persists.

The hotel closed on June 1, 2008, in order to undergo a six-month renovation that should only make a great thing even more spectacular. Renovations are set to include a grand new entryway, a luxury makeover to the grounds, three new pools, upgraded guest rooms in the main (Historic) building, and new restaurant concepts. Perks include lei greetings, poolside bar service, a romantic luau (Waikiki's best), and one of Waikiki's most intimate and pleasing spas. At press time, the grand reopening was scheduled for January 2009. Check the Web site or call the hotel for the latest.

See map p. 120. 2259 Kalakaua Ave. (at the end of Royal Hawaiian Avenue). ☎ 866-716-8109 or 808-923-7311. Fax: 808-924-7098. www.royal-hawaiian.com. *Valet parking: $26; self-parking: $20. Rack rates: $446–$775 double, from $805 luxury oceanfront room or suite. 2009 Internet rates as low as $329 at press time. Good-value package deals are almost always available — including romance, wedding, and honeymoon packages — so ask. Also inquire about AAA and senior discounts. AE, DC, DISC, MC, V.*

Turtle Bay Resort
$$$$–$$$$$ North Shore

Situated dead center on 5 miles of beautiful beachfront, this resort hotel boasts a prime North Shore location that lets travelers who'd rather eschew Waikiki have it all: a full-service resort in a pleasingly out-of-the-way location. This hotel has a lot more going for it, too, including a fabulous special-occasion restaurant, 21 Degrees North, featuring a contemporary island menu, marvelous martinis, and drop-dead gorgeous views; Ola's, a better-than-expected open-air three-meal beachside restaurant; two top-flight championship golf courses (one designed by Arnold Palmer, the other by George Fazio); a spa; and access to a wealth of activities, including horseback riding, hiking trails, and surfing lessons. In the winter, when the surf's up, you can watch big-wave daredevils in action at the legendary nearby beaches; in summer, the glassy waters of the North Shore make an ideal water playground for everyone. Accommodations, ranging from guest rooms to luxury beach cottages and multibedroom oceanfront condos, offer something for everyone.

The downside is that the guest rooms are way out of date, worn, and in serious need of upgrading. They're sizable but feel almost empty; the only chairs in the room were the two upright chairs at the desk, which were in desperate need of recovering in mine.

The gorgeous beach cottages, set a five-minute walk from the main hotel, are the way to go for couples and small families. These semi-attached cottages are generous studio-style units with vaulted ceilings, sunken living rooms, redwood floors, white marble baths with an oversize soaking tub and separate shower, and a nicely furnished lanai with wonderful ocean views and direct beach access. Freshly done in the last couple of years, they're in very nice shape.

Alternatively, larger families can opt for the beautifully outfitted three- or four-bedroom ocean villas, which are luxurious beachfront condos built for long-term living. Expect all the perks here, including full luxury kitchens (think granite and SubZero), a comfy living room complete with oversize TV and surround sound, plus TVs in every bedroom; washers and dryers; and their own fully furnished private lanais.

See map p. 162. 57–091 Kamehameha Hwy., Kahuku. ☎ *800-203-3650, 808-447-6508, or 808-293-8811.* www.turtlebayresort.com. *Parking: Self-parking is included in the $20-per-night "resort fee"; valet parking is an additional $10. Rack rates: $370–$530 double, $500–$950 suite or beach cottage, from $1,400 3- or 4-bedroom villa. Check Web site or inquire about seasonal, spa, and romance package deals and last-minute "Exclusive" rates (as low as $219 at press time). AE, DC, DISC, MC, V.*

Waikiki Beach Marriott Resort & Spa
$$$$ Mid-Waikiki

I really like this hotel; kudos to Marriott for creating such a delightful place to stay. It's spectacularly located, directly across the street from the newly renovated stretch of Waikiki Beach, with no buildings blocking views or access, and only steps from Kapiolani Park. The 1,300-room hotel is massive, but a tropically furnished open-air lobby adds a sense of cohesion, not to mention an inviting place to lounge with your morning coffee (a Seattle Coffee Roasters is on-site). The hotel is also home to one of Hawaii's most attractive spas, the Spa Olakino & Salon, where you'll feel that you've just stepped into a glorious rain-forest retreat overlooking the sands.

All the guest rooms have been given the royal treatment, with quality furnishings and high-speed Internet access. The fine textiles come in eye-catching tropicals, and the feather beds are more comfy than most available at any price. The 600-square-foot family room sleeps up to six comfortably and features two queen-size beds, two twin beds, and a sitting area; a few even have a second bathroom. More family-friendly perks: Not only can kids stay in their parent's room, but a rollaway or crib is provided free of charge. The staffed Kids Salon playroom offers Mom and Dad both day and evening respite from the little ones. Each of the two towers boasts its own pleasant and popular pool deck; there's also a 24-hour fitness center. The Kuhio Beach Grille is a pleasing and affordably priced place to dine; Sansei and d.k Steak House serve up Waikiki views along with menus designed by D.K. Kodama, one of Hawaii's most acclaimed chefs, who deserves his own kudos for bringing first-rate dining to the heart of Waikiki.

See map p. 120. 2552 Kalakaua Ave. (at Papakalani Avenue just west of Kapiolani Park). ☎ *800-367-5370 or 808-922-6611. Fax: 808-921-5255.* www.marriott waikiki.com. *Parking: $27 valet; $22 self-parking. Rack rates: $340–$560 double* *or family room, $1,500–$2,500 suite. A wealth of romance, spa, sightseeing, and room-and-car or room-and-breakfast packages are usually available. Also inquire about AAA, senior (62+), corporate, government, and other special rates (from $199 at press time). AE, DC, DISC, MC, V.*

Waikiki Parc
$$$ Mid-Waikiki

This sister hotel to the ultradeluxe Halekulani is the ideal choice for travelers looking for impeccable service, high-design chic, and little luxuries at affordable rates, plus a terrific at-the-beach location. Now that the new Beach Walk shopping-and-entertainment redevelopment is complete, the location is better than ever. What's more, you can almost always secure an excellent package that improves an already-good value. A high-concept, media-drenched, nightclub-reminiscent lobby leads to comfy, contemporary guest rooms. Boasting an Asian-tinged island vibe, the stylish rooms feature chic ebony woods and rattan, tile floors, plush carpeting, sitting areas, lanais with louvered shutters (go for an ocean view if you can — they're fabulous), minifridges, flatscreen TVs, bold artwork, and nice-size bathrooms. It's worth paying for a deluxe ocean view if you can score a good rate. Amenities include concierge and room service; a coin-op laundry as well as valet service; and a gracious staff that doesn't skimp on signature Halekulani service. Elevating the Waikiki Parc to must-visit status is **Nobu Waikiki,** the first Hawaii venture from internationally acclaimed Japanese chef Nobu Matsuhisa. The hotel has an outdoor heated rooftop pool, but why bother? The sand is 100 yards away, via a beach-access walkway. Not necessarily for those who don't prize chic.

See map p. 120. 2233 Helumoa Rd. (at Lewers Street, east of the Halekulani). ☎ *800-422-0450 or 808-921-7272. Fax: 808-931-6638 (reservations) or 808-923-1336 (front desk).* www.waikikiparc.com. *Valet parking: $20. Rack rates: $275–$415 double. A bevy of excellent money-saving packages are always on offer, including the Parc Sunrise ($245–$339 double, including parking and breakfast), plus room-and-car and family packages. AE, DC, MC, V.*

The Wyland Waikiki
$$$ Mid-Waikiki

This first artist-themed hotel in Hawaii is a wonderful new addition to the Waikiki hotel scene. Run by Waikiki's hometown hotel brand Outrigger, the property is inspired (and design directed) by ocean artist Wyland, who is world-renowned for his artful expressions of marine life.

Even if you don't know who Wyland is, I encourage you to consider this appealing boutique-style property, which evokes the ocean world at every turn in its attractive contemporary design. A beautiful palm-dotted courtyard with a small but lush and pretty lava rock–walled pool area gives the property a feeling of oasis in bustling Waikiki. In addition to about $4 million of Wyland's work, you'll find water elements throughout the hotel, including a dramatic coral fish tank in the light, open lobby.

Rooms are not huge, but they are fresh, contemporary, and attractive, with a sage-and-cream palette and creative touches from Wyland at every turn, including a kissing fish pattern on the bedcover (custom designed for the hotel) and a Wyland print on the wall. Nice features include plush pillowtop beds, small lanais, an iPod-compatible alarm clock, and minifridges; many rooms have kitchenettes with microwave and wet bar. Unfortunately, the upgraded bathrooms are petite, and all but suites have small showers only.

On-site is a cute Italian restaurant as well as the KimoBean Coffee Company, a sleek coffee bar serving only island roasts. You'll also find an all-new fitness room, a day spa, a business center, and the "Chill" room, featuring an oversize flat-panel TV, Nintendo, and massage chairs free for guests' use. Guests benefit from the standard Outrigger perks, including free Internet access and free local and long-distance calls. You'll have a ten-minute walk to the beach, but this corner of Waikiki is both central and quiet.

See map p. 120. 400 Royal Hawaiian Ave. (at Kuhio Avenue). ☎ *877-995-2638 or 808-954-4000. Fax: 808-954-4047.* www.wylandwaikiki.com *or* www.outrigger.com. *Valet parking: $25. Rack rates: $299–$329 double, $329–$369 double with kitchenette, $389–$429 1-bedroom suite with kitchenette. Better-than-average discounts for AAA and AARP members and seniors (50+), plus corporate, government, and military discounts. 1st-night-free, bed-and-breakfast, room-and-car, and other packages regularly on offer; specials from $205 at press time. AE, DC, DISC, MC, V.*

Arranging for a vacation rental

Ingrid Carvahlo's **Pacific Islands Reservations** (☎ 808-262-8133; www.oahu-hawaii-vacation.com) is my favorite rental agency on Oahu. This lovely lady can also hook you up with a gorgeous Windward Coast vacation rental, as well as a handful of North Shore estates and a number of condos right in the heart of Waikiki.

If you want to stay in the middle of the North Shore's Surf City action, you can also call **Team Real Estate** (☎ 800-982-8602 or 808-637-3507; www.teamrealestate.com). This friendly Haleiwa-based agency manages a fleet of fully furnished vacation homes on the North Shore, from affordable cottages to multibedroom beachfront homes, at rates ranging from $65 to $1,035 per night. Most rates are based on a minimum stay of one week; but shorter stays are available, and you may be able to arrange a discount on longer stays.

Naish Hawaii (☎ 800-767-6068 or 808-262-6068; www.naish.com/lodging.html), which also happens to be Hawaii's premier windsurfing school, can help arrange for accommodations in and around Kailua, Oahu's premier Windward Coast community. Double rooms, cottages, and apartments for two run $50 to $125 nightly, and larger homes range from $150 to $300 nightly, depending on size and location.

Also contact **Hawaii's Best Bed & Breakfasts** (☎ 800-262-9912 or 808-985-7488; www.bestbnb.com) for additional Windward Coast and North Shore options. You may also want to check with **Hawaii Beachfront Vacation Homes** (☎ 808-247-3637; www.hibeach.com) and **Hawaiian**

Beach Rentals (☎ 800-853-0787; www.hawaiianbeachrentals.com). If you'd prefer to cut out the middle man and rent directly from a property owner, check out **Vacation Rentals by Owner** (www.vrbo.com) and **VacationHomes.com** (www.vacationhomes.com).

Dining Out

Hawaii has become a culinary mecca in recent years, attracting world-wide attention for its growing constellation of star chefs and its unique brand of Pacific Rim cooking — known as Hawaii Regional Cuisine, Hawaii Island, or just Island cuisine. Honolulu, as you may expect, is the epicenter of this fabulous foodie revolution, so expect to eat well while you're here. Of course, the good stuff doesn't come cheap, but great affordable choices abound as well.

In the restaurant listings that follow, the emphasis is on Waikiki and Honolulu, because (a) that's where you're likely to spend most of your time, and (b) that's where most of Oahu's restaurants are located. But I also include some excellent options for North Shore and Windward Coast dining.

Each restaurant review is followed by a number of dollar signs, ranging from one ($) to five ($$$$$). The dollar signs give you an idea of what a complete dinner for one person — including appetizer, main course, dessert, one drink, tax, and tip — is likely to set you back. The price categories go like this:

$	Cheap eats — less than $20 per person
$$	Still inexpensive — $20–$35
$$$	Moderate — $35–$50
$$$$	Pricey — $50–$75
$$$$$	Ultraexpensive — more than $75 per person

Of course, cost all depends on how you order, so stay away from the surf and turf or the north end of the wine list if you're watching your budget.

To give you a further idea of how much you can expect to spend, I also include the price range of main courses in the listings. (Keep in mind that prices can change at the whim of the management, so call before you go if you want to confirm the price range.)

The state adds roughly 4 percent in taxes to every restaurant bill. The percentage may vary slightly depending on the county you're in, and may be embedded in the total purchase price or shown as an independent line item on your bill. A 15 to 20 percent tip is standard in Hawaii, just as in the rest of the States.

Restaurants In and Around Waikiki

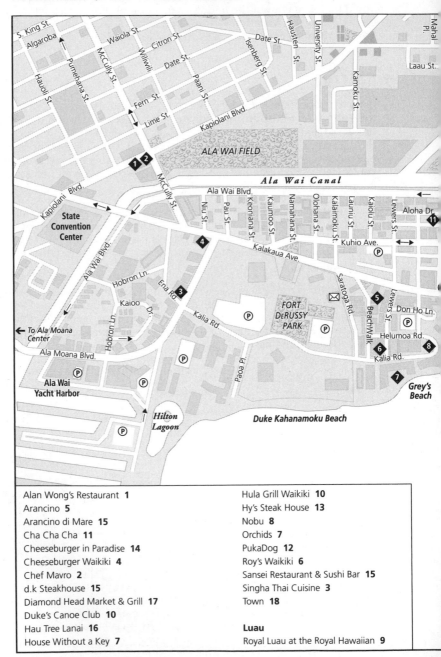

Alan Wong's Restaurant **1**	Hula Grill Waikiki **10**
Arancino **5**	Hy's Steak House **13**
Arancino di Mare **15**	Nobu **8**
Cha Cha Cha **11**	Orchids **7**
Cheeseburger in Paradise **14**	PukaDog **12**
Cheeseburger Waikiki **4**	Roy's Waikiki **6**
Chef Mavro **2**	Sansei Restaurant & Sushi Bar **15**
d.k Steakhouse **15**	Singha Thai Cuisine **3**
Diamond Head Market & Grill **17**	Town **18**
Duke's Canoe Club **10**	
Hau Tree Lanai **16**	**Luau**
House Without a Key **7**	Royal Luau at the Royal Hawaiian **9**

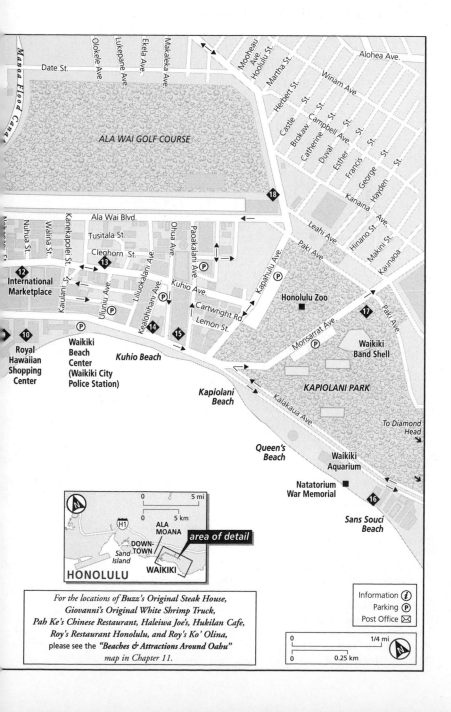

ALA WAI GOLF COURSE

Manoa Flood Canal

Date St.

Olokele Ave.
Lukepane Ave.
Ekela Ave.
Makaleka Ave.
Mooheau Ave.
Hoolulu St.
Martha St.
Herbert St.
Alohea Ave.
Winam Ave.
Castle St.
Brokaw St.
Campbell Ave.
Catherine St.
Duval St.
Esther St.
Francis St.
George St.
Hayden St.
Kanaina Ave.
Hinano St.
Makini St.
Kaunoa

18

Ala Wai Blvd.

Tusitala St.
Cleghorn St.
13
Kanekapolei St.
Walina St.
Nuhua St.
Nkgwoni St.
12
International
Marketplace
Kaiulu St.
Uluniu Ave.
Kealohilani Ave.
Liliuokalani Ave.
Ohua Ave.
Paoakalani Ave.
Kuhio Ave.
P
14
15
Cartwright Rd.
Lemon St.
Kapahulu Ave.
P
Leahi Ave.
Paki Ave.
Honolulu Zoo
17
Paki Ave.
Monsarrat Ave.
P
10
Royal
Hawaiian
Shopping
Center
P
Waikiki
Beach
Center
(Waikiki City
Police Station)
Kuhio Beach
Kapiolani
Beach
KAPIOLANI PARK
Waikiki
Band Shell
Kalakaua Ave.
To Diamond
Head
Queen's
Beach
Waikiki
Aquarium
Natatorium
War Memorial
16
Sans Souci
Beach

0   5 mi
0   5 km
H1
ALA
MOANA
area of detail
DOWN-
TOWN
Sand
Island
WAIKIKI
HONOLULU

For the locations of *Buzz's Original Steak House,*
Giovanni's Original White Shrimp Truck,
Pah Ke's Chinese Restaurant, Haleiwa Joe's, Hukilan Cafe,
Roy's Restaurant Honolulu, and *Roy's Ko' Olina,*
please see the *"Beaches & Attractions Around Oahu"*
map in Chapter 11.

Information (i)
Parking (P)
Post Office ✉

0   1/4 mi
0   0.25 km

Downtown and Ala Moana Restaurants

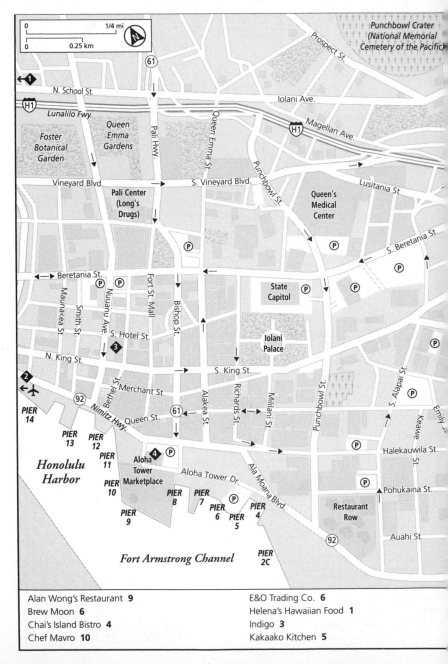

Alan Wong's Restaurant **9**	E&O Trading Co. **6**
Brew Moon **6**	Helena's Hawaiian Food **1**
Chai's Island Bistro **4**	Indigo **3**
Chef Mavro **10**	Kakaako Kitchen **5**

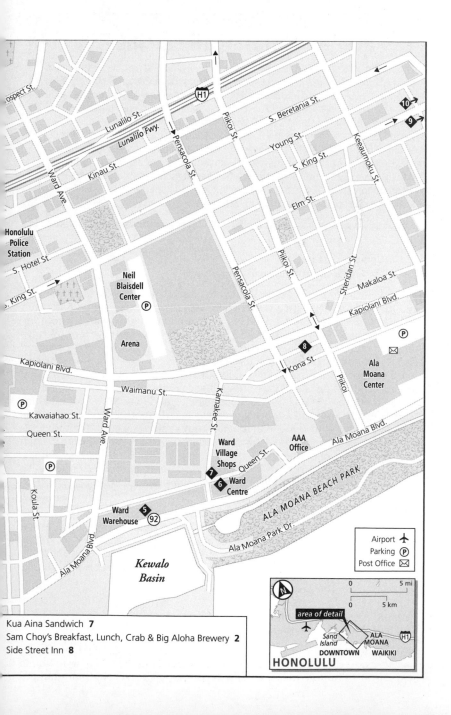

Kua Aina Sandwich **7**
Sam Choy's Breakfast, Lunch, Crab & Big Aloha Brewery **2**
Side Street Inn **8**

In search of Hawaii cuisine

If you're a foodie who really wants an insider's view on island-style dining, don't miss the opportunity to spend a day or an evening with **Hawaii Food Tours** (☎ 800-715-2468 or 808-926-3663; www.hawaiifoodtours.com). Matthew Gray, a former chef, food critic, and restaurant reviewer for Hawaii's largest daily newspaper, offers a trio of excellent tours that let food-obsessed travelers experience true Hawaii cuisine — including the full palate of international cuisines that add color and flavor to the islands. My day spent with Matthew and his lively and knowledgeable partner, Keira (also a former chef), was one of my all-time favorite Hawaii experiences. Tours are usually offered daily from 10 a.m. to 2 p.m., and the $99 per-person cost is well worth it for adventurous foodies. Call or visit the Web site for complete tour details, as well as the other exciting culinary adventures offered by Matthew and Keira.

Alan Wong's Restaurant
$$$$–$$$$$ Honolulu   Hawaii Regional

If there is one master of true Hawaii Regional Cuisine, it is Alan Wong — and his restaurant offers a world-class experience. Koa, rattan, and other tropical touches create a real Hawaiian ambience in the warmly contemporary dining room, which serves as an ideal showcase for Wong's masterful elevation of the local culinary tradition. Expect perfectly prepared island fish bursting with clean, fresh flavors; Asian accents galore (the seaweed-wrapped tempura big-eye ahi with soy mustard is magnificent); and modernist takes on island favorites: Ginger-crusted onaga (red snapper) is adorned with a light miso-sesame vinaigrette, and luau pork accompanies baby romaine, poi, and anchovy dressing in a delightful twist on a classic Caesar. Cap off your meal with a beautifully crafted dessert like the decadent chocolate crunch bars (layers of milk chocolate macadamia crunch and bittersweet chocolate mousse) and a fine selection of island coffees. Service is appropriately sophisticated yet completely unpretentious. No wonder *Gourmet* magazine named this number 8 of America's Top 50 restaurants. Book well in advance.

See map p. 138. 1857 S. King St. (1½ blocks west of McCully Street), 3rd Floor, Honolulu. ☎ *808-949-2526.* www.alanwongs.com. *Reservations highly recommended (online reservations accepted). To get there: Take Kalakaua west from Waikiki and turn right on S. King Street. Main courses: $26–$42. 5-course tasting menu: $75 ($105 with wines); 7-course tasting menu: $95 ($135 with wines). AE, DC, MC, V. Open: Dinner nightly.*

Arancino/Arancino di Mare
$$ Mid-Waikiki   Northern Italian

If Arancino can draw island residents into the heart of Waikiki, you know that it has to be good. This intimate and affordable trattoria-style Italian restaurant is hugely popular with Japanese visitors, mainlanders, and locals alike, all of whom bond over their love of good Italian food. Creative pizzas and pastas, homemade risottos, and fresh island seafood make up a simple but very appealing menu that delivers on all counts. With burnished terra-cotta walls, tile floors, and red-checked cloths on the tables, the charming room is inviting, and friendly service caps it all off. You'll probably find a line when you arrive — but the excellent value is worth the wait. There's now a second location at the Waikiki Beach Marriott, near the Diamond Head end of Waikiki.

See map p. 138. 255 Beach Walk (just south of Kalakaua Avenue), Waikiki. ☎ *808-923-5557.* www.arancino.com. *Also in the Waikiki Beach Marriott Resort & Spa, 2552 Kalakaua Ave., Waikiki.* ☎ *808-931-6273. Reservations not taken. Main courses: $10–$24. AE, DC, DISC, MC, V. Open: Lunch and dinner daily.*

Brew Moon
$$ Ala Moana Eclectic

A comfortable-chic setting, satisfying contemporary pub food, and even better microbrews have made Brew Moon into a comfortable favorite among locals and visitors alike. This trendy spot won't exactly wow the gourmands among you, but the casual eats are nicely prepared and boast a winning island flair. Brew Moon's celebrated handcrafted beers (like the Orion red ale, an amber brew with a robust caramel flavor) wash down offerings like coconut shrimp, fire-roasted ribs, sesame-seared ahi, veggie stir-fry, and thick-crust Luau pizza (topped with smoke-roasted pulled pork, roasted garlic, and Maui onion) perfectly. A full selection of salads, sandwiches, burgers, and creative pizzas complements the array of globe-trotting small plates, making this a good place to come with a group and share. Tiki torches flicker on the pleasant lanai after the sun goes down, and live jazz and R&B set a festive mood every night. Brew Moon is a wi-fi hotspot, so you can check your e-mail during the daily happy hour.

See map p. 140. In Ward Centre, 1200 Ala Moana Blvd. (between Kamakee and Queen streets), Honolulu. ☎ *808-593-0088. Reservations accepted. Sharing plates, sandwiches, and pizzas: $8–$19. Main courses: $18–$26. AE, DC, MC, V. Open: Lunch and dinner daily (bar open late).*

Buzz's Original Steak House
$$–$$$ Windward Coast American

This Windward Coast fixture exudes casual local style — and the food is really good, too, making Buzz's a perennial favorite among visitors and locals alike since 1962. The pleasing restaurant is housed in a little grass shack across from Kailua's gorgeous beach park; a small covered deck with (limited) beach views, a varnished koa bar, rattan furniture, and wood-paneled walls adorned with surf photos set the ideal tropical tone. Lunch is well-prepared, straightforward fare: steak sandwiches, fresh fish (always a beautifully prepared local catch), and teriyaki burgers. Dinner is pricier but worth it; expect traditional steakhouse fare — including well-grilled sirloins, rack of lamb, and teriyaki chicken — plus a soup and salad bar. Service is always welcoming, and the tropical cocktails are everything they should be. Don't pass on starting with the yummy artichoke "surprise" — you won't be disappointed. *Note:* Despite the at-the-beach location, shoes and shirts are required.

See map p. 162. 413 Kawailoa Rd. (across from Kailua Beach Park, just past the bridge that leads to Lanikai Beach), Kailua. ☎ *808-261-4661. Reservations highly recommended for dinner. Main courses: $8–$16 at lunch, $15–$34 at dinner. No credit cards. Open: Lunch and dinner daily.*

Cha Cha Cha
$ Mid-Waikiki Caribbean-Mexican

Finding a great meal in Waikiki without overspending isn't easy, but this tropical charmer does the job well. This small indoor-outdoor restaurant is set back from the street, but establishes a colorful tropical presence on the patio with vibrant red and yellow umbrellas. The kitchen takes Mexican staples and globe-trots them across the tropics — witness such dishes as lava-grilled chicken fajitas, a Jamaican jerk chicken quesadilla, blackened mahi burritos, and the delectable Pacifico quesadilla (grilled mahi in a spinach tortilla, topped with papaya-pineapple salsa). Dishes are always boldly flavored, authentically spiced, and artistically presented, with drizzled sauces on colorful plates. Here you can also find a help-yourself wall of hot sauces for zesty palates, well-blended margaritas, not one but two Happy Hours (4–6 p.m. and again 9–11 p.m.), and a kids' menu.

See map p. 138. 342 Seaside Ave. (between Kalakaua and Kuhio avenues). ☎ *808-923-7797. Reservations not accepted. Main courses: $7.50–$16. MC, V. Open: Lunch and dinner daily.*

Chai's Island Bistro
$$$$ Downtown/Aloha Tower Marketplace Euro/Pacific Rim

Chef/owner Chai Chaowasaree uses this attractive California-style restaurant as an outlet for cross-cultural innovation, and it's an appealing place to dine. The Pan-Asian influences lean heavily on the Thai tradition, as evidenced by organically grown local greens with balsamic tamarind vinaigrette and grilled fresh island mahimahi dressed in a zippy red curry sauce. Those with more timid palates will enjoy the Continental-style plates, such as grilled beef tenderloin in a shiitake-Chianti demi-glace, plus Mediterranean-influenced pastas and risottos. The food is too pricey, but nightly entertainment by some of Hawaii's most celebrated musicians — such as the excellent Olomana and the legendary Brothers Cazimero — softens the blow appreciably.

See map p. 140. Aloha Tower Marketplace, 1 Aloha Tower Dr., just south of downtown Honolulu. ☎ *808-585-0011.* www.chaisislandbistro.com. *Reservations recommended. To get there: Take Ala Moana Boulevard west from Waikiki. Main courses: $13–$32 at lunch, $28–$48 at dinner (most under $40). AE, DC, MC, V. Open: Lunch Tues–Fri, dinner nightly.*

Cheeseburger in Paradise/Cheeseburger Waikiki
$ Diamond Head Waikiki/Ewa Waikiki American

Located just across the street from a prime stretch of Waikiki Beach, Cheeseburger in Paradise is a fun, funky outpost of the wildly successful Maui burger joint (not part of the mainland chain owned by Jimmy Buffett) and the perfect spot for a casual sit-down meal. A second Honolulu branch, Cheeseburger Waikiki, is located at the opposite end of the beach; it's open 24 hours a day to satisfy those late-night munchies. At both restaurants, the tropical-style gourmet burgers are big, juicy, and served on fresh-baked buns. The bar mixes first-rate tropical cocktails — including one of the best piña coladas in the islands — and the attractive retro-Hawaii decor makes for an enjoyable kitschfest. Chili dogs, a tender and healthy chicken breast sandwich, crispy onion rings, coconut shrimp, and spiced fries broaden the menu, and vegetarians can opt for the terrific garden burger, a tofu burger, or a meal-size salad. You can even greet the morning here, with hearty omelets, French toast, eggs Benedict, and other breakfast favorites. The food is universally satisfying.

See map p. 138. 2500 Kalakaua Ave. (at Kealohilani Avenue, 3 blocks west of Kapahulu Avenue), Waikiki. ☎ *808-923-3731.* www.cheeseburgerland.com. *Cheeseburger Waikiki: 1945 Kalakaua Ave. (at the corner of Ala Moana Boulevard).* ☎ *808-941-2400. Main courses: $8.50–$10 at breakfast, $9–$15 at lunch and dinner. AE, DISC, MC, V. Open: Breakfast, lunch, and dinner daily.*

Chef Mavro
$$$$$ Honolulu Hawaii Regional

Marseilles transplant and James Beard award–winner George Mavrothalassitis has long been considered one of Hawaii's finest chefs, and he brings a one-of-a-kind Provençal-Mediterranean accent to the Hawaii Regional table. The menu changes every three months to maximize local ingredients and keep things fresh and exciting for everyone. The onaga (long-tailed snapper) is prepared laulau-style (wrapped in ti leaves along with garlic shoots, fresh water chestnuts, Maui onions, and a fragrant fennel-basil sauce), which results in a deliciously moist fish. A rich roasted Sonoma duckling breast is served with tarragon and yogurt pearl barley and ginger-mango jus.

The menu even goes a delightful step further, matching each and every dish with the perfect glass of wine selected not by a lone authoritarian wine snob but by a vote of the restaurant's entire staff after blind tastings; it's a uniquely democratic system that prevails with every pairing. The clean-lined, candlelit setting is simple, elegant, and romantic, and the sociable, well-informed waitstaff couldn't be more spot-on. A premier dining experience from start to finish. I like Alan Wong's better, but Chef Mavro is an excellent second choice.

See map p. 138. 1969 S. King St. (at McCully Street), Honolulu. ☎ *808-944-4714.* www.chefmavro.com. *Reservations highly recommended. To get there: Take McCully Street north to King Street. 3-course menu: $65 ($98 with wine); 4-course tasting* menu: $71 ($116 with wine); 6-course tasting menu: $104 ($154 with wine). AE, DC, DISC, MC, V. Open: Dinner Tues–Sun.

Diamond Head Market & Grill
$ Honolulu (just north of Diamond Head Waikiki)   Local

This unassuming little takeout joint serves up gourmet plate lunches at a bustling window. Chef/owner Kevin Ro has a rarified pedigree as award-winning chef of the Kahala Moon restaurant and personal chef for former state governor Ben Cayetano. But now he cooks for the masses, serving up local-style main courses, sandwiches, and salads with gourmet flavor and style on takeout Styrofoam. The extensive menu includes such stars as Korean-style kalbi ribs, grilled salmon in a not-too-sweet teriyaki glaze, Chinese-style *char siu* pork, and Ro's famous grilled portobello mushroom. All of the lunch plates come with your choice of white or brown rice, plus a simple garden salad dressed in lemon vinaigrette (a nice change of pace from the usual macaroni salad). Come in the morning hours to dig into delectable coconut pancakes, grilled ahi and eggs, roast pork hash and eggs, or Hawaiian sweet bread French toast. You can enjoy your takeout at the available picnic tables, or carry it back to the beach or to nearby Kapiolani Park. It's also an easy stop before or after a hike up Diamond Head. A wonderful local find. The simple adjacent market is a great place to supplement your picnic basket with bottled water and/or a fine selection of cheeses, deli meats, or after-meal sweets.

See map p. 138. 3158 Monsarrat Ave. (at Campbell Avenue). ☎ *808-732-0077.* www.diamondheadmarket.com. *Reservations not taken. Main courses: $6–$10 at breakfast, $5–$15 at lunch and dinner (most under $11). MC, V. Open: Breakfast, lunch, and dinner daily.*

d.k Steak House
$$$$$ Mid-Waikiki   Japanese/Pacific Rim Seafood

Sushi superstar D.K. Kodama has wowed Hawaii dining with his winning Sansei sushi restaurants (see review later in this chapter) — so he's turned his attention to the venerable steak, another true love of his. Kodama's steakhouse stays true enough to tradition to please classicists, but adds enough creative twists to loosen the mood and suit Waikiki's casual flavor. The steakhouse has its own dry-aging room, which means perfectly tender, dry-aged prime beef. The specialty of the house is the beautifully seasoned, on-the-bone rib-eye, but I also love the melt-in-your-mouth filet mignon, dressed in your choice of a shiitake mushroom demi-glace or the house-made béarnaise. Sides come steakhouse-style; highlights include crispy onion rings and Milanese-style asparagus, broiled with a farm-fresh egg and truffle oil. This being Hawaii, you can expect fabulous surf-and-turf combos. Master sommelier Chuck Furuya has assembled an excellent wine list for all budgets and tastes, including a terrific by-the-glass list. Comfort foods like a yummy burger and Mom Kodama's meatloaf both create more casual options and allow wallet-watchers to keep the bill down. A kids' menu makes d.k's a nice special-dinner choice for families too.

Sit at the bar if you'd like to combine your steakhouse order with some dishes from the adjoining Sansei (see review later in this chapter).

See map p. 138. At the Waikiki Beach Marriott Resort & Spa, 2552 Kalakaua Ave. (at Papakalani Avenue just west of Kapiolani Park), Waikiki. ☎ *808-931-6280.* www.dksteakhouse.com. *Reservations highly recommended. Main courses: $25–$65 (most under $40). AE, DISC, MC, V. Open: Dinner nightly.*

Duke's Canoe Club
$$–$$$ Mid-Waikiki   Steaks/Seafood

Duke's is everything that Waikiki dining should be, complete with sarong-wearing cocktail waitresses, open-air beachfront dining, and Tiki torches in the sand. This inviting restaurant manages to be all things to all people: a kid-friendly choice for families, a romantic lair for lovers, a magnet for Hawaiian music fans, and a hot spot for party hoppers. The menu deserves high marks, too, from the fresh-caught local fish (with a half-dozen preparations to choose from) to the succulent prime rib. I particularly love the poke rolls, made with sushi-grade ruby-red ahi, to start. Duke's is also well-loved for its Barefoot Bar, with a mile-long drink menu, budget-friendly food, and top-notch island music nightly. It's a great place to watch the sunset.

See map p. 138. At the Outrigger Waikiki on the Beach, 2335 Kalakaua Ave. (between the Royal Hawaiian Shopping Center and the Moana Surfrider), Waikiki. ☎ *808-922-2268.* www.dukeswaikiki.com. *Reservations recommended for dinner. Main courses: $5–$14 at breakfast, $20–$30 at dinner (salad bar included). Barefoot Bar menu (served all day): $5–$12. Lunch buffet: $13. AE, DC, DISC, MC, V. Open: Breakfast, lunch, and dinner daily.*

E&O Trading Co.
$$–$$$ Ala Moana   Southeast Asian

This exotic import from San Francisco is a winning addition to the Honolulu dining scene. Styled after an outdoor Pan-Asian marketplace, it garnered two awards from *Honolulu* magazine in 2006: a gold award for best ambience and a silver nod for best new restaurant overall. And the accolades are just: E&O offers all of the elements of a thoroughly enjoyable dining experience. Brightly hued art and accents, including colorful market umbrellas, and warm lighting set a fanciful Eastern tone for a pleasing Pan-Asian family-style dining experience. The menu comprises both small and big plates, good for easy sharing. Menu stars include Indonesian corn fritters in a zesty chili-soy dipping sauce; *char siu*–style smoked *mero,* smoked sea bass prepared Korean barbecue–style; delectable salt-and-pepper-crusted calamari; and a variety of spice-grilled satays and Indian-style flatbreads, including fluffy nan. Inventive, oversize cocktails accent the festive mood; creative virgin "mocktails" are also a delight. Thursday-night diners enjoy live music. A great choice for adventurous families and romance-seeking couples alike.

See map p. 140. In Ward Centre, 1200 Ala Moana Blvd. (between Kamakee and Queen streets), Honolulu. ☎ *808-591-9555.* www.eotrading.com. *Lunch: $7–$20. Dinner: $8–$20 small plates, $17–$28 big plates. AE, DC, MC, V. Open: Lunch and dinner daily.*

Giovanni's Original White Shrimp Truck
$ North Shore   Seafood

In recent years, a uniquely scrumptious cottage industry has arisen in Kahuku, a rural oceanside outpost on the way to the North Shore's surf meccas: the Kahuku shrimp truck. Shrimp farmers cultivate ponds in this region that produce some of the biggest, plumpest, sweetest shrimp you'll ever enjoy. You'll find a string of shrimp trucks along the ocean side of Kamehameha Highway. Best of the bunch is Giovanni's, which specializes in an aromatically delicious shrimp scampi that is far superior to nearby Romy's (which is actually a shrimp shack) in freshness and garlicky goodness. In fact, the scampi is so palette-pleasing that Giovanni's was recently visited by NPR's *The Splendid Table* radio show.

You'll order at the window and receive your generous paper-plate meal to enjoy at an adjoining simple but pleasant covered picnic area. Plates come with two scoops of rice and a dozen shrimp. In addition to scampi, you can also choose lemon and butter or hot and spicy ("Super hot, no refunds!"). Bathrooms are available.

Giovanni's has a second North Shore truck in Haleiwa, just before the junction with Highway 99, next to the Chocolate Gecko Espresso cafe and across from McDonald's.

See map p. 162. On Kamehameha Highway. (on the ocean side of the street, just south of Kahuku Sugar Mill), Kahuku. No phone. Reservations not taken. Shrimp plates: $12. MC, V. Open: Lunch daily.

Haleiwa Joe's
$$–$$$ North Shore/Windward Coast   Seafood

This pleasing seafood grill really embodies the North Shore vibe. It's friendly and easygoing, with a casual, surf-inspired vibe and straightforward, lovingly prepared seafood (fish-phobes can enjoy a tasty grilled steak). The day's catches are served either lightly coated in herbs, bread crumbs, and the house roasted garlic spread, or grilled and served with Asian inspiration in a wonton bowl (called "lumpia" in the islands). The crunchy coconut shrimp, served with a plum and honey mustard dipping duo, is a sweet and sour treat. Main courses come with a salad starter for a mere $3, which adds to the good value. The wine list is also reasonably priced relative to other restaurants on the island. Portions are generous, and the atmosphere is pleasingly unfussy; grab a seat on the harbor-view patio for a genuinely enjoyable and satisfying evening. If you're in the mood to party, come on Friday and stay for the late-night live music (usually starting at 10:30 p.m.). There's an attractive second location in Kaneohe for those staying on the island's Windward Coast, also with live tunes on Fridays.

See map p. 162. 66–011 Kamehameha Hwy., Haleiwa. ☎ 808-637-8005. Haleiwa Joe's Kaneohe: 46-336 Haiku Rd., Kaneohe. ☎ 808-247-6671. www.haleiwajoes.com. Reservations not taken. Main courses: $8–$17 at lunch, $12–$28 at dinner (most under $24). MC, V. Open: Lunch and dinner daily.

Hau Tree Lanai
$$$ Diamond Head Waikiki   Eurasian/Continental

Shaded by an ancient hau tree that twinkles with tiny lights at dinnertime, this informal outdoor terrace on the sand is one of the most romantic beachfront restaurants in all Hawaii. The A-1 location surpasses the food at any time of day — but, frankly, it would be hard for any chef to live up to this magical setting. (Robert Louis Stevenson himself often came here to sit beneath the hau trees and watch the waves roll in.) Breakfast is best: Throw caution to the wind and start the day with the sausage sampler — three kinds of local sausage and a side of fluffy poi pancakes — or the eggs Benedict, which wears a perfect hollandaise. Lunchtime features burgers, sandwiches, and salads, and the fresh island fish preparations are the standouts at dinner. Live music enhances the romantic mood on weekends and during the Friday lunch hour.

See map p. 138. In the New Otani Kaimana Beach Hotel, 2863 Kalakaua Ave. (across the street from Kapiolani Park), Waikiki. ☎ *808-921-7066.* www.kaimana.com. *Reservations recommended. Main courses: $8–$19 at breakfast and lunch, $21–$38 at dinner. AE, DC, DISC, MC, V. Open: Breakfast, lunch, and dinner daily.*

Helena's Hawaiian Food
$ Downtown   Local Hawaiian

This six-decade-old diner may have relocated to new digs in 2002, but the old-time ambience and all the hallmarks of Helena's remain, making this the best place in town to experience genuine island-style eats. Helena's is so renowned for its local fare that the James Beard Foundation has lauded it as a regional classic. Grandson Craig Katsuyoshi now mans the stove while lively 80-something Helena handles the cash register, but all her classic dishes are served, including *pipikaula,* strips of seasoned beef hung to dry and smoked over the stove, moist and tender pulled kalua pork, pork laulau (wrapped and steamed in ti leaves), short ribs, squid luau, fried butterfish collars, and other ethnic island staples. Expect a wait, and don't be afraid to ask these friendly folks for dish descriptions or recommendations. Helena's is a great place to experience Hawaii at its most down-to-earth authentic.

See map p. 140. 1240 N. School St. (near Pohaku Street, north of the H-1 freeway). ☎ *808-845-8044. Reservations recommended for dinner. Main courses: Most less than $12. No credit cards. Open: Lunch and early dinner (to 7:30 p.m.) Tues–Fri.*

House Without a Key
$$$ Waikiki   Eclectic

Everybody in the islands knows that this alfresco beachside lounge is Waikiki's best spot for sunset cocktails, but few realize how good the food is, too. The dinner menu fuses casual dining and elegance without a hitch. Consider starting with premium-grade ahi sashimi or the Maui onion soup gratiné (topped with melted Swiss and Gruyère cheeses) followed by a perfectly grilled Angus beef burger. Or start with casual finger foods (maybe coconut shrimp or peanut-crusted barbecued chicken skewers) and follow with lump crab-crusted mahimahi or a thick-cut New York steak. The mai tais are Hawaii's best, but the bar also excels at nonalcoholic creations; try the tart lime Calamansi soda or a refreshing frozen lemonade. A masterful trio entertains with traditional Hawaiian music nightly, accompanied by an elegant hula dancer of the highest regard (most nights it's Kanoe Miller, a former Miss Hawaii). Romantic, nostalgic, and breathtaking; one of my Waikiki favorites.

See map p. 138. In the Halekulani, 2199 Kalia Rd. (at the beach end of Lewers Street), Waikiki. ☎ *808-923-2311.* www.halekulani.com. *Reservations highly recommended for sunset dining. Main courses: $13–$19 at lunch, $12–$28 at dinner; breakfast buffet $22 adults, $11 kids ages 5–12. AE, DC, MC, V. Open: Breakfast, lunch, and dinner daily.*

Hukilau Cafe
$ North Shore   Local

This super-local North Shore diner was the inspiration for the restaurant featured in the movie *50 First Dates*. The reason to go, though, is not for a movie moment, but for a genuine local experience at this clean, simple, bustling daytime place. The star of the simple menu is the Hukilau burger, topped with cheese, onions, lettuce, tomato, mayo, teriyaki beef (yes, on the burger), and a fried egg. A heart attack on a fresh-baked bun, for sure, but divine nonetheless. Or try one of the mixed plates; my favorites come with teriyaki beef and the local mahimahi, cleanly fried to golden brown. All plates come with the traditional rice and macaroni salad sides. Service is very friendly, but be prepared to move with the flow or wait for a table — whatever the day calls for. A genuine local experience.

See map p. 162. 55-662 Wahinepee St. (off Naniloa Loop), Laie. ☎ *808-293-8616. To get there: From King Kamehameha Highway, at the Laie sign (across from Hukilau Beach), turn mauka (inland, away from the ocean); go three-quarters of the way around the traffic circle at Naniloa Loop and you'll see it at the end of the street (no street sign); look for the surfboard-shaped sign. Main courses: $3.50–$7. No credit cards. Open: Breakfast and lunch Mon–Fri, breakfast only Sat.*

Hula Grill Waikiki
$$–$$$ Mid-Waikiki   Hawaii Regional

I'm thrilled that this Maui favorite has found a second home in Waikiki, on the second floor of the Outrigger Waikiki, above its sister restaurant, Duke's Canoe Club. Styled after a 1920s-era plantation owner's home, the appealing room boasts an airy and sophisticated island ambience with gorgeous ocean and Diamond Head views and a vibe that is significantly mellower than its Maui counterpart, or Duke's downstairs. The midpriced island-style steak-and-seafood menu has something for everyone, including superb wood-grilled or macadamia-crusted fresh island fish, yummy barbecued pork ribs in mango barbecue sauce, Hawaii-style steak Diane with shiitake mushroom cream and lilikoi (passion fruit) butter, or succulent lemon-ginger roasted chicken. Well-blended tropical drinks dressed up with umbrellas round out the carefree island vibe. A nice choice for breakfast, too. All in all, an excellent choice. There's live entertainment nightly from 7 to 9 p.m.

See map p. 138. At the Outrigger Waikiki on the Beach, 2335 Kalakaua Ave. (between the Royal Hawaiian Shopping Center and the Moana Surfrider), Waikiki. ☎ *808-923-4852.* www.hulapie.com. *Reservations recommended for dinner. Main courses: $5–$14 at breakfast, $17–$34 at dinner. AE, DISC, MC, V. Open: Breakfast and dinner daily.*

Hy's Steak House
$$$$ Waikiki   Steaks/Seafood

I just love Hy's — it's the only place in town that still serves a great steak and flaming bananas Foster in true old-world style. This dark and clubby traditional steakhouse is the perfect setting for classics like oysters Rockefeller, beef Wellington, rich and garlicky steak Diane, lamb chops à la Hy's (perfectly broiled and served with tropical fruit chutney), and chateaubriand for two. Or choose from a number of surf-and-turf combos, plus a good selection of seafood options (including calamari, ahi, and kiawe-charred [mesquite-charred] scallops). I suggest starting with the Caesar salad show (prepared tableside with all of the classic flourishes) and crowning the meal with a flambéed dessert, such as cherries jubilee or the aforementioned bananas Foster. More formal and upscale than the new d.k Steak House, it's also mellower in attitude and style. Enjoy live acoustic music Tuesday through Saturday nights, or live island-style ukulele music sets Sunday and Monday nights. Make sure you get seated in the elegant, old-school downstairs dining room; the lame upstairs dining room feels like a Greek diner off the New Jersey Turnpike.

See map p. 138. In the Waikiki Park Heights, 2440 Kuhio Ave. (near Uluniu Avenue). ☎ *808-922-5555.* www.hyshawaii.com. *Reservations highly recommended. Main courses: $29–$63 (most items under $40). AE, DC, DISC, MC, V. Open: Dinner nightly.*

Indigo
$$$ Downtown   Eurasian

This intimate downtown restaurant is a wonderful choice for a romantic midpriced meal. Boasting a casual-chic tropical look, the contemporary main room sets an appealing scene. But call ahead for a table on the magical lanai, which overlooks a charming pocket park; dark woods and rattan, oversize palm fronds, a trickling water fountain, and conspiratorially dim candlelight make this outdoor dining room feel as if it had been transplanted from exotic Thailand or deepest Malaysia. Chef/owner Glenn Chu's East-meets-West menu is best described as Pan-Asian — Chinese and Thai traditions are most apparent — with serious French twists: Witness such taste treats as goat cheese wontons in a four-fruit sauce, and Mongolian lamb chops sauced with minted tangerines. Light eaters or the chronically indecisive can choose to make a meal of dim sum–style plates (lobster potstickers, anyone?). Come early for a relaxed martini, or stay late for some rollicking live music, in the adjacent Green Room lounge.

See map p. 140. 1121 Nuuanu Ave. (between S. King and S. Hotel streets), downtown Honolulu. ☎ 808-521-2900. www.indigo-hawaii.com. *Reservations recommended (accepted online). To get there: Take Ala Moana Boulevard from Waikiki to Bethel Street; turn right, then left on Pauahi Street, then left on Nuuanu Avenue. Main courses: $8–$14 at lunch, $16–$30 at dinner. Lunch buffet with trio of dim sum: $14. DC, DISC, MC, V. Open: Lunch and dinner Tues–Fri, dinner only Sat. Bar menu served until 11:30 p.m. Tues–Wed, to 2 a.m. Thurs–Sat.*

Kakaako Kitchen
$ Ala Moana   Hawaii Local/American

This contemporary dine-and-dash elevates takeout to gourmet status. The huge menu has choices ranging from Chinese *char siu* (barbecue) chicken salad with crispy wontons to an all-American oven-roasted turkey sandwich with sage dressing and mashies. The island-style chicken linguine in chili-hoisin cream is a standout, as is the delectable seared ahi sandwich on taro bread, but you can also come by for a juicy beef or homemade veggie burger, home-style pot roast, sandwiches ranging from seared ahi to grilled pastrami, and daily vegetarian specials. Breakfast stars include omelets, corned-beef hash, and fresh-baked scones. You order at the counter, and then choose a table inside or on the lanai; a server delivers your freshly made meal in short order. Beware the workday lunch hour, which can be maddening. However, it's otherwise hard to dine this well for such low, low prices. A real local gem.

See map p. 140. In the Ward Centre, 1200 Ala Moana Blvd. (entrance 1 block north, on Auahi Street at Kamakee Street), Honolulu. ☎ 808-596-7488. Main courses: $5–$8 at breakfast, $8–$13 at lunch and dinner. AE, MC, V. Open: Breakfast and lunch daily, dinner Mon–Sat.

Kua Aina Sandwich
$ Ala Moana/North Shore   Island Style/American

This North Shore legend has pleased many Honolulu residents — who used to have to drive an hour for the ultimate burger — by opening a second Ala Moana–area location. Cheeseburger in Paradise (see earlier in this chapter) wins on both burger and atmosphere, but Kua Aina (*koo*-ah *eye*-na) runs a close second on the burger and makes for a better quickie meal. The gourmet sandwiches are equally good, especially the mahimahi with a green-chili sauce and cheese. Whatever you order, don't forget a side of the spindly fries, which elevate the fried spud to new levels. Takeout is a good idea at the perpetually packed North Shore location; the larger Honolulu branch offers more indoor and outdoor seating.

See map p. 140. In Honolulu: At Ward Village Shops, 1116 Auahi St. (at Kamakee Street, 1 block inland from Ala Moana Boulevard, directly behind Ward Centre). ☎ 808-591-9133. Open: Lunch and early dinner (to 8 p.m.) daily. On the North Shore: 66–214 Kamehameha Hwy., Haleiwa. ☎ 808-637-6067. Open: Lunch and early dinner (to 8 p.m.) daily. At both locations, sandwiches and burgers: $4.50–$7.50. No credit cards.

Nobu
$$$$$ Mid-Waikiki   Euro-Japanese

In 2007, world-famous chef Nobuyuki Matsuhisa debuted the first Pacific island outpost of his famed Nobu restaurants, and Oahu rejoiced. Deeply rooted in Japanese tradition but heavily influenced by Western techniques, Matsuhisa's cuisine bursts with creative spirit. Unusual textures, impulsive combinations, and surprising flavors add up to a first-rate dining adventure that you won't soon forget. Virtually every creation hits its target, whether you opt for the new-style sashimi; light-as-air rock shrimp tempura; oysters baked in Filo pastry and dressed with caviar; or sublime broiled black cod in sweet miso, the best (and most famous) dish on the menu. You can take a traditional appetizers-and-entrees approach, but most dinners are structured as a series of tasting plates based on your palette and desired level of adventure. Before my recent meal here, I had forgotten how much fun it is to eat at Nobu. The staff is knowledgeable and pleasingly opinionated, and happy to guide you to your ideal meal. The excitement is heightened by the dramatic modern decor and lighting. Come with your mind (and wallet) open, and you're bound to enjoy a stellar Japanese fusion experience. Book well in advance.

See map p. 138. In the Waikiki Parc, 2233 Helumoa Rd. (at Lewers Street). ☎ *808-237-6999.* www.noburestaurants.com. *Reservations essential. Main courses: $15–$43. AE, DC, DISC, MC, V. Open: Dinner daily.*

Orchids
$$$$$ Mid-Waikiki   International Seafood

There's no arguing with the fabulousness of the Halekulani's classic French restaurant, La Mer — but oceanside Orchids is equally fabulous, less expensive, and better suits the Hawaii mood. Everything about Orchids is sigh-inducing: the gorgeous alfresco setting; the spectacular ocean and Diamond Head views; the seamless service; and an impressive surf-and-turf menu that offers time-tested classics to traditionalists and globe-hopping innovations for adventurous spirits. My last dinner here was simply flawless, from the melt-in-your-mouth ahi sashimi appetizer straight through to the beautifully presented coconut cake, white and airy as a cloud. It's very pricey, but if you have something to celebrate, this is a wonderful place to do it. The finest oceanfront dining experience in Waikiki, hands down.

See map p. 138. In the Halekulani, 2199 Kalia Rd. (at the beach end of Lewers Street), Waikiki. ☎ *808-923-2311.* www.halekulani.com. *Reservations highly recommended. Main courses: $8–$20 at breakfast, $16–$24 at lunch, $19–$58 at dinner (chef's tasting menu $57). Sun brunch $49 adults, $28 children. AE, DC, MC, V. Open: Breakfast, lunch, and dinner Mon–Sat; brunch and dinner Sun.*

Pah Ke's Chinese Restaurant
$ Windward Coast   Chinese/Island

This top-flight Chinese restaurant from brothers Raymond and Barry Siu is well worth the 20-minute trip from Waikiki. Pah Ke's serves Hong Kong–style

Chinese food with a local flair thanks to the use of healthy cooking techniques and island-grown ingredients. Specialties of the house include Ka'u orange spinach salad and a steamed fresh local catch, but you can't go wrong with any of the dishes here. Delightful versions of all your Chinese favorites are on the menu, but the staff will be happy to order for you if you'd like to dine creatively with some direction. The brightly lit room bustles with positive energy and happy diners, where seating is both family-style and at private tables for two and four. BYOB if you'd like beer or wine with your meal.

See map p. 162. 46–018 Kamehameha Hwy., Kaneohe. ☎ 808-235-4505. Reservations recommended for dinner. To get there: Take the Likelike Highway (Highway 63) from Waikiki, turn left on Kamehameha Highway (Highway 83), just over 1 mile; Pah Ke's will be on your right. Main courses: $5–$10 (whole duck $22–$28). Fixed-price meals $6–$8 at lunch, $6–$10 at dinner. AE, MC, V. Open: Lunch and dinner daily.

PukaDog
$ Mid-Waikiki Casual American

When irreverent chef and adventure travel rogue Anthony Bourdain, of the Travel Channel's No Reservations, had the opportunity to dine anywhere he wanted in Hawaii, he headed straight for PukaDog. This simple, charming storefront has Hawaiianized the hot dog for unrepentant gourmands in search of local culinary experiences.

PukaDog starts by baking a bun-size loaf of bread from their own house recipe. Once you place your order, they pierce a hole in one end (puka means "hole" in Hawaiian), toast the bun, insert a perfectly grilled Polish-style sausage, and dress it to your taste. You'll customize with your choice of secret sauce — mild garlic-lemon, spicy jalapeño, hot chili pepper, or super-hot habanero — and tropical relish (mango, coconut, banana, pineapple, papaya, or star fruit). Top it all off with the condiment of your choice; my favorite is the lilikoi (passion fruit) mustard. Service is aloha friendly, and a veggie dog is available for those who don't do meat. There are only a few tables, so get your dog to go — and relish in one of the Pacific's most heavenly hot dogs.

See map p. 138. In Waikiki Town Center (on the backside of International Marketplace), 2301 Kuhio Ave., Waikiki. ☎ 808-924-7887. www.pukadog.com. *Reservations not taken. Puka Dogs: $6–$7. No credit cards. Open: Lunch and dinner daily.*

Roy's Honolulu/Roy's Waikiki/Roy's Ko' Olina
$$$–$$$$ East Oahu (Hawaii Kai)/Mid-Waikiki/Leeward Oahu Hawaii Regional

Roy Yamaguchi isn't the sole mastermind behind the Hawaii Regional Cuisine concept, but he is responsible for bringing it an international audience. Roy's has roughly 30 locations worldwide, but his original flagship restaurant, 20 minutes east of Waikiki, is well worth visiting. Roy's hasn't lost its sheen, and there's a bustling, festive buzz every night. You can go whole-hog or keep costs down by ordering from the wide selection of appetizers and creative wood-oven pizzas, most less than $15. The menu changes nightly, but count on such signatures as Szechuan-spiced baby back ribs, crispy crab cakes in spicy sesame butter, and several inventively prepared fresh catches. Roy offers his own private-label ultrapremium sake, which perfectly complements his menu; there's also a wonderful list of creative tropical cocktails. Tables are big and comfortable, and service is friendly and impressively attentive. Kids are welcome, and Roy's is particularly well-suited to groups, making it an ideal choice for a multigenerational family meal. There's also live music Friday, Saturday, and Sunday evenings.

A second Oahu location, Roy's Ko' Olina, which overlooks a lagoon and the 18th hole of the Ko' Olina Golf Club, features the same winning formula. And I'm thrilled that Roy's has now added a third location in the heart of Waikiki as part of the new Beach Walk redevelopment. The three-course prix-fixe meal, featuring Roy's melting-hot signature chocolate soufflé, is the dining bargain of Waikiki at $40 per person; call to see if it's still available while you're in town.

See map p. 138. In Hawaii Kai Corporate Plaza, 6600 Kalanianaole Hwy. (Highway 72 at Keahole Street), east of Honolulu in Hawaii Kai. ☎ *808-396-7697. Roy's Waikiki: 226 Lewers St. (at Kalia Road), Waikiki.* ☎ *808-923-7697. Roy's Ko' Olina: 92–1220 Aliinui Dr., Kapolei, on the Leeward Coast.* ☎ *808-676-7697.* www.roysrestaurant. com. *Reservations recommended. Appetizers and pizzas: $8.50–$16. Main courses: $18–$41 (most under $35). AE, DC, DISC, MC, V. Open: Dinner nightly (Roy's Ko' Olina also open for lunch daily).*

Sam Choy's Breakfast, Lunch, Crab & Big Aloha Brewery
$$–$$$ Honolulu   Hawaii Regional/Seafood

This informal island-style restaurant and crab house is a favorite for its gargantuan portions and fun, energetic atmosphere. I love Sam for his mammoth morning meals and lunches. With appetite ragin' full on, I usually head here straight off my transpacific flight for a piled-high fried poke (ahi) lunch or a monster Lava burger (topped with crabmeat and Swiss cheese). Thoughts invariably turn to crab at dinner: The variety changes with the season, but you can expect a national atlas of choices, from Kona to Alaskan to Maryland crabmeat, in preparations that range from steamed legs to rich chowder to delectable cakes. Service can be slack at times, but it's always friendly.

See map p. 140. 580 Nimitz Hwy. (on the way to the airport), Honolulu. ☎ *808-545-7979.* www.samchoy.com. *Reservations recommended. Main courses: $5.25–$13 at breakfast, $9–$40 at lunch (most less than $13), $21–$45 at dinner (most less than $28). Sat–Sun breakfast buffets $18 adults, $6.95 kids ages 5–12. AE, DC, DISC, MC, V. Open: Breakfast, lunch, and dinner daily.*

Sansei Restaurant & Sushi Bar
$$$–$$$$ Mid-Waikiki   Japanese/Pacific Rim Seafood

Chef D.K. Kodama has wowed Waikiki with this fresh outpost of his Maui sushi palaces. Sansei offers some of the best dining on the island, especially for serious sushi lovers. Composed primarily of Pan-Asian seafood dishes with multicultural touches, Sansei's winningly innovative menu has won raves from fans around the globe. Entrees are available, but I recommend assembling a family-style meal from the adventurous sushi rolls and small plates. Can't-go-wrong menu highlights include the Asian rock shrimp cake in ginger-lime-chili butter, topped with crispy Chinese noodles; the mango crab salad roll in sweet Thai chili vinaigrette; the calamari salad tossed in Korean-inspired *kojuchang* vinaigrette, presented in a pleasing wonton basket; and the beautifully presented flower sushi. Even the desserts are divine at this easygoing, Japanese-style place.

Sit at the bar if you'd like to combine your sushi order with some dishes from the adjoining d.k Steak House (see review earlier in this chapter).

Early-bird diners receive 25 percent off sushi orders placed Tuesdays through Fridays between 5:30 and 6 p.m., and late-night diners enjoy karaoke, drink specials, and 50 percent off the appetizer and sushi menu Fridays and Saturdays between 10 p.m. and 2 a.m.

See map p. 138. At the Waikiki Beach Marriott Resort & Spa, 2552 Kalakaua Ave. (at Papakalani Avenue just west of Kapiolani Park), Waikiki. ☎ *808-931-6286.* www.sansei hawaii.com. *Reservations highly recommended. Sushi and sashimi: $5–$20. Main courses: $11–$43 (most under $30). AE, DISC, MC, V. Open: Dinner nightly.*

Side Street Inn
$–$$ Ala Moana   Local

The popularity of this unassuming sports-and-karaoke bar exploded when locals realized that this is where Honolulu's best chefs gather to nosh after their own kitchens close. This is as hole-in-the-wall as it gets: neon beer signs in the plate-glass windows, long picnic-style tables, TVs turned to the current game, walls long in need of a fresh painting, and no-nonsense service. Chatting, happy crowds dig into heaping family-style plates of tangy Buffalo wings, delectable fried rice chock-full of meat and veggies, *kal bi* (charbroiled Korean-style short ribs), and other diet-defying delights. Many consider the pan-fried pork chops to be the world's best, and they just may be. Also recommended: finger-lickin' good baby back ribs glazed in lilikoi barbecue sauce, and meaty, moist chicken *katsu* (chicken breast coated in panko bread crumbs, a Japanese favorite). Genuine local fun, and some of the best authentic local food on the island. Side Street is also a great choice for late-night dining, because the kitchen is open until 12:30 a.m. daily, as long as the kitchen feels like it (the bar stays open until the wee hours).

See map p. 140. 1225 Hopaka St. (just west of Piikoi Street, 1 block south of Kapiolani Boulevard), Honolulu. ☎ *808-591-0253. Reservations recommended for large parties. To get there from Waikiki: Take Ala Moana Boulevard to Piikoi Street and turn right; turn left on Kapiolani Boulevard; turn left on Pensacola Street; and turn left on Hopaka Street; park on the street where allowed. Main courses: $5–$8 at lunch, $7.50–$21 at dinner (most under $13). AE, DC, DISC, MC, V. Open: Lunch Mon–Fri, dinner daily.*

Singha Thai Cuisine
$$$ Ewa Waikiki   Thai

The imaginative Thai-Hawaiian hybrid cuisine at Singha wins fans among Asian-food addicts and novices alike. Thai-born chef Chai Chaowasaree's complete dinners for two to five are family-style feasts — perfect for introducing first-timers to this rich, flavorful cuisine, as well as elements of Hawaii Regional Cuisine that the chef has incorporated into his cooking. Highlights of the varied menu include yummy blackened ahi rolls; fresh island fish in a light black-bean sauce; a kaleidoscope of curries; and excellent seafood dishes, like the wok-seared jumbo black tiger prawns in spicy ginger-chili sauce. Dishes are presented prettily, and service is first-rate. The graceful Royal Thai Dancers perform nightly, adding to the one-of-a-kind experience. There's free validated parking on the second floor of Canterbury Place (enter from Ena Road).

See map p. 138. 1910 Ala Moana Blvd. (at Kalia Road), Waikiki. ☎ *808-941-2898.* www. singhathai.com. *Reservations recommended. Main courses: $16–$35 (most under $25); complete multicourse dinners (served for 2–5 people) $35 per person. AE, DC, DISC, MC, V. Open: Dinner nightly.*

Town
$$$ Honolulu   Fresh Contemporary

This wonderful contemporary restaurant is well worth seeking out for foodies in the mood for something different. It's only a ten-minute drive from Waikiki, in Honolulu's increasingly stylish Kaimuki district; the restaurant reflects the casual, confident hipness of the area. The atmosphere is spare and loftlike, with enough kitchen-friendly comforts — diner-style tables and chairs, a pastry cabinet serving as the bar — to feel approachable rather than sleek. Town's motto is "Local first, organic whenever possible, with aloha always." Greens come from local island farmers, and fish is caught from island boats most of the time. But the real joy in the food comes in the imaginative marriages and seasonings that create delicate, seamless flavors that are greater than the sum of their parts. Dishes that make memories include a succulent pan-roasted chicken served over a torn bread salad tossed with *tatsoi* (spinach mustard greens), juicy grapes, and savory pancetta. Also consider the grilled monchong filet served with purple Molokai sweet potato, zucchini, Maui onion, and a palette-sparking salsa verde; with so much pan-island origination, it's practically Hawaii on a plate. I recommend starting with the lightly fried Ma'o spring onions. Some consider the service to be snobbish, but I appreciate the clear direction and friendly challenge to dine provocatively and well. The wine list is affordable and inventive, too.

See map p. 138. 3435 Waialae Ave., Honolulu. ☎ *808-735-5900.* www.townkaimuki. com. *Reservations recommended. To get there from Waikiki: Take Kalakaua Avenue toward Diamond Head; turn left at Kapahulu Avenue, go 1 mile to Mooheau Avenue and turn right; go ⅓ mile and turn left on 6th Avenue; go ½ mile to Waialae Avenue, turn right and go ⅓ mile to the restaurant. Use the small lot in the back or park on the street if the lot is full. Main courses: $17–$24. BYO corkage: $10. AE, MC, V. Open: Lunch and dinner Mon–Sat.*

Luau!

None of Oahu's luau are on par with those offered on the neighbor islands, especially Maui's Old Lahaina Luau, but if you're not visiting any of the neighboring islands on this trip, try the **Royal Luau at the Royal Hawaiian** (see map p. 132; 2259 Kalakaua Ave. [at the end of Royal Hawaiian Avenue], Waikiki; ☎ **808-921-4600;** www.royal-hawaiian.com). Prices are $99 for adults (including unlimited cocktails), $55 for kids ages 5 to 12, free for kids age 4 and under; discounts are available for Royal Hawaiian guests, and you can sometimes score online discounts. Reservations are highly recommended. The luau is held every Monday and Thursday at 6 p.m. Note that the event may be canceled or moved to an indoor venue in inclement weather. Furthermore, I wouldn't be surprised if the schedule changes once the Royal Hawaiian opens in late 2008 after its major renovation; call to check for the latest details and prices. This is Waikiki's only luau, and although it's not the most authentic luau in the islands, it is intimate and romantic.

Also consider the nightly (except Sun) luau at the **Polynesian Cultural Center** in Laie; see Chapter 11 for more information.

Sea Life Park also offers the family-friendly **Sea Life Luau** on Wednesday, Friday, and Sunday nights at 6 p.m. It includes a 15-minute dolphin show as well as the usual luau entertainment and traditional *imu* (underground grilled pig) presentation. It's relaxing and fun, and a great way to see the highlights of the park if you don't have a whole day to spare. Prices are $89 for adults, $55 for kids. For advance reservations, call ☎ **866-393-5158,** or visit www.sealifeparkhawaii.com. See Chapter 11 for further details on the park.

Fast Facts: Oahu

American Automobile Association (AAA)

Hawaii's only AAA office is at 1130 Nimitz Hwy., Honolulu (☎ 800-736-2886 or 808-593-2221; www.aaa-hawaii.com). The office is open Monday through Friday from 9 a.m. to 5 p.m., and on Saturday from 9 a.m. to 2 p.m.

American Express

Travel offices are located at 677 Ala Moana Blvd., Honolulu (☎ 808-585-3200), and at the Hilton Hawaiian Village, 2005 Kalia Rd., at Ala Moana Boulevard, Waikiki (☎ 808-947-2607 or 808-951-0644).

Baby Sitters and Baby Stuff

Any hotel or condo should be able to refer you to a reliable baby sitter. See "Traveling with the Brood: Advice for Families" in Chapter 8 for details about renting baby gear on Oahu.

Doctors

Straub Doctors on Call (☎ 808-522-4777 for the 24-hour appointment line; www.straubhealth.org) offers round-the-clock care at its 24-hour health clinic on the ground floor of the Sheraton Princess Kaiulani Hotel, 120 Kaiulani Ave., just north of Kalakaua Avenue in the heart of Waikiki

(☎ 808-971-6000). Straub accepts more than 150 health plans, so pack your insurance card. They can send a van to bring you to their main clinic, or house calls can be arranged. Check the Web site for additional clinic locations throughout Oahu.

Walk-in healthcare is also available at the Urgent Care Clinic Waikiki, 2155 Kalakaua Ave., between Beach Walk and Lewers Street, Suite 308 (☎ 808-924-3399; www.waikikiclinic.org; open daily 8:30 a.m.–7 p.m.). You can call ahead for free taxi pickup from your Waikiki hotel.

Emergencies

Dial **911** from any phone, just like back home on the mainland.

Hospitals

Nearest to Waikiki is Straub Clinic and Hospital, 888 S. King St., at Ward Avenue (Emergency Department: ☎ 808-522-3781; www.straubhealth.org); the Emergency Room entrance is on Hotel Street. Also offering 24-hour emergency care is Queens Medical Center, 1301 Punchbowl St., between Beretania Street and Vineyard Boulevard (☎ 808-538-9011, or 808-547-4311 for the ER; www.queens.org).

Information

The Hawaii Visitors and Convention Bureau operates an office on the seventh floor of 2270 Kalakaua Ave. in the heart of Waikiki (☎ 800-464-2924 or 808-923-1811; www.gohawaii.com). Tons of info is available on the Web site. The Oahu Visitors Bureau, 733 Bishop St., Makai Tower, Ste. 1872, downtown Honolulu (☎ 877-525-OAHU or 808-524-0722; www.visit-oahu.com), offers good island-specific information on its Web site, and you can order a good vacation planner by calling the 877 number.

You can stop into either of these offices while you're in town, or just stop at the airport information desk near Baggage Claim and pick up a copy of *This Week Oahu, 101 Things to Do on Oahu,* and other free tourist publications; they're packed with good maps. All Waikiki's hotels, from budget to deluxe, also overflow with printed info, and the staffs are generally well-informed and helpful.

Newspapers and Magazines

The *Honolulu Advertiser* (www.honoluluadvertiser.com) and *Honolulu Star-Bulletin* (www.starbulletin.com) are Oahu's daily papers. The *Honolulu Weekly* (www.honoluluweekly.com) is the best source for entertainment listings and information on what's happening around town; it's available free at restaurants, clubs, shops, and newspaper racks around Oahu. *Honolulu* magazine is a popular glossy monthly.

Pharmacies

Longs Drugs (www.longs.com), Hawaii's biggest drugstore chain, has convenient locations at Ala Moana Center, 1450 Ala Moana Blvd., next to Sears (☎ 808-941-4433), and elsewhere around the island. You'll find 24-hour stores at 1330 Pali Hwy., at Vineyard Boulevard, downtown Honolulu (☎ 808-536-7302), and 2220 S. King St. (☎ 808-949-4781).

Police

The Waikiki City Police Station is in the Duke Paoa Kahanamoku Building at 2405 Kalakaua Ave., between Kaiulani and Uluniu streets on the ocean side of the street (☎ 808-529-3801). Honolulu Police Department Main Station is at 801 S. Beretania St., west of Ward Avenue (☎ 808-529-3111; www.honolulupd.org). Of course, if you have an emergency, dial **911** from any phone.

Post Offices

The Waikiki Post Office is at 330 Saratoga Rd., just south of Kalakaua Avenue, adjacent to Fort DeRussy Park. Another convenient location is in the Ala Moana Shopping Center. To find the location nearest you, call ☎ 800-275-8777 or visit www.usps.com.

Taxes

Most purchases in Hawaii are taxed at roughly 4 percent; the exact amount will vary depending on the county you're in, and may be embedded in the total purchase price or shown as an independent line item on your bill. Expect taxes of about 11.42 percent to be added to your hotel bill.

Taxis

Oahu's major cab companies offer island-wide, 24-hour radio-dispatched service. Call Star Taxi (☎ 800-671-2999 or 808-942-7827); City Taxi (☎ 808-524-2121); or TheCab (☎ 808-422-2222). Coast Taxi (☎ 808-261-3755) serves Windward Oahu, and Hawaii Kai Hui/Koko Head Taxi (☎ 808-396-6633) serves east Honolulu/southeast Oahu.

See Chapter 8 for wheelchair-accessible transportation.

Transit Info

For information on routes and schedules, call TheBus information office at ☎ 808-848-5555. Point your browser to www.thebus.org for online info.

Weather and Surf Reports

For National Weather Service reports, call ☎ 808-973-4380. For marine conditions and sunrise/sunset times, call ☎ 808-973-4382. For surf reports, call ☎ 808-973-4383 or the Surfline at ☎ 808-596-7873.

Chapter 11

Exploring Oahu

. . . .

In This Chapter

▶ Heading to Oahu's best beaches
▶ Playing in the waves
▶ Seeing the sights
▶ Scoping out the shopping scene
▶ Enjoying Oahu's island nightlife

. . . .

Oahu is the place to rev up and have some fun. This island boasts more than you can see or do in the span of five vacations, much less one — so save the kicking-back portion of your vacation for the next island.

Then again, there are those wonderful white sands and warm turquoise waters. . . .

Enjoying the Sand and Surf

Oahu's warm and wonderful diversity also extends to its wealth of beautiful beaches and ocean activities. Whether you want to bask in the sun or find an ocean thrill, Oahu has the answer for you.

Combing the Beaches

When you're at the beach, maintain a healthy respect for the ocean. Big waves can come seemingly out of nowhere and travel far upshore in a matter of minutes. Never turn your back on the ocean. Take extra care to heed this advice in winter, when the surf is at its least predictable.

Also, never leave valuables in your rental car while you're at the beach. Thieves prey on tourists, and they'll have no trouble getting into your car to take whatever you've left there.

Beaches and Attractions Around Oahu

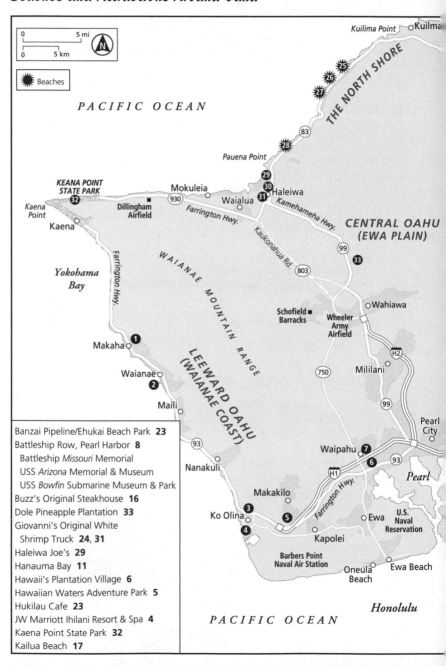

0 5 mi
0 5 km

N

PACIFIC OCEAN

Kuilima Point Kuilima

THE NORTH SHORE

25
26
27

83

28

Pauena Point

KEANA POINT
STATE PARK
32

Kaena
Point
Kaena

Mokuleia

930

Waialua

29
30
31 Haleiwa

Kamehameha Hwy.

Farrington Hwy.

Kaukonahua Rd.

99

803

33

CENTRAL OAHU
(EWA PLAIN)

Wahiawa

Yokohama
Bay

Farrington Hwy.

WAIANAE   MOUNTAIN   RANGE

Schofield
Barracks

Wheeler
Army
Airfield

Makaha

1

Waianae

2

Maili

LEEWARD OAHU
(WAIANAE COAST)

750

Mililani

H2

99

Pearl
City

93

Nanakuli

Makakilo

Ko Olina

3

5

4

Waipahu
7
6

H1

Farrington Hwy.

93

Pearl

Ewa

U.S.
Naval
Reservation

Kapolei

Barbers Point
Naval Air Station

Oneula
Beach

Ewa Beach

Honolulu

PACIFIC OCEAN

Dillingham
Airfield

Beaches

Banzai Pipeline/Ehukai Beach Park **23**
Battleship Row, Pearl Harbor **8**
  Battleship *Missouri* Memorial
  USS *Arizona* Memorial & Museum
  USS *Bowfin* Submarine Museum & Park
Buzz's Original Steakhouse **16**
Dole Pineapple Plantation **33**
Giovanni's Original White
  Shrimp Truck **24, 31**
Haleiwa Joe's **29**
Hanauma Bay **11**
Hawaii's Plantation Village **6**
Hawaiian Waters Adventure Park **5**
Hukilau Cafe **23**
JW Marriott Ihilani Resort & Spa **4**
Kaena Point State Park **32**
Kailua Beach **17**

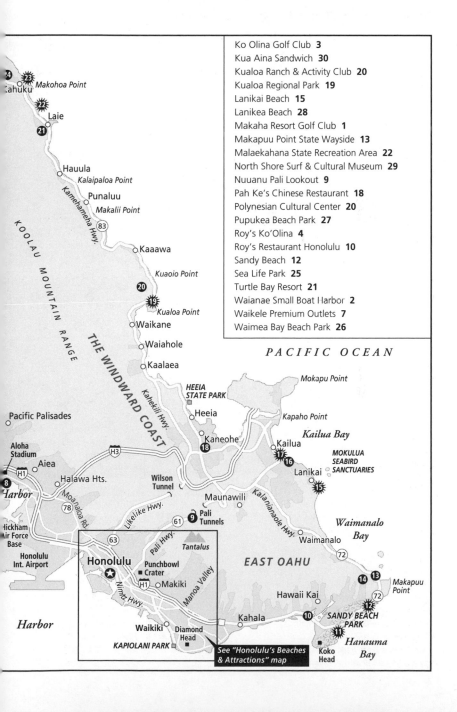

Ko Olina Golf Club **3**
Kua Aina Sandwich **30**
Kualoa Ranch & Activity Club **20**
Kualoa Regional Park **19**
Lanikai Beach **15**
Lanikea Beach **28**
Makaha Resort Golf Club **1**
Makapuu Point State Wayside **13**
Malaekahana State Recreation Area **22**
North Shore Surf & Cultural Museum **29**
Nuuanu Pali Lookout **9**
Pah Ke's Chinese Restaurant **18**
Polynesian Cultural Center **20**
Pupukea Beach Park **27**
Roy's Ko'Olina **4**
Roy's Restaurant Honolulu **10**
Sandy Beach **12**
Sea Life Park **25**
Turtle Bay Resort **21**
Waianae Small Boat Harbor **2**
Waikele Premium Outlets **7**
Waimea Bay Beach Park **26**

Honolulu's Beaches and Attractions

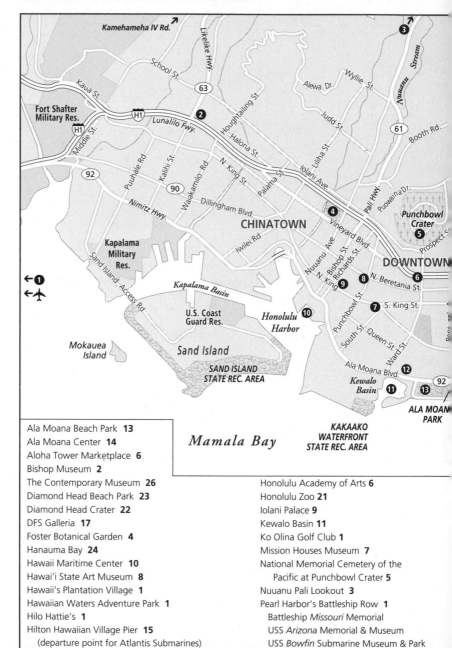

Ala Moana Beach Park **13**
Ala Moana Center **14**
Aloha Tower Marketplace **6**
Bishop Museum **2**
The Contemporary Museum **26**
Diamond Head Beach Park **23**
Diamond Head Crater **22**
DFS Galleria **17**
Foster Botanical Garden **4**
Hanauma Bay **24**
Hawaii Maritime Center **10**
Hawai'i State Art Museum **8**
Hawaii's Plantation Village **1**
Hawaiian Waters Adventure Park **1**
Hilo Hattie's **1**
Hilton Hawaiian Village Pier **15**
　(departure point for Atlantis Submarines)

Honolulu Academy of Arts **6**
Honolulu Zoo **21**
Iolani Palace **9**
Kewalo Basin **11**
Ko Olina Golf Club **1**
Mission Houses Museum **7**
National Memorial Cemetery of the
　Pacific at Punchbowl Crater **5**
Nuuanu Pali Lookout **3**
Pearl Harbor's Battleship Row **1**
　Battleship *Missouri* Memorial
　USS *Arizona* Memorial & Museum
　USS *Bowfin* Submarine Museum & Park

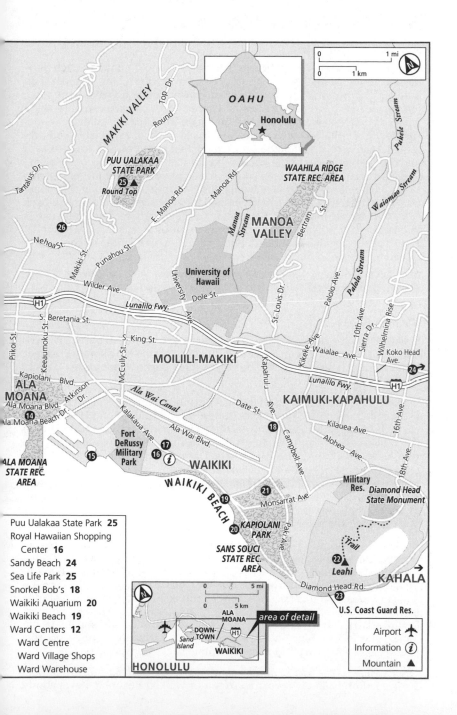

Puu Ualakaa State Park **25**
Royal Hawaiian Shopping
  Center **16**
Sandy Beach **24**
Sea Life Park **25**
Snorkel Bob's **18**
Waikiki Aquarium **20**
Waikiki Beach **19**
Ward Centers **12**
  Ward Centre
  Ward Village Shops
  Ward Warehouse

The Waikiki Coast and East Oahu

Ala Moana Beach Park

Gold-sand Ala Moana ("by the sea") is the city's most popular beach playground for local families, and it's easy to see why. Stretching for more than a mile along Honolulu's coast between downtown and Waikiki, the long, man-made beach is one of the best-sheltered coves on Oahu, so the water's calm and safe year-round, even for little ones. The area called Magic Island, the peninsula that extends from Ala Moana Park, is especially well-protected, thanks to a man-made breakwater that cuts the surf down to zero and offers great views of the Waikiki skyline. The park boasts concessions, lifeguards, bathhouses, tennis courts, a nice paved path for joggers, picnic tables, and wide-open grassy lawns. It's the only beach along this coast that's not lined with high-rise hotels, and the sands are set far enough back from Ala Moana Boulevard that traffic doesn't interfere. The ambience is laid-back on weekdays, whereas a party mood prevails on weekends. Plenty of free parking is at hand; but it fills up on weekends, so come early or catch TheBus to Ala Moana Center.

See map p. 164. Along Ala Moana Boulevard, between Atkinson Drive and Ward Avenue (directly across the street from Ala Moana Center).

Waikiki Beach

Waikiki is center stage for Hawaii's biggest and best beach party. Five million global visitors a year descend onto this 1½-mile-long sunny crescent of sand. Sure, it gets crowded, but that's a big part of what makes Waikiki such a blast.

Waikiki is actually a long, narrow, continuous string of beaches that extends between Ala Wai Harbor to the west and Diamond Head to the east. Each one is wonderful for surfing, swimming, and just frolicking in the mini-swells — and the tight chain of high-rise hotels abutting the beaches actually helps to block street noise and traffic sounds. Every imaginable type of beach toy is available for rent at concessions that line the beach. The sparkling turquoise water is always calm, warm, crystal-clear, and great for floating the real-life stress away. Waves can kick up a bit in the spring, when the south swells come — and the local surfers show up — but it's never so severe that you need to stay out of the water.

Duke Kahanamoku (ka-ha-na-*mow*-koo) **Beach** is the west end of the beach, the section fronting the Hilton Hawaiian Village hotel. Access is off Kalia Road via Paoa Place — or just walk through the hotel grounds. **Waikiki Beach Prime Time Sports** (☎ 808-949-8952; www.primetimesports hawaii.com) operates two excellent beach chair- and gear-rental stands just east of the Hilton and west of the Outrigger Reef, at the edge of Fort DeRussy Park. Prime Time Sports also rents oversize two-person floats, fun aquacycles for paddling on the waves, kayaks, surfboards, boogie boards, snorkel gear, and more. My favorite rental shacks on Waikiki Beach.

Gray's Beach, the arc of sand between the Halekulani and the Moana Surfrider hotels, is my favorite stretch of Waikiki Beach. It's everybody else's, too — particularly the area in front of the historic Royal Hawaiian and Moana hotels — so bring your beach chair and stake a claim because this beach is where the party begins. Waikiki's waters are at their calmest and shallowest here. The beach has a number of access points, including a beach access pathway off Kalia Road, just to the left of the Halekulani and to the right of the Waikiki Parc hotel (as you face the coast); walk to the left to get to the wider sands. (Or, better yet, just parade through one of the hotels.)

The festive party atmosphere continues on **Kuhio Beach,** which begins just to the east of the Moana Surfrider at the end of Kaiulani Avenue. Because fewer hotels separate Kalakaua Avenue from the beach, this one affords the quickest access to the Waikiki shoreline. This is where the majority of concessionaires are set up. (For more on what's available, see the section "Playing in the Surf," later in this chapter.) The swimming is good here; but some deep pools exist (heed the "Watch Out for Holes" signs because you can suddenly find yourself in very deep water), and the surf kicks up a bit a few hundred yards offshore. To the east of the Moana between Kaiulani and Uluniu avenues is Waikiki's newest renovation project, a wonderful parklike area of grassy knolls, winding paths, and Tiki torches — it's an excellent place to watch the sunset. The city regularly hosts sunset entertainment here and occasionally sets up a big outdoor movie screen to show classic films; ask the concierge at your hotel or condo for the current schedule. At the end of Kapahulu Avenue, a seawall marks a favorite boogie boarding spot.

Queen's Beach, directly across from Kapiolani Park (between the zoo and the aquarium), is the easiest place to park along Waikiki. This is also the quietest stretch of beach because no hotels line the road, and a grassy, palm-dotted lawn backs the sand. Head here if you want to get away from the crowds. The facilities include showers, restrooms, barbecue grills, picnic tables, volleyball courts, and a pavilion with a food concession. The middle section of the beach (in front of the pavilion) is a popular gay hangout, but everybody's welcome.

Sans Souci Beach is the easternmost section of Waikiki, the bit that fronts the New Otani Kaimana Beach Hotel and the other small hotels and condos at the foot of Diamond Head. This is the locals' favorite stretch of Waikiki thanks to its beautiful setting (Diamond Head makes a gorgeous backdrop) and intimate, low-key vibe. It's also on the quiet side, with easy-access parking along Kalakaua Avenue and beach showers. The swimming here is excellent — a shallow reef close to shore.

See map p. 164. Lifeguards patrol all Waikiki, and all the hotels have public restrooms and casual beachfront restaurants. For more information, contact the Hawaiian Lifeguard Association (3823 Leahi Ave., Honolulu; ☎ 808-922-3888; www.aloha. com/~lifeguards*).*

Hanauma Bay

Hanauma (ha-*now*-ma) Bay offers the best snorkeling in Hawaii, especially for novices. The curved, gold-sand beach is packed blanket-to-blanket with people year-round — sometimes it seems there are more people than fish in the water — but put on a mask and gaze down into the clear, warm water, and a whole new world opens up to you. Cradled in an old volcanic crater, this marine life conservation district is home to an underwater metropolis of friendly reef fish. (But be sure not to touch or feed the exotic critters here.) The inner reef is calm, clear, and shallow — so much so, in fact, that even nonswimmers can wade and look down. Serious divers come to shoot "the slot" through the reef to Witch's Brew, a turbulent, 70-foot-deep cove featuring coral gardens, turtles, and sharks, but I suggest you stick to the safe, shallow, well-protected inner reef.

A new $13-million Marine Education Center opened in 2002, as extensive improvements were made to the grounds and facilities at Hanauma Bay. The facility features a theater (you will be required to watch a nine-minute video about Hanauma Bay and ocean safety before you enter the park), an education alcove, a gift shop, and food concession at the upper level of the bay; a motorized tram (50¢ to go down the hill, $1 to go up) can take you down the steep road to the beach. Restrooms, outdoor showers, a snorkeling concession, and a new information center are located in the lower bay area. The only food concession is at the top.

Parking at Hanauma Bay costs $1 per car and is severely limited, so go bright and early to snare a spot; arrive after 10 a.m., and you may find yourself shut out. You can also take TheBus no. 22 (marked "Hawaii Kai–Sea Life Park"), which runs down Kuhio Avenue and takes about 45 minutes to reach Hanauma Bay. For information on routes and timetables, call TheBus at ☎ 808-848-5555.

Even though snorkel gear is available at Hanauma Bay, I much prefer to stop by Snorkel Bob's on the way to Hanauma Bay to pick up higher quality gear, which is well worth the extra $2 or $3; see the section "Playing in the Surf," later in this chapter, for details.

See map p. 162 In Koko Head Regional Park, off Kalanianaole Highway (the exit is well marked). ☎ **808-396-4229.** www.co.honolulu.hi.us/parks/facility/hanaumabay. *Admission: $5, free for kids under 12. Parking: $1 per car. Open: Summer: Wed–Mon 6 a.m.–7 p.m. (until 10 p.m. on the 2nd and 4th Sat of each month); closed Tues. Winter: Wed–Mon 6 a.m.–6 p.m. (until 10 p.m. on the 2nd Sat of each month); closed Tues.*

Diamond Head Beach Park

This hidden beach at the foot of Diamond Head is a nice local hideaway, especially if you're ready to escape the crowds of Waikiki but don't feel like venturing too far. A somewhat steep but paved path leads down the sea cliffs to a narrow but pretty golden-sand beach. A rocky shelf forms tide pools that are fun to explore. Snorkeling can be good early in the day; surfers come out later in afternoon, when the waves kick up. *Beware:* There are no lifeguards, and facilities are minimal. The gorgeous open ocean views make this a great whale-watching perch in winter.

See map p. 164. Off Kalakaua Avenue/Diamond Head Road, between Beach Road and the Diamond Head lighthouse. To get there: Drive east from Waikiki on Kalakaua

Avenue; after the road curves around Diamond Head, look for the beach marking on the ocean side of the road, right next to the lighthouse. Park on the street and take the stairs down to the beach.

Sandy Beach

The most famous bodysurfing spot in Hawaii is this beautiful gold-sand beach, which is all the more beautiful for the dramatic desert landscape behind it. This local favorite has starred in countless TV shows, from *Hawaii Five-O* to *Magnum P.I.* In summer, the ocean is fine for swimming and boogie boarding. In winter, the big, pounding waves draw expert body-surfers in droves, but they're simply too dangerous for regular swimmers. If you come to play in the summer waves, boogie boards are fine, but leave any boards with skegs (bottom fins) at home. Be sure to heed the lifeguard warnings and get out of the water if the swells or undertow kicks up. Facilities include restrooms, beach showers, lifeguard, and plenty of parking; a hot food truck usually shows up at lunchtime.

See map p. 164. On Kalanianole Highway. To get there: Drive east on H-1, which becomes Kalanianaole Highway; go past Hawaii Kai, up the hill to Hanauma Bay, past the Halona Blow Hole, and along the coast. The next big, gold, sandy beach you see ahead on the right is Sandy Beach.

Along the Windward Coast

If you have the time, I highly recommend spending a day at the beach along this stunning, uncrowded, residential coast. It's a nice change of pace from Waikiki: Come midweek, and you'll find these beaches pleasantly uncrowded; on weekends, local families set the tone.

Plan on arriving for your day of east shore beach-going early because the windward Koolau mountains block the afternoon sun.

Kailua Beach

The Windward Coast's premier beach park is a 2-mile-long gently sloping golden strand with dunes, palm trees, panoramic views, gentle waves, and a gorgeous green-mountain backdrop. With excellent swimming, water that's about 78°F year-round, and good facilities, it's ideal for families — and your kids will love the bodysurfing and boogie boarding here. Toddlers can splash in the freshwater shallows in the middle of the park, near the mouth of the stream. Facilities include picnic tables, barbecues, restrooms, a volleyball court, a bike path, an open-air cafe (which may be closed on weekdays), and plenty of free parking; lifeguards are usually on hand. Kayak and windsurf rentals are often available, too, because this is also Oahu's premier windsurfing beach.

From Kailua, you can kayak out to the two charmingly petite islets about 1½ miles offshore. Kayaking to the Mokuleias, where you can land on a remote beach for sunning and exploring, is one of my absolute favorite island activities. Local kayaking outfitters provide convenient rentals; see "Ocean kayaking for everyone," later in this chapter.

See map p. 162. At the end of Kailua Road, Kailua. To get there: Take the Pali Highway (Highway 61) to Kailua, where it becomes Kailua Road as it proceeds through town; at Kalaheo Avenue, turn right and follow the coast to the park.

Lanikai Beach

This is one of the most tranquil and beautiful beaches in the entire state — my favorite beach on the entire island. It's almost always excellent for swimming, snorkeling, and kayaking, plus a little easy wave-jumping on occasion. The beach is long and narrow, with gold sand as soft as talcum powder and lightly rippled turquoise water. Two petite offshore islets, called the Mokuleias, provide the perfect panoramic finish. Unfortunately, the trade-off for all this unspoiled beauty is an utter lack of facilities.

See map p. 162. Off Mokulua Drive, Kailua. To get there: Follow the directions to Kailua Beach Park (see preceding entry); just past Kailua Beach Park, turn left at the T intersection and drive uphill on Aalapapa Drive, a one-way street that loops back as Mokulua Drive; park on Mokulua Drive and walk down any of the 8 public access lanes to the shore.

Kualoa Regional Park

Farther north on the Windward Coast is one of Hawaii's most scenic beach parks, a 150-acre coco palm–fringed peninsula on Kaneohe Bay's north shore, at the foot of spiky green mountains. The biggest beach park on the windward side, it has a broad, grassy lawn that's great for picnicking. The long, narrow white-sand beach is ideal for swimming, beachcombing, kite flying, or just enjoying the natural beauty of this once-sacred Hawaiian shore (it's listed on the National Register of Historic Places), but keep in mind that it can get pretty windy out here. The waters are shallow and safe for swimming year-round. It doesn't offer much in the way of facilities, but lifeguards are on duty. Offshore is Mokolii (mow-ko-*lee*-ee), the picturesque mini-isle more commonly known as Chinaman's Hat. At low tide, people like to wade out to the island, which has a small sandy beach; it's just a bad idea to walk on the reef, however, so if you're going to go, swim it instead. Chinaman's Hat is a bird preserve, so tread gently.

See map p. 162. On Kamehameha Highway (Highway 83), Kualoa (about halfway up the coast, north of Waikane). ☎ *808-237-8525. Parking: The beach has a free lot, but there is no access parking or path for visitors with disabilities.*

Malaekahana State Recreation Area

Big, brawny Malaekahana (ma-lie-ka-*ha*-na) Beach is a nearly mile-long white-sand crescent with sheltered waters that are excellent for swimming year-round and waves that are great for beginning bodysurfers in summer. On any weekday, you may be the only one here; should someone intrude on your privacy, however, you can take an easy swim out to Goat Island, a bird sanctuary (you can wade it, but don't — it's bad for the reef). Stands of trees offer daytime shade, and restrooms, barbecue grills, picnic tables, outdoor showers, and tons of free parking are at hand.

Picnicking at Lanikai or Kailua

Both Lanikai and Kailua beaches are ideal places to bring a picnic lunch and camp out for the day. And the perfect place to pack it? **Kalapawai Market,** 306 S. Kalaheo Ave. (☎ **808-262-4359;** www.kalapawaimarket.com), just down the street from Kailua Beach and Buzz's Original Steak House (see Chapter 10). This charming market has evolved into an easygoing gourmet outpost complete with home-style deli sandwiches (including an excellent BLT with avocado spread) and an excellent collection of snacks, soft drinks, wine, and beer. Open daily from 6 a.m. to 9 p.m. There's also a second location in the heart of Kailua town at 750 Kailua Rd., between Hamakua and Hoolai streets, just past the end of the Pali Highway (☎ 808-262-3354). This location keeps the same hours, but also features a wine bar and serves an appealing and moderately priced sit-down dinner from 5:30 p.m. nightly. See map p. 162.

See map p. 162. On Kamehameha Highway (Highway 83), 2 miles north of the Polynesian Cultural Center, Laie. The beach is hidden from the road, so look carefully for the main gate; as soon as you enter you'll come upon the wooded beach park. Parking: There's a free lot.

On the North Shore

This is surf country, where daredevils gather from around the world to ride monster waves in surf season, basically from late September through April. Don't even think about going into the water in winter, because the rip currents along this shore are killers. The North Shore coast is seasonally schizophrenic: The monstrous surf recedes entirely in summer, leaving glassy ponds and idle surfboards.

The waves may kick up even in the fairest months, so don't go near the water in any season if the lifeguards have put out the red warning flags, or if you just suspect that conditions might be too rough.

Banzai Pipeline/Ehukai Beach Park

The Japanese word *banzai* means "10,000 years"; it's used as a toast or battle cry, meaning "go for it." In the late 1950s, filmmaker Bruce Brown was shooting one of the first surf movies ever made, *Surf Safari,* at Ehukai Beach Park when he saw a bodysurfer ride a huge wave. Brown yelled "Banzai!" and the name stuck. The Banzai Pipeline section of the beach is about 100 yards to the left of the Ehukai Beach Park sign as you face the ocean, but you won't need to look hard to find it in surf season. When the winter surf rolls in and hits the shallow coral shelf offshore, the waves that form are so steep that the crest of the wave falls forward, forming a near-perfect tube, or "pipeline," just like in the opening credits of *Hawaii Five-O.* Hang-ten fanatics flock here from around the globe all winter long to master this holy grail of surf challenges, but the wild, wild Pipeline is one tough cookie. If you want to watch top-flight, pro-level wave-riding action, a winter weekend visit to the Pipeline is well worth the long drive from Waikiki — heck, the crowd alone is enough to keep you entertained for hours. Needless to say, head elsewhere to swim.

See map p. 162. Off Kamehameha Highway on Ke Nui Road (which parallels the highway 1 mile north of Pupukea), just south of Sunset Beach. A small lot is available for parking.

Laniakea Beach

This long and narrow white sand beach is a popular surf spot, but it's increasingly well known for something completely different: In recent years, Hawaiian green sea turtles (or *honu*) have taken to crawling onshore to bask in the sun and take midday naps. It's a wonderful sight to behold these prehistorically majestic creatures mosey ashore and settle in, and a great way to get a look at them up close. A wonderful and well-organized group of volunteers known as **Malama Na Honu** (www.malamanahonu.org) mans the beach and surrounds the turtle's napping area with a red rope to keep visitors from getting too close and impinging on the honu's siesta. About 20 resident sea turtles have been tagged and named, so depending on the day, you might see Wooley Bully, Brutus, Oakley, Isabella, or one of their compatriots, who can grow to well more than 3 feet long and regularly live to be 60 or 70 years old. The volunteers are happy to provide visitors with information and insights into the animals. Of course, sea creatures do as they wish, so at any given time it's impossible to say whether you'll find a whole klatch of resting honu or nobody at all. Afternoon hours are best.

Whether volunteers are present or not, please be sure to keep a respectful distance from the turtles, a threatened species that is protected by the Endangered Species Act and Hawaii state law. Do not touch them or disturb them in any way.

See map p. 162. On Kamehameha Highway (Highway 83, between Haleiwa and Waimea Bay beach parks), north of Haleiwa. www.malamanahonu.org. *To get there from Turtle Bay: Drive toward Haleiwa for exactly 9 miles from the resort flag. Limited parking across the street.*

Pupukea Beach Park

This roadside beach park north of Waimea Bay is a wonderful find for snorkelers, who can enjoy a kaleidoscope of marine life when the waves are calm. There are two particularly good separate side-by-side sections here: To the north is **Shark's Cove,** which, despite its name, is not populated by any monsters of the deep. Instead, this large, shallow, protected lava rock cove teems with colorful fish and the snorkelers who seek them. Beware in winter; even though the cove looks protected, the seawall is low, the waves high, and the undertow deadly. There's a small sandy beach down the slope, plus bathrooms and showers near the roadside parking lot. At the south end of the beach is **Three Tables,** a pocket bay offering a wider beach and even easier entry access to great snorkeling around three flat coral "tables" visible just offshore. Bathrooms and showers are available at the Sharks' Cove section.

The hidden section of Pupukea Beach informally known as Ke Iki Beach is a secret gem that's worth seeking out. Ke Iki is hidden from the road by private homes, so most visitors don't know about it. This white-sand beach of sloping dunes is big, wide, open, and virtually empty year-round. Ke Iki is a wonderful place for swimming and wave jumping in summer; as everywhere on the North Shore, stay out of the water entirely in winter, however, when the big swells come. At the lava-dotted east end of the sand is a collection of warm tide pools where you can lie back and take in the natural glory of it all. The downside: no facilities.

See map p. 162. On Kamehameha Highway (Highway 83), Pupukea, north of Haleiwa. To get to Ke Iki Beach: From Haleiwa town, take the 2nd left after the Foodland at Pupukea Road and then turn left again; park along the shoulder and walk down the graded public access path (marked with the "No Parking beyond This Point" sign).

Sunset Beach Park

This surprisingly small beach is one of those legendary surf spots, the kind that draws fearless wave riders from around the world in winter, when the waves grow to huge, thundering peaks — sometimes as high as 15 to 20 feet. Come to watch the board-riding daredevils, who put on a jaw-dropping show. This is a great place to people-watch: It's a blast to eye the local surfers, the sunbathing beauties, and even your fellow vacationers catching a glimpse of the action. Weekends are best for prime spectating. The summer surf is fun for frolicking, and the beach is virtually empty midweek. No facilities are available, save for a small parking lot; join the other cars on the shoulder if it's full.

On Kamehameha Highway (Highway 83), Pupukea. Limited parking.

Waimea Bay Beach Park

This legendary beach is yet another world-famous surfing mecca, a breathtakingly gorgeous one-of-a-kind sandy bowl whose placid fair-weather waves are excellent for swimming, snorkeling, and bodysurfing in summer. But what a difference a season makes: Winter waves pound the narrow bay, sometimes rising a phenomenal 50 feet to the sky. Yes, no-fear brave-hearts (or certifiable nut cases, depending on your point of view) do come to take on these record breakers, and it's well worth the drive to see them in action. Waimea turns into a rollicking beach party when the surf is up and the crowds come to watch. Visit on weekdays to avoid the crowds, weekends to join in. When the surf calms down, there's hardly a better place on the island to chill out and play in the surf — one of my absolute favorites. Facilities include lifeguards, restrooms, and showers. The small lot fills up when the crowds come, so just pull over to the shoulder with everybody else.

See map p. 162. On Kahehameha Highway (Highway 83), just outside the entrance to Waimea Valley Adventure Park, about 3 miles north of Haleiwa. TheBus: no. 52 or 55. A safety tip: Don't get too distracted by the waves and forget to pay attention when parking or crossing the road.

On the remote leeward coast

No matter what time of year you visit remote Kaena Point, check with the lifeguard near the park entrance before you venture into the water. Restrooms and parking are located near the lifeguard stand. This is a remote area that is generally populated by locals, so please respect them and give them their space — and leave *nothing* in your car.

Kaena Point State Park

Tired of the Waikiki crowds? Here's the place for you. Where Farrington Highway ends, the wilderness of Kaena Point State Park begins. Kaena Point is a remote 853-acre coastline park of wide white sands, sand dunes, and desert cliffs overlooking the deep-blue water of Yokohama Bay. When the surf's calm in summer, the beach is pleasant for swimming and snorkeling. When the surf kicks up, stick to the shore, because conditions can be very rough. However, there's good reason to come at any time of year: You can't find a better place onshore to watch spinner dolphins play. The bay is their favorite spot on the island, so it's common to see hundreds on any given day.

If you want to pick up a bite to eat on your way to Kaena Point State Park, stop into **Aloha 'Aina Café,** 85–773 Farrington Hwy., in Waianae, on the ocean side of the highway across from McDonald's, about halfway up the leeward coast (☎ **808-697-8808**). This charming healthy-foods cafe offers excellent breakfasts and lunches for takeout or to eat in. Specialties include Hawaiian sweetbread French toast, taro burgers, zesty chili with a side of sweetbread, kalua pig quesadilla, and Portuguese bean soup, a staple of the local diet. Everything is delicious, and service is as friendly as can be.

See map p. 162. On Farrington Highway (Highway 93), at the end of the road. To get there: Take H-1 west to Farrington Highway and drive up the leeward coast. The drive will take an hour (or slightly more, depending on traffic) from Waikiki.

Playing in the Surf

If you want to rent boogie boards, surfboards, snorkel gear, kayaks, and other beach toys, you won't have a problem doing so on Oahu. In fact, you won't even need to leave Waikiki Beach because beach boys have rental huts set up right on the sand; they'll even take you out on outrigger canoe rides that anybody can join in. For details, see "Catching a wave," later in this section. You can also rent beach chairs, life vests, and boogie boards from **Snorkel Bob's,** which you can read about in the following section.

Snorkeling offshore

Hanauma Bay (see the section "The Waikiki Coast and East Oahu," earlier in this chapter) is not only Oahu's best snorkel spot, but also one of the finest snorkel spots in all Hawaii.

Although you can rent gear right at Hanauma Bay — or on Waikiki Beach if you want to do some fish-finding there — I suggest renting instead from **Snorkel Bob's,** on the way to Hanauma Bay at 700 Kapahulu Ave., at Date Street (across from the Ala Wai Golf Course), Honolulu (☎ **808-735-7944; www.snorkelbob.com**). Snorkel Bob's can rent you much better quality gear than you'll get elsewhere — and it's well worth spending the few extra bucks for a mask that doesn't leak and a snorkel that doesn't fill with water. The best-quality gear — the "Ultimate Truth" — rents for $7.50 a day, or $32 a week ($22 per week for kids) for the mask/snorkel/fins set. For $44, prescription masks (including snorkel and fins set) are available to those near-sighted snorkelers who'd actually like to see the little fishes without getting their glasses wet. Budget travelers can rent the most basic gear for just $9 per week. Snorkel Bob's is open every day from 8 a.m. to 5 p.m. There's no need to reserve in advance, but you can book your gear online if you like to plan ahead or have a special need. The staff can also recommend other local snorkel spots that are currently offering calm conditions and good underwater sightseeing.

One of the best things about renting gear from Bob is that you can rent a set of snorkel gear at the start of your trip, carry it with you as you travel throughout the islands, and then return it to another Snorkel Bob's location on Maui, the Big Island, or Kauai. (All shops offer 24-hour gear return service.) I highly recommend doing this, even if you intend to go on snorkel cruises or kayak trips that provide gear.

Safety is key when snorkeling. See "Ocean Safety," in the Quick Concierge at the end of this book, for snorkeling tips.

All hands on deck: Ocean-cruising adventures

All Oahu's cruise-boat operators combine whale-watching with their regular activities in season (humpback whales migrate to Hawaii's warm waters each winter, roughly Dec–Mar or early Apr). If you're on Oahu during these months, be sure to set out on a cruise — there's nothing like seeing these mammoth creatures up close and personal. Even if you miss out on the whales, keep your eyes peeled for dolphins, flying fish, and sea turtles.

Making reservations is always a good idea for the following cruises and outings.

Online booking and discounts are available for many of the boats listed below through **Tom Barefoot's Tours** (☎ **800-779-6305** or 808-661-5800; **www.tombarefootshawaiitoursactivities.com**), Hawaii's best activities clearinghouse and booking agent.

Captain Bob's Picnic Sail & Snorkeling Cruise

Hop aboard the *Barefoot I,* which shows you Oahu's breathtaking Windward Coast the way it should be seen — from the water. Captain Bob takes you exploring on serene Kaneohe Bay aboard his 42-foot glass-bottom catamaran, which skims across the usually tranquil water — it's just the right mood for this gorgeous turquoise, almost violet-hued surf. You cruise past picture-perfect offshore islands and snorkel a spectacular shallow reef where you can spot a kaleidoscope of tropical fish and, sometimes, turtles. The color of the water alone is worth the price of admission. The boat isn't fancy, but the crew is friendly and accommodating. All in all, the trip is casual, laid-back, and very relaxing; you'll even stop at a sand bar for an easy game of ocean volleyball. The group stays small, which keeps the trip on friendly, casual terms among the guests as well. And one of the nicest things about this trip is that they drop you right on top of the reef for easy snorkeling — no hard-core paddling out to the fishies required. A practice snorkel session makes this a great trip for beginners, but everyone will enjoy it. Plan to spend the whole day with Bob, from roughly 9 a.m. to 4 p.m., but it's a day well spent.

Cruises depart from Kaneohe Bay, Kaneohe. ☎ *808-942-5077. All-day cruise: $83 adults, $63 children 3–12, children under 3 free. Prices include all-you-can-eat barbecue lunch and shuttle from Waikiki. Online booking and discounts available at press time through Tom Barefoot's Tours (*☎ *800-779-6305 or* www.tombarefoots hawaiitoursactivities.com*).*

Dolphin Excursions

Cruise Oahu's little-explored leeward coast in a Zodiac, a motorized inflatable rubber raft, with friendly and extremely knowledgeable owner/guide Victor Lozano, or one of his equally knowledgeable captains, in search of friendly pods of spinner dolphins. These low-slung, intimate boats are great for getting close to the water and the dolphins. The pods of spinner dolphins that live off Oahu's arid west coast are so large that the guides can pretty much guarantee copious sightings every day of the year. The captain always has the best interests of you and the dolphins in mind. If conditions are safe and doing so won't interfere with their actions or behavior, he'll allow the bravest among you to do water "drops" wearing snorkels and masks so that you can watch the dolphins below you in their underwater habitat; decisions are made at the moment based on conditions, but the trip is magic even if you don't get to do this. Excursions are offered daily and last about three hours; expect pickup at your hotel between a bright-and-early 6:30 and 7 a.m. (Later excursions may be available during busy seasons, or can be customized upon request, but afternoon is generally naptime for dolphins, so I recommend sticking with the early hours, which the dolphins consider to be prime playtime.) Book at least a week ahead, more if you don't want to miss out, because the boats carry a maximum of 22 dolphin seekers.

Boats depart from Waianae Small Boat Harbor, Farrington Highway (Highway 93), Leeward Oahu. ☎ *877-257-5579 or 808-239-5579.* www.dolphinexcursions. com. *2½-hour adventure: $105 adults, $75 kids 4–12. Prices include shuttle from Waikiki and lunch; 10 percent discount if you meet the boat at the harbor.*

Ko Olina Ocean Adventures

If you want to take a dolphin-watching cruise but Dolphin Excursions' Zodiac (described earlier in this section) sits a little too close to the action for you, catch a ride aboard Ocean Adventures' more substantial cruiser — the *Pacific Passion,* a powerboat big enough for 30 passengers, complete with onboard restroom and swim-step for easy snorkeling access — which also cruises the western shore in search of playful spinner dolphins. The four-hour trip includes snorkeling and the once-in-a-lifetime chance to swim with the dolphins (the crew is careful to emphasize how to do this nonintrusively). This operator also offers trips aboard the 44-foot rigid inflatable *Ko Olina Explorer* for a more exciting ride; creature comforts include a sunshade and an onboard restroom. There are two morning departures, at 7 a.m. and 11:30 a.m.

Cruises depart from Ko Olina Resort and Marina, Kapolei (off Highway 93, 17 miles west of Honolulu International Airport, a 45-min. drive from Waikiki). ☎ 808-396-2068. www.koolinaoceanadventures.net. Prices: $108 adults, $78 kids. Trip includes breakfast and snacks; Waikiki hotel pickup available for $14 per person. At press time, a free Fuji underwater camera was offered with online reservations.

MaiTai Catamaran

This sleek new 44-foot twin-hulled catamaran prides itself on being the party boat of Waikiki. The *MaiTai* offers 90-minute daytime "Tradewind" and late-afternoon sunset sails right off Waikiki beach. With a built-in bar and 45 of your closest friends aboard, you're bound to have a good time and enjoy some spectacular views while you're at it. Two-hour snorkel cruises are also available. The Friday-night moonlight sails offer a great way to see the weekly fireworks display off Waikiki.

Cruises depart from Waikiki Beach between the Sheraton Waikiki and Halekulani hotel. ☎ 800-462-7975 or 808-922-5665. www.leahi.com. 90-minute afternoon sails $23 adults, $12 kids ages 4–12; snorkel cruise $45 adults, $27 kids ages 4–12; sunset sail and Fri-night moonlight sail $34 adults, $17 kids ages 4–12. Sunset sail includes beverages; drinks are available for purchase on afternoon sails.

Navatek Cruises

For the smoothest ride in the Pacific, hop aboard the *Navatek I,* a high-tech 140-foot SWATH (Small Waterplane Area Twin Hull) vessel that promises even the most perpetually queasy passengers a seasick-free ride. The *Navatek* offers a number of different cruises, from lunchtime whale-watches to the finest dinner cruises on the Waikiki coast (complete with a romantic candlelit setting, a multicourse sit-down dinner, top local entertainers, and an exclusive route along Kahala, Oahu's "Gold Coast," east of Diamond Head). The *Navatek* is operated by Atlantis Adventures Oahu, a company known for submarine dives that feature close-up views of sunken ships and tropical fish; combo packages offer a substantial discount if you want to book both activities.

Cruises depart from Pier 6, Honolulu Harbor, Aloha Tower Drive (just off Ala Moana Boulevard/Nimitz Highway intersection, next to the Aloha Tower Marketplace), Honolulu. ☎ 800-548-6262. www.atlantisadventures.com (click on "Hawaii," then click on "Oahu Dinner Cruises"). Prices: Lunch cruise $56 adults, $28 kids ages 2–12; sunset cruise with entertainment and dinner buffet $77 adults, $52 kids 2–12;

Royal Sunset cruise with entertainment and sit-down steak-and-lobster dinner $108 adults, $71 kids 2–12. Window-seat upgrades and packages including add-on excursions also available.

"Chumming" around with sharks

You're 4 miles out from land, which is just a speck on the horizon, in hundreds of feet of open ocean. Suddenly from out of the blue depths, a shape emerges: the sleek, pale shadow of a 6-foot-long gray reef shark, followed quickly by a couple of 10-foot-long Galápagos sharks. Within a couple of heartbeats, you are surrounded by sharks on all sides. Do you panic? Did you just drop into a scene from *Open Water?* No, you paid $120 to be in the midst of these jaws of the deep. Of course, there is a 6-by-6-by-10-foot aluminum shark cage separating you from all those teeth.

Looking for an unparalleled adventure, snorkelers? **North Shore Shark Adventures** (☎ 808-228-5900; www.hawaiisharkadventures.com) has what you're looking for. Captain Joe Pavsek offers up-close-and-personal encounters with Jaws from the safety of an aluminum cage. Scheduled throughout the day from 7 a.m. to 3 p.m., the two-hour tours take you out from Haleiwa Small Boat Harbor 3 miles offshore in his 26-foot boat, *Kailolo,* where he drops his cage into the cobalt-blue water. To make sure that the predators of the deep appear, Captain Pavsek heaves "chum" — a not very appetizing concoction of fish trimmings and entrails — over the side. It's much like ringing the dinner bell; after a few minutes, the sharks arrive, ready to nosh. Depending on the sea conditions and the weather, snorkelers can stay in the safety of the cage as long as they want, with the man-eaters just inches away. You can expect to see sharks ranging in size from 5 to 15 feet, generally of the gray reef, Galápagos, and sandbar variety. Visibility is so clear — often up to 200 feet — that you can see them swimming in from the deep. The cage can hold two to four snorkelers, who pay $120 per person for the two-hour adventure; children ages 3 to 12 are charged $60 ($45 for riding on the boat only). You're also welcome to view the sharks from a more respectable distance — the boat deck — for just $60. Discounts are available for students and military.

Delving into the deep: Submarine rides

You can dip into Hawaii's spectacular underwater world even if you don't swim by taking a submarine ride with **Atlantis Adventures Oahu** (☎ 800-548-6262 or 808-973-9811; www.atlantisadventures.com; click "Hawaii" then "Oahu"). Atlantis's state-of-the-art subs deliver you a mile offshore and deep beneath the surface to see not only clouds of tropical fish and sea critters, but also sunken ships, the remains of two airliners, and ongoing work on the University of Hawaii's reef enhancement project. Shuttle boats to the sub leave from Hilton Hawaiian Village Pier, on the beach at 2005 Kalia Rd. (at Ala Moana Boulevard). The 90-minute tours cost $80 to $95 for adults, $41 to $48 for kids (children must be at least 36 inches tall), depending on the tour you choose. Online discounts are available; you can also combine a submarine ride with a dinner cruise. A word of warning: The ride is perfectly safe, but skip it if you suffer from serious claustrophobia. On the other side of the coin: If you're a swimmer — even if you just have basic paddle skills — skip this expensive adventure, don a mask, and hit the waves yourself instead for a primo underwater experience.

Catching a wave

Book your surfing lesson, or your windsurfing lesson (see the following section), for early in your stay. That way, if conditions aren't right on your scheduled day, you'll have plenty of time to reschedule.

Learning to surf

If you've always dreamed of learning to surf, Oahu is the perfect place to do it.

Hands down, the best way to learn is with **Hawaiian Fire** (☎ **888-955-7873** or 808-737-3473; www.hawaiianfire.com). In 2000, a group of Honolulu City firefighters, tired of watching visitors get bad surf lessons, decided to start their own surf school that would really teach first-timers how to ride a wave, both with safety and a whole lot of fun — and they do a great job. One of the keys to their success is that they run their lessons at a secluded Leeward Oahu beach, about a half-hour from Waikiki, which has ideal teachable rolling waves for beginners. Group lessons ($99 per person) last two hours and include 45 minutes of on-beach instruction, 75 minutes of in-the-water time, pickup and drop-off at your Waikiki hotel, and all equipment you'll need to ride the waves. Groups average about ten people, and there are at least three instructors in the water for the duration of the lesson, which is a nice student/teacher ratio for learning. If you prefer undivided attention, private lessons are available for $179 ($129 for kids under 12); children ages 10 and under are required to take a private lesson.

At press time, you could save 15 percent on your group lesson by paying the fee in cash at the lesson. When you book, ask if this deal is still available.

Another good option is the **Hans Hedemann Surf School** (☎ **808-924-7778;** www.hhsurf.com), whose pro instructors teach private and group lessons in surfing and body boarding off the Diamond Head end of Waikiki. Hans also has a North Shore location in the Turtle Bay Resort. Prices start at $50 for an hour-long group lesson (five people max), $115 for one hour of private surf instruction and $150 for a two-hour private lesson.

North Shore surf lessons are also offered **Surf-N-Sea** (☎ **800-899-7873** or 808-637-9887; www.surfnsea.com), the North Shore's oldest surf shop. Surf-N-Sea offers customized two-hour group lessons (which often go longer) for beginners daily. Surf-N-Sea also offers two-hour stand-up paddling (also known as beach boy surfing) lessons, which, as anyone who reads *People* magazine knows, is the hot celebrity trend in wave riding. Lessons are $85 per person.

On the Windward Coast, **Kailua Sailboards & Kayaks,** at Kailua Beach Center, 130 Kailua Rd. (☎ 808-262-2555; www.kailuasailboards.com), offers group surf lessons for $89 per person and private lessons for $109, as well as surfboard and boogie board rentals.

If you want to take a more casual approach to learning, the Waikiki beach boys swear that they can teach anybody to stand up on a surfboard and catch a wave, as long as they have basic swimming skills. Go early to the section of Waikiki Beach called Kuhio Beach, next to the Moana Surfrider. Both **Aloha Beach Service** and **Hawaii Beach Boys Services** offer surfing lessons for about $40 an hour, plus affordable surfboard rentals to experienced wave riders (for use on Waikiki Beach only). The small waves are also great for bodysurfing and boogie boarding, and both surf shacks are happy to rent you the appropriate gear. Regular catamaran and outrigger canoe rides are offered from this stretch of sand as well, usually for about 10 or 15 bucks a head; the beach boys will call out for participants when they're ready to go out. (*FYI:* If you're expecting Waikiki's beach boys to be strapping young lads on break between semesters, think again. Most of these perma-tanned fellows haven't been "boys" since the Nixon administration.)

For experienced surfers only

If you're already a skilled surfer, stop at any surf shop to check the latest wave conditions. A good surfing spot for advanced surfers is the Cliffs, at the base of Diamond Head. The 4- to 6-foot waves churn here, allowing for high-performance surfing — and the views of Diamond Head are great. Call or stop at the **Hans Hedemann Surf School** in the Diamond Head Beach Hotel, 2947 Kalakaua Ave. (☎ 808-924-7778; www.hhsurf.com), to rent a board and check conditions, or call and schedule an advanced lesson. Surfboards are also available for rent on the beach at Waikiki. (See Aloha Beach Service and Hawaii Beach Boys Services in the preceding section.)

On the Windward Coast, board rentals are available at **Kailua Sailboards & Kayaks,** at Kailua Beach Center, 130 Kailua Rd. (☎ 808-262-2555; www.kailuasailboards.com).

Of course, if it's winter and you really know what you're doing — or you simply want to watch those who do — visit one of the North Shore beaches. (See "On the North Shore," earlier in this chapter.) Head to **Surf-N-Sea,** 62–595 Kamehameha Hwy., Haleiwa (☎ 800-899-7873 or 808-637-9887; www.surfnsea.com), for board rentals and intermediate and advanced instruction. Lessons are $195 for intermediate and advanced surfers. Skilled surfers can also go out on a half-day safari, which takes in some great hidden surf spots, for $220. Do not — I repeat, do not — get in the water on the North Shore in winter unless you are appropriately skilled to handle the big waves.

Check conditions by calling ☎ **808-973-4383** or the **Surfline** at ☎ **808-596-7873.** You can also check the latest surf report online at www.hawaii.edu/news/weather.

Ocean kayaking for everyone

One of my absolute favorite ocean activities is kayaking to the Mokuleias, the two charmingly petite islets about 1½ miles offshore from Lanikai and Kailua beaches. It's an easy trip that anyone with reasonably good paddle strength can do; I recommend a kayak for two if you're inexperienced or would simply like to share the paddle duties. You can make your first stop for a bit of exploring at the small, flat shelf island that's only about a half-mile offshore. It's another mile or so across the calm bay to reach the beautiful, remote beach for sunning, picnicking, and exploring (landing is allowable only on the near islet; the far islet is off-limits).

The place to launch your kayak is at the north end of Kailua Beach Park; follow the beach path that runs alongside Kalapawai Market. Two local kayaking outfitters provide convenient rentals. **Kailua Sailboards & Kayaks,** at Kailua Beach Center, 130 Kailua Rd., cater-cornered from Kalapawai Market (☎ **808-262-2555;** www.kailuasailboards.com), offers half-day rentals for $39 for a single kayak, $49 for a double kayak. High-performance single kayaks, which are lighter and faster in the water, are also available for $49 for a half-day. If price is not a big concern, I recommend the high-performance kayaks; otherwise, the standard kayaks are just fine. Kayaks are also available for full-day rentals, but a half-day is enough to enjoy this excursion.

If you rent from Kailua Sailboards & Kayaks, reserve your kayaks in advance; kayaks can even be booked online. I recommend touring in the morning for the calmest conditions. You'll have to go to the shop, where you'll watch an instructional video and be assigned equipment and a kayak on a pull cart for an awkward but worthwhile ten-minute walk to the beach. Kailua Sailboards & Kayaks also offers guided kayaking tours for those who want to see more; check the Web site for details.

If you'd rather not drag your own kayak to the launch site, book your kayaks instead with **Twogood Kayaks Hawaii,** in Kailua town at 345 Hahani St. (☎ **808-262-5656;** www.twogoodkayaks.com). You'll have to go to the shop to check in, then drive to the launch site on an estuary at Kailua Beach, where Twogood Kayaks will deliver and help you launch your kayaks. At $25 per person for a half-day tandem rental, Twogood's rental rates are about the same as Kailua Sailboards (see above), but you can get a full-day rental for just $10 more. Twogood Kayaks also offers lessons for all levels of kayakers, from beginning to racers.

Windsurfing and kiteboarding

Kailua Beach, on the Windward Coast, is the best place to learn to windsurf — and the folks at **Naish Hawaii,** 155A Hamakua Dr., Kailua (☎ **800-767-6068** or 808-262-6068; www.naish.com/lessons.html), are just the ones to teach you. Beginning, intermediate, and advanced lessons are available, with prices starting at $75 for one person, $100 for two people for private 1½-hour lessons (includes use of equipment for 1-½ hours following the lesson), and $45 per person for a three-hour group clinic (includes use of equipment for a half-hour following the lesson). Private intermediate or advanced lessons are $65 an hour. There's no minimum age requirement, but you must weigh at least 75 pounds. (Champion and pioneer windsurfer Robbie Naish and his team of instructors have taught kids as young as 8 or 9.) You can expect to be up and sailing (in one direction, anyway) in three to four hours; it takes 12 to 20 hours to become any good at it. They'll also teach you how to kiteboard if you're up to the challenge. Equipment rentals are available for experienced windsurfers and kiteboarders.

Kailua Sailboards & Kayaks, at Kailua Beach Center, 130 Kailua Rd. (☎ 808-262-2555; www.kailuasailboards.com), also offers beginner, intermediate, and advanced windsurfing package that includes hotel pick-up, gear rental, a two-hour lesson, and time to practice afterward for $89 (beginners) and $99 (intermediate and advanced). If you're interested in kiteboarding lessons, call the shop for details.

Scuba diving

Oahu is a wonderful place for wreck diving. One of the more famous wrecks in Hawaii is the *Mahi,* a 185-foot former minesweeper with an abundant marine population that looks like it came straight out of *Finding Nemo.* Schools of lemon butterfly fish, eagle rays, green sea turtles, manta rays, and white-tipped sharks cruise by, and eels slither from the wreck.

For nonwreck diving, **Kahuna Canyon,** a massive underwater amphitheater, is among the island's best offshore summer dive spots. But your smartest bet may be to discuss with your outfitter the best places to go. Whether you're a first-timer in search of a resort course or a veteran diver just looking for a ride, the outfitter to contact is **Aaron's Dive Shop,** 307 Hahani St., Kailua (☎ 888-84-SCUBA or 808-262-2333; www.hawaii-scuba.com), Hawaii's oldest and largest dive shop, in business for more than three decades. Aaron's offers boat and beach dive excursions at all of Oahu's top dive spots, plus night dives, cave dives, photography dives, and more. Prices for two-tank dives start at $125, with all equipment, but check the Web site for online discounts. Aaron's can also offer uncertified introductory dives, or PADI (Professional Association of Diving Instructors) certify you in three days if you're ready to commit. Also in Kailua is **Oahu Dive Center,** 345 Hahani St. (☎ 866-933-3483 or 808-263-7333; www.oahudivecenter.com), which offers instruction, certification, and dive tours at similar rates.

If you don't want to leave Waikiki, **South Seas Aquatics,** 2155 Kalakaua Ave. (near Beach Walk), Ste. 112 (☎ 808-922-0852; www.ssahawaii.com), can meet all your scuba needs, from daily dive trips ($90–$100, including gear) to full PADI open-water certification ($400, including four dives, or $250 if you do your book and pool work at home, before you arrive on Oahu).

Safety is key when diving. See "Ocean Safety," in the Quick Concierge at the end of this book, for diving tips.

Sportfishing

Oahu-based **Sportfish Hawaii** (☎ **877-388-1376** or 808-396-2607; www.sportfishhawaii.com) can book a first-class charter for you out of Kewalo Basin, the main charter-boat marina on Oahu. From Waikiki, take Kalakaua west beyond Ala Moana Center; Kewalo Basin is on the left, across from Ward Centre. On lucky days, the captains display the day's catch after they tuck back into their slips in the afternoon. Prices range from $750 to $938 for a full-day charter just for you and five friends; $550 to $721 for a half-day exclusive; or from $188 for a full-day share charter (you share the boat with five other people). Party-boat trips feature bottom fishing for $63, including a barbecue lunch and transportation from Waikiki hotels. A nighttime shark hunt is $125 per person.

Exploring on Dry Land

You may be able to save money on a few of your big-ticket Oahu activities by booking them through Maui-based **Tom Barefoot's Tours** (☎ **888-621-3601** or 808-661-1246; www.tombarefoot.com), which also books activities on Oahu. Tom Barefoot is a very reliable activities center that's willing to split its commissions with you so that everybody comes out ahead. These discounts may add up to substantial savings, especially if you're bringing the entire family along. At press time, you can save on a number of water adventures recommended earlier in this chapter, plus admission fees to such attractions as Hawaiian Waters Adventure Park, golf greens fees, and more; check the Web site or call for current offerings.

Taking a guided tour

If your mobility is limited, or if you have limited time and want an introductory look at the big picture, you may want to hook up with a guided tour. If you've rented a car and can get around easily, though, I'd recommend going out on your own. Most tour operators do little more than whiz by the major sights in tour buses — including some places where you may actually want to spend some time — or charge you an arm and a leg to take you to places like the *Arizona* Memorial, which is absolutely free to tour if you show up on your own. If you do need to take a guided bus tour try **Polynesian Adventure Tours** (☎ **800-622-3011** or 808-833-3000; www.polyad.com), which offers a range of tours in minivans, big-windowed mini-coaches (good for small groups and big views), and full-size buses; **Roberts Hawaii** (☎ **866-898-2519** or 808-954-8652; www.robertshawaii.com), which offers a similar slate of tours, plus add-ons such as sightseeing cruises, luau, and dinner shows; or **E Noa Tours** (☎ **800-824-8804** or 808-591-2561; www.enoa.com), whose guided minibus tours around the city and the island tend to be smaller than those offered by its competitors, and cheaper, because the tours are intimate enough to allow the driver to serve as your tour guide. Ask about online booking, AARP, and AAA discounts.

 If you intend to visit the **National Cemetery of the Pacific at Punchbowl Crater** (see the section "Visiting Honolulu's top attractions," later in this chapter), don't go with a tour if you want to look around and pay your respects. Tour buses are not allowed to disembark passengers in the Punchbowl; they can merely drive through.

The **Waikiki Trolley** (☎ **800-824-8804** or 808-593-2822; www.waikiki trolley.com), an open-air motorized trolley similar to a San Francisco cable car, offers narrated hop-on, hop-off tours throughout Honolulu and select farther-flung destinations; for complete details, see Chapter 10.

Guided cultural tours

The **Native Hawaiian Hospitality Association** (☎ **808-441-1404**) has outlined a fascinating walk along the **Waikiki Historic Trail.** You'll learn about Hawaii's royal past as you explore the portion of the trail along Prince Kuhio Beach, ending at the Honolulu Zoo. Two-hour guided tours are available only for groups, but you can download a trail guide and map that you can follow on your own self-guided tour at www.waikiki historictrail.com.

If you're a foodie who really wants an insider's view on island-style dining, don't miss the opportunity to spend a day or an evening with **Hawaii Food Tours** (☎ **800-715-2468** or 808-926-3663; www.hawaii foodtours.com); see "Dining Out" in Chapter 10 for details.

Guided eco-hikes

Mauka Makai Excursions (☎ **866-896-0596;** www.hawaiianecotours. net) offers half- and full-day tours revealing a hidden side of Oahu that even most island residents haven't seen. The emphasis is on archaeology and ancient history, but Mauka Makai's full- and half-day tours are also a great choice for nature walkers. There are a variety of distances and difficulties. On the full-day "Legends and Myths" tour, guide Dominic Aki can show you hidden petroglyphs, the ruins of a royal palace tucked away in a bamboo forest, an ancient temple presiding over modern suburbia, and other cultural treasures, complete with fascinating narrative, on an easy 2[bf]1/2-mile hike. "Sacred Sites of the Oahu's North Shore" takes you farther afield on a five-mile, Saturdays-only hike. If you don't want to commit a full day, take the "Sacred Sites Walking Eco Tour," which will show you three or four satisfying ancient sites before noon. Call to inquire about other adventures. Prices range from $50 to $80 for adults, $40 to $60 for kids 6 to 17, including hotel pickup. Discounts are available if you book through **Tom Barefoot's Tours** (☎ **888-621-3601** or 808-661-1246; www.tombarefoot.com; click on "Oahu" and then "Hiking").

Getting "Lost" on Oahu

As any fan of TV's most cryptic series knows, *Lost* is filmed predominately on the island of Oahu — and there are a number of ways to experience the island's Oceanic 815–related hot spots. **Kos Tours** (☎ 808-561-2440; www.hummertourshawaii. com) offers a five-hour guided Hummer tour to top *Lost* locations as well as sites from Oahu-filmed movies such as *50 First Dates, Godzilla,* and *Jurassic Park* for $129 per person (transportation from Waikiki included). Or, go right to the source and book the Movie Sites and Ranch Tour at **Kualoa Ranch** (☎ 800-231-7321 or 808-237-8515; www. kualoa.com), site of many of the show's most famous scenes, such as Hurley's homemade golf course; if you're here at the right time, you might even see cast and crew in action. At $19 per person, it's one of the island's best sightseeing bargains. Or, if you're a do-it-yourselfer, check out **Lost Virtual Tour** (www.lostvirtualtour. com), an episode-by-episode guide of locations around the island, diligently identified and signposted online by what must be the biggest *Lost* fans in Hawaii. It's the ideal source for the Jack and Kate fan with a rent-a-car, a good map, and a Dharma-infused sense of adventure.

Visiting Honolulu's top attractions

Put on your walking shoes, because Oahu boasts the finest collection of sights and attractions in the islands, bar none.

Bishop Museum

If you leave the beach to visit just one museum while you're in Hawaii, make it this one. The state museum of cultural history houses the world's greatest collection of natural and cultural artifacts from Hawaii and the Pacific. If your time is limited, head straight to the Hawaiian Hall, which provides a wonderful introduction to island life and culture. You'll see the great feathered capes of kings, the last grass shack in Hawaii, preindustrial Polynesian art, and even the skeleton of a 50-foot sperm whale. Unfortunately, the Hawaiian Hall is closed for renovation until mid-2009, so call ahead or check the Web site for the opening schedule as well as the updated daily tour, traditional craft-making, and hula show schedules. In the meantime, focus your energy on the Abigail Kinoiki Kekaulike Kahili Room, where some of the museum's famed Hawaiian monarchy collection is on display, as well as the Polynesian Hall, representing the peoples of Polynesia, Micronesia, and Melanesia. The Richard T. Mamiya Science Adventure Center is a cutting-edge interactive facility focused on understanding the fundamentals of Hawaii's natural environment, from oceanography to volcanology. The Hawaiian Sports Hall of Fame is here, too. Call or check the Web site for the current schedule of exhibitions and planetarium shows.

See map p. 164. 1525 Bernice St., just off the Lunililo Freeway (H-1), Honolulu. ☎ *808-847-3511 or 808-848-4136 for planetarium info.* www.bishopmuseum.org. *To get there: From the H-1, take the Houghtailing exit; turn right (toward the mountains); at the 1st light, turn left onto Bernice Street; the museum will be ½ block past Kapalama*

Street on your left. Admission: $16 adults, $13 seniors and kids 4–12. Open: Daily 9 a.m.–5 p.m.

The Contemporary Museum

Housed in the historic Spalding house, a beautiful 1925 estate in one of Honolulu's most exclusive residential communities, TCM is best for fans of modern art (if you want to see Hawaiian art, visit the Honolulu Academy of Arts, listed later in the chapter, instead). Temporary exhibits predominate, filling the main gallery space and changing six to eight times a year, so it's catch as catch can — sometimes terrific, sometimes not so much. (It's best to check the online calendar before you go.) The museum currently doesn't have space to display its entire permanent collection, so exhibitions rotate a selection of highlights, including works from such artists as Jasper Johns, Jim Dine, and William Wegman. David Hockney's postmodern stage sets for Ravel's opera *L'Enfant et Les Sortilèges* are always on display, but they're something of a disappointment; better are the lovely Japanese gardens for strolling, the impressive sculpture garden, and the Contemporary Cafe, one of Honolulu's best-kept secrets for lunch. Docent tours are available daily at 1:30 p.m., the best time to go for the full story on what you're seeing. No reservation is necessary; just meet at the front lanai at about 1:25 p.m. to join in.

The museum also keeps an annex in downtown Honolulu known as **The Contemporary Museum at First Hawaiian Center,** 999 Bishop St., that's open free to the public Monday through Thursday from 8:30 a.m. to 4 p.m., and on Fridays from 8:30 a.m. to 6 p.m.

See map p. 164. 2411 Makiki Heights Dr., Honolulu. ☎ 808-526-1322. www.tcmhi. org. *To get there: Take Kalakaua Avenue to Beretania Street and make a left; turn right on Keeamoku, turn right on Wilder to Makaki Street, turn left, and follow it up the hill; turn left on Makiki Heights Drive and proceed to the museum (which will be on your right). Admission: $5 adults, $3 seniors and students, free for kids 12 and under. Open: Tues–Sat 10 a.m.–4 p.m., Sun noon–4 p.m.*

Diamond Head Crater

Called Mt. Leahi (lee-*ah*-hi) by the Hawaiians, Waikiki's most famous landmark is well worth the climb, if you have the stamina for it. The short but steep 1¼-mile, 1½-hour round-trip climb is a lot of fun — and the 360-degree views from the top are spectacular.

To prepare for your hike to the top, wear a reasonable pair of walking shoes. Rubber-soled shoes with good traction are a must; sneakers or hiking shoes are preferred, but Tevas are fine as long as they're attached to your feet. Bring a bottle of water and a camera; you may also want a flashlight (not a must), since you walk through a few dark tunnels. If you have binoculars, bring them too.

Go early in the day, before the afternoon sun starts beating down. The trail head begins in the parking lot on the crater's inland side and proceeds along a paved walkway (with handrails) that turns rocky as it ascends the slope before it transforms into two very steep staircases (99 and 75 steps,

respectively). You'll pass old World War I and II pillboxes, gun emplace-
ments, and tunnels built as part of the Pacific defense network. Yes, you'll
be climbing lots of steps, but it's well worth the effort — after you reach
the observation post up top, the views are indescribable.

I love this hike, but don't do it if you will not be comfortable with the ver-
tical climb or the exertion.

*See map p. 164. Access road at Monsarrat (also called Diamond Head Avenue) and
18th avenues. To get there: Follow Kalakaua Avenue to Kapiolani Park; turn north on
Monserrat Avenue and follow it around to the back of Diamond Head. Just past
Kapiolani Community College, turn right and go ⅔ mile to the parking lot. Admission: $1
individual walk-in, or $5 per car. Open: Daily 6 a.m.–6 p.m. (last hike start at 4:30 p.m.).*

Foster Botanical Garden

This intimate, leafy oasis amid the high-rises of downtown Honolulu is a
living museum of plants — some rare and endangered — collected from
the tropical regions of the world. Of special interest are 26 "Exceptional
Trees" protected by state law, a large palm collection, a primitive cycad
garden, and a hybrid orchid collection. It's easy to tour the garden in a
half-hour or so, but bring insect repellent because this is a buggy place.
Guided tours are offered weekdays at 1 p.m.; call for reservations.

*See map p. 164. 50 N. Vineyard Blvd. (at Nuuanu Avenue, across the street from Zippy's),
downtown Honolulu.* ☎ **808-522-7066** *or 808-552-7060.* www.co.honolulu.hi.us/
parks/hbg. *Admission: $5 adults, $1 kids 6–12. Open: Daily 9 a.m.–4 p.m.*

Hawaii Maritime Center

If you're interested in Hawaii's rich maritime heritage, or you're just nostalgic for the long-gone cruise-ship days, stop at this harborfront museum
(the maritime branch of the Bishop Museum, listed earlier in this chapter)
for an hour-long visit. The museum tells the islands' complete maritime
story, from the ancient journey of Polynesian voyagers to Hawaii's whaling
era to the high-style Matson Line days of the 1940s and '50s. The full-size
humpback whale skeleton is worth the price of admission alone. Outside,
the famous *Hokulea,* a reconstruction of the double-hulled sailing canoe
that the ancients used to reach Hawaii, is moored next to the *Falls of Clyde,*
a four-masted, fully rigged 1878 schooner. The schooner is closed to visitors as the museum searches for a benefactor to fund $32 million in reno-
vations, but you can still enjoy it harborside.

*See map p. 164. Pier 7, Honolulu Harbor, Aloha Tower Drive (off Nimitz Highway, next
to Aloha Tower Marketplace), Honolulu.* ☎ **808-847-3511.** www.bishopmuseum.
org/exhibits/hmc. *Admission: $7.50 adults, $4.50 kids 6–17. Open: Daily
9:00 a.m.–5 p.m.*

Hawai'i State Art Museum

This new-in-2002 museum houses the largest collection of art by Hawaii-
based artists. All of the contemporary works that are currently on display
were created by artists who live in the islands; in many cases, Western art

forms blend harmoniously with folk art forms fed by the traditions of Hawaii and its many feeder cultures from the Pacific Islands and Asia. The museum is well worth visiting if you want to understand the creative heart that beats within these beautiful islands. Free "Live from the Lawn" music performances are held on the museum's lawn as part of **First Friday,** Honolulu's Downtown Gallery Walk, held on the first Friday of every month from 5 to 9 p.m.

See map p. 164 No. 1 Capitol District Bldg., 250 S. Hotel St. (at Richards Street), 2nd Floor, downtown Honolulu. ☎ *808-596-9958.* www.hawaii.gove/sfca; *select "Hawai'i State Art Museum." Admission: Free! Open: Tues–Sat 10 a.m.–4 p.m.*

Honolulu Academy of Arts

This first-class museum houses one of the finest collections of Asian art in the country, a top-notch collection of American and European masters, and terrific ancient and Pacific art, all in a stunning open-plan, Hawaiian-style building that first opened its doors in 1927. See what's on when you're in town — the temporary exhibits can range from treasures of ancient Egypt to the world's greatest collection of aloha shirts — or just stop by to explore a few rooms of the excellent permanent collection. Highlights include the John Dominis and Patches Damon Holt Gallery of Hawaiian Arts; the Textile Gallery; and the James A. and Mari Michener Gallery, boasting a fantastic collection of Japanese wood block prints tagged with insightful, delightful observances by the author himself. It's easy to spend an hour here, or four — it all depends on your interest level. No matter how long you stay, be sure to spend a few minutes contemplating one of the courtyard Zen gardens — and a few extra perusing the excellent Academy Shop. The museum is a real delight for any art lover! Guided one-hour tours are offered Tuesday through Saturday at 10:15 a.m., 11:30 a.m., and 1:30 p.m.; Sunday at 1:15 p.m.

See map p. 164. 900 S. Beretania St. (between Victoria Street and Ward Avenue), downtown Honolulu. ☎ *808-532-8701 or 808-532-8700.* www.honoluluacademy. org. *Admission: $10 adults, $5 seniors and students, free for kids 12 and under. $5 audio tour. Admission is free on the 1st Wed and 3rd Sun of every month. Open: Tues–Sat 10 a.m.–4:30 p.m., Sun 1–5 p.m. (11 a.m.–5 p.m. on 3rd Sun of month).*

Honolulu Zoo

Located in the heart of Waikiki's lovely Kapiolani Park, this 43-acre zoo is a real charmer. Globe-trotting highlights include the Karibuni Reserve, an African savanna habitat with exotic African mammals roaming around in the open, separated from visitors by hidden rails and moats; a wonderful South American aviary filled with colorful toucans and other eye-catching birds; and the Tropical Forest exhibit, a draw for horticultural buffs as well as animal lovers. The Children's Zoo features friendly critters who love to be petted, including a llama, a monitor lizard, and a potbellied pig.

See map p. 164. In Kapiolani Park, 151 Kapahulu Ave. (at Kalakaua Avenue), Waikiki. ☎ *808-971-7171.* www.honoluluzoo.org. *Admission: $8 adults, $1 kids 6–12, free for kids 5 and under; Family Pass $25. Open: Daily 9 a.m.–4:30 p.m.*

Iolani Palace

I highly recommend visiting this royal palace, the official residence of the last monarchs of Hawaii: King David Kalakaua (ka-la-*cow*-ah) and his sister, Queen Liliuokalani (li-lee-uh-ka-*la*-nee). The good news is that, thanks to a recent expansion of ways to see the palace, it's now easier than ever. You can see the Italian Renaissance structure on a docent-led 90-minute tour, which tells the fascinating story of the coming of Western ways to the islands, the rebirth of Hawaiian culture in the last years of royal rule, and the story of the monarchy's final defeat in a bloodless coup, or on a 50-minute self-guided audio tour, which covers the same ground and tells a similar story a bit less personally but a bit more efficiently.

Very Important: The Iolani Palace Grand Tour (the guided tour), offered in the mornings, sells out regularly, so you must call ahead and reserve your tour spots. Call at least a day ahead, or a few days in advance if you don't want to be disappointed. (It took me three tries before I was able to make my first visit.) Leave the little ones behind, however, because they'll be less than enthralled. It's generally not necessary to pre-book for the 50-minute self-guided Audio Tour, which is offered in the afternoons. This shorter self-guided tour is an ideal alternative for those with limited time, limited budgets, or limited attention spans.

You can also take the self-guided Gallery Tour, which takes you through the lower galleries, which house the Hawaiian crown jewels plus royal gowns, the re-created chamberlain's office, and other period goodies. A real highlight is an ancient feather cloak that was the symbolic trophy won in the battle that united the Hawaiian Islands in the first place. The Gallery Tour does not require reservations. If you opt for the either of the Grand or Audio tours, the galleries will automatically be part of your Iolani experience.

The **Royal Hawaiian Band** plays free concerts on the palace grounds most Fridays at noon. You can confidently expect the band to play *Aloha 'Oe*, which was penned by Queen Liliuokalani around 1890, prior to her deposition and the permanent overthrow of the Hawaiian monarchy. Call to confirm that the band will be playing before you head over.

See map p. 164. 364 S. King St. (at Richards Street), downtown. ☎ *808-522-0832, 808-522-0822, or 808-538-1471 for recorded info.* www.iolanipalace.org. *Grand Tour tickets: $20 adults, $5 kids 5–17; kids under 5 not admitted to Grand or Audio tours. Grand Tour times: Every 20 minutes Tues–Sat 9–11 a.m. Audio Tour tickets: $12 adults, $5 kids 5–17; kids under 5 not admitted. Audio Tour times: Every 10 minutes Tues–Sat 11:45 a.m.–3:30 p.m. Tickets should be picked up 15 minutes before either tour. Both grand and audio tours include a screening of the 16-minute video on the Hawaiian monarchy and the palace. Tickets to Galleries only: $6 adults, $3 for kids 5–17; free for kids under 5. Gallery hours: Tues–Sat 9 a.m.–4:30 p.m.*

Makapuu Point State Wayside

I just love this 1-mile uphill hike, an enjoyable walk through the island's southeastern desert landscape that leads to one of the most spectacular vistas on the island. The trail isn't marked, but it's quite obvious; just follow the directions below until you see the black gate on the ocean side of the highway. It's okay to come through; the gate is just meant to pre-vent cars. Follow the 1-mile paved road up the hill to the lighthouse and lookout; even though it leads uphill, the slope is gradual as it curves around the point, so anyone wearing good-soled shoes and in reasonably good shape can handle it. The contrast between the cactus-dotted land-scape and the deep-blue waves below is reason enough to come; however, the lookout also offers a good place to watch whales between January and March, so bring binoculars. Bring drinking water and wear sunscreen at any time of year. You might also want to pack a picnic lunch, because there are plenty of flat spots for you to enjoy it and the view.

See map p. 162. Take Kalanianaole Highway (Highway 72) past Hanauma Bay and Sandy Beach to Makapuu Head, Oahu's southeastern tip; look for a black gate bear-ing a sign that says "No Vehicles Allowed" on a gate to the right. Park on the side of the highway with the other cars.

Mission Houses Museum

American missionaries set up housekeeping here in the 1820s with the goal of converting the native Hawaiians to Christianity. This museum tells the story of the arrival of Protestant missionaries and the subsequent cultural sea change that swept through the islands. Three restored mission build-ings are open for exploring; they're filled with furnishings and artifacts dating back to this period. One-hour guided tours of the visitor center, frame house, and printing office are offered twice daily.

553 S. King St. (at Kawaiahao Street), downtown Honolulu. ☎ *808-531-0481.* www. missionhouses.org. *Admission: $10 adults, $8 seniors (55+) and military, $6 kids 6–18. Tours are included in the price and offered daily at 11 a.m. and 2:45 p.m. Open: Tues–Sat 10 a.m.–4 p.m.*

National Memorial Cemetery of the Pacific at Punchbowl Crater

This collapsed volcanic cone in the middle of Honolulu — known in Hawaiian as *Puowaina,* roughly translated as "Hill of Sacrifice" — offers some of the most spectacular views in the city. But most people don't come for the views (although you shouldn't miss them; the observation platform is on the ocean side of the crater). They come to honor the more than 48,000 victims, buried over 113 verdant acres, predominantly of three American wars whose theaters were Asia and the Pacific: World War II and the Korean and Vietnam wars. Among the graves are many unmarked ones bearing only the date December 7, 1941, the day Pearl Harbor was bombed and the United States entered the Last Great War. Some of the honorees are destined to be unknown forever; others are world-famous, like WWII war correspondent Ernie Pyle and astronaut Ellison Onizuka, who died in the 1986 *Challenger* explosion. The Courts of the Missing's white stone tablets bear the names of 28,788 Americans missing in action in WWII. You can search for any specific grave locations on the computer in the office, near the entrance, where you'll also find a small tribute to some service-men buried in this hallowed ground.

See map p. 164. 2177 Puowaina Dr. (at the end of the road), Honolulu. ☎ *808-532-3720 or 808-566-1430.* www.interment.net/data/us/hi/oahu/natmem *or* www.cem.va.gov/CEMs/nchp/nmcp.asp. *To get there: Take Ward Avenue north; turn left on Prospect Street; turn right onto Puowaina Drive. Admission: Free. Open: Daily 8 a.m.–6:30 p.m. Mar–Sept; until 5:30 p.m. Oct–Feb.*

Nuuanu Pali Lookout

Sometimes gale-force winds howl through this misty mountain pass, so hold onto your hat. But if you walk up from the parking lot to the precipice, you'll be rewarded with a stunning view of the luxuriant Windward Coast. Bring a jacket or sweater with you because the weather's windy and cool up here year-round, even when it's 85°F and sunny at the beach.

See map p. 164. Near the summit of Pali Highway (Highway 61); take the Nuuanu Pali Lookout turnoff.

Puu Ualakaa State Park

The summit of this 1,048-foot-high hill offers majestic panoramic views over the whole of Honolulu and Waikiki, all the way from Diamond Head to the east to Punchbowl, Pearl Harbor, and beyond to the west. Daytime offers clear viewing, while sunset, with the bright lights of the city below, is pure magic.

See map p. 164. On Round Top Drive. To get there: From Waikiki, take Ala Wai Boulevard to McCully Street, turn right; cross over the H-1 freeway and turn left onto Wilder Street; turn right onto Makiki Street and go onward and upward about 3 miles. Park in the 2nd lot and walk to the viewing platform. Admission: Free. Open: Daily 7 a.m. to sunset.

Waikiki Aquarium

The small but first-class Waikiki Aquarium, part of the University of Hawaii, is a must for anybody who wants to know what they're actually seeing when they're snorkeling. With over 2,500 animals representing more than 420 species and a world-class reputation in coral reef life, the aquarium features tanks full of an amazing variety of marine life found in the offshore waters; a fascinating jellyfish tank; a Hawaiian reef habitat with sharks and eels; a kid-friendly touch tank with urchins and sea cucumbers; and habitats for the endangered Hawaiian monk seal and green sea turtle. Newer exhibits focus on biodiversity and the world's fragile coral reefs. You can watch the monk seals being trained and fed most days; call for the daily schedule.

See map p. 164. 2777 Kalakaua Ave. (across from Kapiolani Park on the ocean side of the road), Waikiki. ☎ **808-923-9741.** www.waquarium.org. *Admission: $9 adults, $6 seniors and students, $4 kids 13–17, $2 kids 5–12, free for kids under 5. Open: Daily 9 a.m.–5 p.m. (last entry at 4:30 p.m.).*

In Pearl Harbor

If you want to see all of Pearl Harbor's sights, arrive early and plan on spending the better part of a day here. To reach Pearl Harbor, drive west on the H-1 freeway or Nimitz Highway (reachable via Ala Moana Boulevard) past the Honolulu International Airport; take the USS *Arizona*

Memorial exit (no. 15-A). Follow the green-and-white highway signs to the free parking lots.

Shuttle service is available from Waikiki daily from 6:50 a.m. to 5:15 p.m. for $11 per person round-trip; to schedule pickup at your hotel, call **V.I.P. Trans.** at ☎ **866-836-0317** or 808-836-0317 24 hours in advance (www.viptrans.com). If you'd rather take TheBus, hop on no. 20 (see Chapter 10 for complete information on TheBus system). Either way, expect the ride to take about an hour from Waikiki. (It's about a half-hour if you drive yourself.)

Security for visitors is tight at Pearl Harbor. At press time, the following items were not permitted *at all:* baby strollers with pockets and compartments, backpacks, diaper bags, fanny packs, camera bags, purses (yes, purses), luggage, shopping bags, and any other items that allow concealment. (Remember, this is an active military base.) Storage units are available in the parking lot of the USS *Arizona* for rent from a private vendor so visitors can check their prohibited items for a $2 fee; size restrictions apply (no bigger than 30 inches by 30 inches by 18 inches), and large luggage cannot be accepted. The concierge at your hotel or condo should have the latest information; you can also call ☎ **808-422-0561** or check the National Parks Web site at www.nps.gov/usar for the latest restrictions.

It's never a smart idea to leave valuables in your rental car, and Pearl Harbor is a high-crime area — so that piece of good advice goes double here.

See the "Honolulu's Beaches and Attractions" map on p. 164.

USS Arizona Memorial and Museum

On December 7, 1941, while moored in Pearl Harbor, this 608-foot battleship was bombed in a Japanese air raid. The USS *Arizona* sank in nine minutes without firing a shot, taking 1,177 sailors and Marines to a fiery death and plunging the United States into World War II. Today, boat launches take you out to the stark white 184-foot memorial that spans the sunken hull of the *Arizona,* which lies 6 feet below the surface of the sea. The memorial contains the ship's bell, recovered from the wreckage, and a room with the names of the dead carved in stone.

Try to arrive early at the visitor center (which is operated jointly by the National Parks Service and the U.S. Navy) to avoid the huge crowds because advance reservations are not taken and waits of an hour or two are common. Sometimes, if crowds are big, they stop selling tickets entirely at noon. While you're waiting for the shuttle to take you out to the ship — you'll be issued a number and time of departure, which you must pick up yourself — you can explore the small but arresting museum, which features personal mementos, photos, and historic documents. An informative and moving 20-minute film precedes your trip to the ship. Allow about three hours for your visit and be sure to remain respectfully silent when you're on the actual memorial.

See map p. 162. On Battleship Row, Pearl Harbor. ☎ *808-422-0561.* www.nps.gov/ usar. *Admission: Free. Shirts and shoes required; no bathing suits. Open: Daily 7:30 a.m.–5 p.m. (boat shuttles and programs run 8 a.m.–3 p.m.).*

USS Bowfin Submarine Museum and Park

The USS *Bowfin* is one of only 15 World War II submarines still in existence today. You can go below deck of this famous submarine — nicknamed the "Pearl Harbor Avenger" for its successful retaliatory attacks on the Japanese — and see how the 80-man crew lived during wartime. The museum holds an impressive collection of submarine-related artifacts, the Waterfront Memorial honors submariners lost during World War II, and the mini-theater shows a constant run of sub-related videos.

 If you're planning to visit both the USS *Bowfin* and the Battleship *Missouri* (see the next listing), purchase a combination ticket, which will save you a few dollars.

See map p. 162. 11 Arizona Memorial Dr. (next to the USS Arizona Memorial Visitor Center), Pearl Harbor. ☎ *808-423-1341.* www.bowfin.org. *Admission to sub and museum: $10 adults, $6 seniors and military, $4 kids 4–12 (kids under 4 are not allowed on the submarine, but can visit the museum and mini-theater). Admission to museum only: $5 adults, $3 kids. Open: Daily 8 a.m.–5 p.m. (last tour at 4:30 p.m.). Combination tickets available for the Bowfin plus an unguided tour of the Missouri: $20 adults, $10 kids.*

Battleship Missouri Memorial

The newest addition to Pearl Harbor's Battleship Row memorial fleet is this 58,000-ton, 887-foot battleship — the last one the U.S. Navy built — which served in three wars, but is most famous for being the site of Japanese surrender to Douglas MacArthur and the Allied forces in 1945. Decommissioned in 1955, the *Missouri* went back into action to the Gulf War before its final retirement to Hawaii in 1998. After you check in at the visitor center at the USS *Bowfin* (see previous listing), you'll be shuttled by trolley to Ford Island for ship boarding. You're free to explore the mammoth battleship from bow to stern after you watch a short informational film, which is a blast: You can see the biggest guns the Navy ever built, climb up the flying bridge, visit the officer's quarters, and experience how sailors lived at sea. I highly recommend hooking up with one of the hour-long guided tours led by retired military veterans, which offer the best insights; you can pair this with a two-hour AcousticGuide tour for the complete experience, or choose to take the AcousticGuide tour only. For the premier battleship experience, opt for the Explorer's Tour, a 90-minute tour that goes behind the scenes to explore the fire rooms, battery rooms (housing the vintage computers that controlled the massive gun turrets), machinery, crew berthing areas, and working rooms. Allow about three hours total for your visit if you plan on working in a tour. Hard-core military junkies should inquire about other specialty tours, including the overnight Encampment Tours.

The battleship is scheduled to be dry-docked for repairs — including sand-blasting and repainting of the hull and teak deck replacement — for two to three months in 2009. Therefore, call ahead to be sure the battleship is open to visitors before you go.

See map p. 162. On Battleship Row, Pearl Harbor; check in at the Visitor's Center of the USS Bowfin, where a trolley will take you for the 7-minute ride to the battleship. ☎ *877-MIGHTY-MO (877-644-4896) or 808-423-2263.* www.ussmissouri.com. *Admission: $16 adults, $8 kids 4–12. Hour-long Guided Tours or 2-hour-long AcousticGuide tour $22 adults, $15 kids. Premium 90-minute Explorer Tours $45 adults, $20 kids. Advance tickets are available online for purchase; reservations are also taken via phone. Reservations are recommended for the Explorers Tour. Open: Daily 9 a.m.–5 p.m. (ticket window closes at 4 p.m.).*

In nearby East Oahu

Sea Life Park

This marine-themed park is Hawaii's very own version of SeaWorld, and it's lots of fun, especially for families. Highlights include a sea lion feeding pool; the quarter-million-gallon Hawaiian Reef Tank, brimming with tropical fish plus a few sharks and stingrays; performing seals, dolphins, and penguins strutting their smarts and skill in choreographed shows, which run every 45 minutes (it takes about two hours to see all four shows); and a pirate-themed play area for the little ones. The chief curiosity, though, is the world's only "wholphin," a genuine genetic cross between a false killer whale and an Atlantic bottle-nosed dolphin. On-site marine biologists operate a recovery center for endangered marine life that allows you to visit with rehabilitated Hawaiian monk seals and seabirds.

Sea Life Park offers a full variety of interactive programs that allow you to get up-close-and-personal with the park's residents according to your age, budget, interest, and swimming ability. The **Hawaiian Ray Encounter** lets you snorkel with stingrays for a $15 add-on fee. **Sea Trek Adventure** gives you the opportunity to actually dive into the Hawaiian Reef Tank with a guide for 40 minutes (including orientation). No previous diving experience necessary; the cost on top of park admission is $59 per person, and you must be 12 or older to participate. The **Dolphin Aloha** allows you a brief 15-minute interaction with dolphins in a poolside environment (read: no swimming); you'll learn communication techniques and even be allowed to kiss your new friends. The cost is $69 for adults, $59 for kids ages 5 to 12 (kids under age 5 participate free; all children under age 8 must be accompanied by an adult). The 45-minute **Dolphin Encounter** allows for shallow-water interaction with the dolphins. The cost is $99 for adults, $69 for kids 6 to 12. A more in-depth 45-minute **Dolphin Royal Swim** that includes an exciting dual-dolphin dorsal fin ride is $149 (no kids under age 12). If sea lions are more your style, try the 30-minute **Sea Lion Discovery** swim program for $99 adults, $69 kids 8 to 12 (no kids under 8). Park admission is included in all dolphin and sea lion interaction programs. Not surprisingly, all of the animal interaction programs are in high demand, so reserve your spots in advance. Bring towels if you're planning to participate in any of these. For details on these and a half-dozen other cool special programs, visit the Web site or call ☎ **808-259-2500.** Space is limited, so reserve in advance to avoid disappointment.

Sea Life Park also offers the family-friendly **Sea Life Luau** on Wednesday, Friday, and Sunday nights that includes a 15-minute dolphin show as well as the usual luau entertainment. It's relaxing and fun, and a great way to see the highlights of the park if you don't have a whole day to spare. For further details, see Chapter 10 or contact the park directly.

See map p. 164. 41–202 Kalanianaole Hwy. (Highway 72), Waimanalo. ☎ *808-259-7933.* www.sealifeparkhawaii.com. *To get there: Take H-1 east to Highway 72; after the road has narrowed to 2 lanes, it's just past Sandy Beach on the left. Parking: $3. Admission: $29 adults, $19 kids 4–12. Park admission is included in some animal interaction programs. Open: Daily 9 a.m.–5 p.m.*

Exploring the rest of the island

Oahu has so much to offer that you'll certainly never lack for things to do. The following are standouts beyond Honolulu that you won't want to miss.

Hawaiian Waters Adventure Park

This 25-acre water-theme amusement park is the place to play if the beach just isn't enough for you. Highlights include an inner-tube cruise along an 800-foot "river," two phenomenal seven-story water slides, a multilevel play pool that's fun for the whole family, mind- and body-bending tube slides and rides, and a wave pool that's as big as a football field (and better for bodysurfing, I might add). Adults have their own "spa" area for relaxing and hot-tubbing. There's something for even the littlest ones here, but you have to be at least 48 inches tall to enjoy everything. Locker rooms, changing rooms, showers, and a well-endowed food court are on hand. Use of life jackets, tubes, and floats is free, but there's a charge for towels, boogie boards, and lockers.

You can order a package ticket that includes round-trip bus transportation to Hawaiian Waters from Waikiki by calling ☎ **808-674-9283,** ext. 107.

See map p. 162. 400 Farrington Hwy. (Highway 93), Kapolei. ☎ *808-674-9283.* www.hawaiianwaters.com. *To get there: Take H-1 west to exit no. 1 (Campbell Industrial Park/Barbers Point Harbor). Admission: $36 adults, $15 seniors (60+), $26 kids 3–11, free for kids under 3. Open: Daily from 10:30 a.m.; closing times vary between 3:30 and 6 p.m., depending on day and season. Closed Tues–Wed in spring.*

Hawaii's Plantation Village

This impeccably restored 50-acre outdoor museum offers a genuine look back to the days when sugar planters from America — and field workers from Japan, China, Portugal, the Philippines, Puerto Rico, and Korea — shaped the land, economy, and culture of territorial Hawaii. You can explore the village only on an hour-long guided tour, which takes you through more than two dozen faithfully restored camp houses, a Buddhist temple and a Shinto shrine, a plantation store, and even a sumo-wrestling ring.

See map p. 162. In the Waipahu Cultural Garden Park, 94–695 Waipahu St. (at Waipahu Depot Road), Waipahu. ☎ *808-677-0110.* www.hawaiiplantation village.org. *To get there: Take H-1 west to the no. 7 (Waikele) exit; turn south onto Paiwa Street, pass 4 traffic signals, turn right onto Waipahu Street, and go ¾ mile. Admission: $13 adults, $10 seniors (62+), $7 military, $5 kids 4–11. Open: Mon–Sat 10 a.m.–4:30 p.m.; escorted tours offered hourly on the hour, last tour at 2 p.m.*

Kualoa Ranch & Activity Club

This 4,000-acre formerly working cattle ranch is now a gorgeous outdoor playground (parts of *Jurassic Park* were filmed here, and *Lost* regularly films on the ranchland; you might even spot Hurley's makeshift golf course while you're here). A range of half- and full-day adventure packages are on offer, including such activities as horseback riding, ATV rides, rifle shooting, a movie-set and ranch tour, a jungle tour aboard a 6-wheeled Swiss Pinzauer, catamaran sailing, and more, including hiking and garden tours. You can mix and match activities to design your ideal day at the ranch. Reservations are required, and you'll need to talk to an agent in advance to sort out the package that's right for you. Individual activities can also be booked if you don't want to spend the whole day here. (Travelers with disabilities, note: There's a special horseback riding program geared for you; inquire about availability.)

See map p. 162. 49–560 Kamehameha Hwy. (Highway 83), Kaaawa. ☎ *800-231-7321, 808-237-7321, or 808-237-8515.* www.kualoa.com. *To get there: Take H-1 to the Likelike Highway (Highway 63); turn left at Kahekili Highway (Highway 83) and continue on to Kaaawa. Full- and half-day activity packages: $59–$129 adults, $29–$69 kids 3–11. Single-activity prices $19–$89 adults and children, depending on activity. Open: Daily 9 a.m.–3 p.m.*

Haleiwa

Little more than a collection of clapboard storefronts with a picturesque harbor, the North Shore town of Haleiwa (ha-lay-*ee*-va) is the unofficial capital of Hawaii's surf culture and a major roadside attraction filled with art galleries, restaurants, surf shops, and boutiques. This beach town really comes alive in winter, when the timid summer waves swell to monster proportions and draw big-wave surfers — and the people who love to watch them risk their necks — from around the world.

Haleiwa is definitely worth a stop to soak in some surf-style atmosphere. Shoppers will find an hour or two worth of good browsing to be had, and your kids will love the wild and wacky surf shops. For directions on getting here, see Chapter 10. Here are a few of the best places to visit:

✔ **Dole Pineapple Plantation:** If you're heading up to the North Shore via the Central Oahu route, you may want to make a pit stop here, 64–1550 Kamehameha Hwy. (Highway 99), Wahiawa (☎ 808-621-8408; www.doleplantation.com). The two draws of this ticky-tacky tourist attraction have long been (a) the world's largest maze (pineapple shaped, no less), which you can take a shot at navigating for $6 adults, $4 kids; and (b) three words: pineapple ice cream. The shop is open daily from 9 a.m. to 6 p.m. (maze until 5 p.m.). Other features include a 20-minute train ride through the grounds ($8 adults, $6 for kids) and a Plantation Garden tour ($4 adults, $3.25 kids).

✔ **North Shore Surf and Cultural Museum:** Tucked into the North Shore Marketplace at 66–250 Kamehameha Hwy. (across from Twelve Tribes) in Haleiwa (☎ 808-637-8888), Oahu's only surf museum is a fun place to spend 20 minutes. The collection of memorabilia includes everything from vintage surfboards to old beach movie posters to trophies won by surfing's biggest legends. Admission is free, but donations are gladly accepted. The museum is open Tuesday to Sunday from about 11 a.m. to 6 p.m., but call ahead because "once in awhile somebody doesn't make it" to open up. Surf's up, anyone?

✔ **Strong Current Surf Design:** This is the place for surf memorabilia and gear. You can't miss Strong Current — just look for the vintage Woody station wagon parked in front of the store. Strong Current has two locations in Haleiwa: in the North Shore Marketplace, at 66–214 Kamehameha Hwy. (☎ 808-637-3406; www.strong currenthawaii.com), and at 66–208 Kamehameha Hwy. (just down the block past Kua Aina Sandwich; ☎ 808-637-3410).

✔ **Matsumoto's:** To really get into the surf city groove, stop into this simple general store at 66–087 Kamehameha Hwy. in Haleiwa (☎ 808-637-6827; www.matsumotoshaveice.com) for a taste of Hawaii's favorite sweet treat: shave ice (never "shaved ice"), the island version of a snow cone. Shave ice comes in a generous cup (don't get the cone — you'll be sorry!) sweetened with your choice of syrup: strawberry, root beer, banana, passion fruit — it really doesn't matter, because they all come out rainbow-colored and tasting vaguely the same. I highly recommend doing as the locals do and ordering yours with a scoop of ice cream and sweet red *azuki* beans nestled in the middle — yum! I never pass up an opportunity to visit Matsumoto's, and you shouldn't, either. Don't be daunted by the long line — it moves fast.

If you're coming up to the North Shore in winter to catch the surfers in action — and you should, if you're on the island — you'll want to head to Waimea Beach Park, the Banzai Pipeline, and Sunset Beach; see "Combing the Beaches," at the start of this chapter, for details.

For recommendations on where to head for food and sunset cocktails while you're in the Haleiwa area, see Chapter 10.

Polynesian Cultural Center

This remarkable cultural theme park allows you to tour the vast Pacific in just a single day. Seven Pacific island villages (representing Fiji, New

Zealand, Marquesas, Samoa, Tahiti, Tonga, and Hawaii) let you experience firsthand each island or island group's lifestyle, traditions, songs, dance, costumes, and architecture as you tour the 42-acre park.

You can "travel" through this living-history museum/theme park either on foot or in a pole boat navigated along a man-made freshwater lagoon system. Each village is "inhabited" by native students from Polynesia who attend Brigham Young University–Hawaii. Operated by the Mormon Church, the park also features a variety of stage shows celebrating the music, dance, history, and culture of Polynesia. An IMAX theater offers a gorgeous movie focusing on the need to preserve the earth's fragile coral reefs. An all-you-can-eat luau is served every evening (sorry, no alcohol), capped by a two-hour Polynesian entertainment extravaganza.

The whole thing may sound hokey, and it is — to a degree. But it's extremely well done and teaches a fascinating cultural lesson about the peoples of Polynesia and their cultural distinctions. Still, it's a lot to take in, and many people will find that the regular daytime activities are satisfactory. My recommendation is that you come for just the day and save your luauing for a neighbor island, especially if you're going to Maui, where the Old Lahaina Luau feast is of better quality, and you won't be required to maintain your theme-park stamina from noon 'til night. If you do want to stay for the entire affair, you'll have to choose between the different price packages, whose options include quality of food, quality of seating, and souvenirs. Because a visit is an all-day affair even if you don't stay for the evening show (straight-admission guests are kicked out at 6 p.m.), plan to arrive before 2 p.m.

Even if you have a rental car, you may want to take an alternate method of transportation to the Polynesian Cultural Center if you're planning to spend the day and evening; the drive back to Waikiki at 10 p.m. can be a real drag after an exhausting day at the park. You can book bus, minibus, and limo transportation starting at $15 per person through the PCC by calling ☎ **800-367-7060.**

See map p. 162. 55–370 Kamehameha Hwy. (Highway 83), Laie. ☎ *800-367-7060, 877-722-1411, or 808-293-3333.* www.polynesia.com. *To get there: Take the Pali Highway (Highway 61) or the Likelike Highway (Highway 63) to the Windward Coast and turn left on Kamehameha Highway (Highway 83). Basic admission: $43 adults, $33 kids 3–11. Basic admission plus evening show: $58 adults, $47 kids 3–11. Buffet, IMAX, evening show, and luau packages: $83–$215 adults, $59–$165 kids, depending on which package you choose. Open: Mon–Sat 12:30–9:30 p.m. (box office and lunch buffet open at noon); regular exhibits close at 6 p.m.*

Hitting the links

Oahu has a handful of championship courses, but hard-to-get tee times and inaccessibility from Waikiki make this my least favorite island for teeing off. Still, if you're on Oahu and in the mood, these courses are your best bets.

For last-minute and discounted tee times, try calling **Stand-by Golf** (☎ 866-224-BOOK; www.stand-bygolf.com). This reservation agency can offer as much as 50 percent off greens fees when courses are anxious to fill tee times. Also check out the deals available through discounter **Tee Times Hawaii.com** (☎ 888-675-GOLF; www.teetimeshawaii.com).

Another great information resource on Oahu's golf courses is **808Golf. com** (☎ 808-791-4591; www.808golf.com), whose extensive Web site offers comprehensive course descriptions and the opportunity to book advance tee times at some courses online. 808Golf.com can even grant you discounts at select courses.

Ko Olina Golf Club

Located on Oahu's arid west side, this 6,324-yard, par-72 Ted Robinson–designed course is a standout with rolling fairways, multitiered greens, and no fewer than 16 water features. The signature hole is the picturesque 12th, a par-3 with an elevated tee sitting on a rock garden, plus its very own cascading waterfall. Wait until you get to the 18th hole; you'll see and hear water all around you. You'll have no choice but to play to the left and approach the green over the water. This course isn't overly difficult, but you'd better be on your game as soon as the wind picks up. Facilities include a driving range, locker rooms, Jacuzzi/steam rooms, and a restaurant and bar. Book in advance because the course is always crowded. Men are asked to wear collared shirts.

See map p. 162. 92–1220 Aliinui Dr., Ewa Beach. ☎ *808-676-5300.* www.koolina golf.com *or* www.koolina.com. *To get there: Take H-1 west until it becomes Farrington Highway (Highway 93); exit at Ko Olina and turn left onto Aliinui Drive. Greens fees: $170 ($145 for J.W. Marriott Ihilani resort guests), $110 after 1 p.m. in winter or 2:30 p.m. in summer ($95 for Ihilani guests).*

Makaha Resort Golf Club

Ask any local duffer, and he's bound to name this course as one of his favorites on the island — everybody does. In fact, *Honolulu* magazine recently celebrated this course as Oahu's best. Designed by William Bell, the challenging par-72, 7,077-yard course is one of Oahu's longest, most difficult, most beautiful, and best maintained. But don't let the rugged beauty of wrinkled cliffs or the luxurious valley setting distract your attention from the challenges: eight water hazards, 107 bunkers, and frequent and brisk winds that you'll have to play into on three holes, minimum. Facilities include a pro shop, a driving range, bag storage, and a particularly fine clubhouse with food service.

See map p. 162. 84–626 Makaha Valley Rd., Waianae (45 miles west of Honolulu). ☎ *808-695-7111.* www.makahavalleycc.com. *To get there: Take H-1 west until it turns into Highway 93, which will wind up the leeward coast; turn right on Makaha Valley Road and follow it to the fork, and the course will be on the left. Greens fees: $65 weekdays, $75 weekends ($85 for non-U.S. residents).*

Turtle Bay Resort Courses

Situated on the gorgeous North Shore, the Arnold Palmer and Ed Seay–designed **Palmer Course** is the most spectacular golf course on the island. With rolling terrain, only a few trees, and lots of wind, the front nine holes play like a Scottish course, whereas the back nine have narrower tree-lined fairways and lots of water (including wonderful ocean views from the 17th hole). Several holes skirt a wetlands preserve, giving the course a tranquil vibe and beautiful native flora and fauna. This course is a really fun place to play, and five sets of tees on every hole accommodate golfers of all abilities. No wonder senior PGAers like Chi Chi Rodriguez and Hale Irwin consider this place to be one of their favorite stops on the annual Senior PGA tour. Turtle Bay is also home to the **Fazio Course,** renowned course architect George Fazio's only course in the islands. This nine-holer can be played twice for a regulation par-71, 6,200-yard course. It's known for its generous fairways, deep bunkers, and immaculately shaped greens. Two sets of tees — one designed for men, one for women — let you enjoy a slightly different game the second time around. Facilities include a pro shop, driving range, putting and chipping green, and snack bar.

See map p. 162. 57–049 Kuilima Dr., Kahuku. ☎ *808-293-8811.* www.turtlebay resort.com. *To get there: Follow directions to Haleiwa outlined in Chapter 10; proceed through town and follow Highway 83 to the Turtle Bay Country Club. Greens fees: $195 at the Palmer Course ($155 for resort guests); $160 at the Fazio Course ($125 for resort guests). Awinata fees (noon to 2 p.m.): $150 at the Palmer Course ($125 for resort guests), $135 at the Fazio course ($105 for resort guests). Ahiahi fees (2 p.m. and later): $110 at the Palmer course ($100 for resort guests); $90 at the Fazio course ($80 for resort guests). Junior rates available.*

Shopping the Local Stores

Most of the city's shopping is conveniently concentrated in a few big malls and shopping centers. Additionally, browsers shouldn't neglect Waikiki's main drag, **Kalakaua Avenue,** as well as Kuhio Avenue 1 block to the north. Both avenues and the side streets that connect them are lined with an eclectic mix that ranges from haute couture boutiques to tacky souvenir stalls. Kalakaua is becoming the Rodeo Drive of Hawaii, lined as it is with shops like **Prada, Burberry, Versace, Bulgari, Celine,** and others. These runway names cater largely to the Japanese crowd, who apparently find this stuff affordable compared with what they pay in Tokyo. Many of the stores along Kalakaua are open until late into the evening.

Shopping malls

Honolulu is the crux of commerce in the Pacific — people fly in from as far away as Tahiti to do their Christmas shopping at the finest collection of malls in the Pacific.

Ala Moana Center

This monster-size mall is the largest open-air shopping center in the United States. With a selection of stores that ranges from **Sears** and **Foot Locker** to **Fendi** and **Gucci,** there really is something for everybody here. Among the standouts are the department stores: **Macy's** (which features a wonderful Hawaiian crafts department), **Shirokiya** (a Japanese department store with a divine food department), **Neiman-Marcus** (bastion of high-society elegance), and new in 2008, Nordstrom. The mall is home to everything from **LensCrafters** to the U.S. Post Office to a massive food court. You can shop for aloha wear at **Reyn's** and **Tori Richard** (two of my favorites for island prints), find affordable gifts for the folks back home at **Hilo Hattie,** and meet just about any other need.

A whole fleet of new and exciting stores and restaurants will be installed at Ala Moana by the time you read this. Look for **Blue Hawaii Surf** for edgy surf and skate wear; **Lush,** the handmade British cosmetics brand; **Harry Winston** for glam wedding and engagement jewelry; **Ruehl No. 925,** the hot clothing and accessories brand from Abercrombie & Fitch; **Islands,** for terrific two-fisted burgers from the Southern California–based chain; and **Pacific Place Tea Garden Café,** for traditional and Hawaii-style afternoon tea service and accouterments, among others. Be sure to check out the new **Tsukiji Fish Market and Restaurant,** modeled after Tokyo's world-famous fish market; it features a sushi bar, a yakitori bar, a Japanese buffet, and an incredible assortment of fresh fish from local waters and exotic locales. Ala Moana is a must for mall lovers.

1450 Ala Moana Blvd. (between Piikoi Street and Atkinson Drive), Honolulu. ☎ *808-955-9517.* www.alamoana.com.

Aloha Tower Marketplace

This waterfront restaurant and dining complex is better for dining (**Chai's Island Bistro** is here; see Chapter 10) and views than it is for actual shopping — most of the stores are ticky-tacky. The choices (lots of gift boutiques and T-shirt shops) are more tourist-oriented than those at neighbors Ala Moana Center, Ward Centre, and Ward Warehouse. It's a great place to stroll, but don't expect the find of a lifetime. The few standouts include **Ang Namsilk** for original women's tropical wear and handbags in exotic silks, and **Honolua Surf Co.** for surf apparel. TheBus and the Waikiki Trolley stop here (consider taking public transportation; parking here is tough).

At Honolulu Harbor between piers 8 and 11 (just past the point where Ala Moana Boulevard meets Nimitz Highway), Honolulu. ☎ *808-566-2337* or *808-528-5700.* www.alohatower.com.

DFS Galleria Waikiki

This three-story shopping emporium in the heart of Waikiki lures big spenders with an array of upscale boutiques (think Prada and Burberry). The main level features Hawaiian food-product outlets where you can pick up Kona coffee and the like. The brand names line the second and third floors, where you'll find everything from designer cosmetics and fragrances to fashion and luggage. The main **Waikiki Trolley** customer service desk is located at the mall. *Beware:* Certain duty-free shopping areas are off-limits to mainland shoppers. There's free live entertainment every evening at 7 p.m., often featuring hula.

330 Royal Hawaiian Ave. (at Kalakaua Avenue), Waikiki. ☎ *808-931-2700.* www.dfs galleria.com.

Royal Hawaiian Shopping Center

Located in central Waikiki, this mall recently underwent a massive $84-million upgrade, making it the extravagant heart of Honolulu's European designer shopping. It's where you'll find **Fendi, Bulgari, Hermès, Furla, Cartier,** and other big-ticket boutiques. In addition, you'll find fresh-faced couture brands and chic mass-marketers such as **Kate Spade, Juicy Couture, Tourneau,** and **White House Black Market.** A new **Hilo Hattie's** megastore, slated to be the chain's flagship location, will be open by the time you arrive. You'll find a Waikiki Trolley ticket and information kiosk here as well (see Chapter 10).

2201 Kalakaua Ave. (at Seaside Avenue), Waikiki. ☎ *808-922-0588.* www.royal hawaiianshoppingcenter.com.

Waikele Premium Outlets

This top-flight outlet mall in west Oahu offers one of the island's best rainy-day activities. Options run from the ultrachic (Barneys New York, Brooks Brothers, Calvin Klein, Kenneth Cole, Coach, Max Mara) to the comfort-casual (Banana Republic, Jockey, Skechers). The outlets are well worth the 20-minute drive if you're a discount-shopping fan.

If you're a shopper without a car, contact **E Noa Tours** (☎ 808-591-2561; www.enoa.com) and **All Occasion Transportation** (☎ 800-454-1380), both of which offer excursions to the outlets.

94–790 Lumiaina St., Waipahu (about 20 miles west of Waikiki). ☎ *808-676-5656.* www.premiumoutlets.com. *To get there: Take H-1 west toward Waianae and turn off at exit 7.*

Ward Centers

What used to be two simple two-story sister shopping centers has bloomed into a six-center mini-empire of quality midpriced shopping occupying 4 city blocks and hosting 120 shops and 23 restaurants. Of the two original malls, Ward Centre is largely dedicated to dining, but has a few standouts, most notably **Borders,** which boasts an excellent Hawaiian music department; **The Gallery at Ward Centre,** which carries a notable collection of works by Hawaii artists; and the **Honolulu Chocolate Company,** makers of fine island-made chocolates from island-grown cocoa beans. **Ward Warehouse**'s good choices include the **Nohea Gallery,** a constant favorite for its terrific collection of high-quality Hawaii-made crafts;

Island Guitars, for new, used, and vintage instruments; and **Mamo Howell,** for both traditional and contemporary muumuu in Mamo's wonderful signature fabrics. At the Ward Gateway Center, **Mauka to Makai** hosts a terrific collection of outdoor gear, Hawaii-style. There's much, much more, even a tropical farmers' market, a state-of-the-art 16-screen movie multiplex, and a wealth of good restaurants, including **Brew Moon Restaurant & Microbrewery, Kakaako Kitchen,** and **Kua Aina Sandwich** (all reviewed in Chapter 10).

Attention, diners: Stop by the concierge desk on the mezzanine level in front of the movie theater, where the concierge can show you menus, make dinner reservations for you, and even present you with coupons.

Ala Moana Boulevard and Auahi Street (1 block inland from Ala Moana Boulevard) between Ward Avenue and Queen Street, just west of the Ala Moana Center. ☎ *808-591-8411.* www.victoriaward.com.

Other shopping of note

Hilo Hattie has been Hawaii's first name in aloha wear for decades, and I'm happy to report that both the quality and the selection are better than ever. There's a ginormous location out toward the airport at 700 N. Nimitz Hwy., at Pacific Street (☎ **888-526-0299** or 808-535-6500; www. hilohattie.com). You'll find a big children's department, as well as macadamia nuts, Hawaii-grown coffees, contemporary Hawaiian music, and lots of other souvenirs to choose from. The chain's flagship megastore in the Royal Hawaiian Shopping Center should be open and active by the time you read this. A more manageable location is at Ala Moana Center, where the selection tends toward the high end (☎ **808-973-3266**).

For the best selection of vintage aloha shirts, visit **Bailey's Antiques and Aloha Shirts,** 517 Kapahulu Ave. (across from the Ala Wai Golf Course), north of Kapiolani Park in the Kapahulu section of Honolulu (☎ **808-734-7628;** www.alohashirts.com). A '50s-era cotton or silkie in A-1 condition can cost upwards of $600 or more, but some cheapies are on hand, too; prices begin around $20. You'll also find hula-girl lamps, vintage costume jewelry, and other bits of kitsch, all priced at top dollar — but a joy to discover, anyway.

For one of the best collections of contemporary aloha wear, visit **Moonbow Tropics,** located at the Westin Moana Surfrider, 2365 Kalakaua Ave. (☎ **808-924-1496;** www.moonbowtropics.com). You'll find gorgeous men's and women's wear from such brands as Tori Richard, Tommy Bahama, Kahala, and Nat Nast, tailor to the King (Elvis that is). **Tori Richard** also has its own wonderful brand store in Waikiki at 2424 Kalakaua Ave. (☎ **808-924-1811;** www.toririchard.com); there's a second store in Ala Moana Center.

Wonderful prints and styles are made by **Reyn's** (www.reyns.com), which has a number of boutiques throughout Hawaii, including one at the Ala Moana Center (☎ **808-949-5929**), plus a charming shop on the lobby level of the Sheraton Waikiki hotel (☎ **808-923-0331**).

Innovative expressions of aloha

Art hounds will enjoy strolling the burgeoning gallery scene of downtown Honolulu, where galleries, studios, and other art venues are flourishing in the tight square near Chinatown occupied by Nuuanu Avenue, Pauahi Street, Hotel Street, and Smith Street. Highlights include **The ARTS at Marks Garage,** 1159 Nuuanu Ave. (☎ 808-521-2903; www.artsatmarks.com), a collaborative gallery and performance space (call ahead to see what's going on while you're in town); **Bethel Street Gallery,** 1140 Bethel St. (☎ 808-524-3552; www.bethelstreetgallery.com), showcasing the excellent contemporary works of its collective of owner-artists; the **Pegge Hopper Gallery,** 1164 Nuuanu Ave. (☎ 808-524-1160; www.peggehopper.com), whose distinctive paintings of island women are justifiably world famous; **thirtyninehotel,** 39 Hotel St. (☎ 808-599-2552; www.thirtyninehotel.com), the domain of painter Gelareh Khoie and DJ Harvey Bassett, who have come together to create a cutting-edge performance and gallery space; and the **Louis Pohl Gallery,** 1111 Nuuanu Ave. (☎ 808-521-1812; www.louispohlgallery.com), for dynamic island-themed art.

A great time to stroll and celebrate the exciting scene is during **First Friday,** a monthly event during which all of the galleries welcome browsers with refreshments and live entertainment. First Friday takes place on the first Friday of every month from 5 to 9 p.m. For more information — and a comprehensive list of galleries and other art venues in the neighborhood — visit www.firstfridayhawaii.com or call ☎ 808-739-9797.

Attention, late-night revelers: You'll also find a growing list of coolly creative bars and entertainment spaces with a twist in this neighborhood, such as **Mercury Bar,** 1154 Fort Street Mall (☎ 808-537-3080); **Bar 35,** 35 N. Hotel St. (☎ 808-537-3535; www.bar35hawaii.com), catering to the style-savvy beer connoisseur; **NextDoor,** 43 Hotel St. (☎ 808-548-6398; www.myspace.com/nextdoorhi), Chinatown's art-house concert and movie hall; and **Indigo,** 1121 Nuuanu Ave. (☎ 808-521-2900; www.indigo-hawaii.com), the terrific Eurasian restaurant (see review in Chapter 10) that also boasts the seductive Green Room lounge, where you'll find terrific live music or DJs spinning a creative music mix Tuesdays through Saturdays.

Some of the finest stops for Hawaiian-made gifts are museum shops: The **Academy Shop** at the Honolulu Academy of Arts, 900 S. Beretania St., between Victoria and Ward avenues in downtown Honolulu (☎ 808-532-8703), and both **Native Books and Beautiful Things** and **Shop Pacifica** at the Bishop Museum, 1525 Bernice St. at Kalihi Street, also downtown (☎ 808-847-3511). The Academy Shop, Native Books, and Shop Pacifica are great choices for traditional Hawaiiana, crafts, and books. Native Books and Beautiful Things also has a larger gallery-style location at Ward Warehouse, 1050 Ala Moana Blvd. (☎ 808-596-8885). Another first-class showcase for island crafts and gifts in the Ward Warehouse is the **Nohea Gallery** (☎ 808-596-0074).

A wonderful new addition to the Oahu shopping scene is **Muumuu Heaven,** on the windward side of the island in the Davis Building, 767

Kailua Rd. (☎ **808-263-3366;** www.muumuuheaven.com). This family-run business uses vintage muumuu fabrics and remakes them as casually gorgeous, one-of-a-kind skirts, tops, dresses, and bags for women. To get there, take the Pali Highway into Kailua; as you enter into town, turn right into the first driveway after Hamakua Road.

Nothing says "aloha" like a lei. For the best selection and prices, head to Chinatown, in downtown Honolulu, where the aroma of flowers being woven into beautiful treasures fills the air. The stretch of Maunakea Street between Beretania and King streets and the adjacent block of Beretania Street are lined with lei shops on both sides of the street. The designs of the leis made here are almost always exceptional. Wander through all the shops before you decide which lei you want and feel free to ask questions about any unfamiliar tropical flowers and styles. Worth seeking out, for both selection and friendliness, are **Cindy's Lei and Flower Shoppe,** 1034 Maunakea St. (☎ **808-536-6538**); **Lin's Lei Shop,** 1017A Maunakea St. (☎ **808-537-4112**); and **Lita's Leis,** 59 N. Beretania St. (☎ **808-521-9065**).

Living It Up after Dark

Your best bet for finding out what's going on around town is to pick up a copy of *Honolulu Weekly* (www.honoluluweekly.com), available free at restaurants, clubs, shops, and newspaper racks around Oahu; the "Happenings" section can tell you what's on tap for the week. Also check the daily papers, particularly *Honolulu Advertiser* (www.honolulu advertiser.com); Friday's "TGIF" section is a prime source for what's going on around town, and you can often find it as its own freebie publication around town, called "TGIWaikiki." But most important, don't forget to make use of your hotel concierge.

If the Brothers Cazimero are putting on a show while you're in town, don't miss it. This legendary musical duo is one of Hawaii's most beloved and gifted acts. Check the papers or ask your concierge if they're playing anywhere in town. At press time, they were appearing most Wednesdays at **Chai's Island Bistro** (☎ **808-585-0011;** www. chaisislandbistro.com) in the Aloha Tower Marketplace. You can also check the brothers' calendar at www.mountainapplecompany.com/ Cazimeros.aspx. Also try to catch the beautiful, contemporary island music by the inspired duo Hapa.

A number of gallery/performance spaces and new nightlife spots, such as **Bar 35** and **thirtyninehotel,** have begun to flourish as part of down-town Honolulu's burgeoning creative arts and nightlife scene. What's more, the whole downtown gallery scene becomes its own street party on the first Friday of every month. For details, see the box "Innovative expressions of aloha," earlier in this chapter. If you're in the party mood and ready to luau, see the listing for the Polynesian Cultural Center, ear-lier in this chapter, or check out Chapter 10.

Of course, one way to enjoy the evening is to participate in an old school luau. The island has a variety of choices; my favorite family-friendly one is the **Sea Life Luau** at Sea Life Park. For details on this and other lively luau nights, see "Luau!" in Chapter 10.

The really big shows

The shows listed in this section are Waikiki staples. Still, schedules, prices, and other parameters do change; so always call ahead.

Magic of Polynesia

This extravaganza is downright Vegas-worthy. Master illusionist John Horikawa performs mind-boggling feats of magic on an elaborate stage set, aided by a large cast and state-of-the-art lighting and sound. This production is first-class, and the audience usually eats it up (although I've also run into show-goers who've walked away less than dazzled). Reserve seats a day or two in advance. I recommend skipping dinner (especially the overpriced deluxe dinner options). Note that Michael Villoria performs on Sundays and Mondays to give John Horikawa some time off.

At the Waikiki Beachcomber hotel, 2300 Kalakaua Ave. (at Duke's Lane), Waikiki. ☎ *888-349-7888, 808-971-4321, or 808-356-1800.* www.magicofpolynesia.com. *Showtimes: Nightly at 8:20 p.m. (dinner seating begins at 7 p.m.; show seating begins at 8 p.m. if you do not opt for dinner). Tickets: $48 adults, $32 children for show only; $76–$130 adults, $52–$66 children for dinner show. Online discounts available.*

Society of Seven

Waikiki's longest-running nightclub act still puts on one of the best shows in Waikiki. Expect a lively blend of skits, impersonations, show tunes, '50s and '60s pop hits, and more.

Stop by any Outrigger or Ohana hotel in Waikiki and ask the activities agent to arrange your Society of Seven tickets; if there's a special running, you may save some money. Online discounts are also available. (As with the other shows, I'd skip the overpriced dinner buffet options.)

In the Outrigger Main Showroom, Outrigger Waikiki on the Beach, 2335 Kalakaua Ave. (between the Royal Hawaiian Shopping Center and the Moana Surfrider), Waikiki. ☎ *888-349-7888, 808-356-1800, or 808-923-7469.* www.outriggeractivities. com. *Showtimes: Tues–Sun at 8:30 p.m. (additional shows at 6:30 p.m. on Tues and Fri). Tickets: $37 adults, $24 children for show only; $53 adults, $43 children for dinner show.*

Cocktails, music, and dancing

Hands down, my favorite spot for sunset cocktails is the **House Without a Key** at the Halekulani hotel, 2199 Kalia Rd. (at the beach end of Lewers Street), Waikiki (☎ **808-923-2311;** www.halekulani.com). On an oceanfront patio shaded by a big kiawe tree, you can sip the best mai tais on the island, listen to masterful steel guitar music, and watch a traditional hula dancer — often former Miss Hawaii Kanoe Miller — sway with the palms. It's romantic, nostalgic, and simply breathtaking. (Also consider the House Without a Key for a casually sophisticated alfresco dinner; see Chapter 10.) Afterward, move indoors to the Lewers Lounge, where light jazz continues the romantic tone.

Another top spot for Hawaiian music and orchid-adorned cocktails is the oh-so-romantic **Banyan Veranda** at the Moana Surfrider, 2365 Kalakaua Ave. (on the beach, across from Kaiulani Street), in the heart of Waikiki (☎ 808-922-3111; www.moana-surfrider.com). I just love this Victorian-style beachfront hotel, situated around a 100-year-old banyan tree — the perfect setting for some soft island sounds.

Nothing separates you from the sand at the **Royal Hawaiian's Mai Tai Bar,** 2259 Kalakaua Ave., at the end of Royal Hawaiian Avenue (☎ 808-923-7311), giving this one of the most lovely views of Waikiki Beach. The Mai Tai Bar maintains an all-Hawaiian music program nightly from 4:30 to 10:30 p.m.

Lively **Duke's Canoe Club,** at the Outrigger Waikiki on the Beach, 2335 Kalakaua Ave. (between the Royal Hawaiian Shopping Center and the Moana Surfrider), Waikiki (☎ 808-922-2268; www.dukeswaikiki.com) is the quintessential beachfront bar and restaurant, with Tiki torches in the sand, a tropical party vibe, and a mammoth drink menu. The Hawaiian entertainment is always top-notch, and usually starts around 4 p.m.

The Sheraton Waikiki, 2255 Kalakaua Ave. (at Royal Hawaiian Avenue, west of the Royal Hawaiian), Waikiki (☎ 808-922-4422), is home to **RumFire** (☎ 866-952-3473; www.rumfirewaikiki.com), a sharp, sexy, cavernous nightspot offering the largest vintage rum selection in the United States. You'll find an oceanfront setting, a generous tapas menu, and a lively scene. Open until midnight Sunday through Thursday, until 2 a.m. on Friday and Saturday.

If you're at the Diamond Head end of Waikiki, head to the **Sunset Lanai** at the New Otani Kaimana Beach Hotel, 2863 Kalakaua Ave., across the street from Kapiolani Park (☎ 808-923-1555). Shaded by a giant light-festooned hau tree, it's no wonder that this magical spot is a favorite Waikiki watering hole. Live Hawaiian music heightens the ambience at sunset hour Monday, Tuesday, Friday, and Saturday.

Hawaii's finest musicians operate at two top Aloha Tower Marketplace venues: **Chai's Island Bistro,** Aloha Tower Marketplace, 1 Aloha Tower Dr., just south of downtown Honolulu (☎ 808-585-0011; www.chais islandbistro.com), where it's more than worth paying for the pricey dinners to see some of the finest names in Hawaiian entertainment (including Robert Cazimero, half of the justifiably legendary Brothers Cazimero duo). The calendar here is always jampacked with top-quality talent, so don't miss it. Another terrific stop in the Marketplace for contemporary talent is **Don Ho's Island Grill** (☎ 808-528-0807; www.donho. com/grill), which also transforms into a hip-shakin' dance club as the weekend evenings wear on.

The locals' best-loved venue for live music is **Anna Bannanas,** 2440 S. Beretania St. (☎ 808-946-5190; www.annabannanashonolulu.com). Music can run the gamut from reggae to blues to rock at the easygoing bar and club, so call or check the Web site to see what's on.

Rumours Nightclub, at the Ala Moana Hotel, 410 Atkinson Dr. (☎ 808-955-4811), is a great place to hit the dance floor on Tuesday, Friday, and Saturday nights, especially if you're into Top 40 and the pop sounds of the 1960s, '70s, and '80s. Locals like to hit the dance floor every night of the week at **Venus,** an upscale dance club near the Ala Moana Shopping Center at 1349 Kapiolani Blvd. (☎ 808-951-8671). Expect house, hip hop, and radio-friendly dance music mixed by some of the island's best DJs, plus occasional special events.

Nostalgists may want to take an excursion to Honolulu's last genuine Tiki bar, **La Mariana Sailing Club,** 50 Sand Island Access Rd. (☎ 808-848-2800). Going strong since 1955, La Mariana is hidden in a decidedly unsexy industrial area near the airport, but it's worth the hunt if you want a genuine slice of a long-gone Hawaii. This is the real deal, not for those looking for pristine conditions or a fussy cocktail menu. Last time I was here, a man played pop classics on a slightly out-of-tune piano while a dog sat on a table, and Honolulu's most colorful characters gathered to enjoy the island's best mai tais and fried pupus. The harbor view is appealing, but come after dark to experience maximum retro magic. To get there from Waikiki, take Ala Moana Boulevard until it turns into Nimitz Highway; turn left on Sand Island Access Road, follow it to the bend in the road and turn right at the sign; park on the street where signs allow.

Sailing into the sunset

Nothing closes a perfect day in paradise like a sunset cruise, and there's no better place for it than Oahu, where the Waikiki skyline and Diamond Head come together in an unforgettable backdrop. **Star of Honolulu** (☎ 800-334-6191 or 808-983-7827; www.starofhonolulu.com) offers sunset dinner cruises for a range of budgets. *Navatek I* and the *MaiTai* **Catamaran** also offer sunset and dinner options to choose from; see the section "All hands on deck: Ocean-cruising adventures," earlier in this chapter, for complete details.

Part IV
Maui

The 5th Wave
By Rich Tennant

"Did you want to take the Schwinn bicycle dive, the Weber gas grill dive, or the Craftsman riding lawn mower dive?"

In this part . . .

Majestic Maui is such a wildly popular destination that it's doubly important to do some smart trip planning before you leave home. The chapters in this part help you map out everything you need for an unforgettable Valley Isle vacation — whether you're after heart-pounding adventure or simply a week (or more, if you're especially lucky) of lounging blissfully on the soft white sands.

Chapter 12

Settling into Maui

In This Chapter

▶ Getting from the airport to your hotel without a hassle
▶ Finding your way around Maui and its major resort areas
▶ Choosing among the island's top accommodations
▶ Discovering Maui's best restaurants
▶ Arranging for a luau

*S*ee the inside back cover for a color map to get you acquainted with Maui; it's slightly more difficult to navigate than the other islands, but not overly complicated. With a good map in hand, you're golden.

You'll most likely arrive at the island's centrally located main gateway, Kahului (ka-hoo-*loo*-ee) Airport, in Central Maui.

Arriving at Kahului Airport

Kahului Airport (☎ **808-872-3893;** www.state.hi.us/dot/airports/maui/ogg) is conveniently located 3 miles from the town of Kahului, Maui's main community, at the end of Keolani Place (just west of the intersection of Dairy Road and the Haleakala Highway).

Hawaiian Airlines provides both interisland and direct mainland services to Kahului. **American, Air Canada, Continental, Delta, United,** and **US Airways** all serve Kahului directly from the mainland as well. And, in addition to Hawaiian, recent entry **go! Airlines** also connects Maui with Hawaii's other islands. Nearly all the island's highways are accessible just outside the airport.

Open-air Kahului Airport is easy to negotiate. The airport is relatively small, and the route from your gate to Baggage Claim is clearly marked.

Although almost everyone arrives at Kahului Airport, Maui does have two single-strip airports served by commercial propeller carriers — one in Kapalua (West Maui) and another one in Hana. If you're interested in avoiding Kahului altogether, contact **Island Air** (☎ **800-652-6541** or 808-484-2222 from elsewhere; www.islandair.com) or **Pacific Wings** (☎ **888-575-4546** or 808-873-0877; www.pacificwings.com).

Getting from the Airport to Your Hotel

All the big car-rental names have cars available at Kahului, and I suggest that you arrange for one in advance. (For more on this subject, see Chapter 6.) If you'd rather not drive yourself, I give you some alternative transportation options in this section.

Driving yourself

Step outside to the curbside rental-car pickup area at the ocean end of the terminal (to your right as you exit the building). Either go over to the counter, if your rental company is represented, or wait for the appropriate shuttle van — they circle the airport at regular intervals — to take you a half-mile away to your rental-car checkout desk.

All the rental-car agencies offer map booklets that are invaluable for getting around the island.

Getting from the airport to your hotel can be a bit of a trial because Kahului is Maui's main business district, and all of Maui's main highways intersect just outside the airport.

If you're heading to **West Maui,** take the Kuihelani (koo-ee-hay-*la*-nee) Highway (Highway 380) to the Honoapiilani (ho-no-ah-pee-ee-*la*-nee) Highway (Highway 30). The Honoapiilani Highway curves around the knob that is West Maui, leading to Lahaina, Kaanapali, Kahana, Napili, and finally Kapalua. To pick up the Kuihelani Highway, exit the airport at Keolani Place and turn left onto Dairy Road, which turns into the highway you want. Expect it to take 30 minutes to reach Lahaina, 40 minutes to reach Kaanapali, and 50 to 60 minutes to reach Kapalua, maybe a little longer if the traffic's heavy.

If you're heading to **South Maui,** exit the airport at Keolani Place, turn left onto Dairy Road, and then left onto Puunene (poo-oo-*nay*-nay) Avenue (Highway 350), which takes you immediately to the Mokulele (mow-koo-*lay*-lay) Highway (Highway 311), which leads directly south. Just north of Kihei, the Mokulele ends; you can choose to continue on the highway — now called Piilani (pee-ee-*la*-nee) Highway (Highway 31) — which takes you through Kihei and to Wailea along the speediest route, with frequent exits along the way. If you're staying at the north end of Kihei, though, exit the Mokulele Highway onto South Kihei Road, Kihei's main drag.

Taking a taxi

As long as you arrive before 10 p.m., you can just go out to the well-marked curbside area and hop into the next available cab.

If you want to arrange for pickup ahead of time, call **Maui Airport Taxi** (☎ 808-281-9533; www.nokaoitaxi.com), **Kihei Taxi** (☎ 808-879-3000), **Wailea Taxi** (☎ 808-874-5000), or **Maui Taxi Service** (☎ 808-276-9515; www.mauipleasanttaxi.com). The mandated fare on Maui is $3 per mile, accommodating one to six people. Expect to pay $65 to $105 depending on your West Maui destination and about $42 to $55 to the Kihei/Wailea area; plus the customary 10 to 15 percent tip. For limousine service, contact **Star Limousine** (☎ 877-875-6900 or 808-669-6900; www.limohawaii.com) or **Maui Executive Transportation** (☎ 800-833-2303; www.mauishuttle.com).

Catching a shuttle ride

If you're not renting a car, the cheapest way to get to your hotel is via airport shuttle. **SpeediShuttle** (☎ 877-242-5777 or 808-242-7777; www.speedishuttle.com) can take you between Kahului Airport and any of the Maui resort areas between 6 a.m. and 11 p.m. daily. Rates vary depending on your destination, but figure on $38 to Wailea (one-way) and $54 one-way to Kaanapali. (Rates also change based on the number of people traveling together.) You can either set up your airport pickup in advance (which allows you to snag a 10 percent online booking discount on your return trip) or use the courtesy phone in Baggage Claim to summon a van (dial 65). Call at least 24 hours before your departure flight to arrange pickup.

Choosing Your Location

The commercial hub of Maui is **Kahului** (ka-hoo-*loo*-ee). Just east of Kahului is **Wailuku,** Maui's appealingly funky county seat (and a burgeoning antiques center). These two Central Maui communities are Maui's largest, but despite their central-to-everything convenience, they aren't really vacation destinations.

Instead, most visitors stay on one of Maui's two major resort coasts: West Maui and South Maui. Both comprise smaller beach resorts and communities, each with its own distinct personality.

West Maui

The West Maui coastline is a little greener in winter — and a little wetter — than the South Maui coast. Some of the best beaches on the island fringe West Maui; eastward, the beautifully jagged mountain peaks of the West Maui mountains rise in the distance.

Of the communities along this resort coast, only Lahaina is a real town. The others are really just a collection of condos or hotels anchored by a few fancy resorts or a high-end mini-mall. The communities described in the rest of this section start at the southern end of West Maui and move northward along the Honoapiilani (ho-no-ah-pee-ee-*la*-nee) Highway (Highway 30).

The port town of **Lahaina** (la-*ha*-nah) still has a historic heart, but has superseded Waikiki as the tacky tourist center of Hawaii. The blocks are lined with bustling waterfront restaurants, touristy galleries and shops, and activity centers that sometimes catcall onto the street. The predominant vibe is that of one big, surf-oriented street party. Lahaina has three more things going for it: some of Maui's best accommodations values, some very good restaurants, and an extremely convenient location. Lahaina has a couple of beaches that will do in a pinch, but it's a bit of a drive to the best ones.

Three miles north of Lahaina is **Kaanapali** (kah-na-*pa*-lee), Hawaii's first master-planned family resort, and a real favorite of mine. Kaanapali's chain of resort hotels and condos fronts a gorgeous golden beach and exudes a nice sense of continuity. All are linked by a landscaped parkway and a walking path along the sand, with a very nice shopping and dining complex sitting at its midpoint. Kaanapali is pricey, but not quite as expensive as Kapalua or Wailea; in fact, it's home to my favorite mid-priced resort, the **Kaanapali Beach Hotel,** and some of Maui's best midrange condos.

Two condo communities, **Kahana** and **Napili,** sit off the highway a few minutes north of Kaanapali, offering great deals for those who want an affordable place to stay and an oceanfront setting. Restaurants and supermarkets are right at hand. The only downside is a lack of personality — expect homogeneous, rather generic condo complexes.

North of Kahana is Hawaii's most beautiful master-planned community, **Kapalua,** the exclusive domain of a gracious Ritz-Carlton as well as some luxurious condos, fabulous gold-sand beaches, and world-class golf. Kapalua is a marvelous place to settle in and unwind, if you have the bucks to do it. But keep in mind that, situated as it is at the north end of the Honoapiilani Highway, Kapalua isn't the most convenient base. Kapalua also tends to get more rain than other Maui resorts. Still, the glorious setting can be well worth the trade-off.

South Maui

South Maui is the island's hottest, driest, and sunniest coast. Actually western-facing, but well-protected from the elements by peninsula-like West Maui, South Maui receives only about 15 inches of annual rainfall, and temperatures stay around 80°F year-round.

If you drive south along Piilani Highway (Highway 31) or Kihei Road (Highway 310), you first reach Kihei and then Wailea. Which one you choose depends entirely on your budget.

Centrally located **Kihei** (*key*-hay) is Maui's bargain coast. Its main drag is South Kihei Road, which is bordered by a continuous string of condos and mini-malls on one side and a series of sandy beaches on the other. Kihei isn't charming or quaint, but what it lacks in physical charm it more than makes up for in sunshine, affordability, and convenience.

Just a few minutes south of Kihei, **Wailea** (why-*lay*-ah) is upscale all the way. This ritzy, well-manicured neighborhood is home to Maui's best luxury resort spreads, a host of championship golf courses, five out-standing beaches, the elegant Shops at Wailea, and the Wailea Tennis Center. The strip is well-developed and tightly packed, but my favorite Wailea resorts remain worlds unto themselves. Even though Kapalua is more beautiful, Wailea is no slouch — and I prefer its more accessible location and wider range of hotel choices. You'll even find some midrange and upscale condos in this appealing neighborhood.

East Maui and Hana

The gateway to east Maui is the funky-charming Paia (pa-*ee*-ah), a hip little surf town about ten minutes east of Kahului that has three main draws: some hip and artsy boutiquing, some of the island's best-value restaurants, and the best windsurfing beach in the world, Hookipa Beach Park, which I discuss in Chapter 13.

Some visitors like to stay way out in Hana for the ultimate escape. In Hana, you can relax in a lush, green, rural setting with access to wonderful beaches. Hana tends to receive more rain than the dry South Maui coast, but the luxurious green vegetation compensates. Hana is a sleepy area, where the accommodations tend to be intimate, but not laden with facilities.

You can see this beautiful area on a day's drive from the major resort coasts (see Chapter 13), but if you have the time and the budget for it, I recommend doing the drive at a leisurely pace and staying overnight at the gloriously renovated **Hotel Hana-Maui** (reviewed later in this chapter). More affordable, bed-and-breakfast–style options are also available. It's a wonderful departure from the bustle of South and West Maui — a step back into Hawaii's simpler days.

Getting Around Maui

To really see the Valley Isle, you have to drive it yourself. Maui has only a handful of major roads; but they all meet in a complicated web in the center of the island, and untangling them can take some effort. Be sure to study a good island map and know exactly where you're going before you set out.

 Maui traffic can be challenging at times. Try to allow yourself extra time to get where you're going during rush hours, especially in the Central and South Maui areas.

Navigating your rental car around the Valley Isle

 If you get in trouble on Maui's highways and you don't have your cell-phone with you, look for the flashing blue strobe lights on 12-foot poles; at the base are emergency call boxes (programmed to dial 911 as soon as you pick up the handset).

Starting out in Central Maui

Kahului, in Central Maui, is where you'll land at the island's major airport. Kahului isn't a vacation destination, but a real town with Wal-Marts, car lots, malls, and so on. Still, you will occasionally find yourself in Kahului as you head to other areas of the island because this area is where Maui's highways intersect.

Kahului's main drag is **Kaahumanu** (ka-ah-hoo-*ma*-noo) **Avenue** (Highway 32). If you're heading to the town of Wailuku, either for some antiquing or a visit to scenic Iao Valley, just follow Kaahumanu Avenue west for about ten minutes and — *voilà* — you're there.

Reaching the West and South Maui resorts

If you're heading to any of Maui's beach resort areas, in either West Maui or South Maui, you first have to head south through the Central Maui corridor (often referred to as Maui's "neck").

To reach West Maui, you take the **Kuihelani Highway** (Highway 380) south from Kahului to the **Honoapiilani Highway** (Highway 30). The Honoapiilani Highway actually starts in Wailuku (it meets up with the end of Kaahumanu Avenue to make a neat inverted "L" there) and runs directly south to Maalaea (mah-*lay*-ah), a windy harborfront village at the south end of Central Maui — where you may be picking up a snorkel cruise to Molokini or visiting the state-of-the-art Maui Ocean Center aquarium. Past Maalaea, the southbound Honoapiilani Highway begins to follow the curve of the land, turning abruptly west and north along the coast toward Lahaina.

All West Maui's resort communities lie directly off the Honoapiilani Highway on the ocean side of the road. As you go from south to north, you'll first reach the old whaling town of Lahaina; then Kaanapali, Hawaii's first master-planned beach resort; then two quiet beachfront condo communities, Kahana and Napili; and, at the end of the road, the Kapalua resort, a stunning manicured beauty. It's about a half-hour of easy highway driving from Lahaina to Kapalua.

Be alert as you drive the Honoapiilani Highway (Highway 30); drivers who spot whales in the channel between Maui and Lanai sometimes slam on the brakes in awe, precipitating tie-ups and accidents.

From Kahului, South Maui is basically a straight shot. The **Mokulele Highway** (Highway 311) heads straight south across the Central Maui corridor from Kahului to the north end of Kihei, west of the Kuihelani Highway, Highway 380.

At the end of the Mokulele Highway, you have two choices: You can either pick up South Kihei Road, Kihei's main drag, which is what you should do if you're heading to a destination in the north portion of Kihei or if you're looking for a supermarket or gas station; or, if you're on your way to the southern portion of Kihei — to Wailea or to Makena — stick to the right as the Mokulele ends and pick up the **Piilani Highway** (Highway 31), which continues south to Wailea. Near the end of the Piilani Highway, you'll veer right onto the coastal road to reach the Wailea resorts or Makena.

The Mokulele Highway (Highway 311) is often the scene of crashes involving intoxicated and speeding drivers, so be extra careful.

If you're traveling from South Maui to West Maui, or vice versa, you don't need to travel all the way back to Kahului to pick up the appropriate road. **Highway 310** (North Kihei Road) connects the Mokulele Highway (Highway 311, the road to South Maui) to the Honoapiilani Highway (Highway 30, the road to West Maui), running east–west at the south end of Maui's "neck."

Going Upcountry and to East Maui

The giant volcanic crater that dominates the main body of the island is Haleakala (ha-lay-ah-*ka*-la), officially preserved as **Haleakala National Park.** The distance from Kahului to the summit of Haleakala is only about 38 miles, but the drive takes about 1½ hours because of its curving nature and steep ascent (to about 10,000 ft.). The drive is called the **Haleakala Highway,** which is Highway 37 as it passes through open flatlands, past turnoffs for groovy rural towns like Haliimaile (ha-lee-ee-*my*-lee; home to **Haliimaile General Store,** one of Maui's finest restaurants; see later in this chapter) and Makawao (a charming shopping stop). Then, just past Makawao Avenue, the Haleakala Highway becomes Highway 377 — so be sure to take the turn for it. After you pass through the little town of Kula, turn onto **Haleakala Crater Road** (Highway 378), which delivers you to the summit.

If you don't take the Haleakala Crater Road turnoff, you'll continue south on Highway 377, which soon connects up with Highway 37 again, here called the **Kula Highway.** If you stay on this road, it will eventually take you all the way to Hana, the small, isolated town at the east end of the island.

If you're trying to get to Hana, the more popular route is the **Hana Highway** (Highway 360), which hugs the north cliffs of Maui for about 52 miles east of Kahului. **The Heavenly Road to Hana,** as it's often called, is a winding drive that borders on treacherous in each direction, crossing more than 50 one-lane bridges in the process. Still, it's one of the most spectacular scenic drives you'll ever take in your life. I guide you through it, mile by mile, in Chapter 13. Early in your drive to Hana, make a pit stop in charming Paia, which has a number of restaurants and cafes offering breakfast and picnic lunches to Hana goers.

The south route to Hana — which is officially Highway 31, but most folks call it the **Kaupo** (*cow*-po) **Road** — was closed at press time due to 2006 earthquake damage. If you're interested in checking it out, check with your hotel or rental car company regarding potential reopening and current road conditions. It's usually fine if the weather has been clear, but

Maui Orientation & Accommodations

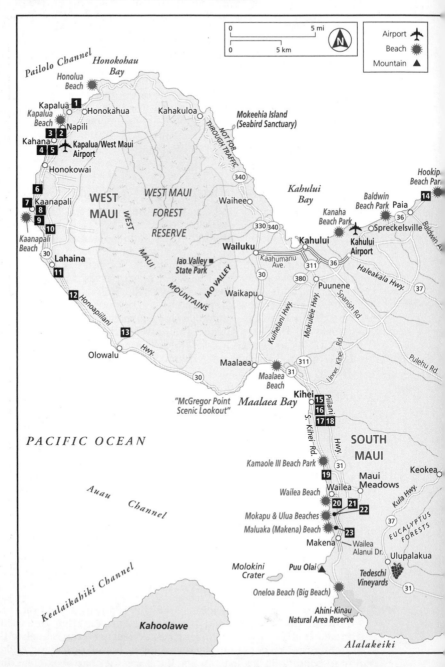

0 ___ 5 mi
0 ___ 5 km

Airport ✈
Beach ✳
Mountain ▲

Pailolo Channel
Honokohau Bay
Honolua Beach
Kapalua **1** ○Honokahua
Kahakuloa
Mokeehia Island (Seabird Sanctuary)
Kapalua Beach
Napili
3 **2**
Kahana **4** **5** Kapalua/West Maui Airport
Honokowai
6
WEST MAUI
WEST MAUI FOREST RESERVE
7 Kaanapali
8
9
10
Kaanapali Beach
30
Lahaina
11
12 Honoapiilani
Hwy.
13
Olowalu
30
Waihee
340
330 340
Kahului Bay
Baldwin Beach Park
Kanaha Beach Park
Paia
Hookip Beach Par
14
36
Spreckelsville
Baldwin Av.
Wailuku
Kahului
Kahului Airport
Iao Valley State Park ■
Kaahumanu Ave.
311
36
37
Haleakala Hwy.
IAO VALLEY
WEST MAUI MOUNTAINS
30
Waikapu
380
Puunene
Kuihelani Hwy.
Mokulele Hwy.
Spanish Rd.
Pulehu Rd.
Maalaea
311
31
Maalaea Beach
Kihei
Piilani
15
16
17 **18**
"McGregor Point Scenic Lookout"
Maalaea Bay
S. Kihei Rd.
Piilani Hwy.
SOUTH MAUI
Keokea
PACIFIC OCEAN
Kamaole III Beach Park
19
31
Maui Meadows
Kula Hwy.
Auau Channel
Wailea Beach
Wailea
20 **21**
22
37
Mokapu & Ulua Beaches
Maluaka (Makena) Beach
Makena
23
Wailea Alanui Dr.
Ulupalakua
EUCALYPTUS FORESTS
Molokini Crater
Puu Olai ▲
Oneloa Beach (Big Beach)
Tedeschi Vineyards
31
Kealaikahiki Channel
Ahini-Kinau Natural Area Reserve
Kahoolawe
Alalakeiki

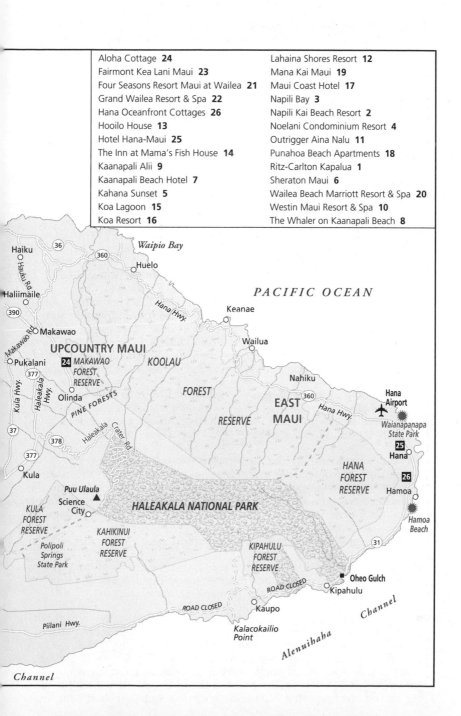

Aloha Cottage **24**

Fairmont Kea Lani Maui **23**

Four Seasons Resort Maui at Wailea **21**

Grand Wailea Resort & Spa **22**

Hana Oceanfront Cottages **26**

Hooilo House **13**

Hotel Hana-Maui **25**

The Inn at Mama's Fish House **14**

Kaanapali Alii **9**

Kaanapali Beach Hotel **7**

Kahana Sunset **5**

Koa Lagoon **15**

Koa Resort **16**

Lahaina Shores Resort **12**

Mana Kai Maui **19**

Maui Coast Hotel **17**

Napili Bay **3**

Napili Kai Beach Resort **2**

Noelani Condominium Resort **4**

Outrigger Aina Nalu **11**

Punahoa Beach Apartments **18**

Ritz-Carlton Kapalua **1**

Sheraton Maui **6**

Wailea Beach Marriott Resort & Spa **20**

Westin Maui Resort & Spa **10**

The Whaler on Kaanapali Beach **8**

stay away if it's been raining because unpaved sections of the road can wash out. And check with your rental-car company before you set out; many rental contracts actually *forbid* customers from driving their cars on Kaupo Road.

Getting around without wheels

Operated by Roberts Hawaii, the **Maui Bus** public transit service (☎ 808-871-4838; www.co.maui.hi.us/bus) runs 11 bus routes between Kahului, West Maui, South Maui, Paia, Haiku, and Upcountry Maui. Both the upcountry and Paia/Haiku routes stop at the Kahului Airport; however, keep in mind that only one medium-size suitcase is allowed per passenger. The fare is $1 per boarding. Routes run generally from 5 a.m. to 10 p.m., but you should call or check the online route map to figure out your most suitable route and schedule.

Maui does have islandwide taxi service. The meter can run up fast, but a taxi will get you where you need to go if you don't have your own wheels. Call **Alii Cab** (☎ 808-661-3688), **Maui Airport Taxi** (☎ 808-281-9533; www.nokaoitaxi.com), **Kihei Taxi** (☎ 808-879-3000), **Wailea Taxi** (☎ 808-874-5000), or **Maui Taxi Service** (☎ 808-276-9515; www.maui pleasanttaxi.com). The mandated fare on Maui is $3 per mile, accommodating one to six people. For limousine service, contact **Star Limousine** (☎ 877-875-6900 or 808-669-6900; www.limohawaii.com) or **Maui Executive Transportation** (☎ 800-833-2303; www.mauishuttle. com). Taxis also cruise Lahaina in the evening, should you have an extra tipple or two and require a sober driver to take you back to the condo.

If you're going to skip renting a car on Maui, a good bet is to base yourself in Lahaina, where restaurants, shops, and attractions are right at hand. Your beach enjoyment will be limited, though; Lahaina does have a beach, but it's not the greatest.

An even better alternative for auto-free visitors is basing yourself in Kaanapali — the beach is excellent here, and restaurants and shops are right at hand in Whalers Village. A free resort shuttle connects hotels, golf, and other attractions within the resort, but most of Kaanapali's attractions are within walking distance of one another. Ask the concierge or front desk staff at your hotel for details on the Kaanapali Resort Shuttle, which provides free transportation throughout the resort daily from 9 a.m. to 11 p.m.

Kapalua and Wailea also have local resort shuttles that you can rely upon to transport you between destinations within the resort: to the golf course, to local restaurants, and to resort shops.

If you're coming to Maui and not renting a car, ultimately, your best bet may be to call the concierge at the hotel where you'll be staying before you leave home. He or she will be able to give you a clear heads-up on how convenient the hotel or resort is to nearby restaurants, shopping, and the beach, as well as what kinds of transport are readily available for you to get to other destinations on the island. Also see Chapter 13 for info on bus tours that can pick you up and drop you off at your hotel.

Staying in Style

Ever-popular Maui boasts a terrific crop of resorts. But high demand means that both resort hotels and condos can — and do — garner ridiculously high rack rates. Take heart, however: Some good bargains are available, especially in the condo market. I've reviewed some of the best values in the pages that follow. Those of you who want an even wider array of budget-friendly options should contact one of the condo-rental agencies listed at the end of this section.

 You may be able to save more money on Maui than anywhere else in Hawaii by purchasing a value-added package deal, especially if you're looking for an upscale vacation. Packagers scoop up huge numbers of Maui hotel rooms, and because they're buying rooms in bulk, they can negotiate substantial price breaks and pass the savings on to you in combination with airfares, car rentals, and the like. (Some packagers can arrange land-only vacations if you already have your plane tickets covered.) See Chapter 5 for tips on where to look for package deals.

Maui's best accommodations

In the following listings, each property is followed by a number of dollar signs, ranging from one ($) to five ($$$$$). Each represents the median rack-rate price range for a double room per night, as follows:

$	Cheap — less than $150 per night
$$	Still affordable — $150–$225
$$$	Moderate — $225–$325
$$$$	Expensive but not ridiculous — $325–$450
$$$$$	Ultraluxurious — more than $450 per night

 Don't be scared off by the "rack rates" listed in these hotel reviews. You almost never *need* to pay the asking price for a hotel room. See Chapter 7 for tips on how to avoid paying full price.

Also, don't forget that the state adds 11.42 percent in taxes to your hotel bill.

Aloha Cottage
$$–$$$ Upcountry Maui

Ron and Ranjana Serle, refugees from Philadelphia who made Upcountry Maui their permanent home some years ago, have crafted a jungle oasis on the slopes of Haleakala for romance-seeking couples. They have built two gorgeous studio-style vacation-rental cottages on their lush upcountry acreage, which is dense with eucalyptus, bamboo, banana trees, and fragrant tropical blooms. Ron and Ranjana have transported their love of Thai and Southeast Asian architecture to the cottages — literally. The Thai

Tree House is a copy of a Chiang Mai river house, reinvented for jungle living. The spacious vaulted-ceiling cottage is outfitted with imported furniture and materials. Exotic Thai details are everywhere, from the teak floors to the kitchen cabinetry to the oriental carpets. The luxuriant king bed, with its leaded glass headboard, is the centerpiece of the cottage. Your other option is the Bali Bungalow, an octagonal cottage with a glorious interior rich with Balinese influence. Lovely touches include the gorgeous silk bedspread, the overhead skylight that's perfect for bedtime stargazing, a marble shower with a dual-head shower system for two, and Asian-style dining, on sofas with a low table. Both beautiful cottages feature full, well-outfitted kitchens (the Bali Bungalow's is the larger of the two); a large lanai with a soaking tub for two; TV with VCR; and plenty of privacy. Really, it's hard to get more romantic than this — perfect for honeymooners. In fact, Ranjana can host small weddings on the gorgeous grounds, cater romantic meals for two in the Lotus House meditation cottage, arrange for an in-cottage massage, or teach a private yoga session for two (she's a certified instructor).

See map p. 229. 1879 Olinda Rd., Makawao (5 minutes uphill from town). ☎ *888-328-3330 or 808-573-8500 Fax: 808-573-2551.* www.alohacottage.com. *Parking: Free. Rack rates: $260–$295; $215–$230 per night for stays of 7 nights or more. Additional maid service charge for stays of less than 7 nights. MC, V.*

Fairmont Kea Lani Maui
$$$$$ South Maui (Wailea)

This fanciful Moorish palace is just as pricey as Maui's other luxury resorts, but it gives you so much more room for your money. Spread out and enjoy a giant one-bedroom suite, complete with a gorgeous living room with a full entertainment center (CD and DVD players, plus a second TV in the bedroom); a wet bar with coffeemaker and microwave; a mammoth marble bathroom with a soaking tub big enough for two, double sinks, separate shower, and terrific toiletries; and a furnished lanai. The two- and three-bedroom villas are even more luxurious, each boasting a gourmet kitchen, a washer and dryer, a gas barbecue and plunge pool on the private patio, and a prime on-the-sand location. Amenities include three swimming pools (one for adults only), two Jacuzzis, an excellent spa (second only to the neighboring Grand Wailea's), a fitness center, a full beach activities center, and a wealth of daily activities and kids' programs. It's a first-rate choice on every level.

See map p. 227. 4100 Wailea Alanui Dr., Wailea. ☎ *800-441-1414 or 808-875-4100. Fax: 808-875-1200.* www.kealani.com. *Valet parking: $18. Self-parking: Free. Rack rates: $450–$1,200 suite; $1,100–$2,500 2- or 3-bedroom villa. Golf and spa packages and breakfast-inclusive deals available. AE, DC, DISC, MC, V.*

Four Seasons Resort Maui at Wailea
$$$$$ South Maui (Wailea)

I personally prefer the neighboring Fairmont or Grand Wailea, but there's no doubting the Four Seasons brand for a premier luxury experience.

Lahaina and Kaanapali Accommodations & Dining

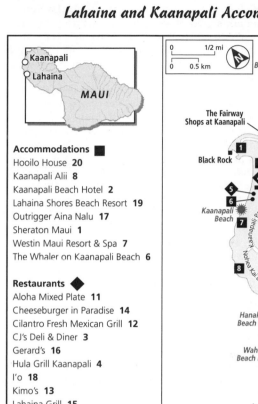

Accommodations ■
Hooilo House **20**
Kaanapali Alii **8**
Kaanapali Beach Hotel **2**
Lahaina Shores Beach Resort **19**
Outrigger Aina Nalu **17**
Sheraton Maui **1**
Westin Maui Resort & Spa **7**
The Whaler on Kaanapali Beach **6**

Restaurants ◆
Aloha Mixed Plate **11**
Cheeseburger in Paradise **14**
Cilantro Fresh Mexican Grill **12**
CJ's Deli & Diner **3**
Gerard's **16**
Hula Grill Kaanapali **4**
I'o **18**
Kimo's **13**
Lahaina Grill **15**
Leilani's on the Beach **5**
Mala, An Ocean Tavern **9**

Luaus
The Feast at Lele **18**
Old Lahaina Luau **10**

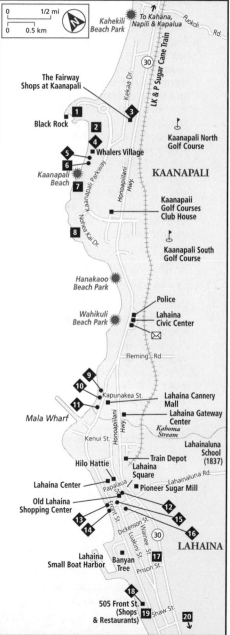

Averaging an extra-large 640 square feet (although the Kea Lani's suites are even more spacious), the guest rooms here are done in soft, warm tones and feature cushy furnishings, grand and gorgeous bathrooms (among the best in Hawaii), and big lanais. About 80 percent have ocean views, but beware those that overlook the driveway — it's a real mood killer. You're better off with a gardenview room overlooking the lovely sculpture gardens and waterfalls. The mountainview rooms are a good value for pricey Maui, considering the quality of the accommodations and service. The gorgeous grounds overflow with first-rate facilities — including the only Hawaii branch of Wolfgang Puck's legendary Spago restaurant and a sublime spa. The beach is one of Maui's finest, and the service is exceptional. If you prefer to lounge poolside, you can recline in comfort under a shaded cabana or on a grassy lawn; a pool attendant will even bring you chilled towels and spritz you with Evian. The kids will be duly pampered in an excellent activities program.

See map p. 227. 3900 Wailea Alanui Dr., Wailea. ☎ *800-334-6284 or 808-874-8000. Fax: 808-874-6449.* www.fourseasons.com/maui. *Rack rates: $475–$1,005 double, $1,045–$5,510 suite. Valet parking: $18. Multiple package deals almost always on offer, including room-and-car, bed-and-breakfast, golf, spa, and others. Also ask about 5th-night-free deals and special family rates. AE, DC, DISC, MC, V.*

Grand Wailea Resort & Spa
$$$$$ South Maui (Wailea)

Now part of the prestigious Waldorf=Astoria collection of luxury hotels, this monument to moneyed excess won me over with its lush, art-filled grounds (boasting works by such masters as Botero, Legér, Picasso, and Warhol) and its exclusive tropical-theme-park vibe. The fantastic 50,000-square-foot Spa Grande is the island's ultimate temple to the pampered life, whereas the pool complex is Hawaii's best water playground, a fantasy of falls, rapids, slides, grottos, hidden hot tubs, and swim-up bars, plus the world's only water-powered elevator. Rooms are huge and elegantly appointed, with luxurious marble bathrooms. If you can afford it, stay in the Napua Tower; this exclusive 100-room hotel-within-a-hotel offers personalized concierge service plus free continental breakfast. Restaurants, shops, and lounges abound, and both food and service are first-rate. And bring the kids — they'll think that they've died and gone to heaven, especially after they see the whopping 20,000-square-foot kids' camp. Despite the resort's grandness, you'll still feel comfortable roaming around in your beach togs. This elegant fantasyland is an ideal place to tie the knot, too, because it's home to a picture-perfect seaside wedding chapel. Minimalists, on the other hand, should book elsewhere.

See map p. 227. 3850 Wailea Alanui Dr., Wailea. ☎ *800-888-6100 or 808-875-1234. Fax: 808-874-2442.* www.grandwailea.com. *Valet parking: $20. Rack rates: $625–$1,180 double, $1,900 and way up suite. Mandatory $25-per-night "resort fee" for "free" self-parking, "free" local and 800 calls, in-room coffee, daily fitness classes, and other resort extras. Numerous packages are usually available, including bed-and-breakfast, seventh night free, spa, golf, kids, and more; from $499 at press time. AE, DC, DISC, MC, V.*

Kapalua, Napili, & Kahana Accommodations & Dining

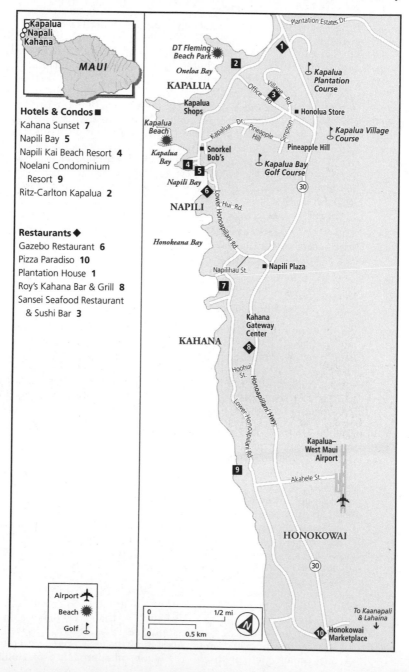

MAUI

Kapalua
Napili
Kahana

Hotels & Condos ■

Kahana Sunset **7**
Napili Bay **5**
Napili Kai Beach Resort **4**
Noelani Condominium
  Resort **9**
Ritz-Carlton Kapalua **2**

Restaurants ◆

Gazebo Restaurant **6**
Pizza Paradiso **10**
Plantation House **1**
Roy's Kahana Bar & Grill **8**
Sansei Seafood Restaurant
  & Sushi Bar **3**

Plantation Estates Dr.

DT Fleming
Beach Park

Oneloa Bay

KAPALUA

Kapalua
Shops

Kapalua
Beach

Kapalua
Bay

Napili Bay

Office Rd.

Village Rd.

Kapalua Dr.

Pineapple
Hill

Simpson

Kapalua
Plantation
Course

Honolua Store

Kapalua Village
Course

Pineapple Hill

Kapalua Bay
Golf Course

Snorkel
Bob's

NAPILI

Lower Hui Rd.

Honokeana Bay

Lower Honoapiilani Rd.

Napilihau St.

Napili Plaza

Kahana
Gateway
Center

KAHANA

Hoohui St.

Honoapiilani Hwy.

Lower Honoapiilani Rd.

Kapalua–
West Maui
Airport

Akahele St.

HONOKOWAI

Airport ✈

Beach ✺

Golf ⚑

0   1/2 mi

0   0.5 km

To Kaanapali
& Lahaina
↓

Honokowai
Marketplace

Hana Oceanfront Cottages
$$$ Hana

Housed in two plantation-style buildings built by friendly California refugees Dan and Sandi Simoni, these two marvelous one-bedroom units are fully outfitted for Hana living. Each comes complete with a living room, a fully appointed gourmet kitchen, supercomfortable furniture (including beautifully made beds), a full bath, a TV with VCR and DVD player, a CD player, and a big lanai with ocean views. The Beach Suite gives you a bit more space, while the Beach Cottage gives you a bit more privacy and puts you closer to the surf. The property boasts lush, mature tropical grounds. Best of all, paradise-like Hamoa Beach, East Maui's finest swimming spot — which James Michener called "the most beautiful beach in the world" — is just steps away. A simply delightful place to stay, whether or not you can afford the luxurious Hotel Hana-Maui down the road. Say hello if you see Dan and Sandi's next-door neighbor — Oprah Winfrey owns the adjacent 4 acres.

See map p. 218. Hana Highway, Hana. ☎ *808-248-7558. Parking: Free. Rack rates: $250–$275. 10 percent discount available for weeklong stays; 3-night minimum for stays booked within 2 months of arrival, 4-night minimum for more advanced bookings. $75 cleaning fee. MC, V.*

Hooilo House
$$$$ West Maui (Lahaina)

Perched on a breezy hill above the West Maui coast is this elegant bed-and-breakfast, coined Hooilo ("winter") House by its innkeepers, who sought refuge from the colder climes of the Pacific Northwest and Alaska and chose Maui as their ultimate escape. Each of the six guest suites features a comfortable custom king bed, an extra-large marble bathroom with a tub and a private outdoor shower lined in lava rock, and a lanai furnished for lounging with tranquil garden or ocean views.

The house is designed and decorated in the Balinese style. Practically every wall is a window that opens to the breeze; the hallways are open-air bridges that cross koi-filled riverlets, and each guest room is entered through an imported Balinese door inlaid with Mother of Pearl that sets the mood for something special, including such creative details as shower heads crafted from stone-carved masks and bamboo. The owners live in an adjacent cottage, so guests feel free to lounge or play a board game in the house's common area, which overlooks a lovely 4-foot-deep pool with panoramic ocean views. This is the site for the morning buffet spread, which you can enjoy at your leisure. I also like the full daily maid service, which isn't a given at all home-style accommodations. However, I do have a few quibbles: The bedrooms are a hair's-breadth smaller than I wish they were. The outdoor shower is delightful, except when the wind kicks up; I wish I had a shower option indoors. In a place with this much attention to detail, I don't understand why the small TVs have VCRs rather than DVD players. In a luxury B&B designed for romance, there should really be a hot tub, as well as a pool designed for more than dipping. And I think the innkeepers are a bit too aloof — but you may actually prefer the hands-off approach. Still, Hoolio House

South Maui Accommodations & Dining

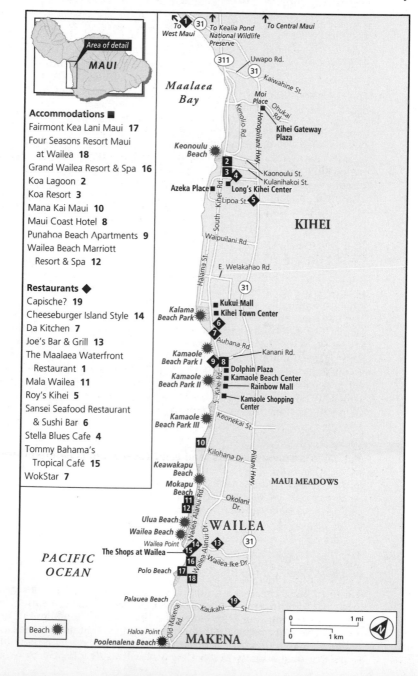

Accommodations ■

Fairmont Kea Lani Maui **17**

Four Seasons Resort Maui
at Wailea **18**

Grand Wailea Resort & Spa **16**

Koa Lagoon **2**

Koa Resort **3**

Mana Kai Maui **10**

Maui Coast Hotel **8**

Punahoa Beach Apartments **9**

Wailea Beach Marriott
Resort & Spa **12**

Restaurants ◆

Capische? **19**

Cheeseburger Island Style **14**

Da Kitchen **7**

Joe's Bar & Grill **13**

The Maalaea Waterfront
Restaurant **1**

Mala Wailea **11**

Roy's Kihei **5**

Sansei Seafood Restaurant
& Sushi Bar **6**

Stella Blues Cafe **4**

Tommy Bahama's
Tropical Café **15**

WokStar **7**

Beach ✺

is a tranquil, romantic retreat, and a convenient drive to beaches and the restaurants and nightlife of Lahaina. Not suitable for children.

See map p. 223. 138 Awaiku St. (off Kai Hele Ku Road, a mile uphill from Honoapiilani Highway, Highway, Highway 30), Lahaina. ☎ 808-667-6669. www.hooilohouse.com. Parking: Free. Rack rates: $345 double. 15 percent discount for stays of 5 nights or longer. AE, MC, V.

Hotel Hana-Maui
$$$$$ Hana

The Hotel Hana-Maui, a breathtaking oceanfront property that had languished in disrepair for too many years, was gloriously reborn a few years ago, I'm happy to report. The same folks behind Big Sur's amazing Post Ranch Inn have transformed this property into one of Maui's most magical resorts, making it reason enough to cruise to Maui's remote eastern shore. The small hotel has just 66 rooms and suites nestled in one-story Hawaiian-style cottages; its expansive and meticulously landscaped grounds slope gently down to glorious Hana Bay, allowing for plenty of privacy and quiet relaxation. Both the setting and the warmhearted staff exude an old-Hawaii feeling. Accommodations boast only the most luxe comforts: Warm and welcoming designer-stylish interiors featuring indigenous island materials, textiles, and patterns. The duplex Sea Ranch cottages are the most luxurious, with cathedral ceilings, gorgeous oversize bathrooms, and private lanais; about half have patio Jacuzzis. But you can't go wrong with the lowrise Bay View suites a little farther up the slope if your wallet is tighter. A lack of TVs, radios, and air-conditioning (you don't need it out here) suits the mood perfectly; no one travels to the end of the road in Hana to watch CNN. (The common Club Room has a giant-screen TV and Internet access if you really need a fix.) A wealth of marvelous outdoor activities — from cultural walks and horseback riding to sunbathing at Hamoa Beach, which James Michener once called the most beautiful beach in the world — will keep you content, as does the utterly pampering and peaceful Honua Spa. The one downside: You may get tired of the cuisine after a time, since there are no other restaurants in Hana other than the hotel's own.

See map p. 218. At Hana Ranch, Hana Highway, Hana. ☎ 800-321-HANA or 808-248-8211. Fax: 808-248-7202. www.hotelhanamaui.com. Valet parking: Free. Rack rates: $495–$525 Bay cottage for 2, $650–$1,625 Sea Ranch cottage for 2, $1,675 2-bedroom suite, $4,000 2-bedroom Plantation guesthouse. Numerous value-added packages available, with oceanview Sea Ranch cottages from $495 at press time; call or check Web site for current offers. AE, DC, DISC, MC, V.

The Inn at Mama's Fish House
$$ East Maui: On the Road to Hana

These tropical cottages on one of Maui's most gorgeous oceanfront lots are ideal for those who want a quiet but still-central location. Nestled in a coconut grove on secluded Kuau Cove — just a ten-minute drive from the airport — six beautifully outfitted vacation rentals feature rattan furnishings, lovely local artwork, terra-cotta floors, and complete kitchens (even dishwashers). Extras like big TVs with DVD, CD players, Weber gas

Paia & Upcountry Maui Orientation, Accommodations & Dining

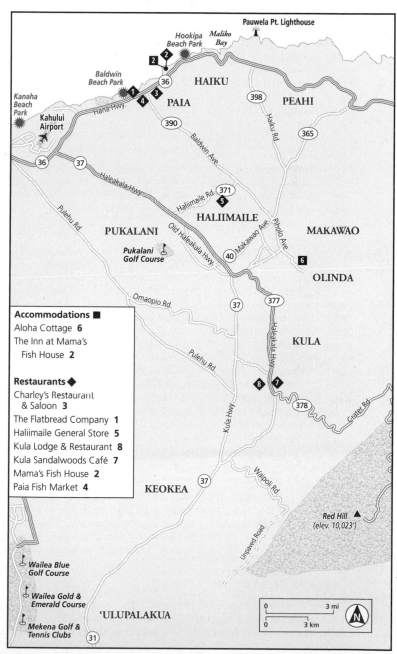

Pauwela Pt. Lighthouse

Hookipa Beach Park
Maliko Bay

Baldwin Beach Park

HAIKU

36

PAIA

398

PEAHI

Kanaha Beach Park

Kahului Airport

Hana Hwy

390

Baldwin Ave

Haiku Rd

365

36

37

Haleakala Hwy

Haliimaile Rd

371

5

Pulehu Rd

PUKALANI

HALIIMAILE

Old Haleakala Hwy

Makawao Ave

Piiholo Ave

MAKAWAO

Pukalani Golf Course

40

6

OLINDA

Omaopio Rd

37

377

Haleakala Hwy

KULA

Accommodations ■
Aloha Cottage **6**
The Inn at Mama's
 Fish House **2**

Pulehu Rd

8

7

378

Crater Rd

Restaurants ◆
Charley's Restaurant
 & Saloon **3**
The Flatbread Company **1**
Haliimaile General Store **5**
Kula Lodge & Restaurant **8**
Kula Sandalwoods Café **7**
Mama's Fish House **2**
Paia Fish Market **4**

Kula Hwy

Waipoli Rd

KEOKEA

37

Red Hill ▲
(elev. 10,023')

Unpaved Road

Wailea Blue Golf Course

Wailea Gold & Emerald Course

Mekena Golf & Tennis Clubs

'ULUPALAKUA

31

0   3 mi
0   3 km
N

barbecues, laundry facilities, and tons of beach toys make this a great place to stay with friends or family. The one-bedrooms can sleep up to four — Mom and Dad on the queen-size bed in the bedroom, two kids on the sleeper sofa. The two-bedrooms can sleep up to six: One bedroom has a queen-size bed, and the second has a full bed or two twin beds, plus a sleeper sofa in the bedroom. Two-bedrooms also benefit from a prime beachfront location, and the one-bedrooms are just steps from the beach nestled in colorful tropical foliage. Service is thoughtful, friendly, and efficient. The divine Mama's Fish House — my favorite Maui restaurant (see review later in this chapter) — is next door, and inn guests benefit from discounts at lunch and dinner. Just down the road is hip-as-can-be Paia, the fun 'n' funky surf town that serves as the gateway to the road to Hana. The only downside? Despite the on-the-beach location, only the luxury beachfront cottage has an ocean view.

See map p. 229799 Poho Place (off the Hana Highway in Kuau), Paia. ☎ *800-860-HULA or 808-579-9764. Fax: 808-579-8594.* www.mamasfishhouse.com. *Parking: Free. Rack rates: $175 garden studio, $225 garden 1-bedroom unit, $325 garden 2-bedroom unit, $525 luxury beachfront unit. 3-night minimum stay. AE, DISC, MC, V.*

Kaanapali Alii
$$$$–$$$$$ West Maui (Kaanapali)

If you want luxury living and condo conveniences, this high-rise beachfront complex is the place for you. These are Maui's finest (and priciest) condos, but they're worth it. Each condo is privately owned, so decor varies, but owners are held to a high standard. The one- and two-bedroom apartments are universally large (between 1,500 and 1,900 sq. ft.) and come with a fully equipped gourmet kitchen, huge living room and dining room, two TVs and VCR, two full bathrooms (even in the one-bedrooms), washer/dryer, and private lanais. The luxuriant grounds feature a fitness room, tennis, a smallish heated pool with hot tub and poolside snack service plus a separate kids' pool, a beach activities center, and poolside gas grills for fun family meals. Among the resortlike amenities are daily maid service; concierge, bell, valet, and room service; complimentary kids' club activities in summer; yoga classes; and even grocery delivery and a resident tennis pro. Service is friendly and accommodating. Best of all, the location — oceanfront at the southern end of fabulous Kaanapali Beach — simply can't be beat. An excellent choice on all fronts.

See map p. 223. 50 Nohea Kai Dr., Kaanapali. ☎ *800-642-6284 or 808-661-3339. Fax: 808-667-1145.* www.classicresorts.com. *Parking: Free. Rack rates: $425–$695 1-bedroom, $590–$975 2-bedroom. 3- to 5-night minimum stay, depending on the date. Numerous deals are usually on offer, including 5th-night-free, room-and-car, and romance packages; 1-bedrooms from $316 at press time. AE, DC, MC, V.*

Kaanapali Beach Hotel
$$–$$$ West Maui (Kaanapali)

The Kaanapali Beach is the last hotel left in Hawaii that gives you a real resort experience in this price range. It's older and it's not luxurious, but it boasts a genuine spirit of aloha that's absent in many other hotels. Set beachfront around a wide, grassy lawn with a whale-shaped pool, three low-rise wings house spacious, well-maintained rooms. They may be rather motel-like, but they're nevertheless perfectly comfortable and feature all the conveniences, plus lanais overlooking the pretty yard or beach. Tiki torches, hula, and music create an irresistible Hawaiian ambience every evening, and the service is some of the friendliest around. An extensive Hawaiiana program goes beyond the standard hula lessons to include Lauhala weaving, lei making, and cultural tours. A kids' program, three just-fine restaurants, and a coin-op laundry are also on-site. This hotel is one of my all-time favorites, and one of *Travel + Leisure*'s too: The magazine has dubbed the Kaanapali Beach Hotel as Hawaii's top hotel for value, and second-best hotel in the world for less than $200 a night. Unfortunately, rates have begun to climb, but they remain relatively affordable considering the excellent location and warm spirit of the place.

See map p. 223. 2525 Kaanapali Pkwy., Kaanapali. ☎ *800-262-8450 or 808-661-0011. Fax: 808-667-5978.* www.kbhmaui.com. *Self-parking: $9. Valet parking: $11. Rack rates: $199–$355 double, $277–$485 suite. Free-car, free-night, golf, and romance packages are almost always available, as well as senior (50+) and corporate discounts and Internet specials. AE, DC, DISC, MC, V.*

Kahana Sunset
$$–$$$ West Maui (Kahana/Napili)

These oceanfront condos are an excellent value, one of Maui's best. The attractive wooden complex stair-steps down pretty terraced grounds to a petite but perfect swimming cove fringed with white sands. The apartments are roomy enough to accommodate families, especially the two-bedrooms, which boast two full bathrooms. Every unit has attractive island-style furniture; a complete kitchen with dishwasher, microwave, and even an icemaker in the fridge; washer/dryer; DVD player and sleeper sofa in the living room; and big lanais with terrific views. Nestled between the coastline and the road above, the complex is much more private than many on this condo coast. On-site are a lovely heated pool and Jacuzzi, a separate kids' pool, barbecues, and beach showers. What's more, daily maid service (not a given in condos) makes it actually feel like vacation.

See map p. 225. 4909 Lower Honoapiilani Hwy., at the northern end of Kahana (8 miles north of Lahaina). ☎ *800-669-1488, or 808-669-8700. Fax: 808-669-4466.* www.kahanasunset.com *or* www.premier-hawaii.com. *Parking: Free. Rack rates: $165–$290 1-bedroom, $225–$465 2-bedroom. 2-night minimum. Car-and-condo packages, special rates, and Internet offers often available. AE, MC, V.*

Koa Lagoon
$$ South Maui (Kihei)

This delightful condo complex just may be the top bargain of the Kihei coast. This midrise building has 42 units — all with a breathtaking oceanfront setting with views that most visitors have to pay much more to enjoy. Each large one-bedroom (700 sq. ft. plus lanai) or two-bedroom (975 sq. ft. plus lanai) apartment is nicely decorated and smartly outfitted. Features include large furnished lanais, a full all-electric kitchen with dishwasher and microwave, a washer/dryer, a TV with VCR or DVD, a sofa bed in the living room, and air-conditioning (not the best, but you're unlikely to need it). Unlimited free local calls and free high-speed Internet access are nice pluses. On the impeccably maintained grounds you'll find a heated pool and gas barbecues to share with your fellow residents — plus those wonderful ocean views, which come alive with whale sightings in the winter months, and nightly year-round at the sunset hour (the building is western facing). Unit 503 is particularly popular thanks to its spectacular sightlines. The whole place is consistently clean and well taken care of, with friendly and professional service. I also like the location at the north end of Kihei, which is relatively quiet and convenient to the rest of the island's sights and attractions. All in all, one of Maui's finest values.

See map p. 227. 800 S. Kihei Rd., Kihei. Reservations c/o Bello Realty. ☎ *800-367-8030 or 808-879-3002. Fax: 808-874-0429.* www.koalagoon.com. *Parking: Free. Rack rates: $140–$180 1-bedroom, $170–$210 2-bedroom. AE, MC, V.*

Koa Resort
$ South Maui (Kihei)

These condos aren't fancy, but they sit right across the street from the ocean, and they make a good choice for active families on tight budgets: On-site are two tennis courts, a very nice swimming pool, a hot tub, and an 18-hole putting green. The spacious, privately owned one-, two-, and three-bedroom units are fully equipped and have plenty of room for even a large clan. Each comes with a full kitchen (complete with dishwasher, microwave, and coffeemaker), a large lanai, ceiling fans, and a washer/dryer. The majority of two- and three-bedroom units have multiple bathrooms. The smaller units have showers only, so ask for one with a tub if it matters to you. Also, for maximum peace and quiet, ask for a unit removed from Kihei Road.

See map p. 227. 811 S. Kihei Rd. (between Kulanihakoi Street and Namauu Place), Kihei. Reservations c/o Bello Realty. ☎ *800-541-3060 or 808-879-3328. Fax: 808-875-1483.* www.bellomauivacations.com. *Parking: Free. Rack rates: $99–$115 1-bedroom, $100–$140 2-bedroom, $160–$240 3-bedroom. AE, MC, V.*

Lahaina Shores Resort
$$–$$$ West Maui (Lahaina)

This dated but pleasant plantation-style complex of studios and one-bedroom suites sits right on the sand at the quiet end of Lahaina, within easy walking distance of restaurants, shopping, and entertainment, but nicely out of the noisy fray. The hotel is more basic than stylish, but the units are comfortable and decently outfitted, and the price is right, especially considering the on-the-beach location. Even the smallest unit is a spacious 550 square feet. Every one comes with a fully equipped kitchen (with microwave), sitting and dining areas, and a furnished lanai. Obviously, those units overlooking the waves and the island of Lanai across the channel are best, but the mountain views aren't shabby here either; still, given the all-around good value, splurge on an ocean view if you can. Do know, however, that individually owned units can vary in quality; some have been recently updated, while others need attention. When you book, inquire about the specific quality and features of your unit. Outside is a lovely grassy lawn with a small pool, hot tub, and lounge chairs; just beyond it is a narrow stretch of swimming beach. (First-time surfers often learn on the low-riding waves here.) Other pleasantries include on-site laundry facilities, and tennis courts just across the street. Best for those who want a good price on an in-town, close-to-conveniences location. Note that units can be rented through two different brokers (see below), so I highly recommend that you price compare.

See map p. 223. 475 Front St. (near Shaw Street), Lahaina. ☎ *800-367-5242 (Condominium Rentals Hawaii), 800-642-6284 (Classic Resorts), or 808-661-4835. Fax: 808-667-1145.* www.crhmaui.com *or* www.lahainashores.com. *Parking: $3. Rack rates: $167–$215 studio, $240–$340 1-bedroom, $290–$370 penthouse. $35 reservation fee added to every booking. 7th-night-free and room-and-car specials offered at press time. Discounts available for stays longer than 1 week. AE, MC, V.*

Mana Kai Maui
$–$$ South Maui (Kihei)

Situated on a beautiful white-sand beach with excellent snorkeling, this eight-story hotel-condo hybrid is one of my favorite affordable choices. About half the units are hotel rooms, which are smallish but offer great value. The larger one- and two-bedroom apartments feature full up-to-date kitchens, nice island-style furnishings, well-maintained bathrooms, and open living rooms that lead to small lanais with ocean views. These units are older, but they're clean and comfortable, thanks to daily maid service. A coin-op laundry is located on each floor, a restaurant and lounge are downstairs, and a nice pool and a grassy lawn with beach chairs complement that fabulous beach. Management is friendly and conscientious. But the Mana Kai's real ace in the hole is its location: It lies on Wailea's doorstep, on the prettiest, most quiet end of Kihei, away from the strip-mall fray. Maui Yoga Path operates an open-air studio on the Mana Kai grounds, offering daily classes by the ocean.

See map p. 227. 2960 S. Kihei Rd., Kihei (just before Wailea). ☎ *800-367-5242 (800-663-2101 from Canada) or 808-879-2778. Fax: 808-879-7825.* www.crhmaui.com. *Parking: Free. Rack rates: $120–$201 double hotel room, $205–$377 1-bedroom, $255–$438 2-bedroom. $35 reservation fee added to every booking. 7th-night-free and room-and-car specials offered at press time. Discounts available for stays longer than 1 week. AE, MC, V.*

Maui Coast Hotel
$$ South Maui (Kihei)

This affordable hotel is recommended for its good package deals, and its central (if not terribly attractive) location, about a block from the beach and a short walk away from restaurants, shopping, and nightlife. This isn't the Four Seasons, so don't expect luxury — but the clean, simple rooms feature good-value extras, including sitting areas, coffeemakers, minifridges, Nintendo game systems, and furnished lanais. Add a pretty good restaurant, room service, free use of laundry facilities, a nice pool with poolside service (plus one for the kids), two Jacuzzis, a restaurant, and tennis courts (with lights for night play), and you end up with a full-service hotel at a bargain price. The suites offer families excellent value, especially if you can find a package to suit you.

See map p. 227. 2259 S. Kihei Rd. (at Ke Alii Alanui Drive), Kihei. ☎ *800-895-6284, 800-663-1144, or 808-874-6284. Fax: 808-875-4731.* www.mauicoasthotel.com *or* www.coasthotels.com. *Parking: Free. Rack rates: $215–$245 double or alcove suite, $275–$320 suite. Inquire about breakfast, golf, romance, room-and-car, and 5th-night-free packages (from $195 with a compact car at press time); also ask about AAA, senior (55+), and best-available rates (from $184, suites from $204 at press time). Special holiday rates may apply. AE, DC, DISC, MC, V.*

Napili Bay
$–$$ West Maui (Kahana/Napili)

This excellent bargain sits on Napili's beautiful half-mile white-sand beach. This small, two-story complex is perfect for an affordable romantic getaway; the sound of the waves creates a comfortable and relaxing atmosphere. The studio apartments are definitely small, but still, you have a full kitchen (with fridge and coffeemaker), a queen-size bed, a queen-size sleeper sofa that lets you sleep two more (if you don't mind lots of togetherness), a TV with DVD, CD player, and a spacious lanai where you can sit and watch the sun set. Note that each unit is individually owned, so furnishings can vary, but the quality is consistently good. Louvered windows and ceiling fans keep the units cool during the day. You have plenty of restaurants and a convenience store within walking distance, and you're about 10 to 15 minutes away from Lahaina and some great golf courses. Coin-op washer/dryers and a barbecue are nice features. The beach right out front is one of the best on the coast, with great swimming and snorkeling right out your door. Book early, because this place fills up fast. Also note that you have two sources for booking: You can book through Maui Beachfront Rentals or Aloha Condos, which allows you to book directly from the owners themselves. Both sites feature pictures of available units so you can choose the one you like. ***Attention, Internet addicts:*** Only a few units have high-speed Internet access, so ask for one if you want it.

See map p. 225. 33 Hui Dr. (off Lower Honoapiilani Highway, in Napili). Bookings handled by Maui Beachfront Rentals, 256 Papalaua St., Lahaina. ☎ *888-661-7200 or 808-661-3500. Fax: 808-661-2649.* www.mauibeachfront.com *or* www.aloha-condos.com. *Parking: Free. Rack rates: $120–$280 studio. Check minimum-stay requirements; usually 7 nights minimum, but may vary depending on rental source. MC, V.*

Napili Kai Beach Resort
$$$–$$$$ West Maui (Kahana/Napili)

Make yourselves right at home at this complex of bright one- and two-story units embracing its own, wonderful white-sand snorkeling beach. There are a handful of basic hotel rooms with minifridges and coffeemakers, but most units have lovely tropical-modern decor, a large lanai, a DVD player, and kitchenettes (all with microwave, some with dishwasher). The one-bedrooms have sleeping accommodations in both rooms — usually a king-size bed in one room, two twin beds in the other — making this a great configuration for families; some even have a second bathroom. The two-bedrooms can sleep as many as six or seven, and all have a second bathroom. The Khaka suites unite two or three adjoining hotel rooms or studios in one value-priced package for families or shares. Most, but not all, units offer air-conditioning, so ask if you want it (you'll need it only in summer); otherwise, ceiling fans do the trick. The complex has a restaurant and bar with a great view; however, I've heard too many complaints that it's overpriced for what you get, and most guests don't dine here more than once. The beach pagoda serves daytime snacks and drinks and doles out snorkel gear for your free use. There's also daily maid service, four pools and a hot tub, barbecues, a fitness room, an 18-hole putting green, and a basic spa. During family seasons (Easter/spring break, summer, and Christmas), kids ages 6 to 10 can enjoy the supervised Keiki Club, with two hours of activities daily (except Sun), plus Wednesday-night movies. All in all a nice place to stay, if not a bargain.

See map p. 225. 5900 Honoapiilani Rd., Napili (at the extreme north end of Napili, next to Kapalua). ☎ *800-367-5030 or 808-669-6271. Fax: 808-669-0086.* www.napili kai.com. *Parking: Free. Rack rates: $230–$280 hotel room double, $285–$385 studio, $430–$700 1-bedroom or 2-room Keaka suite, $625–$1,050 2-bedroom or 3-room Keaka suite. Room-and-car, 5th-night-free, bed-and-breakfast, and spa packages often available. AE, MC, V.*

Noelani Condominium Resort
$–$$ West Maui (Kahana/Napili)

I stand by all my recommendations, but that doesn't mean I don't get a teensy bit nervous when my boss says that she's going to take me up on one. So I was thrilled when she came home from Maui confirming my own observations — that this top-notch oceanfront condo is a stellar value and a great place to stay. All the well-maintained apartments sport kitchens, VCRs, ceiling fans (no air-conditioning), and spectacular ocean views; all but the studios have dishwashers and washer/dryers too (self-service laundry facilities are available for studio dwellers). Best is the Antherium building, where apartments have ocean-facing lanais just 20 feet from the surf. Concierge and midweek maid service, two freshwater pools (one heated for night swimming), and an oceanfront Jacuzzi round out the good value. You're invited to a continental breakfast orientation on the first day of your stay, and mai tai parties in the evenings; oceanfront barbecues are ideal for family outings. Next door is a sandy cove that's popular with snorkelers, but you may find yourself driving to a prettier beach — at these prices, you won't mind. All in all, one of the best values the island has to offer.

See map p. 225. 4095 Lower Honoapiilani Rd., Kahana. ☎ *800-367-6030 or 808-669-8374. Fax: 808-669-7904.* www.noelani-condo-resort.com. *Rack rates: $125–$175 studio, $175–$197 1-bedroom, $240–$290 2-bedroom, $330–$357 3-bedroom. 3-night minimum. Parking: Free. Check for 5 percent Internet booking discount, weekly discounts for seniors and AAA members, and honeymoon specials. AE, MC, V.*

Outrigger Aina Nalu
$$–$$$ West Maui (Lahaina)

Run by Outrigger, the value-minded, Hawaii-based hotel chain, this well-managed plantation-style complex makes a nice place to stay, especially when you can score a good deal (which you usually can). The newly redeveloped property offers petite studios and more spacious one- and two-bedrooms with fresh, contemporary island-style decor that is more attractive than you might expect; Outrigger did a very nice job here. Studios have a microwave and minifridge; all other units have fully outfitted kitchens. All units have lush garden views, air-conditioning, and video games. The one- and two-bedroom apartments have dishwashers, sofa beds, and their own washer/dryers. Note that bathrooms have showers only, no tubs. The well-manicured grounds feature barbecues, a hot tub, and a nice pool. The larger units are perfect for families; your kids will love the heart-of-Lahaina location, and you'll appreciate the tranquil ambience that results from a peaceful side-street location (a rarity in Lahaina). The complex is very quiet in general, but ask for a unit away from the highway for minimum intrusion. Note that this two-story building has no elevators.

See map p. 223. 660 Wainee St. (between Dickenson Street and Prison Street), Lahaina. ☎ **800-688-7444** *or 808-667-9766. Fax: 808-661-3733.* www.outrigger. com. *Parking: $15. Rack rates: $229–$265 studio, $299–$335 1-bedroom, $369–$415 2-bedroom. 2-night minimum. Better-than-average discounts for AAA and AARP members and seniors (50+), plus corporate, government, and military discounts; from $129 at press time. Ask about bed-and-breakfast, room-and-car, and other package deals. AE, DC, DISC, MC, V.*

Punahoa Beach Apartments
$$ South Maui (Kihei)

With the best location in Kihei, this friendly little complex is a bona fide beachfront bargain. The setting — off noisy, traffic-congested Kihei Road, on a quiet side street that faces the ocean — is fabulous: A grassy lawn extends down to the sand, where great offshore snorkeling awaits, and a popular surfing spot sits just next door. A coin-op laundry is on-site, and markets and restaurants are but a stroll away. The apartments aren't fancy, but they're nicer than you'd expect for the money; each has a fully equipped kitchen and a lanai with great ocean views. Studios have Murphy-style queen beds, one-bedrooms have king beds, and corner-unit two-bedrooms have a queen in the master and twin beds in the second bedroom. Only a few units have air-conditioning, but ceiling fans draw in the trade winds. Guests keep coming back, so reserve your bargain unit as far in advance as possible.

See map p. 227. 2142 Iliili Rd. (off South Kihei Road, near Kamaole Beach Park I), Kihei. ☎ **800-564-4380** *or 808-879-2720. Fax: 808-875-9147.* www.punahoabeach. com. *Parking: Free. Rack rates: $116–$150 studio, $160–$231 1-bedroom, $198–$263 2-bedroom. 5-night minimum. 10 percent discount on stays of 10 nights or more Apr to mid-Dec; 15 percent discount on stays of 21 nights or more year-round. AE, DC, DISC, MC, V.*

Ritz-Carlton Kapalua
$$$$$ West Maui (Kapalua)

Situated at the end of the road in glorious Kapalua, Maui's most gorgeous planned community, the Ritz is a destination resort by virtue of its location alone. But you won't need to hop in the car every day in search of fun, because everything is right at hand: a small but fabulous beach and activities galore, including Kapalua's 54 holes of world-class, tournament-quality golf, as well as its justifiably renowned art school for vacationers who want to feed a creative appetite. The natural setting — on 50 terraced oceanfront acres, surrounded by century-old Norfolk pines and ironwood trees — is breathtaking.

Thanks to a multimillion-dollar renovation completed in early 2008, the hotel is more glorious than ever. Designed to look like a grand plantation house, the hotel is airy and graceful, with a gracious pool area, two hot tubs, and a professional croquet lawn. The spacious and tropically gorgeous rooms surpass the chain's usual high standard with heavenly featherbeds, extra-large marble bathrooms, and gorgeous island-inspired decor. The dining is excellent, especially the superb sushi bar, Kai, and the gorgeous, Asian-inspired Banyan Tree restaurant. The amenities are extensive (including a full-service spa that was dramatically expanded and upgraded as part of the renovation, a new state-of-the-art fitness center, the outstanding Ritz Kids program as well as an environmental education center for kids and teens, and a full-time cultural advisor who imbues the service and programming with genuine respect for the culture), and the service is unsurpassed. Still, some may find it a tad too formal for Hawaii. Furthermore, you might expect an on-the-beach location for these prices, but the hotel is situated slightly uphill. You may find it worthwhile to spend a few extra dollars for a club-level room; club guests enjoy individualized concierge service and five — yes, five — complimentary food presentations throughout the day, including a generous morning continental spread. Ask about the brand-new one- and two-bedroom residential suites, if you can afford to do so.

See map p. 225. 1 Ritz-Carlton Dr., Kapalua. ☎ **800-542-8680** *or 808-669-6200. Fax: 808-669-1566.* www.ritzcarlton.com. *Self-parking: Free. Valet parking: $15. Rack rates: $499–$699 double, $799–$1,500 suite. Mandatory $20-per-night "resort fee" covers such amenities as shuttle service, use of fitness center, wireless Internet access, kids' program, and other extras. Romance, golf, room-and-car, and other packages often available; rates from $395 at press time. AE, DC, DISC, MC, V.*

Sheraton Maui
$$$$$ West Maui (Kaanapali)

This expansive resort hotel boasts the best location on Kaanapali Beach: on a spectacular stretch of sand at the foot of Black Rock, one of Maui's best offshore snorkel spots. Much like its Kauai sister, this Sheraton is ideal for those who don't care for the forced formality or over-the-top excesses that often go hand-in-hand with resort vacations. The Sheraton Maui has an easygoing, open style, and great facilities for families and active types, including a nice fitness center and an open-air spa. The lagoon-like pool features lava-rock waterways, wooden bridges, and an open-air whirlpool. You're greeted with a lei upon arrival, and then the valet takes you and your luggage straight to your room so you don't need to stand in line — a smooth, personalized touch. The big, island-style rooms are attractive and comfortable, with nice features like the justly named Sheraton SweetSleeper bed, flat-panel TVs, minifridges, coffeemakers, and a private lanai. Building 6 is the place to be during whale-watch season; the rooms directly overlook one of the whales' favorite playpens. A class of oversize two-room Ohana suites is designed with families in mind; the junior suites can also suit families well, or make a great splurge for couples looking for room to spread out in luxury. Restaurants and bars (including the fun and flavorful Teppan-yaki Dan's for Benihana-style dining), a nightly torch-lighting and cliff-diving show, a terrific year-round kids' program, a spa, tennis courts, and lots of other extras further the appeal, and the location just can't be beat. A terrific hotel from start to finish — it's no surprise that this was Sheraton's North American "Hotel of the Year" in 2007.

See map p. 223. 2605 Kaanapali Pkwy., Kaanapali. ☎ *800-782-9488 or 808-661-0031. Fax: 808-661-0458.* www.sheratonmaui.com. *Valet parking: $12. Self-parking: Free. Rack rates: $500–$770 double, $900–$1,000 family or junior suite, $1,100–$5,000 luxury suite. Mandatory "resort fee" of $20 per day for "free" self-parking, local and toll-free phone calls, high-speed Internet access, yoga and pilates classes, and free dining for kids under 5, plus dining discounts for kids 6–12. Special rates and/or package deals are almost always available, including family, romance, 7th-night-free, and rental-car deals. Also ask for AAA-member and senior discounts, and look for Internet specials, which were as low as $299 at press time. AE, DC, DISC, MC, V.*

Wailea Beach Marriott Resort & Spa
$$$$$ South Maui (Wailea)

This appealing property has an airy, comfortable feel, and it's looking better than ever after a $60-million total renovation was completed in 2006. Eight buildings, all low-rise except for an eight-story tower, are thoughtfully spread over 22 gracious acres, with lots of open parklike space and a half-mile of prime oceanfront. The spacious guest rooms have all been completely redecorated with a more sleek and elegant look. There's a comprehensive kids' program for *keiki* ages 5 to 13, plus five pools — including a kid-friendly water activities playground complete with a pair of water slides — and a terrific beach out front. A good indoor/outdoor restaurant and nightly Hawaiian entertainment, a coin-op laundry, a fitness center, and the full-service Mandara Spa and salon make life easier for the grown-ups in your group, too. My biggest complaint is that the resort fee is too high, and it irks me to have to pay even more extra to access the Internet — but if you leave your computer at home, you won't notice.

See map p. 227. 3700 Wailea Alanui Dr., Wailea. ☎ *888-228-9290 888-236-2427 or 808-879-1922. Fax: 808-874-7888.* www.marriotthawaii.com. *Valet parking: $18. Self-parking: Free. Rack rates: $350–$525 double, $450–$3,250 suite. Mandatory "resort fee" of $30 a day includes discounts on hotel services, spa services and dining, unlimited local and long-distance calls to the U.S. and Canada, and self-parking; Internet access is an extra charge. Seniors (62+) receive 15 percent* *discount. AAA, government, and military discounts plus Hertz rental-car upgrades available. Marriott Rewards members also qualify for special discounts (25 percent off plus a $25-per-day resort credit at press time). Also check for packages, which usually abound. AE, DC, DISC, MC, V.*

Westin Maui Resort & Spa
$$$$$ West Maui (Kaanapali)

This hotel isn't quite as fabulous as the Grand Wailea (reviewed earlier in this chapter), but it's often cheaper, and your kids will be in water-hog heaven here, too, thanks to an 87,000-square-foot "Aquatic Playground" complete with swim-through grottoes, waterfalls, and a 128-foot water slide. (Fear not, grown-ups: You get to play in an adults-only pool and a secluded Jacuzzi.) Rooms are on the smallish side, but they're stylishly contemporary. Each and every one boasts a celestial Heavenly Bed, which will keep me coming back to Westin every time. The Heavenly Shower adds to the luxury in the bathroom, and your youngest ones can enjoy Westin's own plush-as-can-be Heavenly Cribs. A prime stretch of Kaanapali Beach and a wealth of facilities are on hand, including a well-outfitted fitness center with an array of classes, a gorgeous 13,000-square-foot spa, and a full children's program. The stylish Tropica restaurant isn't the best on Maui, but the innovative fare is just fine, and the oceanfront setting is both designer-sleek and romantic at the same time. Beware the timeshare sales-person in the lobby; if you get suckered in, don't say I didn't warn you.

See map p. 223. 2365 Kaanapali Pkwy., Kaanapali. ☎ *866-716-8112 or 808-667-2525. Fax: 808-661-5764.* www.westinmaui.com. *Valet parking: $10. Self-parking: Free. Rack rates: $515–$795 double, $1,000–$3,500 suite. Mandatory "resort fee" of $20 per day for "free" self-parking, high-speed Internet access, shuttle service, bottled water (2 per day, replenished daily), an outdoor portrait sitting and free 4x6 photo, and fitness center access. Inquire about family, golf, wedding and honeymoon, and other packages, as well as special promotions that may include a rental car. Promotional rates from $350 at press time. AE, DC, DISC, MC, V.*

The Whaler on Kaanapali Beach
$$$–$$$$$ West Maui (Kaanapali)

Not only would I stay at this beachfront mid-rise condo complex again, but I'd move in here if I could. The Whaler was built in the '70s and still sports a few "Me Decade" hallmarks, but in a good way — it feels like the kind of place where Jack Lord would keep his neighbor-island bachelor pad. The relaxing atmosphere starts in the clean-lined, open-air lobby and continues in the impeccably kept apartments. They're privately owned and individually decorated, but all have fully equipped kitchens, VCRs, marble bathrooms, and big, blue-tiled lanais. Many one-bedrooms have two full bathrooms, making them great for small families or shares. Most units have some kind of ocean view, but the garden views are also pleasant. Luxuries include daily maid service, plus bell and concierge services. The grounds are private and well-manicured, and on-site extras include an oceanfront pool and spa, five tennis courts, an exercise room, and great dining and shopping at neighboring Whalers

Village. Both property managing agents are reliable, so go with the best rate; I often find that ResortQuest has the best deals.

See map p. 223. 2481 Kaanapali Pkwy., Kaanapali. ☎ *808-661-4861. Fax: 808-661-8315. Parking: $12. Rack rates: $315–$345 studio, $305–$455 1-bedroom, $400–$880 2-bedroom. Car-and-condo packages and other bargains often available through both booking agents, so always mine for specials and off-season discounts. Ask for AAA, senior (50+), and corporate discounts, and other special rate programs. AE, DC, MC, V. Reserve through either of the following companies:* **Premier Resorts:** ☎ *800-367-7052,* www.the-whaler.com, *or* **ResortQuest:** ☎ *877-997-6667,* www.whalerkaanapali.com *or* www.resortquesthawaii.com.

Home sweet vacation condo

Well-developed Maui abounds with condo developments. I review my favorites in this chapter, but there are many more. Many complexes aren't handled by a single management company; instead, real-estate agencies tend to manage individual units throughout a variety of complexes in a given area. So if you want to expand your choices, contact one of the following agencies, which can match you up with the unit that meets your needs and budget.

For a complete selection of upscale condos throughout sunny, luxury-inded Wailea, reach out to **Destination Resorts Hawaii** (☎ **866-384-1365** or 808-891-6249; www.destinationresortshi.com). Prices start as low as $225 or so for a one-bedroom and up for a spacious oceanfront four-bedroom. Value-add packages such as fifth-night-free and car-condo deals are regularly available.

 Although all of their condos make pleasing choices, Destination Resorts' **Wailea Beach Villas** (☎ **866-901-5207** or 808-891-4500; www.waileabeach villas.com) have set a new standard for condominium luxe on Maui. New to the market in June 2006, these 98 glorious villas and "penthouses" blend luxurious, home-style comforts with first-class resort services (even fully stocked kitchens and personal chef services, if you wish) and a wonderful Wailea Beach location. Rates run $880 to $3,000 nightly for the 1,900- to 3,100-square-foot residences, with a five-night minimum stay.

 If you like the sound of the tranquil Kapalua resort but the Ritz-Carlton's luxury hotel rates are out of your league — or you simply prefer home-style amenities and privacy — consider renting an elegant condo or vacation home through **Kapalua Villas** (☎ **800-545-0018,** 800-227-6054, or 808-665-5400; www.kapaluavillas.com). Nightly rates range from $279 for a one-bedroom apartment with a fairway view to $759 for an oceanfront two-bedroom. Golf, tennis, rental-car, and romance packages are available.

 Bello Realty (☎ **800-541-3060** or 808-879-3328; www.bellomaui vacations.com) represents affordable condos throughout the Kihei/Wailea area, with prices starting as low as $99 in the low season, $115 in the high season. Be sure to check out **Koa Resort** and **Koa Lagoon,** two of Maui's best bargains (reviewed earlier in this chapter). **Condominium Rentals Hawaii** (☎ **800-367-5242** or 808-879-2778; www.crhmaui.com) has moderately priced condos throughout Maui, with a concentration in

Staying off the beaten path

Situated at the far east end of the winding Hana Highway (Highway 36/360), isolated from the rest of the island by a three-hour drive, **Hana** makes a dreamy place to kick back and stay awhile, surrounded by little but lush natural beauty. One of Maui's most popular attractions is the drive along the winding 50-plus-mile route, one of the most beautiful scenic drives in the world. (I cover it in detail in Chapter 13.)

Most people drive to Hana and back again in a day, which is an entirely doable trip. It makes for one long day, however, because the curving highway has only one lane in each direction and 50 or so one-lane bridges. What's more, because the drive itself boasts so many wonderful stops, simply getting there can turn into an all-day event. So consider making it a leisurely trip by booking a place to stay at the end of the road in lush and lovely Hana for a couple of nights. It's a good idea, except for a few downsides: Many of the area's B&Bs and rentals require a two-night stay at least (sometimes longer), and, in general, Hana accommodations aren't cheap.

If you would like to stay in Hana but you can't afford the gloriously reinvented Hotel Hana-Maui or you can't get into Hana Oceanfront Cottages (both reviewed earlier in this chapter), I recommend contacting **Hawaii's Best Bed & Breakfasts** (☎ 800-262-9912 or 808-885-4550; www.bestbnb.com), which has a wonderful selection of B&Bs, inns, and vacation rentals. The company has inspected and approved the fine choices in Hana as well as other off-the-beaten-path areas of the island. Hawaii's Best holds all of the property owners it represents to a very high standard, so you can be assured of quality lodgings if you book with the company.

Kihei, and handles the **Mana Kai** (reviewed earlier in this chapter). The car-and-condo packages and other regular specials can really up the value-to-dollar ratio on their units.

You can choose from a range of good-value apartments along West Maui's condo coast through **Maui Beachfront Rentals** (☎ 888-661-7200 or 808-661-3500; www.mauibeachfront.com). One of their best deals for budget-minded couples is the studios at the **Napili Bay,** which start out between $145 and $167. They may even be able to save you a few dollars at two of my favorite Kaanapali Beach condo complexes, **The Whaler** and **Kaanapali Alii** (reviewed earlier in this chapter). Ask about packages that include a free night or a rental car.

A Southern California–based agency, **Hawaii Condo Exchange** (☎ 800-442-0404 or 323-436-0300; www.hawaiicondoexchange.com), acts as a consolidator for condo properties throughout the islands. They represent a number of excellent properties on Maui.

You can cut out the middle man and rent directly from the owner at a number of quality condo resorts on Maui, including the terrific **Napili Bay, The Whaler,** and a few other good-quality condo resorts by visiting **Aloha Condos Hawaii** (www.alohacondos.com), a cooperative of owner-managed units; links on the site will connect you directly to the owner.

Dining Out

Maui's dining scene is excellent. The lovely and charismatic Valley Isle has attracted so many top chefs from around the globe that it's tough to choose among their outposts.

But be prepared to pay for the privilege of dining on Maui. Generally speaking, you can expect to spend more for dinner here than you will on the other islands. Maui is overflowing with restaurants, so choice isn't a problem; but you'll have to navigate a minefield of overpriced, mediocre-quality restaurants in order to get value for your dollar. The listings in this chapter offer a recommendable course of action, whether you're looking for a splurge-worthy special-occasion restaurant or a satisfying casual meal that relieves the pressure on your wallet.

Lahaina, on Maui's west shore, is the heart of the island's dining scene. Luckily, it's quite convenient — no more than a half-hour's drive or so from any of the beach resorts (45 minutes from Wailea). Many of its restaurants — even the affordable ones — boast front-row, on-the-water seats for spectacular sunset watching. But nowhere else is the minefield of mediocrity more explosive, so choose carefully.

In the restaurant listings that follow, each restaurant name is followed by a number of dollar signs, ranging from one ($) to five ($$$$$). The dollar signs are meant to give you an idea of what a complete dinner for one person — with appetizer, main course, dessert, a drink, tax, and tip — is likely to cost. The price categories go like this:

$	Cheap eats — less than $20 per person
$$	Still inexpensive — $20–$35
$$$	Moderate — $35–$50
$$$$	Pricey — $50–$75
$$$$$	Ultraexpensive — more than $75 per person

 If you're on a budget, skip the really expensive entrees and bottles of wine so that you can still enjoy yourself at the pricier restaurants. To give you a further idea of how much you can expect to spend, I also include the price range of main courses in the listings. (Prices can change at any time, of course, but restaurants usually don't raise their prices by more than a dollar or two at any given time.)

 The state adds roughly 4 percent in taxes to every restaurant bill. The percentage may vary slightly depending on the county you're in, and may be embedded in the total purchase price or shown as an independent line item on your bill. A 15 to 20 percent tip for the server is standard, just like on the mainland.

Aloha Mixed Plate
$ West Maui (Lahaina)   Local Hawaiian

This charming, cheap patio restaurant specializes in traditional pan-cultural foods of Hawaii: great saimin (ramen noodle soup), teriyaki chicken, finger-lickin' Korean-style kalbi barbecue ribs, coconut shrimp, mahimahi sandwiches, stir-frys, and other local staples, plus burgers (both taro and beef) and a succulent kalua pig sandwich. Succulent roast duck, stir frys and chow fun noodle dishes reveal the Chinese influence. Most dishes are served as complete meals (a style called "plate lunch") accompanied by "two scoop" rice and a scoop of macaroni salad; they can be ordered mini, regular, or sumo-size to customize to your appetite. Brought to you by the people behind the Old Lahaina Luau (the top luau in the islands, described later in this chapter), this colorful place serves up the best local food around. Don't expect gourmet — this is Hawaii's version of paper-plate eats, and the setting is super-casual but island colorful and friendly. But you will get real value — and in an oceanfront setting to boot! The restaurant even has a bar, so you can celebrate the sunset with a tropical cocktail or wash down your hearty meal with an ice-cold beer as long as you take a seat on the upper deck; both levels have lovely ocean views. Fruit juices and smoothies are available, too. Corn dogs and grilled cheese are available for *keiki* (kids), but the mini-size plate lunches suit smaller appetites, too.

See map p. 247. 1285 Front St. (across from Lahaina Cannery Mall), Lahaina. ☎ *808-661-3322.* www.alohamixedplate.com. *Reservations not taken. Main courses and plate lunches: $4–$13. MC, V. Open: Lunch and dinner daily.*

Capische?
$$$$$ South Maui (Wailea)   Mediterranean-Italian

Nestled in a little-known hilltop resort that caters largely to Japanese guests, this dreamy hideaway is one of Maui's true hidden gems. Capische? boasts majestic coastal vistas, an ultraromantic ambience, and service that's both friendly and professional. The menu showcases the culinary delights of the Mediterranean. Book a table on the lanai or the lovely alfresco terrace and come for sunset to maximize the views and your enjoyment. I find the starters to be the stars of the menu; begin with the delectable quail saltimbocca wrapped in apple-smoked bacon, the to-die-for *kabocha* pumpkin gnocchi in sage brown butter, or a garden-fresh *caprese* salad of buffalo mozzarella, sweet baby basil, and local Kula tomatoes. Follow with a seafood-rich cioppino, a Gorgonzola-crusted filet mignon with Maui onion jus, or one of the delightful daily specials. A pianist often adds to the ambience, sometimes accompanied by a sultry jazz singer. There's also a sexy martini lounge if you're in the mood for something shaken or stirred. Winner of the *Wine Spectator* Award of Excellence for four years running, Capische? also received Chef of the Year for owner-chef Brian Etheredge and Most Romantic restaurant kudos from readers of the *Maui No Ka Oi* magazine in 2008. This really is the most romantic spot on Maui.

Maui's Restaurants

Aloha Mixed Plate **10**
Capische? **30**
Charley's Restaurant & Saloon **35**
Cheeseburger in Paradise **14**
Cheeseburger Island Style **27**
Cilantro Fresh Mexican Grill **9**
CJ's Deli & Diner **6**
Da Kitchen **25, 32**
The Flatbread Company **33**
Gazebo Restaurant **3**
Gerard's **15**

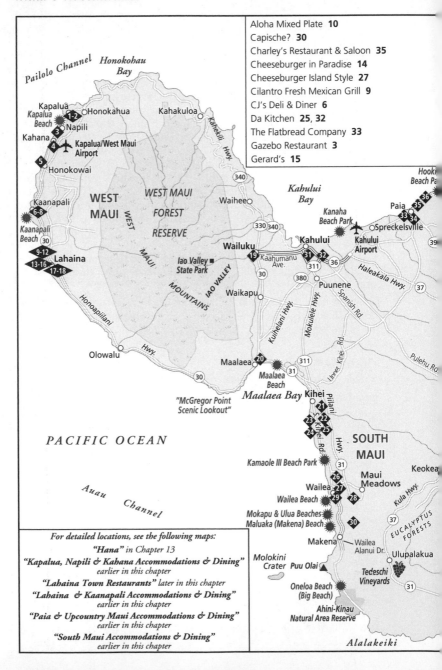

For detailed locations, see the following maps:
"Hana" in Chapter 13
"Kapalua, Napili & Kahana Accommodations & Dining" earlier in this chapter
"Lahaina Town Restaurants" later in this chapter
"Lahaina & Kaanapali Accommodations & Dining" earlier in this chapter
"Paia & Upcountry Maui Accommodations & Dining" earlier in this chapter
"South Maui Accommodations & Dining" earlier in this chapter

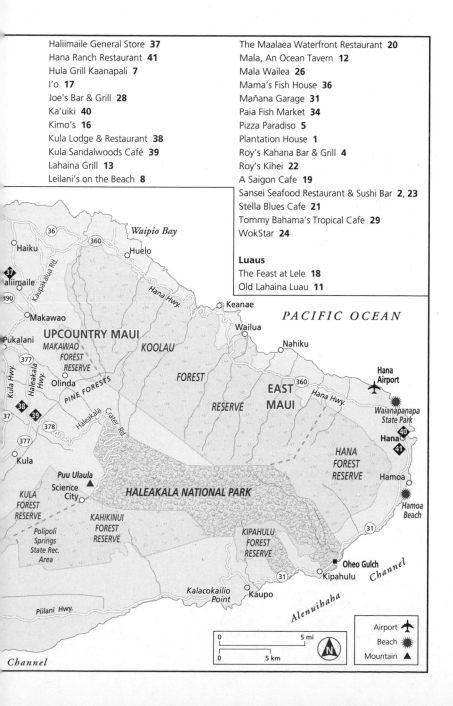

If you're in the mood for the ultimate splurge, consider a private dining, personal chef and wine pairing experience at Il Teatro at Capische; call for details.

See map p. 227. In the Diamond Hawaii Resort & Spa, 555 Kaukahi St., Wailea. ☎ *808-879-2224.* www.capische.com. *Reservations recommended. Main courses: $32–$45. AE, DC, MC, V. Open: Dinner nightly.*

Charley's Restaurant & Saloon
$–$$ **Central Maui (Paia)   American/International**

Before I set out on any drive to Hana, I always make time for a hearty breakfast at Charley's (named after the owner's Great Dane). This is my favorite breakfast place on Maui, thanks to overstuffed breakfast burritos, fluffy omelets, mac-nut pancakes, and eggs Benedict with perfectly puckery hollandaise. Lunch and dinner bring burgers, kiawe-smoked (mesquite-smoked) ribs and marlin, calzones baked fresh to order, and a variety of vegetarian delights, from veggie lasagna to bounteous salads and stir-frys. Expect nothing in the way of ambience, but service is friendly and prices are low, making Charley's worth the half-hour drive from Kihei for an affordable and unpretentious meal, even if you're not heading to Hana. The adjacent roadhouse-style bar serves up a good selection of microbrews.

See map p. 229. 142 Hana Hwy. (at Baldwin Avenue), Paia. ☎ *808-579-9453. Reservations not taken. Main courses: $6–$14 at breakfast and lunch, $12–$26 at dinner. AE, DC, DISC, MC, V. Open: Breakfast, lunch, and dinner daily.*

Cheeseburger in Paradise/Cheeseburger Island Style
$–$$ **West Maui (Lahaina)/South Maui (Wailea)   American**

This oceanfront burger joint (not affiliated with singer Jimmy Buffett's mainland chain, but sister to the Waikiki locations) is a perennial favorite thanks to an always-lively atmosphere, consistently terrific food, and million-dollar views, all at bargain-basement prices. At the original Lahaina location — the first in the burgeoning mini-chain — the second-level open-air room offers a prime ocean view from every seat. The Wailea location is set back farther from the surf, but an upstairs location gives it its own terrific ocean vistas, and the retro-hip decor sets just the right mood. No matter which location you choose, the tropical-style burgers are first-class all the way — big, juicy mounds of natural Angus beef, served on fresh-baked buns, and guaranteed to satisfy even the most committed connoisseur. Chili dogs, fish and chips, crispy onion rings, and spiced fries broaden the menu. Vegetarian options include the excellent garden and tofu burgers and a meal-size salad, all good for the dieter as well, who might also choose the lean chicken breast sandwich. Two full bars boast a festive, first-rate menu of tropical drinks (including one of the best piña coladas in the islands). Lively music every night rounds out the party-hearty appeal at both locations. You can even launch your day oceanside with hearty omelets, French toast, eggs Benedict, and other morning faves.

Lahaina Town Restaurants

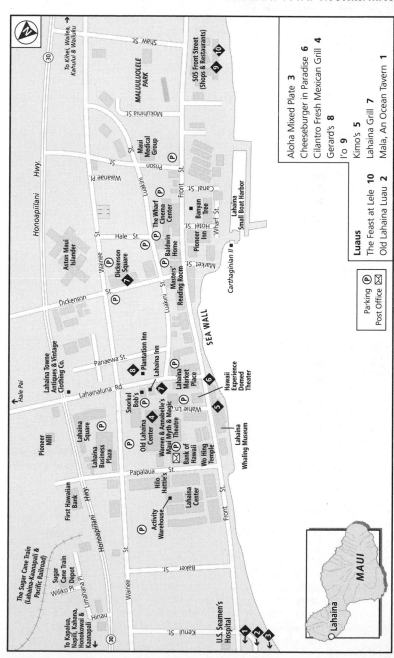

Aloha Mixed Plate **3**
Cheeseburger in Paradise **6**
Cilantro Fresh Mexican Grill **4**
Gerard's **8**
I'o **9**
Kimo's **5**
Lahaina Grill **7**
Mala, An Ocean Tavern **1**

Luaus
The Feast at Lele **10**
Old Lahaina Luau **2**

Parking ℗
Post Office ⊠

See map p. 223/227. *In Lahaina:* 811 Front St. (oceanside near the end of Lahainaluna Road), Lahaina. ☎ *808-661-4855. In Wailea:* At the Shops at Wailea, 3750 Wailea Alanui Dr., 2nd floor. ☎ *808-874-8990.* www.cheeseburgerland.com. Reservations not taken. Main courses: $9–$14. AE, DISC, MC, V. Open: Breakfast, lunch, and dinner daily.

Cilantro Fresh Mexican Grill
$ West Maui (Lahaina)   Mexican

Cilantro Grill promises "a fresh take on Old Mexico" — and it delivers the goods at incredible prices. Here's living proof that fast food doesn't have to be unhealthy and overprocessed. Chef Paris Nabavi has re-created authentic recipes from Mexico's heartland, and reinvented them with local island ingredients (for example, combining a dash of grilled pineapple salsa with the succulent adobo roasted pork found in the *tacos al pastor*). Each dish is bursting with flavor. Tired of plain old guacamole? Then try Cilantro Grill's guacamole tom-tom, which combines chopped tomatoes and tomatillos with avocados and onions and livens things up with the zing of lime, cilantro, and Serrano chili. The clean-lined, zesty-hued interior is a step up from other quick-service restaurants, too.

See map p. 223. In the Old Lahaina Shopping Center, 170 Papalaua Ave., Lahaina. ☎ *808-667-5444.* www.cilantrogrill.com. *Reservations not taken. Most items $3.50–$10. MC, V. Open: Lunch and dinner daily.*

CJ's Deli & Diner
$ West Maui (Kaanapali)   American

"Comfort food at comfort prices" — that's the motto at CJ's, and this cheap-chic diner keeps its word. An extensive chalkboard menu hangs from the brightly colored wall above the open-air kitchen. Menu items include generous farmer-style breakfasts, hearty veggie-packed salads, half-pound burgers, classic Reubens, roasted chicken, pot roast, and fresh-grilled fish. There's a pleasing local flair to the offerings, including a host of homemade baked goodies. Don't miss the hot *malasadas,* a light and flaky sweet pastry, sort of like a powdered-sugar–covered donut hole, which is one of the islands' favorite sweet treats. Food can be prepared for takeout or plated to enjoy in the casual, colorful dining room; you can even order one of their "chefs to go" meals that's completely prepped to be thrown on the grill when you get back to the condo. There's even an Internet-connected computer so you can check your e-mail while you wait. Stop by for a box lunch to go if you're heading to Hana, Haleakala, or the beach. There's also a kids' menu on hand. A great choice for wallet-watchers.

See map p. 223. At The Fairway Shops at Kaanapali, 2580 Keka'a Dr. (facing Honoapiilani Highway, on the access road), Kaanapali. ☎ *808-667-0968.* www.cjs maui.com. *Reservations not accepted. Main courses: $8–$15. MC, V. Open: Breakfast, lunch, and early dinner (to 8 p.m.) daily.*

Da' Kitchen
$ South Maui (Kihei)/Central Maui (Kahului)   Local Hawaiian

Da' Kitchen is the place to come for local grinds. The simple but comfortable Kihei closet is the original; come for the food, not the mood. Place your order at the counter and then grab one of the handful of tables to chow down on the extra hearty eats. All the classic Hawaiian plate lunches come with two scoops of rice, plus potato *and* macaroni salad (you can request a green salad instead) — trust me, you won't leave here hungry. Good choices include pulled kalua pork, slow-cooked until tender and seasoned with Hawaiian salt; chicken *katsu,* breaded in panko crumbs and served with Japanese barbecue sauce; and loco moco, a hamburger patty grilled, topped with two fried eggs, and smothered in gravy (a dieter's delight!). Also recommended are a yummy lemon chicken and a couple of teriyaki dishes for more mainstream tastes, plus big Asian-style noodle bowls, hamburgers, and a better-than-you'd-expect Chinese chicken salad. Some locals complain that this is local food "for tourists," but I continue to see plenty of locals here, especially at the Kahului location. The colorful Kahului location is more cafe-style, with full table service.

*See map p. 227. **In Kihei:** In Rainbow Mall, 2439 S. Kihei Rd. (at the south end of town).* ☎ *808-875-7782. Reservations not taken. **In Kahului:** In Triangle Square, 425 Koloa St. (off Dairy Road).* ☎ *808-871-7782.* www.da-kitchen.com. *Reservations not taken. Open: Late breakfast (from 9 a.m.), lunch, and dinner daily in Kihe; lunch Mon–Sat and early dinner Mon–Fri in Kihei. Main courses $7–$12. No credit cards.*

The Flatbread Company
$–$$ Paia   Pizza

This utterly delightful new entry to the Maui dining scene is well worth the drive to Paia (about ten minutes east of Kahului along the Hana Highway) for its terrific value, excellent fare, and all-around satisfying dining experience. As you might expect, The Flatbread Company specializes in pizza. Their all-natural, wood-fired pizzas are baked right in the center of the colorful, high-rafted open dining room, in a massive clay oven. You can watch the night's baker (a small chalkboard announces his name — ours was Bob) nurture the flatbreads and other dishes to kiawe-charred perfection. All ingredients that can be organic and/or island grown are, including free-range and chemical-free meats; the dough is even made fresh daily from 100 percent organically grown wheat.

The menu features two main sections: salads and flatbreads. However, the wide variety of combinations will keep everyone in your party engaged. You can choose from one of the creatively designed pizzas — such as Mopsy's Kalua Pork, topped with smoked free-range pork shoulder, homemade organic mango barbecue sauce, organic red onions, Maui pineapple, local Surfing Goat Dairy chèvre, Maui Sprout Farm scallions, premium mozzarella, imported Parmesan, and herbs — or design your own. Pizzas come 12- and 16-inch, while salads can be built appetizer or entree size, depending on what you dress yours with. I've found that a salad with a few add-on items and a 16-inch pie is plenty for two hungry diners.

Both the room and service are colorful and very friendly, with a contemporary surfer-hippie vibe that's just right for Paia. There's a full, very competent bar that makes a convivial place to sit should you have to wait a few minutes for your table, plus an affordable list of wines by the bottle or glass. Great for families, too. From start to finish, my new favorite spot on Maui.

See map p. 229. 89 Hana Hwy., Paia. ☎ *808-579-8989.* www.flatbreadcompany. com. *Reservations not taken. Pizzas: $10–$20. AE, MC, V. Open: Lunch and dinner daily.*

Gazebo Restaurant
$ West Maui (Napili)   Local

Tucked in the back of the Napili Shores Resort, this simple, oceanfront gem is well worth waiting in line for. Breakfast and lunch are served simultaneously throughout the morning and lunch hour in a simple open-air setting offering stunning views and service brimming with aloha. Happy diners are glad to stand in line, chat, and enjoy the views while they wait for a table and the opportunity to dig into macadamia nut pancakes dressed with the restaurant's own dream-worthy whipped cream and coconut syrup; hearty omelets served with Portuguese sausage, an island breakfast staple; island-style lunch plates starring such local favorites as kalua pork slow-cooked in traditional luau style; and burgers and salads. This is good, simple food made with care. The kitchen moves quickly, so the line does, too. One of the island's best — and one of its best dining bargains, too.

See map p. 225. In the Napili Shores Resort, 5315 Lower Honoapiilani Hwy., Napili. ☎ *808-669-5621. Reservations not taken. Main courses: $7–$11. MC, V. Open: Breakfast and lunch daily.*

Gerard's
$$$$–$$$$$ West Maui (Lahaina)   French

This traditionalist's haven boasts an ultra-romantic setting that includes a charming, slightly frilly dining room, tables on the lanai, and a lovely garden patio. A regular winner of the *Wine Spectator* Award of Excellence and named "Maui's little French jewel" by *Bon Appétit* magazine, Gerard's offers refined cuisine that seldom disappoints, as long as you're not paying too much attention to price. Gerard Reversade excels at seeking out the freshest local ingredients and preparing them in traditional Gallic style. My favorite among the starters is the shiitake and oyster mushrooms in puff pastry, but the foie gras terrine is a must for those who indulge. A wealth of meat and poultry dishes is at hand (including a terrific rack of lamb in mint crust), plus divine daily fresh fish preparations that depend on what the boats bring in. Inventive desserts provide a memorable finale, unless you opt for a cheese plate, served with toasted country bread and poached pears. Service is appropriately attentive. Very expensive, but a nice choice for special-occasion diners who prefer the classics over contemporary dining experiences.

See map p. 223. In the Plantation Inn, 174 Lahainaluna Rd. (between Wainee and Luakini streets), Lahaina. ☎ 808-661-8939. www.gerardsmaui.com. *Reservations highly recommended. Main courses: $35–$50. AE, DC, DISC, MC, V. Open: Dinner nightly.*

Haliimaile General Store
$$$$ Upcountry Maui   Hawaii Regional

This attractive plantation-style restaurant continues to be one of the best not only in Maui, but all of Hawaii — and my top recommendation for those who prefer to sample top-quality island-style cooking in a refreshingly casual and pretension-free setting. Star chef Bev Gannon, the queen of Hawaii Regional Cuisine, presents a heartier-than-average Hawaii Regional menu full of American home-style favorites prepared with an island spin and a few generous dashes of fun. I love to start with the rock shrimp tempura, served in a Chinese "to go" with popcorn (popcorn shrimp — get it?), and accompanied by a trio of dipping sauces that include a heavenly truffle honey. On the main course menu, look for such signature satisfiers as succulent barbecued pork ribs; long-simmering coconut fish and shrimp curry; and New Zealand rack of lamb prepared Hunan-style. No matter what you order, you won't be disappointed. The desserts — created by Bev's daughter Teresa Gannon, now a well-known chef in her own right — are better than Mom used to make; I never miss the light and tangy lilikoi (passion fruit) tart. The *keiki* menu even comes complete with kid-friendly "cocktails." Well worth the 45-minute drive Upcountry; Bev never disappoints. (If you're in South Maui, you can head to sibling restaurant Joe's Bar & Grill for a different type of experience; see review later in this chapter.)

See map p. 229. 900 Haliimaile Rd., Haliimaile. From the Hana Highway (Highway 36), take Highway 37 for 4½ miles to Haliimaile Road (Highway 371); turn left and drive 1½ miles to the restaurant. ☎ 808-572-2666. www.bevgannonrestaurants.com. *Reservations recommended. Main courses: $10–$24 at lunch, $24–$42 at dinner. AE, DC, MC, V. Open: Lunch Mon–Fri, dinner nightly.*

Hula Grill Kaanapali
$–$$$ West Maui (Kaanapali)   Steaks/Seafood

This attractive and bustling Kaanapali restaurant features a killer beachfront setting and a midpriced island-style steak-and-seafood menu brought to you from the people behind Waikiki's renowned Duke's Canoe Club. Kissed by the trade winds, the patio is the ideal setting for sunset watchers, and Tiki torches make for after-dark magic. The wide-ranging menu has something for everyone, including superb wood-grilled or macadamia-crusted fresh island fish, yummy barbecued pork ribs in mango barbecue sauce, or succulent lemon-ginger roasted chicken. Those on a budget can stick to the bar menu, which features Merriman's famous poke rolls (filled with seared fresh ahi), kiawe-fired pizzas, and creative salads and sandwiches. Hawaiian music, hula dancing at sunset, and well-blended tropical drinks dressed up with umbrellas round out the carefree island vibe. If you want a patio table, you should request one when you book. The more casual Barefoot Bar invites you to sit with your toes in the sand while you enjoy burgers, fish, pizza, and salads.

See map p. 223. In Whalers Village, 2435 Kaanapali Pkwy., Kaanapali Beach. ☎ *808-667-6636.* www.hulagrill.com. *Reservations recommended for dinner. Main courses: $20–$35 at dinner (most less than $25). Barefoot Bar menu (served all day): $9–$18. AE, DC, DISC, MC, V. Open: Lunch and dinner daily.*

I'o
$$$$ West Maui (Lahaina) New Pacific

You can't get closer to the ocean than I'o's alfresco tables, some of which sit just feet from the surf (request one when you book). Overseen by award-winning chef James McDonald, I'o is a multifaceted joy, with winningly innovative fusion cuisine, first-rate service, and a top-notch wine list that has won the *Wine Spectator* Award of Excellence. The seafood-heavy menu features copious Pacific Rim accents, plus a few creative twists courtesy of the Western Hemisphere: Maine lobster tails are stir-fried and served with sweet potatoes flamed in a dark rum and mango Thai curry sauce; the grilled lamb chop is spiced with madras curry and topped with a pineapple demi-glace; and the fresh catch gets a crust of foie gras for the ultimate decadence. Each dish is paired with a recommended wine for easy ordering. Skip the silken purse appetizer, though — it's an overrated signature. A full, friendly bar (including a tempting array of specialty martinis) makes this restaurant an all-around terrific choice.

See map p. 223. 505 Front St. (on the ocean at Shaw Street), Lahaina. ☎ *808-661-8422.* www.iomaui.com. *Reservations recommended. Main courses: $29–$34 ($66 for lobster tails). AE, MC, V. Open: Dinner nightly.*

Joe's Bar & Grill
$$$$ South Maui (Wailea) New American/Hawaii Regional

Joe's is a little slicker than its Upcountry sibling, Haiilimaile General Store, but serves a similarly pleasing menu of American home cooking with an island-regional twist, this time without the strong Asian influence. Top choices include the signature grilled applewood salmon, smoky and sublime; pumpkin-seed-crusted fresh catch accompanied by chipotle honey butter and whipped potatoes; and innovative preparations of such classics as meatloaf, rack of lamb, and center-cut pork chops. Specialty martinis are concocted behind the handcrafted 43-foot copper bar. The wood-paneled room is casual and welcoming, rock-and-roll memorabilia lines the walls (Joe Gannon, husband of acclaimed chef Bev Gannon, managed Alice Cooper for years), and open-air views take in the tennis action below. At night, low lighting and well-spaced tables make for a surprisingly romantic ambience, but the room takes on a laid-back liveliness after it fills up. The service is top-notch.

See map p. 227. At the Wailea Tennis Center, 131 Wailea Ike Place (between Wailea Alanui Drive and Piilani Highway), Wailea. ☎ *808-875-7767.* www.bevgannon restaurants.com. *Reservations recommended. Main courses: $23–$42. AE, DC, DISC, MC, V. Open: Dinner nightly.*

Ka'uiki
$$$$ East Maui (Hana)   Continental/Island Fusion

Now under the guiding hand of executive chef John Cox, the Hotel Hana Maui's main dining room reigns supreme as the best restaurant on this part of the island. Christened Ka'uiki, the restaurant marries fresh island ingredients with sophisticated, contemporary preparations. Chef Cox works closely with local farmers and fisherman in his never-ending quest to procure the finest ingredients on Maui; the menu changes daily to reflect what's fresh and in season. The high-quality cuisine is a perfect match for the simple elegance of the dining room, with gleaming hardwood floors, well-spaced tables, and glorious ocean views. The room is graced with original island-inspired art that includes the breathtaking *Red Sails* painting, with its imagery of the first Hawaiians voyaging to the islands. Come for dinner on Friday to enjoy a Hawaiian buffet dinner accompanied by live island-style music and dance.

 If you're coming for light fare or cocktails in the adjacent Paniolo Lounge, please adhere to the restaurant's dress code: collared shirts and slacks or dress shorts for men, skirts or slacks for women.

See map p. 244. In the Hotel Hana-Maui, Hana Highway, Hana. ☎ *800-321-4262 or 808-248-8211.* www.hotelhanamaui.com. *Reservations recommended for dinner. Main courses: $12–$20 at breakfast and lunch, $28–$42 at dinner. Friday dinner buffet: $50 adults, $35 kids 12 and under. AE, DC, MC, V. Open: Breakfast, lunch, and dinner daily.*

Kimo's
$$$ West Maui (Lahaina)   Steaks/Seafood

This casual waterfront restaurant boasts a winning combination of affordable prices, good food, and great ocean views. The menu isn't quite as innovative as that of sister restaurant Hula Grill, but it still offers a reliable and satisfying selection of fresh fish preparations (a good half-dozen are available to choose from), hefty sirloins served with garlic mashed potatoes, and island favorites like kalua pork ribs with plum barbecue sauce. With Caesar salads and sides included, dinners make for a very good deal, and there's nightly entertainment to boot. Dessert lovers should save room for Kimo's own Hula Pie: macadamia-nut ice cream in a chocolate-wafer crust with fudge and whipped cream — a decadent island delight. The open-air patio is a great place for better-than-you'd-expect sunset cocktails and pupus.

See map p. 223. 805 Front St., Lahaina. ☎ *808-661-4811.* www.kimosmaui.com. *Reservations recommended for dinner. Main courses: $8–$13 at lunch, $18–$32 at dinner (most under $25). AE, MC, V. Open: Lunch and dinner daily.*

 ### Lahaina Grill
$$$$–$$$$$ West Maui (Lahaina)   New American/Hawaii Regional

This nearly perfect restaurant is a bastion of warm island sophistication in ticky-tacky, party-hearty Lahaina, racking up numerous awards and stellar ratings from dining bible *Zagat's*. Both locals and visitors have regularly

---

Another dining option in Hana

Hana's other option is the more casual and affordable **Hana Ranch Restaurant** ($–$$$), in town on the mountain side of Hana Highway (☎ **808-248-8255** or 808-270-5280). At lunchtime, choose between the informal takeout window (serving up local fare like teriyaki chicken and hot dogs that you can enjoy at outdoor picnic tables) and a casual sit-down lunch menu inside (burgers and sandwiches for $9–$15). The restaurant is also open for sit-down dinner on Wednesday and Friday evenings for such fare as New York strip steaks, burgers, and grilled fish ($14–$20; reservations highly recommended).

---

named it as their Maui favorite since it opened its doors in 1990 — and I'm thrilled to report that even though David Paul's name is no longer on the door, it's still as divine as ever. In actuality, David Paul hasn't been involved in the restaurant for nearly a decade now; chef/owner Jurg Munch continues Paul's culinary tradition, and continues to steward the restaurant to success.

The dining room is one of Hawaii's prettiest. It's stylish yet delightfully homey, with high pressed-tin ceilings, elegantly dressed tables, golden wood floors, vibrant original art by spirited Maui colorist Jan Kasprzycki, and a generous bar at the center of the room that adds just the right amount of lively bustle to the scene. The kitchen excels at distinctive flavors that are bold without being overpowering. Signature dishes remain the stars of the menu, including kalua duck, a duck confit leg bathed in reduced plum wine sauce — rich, fork-tender, and greaseless. I'm also wowed by the Kona coffee–roasted rack of lamb dressed in a light cabernet demi-glace. Lahaina Grill also shines with seafood; start with the Cake Walk, a delectable trio of Kona lobster crab cake, zesty Louisiana rock shrimp cake, and seared ahi cake. The celestial seared ahi and foie gras pairing with fig compote will prove that foie gras is far from passé. The wine list is excellent, and the all-pro waitstaff offers welcome relief from Lahaina's usual surfer style.

See map p. 223. At the Lahaina Inn, 127 Lahainaluna Rd. (1 block inland from Front Street), Lahaina. ☎ *808-667-5117.* www.lahainagrill.com. *Reservations highly recommended. Most main courses: $33–$48. Chef's tasting menu: $78 per person. AE, DC, DISC, MC, V. Open: Dinner nightly.*

Leilani's on the Beach
$$$ West Maui (Kaanapali)   Steak/Seafood

The Hula Grill's next-door sister restaurant is a very nice alternative for diners who want good-quality steak-and-seafood fare in an equally lovely oceanfront setting that's a bit more relaxed and suitable for quiet conversation. Downstairs, the Beachside Grill serves an affordable all-day menu similar to that at the Hula Grill's Barefoot Bar. Upstairs is Leilani's, a spacious and comfortable open-air dining room that's dressed in dark woods and simple ornamentation; the fantastic beach and ocean views offer all of the necessary window dressing. On my last visit, I was extremely pleased with the quality of my filet mignon, which was crusted in cracked Hawaiian sea salt and pepper, flash-grilled to keep the juices in, and served with a delectable papaya béarnaise. My husband, a prime-rib connoisseur, was equally pleased with his slow-roasted version, with accompanying au jus and horse-radish crème for dipping. Of course, fresh catches are always available in a variety of preparations; my favorite is the straightforward broil, dressed in grilled pineapple salsa and cilantro lime vinaigrette. Service is casual, friendly, and prompt. The cocktails are everything they should be, as are the sunset views.

See map p. 223. Whalers Village, Kaanapali. ☎ *808-661-4495.* www.leilanis.com. *Reservations recommended for dinner. Main courses $10–$20 at Beachside Grill; $19–$32 for dinner at Leilani's. AE, DC, DISC, MC, V. Open: Beachside Grill lunch and dinner daily; Leilani's dinner only daily.*

The Maalaea Waterfront Restaurant
$$$$ South Maui   Continental/Seafood

Family-run for many years, this decidedly unhip seafood restaurant is a traditionalist's delight, and continues to please diners year after year. The European-style waitstaff serves every dish with a professional flourish, and the restaurant regularly wins the annual "Best Service" and "Best Seafood" awards from the *Maui News*. A half-dozen fresh catches — delivered straight off the boat from local fishermen — are usually on hand, and you can choose the preparation you'd prefer. Your choices include à la meunière; baked and stuffed with Alaskan king crabmeat; Provençal-style (sautéed with olives, peppers, and tomatoes in garlic and olive oil); and Cajun spiced. But my absolute favorite is the *en Bastille,* in which the fish is "imprisoned" (get it?) in grated potato and sautéed and then crowned with scallions, mushrooms, tomatoes, and meunière sauce — yum! Meat and poultry are on hand for non–seafood eaters, including a well-prepared steak Diane and slowly simmered pork *osso buco.* The bread comes with a delectable beer cheese spread (how retro is that?), and your server will prepare your Caesar salad tableside if you ask. Book a table on the lanai before sunset for pretty harbor views.

See map p. 227. In the Milowai Condominium, 50 Hauoli St., Maalaea (north of Kihei). ☎ *808-244-9028.* www.waterfrontrestaurant.net. *Reservations recommended. To get there: From Highway 30, take the 2nd right into Maalaea Harbor and then turn left. Main courses: $19–$38 (some seafood at market price). AE, DC, DISC, MC, V. Open: Dinner nightly.*

Mala, An Ocean Tavern
$$$–$$$$ West Maui (Lahaina)   Healthy Eclectic

The Valley Isle has applauded the return of hometown chef Mark Ellman to the gourmet dining fold. After shutting the doors on Avalon a few years back, Ellman focused his energy on expanding his successful Maui Tacos quick-service chain, and otherwise stayed out of sight. In 2006 he re-entered full-service restaurant business with a bang. *Mala* means "garden" in the Hawaiian language; it's an apt moniker thanks to the restaurant's bounteous menu, which bursts with exciting choices. The menu is built around small plates and sharing, so you can enjoy a variety of taste sensations in the course of your meal. The focus is on healthy eating, so expect whole grains and organic whenever possible. This won't dull your pleasure; highlights from the regular menu include a divine Kobe beef cheeseburger with applewood smoked bacon and Maytag blue cheese, a wok-fried *moi* (a fish once reserved for Hawaiian royalty) sautéed in a delectable black bean sauces, and an exotic Indonesian stir-fry with fresh island fish. However, the real treat is the daily specials menu, where Mark puts his creativity to full use, making the most of what's market fresh that day. Vegetarians will feel well cared for.

Mala boasts a delightfully casual-contemporary setting where you can feel perfectly comfortable showing up in your shorts; with its over-the-water location and waves crashing just below, the Tiki torch–lit lanai is one of Maui's most thrilling open-air dining rooms. Start your meal with a house special mojito or sangria, and the evening is yours. Weekend brunch is its own delight.

Mala now boasts a sister location in South Maui, Mala Wailea, at the Wailea Beach Marriott Resort & Spa, 3700 Wailea Alanui Dr., Wailea (☎ **808-875-9394**), which boasts its own wonderful oceanfront setting. It's open for breakfast and dinner daily.

See map p. 223. 1307 Front St., Lahaina (at the north end of town; take the Front St. exit off Highway 30). ☎ 808-667-9394. www.malaoceantavern.com. *Reservations recommended. Main courses: $8–$15 at lunch, $15–$28 at dinner, $8–$16 at brunch. AE, DC, DISC, MC, V. Open: Lunch and dinner daily, brunch Sat–Sun.*

Mama's Fish House
$$$$$ **Central Maui   Seafood**

Okay, it's true: Mama's Fish House is slightly touristy, and you'll have to pay through the nose. Yet despite those caveats, Mama's is my hands-down favorite restaurant on Maui, and one of my all-time favorite Hawaii restaurants — and one of its most popular too. The Tiki-room setting is an archetype of timeless Hawaii cool, and fresh island fish simply doesn't get any better than this; it's all caught locally, with the provenance indicated on the menu. ("Opakapaka caught by Earle Kiawi bottom-fishing outside his home-port of Hana Bay.") The beach-house dining room has ambience in excess, with lavish tropical floral arrangements, sea breezes ruffling the tapa table-cloths, soft lighting, and gorgeous views galore. The day's catches are the stars of the show, and you choose from four preparations. My favorite is the Pua Me Hua Hana, two of the day's fresh catches steamed gently and served traditional luau-style with purple Molokai sweet potato, baked banana, fresh island fruit, and a fresh young coconut — plates just don't get prettier than this. The service is sincere if a bit serious ("And what will the lady have?"), but, somehow, it suits the mood. A lengthy list of tropical drinks (dressed with umbrellas, of course) completes the tropical-romantic picture. A kids' menu is on hand for families. A real island-style delight.

See map p. 229. 799 Poho Place, Paia (just off the Hana Highway, 1½ miles past Paia town). ☎ *808-579-8488.* www.mamasfishhouse.com. *Reservations recommended for lunch, required for dinner. Main courses: $25–$35 at lunch, $32–$49 at dinner. AE, DC, DISC, MC, V. Open: Lunch and dinner daily.*

Mañana Garage
$$ Central Maui (Kahului)   Latin American

Locals and visitors alike flock here from all corners of the island, drawn by a winning indoor/outdoor setting and creative, nicely prepared Latin American cuisine that scores on all fronts. The boldly colored decor could be described as retro-industrial; it's cute and fun, but the groovy patio is the place to be. Having to pay for chips and salsa is kind of a drag, but all is forgiven after the basket arrives with its trio of zesty "samba" salsas. Everything just gets better from there. At lunchtime, I like the adobo barbecued duck and sweet-potato quesadilla, mildly spiced with delicate green chilis, and the classic pressed Cuban sandwich. At dinner, you might start with green tomatoes, fried just right with smoked mozzarella and slivered red onions, or zesty ceviche, made with fresh island fish. For your main course, consider the citrus-jalapeño glazed salmon, a pepper-cumin-rubbed New York strip steak grilled with chipotle-wine demi-glace, or the skewered jumbo prawns glazed with pineapple rum and served with mashed sweet potatoes. You can't go wrong with anything on the menu; every Pan-Latin dish sings with flavor. No wonder Rachael Ray named Mañana Garage a Maui favorite on her Food Network "$40 a Day in Maui" show. A real winner!

See map p. 244. 33 Lono Ave. (at Kaahumanu Avenue), Kahului. ☎ *808-873-0220. Reservations recommended, especially for Fri–Sat dinner. Main courses: $7–$14 at lunch, $16–$28 at dinner. AE, DC, DISC, MC, V. Open: Lunch and dinner Mon–Sat, dinner only Sun.*

Paia Fish Market
$–$$ Paia   Seafood

This hugely popular restaurant serves some of the freshest and best-prepared seafood on the island. It's nothing fancy — colorful and crowded, with happy diners elbow to elbow at picnic tables, chowing down on whatever's fresh off the day's boat, served on disposable dishware. But whatever you order, it's bound to be fresh, well prepared, and delicious. Place your order at the counter, then find a seat. The mahimahi fish and chips is always lightly breaded and perfectly crisp, and the generous portion is a bargain at $13. The charbroiled fish is always what it should be; if ono is in season, don't miss the opportunity to enjoy this firm and moist local fish. Even though the house specialty is seafood, the chicken selection or burger (also locally supplied, by the Maui Cattle Company) are also well prepared. There's a good beer and wine selection, too. Well worth a drive, especially if you're tired of resort prices.

See map p. 229. 100 Hana Hwy. (at Baldwin Avenue), Paia. ☎ *808-579-8030.* www.
paiafishmarket.com. *Reservations not taken. Main courses: $9–$21. MC, V.
Open: Lunch and dinner daily.*

Pizza Paradiso
$ **West Maui (Honokowai, Kaanapali)   Italian**

This sit-down pizzeria serves up top-quality pies that manage to wow even
skeptical New Yorkers (really!). In addition to a long list of create-your-own
traditional toppings, Pizza Paradiso also offers a variety of theme pies,
from the Maui Wowie (with ham and pineapple) to the Jimmy Hoffa (mozzarella buried under tons of pepperoni); pastas; fresh, bounteous salads;
and surprisingly good desserts (including a lovely homemade tiramisu).
This pizzeria is a terrific choice for bargain-hunting families or anybody
who needs a break from high-priced ahi for a while. The Kaanapali location is an express takeout joint, but you can enjoy your pie at a table in
the adjacent Whalers Village food court. Both locations offer free delivery
in the immediate area.

*See map p. 244. In Honokowai: In the Honokowai Marketplace (next to the Star
Market), 3350 Honoapiilani Rd., Honokowai (south of Kahana).* ☎ *808-667-2929. Full-
size pizzas: $12–$26. Pastas and sandwiches: $6–$12. MC, V. Open: Lunch and dinner
daily.*

The Plantation House
$$$$–$$$$$ **West Maui (Kapalua)   Hawaii Regional/Mediterranean**

Overlooking luxuriant golf greens and the stunning Kapalua coastline
beyond, the absolutely wonderful Plantation House may have the most
glorious setting on Maui. The open, airy, country club–style dining room
features crisp white linens, teak-wood chairs hand-carved with a pineapple motif, and soft tropical colors; at night, a glowing fireplace adds to the
romance. Chef Alex Stanislaw and his team have crafted a one-of-a-kind
Asian-Mediterranean fusion menu that changes frequently to take advantage of fresh seasonal produce. Expect to find dishes such as Tuscan-style
rib-eye steak with garlic mashed potatoes and goat's milk Gorgonzola
cheese; macadamia nut and goat-cheese salad with Kula greens, Kalamata
olives, and passion fruit vinaigrette; or roasted Molokai pork tenderloin
with caramelized Maui onions. Fresh-caught island fish is the star of the
menu, with several preparations available, including the divine Rich Forest
option (the fish is pressed with bread crumbs and porcini mushroom
powder, sautéed, and nestled in garlic-braised spinach and mashed potatoes). Chef Alex even lends his descriptive thoughts to the impressive wine
list, one of the finest on the island. I've heard some complaints recently
that the service can be pretentious, but I haven't had a problem. Book a
terrace table and come at sunset for maximum enjoyment.

See map p. 244. In the Plantation Course Clubhouse, 200 Plantation Club Dr., Kapalua.
☎ *808-669-6299.* www.theplantationhouse.com. *Reservations highly recommended for dinner. Main courses: $8–$18 at breakfast and lunch, $26–$42 at dinner.
AE, DC, MC, V. Open: Breakfast, lunch, and dinner daily.*

Roy's Kahana Bar & Grill/Roy's Kihei

$$$–$$$$ West Maui (Kahana)/South Maui (Kihei)   Hawaii Regional

Roy Yamaguchi is the most famous name in Hawaii Regional Cuisine. There's hardly any difference between these two bustling siblings, one in South Maui and one in West Maui. They share the same executive chef, the same basic menu, and the same lively, sophisticated vibe. Thanks to an oversize menu of dim sum, appetizers, and *imu*-baked pizzas (an *imu* is the underground oven traditionally used to roast the whole pig at a luau), you can easily eat affordably in either dining room. The daily menu revolves around a few standards, such as sublime Szechuan baby back ribs and blackened ahi with a delectable soy mustard butter. The service is always attentive, even when the dinner hour is packed and buzzing, and Roy's well-priced private-label wines are an excellent value (though you may be tempted to sample the outstanding private-label sakes instead).

See maps p. 225 and 227. **Roy's Kahana:** *In the Kahana Gateway Shopping Center, 4405 Honoapiilani Hwy. (Highway 30), Kahana.* ☎ **808-669-6999.** **Roy's Kihei:** *In the Piilani Shopping Center, 303 Piikea Ave., Kihei.* ☎ **808-891-1120.** www.roys restaurant.com. *Reservations highly recommended. Appetizers and pizzas: $8.50–$16. Main courses: $18–$41 (most under $35). AE, DC, DISC, MC, V. Open: Dinner nightly.*

A Saigon Cafe

$$ Central Maui (Wailuku)   Vietnamese

This family-run restaurant serves up outstanding Vietnamese cuisine that's worth seeking out, especially if you're looking for a high-quality culinary return on your dollar. The wide-ranging menu features a dozen different soups (including a terrific lemon-grass version), a complete slate of hot and cold noodle dishes, and numerous wok-cooked Vietnamese specialties starring island-grown produce and fresh-caught fish. Expect a taste sensation no matter what you order; every authentic dish bursts with piquant flavor. Ambience is minimal, but the quality of the food, low prices, and caring service more than compensate.

See map p. 244. 1792 Main St. (between Kaniela and Nani streets), Wailuku. ☎ **808- 243-9560.** *Reservations recommended for 4 or more. To get there: Take Kaahumanu Avenue (Highway 32) to Main Street; it's the white building under the bridge. Main courses: $7.50–$17. DC, MC, V. Open: Lunch and dinner daily.*

Sansei Seafood Restaurant & Sushi Bar

$$$$ West Maui (Kapalua)/South Maui (Kihei)   Japanese/Pacific Rim Seafood

Both of chef D.K. Kodama's Maui sushi palaces offer some of the best dining on the island, especially for serious sushi lovers. Composed primarily of Pan-Asian seafood dishes with multicultural touches, Sansei's winningly innovative menu has won raves from fans around the globe. Entrees are available, but I recommend assembling a family-style meal from the adventurous sushi rolls and small plates: The rock shrimp cake in ginger-lime-chili butter, topped with crispy Chinese noodles, and Thai ahi carpaccio in a red pepper–lime sauce are both standouts. For premier sushi service, cozy up to the bar at the bustling Kihei location — you won't be disappointed. Even the desserts are divine at this easygoing place. There's late-night dining and live karaoke from 10 p.m. to 1 a.m. on Thursday and Friday evenings (Sat as well at the Kihei location), and early-bird and late-night specials can take the sting out of the bill.

See map p. 227. In Kapalua: 600 Office Rd. (near the Honolua Store). ☎ *808-669-6286. In Kihei: Kihei Town Center (near Foodland), 1881 S. Kihei Rd.* ☎ *808-879-0004.* www.sanseihawaii.com. *Reservations highly recommended. Sushi and sashimi: $3–$24. Main courses: $11–$43. AE, DISC, MC, V. Open: Dinner nightly; late-night dining (to 1 a.m.) Thurs and Fri at Kapalua, Thurs–Sat at Kihei.*

Stella Blues Cafe
$$–$$$ South Maui (Kihei)   New American

Stella Blues began life as a Deadhead-themed deli, but it has reinvented itself in recent years as a stylish and sophisticated grown-up restaurant. The rock-and-roll memorabilia still dresses the walls, but now it adds a pleasingly funky touch to an open, airy dining room dressed in rich colors and warm woods. There's an open stainless-steel kitchen and a big, back-lit bar; Tiki torches add romance to the outdoor patio after dark. But the great thing about Stella Blues is that it's still friendly, unpretentious, and affordable. You'd be hard-pressed to find another restaurant in the islands that offers this much panache and good cooking at such affordable prices. Start your day with a hearty create-your-own omelet and then move on to a French dip or another hefty sandwich at lunch. The place really comes alive at dinner: Start with the delectable homemade hummus served with hot pita, or the funky nachos (blue and yellow corn chips layered with mahimahi, ahi, jalapeños, jack cheese, and guacamole). Choose from a range of creative pizzas, pastas, and big plates for your main course; the New York steak (homegrown by the Maui Cattle Company) is as good as most that cost twice the price. Late-night dining (until midnight weekdays, to 1:30 a.m. Fri and Sat nights) is another plus.

See map p. 227. In Azeka II Shopping Center, 1279 S. Kihei Rd. (at the north end of Kihei). ☎ *808-874-3779.* www.stellablues.com. *Reservations not necessary. Main courses: $6–$15 at breakfast and lunch, $12–$28 at dinner. DISC, MC, V. Open: Breakfast, lunch, and dinner daily.*

Tommy Bahama's Tropical Cafe
$$$$ South Maui (Wailea)   Caribbean

Housed in the Tommy Bahama's fashion emporium at the Shops at Wailea, this delightful restaurant perfectly embodies the tropical haberdasher's breezily sophisticated style. The open-air room is a mélange of bamboo, rattan, and tropical prints that come together in a postmodern plantation style. While the food is very well prepared, it's too expensive — but that's the story of this pricey resort coast. I love Tommy Bahama's best for cocktails, which are some of the island's most creative and satisfying, or a relaxed lunch, when the menu focuses on Caribbean-inspired sandwiches

---

Going for a post-Haleakala-sunrise breakfast

Rising at 3 a.m. and driving two hours Upcountry to catch the glorious sunrise from atop Haleakala crater is one of Maui's most popular experiences (see Chapter 13). Another treat comes after, in the form of a hearty breakfast at the base of the mountain in the tiny town of Kula, which you'll pass through on your way back to the beach.

Kula Sandalwoods Cafe, 15427 Haleakala Highway ($; Highway 377; ☎ 808-878-3523; www.kulasandalwoods.com; see map p. 229), is a family-run restaurant that starts serving home-baked and farm-fresh goodies at 7:30 a.m.; it's open for breakfast and lunch Monday through Friday, and breakfast only on Sunday. For slightly more upscale dining, head down the road apiece to **Kula Lodge & Restaurant** ($$; ☎ 800-233-1535 or 808-878-1535; www.kulalodge.com; see map p. 229), whose cozy lodgelike dining room features a big stone fireplace; breakfast is served from 6:30 a.m. Picture windows offer lush panoramic views — a suitable setting for enjoying their justifiably famous banana–macadamia nut pancakes.

---

and bounteous entree-size salads. Pleasing choices include the Habana Cabana pulled-pork sandwich, finished with the restaurant's own blackberry brandy barbecue sauce; and the Aruba Arugula salad, tossed in a tamarind vinaigrette and garnished with Caribbean-zested shrimp and scallops. Dinner brings more substantial fare, like maple-brined and char-grilled pork tenderloin topped with a dried berry merlot chutney, and pan-seared sashimi-grade ahi dressed in sweet chili oil, cilantro, and lemon grass. As good as the food is, Tommy Bahama's Tropical Cafe is really about soaking up the carefree mood along with a few fruity cocktails. Come early for dinner to enjoy the gorgeous sunset views.

See map p. 227. At the Shops at Wailea, 3750 Wailea Alanui Dr., 2nd floor. ☎ 808-875-9983. www.tommybahama.com. Reservations recommended. Main courses: $16–$21 at lunch, $32–$40 at dinner. AE, MC, V. Open: Lunch and dinner daily.

WokStar
$ South Maui (Kihei)   International Noodles

This cheerful new spot has brought welcome color, flavor, personality, and dining value to the Kihei scene. It's situated in a cute plantation-style cottage, with most of the restaurant residing on the covered patio. Place your order at the inside counter, take a seat, and your food will be brought to you by an attentive waitstaff. The menu comprises an international array of noodle bowls, from an Indonesian peanut stir-fry — freshly sautéed veggies in a spiced peanut sauce with thick egg noodles, topped with cilantro and sprouts — to a great version of the local favorite saimin, chow mein noodles in a miso broth, topped with barbecued pork, fried Spam (an island favorite, and tastier than you'd think), fish cake, and boiled egg. I also like the Maui fried rice, a local version of the classic with sweet onion and island pineapple, and the yummy Thai red curry. Beef, pork, chicken, shrimp, or tofu can be added to any dish. You can start your meal with chicken satay or pan-fried potstickers, and follow with banana *jaffel,* an Indonesian toasted sandwich with peanut butter, banana, and honey on Hawaiian sweet bread. Breakfast *jaffels* means you can start your day here, too.

See map p. 227. 1913-D S. Kihei Rd. (just south of Kihei Town Center and Foodland), Kihei. ☎ *808-495-0066. Reservations not taken. Main courses: $5–$9. AE, DISC, MC, V. Open: Breakfast, lunch, and dinner daily.*

Luau!

Maui is Hawaii's hands-down winner in the luau department. If you're going to attend just one, do it on this island.

Reservations are required for both luau listed in this section. Make reservations as far in advance as possible — preferably before you leave home — because all these first-rate beach parties are often fully booked a full week or more ahead of time, sometimes two.

Don't give up if you're trying to make last-minute plans, though; it never hurts to call and ask whether any spots have opened up due to cancellations. Also, if you're booking at the last minute or you want more island luau to choose from, check with **Tom Barefoot's Tours** (☎ **888-222-3601;** www.tombarefoot.com), a very reliable Maui-based activities center that can hook you up with a number of other luau on Maui, and, sometimes, even save you a few bucks in the process.

The Feast at Lele

Here's a winning new concept in luau, and it's ideal for those who don't mind paying more for a more intimate oceanfront setting and a private table. Here you'll enjoy an excellent five-course meal, prepared by a skilled chef and served at your own table. You'll experience a lovely flower-lei greeting, but no traditional *imu* ceremony or craft demonstrations, like at the Old Lahaina Luau. The performance troupe is smaller than Old Lahaina's, but it's held to the same exacting standards. This feast celebrates not only Hawaii but three more Polynesian islands: Tonga, Tahiti, and Samoa. Each course is dedicated to an island culture, composed of gourmet versions of foods from the native cuisine, followed by a native song and dance performance.

Although the Feast at Lele welcomes all visitors, it tends to cater to a more sophisticated, kid-free, grown-up crowd than most luau, making it an ideal choice for romance-seeking couples or anyone wanting a more refined experience. A full wine list and tropical cocktail menu are on hand in addition to the included well cocktails, and you can expect your two dedicated servers to be friendly, knowledgeable, and attentive.

See map p. 247. 505 Front St. (on the ocean at Shaw Street), Lahaina. ☎ *866-244-5353 or 808-667-5353.* www.feastatlele.com. *Nightly at 6 p.m. (at 5:30 p.m. Oct–Mar). Admission: $110 adults, $80 kids 2–12. Cocktails are included, but tax and tips are not.*

Old Lahaina Luau

Old Lahaina Luau is Hawaii's must authentic and acclaimed luau, and my absolute favorite. The oceanfront luau grounds provide a stunning setting, both the luau feast and riveting entertainment serve as a wonderful introduction to genuine island culture, and the staff exudes aloha. When you book, choose between Hawaiian-style seating, on mats and cushions set at low tables at the foot of the stage, or traditional seating, at generously proportioned common tables with comfortable wooden chairs.

You'll be welcomed with a fresh flower lei and greeted with a tropical cocktail. Arrive early so that you'll have plenty of time to stroll the grounds, watching craftspeople at work and taking in the gorgeous views. After dinner, the excellent show features authentic hula and traditional chants accompanied by an intelligent narrative charting the history of Hawaii from the first islanders to modern day. Don't mistake this show for a deadly dull history lesson; it's compelling entertainment, and both the male and the female dancers are first-rate performers. (Don't expect fire dancers, though, because ancient Hawaiians didn't play with fire.) It's well worth the money, and is a joy from start to finish — an excellent choice for families, groups, and couples alike.

See map p. 247. 1251 Front St. (on the ocean side of the street, across from Lahaina Cannery Mall), Lahaina. ☎ *800-248-5828 or 808-667-1998.* www.oldlahaina luau.com. *Nightly at 5:45 p.m. (at 5:15 p.m. Oct–Mar). Admission: $92 adults, $62 kids 2–12. Cocktails included; tax and tips are not.*

Fast Facts: Maui

American Automobile Association (AAA)

Roadside service is available to members by calling ☎ 800-AAA-HELP; however, the only Hawaii office is on Oahu (see Chapter 10).

American Express

There's an office in Kaanapali at the Westin Maui, 2365 Kaanapali Pkwy. (☎ 808-661-7155; www.americanexpress.com).

Baby Sitters and Baby Stuff

Any hotel or condo should be able to refer you to a reliable baby sitter with a proven track record. If yours can't, contact Happy Kids (☎ 888-669-1991 or 808-667-5437; www.happykidsmaui.com), The Nanny Connection (☎ 808-875-4777 or 808-667-5777; www.thenannyconnection.com), or Nana Enterprises (☎ 888-584-6262 or

808-879-6262; www.nanaenterprises.com). See "Traveling with the Brood: Advice for Families," in Chapter 8, for details about renting baby gear on Maui.

Doctors

West Maui Healthcare Center, Whalers Village, 2435 Kaanapali Pkwy., second floor (behind Leilani's), Kaanapali (☎ 808-667-9721), takes walk-ins daily from 8 a.m. to 9 p.m.; note that there is an additional charge for visits after 6 p.m. In Kihei, call Urgent Care Maui, 1325 S. Kihei Rd., Ste. 103 (at Lipoa Street, across from Star Market), Kihei (☎ 808-879-7781), which is open daily from 7 a.m. to 10 p.m. Doctors on Call (☎ 808-667-7676) takes appointments at the Hyatt Regency in Lahaina, at the Westin Maui in Kaanapali, and at the Ritz-Carlton in Kapalua. In Hana, contact the

Hana Community Health Center, 4590 Hana Hwy. (☎ 808-248-8294). The concierge or front-desk staff of your hotel should also be able to direct you to a reliable doctor in the immediate area.

Emergencies

Dial **911** from any phone, just as you would in the rest of the United States.

Hospitals

Round-the-clock emergency care is available from Maui Memorial Medical Center, 221 Mahalani St., Wailuku (☎ 808-244-9056; www.mmmc.hhsc.org), in Central Maui. This is the island's only full-service hospital.

Information

The Maui Visitors Bureau is located in Central Maui at 1727 Wili Pa Loop, Wailuku, HI 96793 (☎ 800-525-6284 or 808-244-3530; www.visitmaui.com), but it's not really designed as a walk-in office. Call before you leave home to order your free Maui travel planner, or check the Web site for a wealth of information. Some of Maui's resort areas have dedicated visitor associations that provide information, including the Kaanapali Beach Resort Association (☎ 808-661-3271; www.kaanapaliresort.com), and the Kapalua Resort (☎ 800-527-2482; www.kapaluamaui.com).

After you land at Kahului Airport, stop over at the state-operated Visitor Information Center while you're waiting for your baggage and pick up a copy of *This Week Maui, 101 Things to Do on Maui,* and other free tourist publications. If you forget, don't worry; you'll find them at malls and shopping centers around the island.

In addition, all the big resort hotels are overflowing with printed info. Even if your hotel or condo doesn't have a dedicated concierge, they should be happy to point you in the right direction, make recommendations, and give advice.

Newspapers and Magazines

The *Maui News* (www.mauinews.com) is the island's daily paper; its Web site can provide you with a great source of information before you leave home. Additionally, a number of free weeklies, such as *Maui Time* and the *Maui Weekly,* are available from racks around town.

Pharmacies

Longs Drugs (www.longs.com), Hawaii's biggest drugstore chain, has a branch in Central Maui at the Maui Mall, 70 Kaahumanu Ave. (between Puunene Avenue and the Hana Highway), Kahului (☎ 808-877-0041). If you're in West Maui, head to the branch at Lahaina Cannery Mall, 1221 Honoapiilani Hwy. (between Kapunkea and Kenui streets), Lahaina (☎ 808-667-4384). In South Maui, head to Longs Kihei Center, 1215 S. Kihei Rd. (just north of Lipoa Street), Kihei (☎ 808-879-2259).

Police

The main headquarters of the Maui Police Department are in Wailuku at 55 Mahalani St., near Maui Memorial Medical Center (☎ 808-244-6300). District stations are located next to the Lahaina Civic Center, 1760 Honoapiilani Hwy., on the mountain side of the highway, just north of Lahaina (☎ 808-661-4441); and in Hana on the Hana Highway, near Ua Kea Road (☎ 808-248-8311). Of course, if you have an emergency, dial **911** from any phone.

Post Offices

In West Maui, a big branch office is next to the Lahaina Civic Center at 1760 Honoapiilani Hwy. between Kaanapali and Lahaina (on the mountain side of the highway, it's easy to spot; ☎ 808-661-8227); and in downtown Lahaina adjacent to the Lahaina Shopping Center, 132 Papalaua St. (between Front and Wainee streets; ☎ 808-661-0904). In South Maui, you'll find a post office at 1254 S. Kihei Rd., across the street from Longs Kihei

Center (☎ 808-874-9143). Satellite post offices are located around the island; to find the one nearest you, call ☎ 800-275-8777 or visit www.usps.com.

Taxes

Most purchases in Hawaii are taxed at roughly 4 percent; the exact amount will vary depending on the county you're in, and may be embedded in the total purchase price or shown as an independent line item on your bill. Expect taxes of about 11.42 percent to be added to your hotel bill.

Taxis

Call **Maui Airport Taxi** (☎ 808-281-9533; www.nokaoitaxi.com), **Kihei Taxi** (☎ 808-879-3000), **Wailea Taxi** (☎ 808-874-5000), or **Maui Taxi Service** (☎ 808-276-9515; www.mauipleasanttaxi.com). The mandated fare on Maui is $3 per mile, for one to six people.

Weather and Surf Reports

For Maui's current weather and forecasts, call ☎ 866-944-5025. For wind and surf reports, call ☎ 808-877-3611.

Chapter 13

Exploring Maui

In This Chapter
- Locating Maui's best beaches
- Playing in the waves
- Exploring Maui's top attractions
- Scoping out the shopping scene
- Enjoying Maui's lively island nightlife

Maui is much like a smorgasbord: Even if you have no intention of sampling everything it has to offer, you'll be wowed by the bounty of choice — and your plate is bound to be full well before you satisfy all of your cravings.

This action-packed island has something for everyone — and then some — so staying active and happy will *not* be a problem on Maui. Your biggest dilemma will likely be just trying to fit everything you want to see and do into your vacation calendar. Just remember: It's equally important to reserve a big chunk of time for lying on the sands and doing nothing at all!

Check with the excellent Maui-based activity center **Tom Barefoot's Tours,** 250 Alamaha St. (at Wakea Street, south of the Hana Highway), Kahului (☎ **800-621-3601** or 808-661-1246; www.tombarefoot.com), which may be able to save you a few valuable dollars on many of Maui's activities on land and sea. You're welcome to visit the store, but you don't have to; all business can be conducted over the phone or online, even before you arrive in the islands (which I recommend to ensure that you don't miss out on an activity that matters to you).

Enjoying the Sand and Surf

Maui wouldn't be such a glamour girl without its breathtaking array of beaches. All of Maui's fabulous beaches (even those that front exclusive resorts) are open to the public. Although resorts may restrict certain areas of private property for their guests' use only, most hotels welcome nonguests to their facilities. Though they frown on visitors using the beach chairs reserved for guests, they're generally happy to rent you beach gear or sell you refreshments.

Combing the beaches

Never leave valuables in your rental car while you're at the beach. Knowledgeable thieves like to prey on tourists, and they know how to get into your interior, trunk, and glove box in no time flat. Be especially diligent about leaving your stuff behind at your condo or in your hotel safe when you're heading off to a remote beach.

Also, when it comes to safe swimming conditions, do your homework: Check out the following beach descriptions and, after you're on Maui, make inquiries about local surf conditions. At beaches without life-guards, keep an eye out for posted signs warning of dangerous currents or conditions. If you see a red flag hoisted at any beach, don't venture into the water; the flag indicates that conditions are unsafe for swim-mers. Even if the waves look placid, trust the warning. And never turn your back on the ocean; big waves can come out of nowhere in a matter of minutes.

In West Maui

These fine beaches are easily accessible from the Honoapiilani Highway, which connects the island's commercial heart, Kahului, to Lahaina, Kaanapali, and Kapalua. Each one offers excellent opportunities for whale-watching in humpback season.

Honolua/Mokuleia Bay Marine Life Conservation District

Snorkelers love this gorgeous cove for its smooth surf, clear waters (which are protected as a marine-life conservation district), excellent coral for-mations, and abundance of tropical fish, especially on the west side of the bay. The beige-sand crescent is lovely, and never too crowded, but there are no facilities. In winter, stay out of the water; come instead to watch daredevil surfers ride some of the finest breaks in the islands.

See map p. 268. At the northernmost end of Honoapiilani Highway (Highway 30), about 2 miles past Office Road (the turnoff for Kapalua); park with the other cars in the available spaces or along the roadside and walk 200 yards down the stairs and to the beach.

Kapalua Beach

This gorgeous golden crescent bordered by two palm-studded points is justifiably popular for sunbathing, swimming, and snorkeling. The sandy bottom slopes gently to deep water that's so clear you can see where the gold sands turn to green, and then deep blue. Well-protected from strong winds and currents, Kapalua's calm waters are usually great for swimmers of all ages and abilities year-round, and waves come in just right for easy riding. The rocky points offer good fish-communing opportunities for both snorkelers and offshore divers. The beach is also great for off-shore whale-watching in winter, too. The inland side of the beach is edged by a shady path and cool lawns. Facilities include indoor and outdoor

Maui's Best Beaches and Attractions

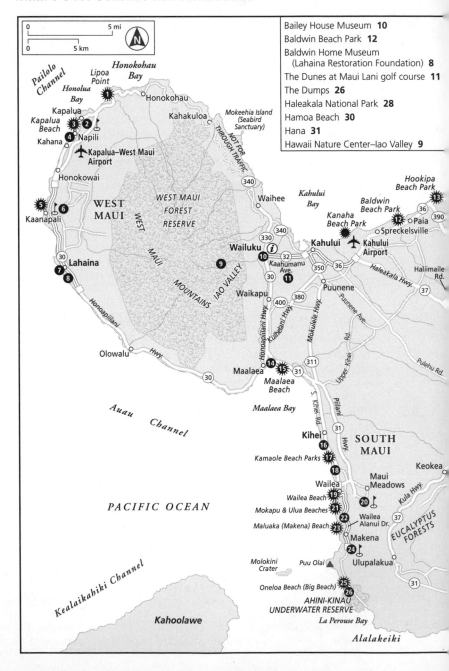

Bailey House Museum **10**
Baldwin Beach Park **12**
Baldwin Home Museum
(Lahaina Restoration Foundation) **8**
The Dunes at Maui Lani golf course **11**
The Dumps **26**
Haleakala National Park **28**
Hamoa Beach **30**
Hana **31**
Hawaii Nature Center–Iao Valley **9**

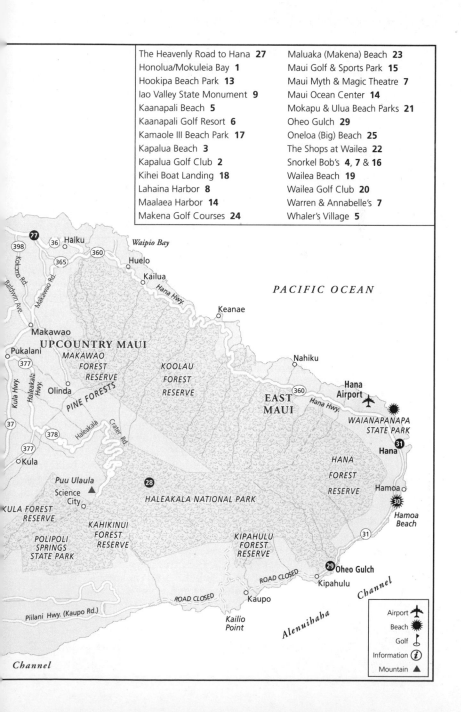

The Heavenly Road to Hana **27**
Honolua/Mokuleia Bay **1**
Hookipa Beach Park **13**
Iao Valley State Monument **9**
Kaanapali Beach **5**
Kaanapali Golf Resort **6**
Kamaole III Beach Park **17**
Kapalua Beach **3**
Kapalua Golf Club **2**
Kihei Boat Landing **18**
Lahaina Harbor **8**
Maalaea Harbor **14**
Makena Golf Courses **24**

Maluaka (Makena) Beach **23**
Maui Golf & Sports Park **15**
Maui Myth & Magic Theatre **7**
Maui Ocean Center **14**
Mokapu & Ulua Beach Parks **21**
Oheo Gulch **29**
Oneloa (Big) Beach **25**
The Shops at Wailea **22**
Snorkel Bob's **4, 7** & **16**
Wailea Beach **19**
Wailea Golf Club **20**
Warren & Annabelle's **7**
Whaler's Village **5**

showers, restrooms, and a rental shack. The small parking lot is limited to about 30 spaces, so arrive early.

See map p. 268. On Lower Honoapiilani Road at the south end of Kapalua, just before the Napili Kai Beach Club. To get there: From Honoapiilani Highway, turn left just past mile marker 30, go ¾ mile to Lower Honoapiilani Road; turn left and go ¾ mile to the access point.

Kaanapali Beach

Maui's first resort developers were drawn to build on this beach for a good reason: It's absolutely fabulous. Hotels and condos (almost approaching the density of Waikiki) now line Kaanapali's 4 miles of grainy, gold sand, but the not-too-wide beach tends to be populated only in pockets; you can usually find an uncrowded area to spread out your towel even when the hotels are at capacity. Swimming and wave jumping are excellent, but beware of the rough winter shore-break (where the waves break on the shore), which can really kick up.

At the beach's north end, in front of the Sheraton, is Black Rock, the best offshore snorkel spot on Maui. The water is clear, the area is well-protected from rough surf (most of the time), and the clouds of tropical fish are used to finned folks. Well worth seeking out; mornings tend to be calmest and clearest.

A paved beach walk links the hotels and the open-air Whalers Village shopping and dining complex — a great place to cure the midday munchies or sip a tropical cocktail while scanning for whales or watching the sun set over the Pacific. Lifeguards and beach boys from the resorts man the beach, beach-gear rental shacks are set up right on the sand, and most hotels have outdoor showers (and sometimes restrooms) you can use; restrooms are also available at Whalers Village.

The only downside is that parking is difficult for those who are not staying in the area. Whalers Village has a paid lot, but beachgoers are discouraged from using it by a "No Beach Parking" sign; if you do, be sure not to be unloading a giant cooler, beach umbrella, or set of chairs from your car, and be sure to buy lunch (or at least some sunscreen) from one of the vendors in the center to count as a shopper. Park with care here, lest you be towed. Another alternative is to pay to park as a visitor at one of the resorts, and do so legitimately by starting your day with a meal there.

There is a small free parking lot for public beach access in the Sheraton Maui's parking structure. Follow the main resort road down to the north end; the entrance is right before the main entrance to the resort itself, on the lower level of the structure at its south end (nearest to the Kaanapali Beach Hotel). Look for the sign that says "Beach Access Parking," park and follow the beach access path between the Kaanapali Beach Hotel and the Sheraton. The lot is open daily from 7 a.m. to 7 p.m.; come early to snare your spot in this tiny lot.

See map p. 268. Kaanapali Parkway, off Honoapiilani Highway (Highway 30), Kaanapali.

Along the South Maui Coast

These fabulous beaches are located along Maui's sunny southwest-facing shore, where you find the resort areas of Kihei and Wailea.

Kamaole III Beach Park

Three popular beach parks — Kamaole I, II, and III — face the waves across from South Kihei Road in mid-Kihei. The biggest and best is Kamaole III (or Kam-3, as the locals call it), which boasts a playground and a grassy lawn that meets the finely textured golden sand. Swimming is generally safe, but parents should make sure that little ones don't venture too far out because the bottom slopes off quickly. Families may prefer the grassy end of the beach with shade trees, where the ocean bottom has a fairly gentle slope. Both the north and south ends have rocky fingers that are great for snorkelers, and the winter waves attract bodysurfers. This west-facing beach is also an ideal spot to watch the sun go down or look for whales offshore in winter. Facilities include restrooms, showers, picnic tables, barbecues, volleyball nets, and lifeguards. Food and beach-gear rentals are available at the malls across the street, but be careful crossing busy Kihei Road!

See map p. 268. On South Kihei Road just south of Keonekai Street (across from the Maui Parkshore and Kamaole Sands condos), Kihei.

Mokapu and Ulua Beach Parks

Situated at the north end of Wailea, these lovely side-by-side sister beaches boast pretty golden sand, good grassy areas for sandless picnicking, and nice facilities, including restrooms and a freshwater shower pole. The ocean bottom is shallow and gently slopes down to deeper waters, making swimming generally safe; snorkelers will find Wailea's best snorkeling at the rocky north end. When the surf kicks up, the waves are excellent for bodysurfers. Although these gems are popular with the nearby upscale condo crowd, the sand rarely gets too crowded; the parking lot is tiny, though, so come early.

See map p. 268. On Wailea Alanui Road at Hale Alii Place, between the Wailea Marriott to the south and the Wailea Ekahi Village condos to the north (directly across from the Palms at Wailea condos), Wailea.

Wailea Beach

The ultrafine gold-sand beach is big, wide, and protected on both sides by black lava points with a sandy and sloping bottom, making the clear waters excellent for swimming (and okay for snorkeling too). The year-round waves are just right for easy board riding or bodysurfing, but trade winds can kick up in the afternoon, so come early. The view out to sea is gorgeous, with the islands of Kahoolawe and Lanai framing the view; this beach is an ideal spot to watch for humpback whales in winter. This stretch of shoreline may feel like it belongs to the ultradeluxe resorts that line it, but it doesn't; just look for the blue "Shoreline Access" signs for easiest access. Restrooms and showers are available.

See map p. 268. Fronting the Grand Wailea and Four Seasons resorts, Wailea. To get there: The blue "Shoreline Access" sign is between the 2 resorts on Wailea Alanui Drive.

Maluaka (Makena) Beach

This wonderful beach park fronting the Maui Prince Hotel offers a pleasing off-the-beaten-path experience for those in search of a first-rate snorkel experience, or for anybody who wants a break from Maui's ever-present crowds. Short, wide, and palm-fringed, this unspoiled crescent of golden, grainy sand is set between two protective lava points and bounded by big, grassy sand dunes. Snorkelers will find surprisingly colorful coral and an impressive array of vibrantly hued reef fish at the rocky south end of the beach, past the lava point. Sunbathers and casual swimmers will want to stick to the beautiful strand closer to the hotel, which is virtually empty on weekdays. Facilities include restrooms and showers.

See map p. 268. Makena Road, Makena (south of Wailea). To get there: Follow Wailea Alanui Drive south through Wailea to Makena (where it becomes Makena Alanui Road); go past the Maui Prince Hotel, turn right on Makena Road (where it wraps around) and look for the "Shoreline Access" sign near the hotel for public access parking.

Oneloa Beach (Big Beach)

Oneloa means "long sand" in Hawaiian, and locals call it Big Beach. It comes by its name honestly — this gorgeous crescent of white sand is 3,300 feet long and more than 100 feet wide. Oneloa is a beautiful spot for swimming, sunbathing, surfing, body or boogie boarding, or just hanging out for the day, strolling along the picture-perfect shoreline. And, true to its nickname, Oneloa is so big that even when it's crowded it doesn't *feel* crowded — so bring your beach chair and plan to stay a while, playing in the gorgeous surf and light waves. Snorkeling is a bit better down the road, but you'll find decent fish-watching near the north. In winter storm season, beware of fierce waves and a strong rip current that sweeps the sharp drop-off. The area has no facilities except portable toilets, but plenty of parking is available. Well worth seeking out for a picture-perfect Maui day.

See map p. 268. Off Makena Road, 1⅓ miles south of the Maui Prince Hotel. To get there: Drive past the Maui Prince Hotel 1⅓ miles, where a paved road leads to the parking lot and beach. A second parking lot is available just to the north.

The Dumps

It's not a sexy name, I know, but the Dumps makes a great spot for serious snorkelers in search of an off-the-beaten-path experience. This locals' favorite is part of the Ahihi-Kinau Natural Area Reserve. The Dumps isn't a beach, really; just an exposed cove with a bit of black sand, lots of lava rock, and a wealth of mature coral offering some very good snorkeling when the winds are down and the turquoise water is clear.

Beach Eats

Hanging out at a perfect spot like Oneloa all day can sure make a vacationer hungry. If you find yourself in such a state, head south on Makena Road just a bit to **Makena Grill**, a simple lunch cart on the inland side of the road serving up fantastic fish tacos with pineapple salsa, beautifully wood-grilled chicken and beef kabobs dressed in a pineapple-teriyaki glaze, and one or two other lunch plates, depending on what's fresh and available. The proprietor is a bit Soup Nazi-ish, but her food is great — supposedly, Tony Hawk calls this the best food on Maui. I don't know if I'd go that far, but it's sure good. There's a small but pleasant picnic area where you can enjoy your eats. Makena Grill is usually open daily from 11 a.m. to "4ish" — but it's just a lady with a cart and a few propane tanks, so don't blame me if she's decided to take the day off.

Only confident swimmers should explore the Dumps, and then only early in the day, when winds are down and visibility is best. Don't get in the water if the winds are kicking or there's rough surge near the shoreline (folks have been known to be blown out to sea on windy days). Also, be sure to wear reef shoes or other sturdy foot covering for your walk out to the shoreline.

See map p. 268. Off Makena Road, just south of Ahihi Cove, just before the lava fields begin; park along the roadside.

Central and East Maui

These glorious sands are accessible from the Hana Highway, which runs along the island's lush north shore.

Baldwin Beach Park

Despite the beauty of this gorgeous north shore beach park — a long ribbon of powdery white sands backed by swaying palms and fringed by white-crested turquoise waves — it's not usually crowded, except on weekends when local families come. The beach stretches for a good mile, so it has plenty of room for everybody, especially because only locals and intrepid visitors generally end up here. This is a terrific spot for swimmers and body boarders, because the water is silky, warm, and gorgeous. But be careful before venturing into the water and always heed the lifeguard, because the undercurrent can be strong at times — and it's best to stay out of the water altogether in the rough winter months. The winter water's not for inexperienced swimmers — but everybody can enjoy the beautiful setting at any time of the year. Facilities include restrooms and showers.

See map p. 268. On the Hana Highway (Highway 36), just east of Paia.

Hookipa Beach Park

Possibly the most famous windsurfing beach in the world, this small, gold-sand beach at the foot of a grassy cliff attracts top windsurfers and wave jumpers from around the globe with hard, constant winds and endless waves that result in near-perfect wave-riding conditions. Come on weekday afternoons (surfers ride the waves until noon) to watch the local experts fly over the waves with their colorful sails; winter weekends host regular competitions. When the winter waves die down, snorkelers and divers explore the reef. Even then, you should be extremely careful because these waters are rough year-round; summer mornings are best. Facilities include some rustic restrooms and showers, plus pavilions, picnic tables, and barbecues. The lower parking lot is generally reserved for windsurfers and their equipment, so park in the upper lot (see the following directions), where the high, grassy bluff offers a better perch for watching the action, anyway.

See map p. 268. Off Hana Highway (Highway 36), 2 miles east of Paia, about 6 miles east of Haleakala Highway (Highway 37). To get there: Drive past the park and turn left at the entrance at the far side of the beach, at the "Hookipa Lookout" sign.

Hamoa Beach

This remote, half-moon-shaped beach near the end of the Hana Highway is one of the most breathtakingly lovely beaches in all Hawaii, celebrated in writing by no less than James Michener for its singular beauty. The Hotel Hana-Maui likes to maintain the beach as its own, but it has to share; so feel free to march right down the steps from the lava-rock lookout point and stake out a spot on the open sand. Even if you don't want to swim or sunbathe, come to peek at this stunner from above: You'll find surf that's the perfect color of turquoise, golden-gray sand, and luxuriant green hills serving as the postcard-perfect backdrop. The beach is generally good for swimming and wave riding in the gentle seasons, but stick close to the shore because this is open, unprotected ocean; in winter, staying out of the water entirely is best. The hotel maintains minimal facilities for nonguests, including a restroom.

See map p. 268. Off the Hana Highway (Highway 36), about 2½ miles past Hana town. To get there: Turn at the small white sign that says "Hamoa Beach" and go about 1½ miles to the lava-rock lookout point; you can park on the roadside or in the dirt area across the street. The stairs are just beyond the lookout point (if you reach the steep service road to the beach, you've gone too far).

Playing in the surf

If your hotel or condo doesn't provide beach gear or beach toys, you won't have a problem finding a place to rent these items. In addition to top-quality snorkel gear, **Snorkel Bob** rents boogie boards, beach chairs, and umbrellas at its three Maui stores (see the following section, "Snorkeling"), and rental shacks on popular beaches like Kaanapali and Kapalua can rent you whatever you need while you're there.

Snorkeling

Maui is justifiably famous for its snorkel cruises to Molokini and Lanai (see the following section), both of which offer first-class fish spotting — some of the best in the state. But anybody who's already perused the "Combing the beaches" section, earlier in this chapter, knows that the island offers a wealth of terrific snorkel spots that are accessible from shore. Probably the best of these is **Black Rock** at the north end of **Kaanapali Beach.** Also excellent are **Honolua Bay,** north of Kapalua; **Mokapu** and **Ulua Beaches,** in Wailea; and one of my lesser known favorites, **Maluaka** (sometimes called **Makena**) **Beach,** south of Wailea in Makena. Additionally, many of the island's hotels and condo complexes sit on coves that are excellent for snorkeling — and not just the superexpensive ones. The affordable Mana Kai Maui in Kihei, for example, fronts a gem of a snorkeling area. Your hotel staff is sure to have nearby recommendations.

If you want to take advantage of Maui's offshore snorkeling opportunities, you'll likely need to rent some gear. My favorite rental-gear supplier in Hawaii is **Snorkel Bob's;** it rents the best-quality gear, with friendly service and a refreshing dose of snarky good humor thrown in for good measure. Snorkel Bob's maintains four Maui locations, with two in West Maui. One is at Dickenson Square, at the corner of Dickenson and Wainee streets in Lahaina town (☎ 808-662-0104). There's another West Maui store almost to Kapalua in Napili Village, 5425 Lower Honoapiilani Hwy. (☎ 808-669-9603). In South Maui, you'll find Bob's at the Kamaole Beach Center at Kihei Marketplace, 2411 S. Kihei Rd., between Rainbow Mall and Dolphin Plaza, across from Kamaole I Beach Park and not too far from Wailea (☎ 808-879-7449). In North Kihei, there's yet another store at Azeka Place 2, 1279 S. Kihei Rd. (☎ 808-875-6188). The best-quality gear — the "Ultimate Truth" — rents for $8 a day, or $32 a week ($22 per week for kids) for the mask/snorkel/fins set. For $12 more, near-sighted snorkelers can opt for prescription masks (including snorkel and fins set). Budget travelers can rent basic gear for just $9 per week. You don't need to reserve gear in advance, but you're welcome to book your gear over the phone at ☎ 800-262-7725 or online at www.snorkelbob.com. The shops are open daily from 8 a.m. to 5 p.m.

Safety is key when snorkeling. See "Ocean Safety," in the Quick Concierge at the end of this book, for general snorkeling tips. On Maui, make mornings your offshore snorkel time because the winds often start to kick up around noon, making surf conditions rougher and less conducive to fish spying.

Ocean cruising to Molokini and Lanai and other on-deck adventures

Maui boasts two top day-cruising destinations: the sunken offshore crater **Molokini,** which is hugely popular among snorkelers and divers; and the island of **Lanai,** terrific for snorkelers and sunbathers alike. (Note that only Trilogy and Paragon take their guests onshore at Lanai; other operators just anchor offshore for snorkeling in the surrounding waters.) Although both options offer excellent snorkeling opportunities,

I recommend prioritizing a Lanai cruise in whale-watching season (from mid-Dec through Apr), because the channel that separates Maui from Lanai is a favorite hangout for wintering humpback whales.

Dramamine or nausea-prevention wristbands are an excellent idea if you're prone to seasickness. *Very important:* If you opt for Dramamine, be sure to take it with plenty of time for it to work, including *before* the boat gears up for the return trip to Maui. After the return sail is underway, it's too late for the drug to do any good.

The outfitters listed in this section hardly scratch the surface of the glut of cruise operators that sail from Maui. I consider these to be the best. If you want additional options, contact the island's most reliable activity center, **Tom Barefoot's Tours,** 250 Alamaha St. (at Wakea Street, south of the Hana Highway), Kahului (☎ **888-222-3601** or 808-661-1246; www.tom barefoot.com), which can also save you a few bucks by booking you with some of the operators that I list.

All the sail-snorkel cruises I recommend are family-friendly, but Trilogy boasts the kid-friendliest crew of them all.

Blue Water Rafting

Blue Water's cruises are distinct for four reasons. First, this outfit takes small groups of guests (no more than 24) out on fast-flying, rigid-hulled inflatable boats for an exciting ride. Second, its Molokini Express cruises arrive at Molokini in between the big boats' trips, so passengers have the perpetually overpopular crater largely to themselves. Third, the speed and maneuverability of its boats allow Blue Water to take you to South Maui's otherwise untouristed Kanaio Coast beyond Makena, where you'll visit sea caves and snorkel in pristine areas favored by sea turtles and spinner dolphins on both Kanaio-only and Molokini-combination tours. And last, the low-to-the-water boats put you as close as possible to turtles and dolphins, as well as humpback whales in winter. This cruise is an excellent choice for adventure seekers in search of something different.

Cruises depart from Kihei Boat Landing, on South Kihei Road just south of Kamaole III Beach Park (between Keonekai Street and Kilohana Drive), Kihei. ☎ *808-879-7238.* www.bluewaterrafting.com. *2- to 5½-hour raft cruises: $55–$119 adults, $45–$99 kids under 12. Prices include deli lunch, plus continental breakfast on the 5½-hour tour.*

Maui Classic Charters

This company can offer you Molokini snorkel-sail experiences on two great boats: The *Four Winds II,* a modern 55-foot, 149-person–capacity catamaran featuring a glass-bottom hull for on-ship viewing, a water slide and three swim ladders, and barbecues; and the *Maui Magic,* a superfast state-of-the-art 54-foot, 71-passenger power catamaran with similarly cool features in a more intimate environment. The *Maui Magic* cruises also include some dolphin spotting on most trips. A naturalist accompanies the whale-watching trips in season.

Cruises depart from Maalaea Harbor (at the Highway 30/130 junction), Maalaea. ☎ 800-736-5740 or 808-879-8188. www.mauicharters.com. 3½- to 5-hour cruises: $42–$99 adults, $30–$79 kids 12 and under. Prices include continental breakfast and barbecue lunch on longer cruises; beer, wine, and soda on all cruises. 15 percent online 7-day-advance-booking discount available at press time.

Pacific Whale Foundation Eco-Adventures

If you consider yourself to be ecologically minded, you can't do better than to give your snorkel-cruise dollars to the Pacific Whale Foundation. This nonprofit organization has been at the forefront of Maui-based whale research, education, and conservation since the 1970s, and it also happens to host very fine cruises. Its first-rate modern catamaran fleet offers some of the best tours of Molokini and offshore Lanai. Its 5½-hour Lanai snorkel-sail takes in the island's less visited bays and includes a search for wild dolphins in its regular itinerary. The five-hour Molokai trip is as fine as any and includes a visit to a second snorkel spot, Turtle Arches. Not only is a naturalist (at least one) always onboard, but the entire crew is knowledgeable, eco-conscious, and friendly; the boats (each of which carries 100 people maximum) even burn eco-friendly fuel. What's more, the cruises are great for beginning snorkelers because guides lead fish talks and reef tours, and a wide variety of flotation devices are available. The winter whale-watching cruises are unparalleled, of course. You can't go wrong with these folks.

Departures from Maalaea Harbor (at the Highway 30/130 junction), Maalaea, and Lahaina Harbor, on Front Street, Lahaina, depending on cruise. ☎ 800-942-5311 or 808-249-8811. www.pacificwhale.org. Cruises: $50–$110 adults, $40–$70 kids 3–12. Kids age 2 and under sail free, except on dinner cruise. Some cruises include continental breakfast and/or deli lunch.

Paragon Sailing Charters

Paragon is most notable for its state-of-the-art, high-performance catamarans, intimate gatherings (only 24–38 passengers, depending on the trip), and landing rights at Manele Bay, which give its Lanai trip a special edge. (Trilogy is the only other outfitter that lands on Lanai, and the only one that will take you on a tour of the island.) This quality outfitter is a nice choice if you want to embark on a Molokini cruise, an easy afternoon snorkel cruise, or a champagne sunset sail from Lahaina, too.

Departures from Maalaea Harbor (at the Highway 30/130 junction), Maalaea, and Lahaina Harbor, on Front Street, Lahaina, depending on cruise. ☎ 800-441-2087 or 808-244-2087. www.sailmaui.com. Cruises (which include drinks and hors d'oeuvres or full meals, depending on the outing you choose): $55–$154 adults, $28–$104 kids ages 4–12. Usually free for children 3 and under, but $20 fee applies to some cruises. 15 percent online advance-booking discount available at press time.

Trilogy Excursions

Book these trips in advance because Trilogy (the Mercedes of Maui snorkel-sail operators) offers the island's most popular snorkel-sail trips, hands down. They're the most expensive, too, but the quality is high. The trips feature first-rate catamarans, top-quality equipment, great food, and the best crew in the business. What's more, Trilogy is the only Lanai cruise operator other than Paragon (above) that's allowed to land on the island's Hulopoe Beach, a terrific marine preserve that's one of the best snorkel and dolphin-watching spots in Hawaii, for a fun-filled day of sailing and snorkeling. It's also the only operator that can offer a ground tour of the island (as part of the deluxe "Ultimate Seafari"). Certainly a quality experience, but I've heard some complaints recently that Trilogy has become a little too slick and commercial for some tastes; book with a smaller operator, like Paragon, if you want a more intimate experience.

Departures from Maalaea Harbor (at the Highway 30/130 junction), Maalaea; Lahaina Harbor, on Front Street, Lahaina; or Kaanapali Beach, Kaanapali, depending on cruise. ☎ *888-225-6284 or 808-874-5649.* www.sailtrilogy.com. *Full-day Lanai cruises: $208 adults, $104 kids 3–15, including barbecue lunch and island tour. (Deluxe "Ultimate Seafari" version with Jeep safari and champagne return sail: $219 adults, $110 kids.) Half-day Molokini or Kaanapali cruise: $121 adults, $61 kids. Scuba add-ons available. Shorter Kaanapali sunset cruise: $65 adults, $33 kids; 2-hour Kaanapali whale-watching cruise: $43 adults, $22 kids. 10 percent online-only 7-day advance-booking discount available at press time.*

Delving into the deep: Submarine rides

There's a way to see Maui's spectacular underwater world even if you don't swim: Take a submarine ride with **Atlantis Adventures Maui** (☎ **800-548-6262** or 808-667-6604; www.goatlantis.com). From Lahaina Harbor, you'll go 125 feet beneath the surface in one of Atlantis's state-of-the-art subs to see a whole new world of sea critters, including — if you're lucky — humpback whales in season. The 90-minute tours cost $84 for adults, $42 for kids (children must be at least 36 inches tall). *A word of warning:* The ride is perfectly safe, but skip it if you suffer from serious claustrophobia. You can also bypass this expensive adventure if you have even the most basic swimming skills — just don a mask and snorkel and hit the waves yourself instead for a primo (and much more affordable) underwater experience.

At press time, Atlantis Adventures was offering a 10 percent discount for online bookings.

Ocean kayaking

My favorite kayaking trips are offered by **Maui Eco Tours** (☎ **808-891-2223;** www.mauiecotours.com), which offers a range of wonderful guided kayak tours for both beginning and more experienced kayakers and snorkelers. I've found their guides to be some of the best out there; ours got in the water with us at snorkel time and knowledgably narrated our underwater tour for a genuinely rich experience, rather than just leaving us to our own devices to look-see. The three-hour Discovery tour, which departs from South Maui's Makena Landing, is ideal for first-time kayakers and first-time-to-Maui kayakers alike; it's $74 for adults and $37 for kids under 12; there's also an advanced adults-only Makena-area tour called the Xplorer for $84 per person. Summer visitors might consider the terrific Escapade trip, which explores gorgeous Honolua Bay in Kapalua; this adults-only trip is $89 per person. Whale-watching trips are also offered in winter — and there's no getting closer to the magnificent mammoths than on a kayak. Check online for Web specials and on-sale dates, which can save you as much as 25 percent.

Another good kayaking outfitter for beginners and accomplished kayakers alike is **South Pacific Kayaks & Outfitters** (☎ **800-776-2326** or 808-875-4848; www.southpacifickayaks.com). South Pacific offers a range of kayak tours that launch from both South and West Maui and incorporate whale-watching in winter. The excellent guides are all very knowledgeable and ecology minded. What's more, both single and double kayaks are available, which is not always the case when you take a guided tour (doubles are most common); let them know your preference when you book. Tour prices run from $65 to $139 per person, with custom options available.

If you're an experienced kayaker capable of setting out on your own, South Pacific can rent you single or double kayaks for $40 or $60 a day, respectively. They'll meet you at Makena Landing in South Maui at 7 a.m., and be there at noon to pick your kayak back up from you; call at least a day in advance to reserve. Weekly rates and islandwide delivery (for an additional charge) are also available.

Winter whale-watching

More than any other Hawaiian island, Maui is your best perch for spotting Pacific humpback whales in winter. Virtually every boat that operates from Maui combines whale-watching with their regular adventures from December through April, and a good number offer dedicated whale-watching cruises in season, most notably the Pacific Whale Foundation. (See the section "Ocean cruising to Molokini and Lanai and other on-deck adventures," earlier in this chapter.) The channel separating Maui from Lanai and Molokai is a whale-watching hot spot, so Lanai cruises, in particular, are always an excellent bet.

You don't have to shell out the bucks for a pricey cruise to see whales. In season, you can spot them right from shore. Just look out to sea; just about any west-facing beach offers you a prime whale-watching opportunity. Follow these tips to increase your humpback-spotting chances:

✔ **After you see a whale, keep watching in the same vicinity.** They often stay down for 20 minutes or so and then pop back up to take in some air and play a little. Be patient, and you're likely to be rewarded.

✔ **Bring your binoculars from home.** You'll see so much more with a little magnification.

✔ **Anywhere along the West Maui coast is a good bet for whale-watching.** A great place to park yourself is **MacGregor Point Scenic Overlook,** a scenic lookout at mile marker 9 on the Honoapiilani Highway (Highway 30), on the way to Lahaina from Maalaea. Another good West Maui whale-watching perch is the straight part of Honoapiilani Highway between MacGregor Point and Olowalu. However, do yourself — and everybody else — a favor and pull over to the side of the road before you look out to sea, because whale-spotting along here has caused more than a few accidents.

 The nonprofit Pacific Whale Foundation (see the section "Ocean cruising to Molokini and Lanai and other on-deck adventures," earlier in this chapter) operates a **Whale Information Station** at MacGregor Point that's staffed by friendly and knowledgeable whale-expert naturalists, daily from 8:30 a.m. to 3:30 p.m. from December through April. Just stop by — they even have high-powered binoculars you can use and they're happy to share whale-watching tips and facts galore. And it's all free. Call ☎ **800-WHALE-1-1** (800-942-5311) or 808-249-8811 or visit www.pacific whale.org for further details.

Catching a wave

Book your surfing or windsurfing lesson (the upcoming sections give you more information on how to do that) for early in your stay. That way, if conditions aren't right on your scheduled day, you'll have plenty of time to reschedule.

Learning to surf

 If you've always wanted to learn to surf, Maui is a great place to fulfill the dream because it's known for having the easiest learning surf in Hawaii. The motto at the **Nancy C. Emerson School of Surfing** (☎ **808-244-7873;** www.mauisurfclinics.com) is "If a dog can surf, so can you!" A pro international surfing champ, an instructor since 1973, a stunt performer in movies like *Waterworld,* and a surf teacher to such celebs as Kiefer Sutherland and Beau Bridges, Nancy has pioneered the technique of teaching completely unskilled folks to surf in one two-hour lesson. You can, really — I've seen it happen firsthand. The instructors are professional and personable; you'll probably have your lesson on the beach behind 505 Front St. in Lahaina, where the surf breaks are big enough to learn on but not overwhelming. A beginning lesson starts at $110 per person for a one-hour private lesson, $95 per person for two hours with a group; I recommend going for the group option. Experienced surfers can take full- and multiday private lessons and group clinics with Nancy's skilled instructors (or Nancy herself, whose time is worth top dollar; check the Web site or call for rate schedules).

Action Sports Surf School (☎ **808-871-5857;** www.actionsports maui.com), with one location near the Kahului airport and one in Kihei, offers everything from kiddie lessons to extreme tow-in and strap surfing lessons for experienced board riders; beginning lessons start at a very reasonable $69 for a two-hour lesson.

For experienced surfers only

Expert surfers visit Maui in winter when the surf's really up. The best surfing beaches include **Honolua Bay,** north of Kapalua; **Maalaea,** just outside the breakwall of the Maalaea Harbor; and **Hookipa Beach Park** in Paia, where surfers get the waves until noon, when the wind-surfers take over. If you have a bit of experience but don't want a serious challenge, head to the **505 Front Street Beach,** next to Lahaina Harbor in Lahaina, where even long-surfing locals regularly catch the easy waves.

Second Wind Sail & Surf, 111 Hana Hwy. (between Dairy Road and Hobron Avenue), Kahului (☎ **800-936-7787** or 808-877-7467; www. secondwindmaui.com), has the best fleet of rental boards on the island ($20 per day, or $110 for a week), and friendly service to boot.

For daily reports on wind and surf conditions, call the **Wind and Surf Report** at ☎ **808-877-3611.**

Windsurfing and kiteboarding

Expert windsurfers will want to head to Paia's world-famous **Hookipa Beach,** known all over the globe for its brisk winds and excellent waves, after noon, when the surfers relinquish the waves. When the winds turn northerly, **Kihei** is the spot to be; some days, you can see whales in the distance behind the windsurfers. The northern end of Kihei is best: At **Ohukai Park,** the first beach along South Kihei Road, the winds are good, the water is easy to access, and a long strip of grass is available to assemble your gear. If you have enough experience to head out on your own but you want manageable waves, head to **Kanaha Beach Park** near the airport in Kahului, which is where all the top schools take their students to learn.

Top-quality rental gear for windsurfing and kitesurfing can be had from **Second Wind Sail & Surf,** 111 Hana Hwy. (between Dairy Road and Hobron Avenue), Kahului (☎ **800-936-7787** or 808-877-7467; www. secondwindmaui.com). They're also an excellent contact if you want to arrange for windsurfing lessons, for beginners and experienced wind-surfers alike, as well as kiteboarding lessons for experienced wave riders. **Action Sports Maui** (☎ **808-871-5857;** www.actionsports maui.com) also offers lessons in both windsurfing and kiteboarding, as well as paragliding for high-soaring adventurers.

Scuba diving

Molokini is one of Hawaii's top dive spots thanks to calm, clear, protected waters and an abundance of marine life at every level, from clouds of yellow butterfly fish to white-tipped reef sharks to manta rays. This crescent-shaped crater has three tiers of diving: a 35-foot plateau inside the crater basin (used by beginning divers and snorkelers), a wall sloping to 70 feet just beyond the inside plateau, and a sheer wall on the outside and backside of the crater that plunges 350 feet below the surface.

Other top dive spots include the pristine waters off the island of **Lanai,** whose south and west coasts are a dream come true for divers looking for a one-of-a-kind setting.

You need to book a dive boat to get to Molokini or Lanai. **Lahaina Divers** (☎ **800-998-3483** or 808-667-7496; www.lahainadivers.com) is a five-star PADI (Professional Association of Diving Instructors) facility that has been lauded as one of Hawaii's top dive operators by publications like *Scuba Diving* magazine. Lahaina Divers can take certified divers to Molokini or Lanai aboard one of its big, comfortable dive boats for two-to four-tank dives ranging in price from $109 to $209; West Maui dives start at $109. Instruction is available for divers of all experience levels, and the "Discover Scuba" package for beginners starts at just $139 (check for Internet specials). Full open-water training packages are also available, as well as specialty training in deep diving, underwater photography, and more. Lahaina Divers is happy to take divers with disabilities out, too. They'll also direct experienced, certified divers to Maui's best beach dives.

Or contact **Ed Robinson's Diving Adventures** (☎ **800-635-1273** or 808-879-3584; www.mauiscuba.com/erd1.htm), which caters to certified divers from his South Maui base. A widely published underwater photographer, Ed is one of Maui's best, and most of his business is repeat customers. Ed offers personalized two-tank dives, three-tank adventures, Lanai trips, and sunset and night dives; prices start at $130. Custom dives are also available, plus discounts for multiple-day dives.

Also recommendable for two-tank boat dives to Molokini and nearby Maui waters is **Mike Severns Diving** (☎ **808-879-6596;** www.mike severnsdiving.com), which takes 12 divers at a time out from Kihei in two groups of six for a quiet and crowd-free experience. The price is $145, including gear, with discounts available if you have your own equipment or schedule multiday dives. Private charters are also available.

If you've never scuba dived before but want to learn, contact either Lahaina Divers or **Bobby Baker's Maui Sun Divers** (☎ **877-879-3337** or 808-879-3337; www.mauisundivers.com). This outfit specializes in training beginners in small groups, and it offers introductory two-tank dives for $110 and multiple-day starter and certification programs.

Sportfishing

Ready to head out on the open waves in search of big-game fish like marlin, tuna, and wahoo? **Hawaii Fishing Adventures and Charters** (☎ **877-388-1376;** www.sportfishhawaii.com) can book a first-class charter for you out of Maalaea or Lahaina harbors on Maui. Half-day private charters start at $600.

Exploring on Dry Land

Maui is home to two of Hawaii's most renowned attractions: **Haleakala National Park,** a remarkable crater at the heart of the island that offers some of the best sunrise watching in the world, not to mention one-of-a-kind hiking and biking fun; and the **Heavenly Road to Hana,** one of the most well-known scenic drives in the United States.

 If you need a little personal assistance in choosing among Maui's wealth of activity options, you can get it. The best and most reliable activity booker on Maui is **Tom Barefoot's Tours,** 250 Alamaha St. (at Wakea Street, south of the Hana Highway), Kahului (☎ **800-621-3601** or 808-661-1246; www.tombarefoot.com). Unlike most other so-called "activity centers" on Maui, this professional operation has nothing to do with timeshares — activities are its business, and I've found the salespeople's recommendations to be consistently good ones. You can book discounted activities before you leave home via their Web site or toll-free number.

 Do yourself a favor and avoid those activities bookers that are trying to sell you a timeshare. Believe me, spending a half-day of your precious vacation time warding off the hard-sell advances of a salesperson trying to force you to buy a timeshare you don't need in exchange for a "free" snorkel cruise on a cut-rate operator is simply not worth it.

Taking a guided van or bus tour

If you've rented a car and can get around easily on your own, driving yourself around the island is definitely the preferable way to go.

But you might want to hook up with a guided tour if your mobility is limited, if you're traveling solo and don't want to make the drive to Hana on your own, or if you just want to kick back and let somebody else take the wheel. The downside is that with a guided tour, you'll have little or no control over where you go and how long you stay, and your time communing with nature will be limited. Still, for some people, a guided tour is the best way to see Haleakala National Park and take in the glories of the Heavenly Road to Hana.

For small-scale, local-led van tours of the Heavenly Road to Hana and Haleakala National Park's sunrise extravaganza, book your guided trip with family-owned **Ekahi Tours** (☎ **888-292-2422** or 808-877-9775; www.ekahi.com). One of the great advantages of its Hana tour is that it's a circle island tour when weather permits; if the going's good, you'll not only drive the road to Hana, but also experience the desert landscape of the little-traveled back road on the return trip, which takes you along the south coast and around the back side of the Haleakala volcano. Ekahi can take you not only to Hana but also to hidden Keanae, a halfway-to-Hana tour that offers an insightful look at Maui's rural past and present. Sunrise tours of Haleakala Crater are also on offer. Ekahi tour prices range from $101 to $130 adults, $75 to $99 kids under 11, depending on the tour you choose; prices include a deli lunch. Discounts are available for seniors over age 60.

Polynesian Adventure Tours (☎ **800-622-3011** or 808-833-3000; www.polyad.com) offered the very first guided bus tours along the Heavenly Road to Hana, and it's still going strong in this department. In addition to the Hana option, it offers both Haleakala sunrise and Iao Valley tours in minivans, big-windowed mini-coaches, and full-size luxury buses. Prices run $76 to $99 for adults, $52 to $60 for kids ages 3 to 11. Book your Polynesian Adventure Tour online to get a 10 percent price break.

If you choose to visit Haleakala National Park on a guided tour, remember to dress warmly, because it gets *cooooold* at 10,000 feet. For more on Haleakala's weather, see the complete section on the park later in this chapter.

Enjoying guided nature hikes

Maui Eco-Adventures (☎ **877-661-7720** or 808-661-7720; www.ecomaui.com) was recognized as Hawaii's Eco-Tourism Operator of the Year in 2005, and deservedly so. This well-run operation specializes in guided cultural and hiking adventures that explore untrammeled areas of the Valley Isle — including the little-known Maunalei Arboretum; Kahakuloa Village, a rare vestige of old Hawaii; and Nakele Point, the northernmost point on Maui — on a variety of compelling journeys for intrepid travelers of all hiking abilities. A selection of wonderful waterfall hikes can make your island dreams come true; the six-hour Rainforest/Waterfall hike is my favorite for the access it provides into the breathtakingly lush, otherwise hidden heart of Maui. A Haleakala crater hike really brings the majestic yet barren landscape to life. Hike/kayak combos are also available for those who want a multifaceted experience, as are custom-designed tours that can add helicopter tours, sailboat adventures, and four-wheeling into the mix. Prices run $80 to $160 per person, including continental breakfast, lunch, a day's supply of water, and pickup from West Maui hotels (expect to pay more for a custom-designed tour). An excellent way to see Maui at its natural best.

Maui's oldest guided hiking company is Ken Schmitt's **Hike Maui** (☎ **866-324-MAUI [6284]** or 808-879-5270; www.hikemaui.com), universally lauded for the quality of its hikes. The expert guides are all trained naturalists who really know their stuff. Hike Maui offers an array of hikes from easy to strenuous, but most fall in the moderate category. Two rain forest and waterfall hikes are available, as are two Haleakala Volcano hikes that offer an excellent way to see this splendid national park, which can be difficult to appreciate if you don't know what you're seeing. If you're an accomplished hiker and fit for it, don't miss the longer hike. It takes you all the way to the crater floor — which looks so much like the moon that the lunar astronauts trained here — for an otherworldly experience. Outings range from $75 to $154 per person, including equipment and transportation from the company's Central Maui headquarters, and a simple, healthy lunch of sandwiches and fruit. You can book as late as a couple of days in advance, but your best bet is to call before you arrive on the island.

Maui Hiking Safaris (☎ **888-445-3963** or 808-573-0168; www.maui. net/~mhs) is another reputable company offering guided hikes for all levels, including waterfall hikes and guided hikes of Haleakala. Prices run from $59 to $139 per person.

Maui Hiking Safaris extends 10 percent discounts to hikers who book online and to groups of six or more.

Getting a bird's-eye view

Flightseeing is an excellent way to explore Maui's stunning, untouched natural areas — areas that simply can't be seen by any other means. Maui-based helicopter tours also offer you the opportunity to see a neighbor island — Molokai, Lanai, or even the Big Island — from the air in addition to the Valley Isle itself. There are, however, some considerations. Although the companies that I recommend all feature skilled pilots and helicopters with excellent safety records, the truth of the matter is that flightseeing can be risky business. A few dozen people have died in commercial helicopter crashes in Hawaii over the past decade. Of course, just as with airplane travel, you are more likely to have a car accident than a helicopter crash. Still, you should make informed decisions.

When reserving a helicopter tour with any company, check to make sure that safety is its first concern. The company should be an FAA-certified Part 135 operator, and the pilot should be Part 135 certified as well; the 135 license guarantees more stringent maintenance requirements and pilot training programs than those who are only Part 91 certified. And any time weather conditions look iffy, reschedule.

Blue Hawaiian Helicopters (tours depart from Kahului Airport; ☎ **800-745-2583** or 808-871-8844; www.bluehawaiian.com) is an excellent flightseeing company that's family run by David and Patti Chevalier and a loyal long-employed staff. Blue Hawaiian flies a fleet of superb American Eurocopter AStar 350 helicopters that carry six passengers, providing each with a 180-degree view and a Bose noise-canceling headset that lets you enjoy a surprisingly quiet ride. A world leader in the flightseeing industry, Blue Hawaiian also features Hawaii's only EC-130B4 Eco-Stars; these cutting-edge helicopters lower noise pollution with a superquiet design, and maximize comfort and views with state-of-the-art design, technology, and materials. They offer one phenomenal ride. (You can choose which kind of copter you'll fly; the Eco-Star tours are more expensive, but offer a slightly better viewing range through their bubble-like windows.) A range of available flight options includes some or all of the following spectacular sights: the misty, green West Maui Mountains; impressive Haleakala Volcano; luxuriant, unspoiled East Maui and Hana; and Molokai, where you'll fly by the highest sea cliffs in the world. Tours last from 30 to 90 minutes, and prices range from $173 to $518 per person (kids under 2 fly free; all other children pay full fare).

At press time, Blue Hawaiian was offering a significant price break — about 13 percent — for online bookings.

Visiting Haleakala National Park

Haleakala (ha-lay-ah-*ka*-la) — the House of the Sun — is the massive 10,023-foot-high mountain that forms the core of the island of Maui. It's also Hawaii's second national park (after the Big Island's Hawaii Volcanoes National Park) and Maui's biggest natural attraction. Each year, some 1.5 million people drive to the summit of Haleakala to peer down into the crater of the world's largest dormant volcano. (Its official status is "active but not currently erupting," even though Haleakala has remained silent since 1790.) The crater is impressive: At 3,000 feet deep, 7½ miles long by 2½ miles wide, and encompassing 19 square miles, it's big enough to hold the entire island of Manhattan. More than anything else, it resembles a barren moonscape.

This stark, rugged place is breathtakingly beautiful in its own way: a desolate, otherworldly canyon painted in hues of blue and green and red. Just driving up the mountain is an experience in itself: The road climbs from sea level to 10,000 feet in just 37 miles, and the views are magnificent along the entire route. At first glance, the landscape looks like nothing more than a dry and barren wasteland. But soon, a fascinating, multihued geologic world emerges — a surprisingly fragile one that supports a number of the world's rarest examples of flora and fauna. Among the rare endangered species that call Haleakala home are the nene (*nay*-nay), a gray-brown Hawaiian goose that doesn't migrate, prefers rock-hard lava beds to lakes, and is now protected as the state bird. There's also the silvery-green, porcupiney silversword plant, which grows only in Hawaii, lives for about 50 years, blooms once in a beautiful purple bouquet, and dies.

Haleakala is best known for its mystical sunrise vistas. Crowds of visitors drive here in the dark predawn hours to watch the spectacle of dawn breaking over the crater. If you decide to join the early-morning crowds, stick around after sunrise for some excellent hiking opportunities. Or do what a lot of people do: Hop on a bike and coast down the switchbacked, view-endowed road to the base of the mountain.

Sunrise at Haleakala has become so popular that the park was experiencing theme-park crowds and L.A.-style gridlock in the predawn hours, which was seriously damaging both the mood and the protected natural environment. The National Park Service instituted policies in late 2005 that limited the number of vehicles allowed into the summit parking lots. Note that if lots are too crowded, there's a chance — albeit a small one — that you may be turned away at the entrance gate.

Haleakala National Park

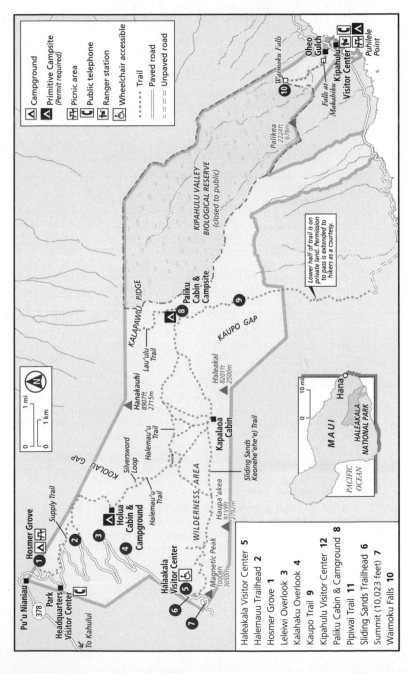

Legend:

- ⚠️ Campground
- ⚠️ Primitive Campsite *(Permit required)*
- 🏕️ Picnic area
- 📞 Public telephone
- 🏢 Ranger station
- ♿ Wheelchair accessible
- ⋯⋯ Trail
- ——— Paved road
- = = = Unpaved road

Lower half of trail is on private land. Permission to pass is extended to hikers as a courtesy.

KIPAHULU VALLEY BIOLOGICAL RESERVE (closed to public)

Waimoku Falls
Oheo Gulch
Falls at Makahiku Kipahulu Visitor Center
Puhilele Point

Palikea 2224ft 678m

Paliku Cabin & Campsite

KALAPAWILI RIDGE

Lau'ulu Trail

KAUPO GAP

Hanakauhi 8907ft 2715m

Haleakal 8201ft 2500m

Silversword Loop

Halemau'u Trail

Kapalaoa Cabin

Sliding Sands Keonehe'ehe'e) Trail

KOOLAU GAP

Supply Trail

Halemau'u Trail

Holua Cabin & Campground

WILDERNESS AREA

Haupa'akea 9159ft 2792m

Magnetic Peak 10008ft 3050m

Hosmer Grove

Pu'u Nianiau

Park Headquarters Visitor Center

378

To Kahului

Halaakala Visitor Center

MAUI

Hana

HALEAKALA NATIONAL PARK

PACIFIC OCEAN

Haleakala Visitor Center **5**
Halemauu Trailhead **2**
Hosmer Grove **1**
Leleiwi Overlook **3**
Kalahaku Overlook **4**
Kaupo Trail **9**
Kipahulu Visitor Center **12**
Paliku Cabin & Campground **8**
Pipiwai Trail **11**
Sliding Sands Trailhead **6**
Summit (10,023 feet) **7**
Waimoku Falls **10**

The legend behind the House of the Sun

The name *Haleakala* actually means "House of the Sun." The story of how this wild-looking volcano got such a magnificent name goes like this: One day, a mom complained that the sun sped across the sky so quickly that her tapa cloth didn't have enough time to dry. So in the predawn hours of the next morning, her thoughtful son, the demigod Maui, climbed to the top of the volcano. When the sun rose above the horizon, Maui lassoed it, bringing it to a halt in the sky.

The sun begged Maui to let go. Maui said he would, on one condition: that the sun slow its trip across the sky to give the island more sunlight. The sun agreed. In honor of the agreement, islanders dubbed the mountain "House of the Sun."

That's the bad news. The good news is that the premium value of getting up in the middle of the night to greet sunrise atop Haleakala is largely a myth. Many believe — including yours truly — that sunset is actually Haleakala's finest hour. The crater is in shadow at sunrise; by sunset, it has positioned itself to bring the colors of Haleakala into their full, vibrant hues. Many consider Haleakala to offer the finest sunsets in Hawaii — and sunset doesn't offer the risk that sunrise holds, because the cloud cover that might block a sunrise view can be difficult to evaluate under cover of darkness. Furthermore, you won't be too exhausted to enjoy the fabulous views.

The park actually contains two separate and distinct destinations: Haleakala Summit and the Kipahulu coast. Lush, green, and tropical, Kipahulu is a world apart from the summit — and accessible only from the east side of the island, near Hana. No road links the summit and the coast, so Hana is a completely separate outing. For a discussion of Kipahulu and its biggest attraction, Oheo Gulch, see the section "Driving the Heavenly Road to Hana," later in this chapter.

See the "Haleakala National Park" map on p. 287 for listings in this section.

Preparing for your visit

For information before you go, contact **Haleakala National Park** at ☎ **808-572-4400** for information on the Haleakala summit (main) area of the park (dial ☎ **808-248-7375** for information and the ranger station at the park's Kipahulu district, near Hana, which is a separate outing I discuss later in this chapter). Or visit the park's official Web site at www.nps.gov/hale. You can also find lots of useful information at an unofficial but excellent site, www.haleakala.national-park.com.

The summit of Haleakala is 38 miles, or about a 1½-hour drive, from Kahului in Central Maui. To get there, take the Haleakala Highway (Highway 37 and then Highway 377) to wiggly Haleakala Crater Road (Highway 378), the heavily switchbacked road that leads you to the

10,000-foot summit. Allow two hours to reach the summit if you're driving from Lahaina or Kihei, 2½ hours if you're arriving from Wailea or Kaanapali, 15 minutes more if you're coming from Kapalua.

For the sunrise time and viewing conditions at Haleakala summit, call ☎ 808-877-5111.

Admission to the park is $10 per car, which allows you to come and go as you please for seven days. It's $5 per person for individual walk-ins.

Keep these tips in mind as you plan your visit to Haleakala National Park:

✔ **If Maui is the first Hawaiian island you're visiting, schedule your sunrise visit for the first full day of your trip.** Your body clock won't be on Hawaii time yet, so it shouldn't be too hard to get up at 3 a.m. It will feel like anywhere from 5 to 9 a.m. if you're from the mainland. If Maui is the last island on your itinerary, schedule your sunrise visit for the final day of your trip, because it's time to reacclimate yourself to the at-home hour anyway. Or, as I've recommended above, simply opt for a visit later in the day, and you won't disturb your normal sleep patterns.

✔ **Dress warmly, in layers, no matter what time of year you visit.** Temperatures at the summit usually range between 40 and 65°F but can drop below freezing any time of year when you factor in the windchill, especially in the predawn hours. Wear a hat and sturdy shoes and bring a blanket if you don't have a warm jacket. The weather is unpredictable at the summit, so be prepared for wind and rain in winter no matter what the time of day; don't be fooled by the coastline conditions. Call ☎ 808-877-5111 for the summit forecast.

✔ **Bring drinking water.** You'll need plenty of water on hand, especially if you plan on hiking.

✔ **Remember that this is a high-altitude wilderness area.** The thinness of the air makes some people dizzy; you may also experience lightheadedness, shortness of breath, nausea, headaches, and dehydration. The park recommends that pregnant women and those with heart or respiratory problems consult a doctor before ascending to high elevations.

✔ **Fill up your gas tank before you head to Haleakala.** The last gas station is 27 miles below the summit at Pukalani. Fill up the night before if you're going for sunrise, because it will be nearly impossible to find an open gas station at 4 a.m.

Arriving at the park and making the drive to the summit

About a mile from the entrance is the **Park Headquarters Visitor Center,** open daily from 8 a.m. to 3:45 p.m. It's a great place to pick up park information, including the latest schedule of guided walks and ranger talks. If, however, you arrive before dawn, all you can do here is use the round-the-clock restrooms; the ones here are much nicer than the ones at the summit, so I highly recommend making a pit stop on the way up. Drinking water is also available.

You'll pass two scenic overlooks on the way to the summit. Stop at the one just beyond mile marker 17, **Leleiwi Overlook,** if only to get out, stretch, and get accustomed to the heights. From the parking area, a short trail leads to a panoramic view of the lunarlike crater. (The other overlook, Kalahaku, is most easily accessible on the descent.)

Continue on, and you'll soon reach **Haleakala Visitor Center,** 11 miles from the park entrance (open daily from 6:30 a.m. to 3:30 p.m.), which offers spectacular views and some bare-bones restrooms. Park rangers also offer excellent, informative, and free naturalist talks daily throughout the day from the center. (Call ahead to confirm the next day's schedule.)

The actual summit — and the ideal sunrise-viewing perch — is beyond the turnoff for the visitor center, at **Puu Ulaula Overlook** (Red Hill). At Puu Ulaula, a triangular glass building serves as a windbreak and the best sunrise viewing spot. After the spectacle of sunrise, you can often see all the way to the snowcapped summit of Mauna Kea on the Big Island if it's clear. Haleakala Observatories (nicknamed Science City), which isn't open to the public, is also located here.

Hiking the park

If you want to hike the park, I strongly suggest going with a guide. This is an outlandishly huge, empty place that is best seen with someone who can lead you in the right direction and help you understand what you're seeing. Park rangers offer a range of free guided hikes; call for the latest schedule (☎ **808-572-4400**) and to find out what to wear and bring (sturdy shoes and drinking water are musts).

Also consider taking one of the guided Haleakala Crater hikes offered by **Maui Eco-Adventures** or **Hike Maui.** I really like the extended views of the crater that professional guides offer on these private tours. See the section "Enjoying guided nature hikes," earlier in this chapter.

If you don't want to bother with a serious hike but just want a glimpse of the park's peculiar brand of natural beauty, take a half-hour walk down the half-mile **Hosmer Grove Nature Trail,** which anybody can do. The trail is well marked, with placards that point out what you're seeing along the way. Ask the ranger at the visitor center to direct you to the trail head.

If you'd like to strike out on your own along the park's more serious trails, preview your options online at www.haleakala.national-park.com (click "Hiking Guide") or call ahead. Rangers are always happy to provide you with complete trail information.

Driving back down the mountain

As you start to head down the volcano, put your rental car in low gear on the way down so that you don't ride your brakes.

Around mile marker 24 is **Kalahaku Overlook,** the best place to spot the spiky, alienlike silversword plant and to take in some fabulous panoramic views.

At the base of the mountain, where you'll turn onto Haleakala Crater Road from the Haleakala Highway, is **Kula,** the closest thing to a gateway town that Haleakala has. Kula is most notable for its two restaurants, Kula Sandalwoods and the Kula Lodge, both of which serve great post-sunrise breakfast and lunch.

Exploring the volcano by horseback

My absolute favorite way to explore Haleakala Crater is with **Pony Express Tours** (☎ **808-667-2200;** www.ponyexpresstours.com), which offers guided trail rides down the crater's Sliding Sands Trail, which descends from the crater rim 2,500 feet to the crater floor, for a majestic 7½-mile round-trip ride. The guides are friendly experts, and the horses are good natured and extremely well taken care of; mine was an agreeable red-haired boy named Leo, and my day exploring Haleakala with him was the highlight of my last trip to Maui. These all-day Haleakala trail rides are $182 per person, and require you to have at least minimal riding experience; this is strictly a nose-to-tail ride, so as long as you know the basics, you'll be in good shape. Rides start daily at 8:30 a.m., with a second ride offered on days that demand it. A two-hour *paniolo* ranch ride is also offered for $110. Book well in advance — ideally, before you leave home — in order to secure your spots on this terrific trip.

At press time, Pony Express was offering 10 percent off for those who booked their trips online.

Biking down the volcano

Another great way to experience Haleakala is to cruise down it, from summit to base, on a bicycle. The guided ride is quite an experience, with stunning views the entire way. And you don't need to be an expert cyclist to do it; you just have to be able to ride a bike. In fact, you barely have to pedal — you'll coast down at a nice, leisurely pace. (The constant switchbacks keep you from picking up too much speed.)

While these tours used to be offered from Haleakala's summit both at sunrise and throughout the day, the National Park Service has suspended all tours from within Haleakala National Park following a glut of increased traffic. As of this writing, most bike tours start at 6,500 feet elevation, just outside the park entrance. The trips are still quite fun, but you will have to start the day atop Haleakala on your own. I'm sure that the big outfitters will reinstate full service as soon as the National Park Service allows; check the outfitters' Web sites or call for further information.

Maui's oldest downhill company is **Maui Downhill** (☎ 800-535-2453 or 808-871-2155; www.mauidownhill.com). Maui Downhill offers a variety of guided Haleakala bike "safaris" at sunrise, midday, and sunset, running from $125 to $195 per person. Other reliable companies include **Maui Mountain Cruisers** (☎ 800-232-6284 or 808-871-6014; www.maui mountaincruisers.com) and **Mountain Riders** (☎ 800-706-7700 or 808-242-9739; www.mountainriders.com). Prices usually include hotel pickup, transport to the top, all equipment, meals, and drop-off. Generally, riders have to be at least 12 and at least 4 feet 10 inches tall. Younger kids and pregnant women can usually ride along in the van.

At press time, you could save a bundle on most of these tours by book-ing in advance via most of these companies' own Web sites (for example, Maui Downhill was offering $30-per-person discounts on its $125 tours!). The current situation has really kicked the deals into gear.

Driving the Heavenly Road to Hana

No road in Hawaii is more celebrated than the Hana Highway (Highway 36), the supercurvaceous two-lane highway that winds along Maui's northeastern shore, offering some of the most scenic natural sightseeing in the entire state.

The Hana Highway winds for some 52 miles east from Kahului, in Central Maui, crossing more than 50 one-lane bridges, passing greener-than-green taro patches, magnificent seascapes, gorgeous waterfalls, botani-cal gardens, and rain forests before passing through the little town of Hana and ultimately ending up in one of Hawaii's most beautiful tropical places: the Kipahulu section of Haleakala National Park. Kipahulu is home to Oheo (oh-*hay*-oh) Gulch, a stunning series of waterfall pools that tumble down to the sea.

Despite the draws at the end of the road, this drive is about the journey — *not* the destination. The drive from end to end takes at least three hours, but you should allow all day for it. If you race along just to arrive in Hana as quickly as you can, you'll wonder what all the fuss was about. Start out early, take it slow and easy, stop at the scenic points along the way, and let the ride along Hana work its magic. It will, I promise.

Take these points into consideration as you plan your Hana road trip:

> ✔ **Leave early.** Get up just after dawn, have an early breakfast (Charley's Restaurant & Saloon in Paia opens at 7 a.m.; see Chapter 12), and hit the road by 8 a.m. If you wait until midmorning to leave, you'll get stuck in bumper-to-bumper Hana Road traffic, you won't have enough time to enjoy the sights along the way, and you'll arrive at Oheo Gulch too late in the day to take a hike or a dip. It's especially important to make the most of the daylight hours in winter, when days are shortest.

✔ **Consider booking a place to stay in Hana if you'd really like to take your time.** That way, you can head out to Hana against the traffic in the afternoon, stay for a couple of nights so that you have a full day to enjoy East Maui's attractions (including an abundance of peace and quiet), and meander back at your own pace (once again avoiding the traffic) on the morning of the third day. See Chapter 12 for accommodations in Hana.

✔ **Fill up on gas before you set out.** If all else fails, make sure that you stop in Paia, just east of Kahului, because the next gas is in Hana — 44 miles, 50-some bridges, and 200-plus hairpin turns down the road.

✔ **Don't bother if it's been raining heavily.** The Hana Highway is well paved and well maintained but can nevertheless be extremely dangerous when wet — and it's easy to get stuck in muddy shoulders and pull-offs.

✔ **Bring your bathing suit and a towel in warm weather.** You'll find a number of waterfall pools along the way that are ideal for a refreshing dip, and folks love to swim in Oheo Gulch's placid summer pools. (However, don't enter the pools unless the park rangers say conditions are safe. Please take their warnings seriously; visitors have been killed here.) Also bring mosquito repellent, because lush East Maui is a buggy place.

✔ **Leave your mainland road rage on the mainland.** Practice aloha as you drive the Hana Road: Give way at the one-lane bridges. Wave at passing motorists. Let the locals who drive this road with jaw-dropping speed and who pass on blind curves have the right of way; if the guy behind you blinks his lights, let him pass. And don't honk your horn — it's considered rude in Hawaii.

 There's one exception to the no-horn-honking rule: If you reach a blind curve, *do* honk your horn to indicate that you're coming around the bend — and proceed slowly.

See "The Heavenly Road to Hana" map on p. 294 and the "Hana" map on p. 299 for listings in this section.

Highlights worth seeking out along the way

If you'd like some narration to accompany what you're seeing along the Road to Hana, pick up a **Hana Cassette Guide** on your way out of town. The 90-minute tape or CD is $20 at the Hana Cassette Guide shop in Kahului on Dairy Road (Highway 380), next to the Shell Service Station just before the Hana Highway (☎ **808-572-0550**). Your Hana CD guide also gets you a map and flora guide that are useful for along the road; in fact, the detailed map is my favorite part of the trip. I highly recommend using it in tandem with the following text, because it covers many more sights and includes much more background than I have the space for here.

The Heavenly Road to Hana

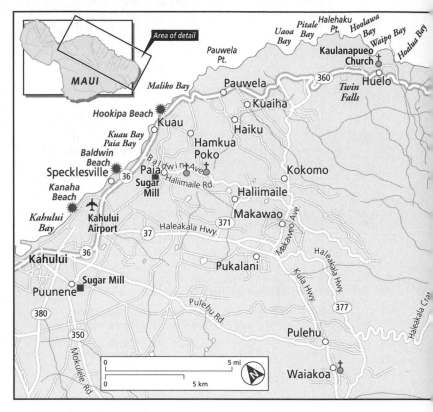

If you want to see the Hana Road but you just don't want to drive it your-self, consider taking a guided van or bus tour. See the section called "Taking a guided van or bus tour," earlier in this chapter, for recom-mended tour operators.

Setting Out: A half-dozen miles east of Kahului on the Hana Highway is Paia (pa-*ee*-ah), a former mill town that's now a neo-hippie, boutique-dotted surf spot. **Charley's Restaurant & Saloon,** at Baldwin Avenue in the heart of town, makes an ideal stop for a hearty breakfast (see Chapter 12); afterward, you can bop around the corner to 30 Baldwin Ave., where **Café Mambo** (☎ **808-579-8021**) offers sandwiches and box lunches for you to take on the road.

Just beyond Paia town is **Hookipa Beach Park,** one of the greatest wind-surfing spots on the planet; see the section "Combing the beaches," ear-lier in this chapter, for details.

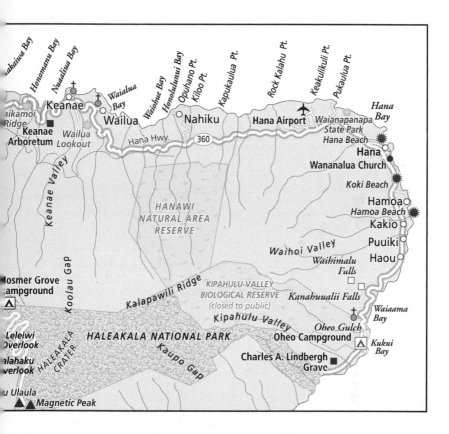

The road narrows to one lane in each direction and starts winding around mile marker 3. But it's at mile marker 16 that the curves really begin, one right after another. Slow down and enjoy the bucolic surroundings. After mile marker 16, the highway number changes from 36 to 360, and the mile markers start again at 0. (I have no idea why.)

At Mile Marker 2: The first great place to stop is **Twin Falls,** on the inland side of the road; the Twin Falls Fruit Stand marks the spot. Hop over the short ladder on the right side of the red gate and walk about three to five minutes to the waterfall off to your left, or continue on another 10 to 15 minutes to the second, larger waterfall. The gate has a "No Trespassing" sign, but you'll see from the crowds that it doesn't bother most folks. If it bothers you, skip Twin Falls altogether; there's plenty more to see farther down the road.

After Mile Marker 4: The vegetation grows more lush as you head east. This area is the edge of the **Koolau Forest Reserve,** where the branches of 20- to 30-foot-tall guava trees are laden with green (not ripe) and yellow (ripe) fruit, and introduced eucalyptus trees grow as tall as 200 feet.

The upland forest gets 200 to 300 inches of rainfall annually, so you'll begin to see waterfalls around just about every turn as you head east from here. The one-lane bridges start, too, so drive slowly and be prepared to yield to oncoming cars.

After Mile Marker 6: Just before mile marker 7 is a forest of waving bamboo. The sight is so spectacular that drivers are often tempted to take their eyes off the road, so be very cautious. Just after mile marker 7, you can pull over at the **Kaaiea Bridge,** which offers a terrific view of the bamboo grove.

At Mile Marker 9: The sign says "Koolau State Forest Reserve," but the real attraction is the **Waikamoi Ridge Trail,** an easy and well-marked ¾-mile loop. This trail makes a great place to stretch your legs; look for the turnout on the right.

Between Mile Markers 10 and 11: At the halfway point, on the inland side of the road, is the **Garden of Eden Botanical Gardens & Arboretum** (☎ 808-572-9899; www.mauigardenofeden.com), featuring more than 500 exotic plants, flowers, and trees from around the Pacific (including lots of wild ginger and an impressive palm collection) on 26 acres. You can drive through the garden in about five minutes, walk its main loop in about 20 minutes, or stay a bit longer and follow any number of nature trails. The garden is open daily from 8 a.m. to 3 p.m., and admission is $10 per person. A fruit-and-smoothie stand offers refreshment at the gate.

At Mile Marker 11: Park at the bridge and take the short walk up the stone wall–lined trail to 30-foot **Puohokamoa Falls,** tucked away in a fern-filled amphitheater surrounded by banana trees, colorful heliconias, and sweet-smelling ginger. The gorgeous pool is a great place to take a plunge.

Just Beyond Mile Marker 12: Kaumahina State Wayside Park has portable toilets and picnic tables at the large parking area, plus a gorgeous view of the rugged coastline across the road.

Just Beyond Mile Marker 14: One of my favorite stops on the entire drive is **Honomanu Bay,** a stark rocky beach popular with net fishermen that faces a beautiful bay. Tear your eyes away from the water, and you'll find incredible golden-green cliffs forming an intense backdrop as you look inland and up. The turnoff is on the left, at the stop sign just after the mile marker; don't attempt the rutted and rocky road if it has been raining recently.

Just Beyond Mile Marker 17: Keanae Lookout is a wide spot on the ocean side of the road where you can see the entire Keanae Peninsula jutting out into the sea, with its checkerboard pattern of green taro fields and its ocean boundary etched in black lava. If time is precious, though, wait to stop after mile marker 19, where the view from the **Wailea Valley** viewpoint is even better.

At Mile Marker 18: The road widens, and fruit and flower stands begin to line the road. Many of these stands operate on the honor system: You select your purchase and leave your money in the basket. I recommend stopping at **Uncle Harry's,** just beyond Keanae School on the ocean side of the road. Harry Kunihi Mitchell was a legend in his time, an expert in native plants who devoted his life to the Hawaiian-rights and nuclear-free movements.

A Quarter-Mile after Marker 19: For the best view of the **Wailua Peninsula,** stop at the lookout and parking area on the ocean side of the road, where sun-dappled picnic tables serve up great views.

A bit farther down the road, just before the bridge on the inland side, is a pretty waterfall view.

Between Mile Markers 22 and 23: At **Puaa Kaa** (poo-*ah*-ah *ka*-ah) **State Wayside Park,** the splash of waterfalls provides the soundtrack for a small park area with restrooms and a picnic area. On the opposite side of the road from the toilets is a well-marked and paved path that leads through a patch of sweet-smelling ginger to the falls and a swimming hole.

After Mile Marker 25: After the mile marker, turn toward the ocean at the steep turnoff just before the one-lane bridge and follow the well-paved but winding road 2½ miles down to the **Old Nahiku Lookout,** one of the very few points along the entire route that lets you get close to the ocean, and the finest picnic spot on the entire route. A small grassy lawn faces rocky lava points and crashing turquoise surf for a breathtaking, up-close view. You can walk down to the rocky beach at the backside of the parking lot.

At Mile Marker 31: Turn toward the ocean on Ulaino Road and go a half-mile to **Kahanu Garden,** one of four National Tropical Botanical Gardens in Hawaii (☎ 808-248-8912; www.ntbg.org). Surrounded by a native pandanus forest (the leaf that lauhala products are woven from), the garden features a remarkable collection of ethno-botanical plants from the Pacific islands (with a particular concentration on plants of value to the people of Polynesia and Micronesia), plus the foundation of Poolanihale Heiau, the largest Hawaiian temple in Hawaii. The self-guided walking tour is $10 (free for kids 12 and under) and takes 30 to 40 minutes to complete; open Monday through Friday from 10 a.m. to 2 p.m. The road that leads to the garden entrance is rough and unpaved, but not bad; still, don't bother if it's been raining.

At Mile Marker 32: The turnoff for 122-acre **Waianapanapa** (wa-ee-na-pa-*na*-pa) **State Park** leads to shiny black-sand **Waianapanapa Beach,** whose bright-green jungle backdrop and sparkling cobalt water make for quite a stunning view. On hand are picnic pavilions, restrooms, trails, and fruit stands lining the road, so come down to take a peek. The beach here is not for swimming, though. A blowhole appears when the winter surf kicks up. This natural hole in the rocks is configured so that when harsh surf kicks up, water shoots through the hole like a spout — quite a neat sight.

Arriving in Hana

Postage stamp–size Hana is a lush and charming little hamlet, but frankly, there's just not much to see in the town itself.

The few attractions include the **Hana Coast Gallery,** on the Hana Highway adjacent to the Hotel Hana-Maui (☎ **808-248-8636;** www.hana coast.com), an excellent showcase for fine arts and island-made products hewn by master craftspeople, including gorgeous woodworks. The quirky **Hasegawa General Store (☎ 808-248-8231)** is worth stopping in for kicks (look for the Spam sushi vending machine near the entrance) or to use the ATM, but the prices on practicals and munchies are better across the road and up the hill at the **Hana Ranch Store (☎ 808-248-8261).** If you want a meal, you might try the casual **Hana Ranch Restaurant,** or the gourmet Hotel Hana-Maui dining room, **Ka'uiki;** for details, see Chapter 12.

History buffs may want to head toward Hana Bay; overlooking the bay is the **Hana Cultural Center and Museum,** 4974 Uakea Rd., near the turnoff to Hana Bay (☎ **808-248-8622;** www.hookele.com/hccm), open daily from 10 a.m. to 4 p.m. (most of the time). This charming museum is dedicated to preserving the history of Hana, with exhibits showcasing traditional Hawaiian quilts and such implements of life as poi boards and fish hooks carved out of the tusks of wild pigs. Also on-site is the Old Hana Courthouse and Jailhouse, plus Kauhala O Hana, four *hale* (living structures) where you can see what it was like to live in the style of Hana's earliest settlers. Admission is $2 (free for kids 12 and under).

If you want to see more of what's available in town, pick up a copy of the **Hana Visitors Guide,** a foldout map and pamphlet that's available free around town. If you don't run across one, stop into Hasegawa's to pick one up.

For those of you spending some time in these parts, a number of active adventures are at hand:

✔ **Hang Gliding Maui (☎ 808-572-6557;** www.hangglidingmaui.com) offers tandem instructional flights aboard its engine-powered ultralight aircraft. Prices are $130 for a 30-minute lesson, $220 for an hour-long lesson.

✔ If you want to explore the lush Kipahulu District on horseback, reach out to **Maui Stables (☎ 808-248-7799;** www.mauistables. com), which offers a taste of real island culture as you explore the gorgeous scenery. Choose a morning or afternoon half-day tour; prices are $150 per person, including a deli lunch (discounts available for kids and seniors). Advance reservations are a must, as are closed shoes and long pants.

Hana

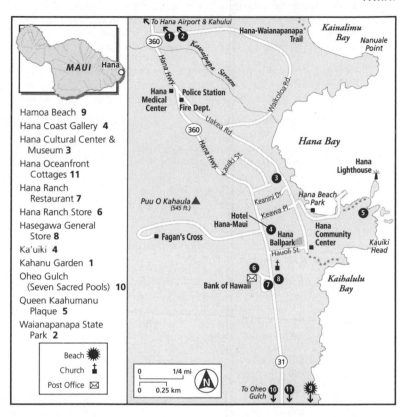

Hamoa Beach **9**
Hana Coast Gallery **4**
Hana Cultural Center & Museum **3**
Hana Oceanfront Cottages **11**
Hana Ranch Restaurant **7**
Hana Ranch Store **6**
Hasegawa General Store **8**
Ka'uiki **4**
Kahanu Garden **1**
Oheo Gulch (Seven Sacred Pools) **10**
Queen Kaahumanu Plaque **5**
Waianapanapa State Park **2**

Beach
Church
Post Office

✔ **Hana Lava Tube** (☎ 808-248-7308; www.mauicave.com) offers the chance to take a 30- to 45-minute self-guided tour ($12 adults, free for kids age 5 and under) through an ancient underground lava-tube system, through which lava flowed two centuries ago when Haleakala was an active volcano. Open Monday to Thursday from 10:30 a.m. to 3:30 p.m.; no reservations are needed, but call a day ahead to confirm that the caves will be open; occasionally, they're open on Sunday, too.

Exploring beyond Hana: Hamoa Beach and Oheo Gulch

About 2½ miles past Hana is the turnoff for Hamoa Beach, one of the most gorgeous beaches in all Hawaii — and great for swimming to boot (in summer, anyway). For details, see the section "Combing the beaches," earlier in this chapter.

About 10 luxuriant miles past Hana along the highway is **Oheo** (oh-*hay*-oh) **Gulch,** a dazzling series of waterfall pools cascading into the sea. Some folks call this the Seven Sacred Pools, even though there are more like two dozen. This area is the Kipahulu district of Haleakala National Park (www.nps.gov/hale), and a **ranger station** located at the back of the unpaved parking lot (☎ 808-248-7375) is staffed daily from 9 a.m. to 5 p.m. Restrooms are available, but no drinking water, so be sure to pick some up in Hana if you're out. Visiting this area of the park is free.

The easy, half-mile **Kuloa Point Loop Trail** leads to the lower pools, where you can take a dip when the weather is warm and the water is placid. This well-marked 20-minute walk is a must for everyone.

Stay out of the Oheo Gulch pools in winter or after a heavy rain, when the otherwise-placid falls can wash you out to sea in an instant, to the waiting sharks below. (No kidding — they actually do hang out in the brackish water at the foot of the falls.) No matter what the season, if you do take a dip, always be extra vigilant — keep an eye on the water in the streams. Even when the sky is sunny near the coast, upland rain can cause floodwaters to rise in minutes, so if the water seems to be running between the pools at all, stay out. A mainland visitor was washed away to sea during a seemingly innocuous Oheo Gulch photo op in May 2002. Don't let this terrible tragedy be repeated; always check with the rangers before you go in the pools.

The 2-mile (each way), moderate **Pipiwai Trail** leads upstream to additional pools and 400-foot Waimoku Falls. The often-muddy but rewarding uphill trail leads through taro patches and bamboo, guava, and mango stands to the magnificent falls. The trail is unmarked but relatively easy to follow. Wear sturdy shoes, bring water, and don't attempt the trek in the rain.

Heading back to the resorts

Before departing Hana, don't forget to check your gas gauge no matter which road west you're traveling. There's nowhere to fill up along either route back to civilization. If you need gas, stop at one of the town's two service stations, Chevron and Hasegawa's Hana Geko Gas, which sit nearly side by side on the right side of the Hana Highway as you leave town. (Prepare for sticker shock at the pump, though!)

More attractions worth seeking out

Here are some more attractions that you may not want to miss.

Central Maui

These attractions are located in and around the commercial heart of the island, Kahului, and nearby Wailuku, the charming county seat. Wailuku offers a few funky places to shop for antiques and Hawaiiana; see "Shopping the Local Stores," later in this chapter.

Bailey House Museum

This 19th-century missionary and sugar planter's home — built in 1833 on a royal Hawaiian site — is a treasure-trove of Hawaiiana that includes a notable collection of precontact Hawaiian artifacts as well as items from post-missionary times. Excellently curated island-themed temporary exhibits are also part of the mix. This little museum is well worth a half-hour stop for history buffs. It boasts lovely gardens and a wonderful gift shop, too, neither of which requires admission.

See p. 268. 2375-A Main St., just west of the Kaahumanu Avenue/Honoapiilani Highway (Highway 32/30) intersection, Wailuku. ☎ *808-244-3326.* www.mauimuseum.org. *Admission: $5 adults, $4 seniors, $1 kids 7–12. Open: Mon–Sat 10 a.m.–4 p.m.*

Hawaii Nature Center — Iao Valley

Before you head into Iao Valley to explore, families will want to stop into this small, kid-centered interactive science center and nature museum located at the gateway of the Iao Valley State Monument. The center features great hands-on exhibits for kids and displays relating to the park's natural history. There's also a nice gift shop if you're in the market for nature-themed toys.

At the gateway to Iao Valley State Monument, 875 Iao Valley Rd. ☎ *808-244-6500.* www.hawaiinaturecenter.org. *Admission: $6 adults, $4 kids under 12. Open: Daily 10 a.m.–4 p.m.*

Call ahead to reserve a spot on Hawaii Nature Center's daily Rainforest Walk through Iao Valley, offered Monday through Friday at 11:30 a.m. and 1:30 p.m., and Saturday and Sunday at 11 a.m. and 2 p.m. Your guide can offer historical, cultural, and natural insight that you just can't gain on a self-guided tour. The price is $30 for adults, $20 for kids (prices include museum admission; children must be at least age 5 to join the Rainforest Walk). Be sure to wear closed-toe shoes suitable for an uneven trail.

Iao Valley State Monument

As you head west to Iao Valley, the transition between town and wild is so abrupt that most people who drive up into the valley don't realize they're suddenly in a rain forest. The walls of the canyon rise, and a 2,250-foot needle pricks gray clouds scudding across the blue sky. This is Iao (*ee-ow*) Valley, a place of great natural beauty and a haven for Mauians and visitors alike. You could easily spend a day here, but you can see everything in an hour or two. Two paved walkways loop the just-over-6-acre park; a leisurely 6-mile loop takes you past lush vegetation and lovely views of the Iao Needle (called Kukaemoku in Hawaiian), a fabulously impressive spire jutting 2,250 feet above sea level. This is the spot of the battle of Kepaniwai, where Kamehameha I conquered the Maui army in 1790 as part of his unification of the Hawaiian islands. An architectural park of Hawaiian heritage houses — including a Japanese teahouse with a lovely koi pond, a Chinese pagoda, a New England–style mission house, a Hawaiian *hale,* and a Portuguese garden — stands in harmony by Iao Stream at Kepaniwai Heritage Garden, near the entrance to the park. It makes an excellent picnic area, because tables are at hand. You'll see ferns, banana trees, and other native and exotic plants in the streamside botanic garden.

See map p. 268. On Iao Valley Road (at the end of Main Street/Highway 32), Wailuku. www.hawaiistateparks.org. *To get there: From Kahului, follow Kaahumanu Avenue east directly to Main Street and the park entrance. Admission: Free. Open: Daily 7 a.m.–7 p.m.*

West Maui: Historic Lahaina town

It may be hard to believe these days, overrun as Lahaina is with contemporary tourist schlock. But any of you who've read James Michener's *Hawaii* know that back in the whaling and missionary days, Lahaina was the capital of Hawaii and the Pacific's wildest port. Now it's a party town of a different kind and has lost much of its historic vibe, but history buffs with an interest can unearth a half-day's worth of historic sites.

Your best bet is to start at the **Baldwin Home Museum,** a beautifully restored 1838 missionary home at the corner of Front and Dickenson streets, where the **Lahaina Restoration Foundation** (☎ **808-661-3262**) is headquartered. Stop in any day between 10 a.m. and 4:30 p.m. to pick up the free self-guided walking tour brochure and map of Lahaina's most historic sites.

South Maui

These terrific attractions are located in Maalaea Harbor Village, at the northernmost end of South Maui.

Maui Golf & Sports Park

This first-class miniature golf play land boasts two courses that have been designed with both fun and duffing precision in mind. The park also offers bumper boats with water cannons (great on a hot day), a rock climbing wall, and an "xtreme" trampoline. All activities carry separate charges, or you can bundle them into a package deal. Tiki torches set the mood after dark, and the staff is very friendly. It's ideal for both family fun and an after-dinner date.

See map p. 268. In Maalaea Harbor Village (at the triangle between Honoapiilani Highway [Highway 30] and Maalaea Road; the entrance is on Maalaea Road), Maalaea. ☎ *808-242-7818.* www.mauigolfandsportspark.com. *Activity prices: $15 for adults, $12 kids for unlimited miniature golf; other activities $9 adults, $7 kids. Package rates available. Open: Daily 10 a.m.–9 p.m.*

Maui Ocean Center

This state-of-the-art aquarium is way too pricey for its own good — it's no Monterey Bay Aquarium, after all. If you can overlook the cost, it's a pretty cool place. All exhibits feature the creatures that populate Hawaii's waters. Start at the surge pool, where you'll see shallow-water marine life like spiny urchins and cauliflower coral; then move on to the reef tanks, a turtle lagoon (where you'll meet some wonderful green sea turtles), a "touch" pool featuring tide-pool critters, a stingray pool populated by the graceful bottom dwellers, and a disappointing whale discovery exhibit (no live creatures). Then you get to the star of the show: the 600,000-gallon main tank, which features tiger, gray, and white-tip sharks, as well as tuna, surgeon fish, triggerfish, and other large-scale tropicals. The neatest thing about the tank is that it's punctured by a clear acrylic tunnel that lets you walk right through it, giving you a real idea of what it might be like to stand at the bottom of the deep blue sea. Allow about two hours for your visit.

See map p. 268. In Maalaea Harbor Village, 192 Maalaea Rd. (at the triangle between Honoapiilani Highway [Highway 30] and Maalaea Road), Maalaea. ☎ *808-270-7000.* www.mauioceancenter.com. *Admission: $24 adults, $21 seniors (ages 65+), $17 kids 3–12. Open: Daily 9 a.m.–5 p.m. (July–Aug daily 9 a.m.–6 p.m.).*

Hitting the links

Always book your tee times well in advance on popular Maui, especially in high season. Weekdays are best for avoiding the crowds and securing the tee times that you want.

The **Maui Golf Shop,** 357 Huku Lii Place, Kihei (☎ **800-981-5512** or 808-875-4653; www.golf-maui.com), can book discounted tee times for you at many of Maui's finest courses (including, at press time, the Dunes, Kaanapali, and Makena, all listed later in this section). If you want to schedule your tee times before you leave home, you can submit your requests online (where you'll also find information and insider tips on playing a wealth of Maui links) up to 30 days in advance. After you arrive, the Maui Golf Shop is the best place on the island to rent clubs and stock up on gear. It's located just off the Piilani Highway (Highway 31) at Ohukai Road (behind Tesoro Gas Express). You can also check out discounter **Tee Times Hawaii.com** (☎ **888-675-GOLF** or 866-927-1453; www.teetimeshawaii.com).

The Dunes at Maui Lani

This dramatic British links–style course was completed in 1997, but it plays like an old pro. Inspired by the old-growth links of Ireland, Honolulu-based course architect Robin Nelson built this public course on the former home of a sand-mining operation, which has allowed the fairways to mature in record time. Several blind and semiblind shots give this all-around enjoyable course an edge. Considering the quality of the course, the rates are a veritable bargain. Private lessons and half-day schools at the PGA pro-taught golf school even make improving your swing a comparatively affordable endeavor.

See map p. 268. 1333 Mauilani Pkwy., Kahului. ☎ *808-873-0422.* www.dunesat mauilani.com. *Greens fees: $99, $75 after 2 p.m.*

Kaanapali Golf Resort

Both of these popular, rolling resort courses pose a challenge to all golfers, from high handicappers to near-pros. In December 2006, the Tournament North Course emerged from a major renovation that slightly retooled the layout and left the course looking better than ever. It's a true Robert Trent

Jones, Jr., design, with an abundance of wide bunkers; several long, stretched-out tees; the largest, most contoured greens on Maui; and one of Hawaii's toughest finishing holes. The par-70, 6,400-yard Resort South Course is an Arthur Jack Snyder design that was renovated in 2005 by renowned course architect Robin Nelson, who added new deep bunkers and landscaping. Although the course still demands challenging shots, the refreshed layout brings the short game and shot selection into play, making it a fun outing for a wide spectrum of players. Facilities include a driving range, putting green, clubhouse, and comprehensive golf academy.

See map p. 268. 2290 Kaanapali Pkwy. (off Highway 30), Kaanapali. ☎ 866-454-GOLF [4653] or 808-661-3691. www.kaanapali-golf.com. *Greens fees: $195–$235 ($150–$290 for Kaanapali resort guests); $75–$95 after 1:30 p.m.*

Kapalua Golf Club

These three spectacularly sited championship courses are worth the sky-high greens fees for the magnificent ocean views alone. Resort golf hardly gets finer; *Hawaii* magazine regularly names the Bay and the Plantation courses as two of the top nine courses in Hawaii. An Arnold Palmer/Francis Duane design, the par-72, 6,600-yard Bay Course is a bit forgiving thanks to generous and gently undulating fairways, but even the pros have trouble with the 5th, which requires a tee shot over an ocean cove. The breathtaking — and breathtakingly difficult — Ben Crenshaw/Bill Coore–designed Plantation Course is prime for developing your low shots and precise chipping; this 7,263-yard, par-73 showstopper is home to the PGA's annual Mercedes Championships. The par-71, 6,632-yard Village Course, a Palmer/Ed Seay design and the most scenic of the three courses, suits beginners and pros alike, but winds can make for a challenging day among the Cook and Norfolk pines. Facilities include locker rooms, driving range, and restaurant. The first-rate **Kapalua Golf Academy** (☎ **877-527-2582** or 808-665-5455), designed with the input of golf legend Hale Irwin, just may be Hawaii's best place to improve the swing of beginners and almost-pros alike.

See map p. 268. Off Honoapiilani Highway (Highway 30), Kapalua. ☎ 877-527-2582 or 808-669-8044. www.kapaluamaui.com. *Greens fees: $215–$295 ($175–$200 for Kapalua resort guests); $185–$255 mid-day (11 a.m.–1:50 p.m.) Apr–Sept; $130–$150 after 2 p.m. Check the Web site for seasonal specials and golf packages.*

Makena Golf Courses

Robert Trent Jones, Jr., was in top form when he designed these 36 holes. The par-72, 7,017-yard oceanside South Course is considered the more for-giving of the two, but has a couple of holes that you'll never forget: Running parallel to the ocean, the par-4 16th has a two-tiered green that slopes away from the player, and the par-5, 502-yard 10th is one of Hawaii's best driving holes. With tight fairways and narrow doglegs, the par-72, 6,914-yard North Course is both more difficult and more spectacular because it sits higher up the slope of Haleakala. Facilities include a clubhouse, a driving range, two putting greens, a pro shop, lockers, and lessons. Additional bonuses include a gorgeous rural setting and spectacular views.

See map p. #268. 5415 Makena Alanui Dr., Makena (south of Wailea). ☎ *808-879-4000 or 808-875-5817.* www.makenagolf.com. *Greens fees: $155–$200 ($125–$130 for Makena resort guests), $135–$155 after 1 p.m.*

Wailea Golf Club

Most difficult among Wailea's courses is the par-72, 7,070-yard Gold Course, home to the Wendy's Championship Skins Game, which features senior golf legends in competition. This classic Robert Trent Jones, Jr., design boasts a rugged layout, narrow fairways, several tricky dogleg holes, daunting natural hazards, and only-in-Hawaii features like lava outcroppings and native grasses. Both the Old Blue and the Emerald are easy for most golfers to enjoy, but the par-72, 6,407-yard Emerald Course — another Trent Jones, Jr., design — is both the prettiest and the easiest for high-handicappers to enjoy. The par-72, 6,700-yard Old Blue Course, an open course designed by Arthur Jack Snyder, has wide fairways that also appeal to beginners, but bunkers, water hazards, and undulating terrain make it a course that all can enjoy. Facilities include two clubhouses, two pro shops, restaurants, lockers, club rentals, and a complete training facility.

Call to inquire about discounted afternoon rates, money-saving triple- and unlimited-play passes, and other specials, including junior golf rates.

See map p. 268. Off Wailea Alanui Drive, Wailea. ☎ *888-328-MAUI, 800-322-1614, or 808-875-7450.* www.waileagolf.com. *Greens fees: $225 ($130 for the Old Blue Course); $180–$190 for Wailea Resort guests; twilight rates $99–$135.*

Relaxing at a Spa

What's the icing on the cake of any vacation? A pampering spa day, of course. Hawaii's spas have raised the art of relaxation and healing to a new level, showcasing Hawaiian products and traditional treatments available only in the islands.

They simply don't come any finer than the luxurious **Spa Grande** at the Grand Wailea Resort (☎ **800-888-6100** or 808-875-1234; www.grand wailea.com), which is regularly recognized as one of the top ten spas in the United States. This 50,000-square-foot temple to the good life boasts a massive East-meets-West spa menu, a first-rate army of therapists, and 40 individual treatment rooms (many with ocean views). There's a full Termé hydrotherapy circuit consisting of a variety of healthful baths (including mud, seaweed, aromatherapy, tropical enzyme, and mineral salt), Roman pools, and Swiss-jet showers that are worth the treatment price of admission alone. (They're included with every treatment, so I recommend coming a full hour or more before your appointment.) Book a full day's package for the ultimate indulgence — you deserve it. Reserve well ahead.

In West Maui, your top choice is **Spa Moana** at the Hyatt Regency Maui (☎ **808-667-4725** or 808-661-1234; www.maui.hyatt.com), a 15,000-square-foot oceanview spa with 15 treatment rooms, a full-service salon with prime views, an open-air relaxation lounge, and an extensive treatment menu that includes some dynamite facials, as well as soothing body work. Two couples suites allow for romantically infused relaxation. The adjacent Moana Athletic Club has the finest views of any fitness center on the island.

If you're in Lahaina and in the mood for some storefront pampering, visit **Lei Spa Maui,** in the 505 Front St. complex, at the far south end of Front Street (☎ **808-661-1178;** www.leispa.com), which carries a wonderful line of fragrant and rejuvenating Hawaii-made bath and body products, and therapists offer massages, body wraps, and facials.

For the ultimate in Upcountry relaxation, contact **Maui Spa Retreat** (☎ **808-573-8002;** www.mauisparetreat.com). Boasting a majestic perch on the slopes of Haleakala, this hidden gem can reward you with one of the finest spa days you'll ever enjoy. The petite spa is also an aromatherapy farm, and the proprietor blends all of her own body scrubs, wraps, and healing oils. If you book the spa as a couple, you'll have it all to yourself; I recommend a three-hour spa package for two, which includes private use of the outdoor spa, sauna, and outdoor showers. A divine day spent here is like having your own private spa, and pampering at the hands of the finest therapists on the island. If you are a spa aficionado, don't miss it.

Shopping the Local Stores

When it comes to shopping opportunities, the Valley Isle is the reigning king among the neighbor islands in terms of quantity. Its status is a bit more dubious when it comes to quality, but you will find some real gems in the eclectic mix.

Central Maui: Wailuku and Kahului

Although Kahului is the island's hub and the place to go for practical items, the historic town of Wailuku, immediately to the west, offers reasonably good hunting grounds for antiques hounds. It's still a mixed bag, but a few quality shops featuring both new and used treasures can be found on North Market Street. To get there, simply go west from Kahului on Kaahumanu Avenue and turn right when you reach Market, in the heart of Wailuku.

Highlights include **Brown-Kobayashi,** 38 N. Market St. (☎ **808-242-0804**), a treasure-trove of graceful Asian antiques (mostly large pieces, but affordable prices make the shipping worth it for committed collectors); and **Bird of Paradise Unique Antiques,** 54 N. Market St. (☎ **808-242-7699**), a jumble of collectible glassware, pottery, and Hawaiiana.

If you're in the mood for a little island music, **Mele Ukulele,** before the old Wailuku bridge at 1750 Kaahumanu Ave. (☎ **808-244-3938;** www.mele ukulele.com), carries Hawaii's largest selection of new and used ukes.

In Kahului, stop by **Hawaiian Island Surf and Sport,** 415 Dairy Rd., Kahului (☎ **800-231-6958** or 808-871-4981; www.hawaiianisland.com), for all of your surfing, body boarding, and water play needs.

West Maui: Lahaina, Kaanapali, and Kapalua

Lahaina's main drag, Front Street, overflows with surf-wear shops, contemporary art galleries, trendy boutiques, cheesy T-shirt shops, and much, much more — you'll tire of browsing well before you run out of places to flex your credit card.

Your best bet is to just start at one end and browse. Highlights include **Serendipity,** 752 Front St. (☎ **808-879-7100;** www.serendipitymaui.com), for casual, island-style women's wear in comfortable, loose-fitting styles. **Honolua Surf Co.,** 845 Front St. (☎ **808-661-8848;** www.honoluasurf.com), carries its own fabulous line of surf wear and gear (you'll find additional locations in Whalers Village, the Lahaina Cannery Mall, Kihei, and the Shops at Wailea). Another excellent stop for surf wear and gear is **Tropix,** 790 Front St. (☎ **808-661-9296**), Maui's homegrown surf company.

Célébrités, 764 Front St. (☎ **800-428-3338;** www.celebrityfineart.com), features art by and about celebrities. It's the height of over-the-top conspicuous consumption, but it's a compelling browse nonetheless. **Vintage European Posters,** 744 Front St. (☎ **808-662-8688;** www.europeanposters.com), boasts a fantastic array of original poster art from 1890 to 1950, mostly European and all in mint condition; prices are excellent considering the quality of the stock. Also worth checking out are the vibrant, three-dimensional natural panoramas of globetrotting photographer Peter Lik, whose **Peter Lik Gallery,** 712 Front St. (☎ **808-661-6623;** www.peterlik.com), is definitely worth a browse.

An island of artistic integrity in the sea of Lahaina kitsch is **Na Mea Hawaii Store,** in the Baldwin Home, 120 Dickenson St., at Front Street (☎ **808-661-5707**), which sells only fine-quality island-made crafts and gifts. That doesn't always mean expensive, though; you'll find a surprising number of affordable prizes among the bounty.

For marine-themed goods and educational gifts for kids, you can't do better than the surprisingly nice nonprofit **Pacific Whale Foundation** store, 612 Front St. (☎ **808-667-7447;** www.pacificwhale.org). Members save 15 percent off all whale- and eco-themed goodies, as well as whale-watching cruises and snorkel tours, which can be booked right at the shop (see the section "Ocean cruising to Molokini and Lanai and other on-deck adventures," earlier in this chapter), so consider joining up for a good cause.

Old Lahaina Book Emporium, 834 Front St. (☎ **808-661-1399;** www.oldlahainabookemporium.com), is a wonderful haunt for used and new fiction, nonfiction, music, and videos.

At the opposite, north end of Front Street are a couple of shopping centers, including **Lahaina Cannery Mall,** 1221 Honoapiilani Hwy. (☎ 808-661-5304; www.lahainacannerymall.com), for practicals. The **Lahaina Center,** 900 Front St. (☎ 808-667-9216; www.lahaina center.com), is a pleasant open-air mall that boasts **Hilo Hattie,** Hawaii's biggest name in affordable aloha wear, and a multiscreen movie theater — perfect for rainy days. Newest on the scene is **Lahaina Gateway** (☎ 808-893-0300; www.lahainagateway.com), a sprawling new complex on the highway featuring such big names as **Barnes & Noble** and **Outback Steakhouse.**

On the beach in Kaanapali, **Whalers Village,** 2435 Kaanapali Pkwy. (☎ 808-661-4567; www.whalersvillage.com), has blossomed into quite an upscale shopping and dining complex, offering a surprisingly appealing open-air shopping experience (after you get past the ordeal of parking). Although it has become the Rodeo Drive of Maui in recent years, with several high-end designer names, it also has some surprisingly excellent midrange boutiques. You'll find two branches of **Honolua Surf Co.,** which I just love for stylish surf gear and wear; **Sandal Tree,** for an excellent collection of women's footwear, sun hats, and handbags; a branch of **Reyn's,** for gorgeous, contemporary aloha wear; **Martin & MacArthur,** for island crafts; **Lahaina Printsellers,** for antique prints, maps, and engravings; **The Body Shop,** in case you need to stock up on eco-friendly sunscreen; and much more.

In Kapalua, stop by the freshly renovated **Honolua Store,** 502 Office Rd. (☎ 808-665-9105), the resort's beloved plantation store, a lone holdover from when this region grew sugar cane and pineapple rather than golfers and sunbathers. In business since 1929, the new Honolua Store has recaptured its vintage feel, marrying it with an ultra-modern selection of wine and locally made gourmet food and gift products. There are also an espresso bar and plate lunch counter.

South Maui: Wailea

The lovely open-air **Shops at Wailea,** 3750 Wailea Alanui Dr. (☎ 808-891-6770; www.shopsatwailea.com), features both practical retailers and elegant gift outlets. Stores run the gamut from **Tiffany & Co., Louis Vuitton,** and **Gucci** to **Gap** and **Banana Republic.** Specialty stores worth seeking out include **Footprints** for an excellent selection of sandals for men, women, and children; **Martin & MacArthur** for handcrafted koa and other Hawaii crafts; **Blue Ginger,** which has brought batik into the 21st century with its bold prints and flowing modern cuts; **Tommy Bahama's Emporium,** whose tropically sophisticated clothing store also boasts a winning oceanview cafe and bar (see Chapter 12); and much more.

Off the beaten path: Paia and Makawao

The hip little surf town of Paia (pa-*ee*-ah), just 15 minutes east of Kahului on the Hana Highway (Highway 36), makes an appealing stop for shoppers looking for funkier goods. The boutiques sprawl in a T shape from the intersection of the Hana Highway and Baldwin Avenue, and the choices range from the sublime to the ridiculous.

Some highlights include **Maui Crafts Guild,** on the ocean side of Hana Highway at no. 43 (☎ 808-579-9697; www.mauicraftsguild.com), an artist-owned cooperative that represents some of the finest fine artists and craftspeople on Maui; you'll find artworks and gifts in all price ranges here. **Moonbow Tropics,** at 20 and 36 Baldwin Ave. (☎ 800-541-9446, 808-579-8775, or 808-579-8592; www.moonbowtropicsmaui.com), offers the finest contemporary aloha-wear lines available.

Also on the Hana Highway, across the street from Maui Hands at no. 83, is **Tamara Catz** (☎ 808-579-9184; www.tamaracatz.com), the first boutique from the Argentine-born, New York–educated Catz, who is married to world windsurfing champ Francisco Goya. The designer specializes in sleek, sexy fashion with a feminine flair for confident women who love body-conscious wear, and has launched Paia as a burgeoning hub of cutting-edge chic in the islands.

From Paia, drive toward the mountain on Baldwin Avenue (Highway 390), and in 7 miles you'll reach Makawao (ma-*ka*-wow), a cowboy town turned New Age village that's another shopper's paradise, especially in the local arts category. Highlights include **The Courtyard,** at 3620 Baldwin Ave., which houses a number of interesting crafts shops of varying quality, including **Maui Hands** (☎ 808-572-5194; www.mauihands.com) — plus a fascinating glass blower's studio that's worth a peek: **Hot Island Glass Studio & Gallery** (☎ 808-572-4527; www.hotislandglass.com).

The true gem of Makawao is the **Hui Noeau Visual Arts Center,** a mile outside of town at 2841 Baldwin Ave. (☎ 808-572-6560; www.huinoeau.com). A tree-lined driveway leads to the 1917 estate (designed by noted Hawaii architect C. W. Dickey) that houses the island's most renowned artists' collective and features rotating exhibits by both established and up-and-coming island artists, plus an excellent shop featuring original works. There's a $2 suggested donation for the exhibit gallery. The artistically inclined among you might also want to inquire about workshops, demonstrations, visiting-artist events, and other short-term opportunities for study.

Living It Up after Dark

Many of the island's restaurants do double-duty as post-dinner hot spots, often hosting lively bar scenes, live music, and dancing. The epicenter of island nightlife is lively Lahaina.

For the most complete calendar of what's happening while you're on Maui, pick up a copy of the weekly *MauiTime Weekly* newspaper, available for free at kiosks all over the island. If you're after the more refined performing arts, look for a copy of *Centerpiece,* the free bimonthly magazine published by the **Maui Arts & Cultural Center;** hotel concierges usually have copies. You can also call the center, located in Kahului, at ☎ 808-242-7469 or visit the Web site at www.mauiarts.org for a current schedule. The diverse calendar might feature big names like Melissa Etheridge or David Sanborn; Maui Film Festival screenings; or performances by Hawaii's most renowned musicians (don't miss Amy Hanaialii Gilliom if she's on the calendar).

The island's best sunset cruises are offered by **Paragon Sailing Charters** (☎ 800-441-2087 or 808-244-2087; www.sailmaui.com). Prices for this two-hour sail, which include hors d'oeuvres and beverages, are $56 for adults, $39 for kids under age 12, but significant discounts are available for online advance bookings.

And, of course, don't forget that Maui is home to the finest examples of the ultimate island form of after-dark entertainment: the luau! I highly recommend planning to participate in one while you're on the Valley Isle. For details, see Chapter 12.

West Maui

All Lahaina takes on a festive atmosphere as sunset nears. The restaurants along oceanfront Front Street boast stellar views and energetic bar scenes, some with live music. Among the best are **Cheeseburger in Paradise,** 811 Front St. (☎ 808-661-4855), a regular forum for live-and-lively music; **Hard Rock Cafe,** 900 Front St. (☎ 808-667-7400); **Kimo's,** 845 Front St. (☎ 808-661-4811); and **Moose McGillycuddy's,** 844 Front St. (☎ 808-891-8600). **Mulligan's on the Wharf,** upstairs at the Wharf Cinema Center in the heart of town, on Front Street across from the banyan tree (☎ 808-661-8881; www.mulligansontheblue.com), offers rollicking live music in its casual Irish pub setting.

Lahaina is also home to two nightly shows that are well worth seeking out. Don't pass up an opportunity to see *'Ulalena,* at the Maui Myth & Magic Theatre, in Old Lahaina Center, 878 Front St. (☎ 877-688-4800 or 808-661-9913; www.ulalena.com). This incredible, Broadway-quality 75-minute live show interweaves the natural, historical, and mythological tales of the birth of Hawaii, using a mix of original contemporary music and dance, ancient chant and hula, creative lighting, gorgeous costumes, and visual artistry (including some mind-blowing puppets). Shows run 6:30 p.m. Tuesday through Saturday; additional shows may be added in high season. Tickets are $60 to $100 for adults, $40 to $70 for kids ages 3 to 12.

For something completely different, spend an evening at **Warren & Annabelle's,** 900 Front St. in Lahaina (☎ 808-667-6244; www.hawaii magic.com). This genuinely fun and surprisingly uncheesy mystery-and-magic cocktail show stars illusionist Warren Gibson and "Annabelle," a ghost who plays a grand piano — and even takes requests. Tickets are $56 per person (with food and drinks available for an additional charge); you must be at least 21 to enter. Dinner packages range from $95 per person. The show is very popular, so book at least a few days in advance to avoid disappointment; no shows performed on Sundays. Inquire about early-evening family-friendly shows, which are sometimes added during major school-holiday periods; call for details.

Kaanapali has its own family-friendly entertainment as well. **Kupanaha** is the terrific magic show at the Kaanapali Beach Hotel (☎ **808-667-0128;** www.kbhmaui.com/recreation/kupanaha.html), starring husband-and-wife illusionists Jody and Kathleen Baran and their daughters, Katrina and Crystal. The show interweaves illusions, Hawaiian hula and chant, and the stories and myths of ancient Hawaii into a show that the whole family will love (really!). Shows are offered Tuesday through Saturday at the family-friendly hour of 4:45 p.m.; dinner is included, and you'll be out by 7:30 p.m. Tickets are $79 to $89 for adults, $55 for teens 13 to 20, $39 for kids 6 to 12, including a three-course dinner; a kids' menu is available. Free for kids under age 6.

For live music in Kaanapali, head to **Whalers Village,** on Kaanapali Beach at 2435 Kaanapali Pkwy., where you can take an open-air seat facing the ocean at the bar at **Hula Grill** (☎ **808-667-6636**), which features Hawaiian music and hula. With Tiki torches flickering and the waves rolling in, you can't go wrong here.

In Napili, the Napili Kai Beach Resort hosts the **Masters of Hawaiian Slack Key Guitar** series (www.slackkey.com) every Wednesday evening. These concerts are a great way to learn more about Hawaiian music and culture. For reservations, call ☎ **888-669-3858** or 808-669-3858. Tickets are $45.

South Maui

South Maui is a tad quieter overall, but boasts a couple of hopping joints; call for schedules because the music can change nightly. Lively **Life's a Beach,** 1913 S. Kihei Rd. (next to Foodland), Kihei (☎ **808-891-8010;** www.mauibars.com), serves up live music nightly, usually starting at 10 p.m.

The casual, easygoing **South Shore Tiki Lounge,** in Kihei Kalama Village, 1913 S. Kihei Rd. (☎ **808-874-6444;** www.southshoretikilounge.com), specializes in first-class mai tais and affordable food in a fun 'n' funky Tiki setting; DJs set a party atmosphere most nights.

In the mood for a taste o' the Emerald Isle while you're on the Valley Isle? Head on over to **Mulligan's on the Blue,** 100 Kauhaki St., on the Wailea Blue Golf Course off Wailea Alanui Drive, across from the Fairmont Kea Lani (☎ **808-874-1131;** www.mulligansontheblue.com). Mulligan's is an genuine Irish pub, complete with Guinness on tap, traditional pub fare, and seven TVs complete with satellite sports channels, plus the kind of panoramic ocean view that only Maui can offer. Pubgoers enjoy high-quality live music nightly, with a Celtic spin on Sundays.

Upcountry Maui

One of the hottest party spots on the island is Upcountry, in the cowboy town of Makawao. The party never ends at the Italian restaurant **Casanova,** 1188 Makawao Ave. (☎ **808-572-0220;** www.casanovamaui. com). After the dinner hour on Wednesday, Friday, and Saturday (plus the occasional Thurs and Sun), attention turns from the good Italian food to socializing around the stage and dance floor. Wednesday is traditionally a ladies' night disco, Fridays and Saturdays bring DJs or live music; expect good blues, rock, reggae, jazz, Hawaiian, and the top names in local and visiting entertainment, which generally starts at 9:45 p.m. and continues to 1:30 a.m.

Part V
Hawaii, the Big Island

FEW MOMENTS IN SAILING COMPARE IN MAJESTY TO THE SHRINERS SUNSET REGATTA.

In this part . . .

The island of Hawaii isn't known as the Big Island for nothing. Measuring 4,038 square miles and roughly the size of Connecticut, the Big Island is more than twice the size of all the other islands combined. You'll do plenty of driving here if you plan to explore the island's many attractions — and I hope that you do. This thrilling island is the land of salt-and-pepper beaches, active lava flows, and tropical rain forests. The chapters in this part help you make the most of your time in this uniquely enchanting place.

Chapter 14

Settling into the Big Island

In This Chapter

▶ Getting from the airport to your hotel
▶ Finding your way around the Big Island and its major resort areas
▶ Choosing the perfect accommodations
▶ Discovering the Big Island's best restaurants
▶ Arranging for a luau

At 4,038 square miles, the Big Island really is *big*. Not only that, but a handful of volcanic mountains dominate the interior, making crossing from coast to coast a challenge, to say the least. If you want to visit all the Big Island's major attractions, I strongly suggest that you choose not one but two places to stay while you're here: one on the hot, arid Kona-Kohala coast, and the other on the lush, rain-forested volcano coast.

You *can* stay just on the Kona side of the island and visit Hawaii Volcanoes National Park on a day trip. It makes for a very long day, however: It takes at least three hours to reach the park from anywhere on the western coast.

 If you're planning to visit both sides of the island, here's a way to cut down on driving time and maximize sightseeing (or relaxation) time. I suggest that you fly in to one side of the island and fly out on the other. Either land at Kona and fly out of Hilo, or vice versa — it really doesn't matter. Doing so may cost you about 50 bucks in car-rental drop-off charges, but can save an extra 3- to 3½-hour drive to return to the coast you started from for your outbound flight, not to mention the cost of gas. Do note that the Hilo airport only accommodates interisland flights; if you want to take a flight to or from the mainland to the Big Island, you'll have to do so from Kona.

Arriving on the West Side at Kona Airport

Kona International Airport at Keahole (☎ **808-329-3423;** www.state. hi.us/dot/airports/hawaii/koa) is located 7 miles north of Kailua-Kona, just off Queen Kaahumanu Highway (Highway 19). Kona is served direct by an increasing number of flights from the mainland; interisland service is provided by **Hawaiian Airlines** and **go! Airlines.** This small,

Big Island Orientation

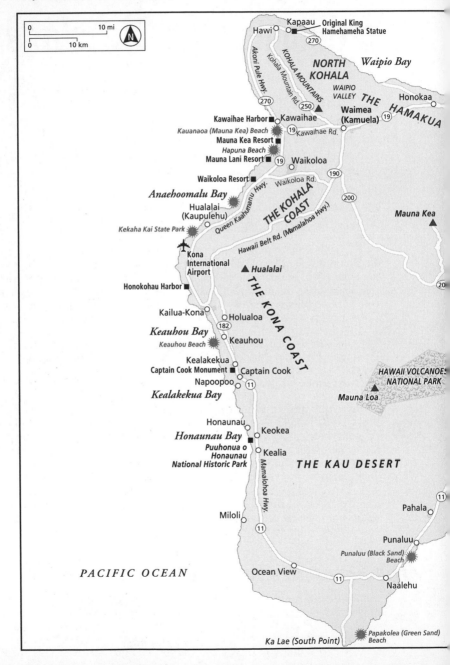

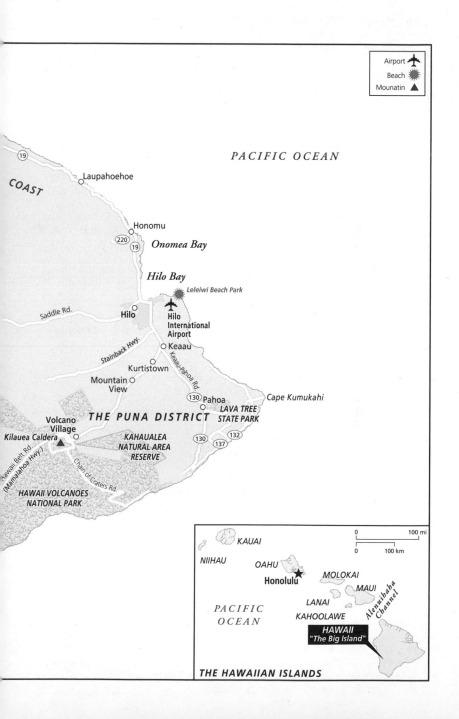

Airport	✈
Beach	☀
Mounatin	▲

PACIFIC OCEAN

(19)

COAST

Laupahoehoe

Honomu

(220) (19)

Onomea Bay

Hilo Bay

Lelelwi Beach Park

Saddle Rd.

Hilo

✈ **Hilo International Airport**

Stainback Hwy.

Keaau

Keaau-Pahoa Rd.

Kurtistown

Mountain View

(130) Pahoa

Cape Kumukahi

LAVA TREE STATE PARK

THE PUNA DISTRICT

Volcano Village

Kilauea Caldera ▲

KAHAUALEA NATURAL AREA RESERVE

(130) (132)

(137)

Hawaii Belt Rd. (Mamalahoa Hwy.)

Chain of Craters Rd.

HAWAII VOLCANOES NATIONAL PARK

KAUAI

NIIHAU

OAHU

Honolulu

0   100 mi

0   100 km

MOLOKAI

MAUI

LANAI

KAHOOLAWE

Alenuihaha Channel

PACIFIC OCEAN

HAWAII "The Big Island"

THE HAWAIIAN ISLANDS

open-air airport is a breeze to navigate. The major rental-car companies have service counters directly across the street, but you'll have to take a shuttle van to a nearby off-site lot to pick up your car.

While you're at the rental counter, be sure to pick up a map booklet from the agent; they're invaluable for getting around the island. They often include money-saving coupons for attractions as well.

If you're heading to the town of **Kailua-Kona,** turn right out of the airport onto Queen Kaahumanu (ka-a-hoo-*ma*-noo) Highway (Highway 19). Clearly marked turnoffs take you down to the town's main drag, Alii (ah-*lee*-ee) Drive, about 7 miles to the south. If you're continuing on to **South Kona** or **Keauhou** (kay-*a*-ho), stay on Highway 19 for another 7 or so miles; for Keauhou, turn toward the coast on Kamehameha III Road.

If you're heading to a **Kohala Coast** resort, turn left out of the airport onto Queen Kaahumanu Highway (Highway 19) and proceed to one of the following locations:

- ✔ **Kaupulehu** (cow-poo-*lay*-hoo), home to the Four Seasons Hualalai and Kona Village, is 7 miles north of the airport, or a ten-minute drive.

- ✔ **Waikoloa** (why-ko-*lo*-ah), home to the Waikoloa Beach Marriott, the Hilton Waikoloa Village, and some very nice luxury condos, is 18 miles north, or a 20- to 25-minute drive.

- ✔ **Mauna Lani,** home to the Fairmont Orchid, the Mauna Lani Bay Hotel and Bungalows, and its own great slate of condo resorts, is about 23 miles north, or a half-hour drive.

- ✔ **Mauna Kea** has its entrance 28 miles north of the airport, or a 40-minute drive.

Look for the gateway to your resort on the ocean side of the road; the only one that's on the right side of the road is the turnoff for the Hapuna Beach Prince Hotel, just before Mauna Kea's entrance. The resort entrances tend to be marked in a rather understated way, so look carefully.

If you're staying at one of the Kohala Coast resorts and don't need a rental car for your entire stay, you can usually arrange for the resort shuttle to pick you up at the airport. Then you can arrange to have a rental car delivered to your hotel only on the day(s) you need it. Call the concierge at your hotel for details before you arrive.

Taxis are also readily available at the airport, so you don't need to arrange for one in advance. If you prefer to, try **Kona Airport Taxi** (☎ 808-329-7779) for personal service. Expect the cost to be about $30 to Kailua-Kona, closer to $60 if you're heading to one of the Kohala Coast resorts. You can also prearrange airport transfers with **SpeediShuttle** (☎ 877-521-2085 or 808-329-5433; www.speedishuttle.com). If you forgot to call SpeediShuttle before you left home, dial "65" from one of the courtesy phones in baggage claim.

If you prefer to have a private car service transport you to your Kohala Coast resort in style, contact **Luana Limousine** (☎ **800-999-4001** or 808-326-5466; www.luanalimo.com); prices are competitive with taxi rates. Be sure to call a couple of days before you leave home to arrange pickup, and check on current rates to your destination.

Arriving on the East Side at Hilo Airport

Hilo (*hee*-low) **International Airport** (☎ **808-934-5840** or 808-934-5838; www.state.hi.us/dot/airports/hawaii/ito) is 2 miles east of downtown Hilo, at the junction of Kamehameha Avenue and Kanoelehua Avenue (Highway 11). It is primarily served by interisland flights on **Hawaiian Airlines** and **go! Airlines.**

Step outside and proceed straight to the rental-car desk. The cars are parked right outside — no rental-car bus to navigate. Be sure to pick up a map booklet at the rental counter.

If you're staying in **Hilo,** turn right out of the airport onto Kanoelehua Avenue (Highway 11), which will lead you right to Banyan Drive and the Hilo Hawaiian and Hawaii Naniloa hotels. To reach downtown and the waterfront, turn left onto Kamehameha Avenue just before Banyan Drive.

If you're heading to **Volcano Village,** turn left out of the airport onto Kanoelehua Avenue (Highway 11). Highway 11 will take you the 27 miles (a 45-minute or so drive) to Volcano Village, at the entrance of Hawaii Volcanoes National Park.

If you're staying in **Pahoa,** turn left out of the airport onto Kanoelehua Avenue (Highway 11), and follow Highway 11 to the Keaau-Pahoa Road (Highway 130); expect a 20-mile, half-hour drive, depending on your ultimate destination.

Taxis line up at the airport's curb, so you don't have to worry about arranging for one in advance. Expect to pay around $15 to a Hilo destination, plus tip. If you need to call a taxi, phone up **Shaka Taxi & Tours** (☎ **808-987-1111**).

Choosing Your Location

The west, or Kona, side of the Big Island is the hot, arid, beachy side, where all the island resorts and condos are located. The misty, luxuriantly green east side is home to the pretty, petite city of Hilo and spectacular Hawaii Volcanoes National Park.

On the west (Kona) side

This hot, dry, almost-always-sunny side of the island is where you go when you want to hit the beach. West Hawaii may come as a shock to some — this is parched, black-lava–covered land fringed by swaying palms, salt-and-pepper sand, and gorgeous Pacific waves. Still, it's a landscape of dramatic, otherworldly beauty. This side is where you'll find some of Hawaii's most gorgeous beaches (and some of the state's most expensive real estate).

The Kohala Coast

This ritzy resort coast stretches for about 30 miles north from Kona International Airport. This is where you'll find the island's most stunning beaches — it's no coincidence that the most upscale resorts chose to build here. No other resort coast in Hawaii boasts luxury spreads this sprawling or fabulously grand; sadly, you won't find many budget-friendly options here. Every hotel along the Kona-Kohala coast is part of a manicured "resort" development — Kaupulehu (cow-poo-*lay*-hoo), Waikoloa, Mauna Lani, and Mauna Kea, in order, from south to north. Each one functions something like a neighborhood, usually encompassing two resort hotels, upscale residential developments, and golf courses. Each resort has a clearly marked gateway off Queen Kaahumanu Highway (Highway 19, the coast's main drag) and its own network of roads, plus public beach access. Waikoloa and Mauna Lani boast their own sizable shopping and restaurant complexes.

When you're making your resort decision, take distance into consideration if you're planning to do lots of running around. Mauna Kea is at least a 30-minute drive from the airport and 40 or 45 minutes from Kailua-Kona town, which can make popping into town for dinner more work than you'd like. Kaupulehu (where the Four Seasons and Kona Village resort hotels are), on the other hand, is only about 10 or 15 minutes from Kailua-Kona and just 7 miles from the airport.

Kailua-Kona

About 7 miles south of Kona International Airport, the town Kailua-Kona is the commercial hub of the island's west side. It's similar to Maui's Lahaina, down to the tacky-touristy shopping and open-air restaurants along Alii (ah-*lee*-ee) Drive that open to spectacular ocean views. Kailua-Kona is a convenient and affordable place to stay, with lots of condo bargains. But the town has been changing in the past few years, with T-shirt shops, chain restaurants, and generic bars proliferating. The town has lost the sleepy, funky charm you'd expect in Hawaii, and traffic has become a bear, especially during the afternoon rush hour, in town and on the adjacent stretch of highway.

If you stay here, you'll have a convenient base for dining, nightlife, and shopping, but you'll have to drive to get to a decent beach. Choose one of the condo complexes south of town if you want better ocean access, great snorkeling, and a respite from crowds and noise. For a truly spectacular beach, you'll have to drive north to the Kohala Coast.

Upcountry Kona

Drive 15 minutes inland and upland from Kailua-Kona, and you'll enter a whole different world. Lush, green, cool, and quiet, this is the world-famous Kona coffee country. Charmingly funky Holualoa has, blessedly, retained the unadulterated vibe of old Hawaii. The village serves as a great alternative to the beach resorts if you're looking to get away from it all. Views are spectacular, the streets are lined with local art galleries housed in restored plantation cottages, and you won't hear much but bird song and the sound of the tropical fruit growing on the trees. It's an excellent choice for off-the-beaten-path types.

South Kona

A ten-minute drive south of Kailua-Kona town is South Kona, a significantly more relaxed and lush territory than Kona central. It's very convenient for dining, shopping, and activities, but it's much more sedate, with a handful of nice hotels and condo complexes, plus an excellent B&B on the slope above the coast, **Horizon Guest House** (see listing later in this chapter).

You'll have wonderful sunset ocean views no matter where you stay in South Kona. However, this stretch of coast has mostly salt-and-pepper pocket beaches, and they tend to be located close to the busy main road. Despite this drawback, South Kona beaches do offer some of the island's best offshore snorkeling, and you're significantly closer to Hawaii Volcanoes National Park than you are if you stay farther north on the coast. If you want a truly fantastic beach, you will have some driving to do — it's a good hour to the Kohala Coast from here, and traffic can be a trial sometimes.

The east (volcano) side

The east side of the Big Island seems like the polar opposite of the Kona side — it's cool, wet, rain-forested, and fragrant with tropical flowers (the Big Island is also known as the Orchid Isle). However, independent types tend to love its genuine local charm and sense of discovery. Stay on this side of the island if you want to dedicate some time to exploring **Hawaii Volcanoes National Park,** but expect a whole different kind of island experience here.

Volcano Village

The gateway to Hawaii Volcanoes National Park is **Volcano Village,** a network of charming B&Bs and vacation rentals tucked into the rain forest just outside the park's gate. Needless to say, Volcano Village makes the best base for exploring the park, but you'll have limited dining and shopping options in this postage stamp–size crossroads.

Hilo

Hawaii's largest city after Honolulu embodies Hawaii the way it used to be: It's a quaint, misty, flower-filled city with a gorgeous half-moon bay, a rustic false-fronted downtown, some beautifully restored Victorian houses, and a real penchant for rain — 128 inches a year makes it one of America's wettest cities. Not everybody loves Hilo, but those of us with a passion for anything retro do. It's just 30 minutes from the national park and offers more dining options, not to mention delightful off-the-beaten-path shopping. B&B lovers will delight in the city's top-notch choices.

Puna District: Pahoa

Want the best of both worlds — the hot, dry, island-style weather you expect, with easy access to Hawaii Volcanoes National Park? Consider this off-the-beaten-path region between Hilo and Volcano. It's not for everyone; there are no tourist services to speak of. The scruffy, offbeat town of Pahoa is still rough around the edges, but a tiny handful of good-quality restaurants and stylish shops have popped up of late. At this writing, the Puna District offered the island's easiest access to Kilauea's current lava flow, which was spilling into the ocean at the end of the road in Kalapana; national park officials had set up a temporary viewing area to accommodate visitors. However, this could change at any moment (see the Hawaii Volcanoes National Park listing in Chapter 15 for details on checking current flow conditions). Puna's best place to stay is the charming, well-run **Coconut Cottage Bed & Breakfast** (see listing later in this chapter).

Upcountry: Waimea

This old Upcountry cowboy town on the northern road between the coasts is nestled in lovely country: rolling green pastures, big wide-open spaces dotted by *puu* (hills), and real Marlboro-smoking cowpokes who ride mammoth Parker Ranch, Hawaii's largest working cattle ranch. It's home to a good number of affordable B&Bs and vacation rentals. It also achieves a nice balance of creature comforts (Starbucks, for example) and ranch-country charm. Although the beach is about a half-hour away and Upcountry weather can be cloudier than it is on the coast, Waimea offers the pleasant advantage of being centrally positioned between the island's Kona and Volcano coasts, but the disadvantage of not really being close to anything. One upside? Some very good dining.

Driving Around the Big Island

You *will* need a rental car on the Big Island. Not having one will leave you dependent on what your resort has to offer — or worse, relegate you to the confines of touristy Kailua-Kona. Distances on this island are just too long to rely on taxis. An island-wide bus system, the **Hele-On Bus** (☎ **808-961-8744;** www.co.hawaii.hi.us; click on "Hele-On Bus Schedule"), is available, but all it really does is transport passengers (mostly locals) between the Kona-Kohala coast and Hilo.

All the major car-rental firms have cars available at both island airports. Arrange for one before you arrive; otherwise, you may find yourself paying top dollar at the airport counter (or run the risk of not getting a car at all if their inventory is depleted).

If your heart's set on some heavy-duty exploring along the Saddle Road, up to the summit of Mauna Kea, or to the southernmost tip of the island (which is also the southernmost point in the United States), you'll need a four-wheel-drive vehicle. For more information, see the upcoming information on Saddle and South Point roads.

If you're not going to rent a car, contact your hotel concierge or condo front desk and ask about local shuttle services. A few shuttles cover the Kailua-Kona area and the South Kona coast. In addition, most of the Kona-Kohala coast resorts offer free resort shuttles that transport guests within the resort, to golf courses, neighboring hotels, shopping and dining complexes, and any other nearby facilities.

For transportation around Kailua-Kona and down to Keauhou, in South Kona, catch a ride on the **Alii Shuttle,** which travels up and down Alii Drive between Kailua-Kona's Kailua Pier to Keauhou, roughly every 1½ hours Monday through Saturday from 8:30 a.m. to 8:30 p.m. If you plan to use the shuttle service, ask your hotel concierge or accommodations booking agent for current details and proximity to the shuttle route from your accommodations.

It's pretty hard to get lost on the Big Island. It has only a handful of main roads, all of which basically stick to the perimeter of the island.

The most important thing to keep in mind is the island's sheer size — they don't call it the Big Island for nothing. Driving from coast to coast takes 3 to 3½ hours; circling the entire island takes between six and seven hours. Distances are often longer than they might seem on a map, so be sure that you have a realistic idea of how far you need to travel before you set out. The concierge or the front-desk staff of your hotel or condo should be able to help you out.

If you arrive at Kona Airport, the first of the Big Island's main highways that you'll encounter is **Queen Kaahumanu Highway** (Highway 19), which runs along the Kona-Kohala coast for 33 miles, from Kailua-Kona at the south to the industrial port of Kawaihae at the north. All the major Kohala Coast resorts and beaches are accessible from this main coastal highway.

The Big Island has one main highway that circles the island: the **Hawaii Belt Road,** also known as the **Mamalahoa Highway,** which is labeled **Highway 11** as it runs south from the sunny, arid resort town of Kailua-Kona around the island's southern tip (a 60-mile drive); another 36 miles through Volcano (gateway to Hawaii Volcanoes National Park); and then about 27 miles north to Hilo, a misty, funky-cool bayfront town that's the second-largest city in the state (after Honolulu). Go north from Hilo, and the road becomes **Highway 19** as it travels north along the misty and ruggedly beautiful Hamakua Coast, then west to the upland cowboy town of Waimea, the heart of the Big Island's ranchland, for a total of 54 miles.

In Waimea, Highway 19 continues directly west, connecting up with the north end of the coastal Queen Kaahumanu Highway, which runs down the Kohala Coast. This roughly 10-mile stretch of east–west road connecting Waimea and the industrial port of Kawaihae (ka-*why*-high) is called **Kawaihae Road.**

An interior road offers a more direct route between Waimea and Kailua-Kona: The continuation of the Hawaii Belt Road (Mamalahoa Highway) is **Highway 190,** a scenic "upper" road that cuts along the western slope of Mauna Kea back to the coast, meeting up with the Queen Kaahumanu Highway (Highway 19) right in Kailua-Kona — thus completing the loop.

 One more road links east to west: **The Saddle Road** (Highway 200) is so named because it crosses the "saddle" between Mauna Kea and Mauna Loa volcanoes as it runs from Highway 190 south of Waimea direct to Hilo; from this road, you can take the access road to the 14,000-odd–foot summit of Mauna Kea. Your rental-car agreement will most likely demand that you avoid the Saddle Road because it's rough and narrow, and the ever-changing weather conditions can be tough to handle (not to mention the locals, who drive like bats out of hell between Hilo and the Kona Coast along this road). So don't take it; stick to the main highways instead. You're also supposed to stay away from **South Point Road,** the road that runs from the Mamalahoa Road at the south end of the island directly south, to the southernmost point in the United States. Although this road is less treacherous, you're best off avoiding it in order to honor the built-in restrictions on your rental-car contract.

If you plan to take on the Saddle Road or the South Point Road, or both, I suggest renting a four-wheel-drive SUV — and check your rental contract first before setting out. If you disregard any disclaimer or restriction in your contract and get stuck on a forbidden road, and your rental-car company then sticks you with a massive tow bill, don't say I didn't warn you.

 Also stay off of the steeply graded **Waipio Valley Road,** at the north end of the Hamakua Coast, which isn't meant for cars — you *will* get stuck here.

For a more complete discussion of the major resort areas as well as Hilo and Volcano, check out the section "Choosing Your Location," earlier in this chapter. If you drive north from the intersection of the Kohala Coast's Queen Kaahumanu Highway and the Kawaihae Road, you'll enter North Kohala, the peninsula that extends off the northern end of the island. The drive north along the **Akoni Pule** (ah-*ko*-nee *poo*-lay) **Highway** (Highway 270) offers a peek at a different side of the Big Island, one where lava cedes to gorgeous rolling ranchlands. It's a beautiful hour-long drive that leads to some wonderful wilderness activities that I discuss in detail in Chapter 15. You can circle back from the town of Hawi (*ha*-vee) at North Kohala's tip along the **Kohala Mountain Road** (Highway 250), ending up back on the Kawaihae Road just west of Waimea.

Staying in Style

The Big Island's best accommodations

In the following listings, each property is followed by a number of dollar signs, ranging from one ($) to five ($$$$$). Each represents the median rack-rate price range for a double room per night, as follows:

$	Cheap — less than $150 per night
$$	Still affordable — $150–$225
$$$	Moderate — $225–$325
$$$$	Expensive but not ridiculous — $325–$450
$$$$$	Ultraluxurious — more than $450 per night

Remember that you almost never need to pay the asking price for a hotel room. Check out Chapter 7 for tips on how to avoid paying for a full-price hotel room. Also see Chapter 5 for advice on how to score an all-inclusive package that can save you big bucks on both accommodations and airfare, and, sometimes, car rentals and activities too.

Also, don't forget that the state adds 11.42 percent in taxes to your hotel bill.

Coconut Cottage Bed & Breakfast
$ **Puna District (Pahoa)**

This darling bed-and-breakfast is a wonderful addition to the Big Island accommodations scene. You don't have to be a budget traveler to enjoy this stylish and comfortable place, whose creature comforts and service surpass what you'd expect at this price point. The low rates come courtesy of the off-the-beaten-path location, which is within 20 miles or so of both Hilo and Hawaii Volcanoes National Park but lacks traditional tourist services.

Innkeepers Jerry and Todd are recent refugees from Orange County, CA, but they have made themselves right at home in this authentic, unspoiled area of the islands. They've imbued their charming yellow cottage with Tommy Bahama–inspired style and a dash of vintage whimsy. The gorgeous gardens and hot tub, housed under a grass-roofed gazebo, add a resortlike feeling.

Three charming and comfortable guest rooms are located in the main house. Even the smallest is spacious, pretty, and well outfitted, with plush bedding, warm island-themed decor, a minifridge with complimentary bottled water, waffle-weave robes, a TV with DVD player (plus full access to the extensive DVD library), access to either a private or shared lanai, and its own private bathroom; the only caveat is that the one for the Royal Hibiscus room is across the hall, but I didn't find it to be a problem when I stayed there. The separate Garden Bungalow adds a kitchenette with full-size fridge and microwave to the list of amenities, plus a sleeper sofa. There's no air-conditioning, but it isn't needed most of the time. The

The Big Island's Accommodations

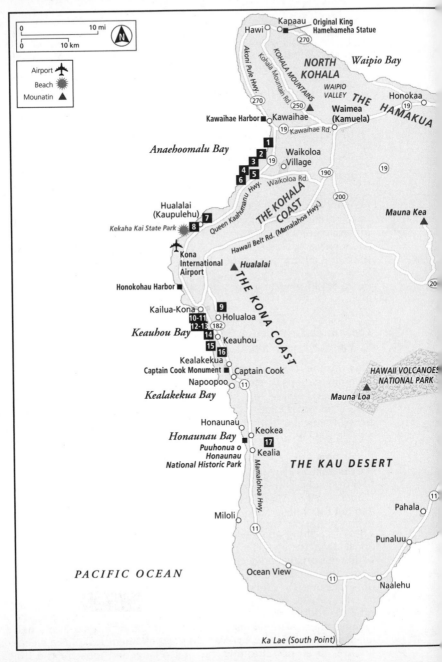

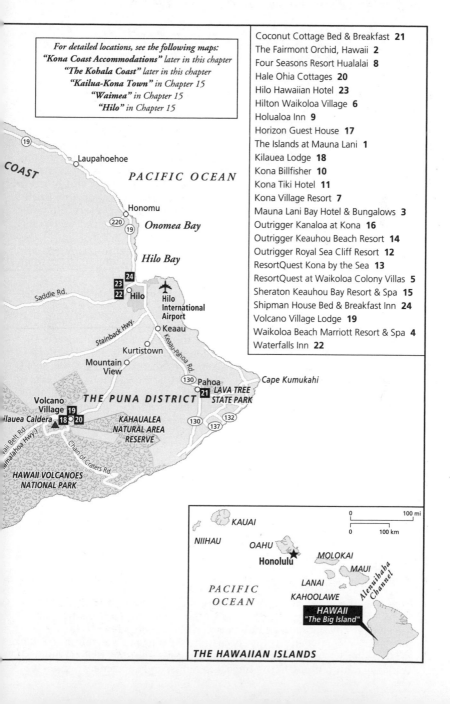

For detailed locations, see the following maps:
"Kona Coast Accommodations" later in this chapter
"The Kohala Coast" later in this chapter
"Kailua-Kona Town" in Chapter 15
"Waimea" in Chapter 15
"Hilo" in Chapter 15

Coconut Cottage Bed & Breakfast **21**
The Fairmont Orchid, Hawaii **2**
Four Seasons Resort Hualalai **8**
Hale Ohia Cottages **20**
Hilo Hawaiian Hotel **23**
Hilton Waikoloa Village **6**
Holualoa Inn **9**
Horizon Guest House **17**
The Islands at Mauna Lani **1**
Kilauea Lodge **18**
Kona Billfisher **10**
Kona Tiki Hotel **11**
Kona Village Resort **7**
Mauna Lani Bay Hotel & Bungalows **3**
Outrigger Kanaloa at Kona **16**
Outrigger Keauhou Beach Resort **14**
Outrigger Royal Sea Cliff Resort **12**
ResortQuest Kona by the Sea **13**
ResortQuest at Waikoloa Colony Villas **5**
Sheraton Keauhou Bay Resort & Spa **15**
Shipman House Bed & Breakfast Inn **24**
Volcano Village Lodge **19**
Waikoloa Beach Marriott Resort & Spa **4**
Waterfalls Inn **22**

COAST

Laupahoehoe

PACIFIC OCEAN

Honomu

Onomea Bay

Hilo Bay

Saddle Rd.

Hilo

Hilo International Airport

Stainback Hwy.

Keaau

Kurtistown

Mountain View

Pahoa

Cape Kumukahi

LAVA TREE STATE PARK

THE PUNA DISTRICT

Volcano Village

Kilauea Caldera

KAHAUALEA NATURAL AREA RESERVE

Chain of Craters Rd.

HAWAII VOLCANOES NATIONAL PARK

KAUAI

NIIHAU

OAHU

Honolulu

MOLOKAI

MAUI

LANAI

KAHOOLAWE

Alenuihaha Channel

PACIFIC OCEAN

HAWAII "The Big Island"

THE HAWAIIAN ISLANDS

0   100 mi
0   100 km

bounteous full breakfast, beautifully prepared by Jerry every morning, is a gourmet treat.

See map p. 326. 13-1139 Leilani Ave., Pahoa. ☎ *866-204-7444 or 808-965-0973.* www.coconutcottagehawaii.com. *Parking: Free. Rack rates: $110–$140 double. Rates include full breakfast. 7th night free. MC, V.*

The Fairmont Orchid, Hawaii
$$$$–$$$$$ Kohala Coast

This elegant, attractive, and thoroughly appealing beach resort boasts gorgeous views and some of the best extras on the coast. The sports facilities are extensive (championship golf, tennis, catamaran rides, and outrigger canoe trips), the oceanside "Spa Without Walls" is as stress-relieving as they come, and the heated oceanfront pool and hot tubs are Tiki-torchlit for maximum romance at night. The resort also offers a wealth of outdoor activities and an excellent Hawaiian program for culture buffs. Brown's Beach House is the coast's most romantic restaurant (see the section "Dining Out," later in this chapter); and eight other bars and restaurants are on the property, including Norio's, a terrific sushi bar and restaurant. The spacious rooms are more boldly colorful than most, with an eye-catching palette, comfy furnishings, and large marble bathrooms. The beach is small but pretty and perfect for well-serviced lounging, snorkeling, and kids at play.

All in all, the Orchid is a tad less opulent and significantly more intimate in size and ambience than other Big Island resorts. The service is top-notch, and even employees at competing resorts admit that the Orchid's concierge staff is the island's best. The only downside is the building's U shape, which gives most of the rooms courtyard or partial-ocean rather than full-ocean views; however, the alternative views are also beautiful. On the Fairmont Gold Floor, guests receive upgraded in-room decor and amenities, a dedicated lounge with free wireless Internet access, an excellent complimentary breakfast, a complimentary cocktail hour, and delightfully personalized concierge service.

See map p. 326. 1 N. Kaniku Dr., Mauna Lani resort. ☎ *800-845-9905 or 808-885-2000. Fax: 808-885-1064.* www.fairmont.com/orchid. *Valet parking: $21. Self-parking: Free. Rack rates: $399–$839 double, $719–$849 Gold Floor room, $1,049–$1,699 suite. Package deals are usually available (including 5th-night-free, golf, honeymoon, spa, and family offers), so be sure to ask. Also ask for AAA-member and senior discounts. AE, DC, DISC, MC, V.*

Four Seasons Resort Hualalai
$$$$$ West Side (Kona Coast)

Here it is: the finest luxury resort hotel in the islands, and the Hope diamond of the glittering Four Seasons chain. Island-style elegance simply doesn't get any better. Low-rise clusters of clean-lined ocean-facing villas are nestled between a lovely sandy beach and a fabulous Jack Nicklaus–designed golf course (for guests only — so start dialing, duffers!). You'll want for nothing in the huge, gorgeous, and supremely comfortable

Kona Coast Accommodations

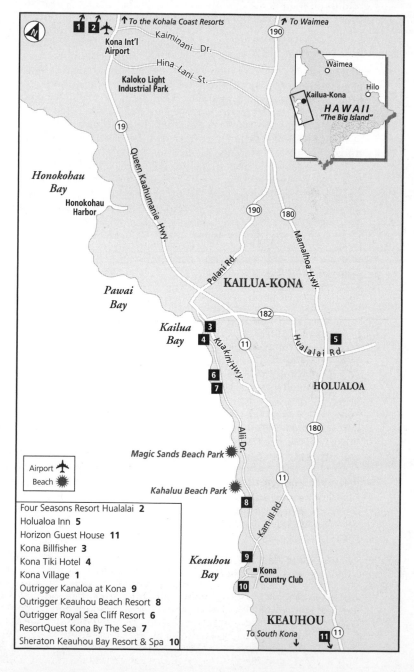

To the Kohala Coast Resorts

To Waimea

190

Kona Int'l
Airport

Kaiminani Dr.

Hina Lani St.

Kaloko Light
Industrial Park

19

Honokohau
Bay

Honokohau
Harbor

Queen Kaahumanie Hwy.

190 180

Pawai
Bay

Palani Rd.

KAILUA-KONA

Mamalhoa Hwy.

Kailua
Bay

182

3

4

11

Hualalai Rd.

5

Kuakini Hwy.

6

7

HOLUALOA

180

Alii Dr.

Magic Sands Beach Park

Kahaluu Beach Park

8

11

Kam III Rd.

9

*Keauhou
Bay*

Kona
Country Club

10

KEAUHOU

To South South Kona

11 11

HAWAII
"The Big Island"

Waimea

Kailua-Kona

Hilo

Airport ✈

Beach ☀

Four Seasons Resort Hualalai **2**
Holualoa Inn **5**
Horizon Guest House **11**
Kona Billfisher **3**
Kona Tiki Hotel **4**
Kona Village **1**
Outrigger Kanaloa at Kona **9**
Outrigger Keauhou Beach Resort **8**
Outrigger Royal Sea Cliff Resort **6**
ResortQuest Kona By The Sea **7**
Sheraton Keauhou Bay Resort & Spa **10**

rooms. Each comes dressed in natural hues and materials — including raffia, rattan, and slate — that set the perfect kick-off-your-shoes Pacific island ambience. Ground-level rooms even have private outdoor showers off the big marble bathrooms, so you can shower au naturel under the sun or stars. Wireless high-speed Internet access is ideal for guests who want to get away from it all without forsaking complete connectivity. The beautiful beach can be too rough for swimming, but no matter — three ocean-front pools more than compensate, including a stocked snorkel pond (with friendly stingrays!) that's ideal for beginners. An exclusive spa (named by *Condé Nast Traveler* as the world's best resort spa), a state-of-the-art fitness center, and sublime beachfront dining round out the experience. Superstar Honolulu chef Alan Wong is the lead chef in the delightful clubhouse restaurant, Hualalai Grille, my favorite place to dine on the Big Island (see review later in this chapter). Who could ask for anything more?

See map p. 329. 100 Kaupulehu Dr., Kaupulehu-Kona (7 miles north of the airport). ☎ *800-332-3442, 888-340-5662, or 808-325-8000. Fax: 808-325-8200.* www.four seasons.com/hualalai. *Parking: $13. Rack rates: $725–$1,000 double, $1,100–$6,800 suite. Ask about romance, golf, spa, 5th-night-free, room-and-car, bed-and-breakfast, and other packages. AE, DC, DISC, MC, V.*

Hale Ohia Cottages
$–$$ Volcano

Condé Nast Traveler named Hale Ohia the top place to stay in Volcano in its February 2004 issue, and the honor is well-deserved. This charming and tranquil assemblage of suites and cottages offers a wonderful opportunity to step into the past and get back to nature. The gorgeous red-shingled 1931 estate boasts an impeccable blend of 1930s Hawaii plantation style and modern-day sophistication. The stunning botanical grounds are the result of more than 30 years' work by a master Japanese gardener. All the accommodations are lovely and comfortable. The Ihilani Cottage is a honeymooner's dream, with its own enclosed lanai with a bubbling fountain, and the three-bedroom Hale Ohia Cottage, with its own full kitchen, is a great deal for families. The transformation of the property's original redwood water tank into Cottage #44, a beautiful and fully outfitted suite (complete with kitchenette and Jacuzzi tub), adds yet another offbeat delight to the retro-romantic collection. The massive Master Suite is a steal if you can snare it. The in-room continental breakfast makes this spot an excellent choice for privacy seekers. Two private, multibedroom vacation rentals are available for families; these are a few minutes' distant from the main property and do not include breakfast.

 At this writing, Hale Ohia's longtime owner had recently sold this delightful property to new owners, and the jury is still out as to whether things will change for the better, worse, or not at all. It's certainly too good an option to remove from this guide, but I highly recommend that you check **Tripadvisor.com** for the latest reader reports before you book.

See map p. 326. On Hale Ohia Road (off Highway 11), Volcano. ☎ *800-455-3803 or 808-967-7986. Fax: 808-967-8610.* www.haleohia.com. *Parking: Free. Rack rates: $119–$189 double, $129 suite; $105–$229 vacation rental (2–6 guests). Most*

The Kohala Coast

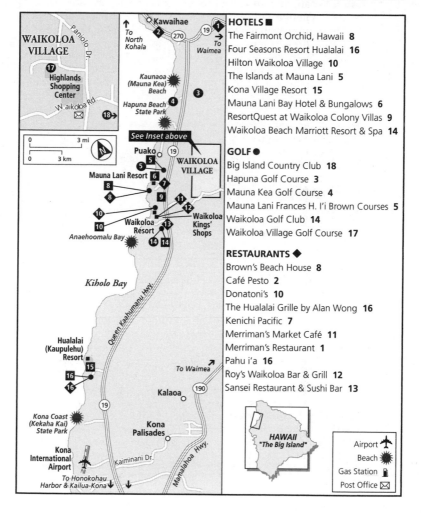

HOTELS ■

The Fairmont Orchid, Hawaii **8**
Four Seasons Resort Hualalai **16**
Hilton Waikoloa Village **10**
The Islands at Mauna Lani **5**
Kona Village Resort **15**
Mauna Lani Bay Hotel & Bungalows **6**
ResortQuest at Waikoloa Colony Villas **9**
Waikoloa Beach Marriott Resort & Spa **14**

GOLF ●

Big Island Country Club **18**
Hapuna Golf Course **3**
Mauna Kea Golf Course **4**
Mauna Lani Frances H. I'i Brown Courses **5**
Waikoloa Golf Club **14**
Waikoloa Village Golf Course **17**

RESTAURANTS ◆

Brown's Beach House **8**
Café Pesto **2**
Donatoni's **10**
The Hualalai Grille by Alan Wong **16**
Kenichi Pacific **7**
Merriman's Market Café **11**
Merriman's Restaurant **1**
Pahu i'a **16**
Roy's Waikoloa Bar & Grill **12**
Sansei Restaurant & Sushi Bar **13**

accommodations require a 2-night minimum stay; expect a $20–$40 surcharge for single-night stays. Rates include continental breakfast for all accommodations except vacation rentals. MC, V.

Hilo Hawaiian Hotel
$$ Hilo

This eight-story waterfront hotel on picturesque Hilo Bay features nice rooms that do the job at a fair price. It's generic but is set on a gracious setting on leafy Banyan Drive, and gets props for being one of the few full-service hotels on this side of the island. There aren't many facilities, but you'll still find a pool and sun deck, a gift shop, a laundromat, and a restaurant and lounge here. Pay the few extra bucks for a bay view if you can swing it; you won't be disappointed. You almost never have to pay rack rate here; check online for frequent money-saving Internet specials.

See map p. 326. 71 Banyan Dr., Hilo. ☎ *800-367-5004 or 808-935-9361. Fax: 808-545-2163. Parking: Free. Rack rates: $190–$240 double, $270–$405 suite. Check for deeply discounted Internet rates (as low as $101 at press time). Also ask about free-car, free-night, and other special packages. AE, DC, DISC, MC, V.*

Hilton Waikoloa Village
$$$$ Kohala Coast

With 1,240 rooms spread over 62 acres, this massive hotel is too big for its own good. Just getting from your room to the lobby is a 15- to 20-minute production, so check in, park yourself, and don't be in any hurry to leave. This is a destination resort of the highest order, Hawaii's very own version of Disneyland. Its high-rise towers, water slide–riddled megapools, dolphin lagoons, and gaggle of restaurants (including the divine Donatoni's; see the section "Dining Out," later in this chapter), bars, and shops are connected by trams, boats, and art-lined walkways. Thanks to so many eye-popping diversions, your kids will think that they've died and gone to heaven. Mom and Dad are bound to be entertained, too, thanks to a tremendous spa and championship golf course — if you don't run screaming from sensory overload first. The rooms are well-appointed, comfortable, and relatively affordable considering the level of luxury and the full slate of amenities that you'll find here. You won't find any sandy beach, though; you have to go next door for that. Stay elsewhere if you won't enjoy the family-friendly vibe.

See map p. 331. 425 Waikoloa Beach Dr., Waikoloa. ☎ *800-HILTONS or 808-886-1234. Fax: 808-886-2900.* www.hiltonwaikoloavillage.com *or* www.hilton.com. *Valet parking: $19. Self-parking: $12. Rack rates: $329–$499 double, suites from $589 (suites must be booked online). Optional daily $15 "resort fee" covers "free" local phone calls, in-room coffee, use of safe, use of spa for 2, and $25 credit toward beach rental and tennis. Advance-purchase online only rates from $215 at press time. A range of packages and special offers are usually available, including romance, golf, and family packages, 7th-night-free deals, and more. Also ask for AAA, AARP, corporate, military, and other discounts. AE, DC, DISC, MC, V.*

Holualoa Inn
$$$ Upcountry Kona

Set on 40 pastoral acres on the slopes above Kailua-Kona, in the charmingly artsy town of Holualoa, this impeccable inn offers the ultimate tranquil escape, yet it's also conveniently located just 15 minutes from South Kona snorkeling and other Kona coast conveniences. Built entirely of golden woods and outfitted in an understated but elegant Asian-inflected island style — all clean lines, rattan, and subtle colors — this gorgeous contemporary Hawaiian home boasts six spacious guest rooms, window-walls that slide away to reveal stunning panoramic ocean views, and an easygoing island vibe. (Note that only the Plumeria Suite has an in-room

TV.) The lovely pool and Jacuzzi overlook a backyard coffee farm and fruit trees (which supply the morning brew and breakfast papayas) and offer spectacular views of the coastline below. Nice extras include a gas grill with all the supplies you need to barbecue a romantic dinner, wonderful common spaces for dining and lounging, guest laundry, and a labyrinth and garden trails where you can wander and contemplate your lucky stars for being here. Even B&B-phobes will feel right at home. As in many island B&Bs, the owners ask that you follow the Hawaiian custom of removing your shoes before entering; it preserves their gorgeous eucalyptus floors and adds to the sense of barefoot elegance.

See map p. 329. 76–5932 Mamalahoa Hwy., Holualoa (a 15-minute drive uphill from Highway 19, along Hualalai Road). ☎ *800-392-1812 or 808-324-1121. Fax: 808-322-2472.* www.holualoainn.com. *Parking: Free. Rack rates: $260–$350 double or suite. Rates include 2-course gourmet breakfast and sunset pupus. Children under 13 not accepted. 2-night minimum stay. 10 percent off for stays of 7 nights or more; also inquire about activity packages. AE, DISC, MC, V.*

Horizon Guest House
$$$ South Kona

This impeccable B&B offers the ultimate in luxurious relaxation. The house is located on 40 acres of lush pastureland at 1,100 feet elevation, offering unparalleled coastline views. The four carefully designed one-room suites are cantilevered off the end of the house for maximum privacy. Each has its own private entry and furnished lanai and is filled with gorgeous island antiques, hand-quilted Hawaiian bedspreads on the king or queen bed, minifridge, coffeemaker, and cushy robes. A dramatic 20-by-40-foot infinity pool (which appears to have no edge) and a romantic hot tub are situated to take full advantage of the breathtaking views. Guests have free use of laundry facilities, a gas barbecue grill, and beach toys galore. Much-beloved innkeeper Clem Classen serves a gourmet buffet breakfast in the artifact-filled main house, which also features a multimedia room with an extensive book and video library and a TV with VCR and DVD. Impeccable personalized service is completely unobtrusive; it's the elegant finish to an all-around excellent stay.

See map p. 329. 86–3992 Hwy. 11 (between mile markers 100 and 101), Honaunau. ☎ *888-328-8301 or 808-328-2540. Fax: 808-328-8707.* www.horizonguest house.com. *Parking: Free. Rack rates: $250 double. Rate includes full gourmet breakfast. Children under 14 not accepted. 15 percent off bookings of 7 nights or more. Inquire about other discounts. MC, V.*

The Islands at Mauna Lani
$$$$$ Kohala Coast

If you're in the market for a two- or three-bedroom condo — be it for a family, sharing couples, or plenty of spreading-out for yourself — you can't do better than the Islands. Light, bright, airy, and gorgeous, these contemporary Mediterranean-style town houses boast a massive 2,100 square feet of living space. On the first floor, you find a gourmet kitchen, full dining and living rooms (both with furnished lanais), and a laundry room with full-size washer and dryer. Upstairs are two (or three) master-size bedrooms, each with a firm, well-dressed king-size bed, its own furnished lanai, and a monster bathroom with an oversize Jacuzzi tub and yards of counter space. Every luxury is at hand, from a cordless phone to a gas grill to daily maid service to your own garage with automatic door opener. The views of the lushly manicured grounds and surrounding fairways more than make up for the lack of ocean vistas. The perks don't end there. On-site is a very nice heated pool and hot tub; what's more, Islands guests can hop the free on-call shuttle to an exclusive beach club, which boasts its own perfect white-sand cove, excellent snorkel reef, gear-rental shack, and restaurant. The shuttle also takes you to and from the Mauna Lani Spa, the island's best. Service is excellent but completely nonintrusive. All in all, an excellent choice, especially when you can score a discounted rate, which is often.

See map p. 331. 68–1050 Mauna Lani Point Dr., Mauna Lani resort. ☎ *800-642-6284 or 808-661-3339. Fax: 808-667-1145.* www.classicresorts.com. *Parking: Free. Rack rates: $459–$680 1- or 2-bedroom, $695–$1,895 3-bedroom. 3-night minimum. Ask about room-and-car packages, spa and golf packages, return-guest packages, and other available discounts; available rates as low as $237 1-bedroom, $321 2-bedroom at press time. AE, MC, V.*

Kilauea Lodge
$$ Volcano

Built in 1938 as a YMCA camp, this popular roadside lodge sits on 10 wooded acres just a stone's throw from the main gate of the national park. The lodge is a real woodsy charmer, with stone pillars and beamed ceilings. Twelve comfortably outfitted rooms offer private bathrooms, attractive artwork by local artists, lovely garden views, and individual heat controls and towel warmers (nice pluses on chilly Volcano nights). A phone, a lending library, games, and a TV set for shared viewing are found in the common room. Two charming cottages are also available, one with two bedrooms and a full kitchen that's great for families, plus a pleasant, newly renovated house on the fairway at the Volcano Golf Course. A complete, satisfying breakfast is served in the restaurant, which is a Volcano favorite for dinner (see the section "Dining Out," later in this chapter). Service is consistently aloha-filled and professional. This is an excellent choice, especially for those who prefer hotel-style anonymity over the intimacy of many of Volcano's B&B-style stays.

See map p. 326. 19–4055 Volcano Rd. (just off Highway 11 at Wright Road), Volcano. ☎ *808-967-7366. Fax: 808-967-7367.* www.kilauealodge.com. *Parking: Free. Rack rates: $160–$215 double, $175–$280 1- or 2-bedroom cottage. Rates include full breakfast. AE, MC, V.*

Kona Billfisher
$ Kailua-Kona

The units aren't fancy, but it's hard to do better for the money — and discounts on longer stays make the rooms practically free. The management company keeps everything neat and reasonably well kept. Each apartment has a full kitchen with all-electric appliances, a large lanai, decent (if dated) furniture, and king-size beds. The one-bedrooms have sliding doors that allow you to close off the living room to make another bedroom, which makes them a real deal for penny-saving families. Air-conditioning is available for $10 a day, but you probably won't need it with those gentle ocean breezes. On-site extras include a pool, barbecues, and a coin-op laundry, and the town is just a walk away. You'll have to drive to a swimmable beach, but at these prices, you won't mind. Beware: The close-to-town location is terrific for walk-to dining and other conveniences, but it can mean late-night noise from vacationing revelers. Book well in advance — this place fills up fast with bargain-hunting travelers.

See map p. 329. On Alii Drive (on the mountain side of the street, across from the Royal Kona Resort), Kailua-Kona, c/o Hawaii Resort Management. ☎ *800-244-4752 or 808-329-3333. Fax: 808-326-4137.* www.konahawaii.com. *Parking: Free. Rack rates: $115–$150 1-bedroom, $135–$165 2-bedroom/1-bath. 3-night minimum. On stays of less than 6 nights, $35 non-refundable cleaning fee for 1-bedrooms, $45 for 2-bedrooms. Discounts available on weekly and monthly stays; also ask about Internet specials (from $67 at press time). DISC, MC, V.*

Kona Tiki Hotel
$ Kailua-Kona

This quirky, friendly family-run motel is one of the best cheap sleeps in the state. Staying here is like stepping into a time warp — one where you can have a reasonable room for two, right on the ocean, for as little as $69 — with breakfast! The rooms are budget-basic on every level, but the beds are firm and comfy, the paint and carpet are fresh, ceiling fans and minifridges are on hand (a few have kitchenettes for just a bit more moola), and every room has a lanai with front-row sunset views over the ocean. A basic continental breakfast is served poolside every morning, making this incredible value that much more astounding. The location is pleasant, away from the hustle and bustle of downtown. It's hard to stay closer to the waves, but beware: Some guests find the crashing of the surf more disruptive than soothing. The ocean here isn't swimmable, so you'll have to drive to the beach; and you'll find no TVs, phones, or coin-op laundry (a local laundry will pick up and deliver). But those are the sacrifices you make for such a bargain. Book way in advance, because people *loooove* this place.

See map p. 329. 75–5968 Alii Dr., Kailua-Kona (a mile south of town). ☎ *808-329-1425. Fax: 808-327-9402.* www.konatiki.com. *Parking: Free. Rack rates: $69–$120 double. Rates include continental breakfast and tax. 3-night minimum. No credit cards.*

Kona Village Resort
$$$$$ Kohala Coast

Hawaii may have fancier and more amenity-laden resorts, but the state's only all-inclusive is truly something special: a superdeluxe version of *Gilligan's Island,* where it feels perfectly natural to tuck a flower behind your ear and sip cocktails out of coconuts. This South Seas paradise of swaying palms and lagoons offers blissful escape, Robinson Crusoe–style: no TVs, phones, or fax machines around to interrupt your tropical reverie for even a minute. You'll stay in your own thatch-roofed *hale,* which is much like a comfortably furnished tropical cabin. The dark-sand beach offers first-rate snorkeling with green sea turtles, who climb up on shore nearly every afternoon for a nap; manta rays hang out in the flood-lit bay after dark, proving that all species love Kona Village. A tenderly attentive staff — one of the best in the islands — is on hand to meet your needs and desires even before you know you have them, and the food is abundant and absolutely terrific at every meal. There's something going on most nights, whether it's dancing to a Hawaiian trio or the terrific Wednesday- and Friday-night luau (see the section "Luau!" later in this chapter). The kids' program is excellent, but for three weeks in May and three weeks in September, the resort is reserved for adults only. Utterly restful, and simply divine, this resort is Hawaii vacationing as it was really meant to be.

See map p. 331. At the Kaupulehu resort, 7 miles north of the airport. ☎ *800-367-5290 or 808-325-5555. Fax: 808-325-5124.* www.konavillage.com. *Parking: Free. Rack rates: $570–$1,300 double. Rates include all meals, in-room refreshments, most activities, children's program, and more. All rates are based on double occupancy; inquire about per-person add-on fees. Deals: Ask about romance and other packages. AE, DC, MC, V.*

Mauna Lani Bay Hotel & Bungalows
$$$$$ Kohala Coast

Hawaiian elders named this section of the sunny lava coast Mauna Lani, or "Mountain Reaching Heaven," and it's an apt name for so heavenly a resort. Mauna Lani has a finer swimming and snorkeling beach than any other Big Island resort hotel. The hotel is designed in the shape of an arrow on the sands to take advantage of its prime coastal location, providing most rooms with substantial ocean views. A vast open-air lobby spilling over with tropical greenery leads to serene and simple rooms that exude island style — teak floors, lauhala headboards, ceiling fans, natural-hued textiles, and lanais. VCRs, opposing vanities, seersucker robes, and twice-daily maid service add a luxury touch. Families can stay in the homelike villas, but those with bottomless bank accounts should opt for one of the incredible bungalows, each of which has its own private pool and a butler who doesn't know the word "no." The historically and culturally sensitive resort features the finest, most Hawaiian spa in the islands, an extensive calendar of daily activities, a first-rate tennis center, and easy access to some of Hawaii's best golf. *One sour note:* Dinner in the celebrated CanoeHouse just isn't what it used to be.

See map p. 331. 68–1400 Mauna Lani Dr., Mauna Lani resort. ☎ *800-367-2323 or 808-885-6622. Fax: 808-885-1484.* www.maunalani.com. *Parking: Free. Rack rates: $445–$935 double, $985–$1,800 suite, from $620–$3,050 1- to 3-bedroom villa, $6,050–$6,850 bungalow: call to reserve a bungalow. Golf, spa, romance, and other packages usually available, plus deals including airfare. AE, DC, DISC, MC, V.*

Outrigger Kanaloa at Kona
$$$ South Kona

Tucked away in a quiet, attractive neighborhood, these big, well-managed oceanfront condos (by the reliable, value-oriented Hawaii-based Outrigger hotel chain) are a cut above the average and ideal for families. Comfortably furnished in quality island style with Hawaiian wood accents, the apartments have all the comforts of home and then some, including dressing rooms, big kitchens loaded with appliances, huge bathrooms (with whirlpools in oceanview suites!), and washer/dryers. Two tennis courts lit for night play, three swimming pools with hot tubs, and playgrounds dot the pleasant, attractively manicured ocean-facing grounds. The coast is lava rock here, however, so you'll have to drive a half-mile to Kahaluu Beach (one of Hawaii's best for snorkeling, though not its loveliest stretch of sand). A big, modern, well-stocked supermarket is just up the hill, and Kailua-Kona's restaurants and shops are a ten-minute drive away. Guests receive discounted rates on 36 holes of championship golf at the neighboring country club.

See map p. 329 78–261 Manukai St., Keauhou. ☎ 800-688-7444, 800-959-5662, or 808-322-9625. Fax: 808-322-3818. www.outrigger.com. *Parking: Free. Rack rates: $249–$309 1-bedroom, $279–$499 2-bedroom. 2-night minimum stay (3 nights during holiday season). Better-than-average discounts for AAA and AARP members and seniors (50+), plus corporate, government, and military discounts. Check for special Internet rates, and ask about 5th-night-free, bed-and-breakfast, room-and-car, and other packages. AE, DC, DISC, MC, V.*

Outrigger Keauhou Beach Resort
$$$ South Kona

This attractive and well-maintained hotel is a great choice for culture buffs, active vacationers, or anybody in search of affordable oceanfront accommodations who doesn't want to mortgage their children to do so. Situated on a tranquil and lovely stretch of coast, the mid-rise structure boasts a central location, lovely views, and a genuine Hawaiian ambience. The island's best snorkeling is right next door at Kahaluu Beach Park, and the hotel's own 10 acres of tropical grounds feature an oceanside pool, a fitness center, and tennis courts lit for night play. The open-air lobby lets the outside in. A grassy oceanfront area is dedicated to the easy life, with hammocks strung between coconut palms, and the on-site Kalona Salon and Spa specializes in first-rate skin-care treatments. Other pleasures include a surprisingly good restaurant and an open-air lounge with live Hawaiian music and glorious golden sunsets. The rooms themselves are less distinctive, but perfectly comfortable. Completely renovated in 2008, you can expect them to be fresh, pretty, and comfortable, with good bedside reading lights, generous counter space, and cushy towels in the bathrooms (some of which have showers only), coffeemakers, free wireless Internet access, and lanais — most with some kind of ocean view. Adjoining rooms make this resort a good family choice, too. All in all, a very nice choice.

See map p. 329. 78–6740 Alii Dr., Keauhou (3 miles south of Kailua-Kona). ☎ 866-326-6803, 800-688-7444, or 808-322-3441. Fax: 808-322-3117. www.keauhoubeachresort.com *or* www.outrigger.com. *Valet parking: $10. Self-parking: $7. Rack rates: $249–$409 double, from $509 suite. Better-than-average discounts for AAA and AARP members and seniors (50+), plus corporate, government, and military discounts. Check for special Internet rates, and ask about air-and-car deals, romance and bed-and-breakfast packages, and other specials. AE, DC, DISC, MC, V.*

Outrigger Royal Sea Cliff Resort
$$ Kailua-Kona

Parents with kids in tow will love these apartments. They're not fancy, but they're large, well outfitted, and older but well cared for and recently upgraded by the reliable Outrigger hotel chain. The big five-story complex steps down a terraced cliff to a black-sand beach. The water's too rough for swimming; but the views are spectacular, and the privacy is unsurpassed. Gardens and hanging bougainvillea give the whole place a pleasant, tropical ambience. The spacious, air-conditioned apartments carry through on the vibe, with lots of rattan, sunny lanais (some with ocean views), full kitchens with microwave, washer/dryer, TV with VCR in the living rooms, and daily maid service, making for easy vacation living. Two pools (one freshwater, one saltwater), a Jacuzzi, sauna, tennis, and barbecues are all on-site. There's a decent beach about a mile away with excellent snorkeling. The location is quiet but convenient to Kailua-Kona town.

See map p. 329. 75–6040 Alii Dr., Kailua-Kona (2 miles south of town). ☎ 800-688-7444 or 808-329-8021. Fax: 808-326-1887. www.outrigger.com. *Parking: Free. Rack rates: $219–$259 studio, $249–$419 1-bedroom apartment, $289–$459 2-bedroom apartment. 3-night minimum stay during the holiday season. Check for special Internet rates. AAA, AARP, senior (50+), government, and military discounts available. Ask about room-and-car and other packages. AE, DC, DISC, MC, V.*

ResortQuest Kona by the Sea
$$$ Kailua-Kona

The units and grounds at this deluxe oceanfront condo complex are a tad more inviting than those at the nearby Outrigger Royal Sea Cliff (see above), but not dramatically so. The bright, spacious, nicely decorated apartments boast complete kitchens with microwave, washer/dryers, daily maid service, and large lanais (most with ocean views). On-site you find an oceanfront freshwater pool, a Jacuzzi, barbecues, and an activities desk that can book your island fun. One of the pluses exclusive to this property is the personal grocery-shopping service — just leave a shopping list with the manager, and your staples are delivered right to your door. The white-sand beach here is lovely but unswimmable, so plan on heading 4 miles south to Kahaluu Beach for first-rate snorkeling or driving a half-hour north to the Kohala Coast for really spectacular sands.

See map p. 329. 75–6106 Alii Dr., Kailua-Kona (2 miles south of town). ☎ 877-997-6667 or 808-327-2300. Fax: 808-327-2333. www.resortquesthawaii.com. *Parking: Free. Rack rates: $280–$395 1-bedroom, $345–$460 2-bedroom. Excellent discounts almost always available. Check the Web site for eSpecial rates, as low as $224 at press time. Ask for AAA, senior (50+), and corporate discounts, and other packages, such as room-and-car deals. AE, DC, DISC, MC, V.*

ResortQuest at Waikoloa Colony Villas
$$$$ Kohala Coast

This peaceful luxury condo complex on the 15th fairway of the Waikoloa Beach Course, in the pleasing Waikoloa resort, is a wonderful choice for families or anybody who wants to enjoy the comforts of home when they come to the islands — and then some. These attractive and well-furnished two-story town home–style units are large and feature a fully equipped kitchen with granite countertops and quality appliances; a big, comfortable, warmly decorated living room; firm, comfortable, well-dressed beds; spacious, well-outfitted baths, with double sinks and separate shower and tub in the master; in-suite washer and dryer; a large patio or lanai with teak furnishings for outdoor dining; and good lighting and art that's more attractive and individualized than you would expect it to be. Units are serviced in basic fashion daily — towels are changed out and trash is picked up — with full maid service every fourth day. The complex features two small swimming pools, a spa, a tennis court, and a small fitness room. Thanks to the creature comforts and room to spread out, this was one of my favorite places to stay on my last trip to the islands. The only downside is that it's near the end of the road in Waikoloa, so it's a short drive just to get out of the resort. A great swim-and-snorkel beach, A-Bay, is a five-minute drive away. Units are quite comparable with the Islands at Mauna Lani, and both resorts make great places to stay; I recommend price comparing.

See map p. 331. 69-555 Waikoloa Beach Dr., Waikoloa. ☎ 877-997-6667 or 808-3886-8899. Fax: 808-886-8898. www.resortquesthawaii.com. *Parking: Free. Rack rates: $350–$425 1-bedroom, $375–$475 2-bedroom, $435–$560 3-bedroom. Excellent discounts almost always available. Check the Web site for eSpecial rates, as low as $221 at press time. Ask for AAA, senior (50+), and corporate discounts, and other packages, such as 4th-night-free and room-and-car deals. AE, DC, DISC, MC, V.*

Sheraton Keauhou Bay Resort & Spa
$$$$ South Kona

Set on a spectacular 22-acre oceanfront lava point on the sunny south Kona Coast is this reliable hotel, reborn from the former Kona Surf in late 2004. Among the appeals are a spectacular open-air lobby, a kid-pleasing pool complex featuring the island's longest water slide, and 530 spacious guest rooms. The hotel isn't perfect — its architecture is still too reminiscent of the 1970s than I'd like it to be, and I wish they had eradicated the popcorn ceilings in the makeover — but it's a fine choice for those who want the comforts and service of a brand-name, full-service resort without the outrageous prices that predominate farther up the coast. Guest rooms feature tropical-modern decor and cloudlike Sheraton Sweet Sleeper beds; many boast spectacular ocean views, but even the mountain views are stunners in this slice of Kona coffee country. The self-contained resort also features an intimate full-service spa with top-notch treatments, including open-air massage; and a Monday-night luau. Don't miss the Crystal Blue bar, where manta rays arrive almost nightly to bask in the ocean spotlights. The location is one of my Big Island favorites, thanks to the lush countryside and the out-of-the-fray convenience to dining, shopping, and a wealth of ocean activities, including snorkel cruises and kayak trips to Kealakekua Bay (one of Hawaii's finest snorkel and dolphin-watching spots). However, as is common on this lava-rock coast, plan to drive to the beach.

See map p. 329. 78–128 Ehukai St., Kailua-Kona (in the Keauhou resort area). ☎ *888-716-8109 or 808-930-4900. Fax: 808-930-4800.* www.sheratonkeauhou.com. *Self-parking: $9. Valet parking: $14. Rack rates: $350–$460 double, from $900–$2,500 suite. Check for online specials and package rates, sometimes as low as $199. AE, DC, DISC, MC, V.*

Shipman House Bed & Breakfast Inn
$$ Hilo

Misty, flower-filled Hilo wows nostalgics with its Victorian homes and charming downtown overlooking a romantic half-moon bay. One of those century-old Victorians is this dreamy B&B. Impeccably renovated and on the National Register of Historic Places, it's right in step with Hilo's old Hawaii vibe. Barbara Ann and Gary Andersen have kept the inn true to its original form, but they haven't lost sight of its present-day purpose. It's full of modern conveniences, including full bathrooms, ceiling fans, minifridges, and kimono robes (but no TVs) in each of the five spacious, impeccably done rooms. Most romantic is Auntie Clara's, a corner room with windows on two walls overlooking a lush rain forest and bay, with a claw-foot tub in the bathroom. (The bathroom for this room is private, but is detached from the bedroom.) The delightful, locally infused breakfast is served on the wide veranda. This B&B is perfect for romance-seeking couples, history buffs, and national park–goers alike (but not a good choice for those traveling with children). Gracious through and through. Smoking and shoes are forbidden inside the house.

See map p. 326. 131 Kaiulani St. (off Waianuenue Avenue), Hilo. ☎ *800-627-8447 or 808-934-8002. Fax: 808-934-8002.* www.hilo-hawaii.com. *Parking: Free. Rack rates: $219–$249 double. Rates include generous continental buffet breakfast. Discounts available for 7-night stays. AE, MC, V.*

Volcano Village Lodge
$$$ Volcano

This divine oasis in the ferns is a dream come true for romance-seeking couples, and one of my favorite places to stay in all of Hawaii. Innkeeper Kay Lee has crafted an impeccable rain forest retreat that makes both an excellent base for exploring the national park and a relaxing haven for kicking back and enjoying your time together.

Pebbled paths wind their way to five cottages built of fragrant white cedar tucked among the magical gardens. Each is oriented just *so,* making you feel like you're alone in a wild, misty world of overgrown orchids, bamboo, and ohia. Each cottage features a luxuriously dressed bed, a gas fireplace, a private bath, a dining area for two, a minifridge and microwave, a flatscreen high-definition TV with a DVD player (there's no TV reception in this part of the forest), a CD player, and a private lanai (ours had rocking chairs for contemplating the natural wonders while I sipped my morning tea). Furnishings are hand-selected for both comfort and one-of-a-kind style. Pricier units add more lounging area and a few extra luxuries to the mix. Kay prepares gourmet breakfast treats (fruit plates, home-baked quiches, and the like), stocks the fridge, and supplies Kona roast and a selection of teas so you can enjoy an intimate breakfast at your leisure. There's a DVD and CD library for borrowing, and a Jacuzzi and a common living room for sharing. Kay has seemingly thought of everything, including flashlights with extra batteries for late-night lava hikes, and loves to share her joy in the natural wonder in which she lives. A blissful escape — I can't wait to go back.

See map p. 326. 19-4183 Road E, Volcano. ☎ *808-985-9500.* www.volcano villagelodge.com. *Parking: Free. Rack rates: $175–$275 double. 2-night minimum; $50 surcharge for 1-night stay with innkeeper's permission. Rates include substantial continental breakfast. AE, DISC, MC, V.*

Waikoloa Beach Marriott Resort & Spa
$$$$ **Kohala Coast**

This Marriott property has a primo location: It's situated on palm-lined A-Bay, one of the island's prettiest white-sand beaches and best bays for watersports. An excellent beach-activities desk provides easy access to snorkeling, diving, kayaking, and windsurfing; championship golf and salon and spa services are also on hand. The smallish rooms evoke a lovely island vibe; nice features include Marriott's genuinely comfortable "Revive" bed, a private lanai, and in-room fridges, coffeemakers, and robes. On-property perks include the full-service Mandara Spa for pampering treatments and a good fitness center; two fantastic championship golf courses are just a shuttle ride away. Considering the cost to stay in neighboring hotels, the Marriott is the bargain of the Kohala Coast (although it's worth comparing prices against Hilton Waikoloa Village, reviewed earlier in this chapter).

See map p. 331. 69-275 Waikoloa Beach Rd., Waikoloa. ☎ *800-922-5533, 800-228-9290, or 808-886-6789. Fax: 808-886-3601.* www.waikoloabeach marriott.com. *Valet parking: $15. Self-parking: $15 (covered by resort fee). Rack rates: $349–$549 double. Mandatory $20 per day resort fee includes high-speed Internet access, local and long-distance calls to the U.S. and Canada, self-parking, and half-day snorkel gear rental. Better-than-average AAA, senior (62+), corporate, government, and military discounts. Bed-and-breakfast and room-and-car packages regularly on offer; pre-paid advance purchase online rates from $219 at press time. AE, DC, DISC, MC, V.*

Waterfalls Inn
$$ **Hilo**

This stately historic home, located in Hilo's most beautiful residential neighborhood, makes a delightful place to stay. The four guest rooms are generously sized and attractively furnished in an island-casual but vintage-inspired style that suits the house perfectly. Each features an elegantly dressed pillow-top bed (queen-size or king-size), comfortable attendant furnishings that include a sitting area, and a beautifully appointed bathroom with either a whirlpool or an antique soaking tub. One room can accommodate families or friends traveling together in a comfortable anteroom. Well-polished wood floors grace the home, which also features a pleasing breakfast room and lush grounds sonorous with bird song, the high-pitched croaks of tree frogs, and the rushing waters of the Wailuku River, which runs behind the house. Innkeepers (and Chicago transplants) George and Barbara Leonard are friendly but not intrusive, and they prepare a pleasing expanded continental breakfast that includes fresh island fruit smoothies. All in all, an excellent choice.

 The Leonards also own a very pleasing oceanfront condo, Hale Kona Kai ($$; www.halekonakai.com), in the heart of Kailua-Kona town. The one-bedroom unit, which can sleep up to four, has been freshly renovated with extras such as mahogany floors, granite countertops, and a flatscreen TV with DVD in the bedroom, and attractive, good-quality patio furniture. The restaurants, shopping, and bustle of Kona town are an easy walk away — and, at $150 to $160 a night, it's hard to do better for on-the-water accommodations. (Plan on an $85 cleaning fee and a three-day minimum stay.) Look for them to add a Pahoa vacation rental to their repertoire in 2009.

See map p. 326. 240 Kaiulani St. (off Waianuenue Avenue), Hilo. ☎ *888-808-4456 or 808-969-3407.* www.waterfallsinn.com. *Parking: Free. Rack rates: $160–$215 double. A surcharge of $20 is added for single-night stays. Rates include generous continental breakfast. AE, MC, V.*

Home, sweet vacation home

Local real-estate agencies offer a wealth of additional condo choices in and around Kailua-Kona and South Kona. One of the more trusted names is **Knutson & Associates** (☎ **800-800-6202** or 808-329-6311; www.kona hawaiirentals.com), a vacation-rental broker representing everything from affordable condos to multibedroom oceanfront houses.

 Hawaii Resort Management (☎ **800-244-4752** or 808-329-3333; www. konahawaii.com) represents a dozen or more condo properties in the Kailua-Kona area (including the Kona Billfisher, listed earlier in this chapter) and is a good source for budget-watching travelers who prize value over perfection — especially if you're looking for oceanfront options at a bargain rate.

If you prefer a luxury rental on the sunny, golf course–riddled Kohala Coast, reach out to **South Kohala Management** (☎ **800-822-4252** or 808-883-8500; www.southkohala.com), which offers first-rate condos and town houses plus a handful of upscale oceanfront homes.

You can cut out the middle man and rent directly from the owner at a number of quality condo resorts on the Big Island, including Kanaloa at Kona and the terrific Keauhou Kona Surf and Racquet Club, by visiting **Aloha Condos Hawaii** (www.alohacondos.com), a cooperative of owner-managed units; links on the site will connect you directly to the owner.

Hawaii's Best Bed & Breakfasts (☎ **800-262-9912** or 808-263-3100; www.bestbnb.com) also represents some excellent vacation homes on the Big Island, as well as delightful B&Bs. The staff can book a room for you in a cozy cottage or a larger home that they have personally inspected and approved, and service is always friendly.

The Web site of **Hawaii Island B&B Association** (www.stayhawaii.com) offers one-stop shopping for charming, affordable island accommodations with no additional charges — and you can book right online. Each of the properties has been inspected and approved by association representatives.

Dining Out

The Big Island is home to some wonderful restaurants, including a handful of special-occasion oceanfront spots that are just right for romance. But you don't have to spend a fortune to eat well; in fact, the Big Island is home to some of my favorite affordable restaurants in the state.

On the downside, things are a little spread out on this oversize rural island, so choose your dining spots carefully; you don't want to make a reservation for dinner only to realize that the restaurant is an hour's drive from where you're staying. I've worked to include the best restaurants in and around all the major resort and visitor areas in which you may be staying. Still, you may find that your choices are limited; the area around Hawaii Volcanoes National Park, for example, has only a small handful of restaurants, period. If you want additional choices, your concierge, front-desk staff, or innkeeper is usually happy to make recommendations.

At the Kohala Coast resorts, you'll find that the resort restaurants are almost universally overpriced. I've included a few worthy local favorites near the hotels, for those of you who'd rather not pay a minimum of 30 bucks for an entree or $16 for a room-service burger that little Johnny isn't going to finish anyway.

In the restaurant listings in this chapter, each review is followed by a number of dollar signs, ranging from one ($) to five ($$$$$). The dollar signs are meant to give you an idea of what a complete dinner for one person — including appetizer, main course, dessert, one drink, tax, and tip — is likely to set you back. The price categories go like this:

$	Cheap eats — less than $20 per person
$$	Still inexpensive — $20–$35
$$$	Moderate — $35–$50
$$$$	Pricey — $50–$75
$$$$$	Ultraexpensive — more than $75 per person

The Big Island's Restaurants

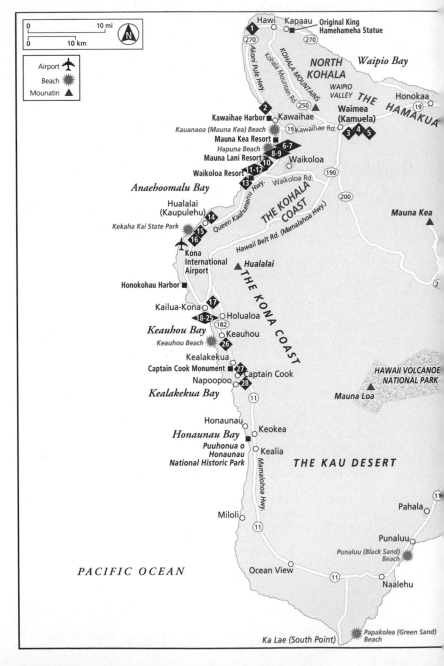

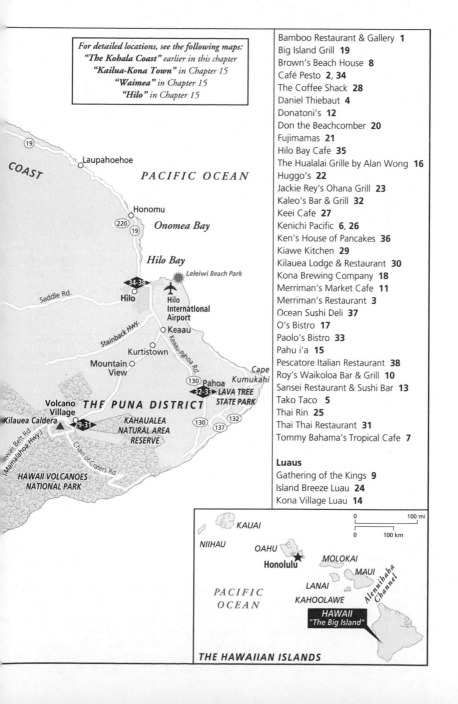

For detailed locations, see the following maps:
"*The Kohala Coast*" earlier in this chapter
"*Kailua-Kona Town*" in Chapter 15
"*Waimea*" in Chapter 15
"*Hilo*" in Chapter 15

Bamboo Restaurant & Gallery **1**
Big Island Grill **19**
Brown's Beach House **8**
Café Pesto **2, 34**
The Coffee Shack **28**
Daniel Thiebaut **4**
Donatoni's **12**
Don the Beachcomber **20**
Fujimamas **21**
Hilo Bay Cafe **35**
The Hualalai Grille by Alan Wong **16**
Huggo's **22**
Jackie Rey's Ohana Grill **23**
Kaleo's Bar & Grill **32**
Keei Cafe **27**
Kenichi Pacific **6, 26**
Ken's House of Pancakes **36**
Kiawe Kitchen **29**
Kilauea Lodge & Restaurant **30**
Kona Brewing Company **18**
Merriman's Market Cafe **11**
Merriman's Restaurant **3**
Ocean Sushi Deli **37**
O's Bistro **17**
Paolo's Bistro **33**
Pahu i'a **15**
Pescatore Italian Restaurant **38**
Roy's Waikoloa Bar & Grill **10**
Sansei Restaurant & Sushi Bar **13**
Tako Taco **5**
Thai Rin **25**
Thai Thai Restaurant **31**
Tommy Bahama's Tropical Cafe **7**

Luaus
Gathering of the Kings **9**
Island Breeze Luau **24**
Kona Village Luau **14**

PACIFIC OCEAN

Laupahoehoe

COAST

Honomu

Onomea Bay

Hilo Bay

Leleiwi Beach Park

Saddle Rd.

Hilo

Hilo International Airport

Stainback Hwy.

Keaau

Kurtistown

Mountain View

Cape Kumukahi

Pahoa

LAVA TREE STATE PARK

Volcano Village

THE PUNA DISTRICT

Kilauea Caldera

KAHAUALEA NATURAL AREA RESERVE

Chain of Craters Rd.

HAWAII VOLCANOES NATIONAL PARK

KAUAI

NIIHAU

OAHU

Honolulu

MOLOKAI

MAUI

PACIFIC OCEAN

LANAI

KAHOOLAWE

Alenuihaha Channel

HAWAII "The Big Island"

0   100 mi
0   100 km

THE HAWAIIAN ISLANDS

Of course, it all depends on how you order, so stay away from the surf and turf or the north end of the wine list if you're watching your budget. To give you a further idea of how much you can expect to spend, I also include the price range of main courses in the listings. (Keep in mind that prices can change at the whim of the management, but restaurants usually don't raise their prices by more than a dollar or two at any given time.)

The state adds roughly 4 percent in taxes to every restaurant bill. The percentage may vary slightly depending on the county you're in, and may be embedded in the total purchase price or shown as an independent line item on your bill. A 15 to 20 percent tip is standard in Hawaii, just as in the rest of the States.

Bamboo Restaurant & Gallery
$$–$$$ North Kohala   Hawaii Local/Pacific Rim

This wonderful restaurant provides the perfect excuse to venture up to pastoral North Kohala. Housed in a delightful plantation-era building and done up in well-worn rattan and retro-tropical prints, Bamboo bubbles over with old Hawaii appeal — like Trader Vic's without the kitsch. The pleasing menu features delicious island cuisine that, refreshingly, doesn't bother with "gourmet" or "culinary" pretensions. This is real food, well prepared with local pride. Almost everything is fresh-caught or locally grown by Kohala fishermen and farmers, and the owners grow their own herbs and flowers. The quality is excellent, portions are generous, and Pacific and Thai influences add zip. Chicken satay potstickers are hand-wrapped and pan-fried in chili oil for a spicy signature treat. Island fish is prepared four winning ways, and a moist and tender 5-ounce filet is flame-broiled and paired with black tiger shrimp and green papaya salad. The lunch menu is simpler but equally satisfying, with offerings like a Hawaiian barbecued pork sandwich. Eggs Bamboo (eggs Benedict with kalua pork and lilikoi [passion fruit] hollandaise) is a winner at Sunday brunch. Passion-fruit margaritas and live slack-key guitar music round out the island appeal. Plan on an early dinner so that you can enjoy the scenic drive in the daylight.

See map p. 344. On Akoni Pule Highway (at Highway 270/250 intersection), Hawi (a 30- to 45-minute drive from most Kohala Coast resorts). ☎ *808-889-5555.* www.bamboo restaurant.info. *Reservations recommended for dinner. Main courses: $9.50–$19 at lunch, $22–$38 at dinner; Sun brunch $5–$15. DC, MC, V. Open: Lunch and dinner Tues–Sat, Sun brunch.*

Big Island Grill
$ Kailua-Kona   American/Local

This local favorite offers huge portions of home-style cooking at retro prices, making it one of the island's most beloved restaurants. And the love shows: The grill is always hopping, from the first cup of coffee at breakfast to the last bite of dessert after dark. Expect American favorites with a local spin, including excellent fresh fish and generous salads and sandwiches; don't miss out on a side of the fabulous mashed potatoes. It's an excellent choice for families. In a hurry? No worries: Head to the drive-up window for coffee, cappuccino, smoothies, fresh-baked pastries, lunch specials, and the like.

See map p. 344 75–5702 Kuakini Hwy., Kailua-Kona. ☎ 808-326-1153. Reservations only accepted for dinner a day or more in advance for parties of 5 or more. Main courses: $9–$23. MC, V. Open: Breakfast, lunch, and dinner Mon–Sat.

Brown's Beach House
$$$$$ Kohala Coast Hawaii Regional

On-the-beach dining experiences don't come finer than Brown's, an excellent alfresco restaurant that consistently shines. The innovative island-inspired cuisine uses the freshest local seafood and produce (you can watch the staff in action in the exhibition kitchen). You might start with ahi poke tossed tableside, or a salad of heirloom tomatoes grown on the nearby slopes, accompanied by passion fruit and a goat cheese panna cotta. Follow with a grilled, spice-rubbed New York strip steak grilled over kiawe (mesquite) and served with Molokai sweet potatoes; or locally farmed sweet lobster and scallops. The food at Hualalai and Pahu i'a (see listings later in this chapter) is better, but the one-of-a-kind ambience here, with nightly entertainment under the stars, is pure magic. What's more, presentation and service are both faultless. Reserve a table close to the spot-lit surf for the ultimate in romance (and bring a light jacket or wrap to ward off the ocean breeze, which can be nippy after dark).

See map p. 344. In the Fairmont Orchid, 1 N. Kaniku Dr., Mauna Lani resort. ☎ 808-887-7368 or 808-885-2000. www.fairmont.com/orchid. *Reservations highly recommended for dinner. Main courses: $16–$28 at lunch, $30–$68 at dinner. AE, DC, DISC, MC, V. Open: Lunch and dinner daily.*

Cafe Pesto
$$ Hilo/Kohala Coast Pizza/Italian/Island

These casual island favorites are a long-standing hit with locals and visitors alike. The well-prepared pastas and Pacific Regional specialties are pleasing, but the pizza is the real star — and the real value — of the menu. Both branches serve top-flight gourmet brick-oven-baked pies featuring fresh organic herbs, island-grown produce, and a thick, slightly sweet golden crust. My favorite is the pizza luau, with kalua-style pork, sweet onions, and fresh pineapple, but you can choose from a full slate of creative combinations or build your own from a list of more than two dozen toppings. I find the food to be consistently better at the original Hilo branch (which also boasts a more appealing and attractive high-ceilinged setting), but the branch at the northernmost end of the Kohala Coast provides a great escape for families tired of feeding on overpriced resort food.

See map p. 344. Hilo: In the S. Hata Building, 308 Kamehameha Ave. (at Mamo Street). ☎ 808-969-6640. The Kohala Coast: In the Kawaihae Shopping Center at Kawaihae Harbor, at Akoni Pule Highway and Kawaihae Road, Kawaihae (at the Highway 19/270 junction). ☎ 808-882-1071. www.cafepesto.com. *Reservations recommended for dinner. Main courses: $7–$20 at lunch, $9–$35 at dinner (most items $10–$21). AE, DC, DISC, MC, V. Open: Lunch and dinner daily.*

The Coffee Shack
$ South Kona   American

This bare-bones roadside charmer prepares some of South Kona's best eats. Take a seat on the pleasant terrace (which boasts ocean views beyond the banana trees) for table service or pony up to the friendly counter to order takeout. You can start the day with first-class eggs Benedict or thick French toast accompanied by a cup of world-class Arabica joe that was grown right on the mountainside below. Come by at lunch for the best sandwiches on the coast. Top-notch fillings range from smoked Alaskan salmon to fresh local veggies to warmed corned beef and Black Forest ham, and you can have them applied to any one of six kinds of fresh-baked bread. The thick-crusted, generously topped pizzas are even better than Cafe Pesto's (see the preceding listing), and when it's time for dessert, lots of homemade pies and baked goods tempt you. The service can be slow, but what's your hurry? You're on vacation. Sit back, take it in stride, and consider it a blessing that you have more time to take in the million-dollar view.

See map p. 344. On Highway 11, between mile markers 108 and 109, a mile south of Captain Cook (about 10 minutes south of Keauhou). ☎ *808-328-9555.* www.coffee shack.com. *Breakfast and sandwiches: $8–$12. Pizzas: $10–$13. MC, V. Open: Breakfast and lunch daily.*

Daniel Thiebaut
$$$$–$$$$$ Waimea   French Asian

Although the food here can be just wonderful, my favorite thing about Daniel Thiebaut is its delightful setting: It's housed in the former Chock In Store, which kept Waimea in staples for nearly all of the 20th century. The wonderful warren of high-ceilinged rooms has been beautifully preserved, and memorabilia from the olden days line the walls and curio cabinets. The food blends island freshness with Thiebaut's own European-style sauces and reductions to pleasing effect. The menu is laden with choices that range from a delectable lobster bisque and a fresh-catch fish in macadamia-nut sauce to lilikoi-glazed barbecue short ribs and a Hunan-style rack of lamb. Word is that the kitchen can be iffy when Chef Daniel isn't in the house, but I've had very good dining experiences here. Sunday brunch is a bounteous treat. Not cheap, but a fairly priced alternative to the Kohala Coast resorts a half-hour down the hill.

See map p. 344. 65–1259 Kawaihae Rd. (Highway 19), Waimea. ☎ *808-887-2200.* www.danielthiebaut.com. *Main courses: $10–$18 at lunch, $21–$45 at dinner; Sun brunch $19. AE, MC, V. Open: Lunch Mon–Sat, Sun brunch, dinner nightly.*

Donatoni's
$$$$–$$$$$ Kohala Coast   Northern Italian

This wildly romantic restaurant replicates the feel of an Italian villa, with tables overlooking a tranquil lagoon and boasting unforgettable sunset views. Make sure to book a table on the twinkle-lit, European-elegant patio.

Excellent choices include a delectable, fall-off-the-bone *osso buco alla Milanese;* delicate and delicious veal scaloppine with sautéed mushrooms in a light asparagus cream sauce; pan-seared Hawaiian snapper with puttanesca sauce; and any of the house-made pastas. But if something else entices you, go for it; I dined with a large party on my last visit, and every dish at the table was a star. Desserts are equally impressive. For something really special, opt for the Venetian Carnival Mask, made of white chocolate and resting atop a lightly bittersweet chocolate marquis with Franjelico sauce. The restaurant offers an excellent (though quite pricey) wine list too — it has garnered multiple *Wine Spectator* Awards of Excellence. Come for sunset because the view is everything it should be.

 Be sure to arrive at the Hilton Waikoloa a full 15 to 20 minutes before your reservation time; it will take you that long to walk (or take one of the resort's silly shuttles) to the restaurant because the Hilton sprawls over a massive 62 acres.

See map p. 344. At Hilton Waikoloa Village, 69–425 Waikoloa Beach Dr., Waikoloa. ☎ *808-886-1234.* www.donatonis.com. *Reservations highly recommended. Main courses: $26–$49. AE, DISC, MC, V. Open: Dinner nightly.*

Don the Beachcomber
$$$ **Kailua-Kona   Island Steak and Seafood**

I'm thrilled with the arrival of Don the Beachcomber to the Kailua-Kona dining scene, which has long been in need of supplement to its few good-quality options. The legendary Donn Beach was the inventor of the mai tai, and one of the originators of the classic Tiki lifestyle; this new restaurant hits all of the right vintage notes, but doesn't sacrifice quality for style. The island-style steak-and-seafood menu is prepared with fresh, top-quality ingredients and an inventive spirit that's creative yet delightfully unfussy. Highlights include a slow-roasted Hawaiian salt-and-pepper-crusted prime rib; the "Sword Fight," a fresh-caught billfish and lobster tail combo; macadamia nut–crusted mahimahi with fresh papaya-mango-lime salsa; and Don's Drunken Chicken, a breast pan-seared in truffle oil and dressed in dark rum and a wild mushroom Marsala sauce. A variety of entree-size salads are on the menu for diners with lighter appetites.

The decor is Tiki perfect, complete with grass-skirted tables in the open-air, oceanfront dining room. The colonnaded bar overlooking the surf is the height of Tiki chic, and the mai tai is everything it should be. Daytime diners can enjoy a generous breakfast buffet or lunch and island-style pupus (coconut prawns, ahi sashimi, honey-mango-glazed baby back ribs) served in the bar throughout the day. Just as Kona should be, and satisfying through and through. *Note:* Bring your parking ticket in for free-parking validation.

See map p. 344. At the Royal Kona Resort, 75-5852 Alii Dr., Kailua-Kona. ☎ *808-329-3111.* www.royalkona.com *(click on "Dining"). Reservations recommended for dinner. Main courses: $14–$19 at breakfast and lunch, $10–$35 at dinner (most $20–$30). AE, DC, DISC, MC, V. Open: Breakfast, lunch, and bar daily, dinner Tues–Sun.*

Fujimamas
$$$ Kailua-Kona   Asian-Inspired/Sushi

Chef Mark Vann has taken the spirit of the original Fujimamas in Tokyo and transported it to a tucked-away corner in Kona town that sizzles with hip, creative energy. The indoor-outdoor restaurant features sexy Southeast Asian details and furnishings, while the rustic outdoor patio twinkles. The food is good, if not consistently great; I really enjoyed the zestily inventive Thai Caesar salad with crispy calamari "croutons" and the mushroom-stuffed pork *tonkatsu* with spicy apple sauce, but found the corn griddle cake under the seared salmon to be a little colder than I would have liked. Most dishes are served family style so everyone can share. The sushi is mostly local caught and creatively prepared, and probably the highlight of the menu; consider the Pink Panther roll (tempura shrimp, *shiso*, avocado, and cucumber wrapped in pink soy paper and accompanied by a spicy aioli) for a fun and flavorful sushi experience. An inspired drinks menu that includes creative cocktails, sake flights, and Asian beers adds to the flair. All in all, a less-than-perfect but fun choice.

See map p. 344. 75-5719 Alii Dr. (at Sarona Road), Kailua-Kona. ☎ *808-327-2125.* www.fujimamas.com. *Reservations recommended for dinner. Main courses: $16–$28, sushi $5–$16; Mon–Fri lunch specials $10–$14. AE, DC, DISC, MC, V. Open: Lunch Mon–Sat, dinner nightly.*

Hilo Bay Cafe
$$ Hilo   Contemporary

One of Hilo's top fine-dining spots is tucked away in a nondescript strip mall a ten-minute drive from downtown, but it's well worth seeking out for its good food at reasonable prices. The contemporary-styled room is simple, with colorful accents to energize the style. Local and organic ingredients drive a modern menu blending dashes of island and Italian inspiration. Winning dishes include macadamia-praline crusted scallops, served on angel hair pasta with smoked bacon, and a nicely grilled local rib-eye with gold mashed potatoes, tomato confit, and smoked green beans. Dishes are generally well prepared and pleasing, and I like how they recommend wine pairings with every main. Service is attentive (if not always as attentive as it should be), and the wine list is affordable. The lunch menu is simpler but no less satisfying. All in all, a nice choice in a dining-basic town.

See map p. 344. In the Waiakea Shopping Center (near Office Max), 315 Makaala St. (at Kanoelehua Street [Highway 11], north of Prince Kuhio Plaza), Hilo. ☎ *808-935-4939.* www.hilobaycafe.com. *Reservations recommended. Main courses: $9–$14 at lunch, $10–$28 at dinner (most under $22). AE, MC, V. Open: Lunch and dinner daily.*

The Hualalai Grille by Alan Wong
$$$$$ Kohala Coast   Hawaii Regional

My favorite restaurant in all of Hawaii is Alan Wong's in Honolulu — until I dined here, that is. The Hualalai Grille strikes all of the same inspiring notes that the original does, but adds the appeal of a gorgeous, casually sophisticated resort setting. The restaurant is housed in the golf course clubhouse at the ultraluxe Four Seasons resort; the floor-to-ceiling windows sweep aside to reveal stunning 18th hole views in one direction, resort and ocean views in the other. The high-ceilinged, haute plantation-style room is outfitted in warm woods and comfortable furnishings, and boasts a stylish but unfussy vibe; the tables are well spaced to allow for plenty of elbow room and private conversation.

If there is one master of Hawaii Regional Cuisine, it is Wong — and his cuisine is exquisite. The island-modern menu maintains the spirit of the original while having a flair all its own. It even wears the glow of the Big Island in such dishes as grilled Kukaiau Ranch beef tenderloin with a warm Hamakua-grown mushroom and Cipollini onion salad, topped with a béarnaise sauce that seems lighter than it must be. The soy-braised short ribs, Wong's own version of Korean kalbi, accompanied by ginger-crusted grilled shrimp and lotus root, was a culinary dream come true for me, but you can't go wrong with any creation on this ethereal menu. I like its joyful spirit, showcased in the "soup and sandwich" appetizer, a grilled cheese, kalua pig, and foie gras sandwich served with a martini glass of chilled tomato soup; I reveled in feeling like the most sophisticated little kid in the room. Service is thoughtful, attentive, and unpretentious, and the cocktails and desserts are everything they should be. The tasting menu is a relative bargain, considering the don't-have-to-choose experience it offers. A world-class wow from start to finish. Book well ahead.

See map p. 344. At the Four Seasons Resort Hualalai, 100 Kaupulehu Dr., Kaupulehu-Kona (7 miles north of the airport). ☎ *808-325-8525.* www.hualalairesort.com *or* www.fourseasons.com/hualalai. *Reservations essential. Main courses: $36–$54 at dinner; tasting menu $70 ($100 with wine pairings). AE, DC, DISC, MC, V. Open: Dinner daily.*

Huggo's
$$$$ Kailua-Kona   Seafood

Happy, hopping Huggo's serves fine seafood to a jovial crowd drawn in by the festive vibe and remarkable Kailua Bay views. Fresh fish — grilled, blackened, sautéed, or steamed — is the specialty, as it should be. The dining room is so close to the surf that the kitchen staff could practically cast a line over the side of the deck; it's virtually impossible to find a more fabulous on-the-water setting, even at twice the price. Some of the preparations can be a bit heavy-handed, smothering the top-quality local catches, so I recommend opting for simpler preparations that let the freshness and flavor shine through. The service is welcoming, friendly, and knowledgeable, and the wine list features a number of good bargains. Ginger orange chicken, New York steak, and wild mushroom pasta are on hand for the fish-o-phobic, and there's macadamia nut pie à la mode to cap things off. All in all, a terrific choice — certainly among the best of Kailua-Kona town's string of waterfront restaurants (although Don the Beachcomber's is giving Huggo's a run for its money).

Next door at the lively, thatch-roofed **Huggo's on the Rocks,** you'll find casual all-day dining and live music nightly. Huggo's also prepares an extensive tropical cocktail menu, making this the perfect place to watch the sunset while the waves crash just a few feet away. The light and affordable menu of burgers, sandwiches, and pupus is served late into the evening. Come extra-early for your sunset perch because the secret's out. From 6:30 to 11 a.m., this same location turns into **Java on the Rocks,** a great place to greet the day.

See map p. 344. 75–5828 Kahakai Rd., off Alii Drive (behind Snorkel Bob's and next to the Royal Kona Resort), Kailua-Kona. ☎ *808-329-1493.* www.huggos.com. *Reservations highly recommended. Main courses: $10–$20 at lunch, $23–$53 at dinner (most less than $35). Light fare at Huggo's on the Rocks $9–$14. AE, DC, DISC, MC, V. Open: Lunch and dinner daily.*

Jackie Rey's Ohana Grill
$$–$$$ Kailua-Kona   Eclectic

Here's a refreshing change of pace; a chance to escape the high-priced resorts and the constant bustle of Kailua-Kona's main drag to rub elbows with the locals. Cheery, colorful, and relaxed, Jackie Rey's is a real neighborhood find with a surprisingly sophisticated menu, warm service, and an impressively talented kitchen staff. Drop in at lunch for beer-battered fish and chips, a kalua turkey wrap with avocado and melted Swiss cheese, or a half-pound cheddar burger with a side of curly fries. Weekday happy hours bring half-price pupus, like the Korean-style short ribs or spicy hoisin chicken wings (not to mention tropical drinks and a nice selection of local microbrews). For dinner, Angie's salad is a lavish composition featuring fresh spinach greens, blue cheese, candied walnuts, papaya, and onions in a raspberry balsamic vinaigrette. The seared ahi with crispy noodles and Asian vegetables is always in demand, as are the sweetly zesty Korean-style beef short ribs, which may be ordered as either an appetizer or an entree. The nightly specials include several fresh catches done with tempting preparations. The desserts are top-notch and a *keiki* (children's) menu makes things easy for Mom and Dad. The wine list is thoughtfully chosen and extremely well-priced. A definite winner — and an excellent value to boot, all things considered. Enjoy an eclectic mix of live music and dancing on weekend nights.

See map p. 344. 75–5995 Kuakini Hwy., Kailua-Kona. ☎ *808-327-0209.* www.jackie reys.com. *Reservations recommended for dinner. To get there: From Alii Drive, turn inland on Lunapule Road. Bear right at Walua Road, then right again on Kuakini Highway. Main courses: $11–$14 at lunch, $13–$28 at dinner (most under $20); pupus and lighter fare $6–$11. AE, MC, V. Open: Lunch and happy hour Mon–Fri, dinner nightly.*

Kaleo's Bar & Grill
$$–$$$ Puna District (Pahoa)   Eclectic

This smart, sophisticated grill has contributed significantly to the upscaling of scruffy little Pahoa. A new-in-2008 addition to the postage stamp–size scene, it has infused the town with a dash of sleek, artful style, while still maintaining the casual, approachable style that an authentic,

---

Another Pahoa Dining Option

If you've dined at Kaleo's and want another quality option in Pahoa, or are simply in the mood for something different, head a few rustic storefronts down to **Paolo's Bistro** ($$), 333 Old Government Rd. (☎ **808-965-7033**), a rustic-charming Italian bistro complete with lace curtains, checkered tablecloths, smoothly attentive service, and a limited but high-quality menu of Tuscan-style favorites, including chicken marsala and pasta puttanesca, plus a sweetly simple Italian-style dessert. Come bearing your own bottle of wine; the BYOB policy also keeps your bill down.

---

untouristed town like this demands. The pretty restaurant boasts rich red walls, white tablecloths, and colorful, well-chosen art. There's live acoustic music most nights. The menu blends straightforward steaks, chops, and burgers with island favorites prepared in creative ways that are the most satisfying options on the menu. I recommend starting with the classic ahi poke, Hawaii's version of ceviche well seasoned with Kukui nut and onions, garnished with fresh-sliced avocado, and served with a dash of élan in a martini glass. Fresh island fish from the deep Big Island waters is presented five ways; I delighted in my pan-fried, coconut-crusted ono dressed in sweet-spicy lilikoi (passion fruit) sauce. Plates are beautifully presented, the full bar mixes a great martini, and service is attentive.

See map p. 344. 15-2969 Pahoa Village Rd. (the main drag in town, also known as Old Government Road), Pahoa. ☎ *808-965-5600. Reservations accepted for dinner. Main courses: $6–$15 at lunch, $10–$26 at dinner. AE, MC, V. Open: Lunch Tues–Sun, dinner nightly.*

Keei Cafe
$$–$$$ **South Kona   Island/Eclectic**

Keei (*kay*-ee) Cafe prepares some of the Big Island's finest food in a casual, low-key environment. A few years back, Keei moved from its previous locale in a former fish market to its present digs, a bit farther north and somewhat more upscale. The ambience remains as comfortable as ever, the service is friendly, and the island-style meals are excellent. Expect hearty Mediterranean- and Asian-slanted dishes in pleasantly light sauces accompanied by fresh, crisp vegetables, such as half-roasted chicken in red Thai curry, or marvelous fresh Kona catches in a puckery piccata sauce. Every dish is made from scratch, and virtually all ingredients are caught, grown, or harvested on the island. Keei Cafe offers one of the best dining values in the state; it's easy to pay a lot more for a lot less elsewhere in Hawaii. Save room for dessert, because both the bread pudding, made with bananas and pineapple, and the coconut flan with lilikoi sauce (secret recipe of the owner's Portuguese mother-in-law) are home-style tropical delights. Complaints about service nearly sunk Keei Cafe after the big move, but the attention and attitude seem to be squarely on the upswing these days.

See map p. 344. On Highway 11 at mile marker 113, Kealakekua. ☎ *808-322-9992. Reservations highly recommended. Main courses: $15–$26. No credit cards. Open: Dinner Tues–Sat.*

Kenichi Pacific
$$$ South Kona/Kohala Coast   Pacific Rim Fusion/Sushi

Master sushi chef Kenichi Kamada, who has already made a splash in Austin and Aspen with his very pleasing Pacific Rim fusion cuisine, has thankfully blessed the Big Island with his hip signature style, his famous sushi bar, and a welcome blast of cool. The setting is Zen-modern, the service is efficient, and the food is usually terrific, making Kenichi Pacific a winner on all fronts. You can enjoy some excellent sushi and sashimi, opt for more traditional appetizer/main-course ordering, or mix it up family-style, if you prefer. If you're a sushi novice or unfamiliar with any of the ingredients or preparations, your server is happy to walk you through the menu. Dishes that make grazing a pleasure include ginger-marinated squid, Saikyo black cod — cured for 48 hours in miso blend and then broiled with a teriyaki glaze until it's melt-in-your-mouth perfection — and Dungeness crab cakes, fresh crab encased in crispy phyllo and dressed in a sambal-pickled ginger sauce. Kenichi's special roast duck with orange hoisin sauce, wrapped moo shu–style and served with tempura asparagus, is a delight. A new Mauna Lani location has both added to the Kenichi empire and happily expanded the Kohala Coast's dining choices — but word on the street is that the quality is now variable in both locations, depending on where you find Kenichi in the kitchen.

See map p. 344. South Kona location: In the Keauhou Shopping Center, Keauhou. ☎ *808-322-6400. To get there: From Highway 11, turn right on Kamehameha III Road (between mile markers 117 and 118) and head downhill to the shopping center. Kohala Coast location: At the Shops at Mauna Lani, 68-1330 Mauna Lani Dr., Mauna Lani.* ☎ *808-885-1515.* www.kenichirestaurants.com. *Reservations recommended for dinner. Main courses: $29–$43. AE, MC, V. Open: Lunch Tues–Fri, dinner nightly.*

Ken's House of Pancakes
$ Hilo   Coffee Shop

The classic coffee shop goes Hawaiian at Ken's, the only round-the-clock joint on the Big Island. This cheery local favorite is an all-American diner, where the comfort food is pleasingly prepared and the old-fashioned service comes with a genuine dash of island-style aloha. Ken's is a three-meals-a-day-plus kind of place with a monster menu that boasts something for everyone. Start your day bright and early with French toast or a macadamia-nut waffle (topped with passion-fruit or coconut syrup, if you want); Ken's has been voted "Best Big Island" breakfast for nine years (and counting), so you won't be disappointed. Come back at noon for a garden-fresh salad or a flame-broiled burger. Later in the day, stop in for a roast turkey, teriyaki chicken, or kalbi rib dinner, or drop by for a late-night piece of pie and a cup of Kona joe. Ken's is also my favorite place on the island for saimin, the ramenlike noodle soup that's an island staple; in Ken's version, the noodles are handmade, as are the yummy chicken won tons. I just love Ken's — it's a great place to experience real local cuisine and aloha spirit.

See map p. 344. 1730 Kamehameha Ave. (at Kanoelehua Avenue), Hilo. ☎ *808-935-8711. Reservations not taken. Main courses: $5–$21 (almost all under $15). DC, DISC, MC, V. Open: Daily 24 hours.*

Kiawe Kitchen
$$–$$$ Volcano Village   Contemporary Italian

I really like this fairly recent addition to the Volcano dining scene (comprising precisely three recommendable restaurants). The simple room with a few cute touches isn't much to look at; in fact, based on what I'd heard about the place, I was surprised to be greeted by some rather dour-looking carpet. Still, I got over any reservations quickly, thanks to very well prepared food, with classier details than I expect in Volcano, and friendly (if a bit too casual) service. The menu isn't strictly Italian, but it wears a distinct Italian flair. It includes good wood-fired pizzas, sandwiches, and elegant salads at lunch, plus fire-roasted fish and meat main courses at dinner. I really enjoyed Kiawe's creative lunchtime Caesar (although I must note that traditionalists may not), made with whole ladle-shaped organic baby romaine leaves, fresh island tomatoes, and a perfectly creamy-tart dressing, accompanied by an exceptionally good French-style baguette (the bread is brought in from Hilo's legendary Suisan market). Preparations across the board are simple but stylish, and feature crisp island-grown vegetables. Not as consistent or broadly appealing as the terrific Kilauea Lodge (see review below), but a bit more spirited.

See map p. 344. 19-4005 Haumani Rd. (at Old Volcano Road, adjacent to the Volcano Store), Volcano Village. ☎ *808-967-7711. Reservations accepted for parties of 5 or more only. Main courses: $10–$16 at lunch, $15–$29 at dinner. MC, V. Open: Lunch and dinner daily.*

Kilauea Lodge & Restaurant
$$$$ Volcano   Continental

My favorite Volcano restaurant is dressed like a cozy old-world hunting lodge and is tucked away in the rain forest just outside the national park. The large, high-ceilinged room is appealingly attractive, with country-style furniture polished to a high sheen and a roaring stone fireplace. The knowledgeable and warmly welcoming servers are dressed in beautiful island prints by renowned Big Island designer Sig Zane (see Chapter 15 for info on where to get your own Sig Zane aloha wear). A skilled bartender mixing up perfect martinis rounds out the picture. Chef-owner Albert Jeyte specializes in hearty old-world cuisine. A well-prepared fresh catch is always on offer (broiled and topped with mango chutney glaze and crushed mac nuts is my favorite of the preparation choices), but Jeyte's heart lies with such richly flavored dishes as duck l'orange, roasted with oranges, pepper, and garlic and coated in a yummy apricot mustard glaze. The leg of ante-lope is sautéed, flamed over an open fire, and dressed in a red wine shal-lot sauce. Dinners come with house-made soup or locally grown salad and fresh-baked bread, which makes the excellent fare an excellent value too.

See map p. 344. 19–4055 Volcano Rd., (just off Highway 11 at Wright Road), Volcano. ☎ *808-967-7366.* www.kilauealodge.com. *Reservations recommended. Main courses: $20–$43 (most less than $35). AE, MC, V. Open: Dinner nightly.*

Kona Brewing Co.
$$ Kailua-Kona   Island/Pizza

Kona Brewing Co. is Hawaii's finest microbrewery, specializing in flavorful handcrafted brews with island-rooted names like Longboard Lager, Fire Rock Pale Ale, and Hula Hefewiezen. You can enjoy them fresh from the tap at this pleasingly casual pub, along with equally well-prepared island-style pub grub. The hand-tossed pizza crusts are topped with top-quality Parmesan and mozzarella, locally grown herbs, and a range of creative ingredients, from traditional pepperoni to lilikoi barbecue chicken. Or you can opt for hearty salads with crisp island-grown veggies, and generously stuffed sandwiches on the brewery's own focaccia. A nice selection of pupus (appetizers) is on hand for those who merely want to pull up to the blond-wood bar for some munchies and a beer. Inside service is available, but snare a table on the pretty tropical patio if you can. Friendly service rounds out the affordable, easygoing appeal.

See map p. 344. 75–5629 Kuakini Hwy., in the North Kona Shopping Center (1 block inland from Alii Drive) and Palani Road. ☎ *808-334-2739.* www.kona brewingco.com. *Reservations taken only for parties of 10 or more. To get there: Heading toward the ocean on Palani Road, turn left on Kuakini Highway, and then right into the shopping center. Sandwiches and salads: $9–$12. Pizzas: $11–$26. DC, DISC, MC, V. Open: Lunch and dinner daily.*

Merriman's Market Cafe
$$–$$$ Kohala Coast   Island Mediterranean

If you'd like to try Peter Merriman's winning fare but don't feel like driving all the way to Waimea — or if you're simply in the mood for something more casual (or more affordable) — visit this pleasing outpost in the Waikoloa Kings' Shops. This casually sophisticated market cafe features Italian- and Mediterranean-style fare simply prepared with fresh local pro-duce, meats, and day-caught local fish that give every dish crisp freshness and a delightful local flair. Highlights include rosemary roasted rack of lamb, served with garbanzo salad and island-grown greens; Portuguese *cataplana,* a delightfully zesty dish of pan-roasted clams with locally made chorizo sausage, garlic, and tomatoes; char-grilled shrimp kebabs; and a hearty homemade meatball sandwich on a house-made hoagie roll at lunch. A bountiful appetizer menu that includes yummy hummus, mini-pizzas, a crisp and flavorful Greek salad, and other Mediterranean treats allows for family-style sharing. The cafe also boasts a good selection of affordable Mediterranean-style wines, including crisp, refreshing whites and light, flavorful reds that pair with their dishes beautifully. A takeout counter features "almost ready to eat" family-style dishes that you can take back to the condo for a gourmet heat-and-serve evening. It's a wonderful place to relax at lunch or enjoy a light dinner.

See map p. 344. In the Kings' Shops, 250 Waikoloa Beach Dr., Waikoloa. ☎ 808-886-1700. Call ahead for preferred seating (first available nearest to your reserved time). Main courses: $10–$16 at lunch, $10–$28 at dinner. AE, MC, V. Open: Lunch and dinner nightly.

Merriman's Restaurant
$$$$ Waimea   Hawaii Regional

One of the original purveyors of Hawaii Regional Cuisine, James Beard–nominated chef Peter Merriman reigns over this cozy and comfortable cowboy-country enclave. Over the years, it has matured into a still-pleasing — and still hugely popular — culinary institution. Residents and visitors alike happily make the long drive Upcountry (20 minutes from the Kohala Coast, about an hour from Kona or Hilo) to feast on Merriman's winning cuisine. Simplicity is the secret to his long-lasting success. Waimea-raised beef and lamb, fish caught daily in Kona waters, and organically grown veggies from nearby family farms are used in uncomplicated yet innovative preparations; the fresh natural flavors of the top-quality ingredients shine through. Wok-charred ahi, Pahoa corn-and-shrimp fritters, and slow-roasted chicken are among the many standouts on the perpetually pleasing menu. Lunch is an especially good bargain.

See map p. 344 65–1227 Opelo Rd., in Opelo Plaza, Highway 19 (at Opelo Road, on the Kona side of town), Kamuela. ☎ 808-885-6822. www.merrimanshawaii.com. *Reservations recommended. Main courses: $9–$18 at lunch, $24–$45 at dinner. AE, MC, V. Open: Lunch Mon–Fri, dinner nightly.*

Ocean Sushi Deli
$$ Hilo   Japanese

Sushi lovers who visit Hilo will enjoy this plain and simple sushi restaurant, which makes the most of the bounty of the sea, both island-caught and flown in fresh from Japan. The fish is skillfully prepared and served with aloha by a young, friendly, and attentive waitstaff. Creative rolls are a forte, and combination plates are a bargain. The restaurant is very popular at dinnertime thanks to the quality and overall value, so make reservations or be prepared for a wait.

See map p. 344. 239 Keawe St. (near Haili Street, next to Pescatore), Hilo. ☎ 808-961-6625. Reservations recommended for dinner. 2-piece sushi and rolls: $3–$9. Sushi boxes: $5–$23. Family platters: $22–$50. DC, MC, V. Open: Lunch and dinner Mon–Sat.

O's Bistro
$$–$$$ Kailua-Kona   Pan-Asian/International

This popular restaurant is the domain of top Hawaii Regional chef Amy Ferguson, who reinvented noodle dishes for discriminating diners. It's

Behind the Scenes of Hawaii Regional Cuisine

Attention, foodies: If you want to enjoy the full agricultural bounty of the Big Island, consider joining a **Merriman's Farm Visits & Dinner** tour, offered Monday through Thursday afternoons in partnership with **Hawaii Forest & Trail**, Hawaii's top tour operator. The half-day adventure takes you behind the scenes of Hawaii Regional Cuisine, to the Big Island's finest and most picturesque small-batch farms, where the emphasis is on sustainable agriculture. Your tour will culminate with a four-course feast at the restaurant. Tours run daily from 2:30 p.m. to 7:30 p.m. and cost $155 per person. For more information, call ☎ **808-464-1993** or visit www.merrimanshawaii.com or www.hawaii-forest.com/adv-farmtour.html.

upscale-casual, with a full list of international beers and fine wines. Creative noodle dishes are the stars of the menu, winning loyalty from locals and visitors alike. The menu runs the gamut from Vietnamese pho (beef noodle soup) to pasta primavera with grilled vegetables to wok-seared ahi noodle casserole. The noodle dishes are significantly cheaper than the full-fledged entrees, which include a well-prepared crispy Peking duck with fresh plum sauce and local-style fish steamed in shiitake, scallion, and sesame *shoyu* (soy sauce). Save room for the scrumptious desserts.

See map p. 344. In the Crossroads Shopping Center (the Safeway Center), 75–1027 Henry St. (at Highway 11 and Palani Road), Kailua-Kona. ☎ 808-327-6565. www.osbistro.com. Reservations accepted for parties of 6 or more. Main courses: $8–$15 at breakfast, $9–$20 at lunch, $12–$34 at dinner. AE, DC, DISC, MC, V. Open: Late breakfast, lunch, and dinner daily.

Pahu i'a
$$$$$ **Kohala Coast   Euro-Pacific Fusion**

Done in an elegant haute-plantation style and open to the trade winds and ocean views, this ultraromantic candlelit dining room (with a brilliant aquarium as its centerpiece) is the Big Island's most beautiful restaurant. The sublime food and faultless service live up to the setting in every respect. The regularly changing menu features only the finest regional ingredients, and both Pacific-born and Continental preparations take inspired turns in the capable kitchen. A thick-cut ahi steak wears a red-wine lobster sauce, and is accompanied by a wonderful Molokai sweet-potato purée. A delicate guava glaze adorns pan-seared scallops, and heartier appetites might opt for prime dry-aged peppercorn steak or a tender roasted rack of lamb. The depth and richness of the truffle and butternut squash risotto is enhanced by wild mushrooms and shaved Parmesan. The dessert menu is a showstopper, with creations such as a ginger–macadamia nut praline mousse served with Kona coffee ice cream. I'm clearly not alone in considering Pahu i'a phenomenal on all fronts; it has won stellar ratings from Zagat, four-diamond status from AAA, and recognition as one of America's top hotel restaurants by *Food & Wine*. I prefer the Hualalai Grille, but there's no denying the sheer romance of this place; still, some come away feeling like it's just a bit too formal and a bit too pricey. Scoring a table can be rather difficult in the busy seasons, so book ahead.

See map p. 344. At the Four Seasons Resort Hualalai, 100 Kaupulehu Dr., Kaupulehu-Kona (7 miles north of the airport). ☎ *808-325-8000.* www.fourseasons.com/ hualalai/dining.html. *Reservations essential. Breakfast buffet $28. Main courses: $31–$46 at dinner. AE, DC, DISC, MC, V. Open: Breakfast and dinner daily (no lunch).*

Pescatore Italian Restaurant
$$–$$$ Hilo   Southern Italian

This old-world restaurant is a consistent performer in old Hilo town, which isn't exactly known for its fine-dining scene. The traditional southern Italian, seafood-heavy menu stars good-quality scaloppines, primaveras, and puttanescas. Dishes are generally well prepared and pleasing: Ahi carpaccio is sliced paper-thin and dressed in extra-virgin olive oil to heighten the fresh flavor, the seafood Fra Diavolo is a spicy bounty of fresh seafood in zesty marinara, and the chicken parmigiana is tender and flavorful. Service is attentive with a dash of personality, and the wine list is affordable. The lunch menu is simpler but still satisfying. A pleasant choice, if not spectacular.

See map p. 344. 235 Keawe St. (at Haili Street), Hilo. ☎ *808-969-9090. Reservations recommended for dinner. Main courses: $5–$8 at breakfast, $7–$14 at lunch, $16–$38 at dinner (most under $28). AE, DC, DISC, MC, V. Open: Breakfast, lunch, and dinner daily.*

Roy's Waikoloa Bar & Grill
$$$–$$$$ Kohala Coast   Hawaii Regional

The Waikoloa branch of Roy Yamaguchi's high-profile, high-end restaurant chain is not quite as winningly casual as the other Roy's establishments throughout Hawaii (particularly my favorite, Roy's Poipu Grill on Kauai), but this brightly lit, bustling restaurant is still a wonderful place to sample the original Hawaii Regional Cuisine nonetheless. Roy's food is more overtly Asian than what you'll find in many other Hawaii Regional restaurants (like Merriman's; see listing earlier in this chapter). The menu changes daily, but usually includes standards such as sublime slow-braised and charbroiled short ribs, blackened ahi with a delectable soy mustard butter, or roasted macadamia-nut mahimahi in lobster cognac butter sauce. You can easily eat affordably here thanks to an oversize menu of dim sum and appetizers; you can never go wrong with Roy's wood-grilled, Szechuan-style baby back ribs. The wines and sakes bottled under Roy's own label are affordable and surprisingly good. The noise level can be high and service is almost a little too attentive; but these are minor quibbles — like complaining that the Moët's too cold, if you know what I mean.

See map p. 344. In the Kings' Shops, 250 Waikoloa Beach Dr., Waikoloa. ☎ *808-886-4321.* www.roysrestaurant.com. *Reservations highly recommended. Appetizers and pizzas: $8.50–$18. Main courses: $18–$41 at dinner (most under $35). AE, DC, DISC, MC, V. Open: Dinner daily.*

Sansei Restaurant & Sushi Bar
$$$ Kohala Coast   Japanese/Pacific Rim Seafood

Chef D.K. Kodama has wowed the Big Island with this fresh outpost of his Maui sushi palaces. Sansei offers some of the best (and best-value) dining on the island. Composed primarily of Pan-Asian seafood dishes with multicultural touches, Sansei's winningly innovative menu has won raves from fans around the globe. Traditional-style main courses are available, but I recommend assembling a family-style meal from the adventurous sushi rolls and small plates. Can't-go-wrong menu highlights include the shrimp Dynamite, crispy tempura shrimp tossed in a creamy-zesty garlic *masago* aioli; the mango crab salad roll in sweet Thai chili vinaigrette; and the calamari salad of local greens tossed in Korean-inspired *kojuchang* vinaigrette, presented in a pleasing wonton basket. But, frankly, it's hard to go wrong with anything here. I love the beautifully presented flower sushi. This easygoing, Japanese-style place is palatable even for more tentative sushi eaters thanks to satisfying, Asian-inspired steak and poultry entrees as well. Not cheap, but you get what you pay for. A real winner, and my choice over nearby Kenichi. My only complaint with this cavernous new space is that it's too brightly lit and lacks the intimacy of the Maui and Oahu outposts — but for food this good, I'll live.

 Early-bird diners receive 25 percent off sushi orders placed daily between 5:30 and 6 p.m., and late-night diners enjoy karaoke and 50 percent off the appetizer and sushi menu Fridays and Saturdays between 10 p.m. and 1 a.m.

See map p. 344. At the Queens' MarketPlace, 201 Waikoloa Beach Dr. (off Highway 19, just inside the entrance to the resort, across from the Kings Shops), Waikoloa Beach Resort. ☎ *808-886-6286.* www.sanseihawaii.com. *Reservations highly recommended. Sushi and sashimi: $5–$19. Main courses: $11–$47 (most under $30). AE, DISC, MC, V. Open: Dinner nightly.*

Thai Rin
$$ Kailua-Kona   Thai

An oasis of good value in a town that falls short more often than not, this affordable and authentic spot features an expansive menu of well-prepared Thai favorites. The noodle dishes and multicolored curries are universally pleasing and include a pad Thai that borders on greatness. Thai Rin's version of chicken with cashew nuts — a dish that can often be pedestrian in lesser restaurants — is light, flavorful, and overflowing with a bounty of fresh veggies. Service is graciously attentive.

Alii Sunset Plaza, 75–5799 Alii Dr., in the heart of Kailua-Kona. ☎ *808-329-2929. Reservations accepted. Lunch specials: $7–$14. Main courses: $8–$20 (most less than $15). AE, DC, DISC, MC, V. Open: Lunch and dinner daily.*

Thai Thai Restaurant
$$ Volcano Thai

I am thrilled that this wonderful Thai restaurant remains a consistent winner in Volcano Village, which doesn't exactly brim with quality dining spots. An attractive high-ceilinged room with Thai decorative touches, pretty table linens, and Thai pop music on the sound system sets the stage for simple, freshly prepared dishes. The menu is on the smallish side, but every dish I tasted was a winner. The tom yum soup was clear and well-spiced with lemon grass and kaffir lime leaves; the *masaman* curry was rich with coconut milk and potatoes; and a stir-fry starred crisp Asian veggies and jumbo shrimp. The green papaya salad makes an excellent way to start a wholly satisfying meal. *Note:* The owners close down once a year for about a month to visit the homeland and bring back cooking spices, so call ahead or check with your innkeeper to avoid disappointment.

See map p. 344. 19–4084 Old Volcano Rd., Volcano. ☎ *808-967-7969. Reservations accepted. Main courses: $10–$26 (most under $20). AE, MC, V. Open: Dinner nightly.*

Tommy Bahama's Tropical Cafe
$$$$ Kohala Coast Caribbean

Housed in the Tommy Bahama's fashion emporium at the Shops at Mauna Lani, this delightful restaurant perfectly embodies the tropical haberdasher's breezily sophisticated style. The open-air room is a mélange of bamboo, rattan, and tropical prints that come together in a postmodern plantation style. While the food is very well prepared, it's too expensive — but that's the story of this pricey resort coast. I love Tommy Bahama's best for cocktails, which are some of the island's most creative and satisfying, or a relaxed lunch, when the menu focuses on Caribbean-inspired sandwiches and bounteous entree-size salads. Pleasing choices include the Habana Cabana pulled-pork sandwich, finished with the restaurant's own blackberry brandy barbecue sauce; and the Aruba Arugula salad, tossed in a tamarind vinaigrette and garnished with Caribbean-zested shrimp and scallops. Dinner brings more substantial fare, like maple-brined and chargrilled pork tenderloin topped with a dried berry merlot chutney, and pan-seared sashimi-grade ahi dressed in sweet chili oil, cilantro, and lemon grass. All in all, a really satisfying dining choice, if you can overlook the tab.

See map p. 344. At the Shops at Mauna Lani, 68-1330 Mauna Lani Dr., Mauna Lani. ☎ *808-881-8686.* www.tommybahama.com. *Reservations recommended for dinner. Main courses: $16–$21 at lunch, $32–$40 at dinner. AE, MC, V. Open: Lunch and dinner daily.*

Tako Taco
$ Waimea Cal-Mex

This quick-service California-Mexican cafe in the heart of Waimea town offers welcome relief from Hawaii's high restaurant prices. The fare — burritos, tacos, quesadillas, salads, enchiladas and combo plates — is well-prepared with high-quality ingredients. Fresh-caught local fish dresses the fish tacos; you can also opt for your choice of spicy ground beef, grilled marinated chicken, grilled steak, chile verde pork, and roasted pork carnitas in most dishes. Choose your meal from the chalkboard, order at the counter, and then take a seat at one of the tables in the bright, pretty, high-ceilinged dining room, where orange plastic chairs add a dash of contemporary pizzazz. After a short wait (everything is prepared fresh) your food will be served up casual style, in baskets. All of the dishes are served pretty mild — even salsas are not particularly fiery — but you can ask for habanero sauce at the counter. Kona beer is on tap and margaritas are available to accompany your meal, but you may just want to opt for the not-too-sweet, hand-squeezed limeade, which offers refreshing accompaniment.

See map p. 344. 64-1066 Mamalahoa Hwy. (at Kamumalu Street). ☎ *808-887-1717.* http://restauranteur.com/treshombres. *Reservations not taken. Main courses: $4–$11. MC, V. Open: Lunch and dinner daily.*

Luau!

My favorite luau on the Big Island has always been the wonderful Kona Village Luau (see later in this chapter) You should make your reservations as far ahead of time as possible (before you leave home) because it can sell out weeks in advance.

Gathering of the Kings

This progressive Polynesian feast under the stars forsakes some of the traditional luau touches (such as the traditional pig roasting) in favor of a more artful, creative approach. The focus is in two places: the stage show and the food. The stage show blends modern choreography and contemporary island-style music to tell the story of the Polynesian people as they journeyed across the great Pacific to Hawaii, with stops in Samoa, Tahiti, and New Zealand along the way. It's a very well done show with a dash of Broadway flair. Some folks love its adventuresome nature, but if you're looking for a more traditional depiction of the culture, look elsewhere. The elegant buffet is arranged in "destination" stations as well (Samoa, Tahiti, Hawaii, New Zealand). This is the closest that any luau comes to a gourmet feast. The open-air grounds are gorgeous, and the service is excellent. All in all, one of the most upscale luau experiences around.

Island Breeze, the folks behind the Gathering of the Kings, also hosts the more traditional-style and affordable **Island Breeze Luau** at King Kamehameha's Kona Beach Hotel in Kailua-Kona Sunday and Tuesday to Friday nights. Tickets are $70 for adults, $35 for kids ages 6 to 12, and free for age 5 and under. For information or reservations, call ☎ **808-326-4969** or visit www.islandbreezeluau.com.

See map p. 344 At the Fairmont Orchid in the Mauna Lani resort, Kohala Coast. ☎ *808-326-4969.* www.gatheringofthekings.com. *Admission: $99 adults, $65 kids 6–12, free for kids 5 and under. Hosted bar for adults. Time: Tues and Sat at 5:30 p.m.*

Kona Village Luau

This ultradeluxe Polynesian-style resort is the ideal place for a luau, and you'd be hard-pressed to find a better one. The food is beautifully prepared and well labeled (so you know what you're eating); and the traditional *imu* (underground pig roasting) ceremony is well narrated, so you get the cultural gist. The South Pacific revue is fast-moving and lots of fun, if not entirely authentic (I don't think that cowboy hulas occurred in old Hawaii). The fire dancer is a showstopper, of course, and everyone involved is a first-rate entertainer. The setting isn't oceanfront, but it's lovely nonetheless; the luau is large-scale, but it manages to feel friendly and intimate; service is attentive and aloha friendly. Wednesday and Friday nights only; reservations are required, so book as far in advance as possible.

See map p. 344. At Kona Village, in the Kaupulehu resort, 7 miles north of the airport on the Kohala Coast. ☎ 800-367-5290 or 808-325-5555. www.konavillage.com. *Admission: $98 adults, $67 kids 6–12, $40 kids 3–5. Rates include show, demonstrations, food, 1 complimentary beverage, and service charge. Free for Kona Village guests. Time: Wed and Fri at 5:15 p.m.*

Fast Facts: Big Island

American Automobile Association (AAA)

Roadside service is available to members by calling ☎ 800-AAA-HELP; however, the only Hawaii office is on Oahu (see Chapter 10).

American Express

American Express has one office on the Big Island, on the Kohala Coast at the Hilton Waikoloa Village, 425 Waikoloa Beach Dr., off Highway 19 in the Waikoloa Resort (☎ 808-886-7958).

Baby Sitters and Baby Stuff

Any resort, hotel, or condo should be able to refer you to a reliable baby sitter with a proven track record. See "Traveling with the Brood: Advice for Families," in Chapter 8, for details about renting baby gear on the Big Island.

Doctors

Hualalai Urgent Care is in Kailua-Kona at 75–1028 Henry St. (behind Borders, across the street from Safeway; ☎ 808-327-4357). In Hilo, contact Hilo Urgent Care Center, 42 Mohouli St., off Kilauea Avenue (☎ 808-

969-3051; www.hilourgentcare.com), which offers walk-in service.

Emergencies

Dial **911** from any phone, just like on the mainland.

Hospitals

Kona Community Hospital, on the south Kona Coast at 79–1019 Haukapila St., off Highway 11, in Kealakekua (☎ 808-322-9311; www.kch.hhsc.org), has 24-hour emergency facilities. On the east side of the island, head to the emergency room at Hilo Medical Center, 1190 Waianuenue Ave. (just west of Rainbow Drive), Hilo (☎ 808-974-4700; www.hmc.hhsc.org). In Waimea, visit North Hawaii Community Hospital, 67–125 Mamalahoa Hwy. (☎ 808-885-4444; www.northhawaiicommunity hospital.com).

Information

The Big Island Visitors Bureau (www. bigisland.org) has two island offices: one on the Kohala Coast at the Kings'

Shops, 250 Waikoloa Beach Dr., Ste. B-15, in the Waikoloa Resort (☎ 808-886-1655); and another in Hilo at 250 Keawe St., at Haili Street (across from Pescatore restaurant), downtown (☎ 808-961-5797).

For information on Hawaii Volcanoes National Park, contact P.O. Box 52, Hawaii National Park, HI 96718-0052 (☎ 808-985-6000; www.nps.gov/havo).

Chances are good that you'll find all the information you need even before you leave the airport. Just wander over to the information kiosks while you're waiting for your baggage and pick up copies of *This Week Big Island* and *101 Things to Do on the Big Island,* and the other free tourist publications and brochures that you'll find there. They're also available all over the island (particularly at malls and shopping centers).

Also, don't hesitate to ask the staff at your resort, condo or bed-and-breakfast for help or advice if you need it. These knowledgeable folks are usually more than happy to point you in the right direction and make recommendations.

Newspapers and Magazines

The Big Island has two daily papers: *West Hawaii Today* (www.westhawaiitoday.com) and the *Hawaii Tribune Herald* (www.hilohawaiitribune.com), which predominantly serves Hilo and environs. In addition, the *Hawaii Island Journal* (www.hawaiiislandjournal.com) is a free weekly newspaper that's a good source for event and entertainment listings; it's easy to find in free racks around the island.

Pharmacies

Longs Drugs (www.longs.com), Hawaii's biggest drugstore chain, has two branches on the Kona Coast: one in South Kona at the Keauhou Shopping Center, 78–6831 Alii Dr., Keauhou (☎ 808-322-5122); and one in the Lanihau Shopping Center, 75–5595 Palani Rd., on the ocean side of Highway 19, Kailua-Kona (☎ 808-329-1380). In Hilo, you'll find Longs at 555 Kilauea Ave., at Ponahawai Street (☎ 808-935-3357); and in the Prince Kuhio Shopping Plaza, 111 E. Puainako St., east of Highway 11 (☎ 808-959-5881).

Police

Hawaii County Police Department headquarters is at 349 Kapiolani St. (between Kukuau and Hualalai streets), Hilo (☎ 808-935-3311; www.hawaiipolice.com). The Kona Police Station is at 74–5221 Queen Kaahumanu Hwy. (Highway 19), just south of Kaloko Light Industrial Park (☎ 808-326-4646). Of course, if you have an emergency, dial **911** from any phone.

Post Offices

The Kona branch offices are at 74–7577 Palani Rd. (past Highway 11, almost to the shoreline), Kailua-Kona, and in the Keauhou Shopping Center, 78–6831 Alii Dr. (near Judd Trail), Keauhou. In Hilo, head to 1299 Kekuanaoa Ave. (past the airport; follow it as it loops around). A downtown branch is at 152 Waianuenue Ave., between Keawe and Kinoole streets. Satellite post offices are located around the island; to find the one nearest you, call ☎ 800-275-8777 or visit www.usps.com.

Taxes

Most purchases in Hawaii are taxed at roughly 4 percent; the exact amount will vary depending on the county you're in, and may be embedded in the total purchase price or shown as an independent line item on your bill. Expect taxes of about 11.42 percent to be added to your hotel bill.

Taxis

On the Kona-Kohala side of the island, call Paradise Taxi (☎ 808-329-1234) or Kona Airport Taxi (☎ 808-329-7779), which serve the Kailua-Kona area, or Luana Limousine (☎ 800-999-4001 or 808-326-5466; www.luanalimo.com). In Hilo, call Ace One (☎ 808-935-8303) or Shaka Taxi & Tours (☎ 808-987-1111).

Weather, Surf, and Volcano Reports

For the current weather, call ☎ 808-961-5582 or 808-935-8555 in Hilo. For the marine forecast, dial ☎ 808-935-9883. For volcano eruption information and weather updates for Hawaii Volcanoes National Park, dial ☎ 808-985-6000; for eruption information and viewing conditions in the Kalapana area outside the park, call ☎ 808-961-8093.

Chapter 15

Exploring the Big Island

. . . .

In This Chapter

▶ Locating the Big Island's best beaches

▶ Enjoying the sun and surf

▶ Exploring Hawaii's top attractions — including an active volcano!

▶ Scoping out the shopping scene

▶ Enjoying yourself on this rural isle after sunset

. . . .

*T*he Big Island's top attraction — and the most spectacular attraction in the entire state — is **Hawaii Volcanoes National Park.** But the Big Island is no one-trick pony; it boasts a wealth of wonderful and one-of-a-kind attractions that you won't want to miss.

Check with the excellent Maui-based activity center **Tom Barefoot's Tours** (☎ **800-621-3601** or 808-661-1246; www.tombarefoot.com), which may be able to save you a few dollars on many of the Big Island's activities on land and sea.

Enjoying the Sand and Surf

Some visitors to the Big Island complain that the island has only ugly dark-sand beaches, not the pretty white ones most people associate with a tropical paradise. The Big Island is the youngest island in the Hawaii chain, geologically speaking; as it matures over the next few millennia, the shores will pumice into the fine white sands you're used to. But if it's unusual-looking beaches you're after, the Big Island features the most eye-popping collection you'll ever see: black-sand ones, salt-and-pepper ones, lava-covered ones, even a green-sand one. And yes, the island also happens to already boast some of the dreamiest white sands in Hawaii, at Hapuna Beach State Park.

Combing the beaches

Safety takes top priority at the beach. Never turn your back on the ocean; big waves can come out of nowhere in a matter of minutes. Some beaches regularly have lifeguards on duty, not all of them. At beaches without lifeguards, keep an eye out for posted signs warning of dangerous currents or conditions. Winter surf is generally rough and unpredictable, although some beaches can be counted on for calm waters in any season. Others have dangerous rip currents year-round, making swimming inadvisable for all but the strongest swimmers. Do your homework: Check out the following beach descriptions and, after you're on the Big Island, make inquiries about local surf conditions.

Also, never leave valuables in your rental car while you're at the beach — not even in the glove box. Thieves can be in and out of your car before you've finished slathering on your sunscreen. Remote beaches, in particular, are magnets for thieves.

Along the Kohala Coast

All these fabulous beaches are located on the dry leeward side of the island, along the Queen Kaahumanu Highway (Highway 19) north of the Kona Airport.

Hapuna Beach State Park

Wow! If forced to choose, I'd name this as my favorite beach in all Hawaii. This big, gorgeous stretch has it all: glorious turquoise surf, a half-mile-long crescent of powdery-fine white sand (backed by green lawns, so you can picnic without getting sand in your lunch), and the best facilities on the coast. Hapuna is simply magical, especially in the gentle seasons when the beach is widest, the ocean is calmest, and crowds — both locals and visitors — come out to swim, play, and ride the easy waves. One of the best things about this stunning beach is that it's a blast even when it's crowded. The Hapuna Beach Prince Hotel is tucked away at the north end, but you barely notice it. Venture nearer to the hotel only if you're looking to snorkel; the cove at its base is your best bet. The excellent facilities include restrooms, showers, pavilions, picnic tables, barbecues, Hapuna Harry's for snacks and beach toys, and plenty of parking. If you're on this coast, don't miss it. Beware the waves in winter, though, when the big surf can be very dangerous.

See map p. 368. Off Queen Kaahumanu Highway (Highway 19), about 27 miles north of Kona Airport (3 miles south of Kawaihae, where Highway 19 turns inland toward Waimea).

Kaunaoa (Mauna Kea) Beach

The Mauna Kea Beach Hotel would like to keep this curving gem all to itself, no doubt. And who can blame them? Kaunaoa (cow-a-*no*-ah) is one of the Big Island's finest and most well-protected cove beaches. But because all Hawaii beaches are public, you can come, too, even if you're not staying at the ritzy resort. The gorgeous beige sands slope gently into the bay, where the calm, warm waters are often populated by schools of colorful tropical fish and green sea turtles, making this a wonderful snorkeling spot (especially near the rocky points). Swimming is excellent year-round. Non–hotel guests are relegated to one small section of the beach, and facilities are limited to restrooms and showers (no lifeguard). Don't be surprised if you're not warmly greeted at the gate; the hotel prefers to keep the public-access crowd small — but you're perfectly entitled to be here.

The Big Island's Best Beaches and Attractions

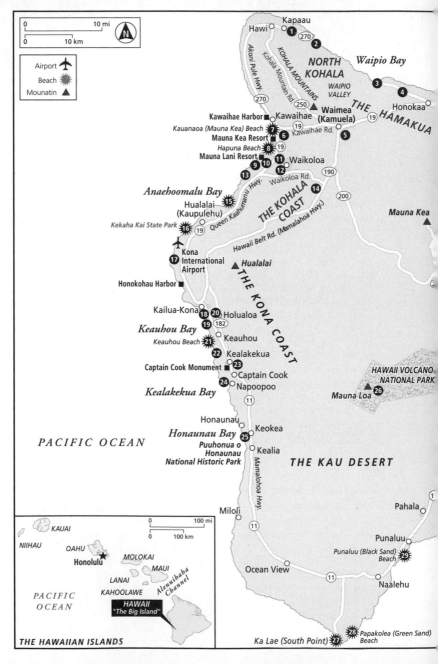

For detailed locations, see the following maps:
"The Kohala Coast" in Chapter 14
"Kailua-Kona Town" later in this chapter
"Waimea" later in this chapter
"Hilo" later in this chapter

Akaka Falls **38**
Anaehoomalu Bay (A-Bay) **15**
Banyan Drive **35**
Big Island Country Club **14**
Coconut Island **35**
Hapuna Beach State Park **8**
Hapuna Golf Course **6**
Hawaii Tropical Botanical Garden **37**
Hawaii Volcanoes National Park **30**
Holualoa **20**
Honokohau Harbor **17**
Hulihee Palace **18**
Imiloa Astronomy Center of Hawaii **32**
Kahaluu Beach Park **21**
Kailua Pier **18**
Kalahuipuaa Fishponds **10**
Kaunaoa (Mauna Kea) Beach **7**
Kealakekua Bay **24**
Keauhou Bay **22**
Kekaha Kai State Park **16**
Kona Historical Society Museum **23**
Leleiwi Beach Park **36**
Liliuokalani Gardens **35**
Lyman Museum **34**
Mana Hale & Puopelu historic homes **5**
Mauna Kea Golf Course **7**
Mauna Lani Frances H. I'i
   Brown Courses **11**
Mauna Loa Volcano **26**
Mokuaikaua Church **18**
Original King Kamehameha Statue **1**
Pacific Tsunami Museum **34**
Panaewa Rainforest Zoo & Gardens **31**
Papakolea (Green Sand) Beach **28**
Parker Ranch Visitor Center
   & Museum **5**
Pololu Valley Lookout **2**
Puako Petroglyph
   Archaeological District **9**
Punaluu (Black Sand) Beach Park **29**
Puuhonua o Honaunau
   National Historical Park **25**
Rainbow Falls **33**
Snorkel Bob's **18**
South Point (Ka Lae) **27**
Waikoloa Golf Club **13**
Waikoloa Village Golf Course **12**
Waipio Valley Artworks **4**
Waipio Valley Lookout **3**

Laupahoehoe
Honomu
Onomea Bay
Hilo Bay
Leleiwi Beach Park
Hilo
Saddle Rd.
Hilo International Airport
Keaau
Kurtistown
Mountain View
Cape Kumukahi
Pahoa
THE PUNA DISTRICT
LAVA TREE STATE PARK
Volcano Village
KAHAUALEA NATURAL AREA RESERVE
Kilauea Caldera
Chain of Craters Rd.
HAWAII VOLCANOES NATIONAL PARK

PACIFIC OCEAN

See map p. 368. At the Mauna Kea Resort, off Queen Kaahumanu Highway (Highway 19), 28 miles north of Kona Airport (about 2½ miles south of Kawaihae, where Highway 19 turns inland toward Waimea). To get there: Turn west at the Mauna Kea Beach Hotel entrance and ask for a beach pass from security; follow the road to the public beach parking area, at the end of the road (through the hotel and past registration).

Anaehoomalu Bay (A-Bay)

This popular beach — called Anaehoomalu (ah-na-ay-ho-o-*ma*-loo), or A-Bay for short — is the most beautiful of the Big Island's salt-and-peppery beaches. It's long and curvaceous, with pretty fine-grained sand and a lovely grove of swaying coconut palms. The beach fronts the Waikoloa Beach Marriott, but it's easily accessible. The beach is wider near the hotel, and narrows into a more intimate, palm-dotted dune closer to the public-access parking lot. The sand slopes gently from shallow to deep water; swimming, kayaking, and windsurfing are all terrific here; and the snorkeling is very good at the end nearest the hotel. At the far edge of the bay is a rare turtle-cleaning station, where snorkelers and divers can watch endangered green sea turtles line up, waiting their turn to have small fish clean them. The hotel's friendly beach boys usually have the area marked so that you can make your way out to see the action. Facilities include restrooms, showers, and plenty of parking (not always a given at resort-adjacent beaches), plus excellent beach-gear rentals at the north (hotel) end of the beach.

See map p. 368. At the Waikoloa Beach Marriott, just off Queen Kaahumanu Highway (Highway 19), 18 miles north of Kona Airport. To get there: Turn west at the stone gate marked "Waikoloa," left at the stop sign, and then follow the road to the parking lot.

On the Kona-Keauhou Coast

These playful beach parks are located on the sunny Kona Coast; they're all accessible from the Queen Kaahumanu Highway (Highway 19).

Kekaha Kai (Kona Coast) State Park

If you really want some sand to yourself, head to this remote beach park, which is separated from civilization by nearly 2 miles of vast lava fields. The road that reaches the beach has been recently repaved — and what awaits at the end is worth the drive for solitude seekers: a half-dozen long, curving, unspoiled gold-sand beaches, with well-protected coves that are great for swimming in the gentle seasons. Even if a few other folks are around, you'll find plenty of stretches of sand that you can have all to yourself. Stay out of the water in winter, when the swells come, but you may want to visit anyway to kick back on the sand and see the surfers in action. Facilities are minimal — nothing more than a few picnic tables and portable toilets — so be sure to bring your own drinking water.

See map p. 368. Off Queen Kaahumanu Highway (Highway 19), 2¾ miles north of Kona Airport. To get there: Turn left at the sign and follow the bumpy road 1¾ miles to the coast. Open: Thurs–Tues 8 a.m.–8 p.m.

White Sands (Magic Sands) Beach

This petite white-sand pocket of beach is an oddity on this lava-rock coast in more ways than one: Not only are darker and coarser beaches more common on this coast, but the beach itself sometimes vanishes completely, washed away by high tides or winter waves or during storms. It usually reappears in short order, just like it never went away. The small waves are great for just-learning boogie boarders and bodysurfers; on calm summer days, the water is good for swimming and snorkeling too. Facilities include restrooms, showers, lifeguards, and a small parking lot. White Sands doesn't warrant a long drive, but it's conveniently situated for those staying in the Kailua-Kona or Keauhou areas.

See map p. 368. Adjacent to Kona Magic Sands condos, 77–6452 Alii Dr., 4½ miles south of Kailua-Kona.

Kahaluu Beach Park

Kahaluu (ka-ha-*loo*-oo) isn't exactly the prettiest beach in the islands: It's narrow, salt-and-peppery, close to the busy road (a situation softened by some coconut palms that serve as a buffer), and almost always blanket-to-blanket crowded. But it's one of the finest snorkeling beaches in all Hawaii, with a shore that gently slopes to shallow, well-protected turquoise pools. The water is so clear and rich with marine life that all you have to do is wade in and look down. If you're a first-time snorkeler, this is the place to learn, but even advanced fish-watchers will be thrilled with the schools of brilliantly colored tropical fish that weave in and out of the well-established reef. The odds are great for spotting sea turtles here. (On my last visit, I spotted ten turtles in the first 20 minutes!) Great facilities are on hand, including a parking lot, beach-gear rentals, a covered pavilion, and a snack bar. Come early to stake out your spot. Riptides sometimes kick up in winter, though, so check the lifeguard warning flags. (Red means stay out of the water.)

See map p. 368. On Alii Drive, 5½ miles south of Kailua-Kona.

On the Hilo-Volcano coast

On the lush windward coast, the island's beaches become fewer and far between, but more breathtakingly unusual.

Leleiwi Beach Park

If you get a beautiful beach day while you're in Hilo, head to picture-perfect Leleiwi (lay-lay-*ee*-vee) Beach. This lovely palm-fringed cove of black-lava tide pools fed by freshwater springs and rippled by gentle waves is a photographer's delight and the ideal place to take a dip. The shallow pools are generally calm and ideal for little ones, especially in the protected inlets at the center of the park. Sea turtles make this beach the locals' favorite snorkel spot; playful spinner dolphins appear on occasion, too. Facilities include restrooms, showers, and picnic pavilions.

See map p. 368. On Kalanianaole Avenue, 4 miles west of Hilo.

Punaluu (Black Sand) Beach Park

If you're driving the south route between Volcano and Kona, stop here if you want to set your eyes on a genuine black-sand beach, the only one that's still accessible. (The others have been blocked by lava flows.) Stay out of the water year-round because the offshore currents are strong (although you're likely to see some daredevil surfers taking on the waves), but the sands are great for sunbathing and picnicking. (Keep your distance from the turtles who often come on shore to nest.) If you do venture into the water, do it in summer and be extremely careful. Picnic pavilions and restrooms are located across the road.

See map p. 368. Off the Hawaii Belt Road (Highway 11), about 30 miles south of Volcano Village. (The turnoff is well marked.)

At land's end

The southernmost point in the United States is Ka Lae, or South Point. There's not much down here, except some rocky cliffs and remarkable ocean views, but I love coming anyway: Standing at this dramatic, desolate, windswept place (hold on to your hat!) actually feels like you're standing at the end of the earth.

Ka Lae (South Point) and Papakolea (Green Sand) Beach

Down at South Point is Green Sand Beach, worth seeing for its olive-green sands (actually crushed olivine, a green semiprecious mineral found in eruptive rocks and meteorites). It's a bear to reach, however, so most people don't bother. You need a four-wheel-drive vehicle and a hearty constitution to traverse the 2½-mile path from the Kaulana Boat Ramp to the cliffs overlooking the beach. You can also walk it, if you wear sturdy shoes and bring water. The trail is relatively flat, but you're usually walking into the wind as you head toward the beach. After about 30 or 40 minutes, you'll see an eroded cinder cone by the water; continue to the edge, where the green sands lie below.

I highly recommend that you simply take in the view from the cliff above the beach (which is actually very good) because the trail to the sand is difficult and treacherous, requiring you to drop down (and climb back up) 4 to 5 feet in spots. If the surf's up, don't even think about it — and stay out of the water anywhere along South Point entirely.

See map p. 368. At the end of South Point Road, 12 miles south of Mamalahoa Highway (Highway 11).

Getting Your Feet Wet

Although the east (Hilo-Volcano) coast does have some accessible beaches (see the preceding section), the west (Kona-Kohala) coast is the exclusive domain of watersports on the Big Island.

If you're coming to the islands to learn to surf, you're better off on Oahu or Maui. Big Island surfing is best left to the experts.

Snorkeling

The Big Island boasts wonderful opportunities for snorkeling, possibly the best in all the islands. One of Hawaii's absolute best snorkel spots is **Kealakekua** (kay-ah-lah-kay-*koo*-ah) **Bay.** The coral in this underwater marine life preserve is the most beautiful I've ever seen, and the calm, clear waters teem with a kaleidoscope of colorful reef fish, octopuses, and moray eels; what's more, a pod of playful spinner dolphins often comes by to say hi. The bay can be reached only by snorkel cruise or kayak, however. For details on getting there, see the section "On-deck adventures — ocean cruising," later in this chapter. Fair Wind is my favorite snorkel-cruise operator. Accomplished kayakers can also paddle their way there; see "Ocean kayaking," later in this chapter.

The Kona and Kohala coasts also boast a bunch of wonderful snorkeling beaches where you can simply wade in and see the colorful aquatic life. The best is **Kahaluu Beach Park,** but you might also have some fish- and turtle-spotting luck at **Anaehoomalu Bay, Kaunaoa Beach, White Sands Beach,** at the north end of **Hapuna Beach,** or even right at the foot of your hotel, if you're lucky enough to be staying at a beachfront resort. (The Mauna Lani Bay Hotel, the Fairmont Orchid, and Kona Village are particularly good choices; see Chapter 14.)

All the Big Island's dive shops arrange snorkel cruises and/or take experienced snorkelers out on their dive trips. Jack's Diving Locker even takes snorkelers out on their night dives with manta rays. See the section "Scuba diving," later in this chapter, for details.

One of the locals' favorite snorkeling spots is in South Kona, in the cove right next to the **Puuhonua o Honaunau National Historical Park.** (See the section "More attractions worth seeking out," later in this chapter.) It's not the kind of place where you'll want to sunbathe all day, but it is a great spot for adventurous snorkelers looking for something different, and has an abundance of colorful reef fish and sea turtles. To get there, follow Highway 11 south from Kailua-Kona to mile marker 103 (about 22 miles); turn right at the sign onto Highway 160 and follow it 3½ miles downslope to the national park and coast. Come early in the day before the waves kick up, bring your own gear, and turn right before you get to the entrance kiosk; the road will take you down to the boat ramp and snorkel area.

You can rent snorkel gear from **Snorkel Bob's** (☎ **808-329-0770;** www. snorkelbob.com) at the south end of Kailua-Kona town (see the "Kailua-Kona Town" map, later in this chapter). The address is 75–5831 Kahakai St., but it's actually on Alii Drive (Kailua-Kona's main drag) right in front of Huggo's restaurant. There's also a second location right near the airport in the Hale Kui Plaza, just north of the boat harbor, at 73-4976 Kamanu St. (☎ **808-329-0771**); turn mauka (toward the mountain) on Hina-lani Street, and follow it to Kamanu Street.

The best-quality gear — the "Ultimate Truth" — rents for $32 a week ($22 per week for kids) for the mask/snorkel/fins set. For an additional $12, nearsighted snorkelers can opt for prescription masks (including snorkel and fins set). Budget travelers can rent basic gear for just $9 per week. You can also rent boogie boards, life vests, wet suits, beach chairs, and so on. The shop is open every day from 8 a.m. to 5 p.m. You don't need to reserve gear in advance, but if you prefer to plan ahead, you can book your gear over the phone at ☎ 800-262-7725 or online at www.snorkelbob.com.

Safety is key when snorkeling. See "Ocean Safety," in the Quick Concierge at the end of this book, for snorkeling tips.

On-deck adventures — ocean cruising

When the Pacific humpback whales make their annual visit to Hawaii from Alaska from December to March, they swim right by the Big Island. In season, virtually all cruise boats combine whale-watching with their regular outings.

If you want to go sportfishing off the world-famous Kona Coast, see the section "Hooking the big one," later in this chapter.

Body Glove Cruises

The 51-foot, 100-passenger trimaran *Body Glove* runs cruises to Pawai Bay, north of Kailua-Kona, a marine preserve with excellent snorkeling and dolphin-watching opportunities year-round. The year-round morning cruise features 2½ hours of snorkel time (total sailing time is 4½ hours), whereas the afternoon cruise (offered Apr–Nov) features 1½ hours of snorkeling. Both the 15-foot water slide and high-dive board will get you into the drink immediately, and they're real kid-pleasers. Scuba upgrades with PADI-certified (Professional Association of Diving Instructors) trainers and dive masters are available as well. In winter, the afternoon sail becomes a three-hour whale-watching excursion, complete with a naturalist onboard.

Cruises depart from Kailua Pier, off Alii Drive, Kailua-Kona. ☎ *800-551-8911 or 808-326-7122.* www.bodyglovehawaii.com. *4½-hour snorkel-sails: $112 adults, $72 kids ages 6–17, free for kids age 5 and under. 3-hour afternoon snorkel-sails or whale-watching trips (offered only Dec–Mar): $66 adults, $44 ages 6–17, free for kids age 5 and under. Scuba rates $61–$81 higher, depending on whether you need gear or instruction. Morning cruises include continental breakfast and buffet deli lunch; afternoon sails include snacks.*

Captain Dan McSweeney's Year-Round Whale-Watch Learning Adventures

Do you have your heart set on whale-watching, even though you missed whale season? Or maybe you're visiting in season, but you just want to spot humpbacks with the most qualified expert around? Then contact Captain Dan McSweeney, a professional whale researcher for more than

25 years, who leads excellent whale-watching tours along the Kona Coast year-round. Sure, you'll only spot the visiting humpbacks from December through April, but you can see pilot whales, sperm whales, false killer and pygmy killer whales, melon-headed whales, and beaked whales, as well as five kinds of dolphins, in any month. Knowledgeable and engaging, Captain Dan and his crew are experts at knowing where to look for these wonderful creatures so that you can watch them, undisturbed, in their natural habitat. (He frequently drops an underwater video camera and/or microphone into the water so that you can see them clearly and listen to their songs.) What's more, he professes to have a 99 percent success rate at finding humpbacks in season. But if, for some reason, you don't see any whales at all on your trip, Captain Dan will take you out again for free — not a bad guarantee! This trip is terrific for visitors of all ages.

See map p. 368. Cruises depart from Honokohau Harbor, off Queen Kaahumanu Highway (Highway 19), 2½ miles south of Kona Airport (between mile markers 97 and 98). ☎ **888-942-5376** *or 808-322-0028.* www.ilovewhales.com. *3-hour cruises: $80 adults, $70 kids under 90 pounds. Prices include snacks. Check for online discounts. No cruises May through early July.*

Captain Zodiac Raft Expeditions

Captain Zodiac leads four-hour snorkel cruises to Kealakekua Bay aboard 16-passenger, 24-foot fiberglass-bottom rubber boats (zodiacs); these inflatables, pioneered by Jacques Cousteau, have minimal environmental impact, sit low to the water, and cruise fast over the waves for a thrill-a-minute ride. On the way to Kealakekua — one of the best snorkel spots in all Hawaii (see the section "Snorkeling," earlier in this chapter) — you'll search for spinner dolphins and green sea turtles (plus humpback whales in season) and then spend more than an hour snorkeling in the bay. On the return, if conditions permit, the captain takes you exploring sea caves that only these small, easily maneuverable boats can reach. This expedition is an excellent choice for adventuresome types. Morning and afternoon cruises are available, as is a three-hour whale-watching trip in season.

See map p. 368 Cruises depart from Honokohau Harbor, off Queen Kaahumanu Highway (Highway 19), 2½ miles south of Kona Airport. ☎ **808-329-3199.** www. captainzodiac.com. *4-hour tours: $110 adults, $85 kids 4–12. Deli lunch included. 3-hour whale-watches (in season): $59 adults, $45 kids 4–12. Check for online discounts ($15 off 4-hour tours at press time).*

Fair Wind Snorkel Cruises & Orca Raft Adventures

Family-owned and -operated since 1971, this absolutely terrific company offers my favorite sail-and-snorkel cruises to Kealakekua Bay, the best snorkel spot in all Hawaii, period. The company's vessels — the *Fair Wind I* and the new state-of-the-art *Hula Kai* — are comfortable and loaded with amenities and the staff is friendly and knowledgeable.

The 60-foot catamaran, the *Fair Wind II,* has room for about a hundred or so passengers. It's an impeccably maintained boat complete with easy-access water stairs (so you can literally walk into the water), a 15-foot water slide, wide-open decks (plus plenty of covered areas if you prefer to stay out of the sun), a barbecue grill for lunchtime burgers, and freshwater showers. The boat (including bathrooms) is fully wheelchair accessible. The smaller, 55-foot *Hula Kai* (built in 2005) is a Teknicraft power catamaran with cushioned seating (the best on any snorkel boat on the islands) and other excellent comfort features, such as state-of-the-art restrooms and freshwater showers. The *Hula Kai* is an excellent choice for those who want a first-class experience in a more intimate sailing environment. Scuba diving is available onboard.

All levels of snorkelers are welcome: Fair Wind provides all manner of floaties and assistance to those who want it and leave experienced swimmers and snorkelers pretty much to do their own thing (within the established boundaries, of course). Fair Wind is also a great way to experience Snuba, a cross between snorkeling and scuba diving that allows you to go as much as 20 feet below the surface of the water without getting certification or carrying cumbersome oxygen tanks.

Book ahead, because these cruises fill up fast.

See map p. 368. Catamaran cruises depart from Keauhou Bay, off Highway 11 at the end of Kamehameha III Road (between mile markers 117 and 118), 10 minutes south of Kailua-Kona. Orca cruises depart from Kailua Pier, off Alii Drive, Kailua-Kona. ☎ *800-677-9461 or 808-322-2788.* www.fair-wind.com. *4½-hour deluxe snorkel cruises: $109–$119 adults, $69–$75 kids 4–12, $29 toddlers on morning cruise, free for toddlers on afternoon cruise. 5-hour snorkel cruise aboard the Hula Kai: $155 adults. 3-hour whale-watching cruise in season aboard the Hula Kai: $75 adults. Morning cruises include continental breakfast and barbecue lunch; deluxe afternoon cruises include barbecue lunch plus beer, wine, and soft drinks on last hour; regular afternoon cruises include snacks. Scuba add-on $65–$75 extra.*

Kamanu Charters

If you want to snorkel in untouristed Pawai Bay but you prefer a more intimate experience than the *Body Glove* offers, go instead with the *Kamanu*, a late-model 36-foot catamaran that limits its crowds to about two dozen per sail. This route is a good choice for first-time snorkelers (instruction and all the necessary gear are provided) and nonswimmers because a wide array of alternative flotation devices is available.

Cruises depart Honokohau Harbor, off Queen Kaahumanu Highway (Highway 19), 2½ miles south of Kona Airport. ☎ *800-348-3091 or 808-329-2021.* www.kamanu.com. *3½-hour cruises: $80 adults, $50 kids 12 and under. Lunch included. Check for online discounts (10 percent off with 10-day advance booking at press time).*

Scuba diving

With calm, warm waters (75–81°F), 100-plus-foot visibility, and an open drop-off that supports a wealth of colorful marine life of all shapes and sizes, the Kona-Kohala coast offers some of the best scuba diving in the world (including excellent opportunities to swim with manta rays). Conditions are so good, in fact, that scuba magazines regularly name it among the best diving destinations in the world.

Jack's Diving Locker, in the Coconut Grove Marketplace, 75–5819 Alii Dr., Kailua-Kona (☎ **800-345-4807** or 808-329-7585; www.jacksdiving locker.com), is consistently chosen by readers of _Rodale's Scuba Diving_ magazine as the best dive shop in the Indo-Pacific, and one of the best in the world. Two-tank boat and shore dives start at $125, and night dives with manta rays are $145. Jack's trips book up fast, so be sure to reserve in advance.

Jack's also offers a full slate of introductory dives and is the best dive shop on the island for kids who want to learn: Skin-diver programs are available for kids ages 8 and up, and open-water instruction is offered to kids 12 and older.

If you have little experience but a yen to learn and become certified, **Big Island Watersports** (☎ **808-324-1650;** www.snubabigisland.com) is an excellent outfitter for those in need of first-time instruction and certification courses.

Red Sail Sports (☎ **877-RED-SAIL** or 808-886-2876; www.redsail hawaii.com), which operates watersports and dive centers from the Hapuna Beach Prince Resort and Hilton Waikoloa Village hotels, hosts two-tank dives and night dives aboard its 38-foot Delta dive boat (the _Lani Kai_) to a number of unique sites accessible from the Kohala Coast; prices run $98 to $155. Red Sail also offers a one-day introductory scuba instruction package — including pool instruction, a one- or two-tank boat dive, and all equipment — for $175 to $190 per person. Check out Red Sail's full slate of snorkel cruises, whale-watching trips, sunset sails, and kayak adventures.

If you want the once-in-a-lifetime experience of night diving with manta rays, contact **Sea Paradise** (☎ **800-322-KONA** or 808-322-2500; www.seaparadise.com). Cruises aboard the company's 46-foot catamaran, the _Hokuhele,_ depart from Keauhou for the short trip to "manta village," where the graceful creatures congregate for feeding at night. Both snorkelers and scuba divers are invited. Snorkelers pay $85 for adults, $59 for kids 4 to 12; certified divers pay $110.

If you want to dive from the volcano side of the island, your best choice is **Nautilus Dive Center,** 382 Kamehameha Ave., between Open Market and the Shell Gas Station, Hilo (☎ **808-935-6939;** www.nautilusdive hilo.com), where dive charter prices start at $85 for both certified divers and beginners.

Also keep in mind that both Body Glove and Fair Wind offer scuba upgrades for divers aboard their cruises to Palani Bay and Kealakekua Bay, respectively; see the section "On-deck adventures — ocean cruising," earlier in this chapter.

Try-it diving for beginners: Snuba

If you've always been interested in trying scuba but haven't gotten around to the hassles and expense of certification, you can sample a very close approximation: Snuba. I highly encourage you to try it if you're so inclined, because Snuba is a marvelous introduction to the kind of underwater exploration that scuba offers, without any necessary preparation.

With Snuba, you wear a mask and a regulator that's connected via a 25-foot-long hose to an oxygen tank that floats on the surface, thereby allowing you to dive deep and simulate the scuba experience without full training (or a heavy air tank attached to your back). A great place to try it is with **Fair Wind Snorkel Cruises** (see the section "On-deck adventures — ocean cruising," earlier in this chapter). All it takes is about 15 minutes of instruction; you'll get about 45 minutes of underwater time. No advance booking is necessary — the Snuba instructor asks on the way out if you're interested in participating. Call ahead to the Fair Wind office to confirm that Snuba will be offered on your cruise if your heart's set on trying it.

If you'd like to skip the snorkel cruise and go directly to Snuba, contact **Big Island Watersports** (☎ 808-324-1650; www.snubabigisland.com); both shore and boat dives are offered daily starting at $89 per person shore dive, $145 boat dive.

Ocean kayaking

Kayaking is another great way to explore Kealakekua Bay, especially if you'd prefer an up-close, unmotorized relationship with the water and the marine life around you. It's quite easy to learn, as long as you know how to swim: Just get on your sit-on-top kayak, find your balance, and paddle.

That said, I highly recommend taking a guided kayak tour if you're inexperienced, because there are nuances to launching your kayak, dealing with surf, and getting on and off your kayak in open water. Even if you're an experienced kayaker, you may find that going out with a guide offers the better experience, because the guides know the best snorkel spots, the history of the area, and where the spinner dolphins like to hang out. Hawaiian-owned and -operated **Aloha Kayak Co.** (☎ 877-322-1444 or 808-322-2868; www.alohakayak.com) offers 2½- to 4-hour guided kayak-and-snorkel tours from Keauhou Bay for $59 to $79 for adults, and $30 to $40 for kids under 12, including all equipment and snacks. Reservations are required at least 24 hours in advance.

If you have some experience under your belt, you can rent single kayaks for $35 a day, tandem kayaks for $60, with all gear (including a cooler and car rack). Friendly guys at the shop will point you to the best launch spots. Half-day and weekly rates are also available, as well as glass-bottom kayaks and snorkel-gear rentals. Most convenient to Kealakekua Bay is the Honalo location, on the ocean side of Highway 11 at 79–7428 Mamalahoa Hwy., across from the 114 mile marker and Teshima's restaurant.

Another great option for kayak tours and rentals is **Ocean Safaris** (☎ 808-326-4699; www.oceansafariskayaks.com), also located at the marina at Keauhou Bay. Prices are similar; bargain hunters and those on the quest of dolphin sightings might consider the Early Riser Dolphin Tour, which leaves at 7 a.m., the prime dolphin activity hour ($35 per person).

Lastly, consider **Kona Boys,** 79-8539 Mamalahoa Hwy., Kealakekua (☎ 808-328-1234; www.konaboys.com), for single-kayak ($47) and double-kayak ($67) rentals. Also give them a call for details on their variety of half-day guided kayak and kayak-snorkel tours.

Hooking the big one

If you want to catch fish, you've come to the right place. Big-game fish (including monster blue, black, and striped marlin), spearfish, tuna (ahi, aku, and albacore), mahimahi, ono (also known as wahoo), and other good eating fish, as well as barracuda and shark, roam the deep, warm "fish-rich" Kona waters. There are no guarantees, but few anglers come away empty-handed. More than 100 charter boats depart from four harbors along the island's west coast, but the epicenter for Hawaii sportfishing is Honokohau Harbor, located off the Queen Kaahumanu Highway (Highway 19) 2½ miles south of the Kona Airport.

The best way to arrange a charter is through a charter boat booking agency before your trip, and the best in Kona is **The Charter Desk at Honokohau Marina** (☎ 888-KONA-4-US or 808-329-5735; www.charter desk.com). The Charter Desk's booking agents are real pros; they know the best boats in Honokohau Harbor, and they'll sort through the more than 50 different available boats, fishing specialties, and personalities to match you up with the boat and crew that's right for you. When you book with the Charter Desk, you can be sure that your boat captain is licensed by the United States Coast Guard, and the boat is fully insured.

Most big-game charter boats carry six passengers maximum. Half-day and full-day charters are available, and boats supply all equipment, bait, tackle, and lures. You don't need a fishing license on a charter boat. Prices start at around $80 to $140 for a half-day share charter (where you share the boat with strangers), $190 for a full day. Private charters range from $300 to $600 for a half-day, $500 to $900 for a full day.

Understand that if you go for a share, you'll have to rotate rods, so you won't get a full four hours of fishing in on a half-day charter. If you're calculating time-for-dollars spent, you're better off booking your own boat, especially if two or three of you are along to split the costs.

One of the best charters on the coast — and an especially good option for first-timers — is the aptly named **Bite Me Sportfishing** (☎ 808-936-3442; www.bitemesportfishing.com). (See the section "On-deck adventures — ocean cruising," earlier in this chapter.) Captain Brian Wargo will take you out on the *Bite Me,* a 40-foot air-conditioned turbo twin diesel Uniflite vessel, in search of blue, black, and striped marlin; yellowfin tuna; mahimahi; and other impressive big-game fish. Wargo has excellent experience catching 500-plus-pound marlin. These are private fishing charters only with a capacity for up to six passengers, running five lines at a time. A full-day charter is $650, and a half-day is $395. A half-day share charter is $109.

In addition, you may also consider booking your boat through **Hawaii Fishing Adventures and Charters** (☎ 877-388-1376; www.sportfish hawaii.com), which represents about close to a dozen boats based at Honokohau Harbor, starting at $395 for a half-day private charter. Or try **Charter Services Hawaii** (☎ 800-567-2650; www.konazone.com). If you're an experienced angler and prefer to book with a boat captain directly, consider chartering the *Anxious* (☎ 808-326-1229; www.aloha zone.com), owned by Captain Neal Isaacs.

If you're interested in light-tackle sportfishing for smaller catches, contact **Reel Action Light Tackle Sportfishing** (☎ 808-325-6811; www.fishkona.org/reel_action.html), which can take you out spinning, bottom-fishing, or trolling for smaller catches. For a real thrill, try ocean fly-fishing for giant tuna or marlin. Rates range from $100 to $200 per person on a shared boat, or $400 to $900 for the whole boat (up to six people) for an eight-hour trip.

Exploring Dry Land

I've said it before, and I'll say it again: Visiting Hawaii Volcanoes National Park is one of the most thrilling things that you can do on the planet. I know that coming within spitting distance of an active volcano was definitely one of the highlights of my life. But the excitement doesn't end there. Do what you can to budget plenty of time to see at least a few faces of this wonderfully multifaceted island.

Sightseeing with a guide

If your mobility is limited, or if you're short on time and you want an introductory look at the big picture, you may want to hook up with a guided tour. But if you've rented a car and can get around easily on your own, driving yourself is definitely the way to see the island. But if you're going to take a guided bus tour of Hawaii Volcanoes National Park, do yourself a favor — take the more detailed one that departs from nearby Hilo, rather than the deadly long Circle Island tour that leaves from Kona and incorporates more than five hours of driving and a good half-dozen stops into an endurance-challenging 9- to 12-hour day (ultimately short shrifting the national park in the process). Or, better yet, if you don't mind a little hiking in your trip, book the 12-hour Volcanoes Adventure offered by conservation-minded outfitter **Hawaii Forest & Trail** (☎ 800-464-1993; www.hawaii-forest.com), which travels full circle from the Kona-Kohala coast and offers more insight into the park and its geology and history than you're likely to glean in a three-day visit on your own. (See the section "Enjoying guided nature tours," later in this chapter.)

Polynesian Adventure Tours (☎ 800-622-3011 or 808-833-8000; www. polyad.com) offers a range of guided tours in minivans, big-windowed mini-coaches (good for small groups and big views), and full-size buses. Their tours tend to be a little more action-oriented than those offered by competing companies. Expect to spend $65 to $79 per person ($44–$53 for kids 3–11), depending on the tour that you choose and your departure point.

Roberts Hawaii (☎ 866-898-2519 or 808-954-8652; www.roberts hawaii.com) is Hawaii's biggest name in narrated bus tours. Roberts offers a circle-island tour for $65 adults, $52 children ages 4 to 11.

I recommend only going out with Polynesian Adventure and Roberts if you have mobility or other issues that prevent you from going on your own.

 Book your Polynesian Adventure or Roberts Hawaii tour online and score a 10 percent price break.

 If you do opt for a guided tour that takes you around the entire island, remember: It will be chillier on the east coast than it is on the west coast, so bring a jacket or sweater for your volcano visit. It's also a good idea to bring along rain gear and/or an umbrella, as well as sturdy closed-toe walking shoes.

Enjoying guided nature tours

If you want to experience the Big Island's natural world, I highly recommend going out with a guide. An expert guide can really help you appreciate the majesty of this fantastic island and even take you into areas that you couldn't otherwise reach on your own. Even if hiking and nature exploring aren't parts of your daily life, don't worry; you won't be required to be in racing shape. All the following terrific tour companies offer adventures for every level of experience and ability.

 My absolute favorite Big Island outfitter is **Hawaii Forest & Trail** (☎ 800-464-1993 or 808-331-8505; www.hawaii-forest.com), named 2006 Ecotour Operator of the Year by the Hawaii Ecotourism Association and recipient of the 2007 Keep It Hawaii Award. I first explored the Big Island with naturalist and educator Rob Pacheco back in 1995, and it was one of the best — and most fun — nature experiences of my life; so I'm thrilled to see his first-rate business growing and widening its options for visitors. I never miss an opportunity to go out with Hawaii Forest & Trail when I'm on the Big Island — you just can't go wrong with these guys.

Both half- and full-day trips are available; they're all personalized to a group's interest and ability levels and often feature easy or moderate walking. (Ask when you book if you're concerned.) Regularly scheduled half-day adventures include the **Kohala Waterfalls Adventure,** which takes you into private lands on the Kohala Coast to discover hidden waterfalls and killer views along a family-friendly 3-mile hike.

Full-day outings include the **Kilauea Volcano Adventure,** a 12-hour trip from the Kona-Kohala coast to the splendid Hamakua Coast and Hawaii Volcanoes National Park that's the best introduction to the active volcano and volcanology that there is. If you have only one day to see the volcano, see it this way.

Another one-of-a-kind eight-hour adventure that makes lifetime memories is the **Mauna Kea Summit & Stars Adventure,** in which your astronomer guide takes you across Parker Ranch pastureland — gorgeous wide-open landscape that you never thought you'd see in Hawaii — to the (often snow-capped) summit of Mauna Kea (at 13,796 ft.), one of the best and most famous stargazing spots in the world, dotted with a world-class array of telescopes from the world's foremost astronomical observatories. At dusk, you'll descend to 9,000 feet for an incredible lesson in astronomical observation in a night sky unlike any other you've ever seen. Dinner is included, and the outing is restricted to adults only (no kids under age 16). This trip is a total blast; everyone on ours agreed that it was the best thing they'd done in Hawaii.

Although you can visit the summit of Mauna Kea on your own, you must have a four-wheel-drive vehicle and approval from the rental company (difficult to get) in order to drive on Saddle Road and the summit road. You'll also need parkas to withstand the icy temperatures at the summit, which the guides issue. Finally, you should be accustomed to driving at high altitudes and need to know a bit about astronomy and the night sky to get anything out of your visit. For these reasons, I highly recommend just going with Hawaii Forest & Trail instead.

PinzTrek Off-Road Adventures combine breathtaking natural sightseeing with exciting off-roading aboard a six-wheel-drive Pinzgauer, a 1970s Swiss Army vehicle. These half-day adventures are great for kids, or even older folks who don't mind the bumpy ride, because the vehicles can reach views and landscapes that are accessible only through arduous hiking (some are not accessible at all, because the company has exclusive access to private lands). Two different routes, both of which include about a mile of walking, are available: the Kohala Wai, which accesses remote North Kohala lands so you can peek into lush valleys and view hidden waterfalls, and the Hualalai Holoholo route, a more rugged volcanic landscape adventure.

A number of **bird-watching adventures** to private lands are also available. Rob, from Hawaii Forest & Trail, is a birder at heart and has exclusive access to various private lands that showcase the ecological diversity of the island, so there's really no one better to go with if you're into bird-watching (or want to learn).

Call or check the Web site for details and schedules for these and other adventures. Prices for half-day trips cost $109 to $135 for adults ($89–$99 for kids, but check to see which adventures are age-restricted). Full-day trips run $155 to $195 per person ($120 for kids under 12; not all trips are appropriate for younger ones). Rates include food and all the gear that you'll need. Prices are high, but you get your money's worth and then some. All trips depart from the Kona-Kohala coast; some include pickup and drop-off, whereas others have a designated meeting point. Reservations should be made at least a week in advance. Note that certain trips have restrictions based on age, weight, or health; be sure to confirm these with the Hawaii Forest & Trail representative when you book. After you arrive, you can also stop at the Hawaii Forest & Trail Headquarters and Outfitting Store at 74–5035B Queen Kaahumanu Hwy. (Highway 19, on the mountain side of the highway across from Honokahou Harbor, behind the Chevron Station), Kailua-Kona, where you can book trips and pick up outdoor equipment and nature-related gear and books.

If, for some reason, Hawaii Forest & Trail doesn't meet your needs or doesn't go where you want to go, try **Hawaiian Walkways** (☎ 800-457-7759 or 808-775-0372; www.hawaiianwalkways.com). This reliable outfitter offers a variety of regularly scheduled full- and half-day hikes led by excellent, enthusiastic guides. The Hawaii Ecotourism Association named them tour operator of the year in 2002. The Waipio Waterfall Adventure, a wonderful half-day hike that takes you along the rim of the Big Island's best-loved unspoiled valley, leaves daily at 9 a.m. You can arrange other trips in advance, including a Kona Cloud Forest Botanical Walk, a Kilauea Volcano Discovery Hike into Hawaii Volcanoes National Park, a Saddle Road Exploration, or just about any part of the island you'd like to visit. Prices range from $95 to $150 per person ($75–$95 kids under 12), depending on the trip you choose; all gear, food, and beverages are provided.

If you can't hook up with Hawaii Forest & Trail for its Mauna Kea Summit and Stars, head to the top with **Mauna Kea Summit Adventures** (☎ 888-332-2366 or 808-332-2366; www.maunakea.com), a company that has been leading Mauna Kea tours exclusively for more than two decades. The price is $190 per person, including dinner, all necessary equipment, and parkas. You can arrange to meet your guide for your seven- to eight-hour adventure in Kailua-Kona, or at the Kings Shops at Waikoloa, or the Saddle Road junction. Reserve two weeks in advance, and you'll save 15 percent.

Getting a bird's-eye view — flightseeing tours

Flightseeing is a great way to explore this large, dynamic isle, which boasts sheer cliffs, pristine valleys, gorgeous waterfalls, expansive lava fields, and remote beaches that are otherwise inaccessible. And, of course, there's no better way to see that spectacular bubbling volcano, especially if the current flow is too far from civilization to see from accessible points in the national park.

Blue Hawaiian Helicopters (☎ 800-745-BLUE or 808-961-5600; www.bluehawaiian.com; 40- to 50-minute tours $177–$214 per person; two-hour tour $380–$428 per person) is an excellent flightseeing company that's run by David and Patti Chevalier and a loyal staff. Blue Hawaiian flies a fleet of American Eurocopter AStar 350 helicopters that carry six passengers, providing each with a 180-degree view and a Bose noise-canceling headset that lets you enjoy a surprisingly quiet ride. Recent additions to the fleet are new technologically advanced Eco-Star copters, which offer even better interior space, comfort, and views; the Eco-Star flights are the most expensive options. For Hilo-based travelers, Blue Hawaiian offers a 45- to 50-minute Circle of Fire volcano tour. From Waikoloa, choose between the gorgeous 45- to 50-minute Kohala Coast Adventure, which shows you the secret fluted valleys, majestic peaks, and rugged coastline of the island's northernmost point; and the Big Island Spectacular, which takes you over the entire island, from rugged coast and misty peaks to rain forest and volcano, all within two hours. Tours depart from Waikoloa Heliport or Hilo Airport.

Book your tour well in advance, and check for substantial online discounts — 15 percent off makes a huge difference at these prices.

You should consider the risks of flightseeing before you sign on. Although all the companies that I recommend feature skilled pilots and helicopters with excellent safety records, the truth of the matter is that flightseeing is a somewhat risky business. Dozens of people have died in commercial helicopter crashes in Hawaii over the past decade. Of course, just getting into your car and driving to dinner is far more dangerous than catching a 'copter ride. Still, you should make informed decisions when booking.

When reserving a helicopter tour with any company, check to make sure that safety is its first concern. The company should be an FAA-certified Part 135 operator, and the pilot should be Part 135 certified as well; the 135 license guarantees more stringent maintenance requirements and pilot training programs than those who are only Part 91 certified. And if weather conditions look iffy, reschedule.

Seeing Hawaii Volcanoes National Park

The top natural attraction in the islands, Hawaii Volcanoes National Park is the only destination in the entire U.S. National Parks system that's home to a live, lava-pumping volcano. This phenomenal park stands testament to 70 million years of volcanic activity, plate tectonics, and evolution. It encompasses two volcanoes, **Mauna Loa** and **Kilauea,** and spans 217,000 acres that reach from sea level to Mauna Loa's towering summit at 13,677 feet, and has both vast fields of black lava and an ancient rain forest.

Both volcanoes are classified as active, but Mauna Loa hasn't erupted since 1984. Kilauea, on the other hand, is the most active volcano in the world. An amazing geological phenomenon, it's been erupting nonstop

Hawaii Volcanoes National Park

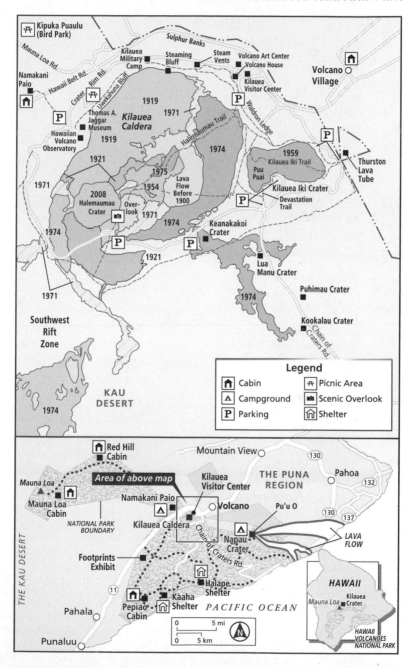

Legend

- 🏠 Cabin
- 🔺 Campground
- P Parking
- 🎋 Picnic Area
- 📷 Scenic Overlook
- 🏠 Shelter

since January 3, 1983. Most volcanic flows last a while — several months, maybe — but going for more than two and a half decades is simply unheard of in the annals of scientific history. Until now, of course.

When most people think of active volcanoes, they think of Mount St. Helens: A calm mountain suddenly blowing its stack, belching out raging, destructive torrents of fire. Hawaii's volcanoes, however, are much more mellow geologic creatures: They're shield volcanoes, which erupt gradually — usually in a sort of gloopy, Jell-O–like fashion — rather than in one big, fiery explosion. Thus, they allow for excellent, safe viewing most of the time, giving you plenty of time to calmly move out of the way if a blob of lava starts inching toward you (if you should be lucky enough for park officials to let you get that close, which they sometimes do). Leave it to Hawaii to have such laid-back volcanoes!

There are two lava flows going at this writing that you'll be able to see, if you're lucky. The primary flow is from the Puu Oo (*poo*-oo *oh*-oh) vent to the sea, where it spills into the ocean in a steaming stream. The hardened lava trail has extended the shoreline seaward, adding new land to the Big Island as it flows. It used to flow into the sea within the bounds of the park, at the end of the park's Chain of Craters Road. However, in July 2007, changes in the eruption triggered the opening of new vents on Kilauea's East Rift Zone, on the park's eastern edge and beyond its bounds, about 12 miles from Kilauea's summit. Lava is (at this writing, anyway) flowing into the ocean at Kalapana, at ocean's edge in the island's Puna Region, about an hour's drive from Volcano Village and 45 minutes or so from Hilo.

To make matters even more exciting, in March 2008, Halemaumau (ha-lay-*mow*-mow) Crater experienced its first explosive eruption since 1924, followed by a second explosion in April, and it continues to emit gases that glow in luminous red and orange in the after-dark hours. This one is located in the heart of the park, overlooked by the Jaggar Museum, which has escaped harm thus far.

At press time, the lava flow was going stronger than ever and, despite an 11-day pause in September 1999, shows no signs of stopping anytime soon, volcanologists say. But neither Mother Nature nor Madame Pele (pell-*ay*), Hawaii's volcano goddess who is said to reside in Kilauea's steaming Halemaumau Crater, runs on a fixed schedule. The volcano could be shooting fountains of lava hundreds of feet into the air, or it could be dormant on the day you arrive in the park (or the day after this book goes to press, for that matter) — there are no guarantees.

What's more, just because the lava is flowing doesn't mean that you'll be able to witness it firsthand. On many days, the lava flows right by accessible roads and within reach of hiking trails; you can get as close as the heat will allow and even watch it dump into the sea — quite a dramatic sight. At other times, the lava changes course, flowing miles away from any accessible points, visible only in the distance (or from the air via helicopter) or not at all (on occasion it sticks to underground lava tubes). Furthermore, the recent flows have been emitting elevated amounts of sulfurous gases and, at times, ash, which have required officials to keep visitors at safe distances from the flow at times, even when it is technically accessible. On my last visit, the closest you could get to the flow was about 2 miles distant due to the violence and toxicity of the current eruption — but it was still a sight to behold even at a distance.

If you hear that the flow is going strong and the viewing is good (word gets around quickly on this side of the island), don't hesitate: Head straight to the end of the road. You won't be disappointed, I promise. And don't put it off until tomorrow, when the situation may be entirely different.

If your visit happens to land during a period when the lava isn't visible at all, don't be too disappointed — or, worse yet, consider your visit a waste. Although I've been lucky enough to have some spectacular lava-viewing experiences, my favorite day in the park was spent without even seeing a speck of red. Trust me on this — visiting Hawaii Volcanoes National Park is a one-of-a-kind, once-in-a-lifetime experience even without the lava show.

Getting ready for your visit

For information before you go, contact Hawaii Volcanoes National Park headquarters at ☎ 808-985-6000, or visit the park's official Web site at www.nps.gov/havo, which features frequent updates on weather and lava flows. The telephone number also serves as a 24-hour eruption update and information hot line. Dial the same number (or visit the Web site) to obtain camping information.

At press time, because the flow had breached the park's boundary, Hawaii County officials had opened a viewing area at the end of Highway 130, the Keaau-Pahoa Road, which connects to Highway 11 south of Hilo in the town of Keaau. If you hear that the flow is still concentrated in the Kalapana/Puna region on your arrival on the Big Island, call ☎ 808-961-8093 for the latest information on the lava viewing area, which was open daily from 2 p.m. to 10 p.m. (last car in at 8 p.m.) at this writing. Be prepared for a long walk over rough lava, depending on where the lava is flowing at the time; good shoes are a must, as are long pants, water, and flashlights (one per person; most local hotels have them available for borrowing). And keep in mind that the story could change dramatically by the time you arrive.

Visit the U.S. Geological Survey's **Hawaiian Volcano Observatory** site at http://hvo.wr.usgs.gov for more complete information on Kilauea's recent eruption activity (including pictures) and past history. Another excellent (albeit unofficial) site for general park information is www.hawaii.volcanoes.national-park.com.

After you arrive on the island, you'll find that most information kiosks are stocked with a free booklet-size official visitor's guide to the park.

I recommend picking one up and reviewing it before your visit, because it's packed with practical details, historical background, and sightseeing information — way more than I am able to supply in these pages.

Hawaii Volcanoes National Park is on the Big Island's east side, about 30 miles southwest of Hilo along the Hawaii Belt Road (Highway 11). The drive from Kailua-Kona is about 100 miles and takes 2½ to 3 hours. For the shortest drive, choose the south route (around South Point) if you're staying to the south of Kailua-Kona, the north route (through Waimea) if you're staying along the Kohala Coast.

The gateway town of Volcano Village, on the north side of the park off Highway 11 just about a mile or so from the park entrance, is your best bet for accommodations and dining (see Chapter 14).

Admission to the park is $10 per car ($5 for pedestrians), which allows you to come and go as you please for seven days.

Keep these tips in mind as you plan your trip to Hawaii Volcanoes National Park:

✔ You really need two or three days to explore the park and environs thoroughly, so I recommend booking yourself a stay in Volcano Village, the park's gateway community; the small and pretty city of Hilo, about a half-hour drive away; or Pahoa, in the Puna Region, which is a good option for more adventurous travelers, especially if the flow is still meeting the ocean at Kalapana. But even if you can't dedicate so much time, don't stay away. You can see a lot of the park in one day if that's all the time you have.

✔ No matter how long you have to visit, do yourself a favor and plan on staying until after dark at least one evening. That's when, if you're lucky, you'll be able to witness nothing less than the miracle of creation as erupting Kilauea volcano spews red-hot, glowing lava. If you stay for after-dark viewing, bring a heavy-duty night lantern, because a standard flashlight tends not to be enough for navigating the walk across the lava fields. (Any hotel or B&B worth its salt lends its guests a good flashlight, but you may want to call ahead or ask via e-mail to be sure.) And be prepared to walk; at my visit before last (in 2006), the lava flow was about 1½ miles from the end of the road, but you were allowed to hike out to it if you were appropriately prepared. You might also consider bringing night-vision binoculars, if you have them.

✔ If you're staying on the west (Kona-Kohala) coast and you can only see the park on a day trip, you might consider visiting with a guide-led nature tour, such as the one offered by **Hawaii Forest & Trail,** or the park hike that **Hawaiian Walkways** offers in order to maximize your volcano experience. Otherwise, without a knowledgeable guide at hand to show you the highlights and explain what you're seeing, you may find that you're unable to get a real handle on the park in just a day. Trust me — an expert guide is well worth the dough you'll spend. Or, if you only want to catch a glimpse of the volcano from your perch on the Kona-Kohala coast, consider taking a helicopter tour that flies over the volcano. See the sections "Enjoying guided nature tours" and "Getting a bird's-eye view — flightseeing tours," earlier in this chapter.

✔ The most adventurous among you may want to rent a four-wheel-drive SUV when you book your rental car on the Big Island, because a few areas of the park are accessible only by four-wheel-drive. If you don't, however, don't sweat it — I never have, and I've seen more of the park than most visitors. You won't feel limited.

✔ I just can't say it strongly enough: I've seen way too many visitors running around the park soaking wet or freezing their buns off in shorts and T-shirts. Remember: It's always colder here than it is at the beach, so dress accordingly. If you're coming from the Kona side of the island in summer, expect it to be at least 10 to 20 degrees cooler at the volcano than it is there; bring a sweater or a light jacket and long pants. It's probably even slightly cooler than it is in Hilo thanks to a higher elevation (4,000 ft.), so anticipate a drop. In the cooler seasons, wear layers, and be prepared for temperatures to be in the 40s or 50s. Always have rain gear on hand, especially in winter. Sturdy closed-toe shoes are a good idea year-round, and a necessity if you're going to walk on the lava flow, because sneakers sometimes melt on the lava.

✔ No matter what the weather forecast may be, always bring a hat, sunglasses, and sunscreen. Take it from me, someone who came away with quite a sunburn on a day that started with a downpour: The weather can change at any time. Bring drinking water too, because it isn't readily available in most areas of the park.

✔ Pregnant visitors may want to skip the national park altogether, because it's not a good idea to expose yourself or your baby to the sulfuric fumes that are ever-present. Those with heart or breathing problems may also want to stay away, although my asthmatic husband has never had a problem in five visits. Otherwise, the park is perfectly safe for visitors. Some people claim that long-term exposure to vog, the smoglike haze caused by the gases released when molten lava pours into the ocean, can cause bronchial ailments, but sulfuric fumes are generally far less dangerous than urban industrial fumes. However, in recent months, vog has proved to be quite an issue around the island thanks to the recent volcanic activity. In fact, in May 2008, South Kona was oppressed by terrible vog, causing scratchy throats and persistent coughs, while Volcano was clear as a bell. It all depends on the winds. If you have any issues that may cause you to worry, I suggest that you check current conditions with your accommodations host.

✔ Lastly, based on current conditions, many areas of the park were closed due to the high level of volcanic activity in mid-2008. Therefore, if you're planning an extended visit to the park, call ahead to check current park status. However, keep in mind that the situation can change on a dime, so don't be disappointed if tomorrow's situation isn't the same as it was when you called yesterday.

Getting your bearings after you arrive

Make your first stop the **Kilauea Visitor Center,** just beyond the park entrance, open daily from 7:45 a.m. to 5 p.m. Here you can get up-to-the-minute reports on the eruption and good viewing points, check out exhibits that show you how volcanoes work and introduce you to the plants and animals of the park, watch a 20-minute film on eruptions (shown hourly), and review a schedule of the day's activities (posted on the bulletin board). While you're there, impress the rangers with your knowledge of Hawaii's volcano vocabulary:

✔ The smooth, ropy lava that looks like swirls of chocolate frosting is called **pahoehoe** (pa-ho-ay-*ho*-ay). It results from a fast-moving flow that curls as it flows.

✔ The rough, chunky lava that looks like a chopped-up parking lot is called **aa** (*ah*-ah). It's caused by lava that moves slowly, pulling apart as it overruns itself.

Check the bulletin board in the visitor center. Each day at 9 a.m., the staff posts a schedule of activities — perhaps a ranger presentation or an easy, guided walk to the summit. The offerings change daily, but always give visitors the chance to learn from the rangers; they're an excellent resource. If the day's activity doesn't suit you, ask the rangers to help you plan your explorations. They're expert at matching you with the trails and activities that are best suited to your fitness level and time constraints.

Be sure to use the restroom before heading into the depths of the park, because facilities are not readily available in the wild.

Exploring the park

For the best park overview, follow 11-mile **Crater Rim Drive,** which loops around the perimeter of Kilauea Crater and serves as the park's main road. As it passes through rain forest and lava desert, it takes you past all of the park's well-marked scenic spots and points of interest. The drive takes about an hour if you don't make any stops, but what's the point in that? Assuming that the drive is open for its full length, allow at least three hours, plus hiking time.

Before you even get in your car at the visitor center to make the drive, walk across the street and through the Volcano House for a railside panoramic view of the **Kilauea Caldera** and its vast, black steaming floor. Before you enter the building, look to your right for the marked steam vents, which illustrate the underground action with a cloud of warm, wet air escaping from the earth. (Notice how all the rain-forest ferns have gravitated to the moisture.)

I recommend following the Crater Rim Drive counterclockwise (west) from the visitor center about 3 miles so that you can stop at the **Thomas A. Jaggar Museum** (open daily 8:30 a.m.–5 p.m.), early in your drive. This little museum is well worth a half-hour of your time for the insight it offers into the park's geologic complexities, island evolution, and volcano observing; there's even a great telling of the Pele legend in murals. (Jaggar was a scientist and volcano observer who arrived to head the observatory in 1912; he was instrumental in both making the Big Island's volcanoes the most closely watched volcanoes in the world and petitioning to establish the area as a national park, a status it achieved in 1916.) The museum overlooks **Halemaumau** (ha-lay-*mow*-mow) **Crater,** which is the legendary home of Hawaii's tempestuous goddess of volcanoes, Pele, and is steaming mightily at this writing.

Natural highlights along the Crater Rim Drive include the **Steam Vents** along the Steaming Bluff, where clouds of warmth rise from vents in the active earth. At **Halemaumau** (ha-lay-*mow*-mow) **Overlook,** walk to the crater's edge and take in an alternate view of the steaming crater. Across the road is **Keanakakoi Crater,** whose short trail leads to colorful eruption fissures — very cool! — and the backside of the Halemaumau Crater. As you drive the road, you'll see that the flows are dated (1959, 1974, 1982), which really brings home the reality of volcanic destruction.

You'll also pass numerous scenic overlooks and trail heads, and I highly recommend that you hit the trail at least once during your visit; the following are some highlights to seek out.

The **Thurston Lava Tube** is the coolest spot in the park. This short (⅓-mile), easy, well-maintained loop trail leads you into a small rain-foresty crater, luxuriant with giant ferns and native birds, and to a cave in the lava flow that hot lava once ran through. (Similar tubes are currently carrying hot lava underground closer to the current rift.) It's all drippy and cool, with naked roots hanging down. You can hike through the short tube and exit out the other side (bring your flashlight if you have one).

My absolute favorite is the **Kilauea Iki Trail,** a 4-mile, two-hour moderate-to-challenging hike that starts across the road from the Thurston Lava Tube and descends about 400 feet to and across the floor of the Kilauea Iki Crater, which last erupted in 1959. Crossing the black, steaming crater floor is a wild, otherworldly, magnificent trip and offers the park's best opportunity to put yourself in the heart of the matter. Be prepared for the hike with good walking shoes, sunscreen, a hat, and plenty of water; remember, conditions can change quickly, so raingear is a good idea even if the sun is high in the sky at the start of the hike.

Another result of Kilauea Iki's 1959 eruption is **Devastation Trail.** This brief and easy half-mile walk with the ominous name shows you what a volcanic eruption can do to a flourishing rain forest. The petrified landscape is quite astounding — it looks like a tree graveyard. Anybody can manage this walk; the trail head is on Crater Rim Drive at Puu Puai Overlook.

If you'd like a respite from all the devastation, follow the **Kipuka Puaulu (Bird Park) Trail,** an easy 1-mile loop that takes you through a thriving forest of native trees. The trail head is off Highway 11 to the northeast of the main park area, on the Mauna Loa Road. (The park map makes it easy to find.)

 Both the Devastation and Kipuka Puaulu trails are excellent walks to take between 4 and 5 p.m., because that's when the park's resident pheasants emerge from their daytime nests to poke around and see what's going on.

The park has enough fascinating hiking trails to keep you busy and interested for days on end. Your best bet is, again, to start your day at the Kilauea Visitor Center, where you can learn about guided walks and day-hike options. Remember to always check conditions with the park rangers before you set out on any hike. If you're interested in getting a preview of accessible trails, visit www.hawaii.volcanoes.national-park.com and click "Hiking Guide."

 After you circle back around to the Kilauea Visitor Center, stop in next door at the **Volcano Art Center** (www.volcanoartcenter.org), which serves as one of the top showcases for island artists. Don't miss it if you're interested in local arts and crafts — from native-wood jewelry boxes to handcrafted jewelry to first-rate paintings and photographs — because the works you'll find here are first-rate.

More attractions worth seeking out

The Big Island certainly has an activity or interest for just about everyone. In this section, I've rounded up some off-the-beaten-path attractions that are worth a visit.

Along the Kona-Kohala coast

In addition to these sights, you may want to head upcountry from Kailua-Kona town on Hualalai Road to the charmingly funky gallery-lined town of **Holualoa,** which offers a nice peek at Kona's world-famous coffee-growing country. See the section "Shopping the local stores," later in this chapter, for further details on what you'll find there.

Hulihee Palace

These days, the ancient port town of Kailua-Kona, lined with waterfront restaurants and touristy shops, is more like a modern mall than anything else. But if you have an interest in Hawaii's history, you may want to take

Kailua-Kona Town

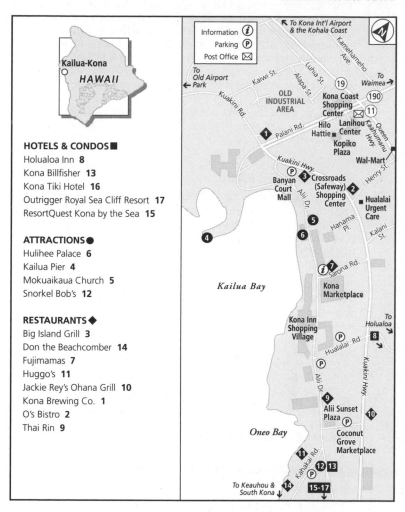

HOTELS & CONDOS ■
Holualoa Inn **8**
Kona Billfisher **13**
Kona Tiki Hotel **16**
Outrigger Royal Sea Cliff Resort **17**
ResortQuest Kona by the Sea **15**

ATTRACTIONS ●
Hulihee Palace **6**
Kailua Pier **4**
Mokuaikaua Church **5**
Snorkel Bob's **12**

RESTAURANTS ◆
Big Island Grill **3**
Don the Beachcomber **14**
Fujimamas **7**
Huggo's **11**
Jackie Rey's Ohana Grill **10**
Kona Brewing Co. **1**
O's Bistro **2**
Thai Rin **9**

15 minutes or so to explore Hulihee Palace. Built in 1838, this beautifully restored two-story New England–style mansion of lava rock and coral mortar served as the vacation home of Hawaii's royalty. It features gleaming koa antiques as well as ancient artifacts collected by the Daughters of Hawaii. There's a cute gift shop too.

At press time, Hulihee Palace was undergoing extensive renovation to repair damage from the October 2006 earthquake that the Big Island experienced. Call the number listed below or Daughters of Hawaii at ☎ **808-595-6291** to learn if the palace has been reopened, as well as for any updated visitor information.

After you're done exploring the palace — or even if you just view it from the streetside — head across the street to handsome **Mokuaikaua Church**, 75–5713 Alii Dr. (☎ 808-329-0655; **www.mokuaikaua.org**), the first Christian church in Hawaii, now housing a Congregational church. The 112-foot steeple is still the tallest structure in Kailua-Kona. Sunday services are offered at 8 a.m. and 10:30 a.m., and services last about an hour; child care and Sunday school are only offered at the early service, but you should call to confirm if you wish to take advantage of these kid-friendly programs.

See map p. 393. 75–5718 Alii Dr., Kailua-Kona (in the heart of town). ☎ 808-329-1877. www.daughtersofhawaii.org. *Admission: $6 adults, $4 seniors, $1 kids under 12. Open: Daily 9 a.m.–4 p.m.*

Kalahuipuaa Fishponds

Scientists still marvel at the ancient Hawaiians' sophisticated aquaculture system, which used brackish shoreline ponds to stock, cultivate, and harvest fish for eating. This picturesque set of seven adjacent 2,000-year-old ponds are of two types: The closed ponds, inshore and closed off from the ocean, were used to raise mullet, milkfish, and shrimp; and ponds that open to the sea have rock-wall barriers and sluice gates that connect them directly to the ocean.

These beautifully preserved oceanfront ponds are a stellar example of the ancient way of life — not to mention a gorgeous place to enjoy a stroll. A palm-lined lava-rock path winds its way around the ponds; the entire walk is an easy 2½-mile loop, dotted with wooden benches that let you take frequent breaks and enjoy the vistas (or watch the flying mullets, which love to leap into the air). Next door is the restaurant at the Mauna Lani Beach Club, where you can enjoy a refreshing beverage after your walk.

See map p. 368. In the Mauna Lani Resort, 23 miles north of Kona Airport. ☎ 808-885-6622 for Mauna Lani Resort. To get there: Take Queen Kaahumanu Highway (Highway 19) to the Mauna Lani turnoff; ask the gate attendant to point you to the fishponds. If you're staying at the resort, the free shuttle can take you there.

Kona Historical Society Museum

This well-organized pocket museum is housed in the historic Greenwell Store, built in 1875 by Henry Nicholas Greenwell out of native stone, with lime mortar made from burned coral. Antiques, artifacts, and photos tell the story of the fabled Kona Coast in the heyday of coffee growing and cattle raising. Serious history buffs should call ahead to inquire about joining one of the museum's first-rate walking or jeep tours, or their living history or other educational programs.

See map p. 368. On Highway 11, ¼ mile south of Kealakekua town (between mile markers 111 and 112). ☎ 808-323-3222. www.konahistorical.org. *Admission: $7 adults, $3 children 5–12, free for kids under 5. Open: Mon–Fri 9 a.m.–3 p.m.*

Puako Petroglyph Archaeological District

Petroglyphs, lava-rock carvings that tell the story of the precontact past (much like the paintings inside the great pyramids of Egypt), serve as a fascinating window to Hawaii's ancient history. These pictures of daily life — dancers and paddlers, families and chiefs, poi pounders and canoes — appear throughout the islands, but most of them are found on the Big Island. The largest concentration is here, at this 233-acre site just north of the Mauna Lani resort. The easy ¾-mile (one-way) dirt **Malama Trail** leads you through a mesquite forest to rock art that's graphic and easy to see. The symbols date from A.D. 800 to 1400; carvers used the blue rocks you see along the path to carve into the harder lava-rock fields. They are very simple figures, and tend to be self-explanatory in nature. The most compelling artwork is at the far (right) end of the petroglyph field, where the carvings overlap; this area is said to have excess *mana,* or supernatural power, which made it a prime canvas. The grave of a young woman, buried with her tea set, is also said to be located at this end of the field. Early morning or late afternoon is best for petroglyph viewing. The petroglyphs are thousands of years old and can be easily destroyed, so don't walk on them (shoes can act as an eraser) or attempt to take a rubbing; stick to photos, please.

See map p. 368. Trail head begins at the Holoholokai Beach Park access parking lot, Mauna Lani resort, 23 miles north of Kona Airport. ☎ 808-885-6622. To get there: Take Queen Kaahumanu Highway (Highway 19) to the Mauna Lani turnoff and drive toward the coast on North Kaniku Drive, which ends at a parking lot; the trail head is marked by a sign and interpretive kiosk.

Puuhonua o Honaunau National Historical Park

If you visit only one historic site while you're in Hawaii, make it this one. No other site better illustrates what ancient life in the islands was like — and, boy, is this place cool.

With its fierce, haunting totemlike idols, this sacred site on the ocean looks mighty intimidating. To ancient Hawaiians, though, it was a welcome sight — especially for defeated warriors and *kapu* (taboo) breakers, because Puuhonua O Honaunau (poo-oo-ho-*noo*-ah oh ho-*now*-now) was a designated sanctuary. A massive rock wall defines the refuge; as long as the troubled Hawaiians made it inside the wall, they were absolved. In addition to the sanctuary itself, this visually stunning ancient site on the black-lava coast is also home to fascinating archaeological preservations and reconstructions, including royal grounds that were home to the *alii* (chiefs) of the Kona Coast in premodern times; an ancient temple re-creation; royal fishponds and burial sites (some pretty powerful chiefs called this area home); and much more. Heck, the old rock wall alone is worth a visit: Separating the royal compound from the *puuhonua* (sanctuary) and standing 10 feet high and 17 feet thick in spots, it was built entirely without mortar, by simply fitting stones together — a remarkable achievement considering that it's been standing since about 1550.

The historic site is tons of fun to explore. At the park entrance, you get a self-guided tour map that leads you to 16 important sites. The trail takes about an hour to follow and serves as a great window into precontact Hawaiian culture — not only in such fierce life lessons as war and sanctuary, but also in basic living, from fish-raising and -netting to the basic rules of *konane* (ancient Hawaiian checkers). Wear shoes or sandals with good traction, and you can crawl around on the ocean-facing lava flats — fun! I highly recommend that you launch your visit, however, with a half-hour ranger-led orientation talk, held in the amphitheater periodically throughout the day. (Call for the current schedule.) Allow two to three hours for your visit.

See map p. 368. At the end of Highway 160, Honaunau (about 22 miles south of Kailua-Kona). To get there: Turn off Mamalahoa Highway (Highway 11) at Highway 160, between mile markers 103 and 104, and proceed the 3½ miles to the park entrance. ☎ *808-328-2288.* www.nps.gov/puho. *Admission: $5 per vehicle, $3 per walk-in individual; admission good for 7 days. Open: Park Mon–Thurs 7 a.m.–8 p.m., Fri–Sun 6 a.m.–11 p.m.; visitor center daily 8 a.m.–5 p.m.*

Off the beaten path: North Kohala

If you look at a map of the Big Island, you see that a mountainous peninsula protrudes from the very top of the island. That's **North Kohala,** the last bastion of plantation life on the Big Island until not too long ago. If you want to experience the old Hawaii vibe, this is the place to do it.

The hour-long drive along the Akoni Pule (ah-*ko*-nee *poo*-lay) Highway (Highway 270) from Kawaihae (at the north end of the Kohala Coast, where Highway 19 turns inland toward Waimea) to the end of the road at the island's north tip is one of my favorite drives in all Hawaii. It takes you past gorgeous rolling ranchlands with remarkable ocean vistas and through two charming old plantation towns, **Hawi** (*ha*-vee) and **Kapaau** (ka-*pa*-ow), both of which have been transformed into small but rewarding shopper's havens. (See the section "Shopping the local stores," later in this chapter, for details.)

As you drive through Kapaau, look to the mountain side of the road, where you can't miss the **Original King Kamehameha Statue** standing guard outside the New England–style courthouse–turned–senior center in the heart of town. This unspoiled territory was the birthplace of King Kamehameha the Great, the great chief who united the Hawaiian Islands as one kingdom back in 1810. This 8-foot, 6-inch bronze statue was cast in Europe in 1880 and was lost at sea before being ultimately rescued and erected here.

After you're finished browsing Hawi and Kapaau, if it's a nice day and you're enjoying your North Kohala drive, continue a few miles to the end of Highway 270, where you'll find the **Pololu Valley Lookout,** a gorgeous scenic overlook that takes in a panoramic view of foaming waves and sheer sea cliffs.

After all this sightseeing, you're bound to be hungry, so don't miss retro-charming **Bamboo,** in Hawi, for lunch; see Chapter 14 for details.

If you want to explore the verdant ranchlands of North Kohala the way they were meant to be seen — from the saddle of a horse — contact **Paniolo Adventures** (☎ 808-889-5354; www.panioloadventures.com), which offers 1½-, 2½-, 3-, and 4-hour rides through 11,000 acres of still-working cattle lands. This is a spirited ride, not a pokey nose-to-tail trailer; even brave beginners often get up to a canter. Beginning, intermediate, and advanced riders alike, ages 8 and up, will enjoy these trips. Rides are $69 to $159 per person. (Be sure to ask about weight restrictions and minimum ages for kids. You'll also need to wear long pants and closed-toe shoes.) Custom-designed private rides (minimum two people) are also available.

The interior: Waimea

Smack-dab in the middle of the north road between the west and east sides of the island is Waimea, the heart and soul of Hawaii's *paniolo* (cowboy) country.

As you drive along Highway 19 east from the Kohala Coast to Waimea, most of the rolling, grassy ranchland that you see is part of **Parker Ranch** (www.parkerranch.com), Hawaii's biggest ranch and one of the largest cattle ranches in the entire United States (rather remarkable, if you think about it).

If you're interested in learning just how cattle roping came to find a home in Hawaii, spend a half-hour at the **Parker Ranch Visitor Center and Museum,** in the Parker Ranch Shopping Center at the junction of highways 19 and 190 (☎ 877-885-7999 or 808-885-7655), which chronicles the ranch's history from 1847 until today, capturing the essence of day-to-day life on the ranch along the way. The museum is open Monday through Saturday from 9 a.m. to 5 p.m. (the last ticket is sold at 4 p.m.). Admission is $8 (ask about discounted prices for kids 12 and under).

The Parker Ranch also has two historic home sites that you can tour: **Mana Hale** and **Puuopelu,** both open Monday through Saturday from 10 a.m. to 5 p.m. (You must arrive by 4 p.m.) These beautifully restored ranch homes (once the home of ranch founding father John Parker and his Hawaiian princess bride) are filled with gorgeous furnishings (lots of native koa in Mana Hale, European heirlooms at Puuopelu). To get there, turn south at the Highway 19/190 junction in Waimea and go ¾ mile to the sign that says "Parker Ranch Historic Homes & Art Collection." Curators are available to show you around and fill you in on ranch history and gossipy lore. Admission is $9 per person; call ☎ 877-885-7999 or 808-885-5433 for more information. Allow an hour or so for your visit.

 You can save $1 per ticket by purchasing dual admission to the Parker Ranch Visitor Center and Museum and the ranch's historic home sites. Just let the ticket agent know at purchase time.

If you want to get out and see the ranch itself, a two-hour *paniolo*-led **Horseback Ride** is offered twice daily at 8:15 a.m. to 12:15 p.m. The trail ride passes through 19th-century stone corrals that still hold the ranch's Herefords on occasion, across vast rolling hills, and to the ranch's rodeo arena and thoroughbred racetrack. If you're lucky, you may even get to see working *paniolo* herding, cutting, holding, roping, throwing, branding, or sorting the cattle. These beginner-friendly rides are $79 per person, and riders as young as 7 years old are accepted, making this a great activity for the entire family. Be sure to book at least a few days in advance by calling ☎ 877-885-7999.

Riders who prefer horseless carriages can opt instead to explore the rolling ranchlands via 4x4 fully automatic ATVs. Rides are offered daily at 8:15 a.m. and 12:15 p.m. The cost is $95 per person, and you must be at least 16 years old to participate. Call ☎ 877-885-7999 or 808-885-7655 to book.

There's even more to do on Parker Ranch than I have space to discuss here. For a full list of events and activities, call ☎ 877-885-7999 or go online to www.parkerranch.com.

The Hamakua Coast

If you drive east from Waimea or north from Hilo (see the following listing), you'll reach more off-the-beaten-path territory: the mist-shrouded Hamakua Coast, where you'll find some wonderful natural attractions and the one-horse town of **Honokaa,** which still boasts a weathered old-plantation charm.

Akaka Falls

Tucked away in a misty, fragrant rain forest, this dramatic 422-footer is one of Hawaii's most scenic waterfalls. You can reach it via an easy mile-long paved loop, which takes you past bamboo and flowering ginger and down to an observation point, where you'll have a perfect view. You'll also see nearby Kahuna Falls, which is a mere 100 feet tall. Be on the lookout for rainbows.

See map p. 368. At the end of Akaka Falls Road (Highway 220), Honomu (8 miles north of Hilo). To get there: From Highway 19, turn left at Honomu and head 3½ miles inland.

Hawaii Tropical Botanical Garden

This lush, Eden-like 40-acre valley makes a magical stop for horticultural buffs, or anybody who wants to experience the extraordinary flora of the Hawaiian Islands. The spectacular collection of more than 2,000 species of tropical plants runs the gamut from delicate orchids to towering torch ginger to 100-year-old mango, coconut, and banyan trees, all of which thrive in the protected valley's rich volcanic soil. Stay for an hour or come to bask in the natural tranquillity of the garden all day.

Waimea (Kamuela)

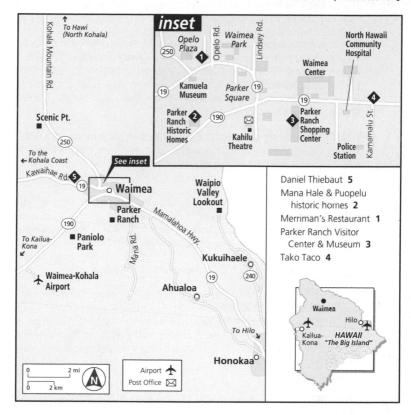

See map p.368. 27-717 Old Mamalahoa Hwy., on the 4-mile Scenic Route off Highway 19, Onomea Bay (8½ miles north of Hilo; look for the blue "4-Mile Scenic Route" sign on the ocean side of the highway). ☎ **808-964-5233.** www.htbg.com. Admission: $15 adults, $5 kids 6–16, free for kids age 5 and under. Open: Daily 9 a.m.–5 p.m. (last admission is at 4 p.m.).

Waipio Valley

This gorgeous tropical valley at the end of the road on the Hamakua Coast is very difficult to reach, which is precisely what makes it so spectacular. From the black-sand bay at its mouth, remote Waipio sweeps back 6 breathtaking miles, boasting intense emerald green taro patches rustling in the wind between sheer cliffs reaching almost a mile high.

You don't have to hike down into the remote valley to admire it. Just take Highway 19 to Honokaa and then turn onto the Kukuihaele Highway (Highway 240), which leads right to the **Waipio Valley Lookout.** This grassy park on the edge of Waipio Valley's sheer cliffs has splendid views of the luxuriantly green valley below. Featuring some old redwood picnic tables and rudimentary facilities, this is the ideal spot to unpack a picnic while you take in the magnificent view.

The more ambitious among you can hike down the paved path into the valley, or catch a ride with the **Waipio Valley Shuttle** (☎ 808-775-7121), which offers a 90-minute narrated four-wheel-drive tour into the valley. The shuttle runs Monday through Saturday at 9 a.m., 11 a.m., 1 p.m., and 3 p.m. Tickets are $55 for adults, $30 for kids under age 11. Reserve your spot in advance.

While you're here, drop in at **Waipio Valley Artworks,** in Kukuihaele Village on Highway 240, 2 miles from the lookout (☎ 800-492-4746 or 808-775-0958; www.waipiovalleyartworks.com). You'll find a good selection of local art, Koa heirloom bowls, furniture, ceramics, and more.

You can also explore the valley aboard a mule-drawn wagon with **Waipio Valley Wagon Tours** (☎ 808-775-9518; www.waipiovalleywagontours.com). This touristy 1½-hour tour is also fully narrated and departs from the Last Chance Store. Tours are offered Monday through Saturday at 9:30 a.m., 11:30 a.m., 1:30 p.m., and 3:30 p.m. Tickets are $55 for adults, $25 for kids ages 4 to 12; free for children under 3.

If you want to explore the lush Waipio Valley on horseback, contact **Naalapa Stables** (☎ 808-775-0419; www.naalapastables.com), which offers 2½-hour nose-to-tail trail rides Monday through Saturday at 9:30 a.m. and 1 p.m. Tickets are $89 per person, and you must be at least 8 years old and weigh less than 230 pounds. Tours leave from Waipio Valley Artworks.

If you want to take one of the guided tours of the Waipio Valley, make advance reservations to avoid disappointment; call a week in advance to book a mule tour.

Don't take your rental car down the steep road that leads into the Waipio Valley; you won't get back up the steeply graded hill. What's more, most rental-car contracts prohibit it, so if you do get stuck, you'll also end up with a hefty tow bill (not to mention a wasted day).

Hilo

I love this pretty bayfront city and its wonderfully nostalgic, if rustic, atmosphere. Although Hilo is Hawaii's second-largest city (after Honolulu), it really feels like a sort of funky old plantation town. Some people, especially those who come to Hawaii to get away from gray skies, just don't understand Hilo's appeal. I've found that you have to be something of a retro-romantic to appreciate it.

Despite Hilo's reputation for rain, you may want to spend a couple of days here. Hilo is a good base from which to explore Hawaii Volcanoes National Park, which is only a 45-minute drive away (see Chapter 14 for

Hilo

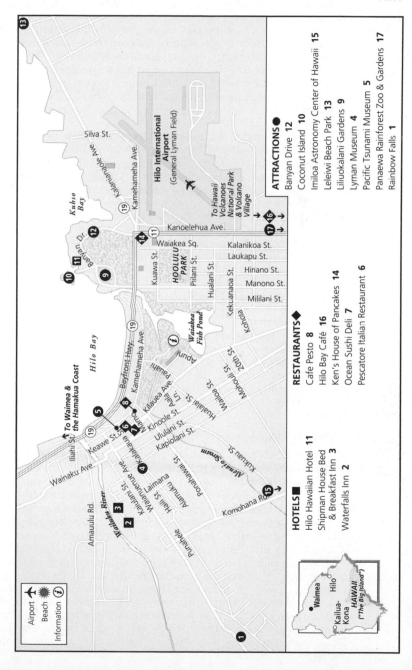

ATTRACTIONS ●
Banyan Drive **12**
Coconut Island **10**
Imiloa Astronomy Center of Hawaii **15**
Leleiwi Beach Park **13**
Liliuokalani Gardens **9**
Lyman Museum **4**
Pacific Tsunami Museum **5**
Panaewa Rainforest Zoo & Gardens **17**
Rainbow Falls **1**

RESTAURANTS ◆
Cafe Pesto **8**
Hilo Bay Café **16**
Ken's House of Pancakes **14**
Ocean Sushi Deli **7**
Pescatore Italian Restaurant **6**

HOTELS ■
Hilo Hawaiian Hotel **11**
Shipman House Bed & Breakfast Inn **3**
Waterfalls Inn **2**

Airport ✈
Beach ☀
Information *i*

HAWAII
("The Big Island")
Waimea
Hilo
Kailua-Kona

hotel recommendations). Hilo also boasts some interesting shopping. (See the section "Shopping the local stores," later in this chapter).

But even if you just drive through on your way to the national park, take a few minutes to cruise or stroll down **Banyan Drive,** the shady lane that curves along the waterfront, offering fabulous Hilo Bay views. (A number of the banyan trees along here were planted as saplings by such celebrities as Amelia Earhart and Babe Ruth.) If it's a clear day, take the short walk across the concrete arch bridge in front of the Hawaii Naniloa Hotel to **Coconut Island,** if only for a panoramic look at this pretty little city.

Also along Banyan Drive is **Liluokalani Gardens,** the largest formal Japanese garden this side of Tokyo. This 30-acre park, named for Hawaii's last monarch, Queen Liluokalani, is postcard-pretty, complete with bonsai, carp ponds, pagodas, and a moon gate bridge. It's free and open 24 hours, so stop by to spend a moment in old Japan.

The following are a handful of additional attractions you may want to seek out while you're in Hilo. If Hilo's charms win you over — and they just might — pick up a copy of the free *Explore Hilo* walking tour pamphlet, which is available all over town and the island. If, for some reason, you don't run across it, pick one up at the **Big Island Visitors Bureau** office at 250 Keawe St., at Haili Street, across from Pescatore restaurant (☎ **808-961-5797;** www.bigisland.org).

If you find yourself intrigued by Hilo, contact the **Downtown Hilo Improvement Association,** 329 Kamehameha Ave., Hilo (☎ **808-935-8850;** www.downtownhilo.com; office hours: Mon–Fri 8:30 a.m.–4:30 p.m.), which has a very informative Web site detailing the history of the town and its attractions. You can also stop by its office for helpful information, or to pick up a copy of its informative self-guided walking tour of 18 historic sites.

Imiloa Astronomy Center of Hawaii

This excellent hands-on museum is focused on telling the story of astronomy through the dual lenses of both science and Hawaiian culture. Visitors get a new understanding of the mysteries of the night sky unraveled through the world's largest and most important collection of observatories, situated above the clouds atop majestic Mauna Kea volcano. The museum also unravels the mysteries of history, telling the story of the sky as the roadmap to Hawaii for the ancient Polynesians — widely considered the world's first astronomers — who sailed across the vast Pacific to find these fair isles. The appealing museum offers hands-on exhibits for everyone, ranging from a kid-friendly introduction to the Big Bang theory to computer banks that allow you to interact with Mauna Kea's telescopes. (The museum treads lightly with cosmic origins stories, focusing more on the "what" than the "how," maintaining appropriate respect for a full range of beliefs on this subject.) The highlight is the signature planetarium show, "Maunakea: Between Earth and Sky," which summarizes the story of the museum in a half-hour show; I recommend starting your visit with the signature show, and follow by exploring the exhibits. There's usually a second "feature" planetarium show on offer that changes periodically; at press time, it was a 3-D feature on the dawn of the space age. Allow two to three hours for your visit, depending on your level of interest.

See map p. 368. At the University of Hawaii at Hilo, 600 Imiloa Place, Hilo. ☎ *808-969-9700.* www.imiloahawaii.org. *To get there: Follow Kanoelehua Avenue (Highway 11) to Puainako Street (at Prince Kuhio Plaza); head west on Puainako Street, go 1¾ miles and turn right on Komohana Street, turn right on Nowelo Street, and turn left on Imiloa Place. Admission: $18 adults, $9.50 kids ages 4–12. Admission includes 1 planetarium show (your choice); additional planetarium show $6 adults, $3 kids. Open: Tues–Sun 9 a.m.–4 p.m. Signature planetarium show at 11 a.m. and 2 p.m.; feature show at 1 and 3 p.m. Check the planetarium schedule for Fri night laser rock shows, usually at 7:30 and 9 p.m.*

Lyman Museum

Composed of two major exhibit halls and a historic missionary home, this museum should be high on the priority list for culture and history buffs. The first-rate Earth Heritage and Island Heritage galleries tell the islands' native natural and cultural story; other permanent collections include notable collections of Hawaiian and Chinese art. Next door is the fully restored 1839 home of David and Sarah Lyman, a hybrid New England/Hawaiian–style house — the oldest wooden house on the island — that perfectly exemplifies missionary times, which transformed Hawaii permanently and served as the foundation for the unique East-meets-West island culture that prevails today. No other site in Hawaii tells the story so well. Excellent guided tours of the Lyman Mission House are offered at 11 a.m., 1 and 3 p.m. Your best bet is to arrive about an hour before your tour time to tour the museum, then follow with the house tour.

See map p. 368. 276 Haili St. (at Kapiolani Street), Hilo. ☎ *808-935-5021.* www.lyman museum.org. *Admission: $10 adults, $8 seniors (60+), $3 kids ages 6–17. Family package: $25 for 2 adults and 2 kids; also ask about AAA discounts; discount coupons are often available in visitor brochures around town, including 2-for-1 admission coupons. Open: Mon–Sat 9:30 a.m.–4:30 p.m.*

Pacific Tsunami Museum

This compelling small museum and education center chronicles the tsunamis (tidal waves) that devastated — and subsequently reshaped — Hilo in 1946 and 1960. Exhibits that tell both scientific and personal stories are on hand; some of the guides are even survivors, with their own tales to tell. The museum — which can add depth and immediacy to your understanding of the massive tragedy that struck Southeast Asia in 2004 — is well worth 45 minutes or an hour of your time.

See map p. 368. 130 Kamehameha Ave., downtown Hilo. ☎ *808-935-0926.* www. tsunami.org. *Admission: $7 adults, $6 seniors, $2 kids ages 6–17, free for kids 5 and under. Open: Mon–Sat 9 a.m.–4 p.m.*

Panaewa Rainforest Zoo & Gardens

This cute-as-a-button 12-acre rain-forest zoo — the only tropical rain-forest zoo in the United States — is a good bet if you have little ones in tow. Some 50 species of birds, reptiles, and mammals are on hand, from Hawaiian owls to Bengal tigers. The tigers are fed daily at 3:30 p.m., which is quite a sight to behold. There's also a petting zoo for the little ones every Saturday from 1:30 to 2:30 p.m.

See map p. 368. On Stainback Highway (off Highway 11), Panaewa (just south of Hilo). ☎ *808-959-9233.* www.hilozoo.com. *Admission: Free. Open: Daily 9 a.m.–4 p.m. except Christmas and New Year's Day.*

Rainbow Falls

This 80-footer isn't quite as towering or dramatic as Akaka Falls (see the section "The Hamakua Coast," earlier in this chapter), but the sight of the waterfall spilling into a pool surrounded by wild ginger is just lovely. Go in the morning, around 9 or 10 a.m., to see Rainbow Falls at its best.

See map p. 368. On Waianuenue Avenue (Highway 200), Hilo. To get there: Follow Bayfront Highway (Highway 19) to Waianuenue Avenue and turn inland; the falls are on the right past the Kaumana Drive intersection.

Hitting the links

The Kohala Coast is home to the top golf courses on the Big Island, and among them are some of the finest golf challenges in the world. This vast island boasts far more golfing opportunities than I can list here; if you want more options, either on this coast or elsewhere around the island, contact the **Big Island Visitors Bureau** (☎ 808-886-1655 on the Kohala Coast, or 808-961-5797 in Hilo; www.bigisland.org).

The **Golf Hawaii Card** (☎ 888-GOLF-918; www.hawaiigolfdeals.com) costs $60 annually, but can pay for itself in just one or two visits to participating courses. Eight courses on the Big Island alone offer significantly lower rates for cardholders, including Hapuna, Mauna Kea, the two Waikoloa courses, Big Island Country Club, and the two courses at the Kona Country Club. Your Big Island card also scores you bonus use at some Oahu and Maui courses. For discounted tee times, also check out the deals available through **Tee Times Hawaii.com** (☎ 888-675-GOLF; www.teetimeshawaii.com).

Probably the best golf course on the Big Island is the Hualalai Golf Course at the Four Seasons Resort Hualalai. Many duffers in the know consider it the finest course in the state. Unfortunately, you have to be a resort guest to play it, but for the committed, this Jack Nicklaus–designed championship course is reason enough to stay there; see Chapter 14 for a review.

Book your tee times well in advance, especially in high season.

Big Island Country Club

The island's newest course is this 6,114-yard Pete and Perry Dye design, situated at 2,500 feet elevation above the Kohala Coast, offering welcome relief from the perennially hot coastal weather. Seven water features come into play along this popular, immaculately kept, dramatically situated, and justifiably popular course. The mountain and ocean views are incredible. An excellent bargain on a pricey golf coast.

See map p. 368. 71–1420 Mamalahoa Hwy. (Highway 190), near Waikoloa Road (at mile marker 20). ☎ *808-325-5044. Greens fees: $169, $109 after noon; $55 for seniors Mon and Thurs. With Golf Hawaii Card, fees are $75.*

Hapuna Golf Course

This 6,029-yard links-style championship course is widely considered one of Arnold Palmer and Ed Seay's finest courses. Boasting indigenous vegetation and a design that blends seamlessly with the surrounding landscape, it has been honored as Most Environmentally Sensitive Course by *Golf Magazine* and Course of the Future by the U.S. Golf Association. The course extends from the coastline to 700 feet above sea level, with pastoral mountain scenery to one side and sweeping ocean views on the other. The elevation changes keep play challenging, as do the higher-elevation winds and a series of daunting bunkers. Facilities include a practice green, driving range, pro shop, restaurant, and fitness center.

See map p. 368. Adjacent to the Hapuna Beach Prince Hotel, 62–100 Kauanoa Dr. (off Highway 19 near mile marker 69). ☎ *808-882-5400.* www.princeresortshawaii. com. *Greens fees: $165 ($125 for hotel guests). Twilight rate $145 available seasonally for tee times after 1 p.m.*

Mauna Kea Golf Course

This 6,365-yard Robert Trent Jones, Sr., grande dame has been around since 1964, but it's still at the top of its game — just ask the editors of *Hawaii* magazine, who recently named it the second-best course in the state (after the Kiele Course at Kauai Lagoons; see Chapter 17). Its combination of breathtaking natural beauty, stunning oceanfront setting, and championship-level challenge make it one of Trent Jones's finest designs anywhere, and one of the best courses in the state. Expect undulating greens, more than 100 well-placed bunkers, and dramatic changes in elevation. The signature hole is the 3rd, a par-3 shocker with 200 yards of ocean standing between tee and green, which the legendary architect called his favorite hole of all time. Facilities include practice green, driving range, lockers and showers, pro shop, and restaurant.

 At press time, the Mauna Kea golf course was in the midst of a major renovation led by Rees Jones, the legendary course designer's son. The renovation is slated to be complete in December 2008 — and don't be surprised if it comes with higher greens fees.

See map p. 368. In the Mauna Kea resort, 62–100 Mauna Kea Beach Dr. (off Highway 19). ☎ *808-882-5400.* www.princeresortshawaii.com. *Greens fees: $200 ($130*

for guests of the Mauna Kea Beach Hotel). Twilight rates available seasonally for tee times after 1 p.m.

Mauna Lani Frances H. I'i Brown Courses

Carved out of rugged black lava flows, both of these 6,335-yard championship courses are real winners. You'll really know that you're playing Big Island golf here; as a matter of fact, the dramatic oceanfront South Course is so otherworldly that it looks like it might be set on the moon. Long home to the Senior Skins Game, it's one of Hawaii's most difficult golf challenges and boasts an unforgettable ocean hole, the 221-yard, par-3 7th. The intense drama of the seasoned North Course is toned down by its rolling greens and wealth of old-growth greenery, which gives it a Scottish feel; don't be surprised if you have to wait for feral goats to clear the fairways before you take your shot. Facilities include two driving ranges, putting green, pro shop with rentals, restaurant, and on-course refreshment carts; pro-instructed golf clinics are available.

In the Mauna Lani resort, 68–150 Hoohana St. (off Highway 19). ☎ **808-885-6655.** www.maunalani.com. *Greens fees (for either course): $210 ($145 for resort guests); twilight rates $90 (times vary).*

Waikoloa Golf Club

You have two spectacular courses to choose from here: The beautiful, sporty par-70, 5,958-yard Beach Course is dramatically set in the lava, and it reflects designer Robert Trent Jones, Jr.'s, motto: "Hard par, easy bogey." Most golfers remember the par-5, 505-yard 12th hole, a sharp dogleg with bunkers in the corner and an elevated tee surrounded by lava. Designed by Tom Weiskopf and Jay Morrish, the par-72, 7,074-yard Kings' Course is a links-style challenge — and a real shot maker's course — with six major lakes and about 75 bunkers that often come into play thanks to ever-present trade winds. Facilities include golf shop, restaurant, practice facility, and golf academy.

See map p. 368. In the Waikoloa Resort, 18 miles north of Kona Airport. ☎ **877-924-5656** *or 808-886-7888.* www.waikoloabeachresort.com. *Greens fees: $195 ($130 for Waikoloa resort guests); $180 for 2-day access to both courses with Golf Hawaii Card.*

Waikoloa Village Golf Course

This semiprivate course on the slopes of Mauna Kea is a real gem, worth seeking out for its beautiful views, great game, and relatively affordable fees. Robert Trent Jones, Jr., designed this 5,490-yard challenge (with a par 72 for each of the three sets of tees) with his trademark sand traps, slick greens, and great fairways. Facilities include pro shop, putting and chipping greens, driving range, locker rooms with showers, restaurant, club rentals, and private instruction.

See map p. 368. On Waikoloa Road, Waikoloa Village (off Highway 19, 28 miles north of Kona Airport). To get there: Turn toward the mountain at the Waikoloa Road traffic light; go 6 miles up the mountain and turn left at Paniolo Drive, and then take another immediate left onto Lua Kula. ☎ *808-883-9621.* www.waikoloa.org/golf. *Greens fees: $80.*

Relaxing at the spa

As you might expect from an island with so many fabulous resort hotels, the Big Island boasts a wonderful collection of spas.

My favorite — perhaps my favorite in all of Hawaii — is the **Mauna Lani Spa,** 68-1365 Pauoa Rd., in the Mauna Lani Resort (☎ **808-881-7922;** www.maunalani.com). Set almost entirely outside and within simple thatched-roof *hales,* this glorious island-style retreat has bathed in accolades: It was named number-one spa in Hawaii and number three in the U.S. by readers of *Conde Nast Traveler* magazine in 2008, and *Travel + Leisure* has called it one of the world's best. Therapies run the gamut from the expected menu of massages and facials to tranquil watsu in a lava-rock, saltwater pool. If you're a spa fan, don't miss it.

Another great choice on the Kohala Coast is the **Spa Without Walls** at the Fairmont Orchid Hawaii, 1 N. Kaniku Dr., in the Mauna Lani resort (☎ **808-887-7540;** www.fairmont.com/orchid). For the ultimate in relaxation, consider the outdoor Awa Earth and Fire treatment, which starts with a Hawaiian-style lomilomi massage with warm coconut oil, followed by a relaxing treatment during which Hawaiian medicinal herbs are compressed into your skin with a warm lava stone to rub any remaining mainland tension away.

Should you find yourself in Volcano and in need of a pampering treatment, seek out **Hale Hoola,** 11-3913 7th St., Volcano Village (☎ **808-756-2421;** www.halehoola.net). The lomilomi massage is to die for, and the prices are reasonable.

Shopping the local stores

For such a rural island, the Big Island has a shockingly good shopping scene. Big Island–based artists and artisans generate some of the best art and crafts in Hawaii, from traditional lauhala weaving (rare to find) to gorgeous koa-wood gifts. But you do need to venture past Kailua-Kona to find it.

Kailua-Kona and South Kona

Kailua-Kona is a carnival of T-shirts, tacky trinkets, and silly souvenirs, with a little beachwear and a few quality gift items thrown into the mix for good measure. **Alii Drive** is the heart of the action; all you need to do is start at one end and browse. The best of what's on offer can be found at the **Kona Inn Shopping Village,** in the heart of town on the ocean side of the road, where one standout among the 50-plus shops is the **Honolua**

Surf Co. (☎ 808-329-1001; www.honoluasurf.com), which has my favorite surf wear in the islands.

Hilo Hattie, Hawaii's biggest name in aloha wear, has an outpost in Kailua-Kona at 75-5597A Palani Rd. (at Kuakini Highway, next to Burger King; ☎ 808-329-7200; www.hilohattie.com). Hilo Hattie is geared to the tourist market, carrying inexpensive, colorful wear that has improved in quality and style in recent years, plus a wide selection of souvenirs like macadamia nuts and Hawaii-grown coffees.

Upcountry Kona: Holualoa

One of my favorite places to shop in all Hawaii is the artsy, funky Upcountry village of Holualoa, sitting 1,400 feet above Kailua-Kona on the slopes of Hualalai mountain. To get there, head south from Palani Road on Highway 11; turn up the mountain at the clearly marked Hualalai Road turnoff. The curving 3-mile drive up the mountain takes about ten minutes; after you reach the top, turn left on Mamalahoa Highway, the coffee country town's gallery-lined main street.

The first shop you'll reach, even before you make the turn onto Mamalahoa Highway, is **Kimura's Lauhala Shop** (☎ 808-324-0053), where the dying Hawaiian art of lauhala weaving still thrives, thanks to Kimura's group of weavers. Look carefully, however, to separate the island-made crafts from the increasing number of Polynesian imports.

Farther along Mamalahoa Highway, the highlights include the **Holualoa Gallery** (☎ 808-322-8484; www.lovein.com/holualoagalleryblue. htm), which showcases original works by a bevy of local fine painters, sculptors, photographers, and jewelers. The **Studio 7 Gallery** (☎ 808-324-1335), a wonderful multiroomed Japanese-style gallery, showcases prints, sculpture, multimedia art, jewelry, and gorgeous pottery and crafts, all with the signature Asian simplicity of artist Hiroki Morinoue.

My favorite gallery in a sea of terrific ones is **Dovetail Gallery and Design** (☎ 808-322-4046), a gorgeous plantation-style building housing a well-curated collection of the island's most exceptional crafts, from hand-turned bowls of rare island woods and hand-painted silks to jewelry, woodcuts, and more. Nearby is the **Holualoa Ukulele Gallery** (☎ 808-324-4100; www.konaweb.com/ukegallery). Another notable stop, the **Shelly Maudsley White Gallery** (☎ 808-322-5220; www.shellymaudsley white.com), focuses on the bold tropical-themed works of a local artist, and the **Ipu Hale Gallery** (☎ 808-322-9069) has virtually single-handedly resurrected the traditional art of gourd carving — a must for fans of indigenous art forms.

If all this top-quality shopping makes you hungry, stop into the **Holuakoa Café** (☎ 808-322-2233) for well-prepared sandwiches, salads, tropical smoothies, and 100 percent Kona joe.

Kohala Coast

Probably the finest one-stop shopping on the island is the **Waikoloa Kings' Shops** (www.waikoloabeachresort.com) an open-air shopping complex at 250 Waikoloa Beach Dr. in the Waikoloa Resort. Highlights include **Blue Ginger** (☎ 808-886-2020; www.blueginger.com), for comfortable and stylish island-style batik wear for women and kids; **Kubuku** (☎ 808-886-8581), for the islands' best selection of gorgeous, creative pareu (also known as sarongs), many of them custom made for the shop; and **Walking in Paradise** (☎ 808-886-2600), for shoes that emphasize both style and comfort. You'll also find such familiar names as **Coach, Louis Vuitton,** and **Tommy Bahama.**

Waikoloa now has a second shopping complex just across the street called the **Waikoloa Queens' MarketPlace,** but I'm generally disappointed with the quality of the shops there.

Giving the Kings' Shops a serious run for its money are the **Mauna Lani Shops** at the Mauna Lani resort (www.shopsatmaunalani.com). Highlights include **Jourabchi** (☎ 808-885-0040), home to gorgeous women's island-style evening wear (and an excellent collection of evening bags) and some of the finest quality men's aloha wear on the market. There's also **Tori Richard by Quiet Storm** (☎ 808-885-4978) for Tori Richard's own understated, upscale aloha wear for men and women; I particularly like the men's line. Also check out **Oasis Lifestyle** (☎ 808-885-8795), specializing in relaxed women's fashions (perfect for the island lifestyle) as well as a creative mix of homewares and jewelry, all attractively displayed. The bigger names are more limited here, but you will find Mauna Lani's own **Tommy Bahama Emporium,** this one featuring one of their winning cafes.

North Kohala

If you're interested in high-quality Hawaiian crafts, especially those made of gorgeous island woods — of which native koa wood is the most highly prized — head up the Akoni Pule Highway (Highway 270) to the North Kohala towns of **Hawi** (*ha*-vee) and **Kapaau** (ka-*pa*-ow). Both towns are worth browsing, and all the stops are right along the highway.

As you shop around the islands, you'll see gorgeous koa-wood boxes, vessels, furniture, and accessories in finer galleries. Prices are high (a small keepsake box can easily run more than $100) thanks to a quickly diminishing supply of the wood. The Big Island has the finest koa craftsmen, because it's home to the largest existing stand of koa.

If you don't mind shelling out big bucks for heirloom-quality crafts carved from koa and other woods, visit the **Ackerman Gallery** in Kapaau (☎ 808-889-5971; www.ackermangalleries.com). Boasting the best selection of woodcrafts in the islands, as well as Gary Ackerman's own Impressionist-style paintings, it's worth a look even if you can't buy. The second location, a little farther up the street across from the King

Kamehameha Statue, is a lovely gift gallery with more affordable wood crafts, plus home accessories and jewelry. (I bought a string of Hawaii-strung Japanese black pearls on my last visit.)

Another excellent stop in Kapaau is the **Kohala Book Shop,** 54–3885 Akoni Pule Hwy. (☎ **808-889-6400;** www.kohalabooks.com), Hawaii's largest used bookstore and one of the most browsable bookshops in the islands, featuring everything from rare out-of-print editions to new books by Hawaii authors to gently used beach reads.

Waimea

Waimea has a bit of offbeat shopping that's worth seeking out. I really like **Antiques By . . .,** housed in a white clapboard cottage at 65-1275 Kawaihae Rd. (☎ **808-887-6466**). There is a wealth of Hawaii-themed treasures to be found. Prices tend to be high, but negotiable.

I'm also intrigued by **Hooked Gallery,** across the street at 65-1298 Kawaihae Rd. (☎ **808-987-0072;** www.hookedgallery.com), which specializes in jewelry and art. I'm not much taken by the art collection, but the selection of New Zealand jade jewelry, Niihau shell leis, and vintage pieces is quite remarkable. Be sure to negotiate.

I also like the **Gallery of Great Things** at Parker Square, 65-1279 Kawaihae Rd. (☎ **808-885-7706;** www.galleryofgreatthingshawaii.com), a warm and friendly gallery chock-full of Hawaiian, Polynesian, and Asian treasures, from primitive to contemporary.

Also make a stop at **Dan De Luz's Woods,** 64–1013 Mamalahoa Hwy., down the road from Parker Center and next to the Lex Brodie tire dealership (☎ **808-885-5856;** www.deluzwoods.com). Dan is a master craftsman who turns some of the finest koa and Norfolk pine bowls in the business; masterworks by other artisans are also shown in the unpretentious showroom.

Hilo

Boasting an appealing mix of fine and funky shops, this charming city is a wonderful place to browse. Shopping is centered in the wooden storefronts along oceanfront Kamehameha Avenue, on Keawe Avenue 1 parallel block inland, and on the side streets in between. Note that many of Hilo's shops are closed on Sunday, so plan accordingly.

 If you want to come home with just one article of aloha wear, buy it at **Sig Zane,** 122 Kamehameha Ave. (☎ **808-935-7077;** www.sigzane.com), whose distinctive, two-color, all-cotton aloha wear is the height of simple style and good taste. The stunningly beautiful fabrics are sold in a variety of clean-lined, easy-to-wear styles, and even off the bolt if you want to take some home. I can't recommend this marvelous shop enough. The leather goods are gorgeous, too.

Aloha-wear queen **Hilo Hattie** has a second Big Island outpost at Prince Kuhio Plaza, 111 E. Puainako St., at Highway 11 in Hilo (☎ **808-961-3077;** www.hilohattie.com) — but if you're going to buy aloha wear while you're in Hilo, I recommend Sig Zane.

Basically Books, 160 Kamehameha Ave. (☎ **800-903-MAPS** or 808-961-0144; www.basicallybooks.com), is your stop for all kinds of Hawaii books and maps. Other Hilo favorites include **Hanahou,** 164 Kamehameha Ave. (☎ **808-935-4555**), for an eye-catching collection of Hawaii-style gifts, both vintage and new, precious and affordable; **The Grove Gallery,** 302 Kamehameha Ave. (☎ **808-961-4420;** www.the grovegallery.com), for a clever collection of island art and crafts; **Dreams of Paradise Gallery,** 308 Kamehameha Ave. (☎ **808-935-5670;** www.dreamsofparadisegallery.com), for a good selection of island-made art; **Koehnen's Interiors,** 76 Kamehameha Ave. (☎ **808-961-4725;** www.koehnens.com), for gorgeous island-style furnishings, which can be shipped back to the mainland; **Burgado's Fine Woods,** in the S. Hata Building at 308 Kamehameha Ave. (☎ **808-969-9663**), for koa-wood crafts and gifts, both affordable and pricey; and **Dragon Mama,** 266 Kamehameha Ave. (☎ **808-934-9081;** www.dragonmama.com), for Asian home wares and textiles, from tatami mats to buckwheat pillows to antique kimonos and much more, all gorgeous.

In the Volcano area

On Highway 11, the road from Hilo to Volcano, you'll find another outpost of **Dan De Luz's Woods** just past mile marker 12 in the town of Mountain View (take the first right past the mile marker; ☎ **808-935-5587;** www.deluzwoods.com), where the master bowl turner creates gorgeous works in koa, sandalwood, mango, and other island woods.

While you're at Hawaii Volcanoes National Park, take a few minutes to stop into the **Volcano Art Center Gallery,** next to the Kilauea Visitor Center (☎ **808-967-7565;** www.volcanoartcenter.org), a marvelous showcase for some of the island's best artists and craftspeople, and a real delight to browse.

Also seek out **Volcano Garden Arts,** 19-3834 Old Volcano Rd., Volcano Village (☎ **808-985-8979;** www.volcanogardenarts.com). This utterly charming farmhouse-turned-gallery is the domain of multimedia artist Ira Ono, and features both his attractive works and those of the artists and artisans from throughout Hawaii and the Pacific, with a few treasures from Southeast Asia in the mix. Many of the pieces are quite affordable. The garden is reason enough alone to visit.

Living It Up after Dark

This marvelous island has a wealth of stuff to see and do — more than you can take in during the course of a single vacation — but it all tends to come to a screeching halt at sunset.

Your best source for finding out what's going on around town, especially if you're interested in live music, is the free weekly *Hawaii Island Journal*.

If you're staying on the west side of the island, make sunset the highlight of your evening with a leisurely dinner at an oceanfront restaurant. The waterfront restaurants in Kailua-Kona all make great sunset perches, as do the Kohala Coast resorts, which offer beachfront spots for sunset cocktails and dinner. See Chapter 14 for recommendations. **Huggo's** is a great place to maximize in-town sunset fun, while **Don's Mai Tai Bar at Don the Beachcomber** serves up the perfect mai tai in a glorious oceanside setting. You'll find that all of Kailua-Kona town boasts a party-hearty atmosphere in the evenings.

On the Kohala Coast, the Hilton Waikoloa Beach's **Malolo Lounge** (☎ 808-886-1234; www.hiltonwaikoloavillage.com) is a wonderful setting, designed to evoke the classic steamships of the 1920s. Drop in for sunset cocktails or live jazz nightly, from 9 p.m. to midnight.

In South Kona, drop by the **Keauhou Shopping Center** (www.keauhou-resort.com), which is home to a multiplex movie theater. You'll also find **Drysdale's Two** (☎ 808-322-0070), a casual bar and grill that's popular with the locals. If there's a big game being played on the mainland, you can catch it here on the giant screens — would you expect anything less from a place named after Dodger great Don Drysdale? Also consider the oceanside **Crystal Blue** bar at the Sheraton Keauhou Bay Resort and Spa, 78-128 Ehukai St. (☎ 808-930-4900; www.sheratonkeauhou.com), which overlooks an area of ocean where manta rays love to congregate after dark, making this a great place for cocktails and pupus.

A top sunset draw on the Kona Coast is **Captain Beans' Polynesian Cruises** (☎ 800-831-5541 or 808-329-2955; www.robertshawaii.com/big-island/capt-beans-dinner-cruise.php). This two-hour sunset cruise sails from Kailua Pier nightly and features dinner, dancing, and a full-scale Polynesian revue aboard a 150-foot catamaran. It's really cheesy, but lots of fun nonetheless. Tickets are $56 to $64 for adults ($32–$40 for kids 4–11) and include your meal, cocktails, the show, and transportation to and from most hotels and condos on the Kona-Kohala coast.

You can save 10 percent by booking your Captain Beans cruise online.

Substantially less touristy are the sunset cruises that **Red Sail Sports** (☎ 877-RED-SAIL or 808-886-2876; www.redsailhawaii.com) operates aboard its 50-foot catamaran, the *Noa Noa,* from Anaehoomalu Bay at the Waikoloa resort on the Kohala Coast. The two-hour sail costs $84 for adults, $51 for kids 3 to 12, including appetizers and a full bar. *An extra plus:* You're likely to spot humpback whales in the winter whale-watching season. A Dinner Sail Cruise leaves at the same time and is a few more dollars.

If you're looking for entertainment that's more culturally enriching, see what's on at the **Kahilu Theatre,** just a half-hour's drive from the Kohala Coast resorts on Highway 19 in Waimea (☎ **808-885-6868;** www.kahilu theatre.org), the island's home for theater, dance, live music, and the performing arts. Entertainment can range from local music masters the Brothers Cazimero (who are well worth catching) to the Dirty Dozen Brass Band to the Kronos Quartet to the Beijing Modern Dance Company. There's also an artsy movie theater attached.

Of course, for the most animated after-dark entertainment, head to — you guessed it — a luau! The Big Island has an excellent Friday-night option; check out Chapter 14 for more information.

 If the volcano is acting up and you're staying on the east side of the island, it's the best show in town. Nighttime is the right time to see the lava pumping — so get yourself to Hawaii Volcanoes National Park and ask the rangers where's the best place for lava watching. See the complete park section earlier in this chapter for details.

Part VI
Kauai

The 5th Wave   By Rich Tennant

In this part . . .

With its lush, tranquil landscapes, sleepy, seductive Kauai is simply one of the most beautiful places on earth. In these chapters, you discover everything this lush and lovely island has to offer, from pristine white-sand beaches to dramatic seaside cliffs to gorgeous tropical gardens.

Chapter 16

Settling into Kauai

In This Chapter

▶ Landing at Lihue Airport and getting to your accommodations
▶ Finding your way around Kauai
▶ Choosing among the island's top accommodations
▶ Discovering Kauai's best restaurants
▶ Arranging for a luau

Kauai is an easygoing, and easily manageable, island. You'll need a rental car to get around, so plan on booking one before you arrive (see Chapter 6). No matter where you're coming from, you'll arrive at Kauai's Lihue (li-*hoo*-ay) Airport.

Arriving at Lihue Airport

Lihue Airport (☎ 808-246-1448; www.hawaii.gov/dot/airports/kauai/lih) sits on Kauai's eastern shore just north of Lihue town, at the end of Ahukini Road (east of Kuhio Highway). Interisland service is provided by **Hawaiian Airlines** and **go! Airlines.** In addition, some transpacific carriers offer direct service to Kauai, including **Alaska Airlines, American Airlines, Hawaiian Airlines, United Airlines,** and **US Airways.**

Open-air Lihue Airport is very small and easy to negotiate. The major rental-car companies have service counters directly across the street from the terminal (in the wooden hut), but you'll take a shuttle van off-site to actually pick up your car. All the rental-car agencies offer map booklets that are invaluable for getting around the island.

 Car-rental lots for National, Alamo, and Thrifty are located significantly off-site from the airport in a poorly signed area that can make returning your rental a challenge. If there is no price repercussion, I suggest booking with another firm.

Kauai Orientation

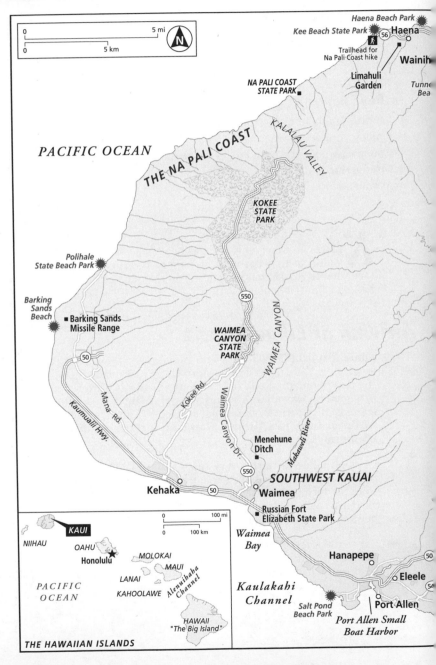

THE HAWAIIAN ISLANDS

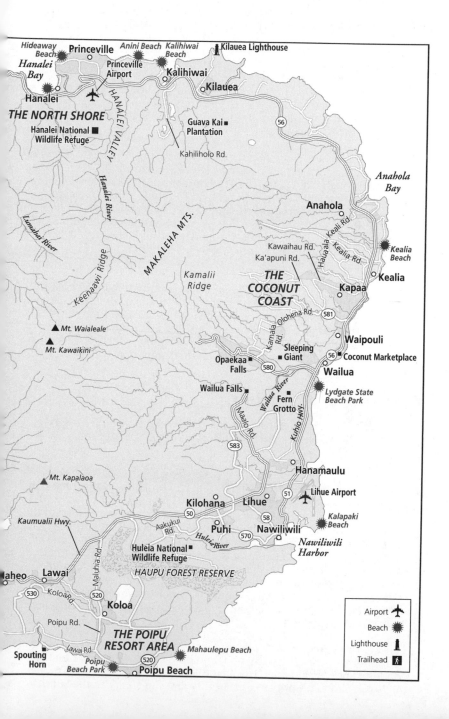

Getting from the Airport to Your Hotel

If you're heading to the Coconut Coast or the North Shore, turn right immediately out of the airport onto Kapule Highway (Highway 51), which eventually merges into Kuhio Highway (Highway 56) a mile down the road. Kuhio Highway leads to the Coconut Coast and the North Shore. Expect the trip to take 10 to 15 minutes if you're headed for the Coconut Coast, and about an hour if you're staying in Princeville or Hanalei on the North Shore.

If you're heading to Poipu Beach or Waimea, follow Ahukini Road out of the airport and turn left onto Kuhio Highway (Highway 56), which will take you through Lihue. Stay in the right lane; in less than a mile, merge right onto Kaumualii Highway (Highway 50), which will take you to the south and southwest areas of the island. The highway doesn't follow the coast, however, so if you're heading to Poipu, turn left on Maluhia Road (Highway 520); it's about 10 miles from where you picked up Highway 50. You can expect about a half-hour trip to reach Poipu; getting to Waimea takes 45 minutes or so.

If, for some reason, you don't have a car, taxis are available at curbside; however, if you know that you're going to need a taxi when you arrive, I recommend arranging one in advance with **Kauai Taxi Company** (☎ 808-246-9554; www.kauaitaxico.com). Expect the fare to cost about $48 to reach Poipu, $25 to $28 to reach a Coconut Coast destination, or $80 to $100 to reach a North Shore destination.

Choosing Your Location

Kauai has three major resort areas: The Coconut Coast, on the East Shore; the North Shore; and Poipu Beach, on the South Shore.

The Coconut Coast

Of all Kauai's resort areas, the island's East Shore makes the most convenient base for exploring the island. The Coconut Coast is just a 10- to 15-minute drive north of **Lihue** (li-*hoo*-ay), Kauai's largest town and the center of island life and commerce, which means that lots of conveniences are right at hand. It's also at the midpoint of the main highway, which connects the North Shore to the South Shore, so it couldn't be more centrally located for sightseeing and beach hopping. A gorgeous mountain backdrop and leftover island-style plantation buildings help to make what could have been a suburban-generic resort coast actually rather charming. And the region's main beach, Lydgate State Beach Park, is a winner.

This area is geared toward value-conscious travelers. Your accommodations choices here are mostly mid- and budget-priced family-friendly condos. However, although the East Shore doesn't get as much rain as the North Shore, it's not as consistently dry and sunny as the South

Shore, either; in winter, you should expect a bit more rain than you
might get in Poipu. Also expect more traffic and noise than what you'd
find in Poipu. On my last trip, I was surprised to encounter some honest-
to-goodness traffic jams in this area.

The North Shore

Kauai's North Shore is as breathtaking as Hawaii gets. It boasts a string
of stunning beaches; two charming towns, **Hanalei** and **Kilauea;** lush
fields of taro as far as the eye can see; and cliffs so beautiful that they
starred as Bali Hai in the film version of *South Pacific.* A sophisticated
and well-manicured resort, **Princeville,** is tucked away on a peninsula
bluff so that you can enjoy it or ignore it as you see fit. No place on the
island is as soothing to the spirit as this verdant, almost magical coast.

So why don't I tell everyone to stay up here, you ask? First of all, the
North Shore is quite removed; Lihue is a full hour's drive away. Second,
the number of accommodations choices is limited. Third, the North
Shore gets lots of rain, especially in winter. Another turnoff is the winter
surf, which can be too turbulent for most swimmers.

Still, the North Shore's stunning natural beauty more than makes up for
its shortcomings, and I highly recommend staying here. Your best bet is
to come in summer or fall, when the weather is usually excellent. Choose
Princeville if you like world-class golf and spa offerings. If resorts aren't
for you, try a B&B or vacation rental in island-charming Hanalei, Kilauea,
Anini Beach, or **Haena.** But if you stay elsewhere, you should set aside at
least a full day to drive here and explore.

The South Shore: Poipu Beach

Excellent year-round weather, great beaches, a wealth of ocean activities, terrific golf and tennis, and an easy-access location make Poipu
Beach a terrific place to stay. This is Kauai's all-around best choice in
terms of convenience, climate, activities, and natural beauty. You can't
go wrong here, no matter what your budget or what kind of accommodations you're looking for.

The beach is particularly family-friendly, and the whole area is surprisingly relaxing considering its popularity. It's one of Hawaii's best resort
areas, simply because it hasn't been overdeveloped. And although Poipu
may not be quite as breathtaking as the North Shore (what is?), its
sunny, vibrant setting — red earth, lush greenery, turquoise waves,
blond sand, clear blue skies — can hold its own in any natural-beauty
category. The only marks in the negative column are the 1½-hour drive
to the North Shore, and tiny Koloa, a one-horse plantation town that's a
bit too ticky-tacky for its own good.

Southwest Kauai: Kalaheo, Hanapepe, and Waimea

Just about a ten-minute drive inland and west from Poipu is **Kalaheo,** a
pleasantly quiet town offering some wallet-friendly, independent-style

accommodations as well as a more locals-only, nonresort location and affordable restaurants.

In a bend in the road a few minutes west of Kalaheo is **Hanapepe,** self-billed as "Kauai's Biggest Little Town." Hanapepe is finally beginning to realize its years-long potential as an arts community, with an increasing number of interesting galleries along its main street, Hanapepe Road. Hanapepe particularly comes alive during its weekly Friday-night art walk.

The southwest town of **Waimea** is a good 45 minutes from Lihue and nearly two hours from the North Shore. Not only is it sunny nearly year-round, but it's also home to one of my favorite places to stay, a charming group of fully restored plantation-era beachfront cottages that will charm the pants off even the most committed modernist. You should know, however, that you'll have to drive to the beach (the surf is rough at Waimea and isn't suitable for swimming), and you'll spend a lot of time in the car if you plan on exploring the island thoroughly. But one of the most beautiful spots on the island, Waimea Canyon, is nearby, as is the departure point for most Na Pali cruises.

Getting Around Kauai

You pretty much have to drive yourself around Kauai. The island has a public transportation system, **Kauai Bus** (☎ 808-241-6410; www.kauai. gov, click on "Transportation" then "Bus Schedules"), but it operates a minimal fleet and is geared to serving locals, not visitors. It provides only limited service to the resort areas, runs only during working hours Monday to Saturday, and you're not allowed to carry anything larger than a shopping bag onboard. Taxis are available; call **Kauai Taxi Company** (☎ 808-246-9554; www.kauaitaxico.com), but they're not really a viable means for regular transport, either.

Kauai is a compact island — only 25 miles long by 33 miles wide — and easy to navigate. Still, it does take some time to get around because no road cuts through the middle of the island, and no road goes all the way around, thanks to the impassable Na Pali Coast at the northwest corner of the island.

The island has two major highways, each beginning in Lihue, Kauai's biggest town and commercial hub. They each run basically around the perimeter of the island — one north, one south — dead-ending at the Na Pali Coast on each side. The entire drive, from end to end, takes about three hours.

The two major highways are

- ✔ **Kuhio Highway** (Highway 56), which follows the coast north from Lihue, leading through the Coconut Coast communities of Wailua, Waipouli, and Kapaa (ka-*pa*-ah) to the North Shore, where it passes by charming Kilauea (turn at the Shell Station, where the sign says

"Kilauea Lighthouse," if you want to explore) and, 5 miles beyond, the carefully manicured Princeville resort. Then (31 miles and about an hour's drive beyond Lihue) Kuhio Highway runs directly through Hanalei (probably my favorite little town in all Hawaii) and Haena (mostly homes and vacation rentals) before ending at Kee (*keh*-eh) Beach, where the Na Pali Coast begins.

✔ **Kaumualii** (cow-moo-a-*lee*-ee) **Highway** (Highway 50) heads south from Lihue, passing through Kalaheo (ka-la-*hay*-oh) and Hanapepe (ha-na-*pay*-pay) before reaching the little cowboy town of Waimea (where you can pick up the road that climbs inward and upward to Waimea Canyon; see Chapter 17 for details); at this point, you will have traveled 23 miles, or about 45 minutes, west of Lihue. After Waimea, the road curves north again before winding up in the far west at Polihale (po-lee-*ha*-lay) Beach, ending at the other side of the Na Pali Coast.

Highway 50 doesn't hug the coast like its northern counterpart — it runs roughly 4 miles inland until Hanapepe — so Maluhia Road (Highway 520) cuts south to reach Poipu (po-*ee*-poo) Beach, Kauai's most popular resort, about 10 miles west of Lihue.

 Kauai's traffic problems definitely aren't in the same league with places like Los Angeles (or even Honolulu, for that matter). Still, because the main highways have only one lane traveling in each direction, traffic can bottleneck in certain spots, especially along the Coconut Coast. The congestion has been getting notably worse in the past couple of years.

What's more, the roads are curvy (especially after you start heading toward the North Shore), and the speed limit doesn't top 50 mph anywhere on the island. So don't let the short distances fool you; it *will* take a full hour to reach the North Shore from Lihue, and 20 minutes or so longer if you're traveling the additional 8 miles beyond Hanalei. Allow 1½ hours to reach Hanalei from Poipu.

 Rates tend to be pretty reasonable on Kauai; in fact, this island features some of Hawaii's best lodging values. Still, Kauai is an increasingly popular destination, and travelers are booking rooms earlier and earlier each year. So try to reserve your accommodations as soon as possible to avoid missing out on your first choice.

Staying in Style

 Remember that you almost never need to pay the asking price for a hotel room. Check out Chapter 7 for details on how to avoid paying for full-price hotel rooms. Also see Chapter 5 for advice on how to score an all-inclusive package that can save you big bucks on both accommodations and airfare, and sometimes car rentals and activities too.

Kauai's Accommodations

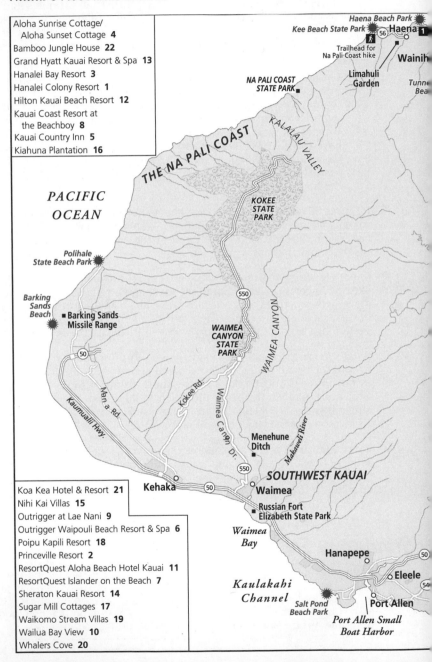

Aloha Sunrise Cottage/
  Aloha Sunset Cottage **4**
Bamboo Jungle House **22**
Grand Hyatt Kauai Resort & Spa **13**
Hanalei Bay Resort **3**
Hanalei Colony Resort **1**
Hilton Kauai Beach Resort **12**
Kauai Coast Resort at
  the Beachboy **8**
Kauai Country Inn **5**
Kiahuna Plantation **16**

PACIFIC
OCEAN

Haena Beach Park
Kee Beach State Park
Haena **1**
Trailhead for
Na Pali Coast hike
Wainih

NA PALI COAST
STATE PARK
Limahuli
Garden
Tunne
Bea

THE NA PALI COAST
KALALAU VALLEY

KOKEE
STATE
PARK

Polihale
State Beach Park

Barking
Sands
Beach
■ Barking Sands
Missile Range

550

WAIMEA
CANYON
STATE
PARK

WAIMEA CANYON

50
Kaumualii Hwy.
Mana Rd.
Kokee Rd.
Waimea Canyon Dr.

Makaweli River

Menehune
Ditch

550

SOUTHWEST KAUAI

Koa Kea Hotel & Resort **21**
Nihi Kai Villas **15**
Outrigger at Lae Nani **9**
Outrigger Waipouli Beach Resort & Spa **6**
Poipu Kapili Resort **18**
Princeville Resort **2**
ResortQuest Aloha Beach Hotel Kauai **11**
ResortQuest Islander on the Beach **7**
Sheraton Kauai Resort **14**
Sugar Mill Cottages **17**
Waikomo Stream Villas **19**
Wailua Bay View **10**
Whalers Cove **20**

Kehaka
50
Waimea
Russian Fort
Elizabeth State Park

Waimea
Bay

Hanapepe
50

Eleele
54

Kaulakahi
Channel
Salt Pond
Beach Park
Port Allen

Port Allen Small
Boat Harbor

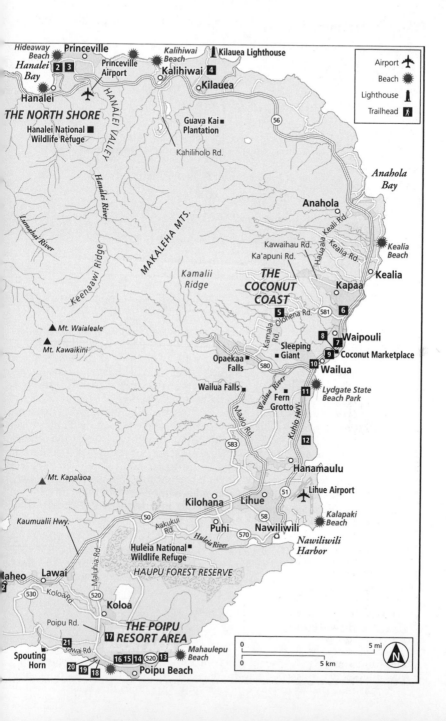

Airport ✈
Beach ☀
Lighthouse ⚲
Trailhead 🚶

Hideaway Beach
Princeville
Hanalei Bay
2 **3** Princeville Airport
Hanalei
THE NORTH SHORE
Hanalei National Wildlife Refuge ■
Lamahai River
Keenaaiwi Ridge
Hanalei River
HANALEI VALLEY
Kalihiwai Beach
Kalihiwai
Kilauea Lighthouse ⚲
4
Kilauea
Guava Kai ■ Plantation
Kahiliholo Rd.
56
Anahola Bay
Anahola
Kawaihau Rd.
Ka'apuni Rd.
Hanalei Keali Rd.
Kealia Rd.
Kealia Beach ☀
Kealia
MAKALEHA MTS.
Kamalii Ridge
THE COCONUT COAST
Kapaa
581
5 Olohena Rd. **6**
▲ Mt. Waialeale
▲ Mt. Kawaikini
Opaekaa ■ Falls
Kamala Rd.
Sleeping ■ Giant
580
8 **7** **Waipouli**
9 ■ Coconut Marketplace
10 **Wailua**
Wailua Falls ■
Wailua River
Fern Grotto
11 Lydgate State Beach Park
Maalo Rd.
Kuhio Hwy.
583
12
▲ Mt. Kapalaoa
Hanamaulu
51
Lihue
Lihue Airport ✈
Kilohana
58
Kaumualii Hwy.
50
Aakukui Rd.
Puhi
570
Nawiliwili
Huleia River
Kalapaki Beach ☀
Nawiliwili Harbor
Huleia National ■ Wildlife Refuge
HAUPU FOREST RESERVE
aheo
Lawai
530
Koloa Rd.
Maluhia Rd.
520
Koloa
Poipu Rd.
17 **THE POIPU RESORT AREA**
21
Lawai Rd.
16 **15** **14** 520 **13**
Mahaulepu Beach ☀
Spouting Horn ■
20 **19** **18**
Poipu Beach

0 _____ 5 mi
0 _____ 5 km
N

Also, don't forget that pesky 11.42 percent in taxes that the state adds to your hotel bill.

You may also want to check with **Hawaii Beachfront Vacation Homes** (☎ **808-247-3637;** www.hibeach.com).

Kauai's best accommodations

In the following listings, each property is followed by a number of dollar signs, ranging from one ($) to five ($$$$$). Each represents the median rack-rate price range for a double room per night, as follows:

$	Cheap — less than $150 per night
$$	Still affordable — $150–$225
$$$	Moderate — $225–$325
$$$$	Expensive but not ridiculous — $325–$450
$$$$$	Ultraluxurious — more than $450 per night

Aloha Sunrise Cottage/Aloha Sunset Cottage
$$ North Shore (Kilauea)

These two darling North Shore cottages are ideal for independent-minded couples with a yen for natural beauty and seclusion. Hidden away near Kilauea on 7 farmlike acres blooming with fruit trees and flowers, each vacation rental is a beautifully outfitted and utterly charming 700-square-foot tropical-style home. Each cottage comes complete with full kitchen, dining table for two, lanai overlooking the expansive lawn and gardens, washer/dryer, VCR with video library (there's no TV reception), stereo with CD player, wireless Internet, barbecue, beach supplies, and more. There's no A/C, but you're highly unlikely to need it. The Aloha Sunset Cottage is on one level, with a spacious master bedroom and a petite but pristine bathroom. The Aloha Sunrise Cottage is on two levels, with the bedroom and living room upstairs and the eat-in kitchen and bath down. The innkeepers are gracious hosts, and are happy to offer you any advice you need. Dining, shopping, and fabulous beaches are a pleasant drive away. A simply delightful choice, especially for romance-seekers. Not appropriate for families with children.

See map p. 424. 4899-A Waiakalua St., Kilauea. ☎ ***888-828-1008** or 808-828-1100.* www.kauaisunrise.com *or* www.kauai-sunset.com. *Parking: Free. Rack rates: $230 cottage; $1,635 per week. 3-night minimum stay, plus 1-time $95 out-cleaning fee. No credit cards.*

Bamboo Jungle House
$–$$ Kalaheo

Lucy and Terry Ryan, transplants from Cape Cod, have transformed what was once only a so-so bed-and-breakfast into one of the most impeccable and charming places to stay on the island. This charming plantation-style mini-estate has all of the hallmarks of a true tropical oasis. The U-shape of the structure creates a sense of secluded comfort; at its heart are a lap pool and a lava-rock Jacuzzi with its own waterfall that creates a soothing sound that pervades the compound. The three guest suites are tucked away in their own wing. Each is spotlessly maintained and boasts a comfortable queen-size bed draped in romantic netting, a well-outfitted private bathroom stocked with local-made toiletries, TV with cable, a CD player, wireless Internet access, and its own private lanai. My favorite is the Bamboo Garden Suite, which features a cozy sitting area and a well-outfitted kitchenette. The common areas are attractively outfitted and welcoming, and the breakfasts are deliciously prepared by chef Terry. Both Lucy and Terry are warm and friendly hosts more than willing to offer local information and advice. Lucy can also arrange for a to-die-for massage in their open-air gazebo; you'll pay a fraction of the cost that you would for an equivalent experience at the Hyatt's spa down the road. An ideal choice for those who want a genuinely local, off-the-beaten-path experience. Especially suitable for romance-seeking couples. The beach is about a ten-minute drive away.

See map p. 424. 3829 Waha Rd., Kalaheo. ☎ ***808-332-5515.*** www.kauai-bedand breakfast.com. *Parking: Free. Rack rates: $130–$160 double. 3- to 5-night minimum stay (depending on the room you choose), plus 1-time $35–$45 out-cleaning fee. MC, V.*

Grand Hyatt Kauai Resort & Spa
$$$$$ Poipu Beach

I have one big complaint about this hotel: I never get to stay here. It's always too full of contented vacationers who adore the high plantation style, the easygoing vibe, the big and beautiful rooms, the excellent service, and the pleasingly sunny South Shore location. The facilities are first-rate — especially the sigh-inducing, open-air 25,000-foot Anara Spa, one of the two best spas in the state. One of Hawaii's best luxury hotels, the Hyatt is fabulous in an understated way; everyone feels comfortable here. The oversize, elegant rooms feature rich wood furnishings, well-chosen tropical fabrics, luxurious marble bathrooms, and spacious lanais (most with ocean views). Because the ocean is rough here, the gorgeously landscaped grounds boast a mega–pool complex that's a total blast without being over-the-top, plus 5 acres of swimming lagoons (with islands and a man-made beach) that are perfect for learning to kayak.

The restaurants and lounges are elegant and satisfying across-the-board, particularly Dondero's for Italian and Tidepools for romantic open-air Pacific Rim–style dining. The kids' program is terrific, including evening "camp" sessions that allow Mom and Dad to enjoy a romantic dinner alone. The fitness center offers a good selection of equipment, plus an array of free classes, and there's also a tennis center with four courts. Next door is the Robert Trent Jones, Jr.–designed Poipu Bay Golf Course, home to the PGA Grand Slam of Golf. You won't want for anything here. It's perfect for honeymooners, families, everybody. Book well ahead.

See map p. 424. 1571 Poipu Rd., Koloa. ☎ *800-55-HYATT or 808-742-1234. Fax: 808-742-1557.* www.kauai-hyatt.com. *Parking: Valet and self-parking included in resort fee. Rack rates: $480–$755 double, $800–$1,200 club floor double; suite from $1,200. Mandatory "resort fee" of $15 per day for "free" local calls, access to the fitness center, parking, and other amenities. Special rates and packages usually on offer; ask about 6th night free; golf, spa, and romance packages; and other special deals, including discounts for AAA members, seniors, and government employees. AE, DC, DISC, MC, V.*

Hanalei Bay Resort
$$$ North Shore

This condo resort is a good North Shore choice, especially for families who require the space and comforts of home. It overlooks the same fabled Bali Hai cliffs and gorgeous golden beach as the ritzy Princeville Resort (see the listing later in this chapter), but for a substantial savings. The apartments boast plenty of room to spread out, plus rattan furnishings and big lanais; however, quality can vary (these are individually owned condos), so if you don't like the one you're assigned, ask to see an alternate unit. Hotel rooms and studios are a spacious 570 feet, while the one-bedrooms are a large 1,100 square feet and come with a fully outfitted kitchen; most also have their own washer/dryer and a DVD player in the living room, but you should inquire about the unit you are renting to avoid disappointment. (There is coin-op laundry available on property if yours doesn't boast its own.) The superlush, terraced grounds feature two terrific freshwater pools, Jacuzzis, and tennis courts, plus easy beach access. The restaurant is just fine, and the lounge is a stellar place to sip a sunset cocktail. The property is part timeshare, so beware; you will be invited to an "orientation" (read: sales) meeting, but you can ignore it.

See map p. 424. 5380 Honoiki Rd., Princeville. ☎ *800-827-4427 or 808-826-6522. Fax: 808-826-6680.* www.hanaleibayresort.com. *Parking: Free. Rack rates: $215–$305 double, $260 studio with kitchenette, $380–$420 1-bedroom suite. Always ask about AAA rates, packages, or other special offers (at press time, there was a 3-night special for $500). Also inquire about discounted greens fees at Princeville area golf courses. AE, DC, DISC, MC, V.*

Hanalei Colony Resort
$$$ North Shore

This small, quiet, low-rise condo resort is an extremely pleasant and affordable place to stay if you're looking to experience Kauai's pristine North Shore in all its lush, tranquil, end-of-the-road glory. It's well past Hanalei town, near the very end of the North Shore highway — perfect if you're looking to get away from it all, less than ideal if you're planning to do lots of exploring. The golden beach that fronts the property is okay, but some of Hawaii's best beaches and most celebrated stretches of sand are close by. The spacious two-bedroom apartments aren't luxurious, but they have recently undergone renovation, and they're very comfortable; some of the woodwork is a bit worn (an outcome of being this close to the sea), but the units are very nicely maintained. Pleasantly furnished in island style, each one has a lanai, a complete kitchen, ceiling fans (air-conditioning isn't necessary), and beautiful views. While the mountain views are nearly as fab as the ocean views, I recommend splurging on an ocean-view unit if you can; after all, this is why you came to Hawaii, right? Twice-a-week maid service is included, and a coin-op laundry is available. The atmosphere is quiet and relaxing — no TVs or phones to interfere with the waves and bird song. The Hanalei Day Spa offers massage, body wraps, yoga classes, and other treatments. Even the kids won't miss the TV; the resort has plenty of beach gear at hand, plus a pool, lawn and board games, and more to keep them happy. There's an appealing restaurant on-site with live entertainment most nights (complimentary wireless Internet access is only available here), plus a pleasant coffee shop next door. Al in all, a delightful place to get away from it all and recharge your batteries. ***Beware:*** The nearest grocery store or restaurant is a 15-minute drive away, so stock up on staples.

See map p. 424. 5–7130 Kuhio Hwy., Haena (2 miles past Hanalei town, near the end of the road). ☎ **800-628-3004** *or 808-826-6235. Fax: 808-826-9893.* www.hcr.com. *Parking: Free. Rack rates: $240–$420 2-bedroom condo. 7th night free; also ask about car-and-condo, honeymoon, and other package deals. AAA, government, senior, and return guests qualify for discounts. AE, MC, V.*

Hilton Kauai Beach Resort
$$$ Coconut Coast

This recent addition to Kauai's limited full-service hotel scene has its pros and cons. It has 350 guest rooms and suites spread over 25 lush, ocean-facing acres. There's a pool complex with two large pools and attractive waterfalls, plus a water slide and sand-bottomed children's pool for the kids, and great ocean views. The freshly renovated rooms are attractive and very comfortable, boasting Hilton's own Serenity bed, travertine marble in the well-appointed bathroom, its own lanai, and touches such as desk-level electrical outlets and curved shower rods. There's a nice spa and fitness center on-site, and the central location is five minutes from the airport and convenient to island attractions on both the north and south shores. However, this location isn't my favorite on the island; the beach is a pleasant place for strolling, but you'll have to drive to a swimmable one. Also, the hotel was converted to a Hilton from a cheaper property, so it doesn't live up to what I expect from a Hilton, and is certainly well below the standard maintained at the Oahu and Big Island properties. Still, it's a fine choice if you prefer a full-service hotel option and can't afford the Grand Hyatt or Princeville; I definitely prefer it over the nearby Marriott.

See map p. 424. 4331 Kauai Beach Dr., Lihue. ☎ **800-HILTONS [445-8667]** *or 808-245-1955. Fax: 808-246-9085.* www.hiltonfamilyhawaii.com *or* www.hilton.com. *Valet parking: $13. Self-parking: $10. Rack rates: $229–$359 double, $800–$1,200 club floor double; suite from $1,200. Optional "resort fee" of $13 per day for local and 800 calls, wireless Internet access, parking, and free coffee in the restaurant 6–7 a.m. Check for bed-and-breakfast specials, net-direct rates, and other special deals; rates from $170 at press time. AE, DC, DISC, MC, V.*

Kauai Coast Resort at the Beachboy
$$ Coconut Coast

This attractive low-rise hotel is a treat through and through for travelers who don't want to pay a fortune, but don't want to sacrifice a beachfront location, either. The sprawling grounds are as Hawaii should be, with swaying palms and expansive lawns leading to a narrow gold-sand beach that's perfect for romantic strolls and sunset watching (just down the road is Lydgate beach for swimming). Accommodations options are large studio-style double rooms or one- and two-bedroom condo-style units. The studio-style doubles feature a king bed, a compact fridge, a microwave, a coffeemaker, and a private lanai with garden view. The one- and two-bedrooms have complete kitchenettes with full-size fridge and dishwasher, plus a king bed in the master bedroom (as well as two twins in the second-bedroom units), a sleeper sofa, and a private lanai with either ocean or garden views. The warm-hued, island-style decor is quite attractive for the price range, and everything is well maintained. Facilities include a small but attractive pool with a waterfall, and a much-better-than-you'd-expect restaurant. The location is one of the finest on the Coconut Coast, central to both south and north shore attractions and adjacent to the Coconut Marketplace, whose shops and restaurants are within walking distance. All in all, a great mid-priced choice. The best value comes in the one-bedrooms, so book one if you can afford to do so.

520 Aleka Loop (at the Coconut Marketplace), Kapaa. ☎ *866-822-0843 or 808-822-3441. Fax 808-822-0843.* www.shellhospitality.com/hotels/kauai_coast_resort. *Parking: Free. Rack rates: $156–$180 double, $240–$300 1-bedroom; call for 2-bedroom rates. Substantial discounts available for 4-night-minimum stays (from $134 at press time). AE, DC, DISC, MC, V.*

Kauai Country Inn
$–$$ Coconut Coast (Kapaa)

Mike and Martina Hough traded in the L.A. rat race for the laid-back island lifestyle, carving out their own special farmland corner of Kauai as their newfound haven. Their Kauai Country Inn is the centerpiece of their 2-acre organic fruit and flower farm, situated 4 miles inland from Kapaa town and the island's Coconut Coast.

The main house features four vacation-rental suites with a private entrance and bathroom, plus a separate three-bedroom cottage. They're all thoughtfully outfitted in Hawaiian style; the one that's right for you will depend on your needs. My favorite is the Green Rose Suite, a spacious upstairs one-bedroom, one-bath suite with vaulted ceilings, hardwood floors, a well-outfitted full kitchen, a comfortable California king-size bed, and its own 500-square-foot lanai with barbecue. The Plumeria Suite is most notable for its big and beautiful bathroom with Jacuzzi tub, as well as its own kitchenette and spacious lanai with barbecue; this one can be converted to a large (1,200 sq. ft.) two-bedroom if your brood requires. The 1,200-square-foot, three-bedroom Country Cottage is best for families (it's the only accommodation that welcomes kids under 12), and a bargain considering the quality and generosity of the living space. The Orchid Suite is a beautiful bargain for wallet-watching couples. All accommodations feature TV with DVD player and their own computer with free Internet access (in all main-house suites), as well as free wi-fi. Beach equipment is on hand for guests, as are free laundry facilities.

The innkeepers are friendly and generous with advice on what to see and where to go. *Attention, Beatles fans:* Ask Mike to show you his private Beatles Museum, whose world-class collection of memorabilia includes Brian Epstein's own Mini Cooper S (open to guests of the inn only).

See map p. 424. 6440 Olohena Rd., Kapaa. ☎ *888-821-0207.* www.kauaicountry inn.com. *Parking: Free. Rack rates: $119–$169 double, $179 2-bedroom suite for 4, $249 3-bedroom cottage for up to 6. 4-night minimum stay; a $35 clean-out fee is added to the final bill. Additional per-person charge for extra guests. No children under 6. AE, MC, V.*

Kiahuna Plantation
$$$–$$$$ **Poipu Beach**

The only Poipu condos that sit right on the sand, this low-rise complex maintains an air of privacy and retro Hawaiian style. Two- and three-story plantation-style buildings pepper 35 spacious, beautiful, gardenlike acres fronting a wonderful stretch of swimmable beach. The individually decorated one- and two-bedroom apartments feature fully outfitted kitchens with microwave and dishwasher, daily maid service (not a given in condos), cooling ceiling fans, and private lanais. A coin-op laundry, barbecues, and a pleasant restaurant and bar are on-site, and a first-class tennis center with pool and another great restaurant (Casablanca, reviewed below), championship golf at the Poipu Bay Course, and Poipu Shopping Village are just across the street. Rack rates are high, but discounts abound; go with whichever of the two reliable management companies can score you the best rate. Outrigger units have free Internet access.

See map p. 424. 2253 Poipu Rd., Poipu Beach. **Outrigger Resorts:** ☎ *800-688-7444 or 808-742-6411. Fax: 808-742-1698.* www.outrigger.com. *Parking: Free. Rack rates: $285–$535 1-bedroom, $435–$585 2-bedroom. 2-night minimum. Better-than-average discounts for AAA and AARP members and seniors (50+), plus corporate, government, and military discounts. 1st-night-free, bed-and-breakfast, room-and-car, and other packages regularly on offer. AE, DC, DISC, MC, V.* **Castle Resorts:** ☎ *800-367-5004 or 808-742-2200. Fax: 808-742-1047.* www.castleresorts.com. *Parking: Free. Rack rates: $285–$420 1-bedroom, $465–$590 2-bedroom; request rates for oceanfront 2-bedroom. Check Web site for special Internet rates (from $199 at press time). Romance and room-and-car packages available, as well as senior and military discounts. AE, MC, V.*

Koa Kea Hotel & Resort
$$$$$ **Poipu Beach**

At this writing, the former Poipu Beach Hotel was on the brink of being reborn as the sleek and sophisticated Koa Kea Hotel and Resort — which, if it lives up to its heady promise, should be an exciting addition to a hotel scene that currently falls short in the modern-luxe category. The hotel will feature clean-lined, ultra-modern design with tropically inspired accents and ocean hues adding the appropriate island warmth. Expect such luxuries as 42-inch flatscreen high-definition TVs, iPod docking stations, plush beds with Italian linens, white-marble bathrooms with L'Occitane amenities, in-room espresso machines, and — of course — a spa.

2251 Poipu Rd., Poipu Beach. ☎ *877-806-2288 or 808-828-8888. Fax 808-332-5316.* www.koakea.com. *Parking: To be determined. Rack rates: $445–$725 double, from $1,625 suite. Inquire about fifth-night-free and breakfast-inclusive deals. AE, DC, DISC, MC, V.*

Nihi Kai Villas
$$–$$$ Poipu Beach

This beautifully maintained Mediterranean-style condo complex, just a block from the finest stretch of Poipu Beach, is an excellent choice on all fronts. It's lovingly and meticulously run, and the tropical-style condo-style apartments are gorgeous. You can choose a one-, two- or three-bedroom condo, ranging from 1,000 to 2,100 square feet. Each boasts a full kitchen (with microwave and dishwasher), ceiling fans, washer/dryer, full cable and VCR, CD player, lots of windows, and at least one lanai (usually two). Bedding is usually a king or queen in the master, with two twins in the extra bedrooms and a sleeper sofa in the living room, but there is some variation across units, since these are individually owned condos. (Most units have high-speed Internet access, but you should inquire to be sure that yours does when you book if you need it.) All units are maintained to a high standard. One of the things I like best is that you can go online, review pictures, features (many have ocean views), and quality level (they're honest about which ones have been recently renovated and which ones have not), and choose the one that best suits your family's needs and budget. The grounds are well landscaped and quiet, boasting two tennis courts, paddle ball, barbecues, and two nice pools. Best of all, world-class Poipu Beach is just a short walk away. There's no daily maid service, but I actually enjoyed it on my last stay; I didn't mind rinsing my own breakfast dishes, and I thoroughly enjoyed not having to worry about the intrusion. All in all, a delightful choice, with options for a range of budgets.

See map p. 424. 1870 Hoone Rd., Poipu Beach. ☎ *800-325-5701, 800-742-1412, or 808-742-2000; direct property phone* ☎ *808-742-1412. Fax: 808-742-9093.* www.parrishkauai.com. *Parking: Free. Rack rates: $145–$244 1-bedroom, $159–$625 2- or 3-bedroom. 5-night minimum stay. $50 non-refundable processing fee. Deals: Discounts on stays over 30 days. AE, DISC, MC, V.*

Outrigger at Lae Nani
$$$ Coconut Coast

I just love this pleasant and unpretentious tropical oceanfront condo complex. It's quiet, easygoing, and situated on a wonderful stretch of beach (and located near the shops and restaurants of the Coconut Marketplace). The individually decorated one- and two-bedroom apartments are comfortable and spacious (800 square feet at minimum), with large living rooms, adjacent dining areas, complete kitchens, cooling ceiling fans, TV with DVD player, and well-furnished lanais; all one-bedrooms and most two-bedrooms have ocean views. The two-bedroom/two-bathrooms can easily accommodate six, as long as two don't mind sleeping in the living room; even my one-bedroom unit had a second bathroom. The well-tended grounds feature a pool, tennis courts, barbecues, and a coin-op laundry, and daily maid service makes it feel like a real vacation. Not the best choice for those who require Internet access, because only dial-up is currently available.

See map p. 424. 410 Papaloa Rd. (next to the Coconut Marketplace), Kapaa. ☎ *800-688-7444 or 808-822-4938. Fax: 808-822-1022.* www.outrigger.com. *Parking: Free. Rack rates: $295–$355 1-bedroom, $315–$425 2-bedroom. 2-night minimum. Better-than-average discounts for AAA and AARP members and seniors (50+), plus corporate, government, and military discounts. 1st-night-free, bed-and-breakfast, room-and-car, and other packages regularly on offer; discounted rates from $215 at press time. AE, DC, DISC, MC, V.*

Outrigger Waipouli Beach Resort & Spa
$$$ Coconut Coast

This shiny new oceanfront condominium resort makes a simply wonderful place to stay. While there are a few standard hotel rooms, the bulk of the accommodations are large (900 to 1,850 sq. ft.) and quite luxurious one-, two- and three-bedroom condo units. With fully equipped designer kitchens (complete with granite counters, dishwashers, and Wolf and Sub-Zero appliances), washer/dryers and daily maid service, you'll enjoy the best of the full-service hotel and home-style living worlds. The decor is contemporary and attractive, and everything is fresh and new, including flatscreen TVs and big, attractive bathrooms. Free wireless Internet access is a nice perk for laptop toters. The heated salt-water pool meanders lagoon-like over two acres and features a terrific set of water slides, waterfalls, and a sandy-bottomed kids' pool; the expansive grounds also feature three whirlpool spas, a fitness center, and a very nice Aveda Spa and Salon. Book into building A or H for the finest views. Note that the beach is great for strolling and sunset watching, but you'll have to drive elsewhere to swim.

See map p. 424. 4-820 Kuhio Hwy., Kapaa. ☎ *800-688-7444 or 808-822-6000. Fax: 808-823-1420.* www.outrigger.com. *Parking: Free. Rack rates: $205 double, $295–$499 1-bedroom/2-bath suite, $425–$709 2-bedroom/3-bath suite. 2-night minimum stay. Deals: Better-than-average discounts for AAA and AARP members and seniors (50+), plus corporate, government, and military discounts. 1st-night-free, bed-and-breakfast, room-and-car, and other packages regularly on offer; from $175 at press time. AE, DC, DISC, MC, V.*

Poipu Kapili Resort
$$$ Poipu Beach

This quiet, upscale cluster of condos is outstanding in every way but one: The ocean is across the street and the nearest sandy beach is a block away, even though the waves are right out your window. Still, I love the home-away-from-home amenities and comforts in these very pleasing apartments, and I hear nothing but good things from those who choose to stay here. The beautifully manicured grounds feature an especially lovely pool, barbecues, tennis courts (lit for night play), and an herb garden (you're welcome to take samples to cook with). The tropical-style apartments are extra-large (one-bedrooms are 1,120 sq. ft., two-bedrooms are a massive 1,900–2,600 sq. ft.). All the one-bedrooms have two bathrooms, and most of the two-bedrooms have three bathrooms, making this an ideal place for family gatherings. The oceanfront two-story, two-bedroom town-house-style units are my favorites because they catch the trade winds. All units have full kitchens, ceiling fans, private lanais, VCRs, CD players, and free high-speed Internet access; the two-bedrooms also have washer/dryers (a coin-op laundry is on the grounds). Towels are changed three times a week, and weekly maid service is offered for longer stays. It's an excellent choice, especially if you want a tranquil, residential-style ambience. All of Poipu's perks, including beaches and restaurants, are a stone's throw away.

See map p. 424. 2221 Kapili Rd., Koloa. ☎ *800-443-7714 or 808-742-6449. Fax: 808-742-9162.* www.poipukapili.com. *Parking: Free. Rack rates: $230–$355 1-bedroom, $345–$480 2-bedroom, $500–$640 deluxe oceanview penthouse suites. 5-night minimum stay (10 nights at holiday time). Your 7th night is free May through mid-Dec. Ask about discounts for longer stays and discounted car-rental rates. Car-and-condo, golf, romance, senior, and other special packages often available. MC, V.*

Princeville Resort
$$$$$ North Shore

This stunning North Shore resort, a member of Starwood's Luxury Collection, is among Hawaii's very best; in fact, it's nearly faultless. The setting is breathtaking (you won't be surprised to learn it's the most popular site on Kauai for weddings), and the tiered hotel steps down the cliffs above Hanalei Bay to take spectacular advantage of the views. A subdued color palette and natural fibers strike the perfect note of comfortable island elegance. Grand and gorgeous public spaces lead to universally sizable rooms that come outfitted with eye-catching original art, oversize windows (no lanais, though), and bedside control panels for everything. Your oversize green-marble bathroom features double sinks and a huge soaking tub, plus a "magic" shower window that you can switch in an instant from opaque to clear, allowing you to take in those awesome views even as you shampoo.

The infinity pool is one of the state's finest and comes complete with a swim-up bar and always-attentive service. Just steps away is a golden-sand beach with a wonderful snorkel reef for beginners and well-practiced snorkelers alike; it remains well protected even when the winter waves kick up. Additional perks include world-class golf (the Prince Course is regularly named best in Hawaii by *Golf Digest*), a first-rate spa and fitness center, a tennis center, a kids' program, a resort shuttle, and excellent dining options. Service is impeccable. It's one of my all-time favorites; needless to say, you'll want for nothing here. Expensive, but divine.

See map p. 425. 5520 Ka Haku Rd., Princeville. ☎ **866-716-8110**, *866-500-8313, 800-325-3589, or 808-826-9644. Fax: 808-716-8110.* www.princevillehotelhawaii.com. *Valet or self-parking: $15. Rack rates: $600–$875 double, $1,000–$5,800 suite. Romance, room-and-car, 7th-night-free, and other packages often available. Endless Escape rates available from $445 at press time. Also inquire about AAA and senior discounts. AE, DC, DISC, MC, V.*

ResortQuest Aloha Beach Hotel Kauai
$$$ Coconut Coast

With a wonderful beachfront location, this former Holiday Inn resort is a good choice for families, or anybody looking for a reasonably priced vacation. What the resort lacks in personality it makes up for in moderate prices and amenities. It fronts Lydgate Beach, the best beach on the Coconut Coast, which has a playground and a protected natural pool that's ideal for young swimmers and first-time snorkelers. On-site extras include two pools, a Jacuzzi, a coin-op laundry, two just-fine restaurants, and a sunset-view lounge. The regular doubles are on the small side and could use some upgrading, so book a suite (with pullout sofa), or — even better — a free-standing family-size two-room beach cottage (with queen-size sleeper sofa in the living room and a kitchenette with a microwave and a toaster) if you're traveling with the kids. If you need to stick with a standard room to meet your budget, pick one with two queen-sized beds (rather than two doubles) — they're a bit larger. All in all, a reasonable beachfront place to stay if you're watching your wallet and can score a good deal, which you usually can.

See map p. 424. 3–5920 Kuhio Hwy., Kapaa. ☎ **888-823-5111** *or 808-823-6000. Fax: 808-823-6666.* www.alohabeachresortkauai.com. *Parking: Free. Rack rates: $250–$340 double or suite, $395–$405 beach cottage. You should never have to pay rack rate here. Available Web rates as low as $99 at press time (cottages from $189); AAA rates, senior rates, bed-and-breakfast and room-and-car packages also available; also inquire about discounts for stays of 7 nights or more. AE, DC, DISC, MC, V.*

ResortQuest Islander on the Beach
$$–$$$ Coconut Coast

This pleasant, plantation-style beachfront hotel complex is a great choice for value-minded travelers, especially if you can score one of the many packages and discounts that are usually there for the taking. The smallish rooms are fresh and attractive, with pretty textiles, firm beds, minifridges, and coffeemakers. (The oceanfront rooms have microwaves, too.) The nicely maintained property still looks attractive following a $10-million renovation a couple of years back. A good swimming beach, a pool and a hot tub, barbecue grills, a coin-op laundry, and the Coconut Marketplace just a stone's throw away add to its allure. Not luxurious, but a nice value. The only downside? Some of the rooms labeled "oceanview" are a stretch, so beware.

See map p. 424. 440 Aleka Place, Kapaa. ☎ **877-997-6667** *or 808-822-7417. Fax: 808-822-1947.* www.resortquest.com. *Parking: Free. Rack rates: $210–$300 double, $325 junior suite. Internet-only eSpecial rates as low as $173 at press time. Ask for*

AAA, senior (50+), and corporate discounts, 4th night free, and other special rate programs, plus air-inclusive packages. AE, DC, DISC, MC, V.

Sheraton Kauai Resort
$$$$$ Poipu Beach

This Sheraton is an excellent choice for visitors who like the advantages that a resort hotel can offer, but who don't care for the forced formality that often goes along with it. The resort brims with aloha spirit and an easygoing style that's reminiscent of old Hawaii. You have a choice of three buildings: one nestled in tropical gardens with koi-filled ponds; one facing a fabulous stretch of palm-fringed, white-sand beach (my favorite, of course); and one ocean-facing wing that boasts great sunset views. Whichever you choose, you'll get a spacious, comfortably decorated room with minifridge; most in the Ocean Wing have sofa beds, making them suitable for small families. Amenities include an oceanfront pool, a kids' pool, and a Jacuzzi; a fitness center with daily classes; tennis courts; a handful of restaurants (one child 12 or under eats free for each paying grown-up in Shells, the signature restaurant); and a glass-walled lounge featuring live Hawaiian music and sunset views. Rack rates are ridiculous, but specials abound.

See map p. 424. 2440 Hoonani Rd., Poipu Beach. ☎ *800-782-9488 or 808-742-1661. Fax: 808-742-4041.* www.sheraton-kauai.com *or* www.sheraton.com. *Valet parking: $8. Self-parking included in the resort fee. Rack rates: $420–$775 double, $800–$3,500 suite. Mandatory "resort fee" of $18 for "free" local and 800-access phone calls, use of the fitness center, wireless Internet access, self-parking, Hawaiian craft and hula lessons, and more. Promotional rates and/or package deals are almost always available, so be sure to ask; value rates from $199 at press time. Also ask about AAA and senior discounts. AE, DC, DISC, MC, V.*

Sugar Mill Cottages
$ Poipu Beach

Attention, shoestring travelers: This simple plantation-style complex of 12 petite studio apartments sits on a pleasant residential parcel that's part of the Poipu Kai resort complex just a five-minute stroll from Brennecke's Beach, everybody's favorite stretch of Poipu sand. Each studio for two boasts cooling slate floors, air-conditioning, an attractive bathroom (shower only), a kitchenette with all the tools to prepare a full meal, a dining table, a TV and VCR, and air-conditioning (almost unheard of at these low rates). Also request the kitchen that's right for you because they vary from petite to nearly full-size. Every three units share a free laundry room, and each unit has its own beach cooler, towels, chairs, mats, and toys, plus access to a swimming pool, a gas grill, and a tennis club with Jacuzzi. This is a simple but solid place to stay in a great neighborhood for budget travelers, but there's no on-site manager, so it's best for independent types. The cottages are available for rent through two agencies (see below), so be sure to price compare. Also, be sure to check Waikomo Stream Villas (see review below), and stay there if prices are similar, as you'll get more space for your money there.

See map p. 424. 2391 Hoohu Rd. (at Pe'e Road), Poipu Kai. Kauai Rents: ☎ *877-430-7543 or 330-317-1333. Fax: 330-262-2707.* www.kauai-rent.com/sugar-mill-poipu/sugar-mill-poipu.htm. *Parking: Free. Rack rates: $95–$149 double (single-night stay $185). AE, DC, DISC, MC, V. Suite Paradise:* ☎ *800-367-8020 or 808-742-7400.* www.suite-paradise.com *(click on "Poipu Kai Studio Cottages"). Rack rates: $86–$131 double. Car-inclusive packages from $137 per night at press time. AE, DC, MC, V.*

Waikomo Stream Villas
$ Poipu Beach

Here's a real gem, perfect for families or anyone hoping for all the comforts of home at bargain-basement prices. These huge (1,100–1,500 sq. ft.), well-managed, and attractive one- and two-bedroom apartments have everything that you could possibly need — fully equipped kitchen, VCR (plus DVD in most), CD player, high-speed Internet access, ceiling fans, a king-size or queen-size bed in the master bedroom and a sofa bed in the living room, washer/dryer, and private lanai, plus a second bathroom and cathedral ceilings in the two-bedrooms — at *very* affordable prices. One of the things I like best is that you can go online, review pictures and quality level (they're honest about which ones have been recently renovated or upgraded to a premium level, and which ones have not), and choose the one that best suits your family's needs and budget. The beautifully landscaped complex boasts both adults' and kids' pools, tennis courts, and a barbecue area; right next door is the Kiahuna Golf Course, designed by Robert Trent Jones, Jr., so pack your irons and woods. The beach is a seven-minute walk away — a worthy sacrifice for the kind of savings you'll realize here. Value-conscious travelers who need their space can't do better for the dough. No daily maid service, but for the savings that you get here, you won't mind pulling the blanket up on the bed or washing your own breakfast dishes.

At press time, 15 percent discounts were being offered in order to compensate for nearby daytime road construction and new development. Guests report that the construction isn't disruptive, especially if you're the type to be out all day, and it may very well be complete by the time you arrive. If you're concerned, I recommend that you call ahead and check on the status (the kind folks at Parrish will be honest with you), and ask for recommendations for a unit away from any current noise.

See map p. 424. 2721 Poipu Rd., Poipu Beach. ☎ *800-325-5701, 800-742-1412, or 808-742-2000. Fax: 808-742-9093.* www.parrishkauai.com. *Parking: Free. Rack rates: $105–$189 1- or 2-bedroom. 5-night minimum stay (7 nights in some units). $50 non-refundable processing fee. Discounts on stays over 30 days. AE, DISC, MC, V.*

Wailua Bay View
$$ Coconut Coast

These one-bedroom, one-bathroom apartments on the beach aren't fancy, but they offer a wonderful value if your budget is tight. Every apartment has at least a partial ocean view, plus a complete kitchen (with microwave and dishwasher), ceiling fans, washer/dryer, TV with VCR, air-conditioning in the bedroom, and a large furnished oceanview lanai. A sleeper sofa in the living room makes each unit spacious enough for a budget-minded family of four who don't mind sharing. You can choose your own unit online; rates vary a bit based on quality and view (I like cute number 205, as well as 309 for its premium views). Facilities include a small pool and barbecues. Apartments closest to the road can be noisy, so book oceanview for maximum quiet. All in all, it's an excellent value if you want cheap, comfortable sleeps. You'll have to make your own bed, but at these prices, who cares?

See map p. 424. 320 Papaloa Rd., Kapaa. ☎ **800-882-9007.** *Fax: 425-391-9121.* www. wailuabay.com. *Parking: Free. Rack rates: $140–$165 double. $95 cleaning fee. Weekly discount rates and discounted car rentals available. MC, V.*

Whalers Cove
$$$$$ Poipu Beach

Condo living hardly gets better than this. The individually decorated apartments are elegant and oversize; each has a full modern kitchen, a large furnished lanai, washer/dryer, and ceiling fans throughout. Most have Jacuzzi tubs in the master bathroom. The units are generally held to a high standard, but are individually owned and renovated at various times; when you book, be sure to inquire as to the state of your unit in detail. The contemporary and stylish water's-edge complex was smartly designed to give each unit a spectacular view of the crashing surf. Hotel-like amenities include bell service, concierge, and daily housekeeping; an elevator (uncommon in condo complexes) is another nice luxury touch. A very nice oceanside pool is on-site, plus a hot tub, a sauna, and barbecues. You'll have to drive to the beach, but there's good swimming and snorkeling (often with sea turtles) from a rocky cove.

See map p. 424. 2640 Puuholo Rd., Poipu Beach. ☎ **800-225-2683,** *800-367-7052, or 808-742-7571. Fax: 808-742-1185.* www.whalers-cove.com. *Parking: Free. Rack rates: $349–$541 1-bedroom, $479–$709 2-bedroom. "Resort fee" of $15 per night. 2-night minimum stay. Room-and-car, romance, and other packages usually available. AE, DISC, MC, V.*

More B&Bs worth writing home about

Tropically tranquil Kauai makes the ideal place to hide away in a B&B. If you're a fan, consider these enticing, and quite affordable, options.

In Lawai, a rural hillside community just a short drive from Poipu Beach, you'll find the much-beloved **Kauai Banyan Inn** ($–$$; ☎ **888-786-3855;** www.kauaibanyan.com), offering five charming and beautifully outfitted suites, a cute brand-new cottage, and a world of off-the-beaten-path aloha. Rates run $130 to $150 per night.

On the Coconut Coast, consider **Inn Paradise Kauai** ($; ☎ **808-822-2542;** www.innparadisekauai.com), whose friendly hosts provide three impeccably kept and thoughtfully outfitted guest suites, all with kitchen facilities. Rates run $85 to $120 per night.

On the North Shore, consider the **Palmwood Inn** ($$$; ☎ 808-631-9006; web.mac.com/eddihenry), a newly constructed luxury inn built in the style of a Japanese mountain ryokan. A unique and utterly elegant place to stay for those who love streamlined Japanese style. Rates are $295 to $325 per night.

For more options, contact **Hawaii's Best Bed & Breakfasts** (☎ 800-262-9912 or 808-263-3100; www.bestbnb.com), which represents some delightful B&Bs on the island. The staff can book a room for you in a Kauai inn that they have inspected and approved, and they offer vacation home rentals too.

Also check out the fine bed-and-breakfast members of the Kauai Visitors Bureau, which can be found online at www.kauaidiscovery.com/accommodations/bed+breakfasts.

Home, sweet vacation home

Kauai has lots of fabulous apartments, condos, and full homes that can be rented by the day, the week, or the month, and many are just steps from the ocean. Vacation rentals can be a fabulous deal. They often cost no more than your average resort room, but for your money, you get a whole house brimming with conveniences and privacy. Sometimes it's even cheaper to rent a home, especially after you factor in the extra bucks you inevitably hand out at resorts for room service, poolside cocktails, and the like. Vacation rentals are also the only available option if you want to base yourself in the North Shore's most appealing residential communities, such as Anini Beach, Hanalei, or Haena. Make sure that you understand payment policies (including any cleaning fees and security deposits) and minimum-stay requirements.

I've had great luck renting through **Kauai Vacation Rentals** (☎ 800-367-5025 or 808-245-8841; www.kauaivacationrentals.com), which handles top-quality vacation rentals all over the Garden Isle. It has a particularly fab selection on the lush North Shore; renting a home on this quiet coast is a great way to commune with nature, especially for those who favor being on their own over the sometimes-smothering atmosphere of a big resort. KVR has something for everybody; prices start at about $850 a week for a cozy cottage for two ($700 for a studio condo) and reach into the thousands for luxurious multibedroom beachfront homes. Check out the complete list of options on the extensive Web site. One of my favorites is the ultracharming Ursula Taylor home, a modern two-bedroom done in traditional plantation style; it's perfectly located, just across the street from idyllic Hanalei Bay and a walk from charming Hanalei town, and it goes for $1,750 a week.

Poipu Beach Vacation Rentals (☎ 800-684-5133 or 808-742-2850; www.pbvacationrentals.com), formerly known as Gloria's Vacation Rentals, offers an excellent selection of vacation-rental cottages, condos, and homes in Poipu and around the island, ranging from $85 to $429 per night. Now that Gloria is retired, the business is run by her son, Amos Merkle; you can expect the same great quality and service that Gloria offered Kauai visitors for 20 years.

Another agency that represents an extensive collection of North Shore vacation rentals is **Hanalei North Shore Properties** (☎ 800-488-3336 or 808-826-9622; www.kauai-vacation-rentals.com). For the best deal in sunny Poipu Beach, on either a condo or a full vacation home, call the **Parrish Collection Kaua'i,** formerly known as Grantham Resorts (☎ 800-325-5701 or 800-742-2000; www.parrishkauai.com). In addition to managing the Nihi Kai Villas and Waikomo Stream Villas (both reviewed earlier in this chapter), Parrish handles a wonderful selection of Poipu-area rental units in a range of other condo developments as well as dozens of Poipu-area houses (including some beachfront homes that turned me pea green with envy on my visit to Poipu). Parrish also rents out Hale Manu, a lovely three-bedroom house on the North Shore, situated on a lush and fragrant flower farm, which goes for $265 to $400 per night (plus a $200 cleaning fee), as well as a wealth of other great rentals around the island. Parrish sets exacting standards for all their rentals; when you rent a Parrish apartment or home, you know that you're getting high quality and top value for your dollar. You can — and should — peruse its full list of properties on the Web. **Hawaii's Best Bed & Breakfasts** (see the section "More B&Bs worth writing home about," earlier in this chapter) also represents some excellent vacation homes on Kauai.

Dining Out

The gorgeous Garden Isle has used its not-so-subtle charms to woo some of Hawaii's finest chefs over to its shores. Still, as you might expect, the dining scene is not quite so broad here as it is on the other islands. For reasons that escape me, Kauai has an excess of quality Italian, zesty island-style Mexican, and great burgers — not that I'm complaining, mind you. Whether you're looking for a romantic candlelit dinner, fresh seafood in an oceanfront setting, or just a great island-style pizza, you'll find some terrific choices.

In the following restaurant listings, each restaurant review is followed by a number of dollar signs, ranging from one ($) to five ($$$$$). The dollar signs are meant to give you an idea of what a complete dinner for one person — including appetizer, main course, dessert, one drink, tax, and tip — is likely to set you back. The price categories go like this:

$	Cheap eats — less than $20 per person
$$	Still inexpensive — $20–$35
$$$	Moderate — $35–$50

$$$$ Pricey — $50–$75

$$$$$ Ultraexpensive — more than $75 per person

Of course, it all depends on how you order, so stay away from the surf and turf or the north end of the wine list if you're on a tight budget. To give you a further idea of how much you can expect to spend, I also include the price range of main courses in the listings.

 The state adds roughly 4 percent in taxes to every restaurant bill. The percentage may vary slightly depending on the county you're in, and may be embedded in the total purchase price or shown as an independent line item on your bill. A 15 to 20 percent tip is standard in Hawaii, just like on the mainland.

Bar Acuda
$$–$$$ North Shore   Contemporary Mediterranean

This newish tapas restaurant and wine bar is a welcome addition to the North Shore dining scene. The restaurant comprises a gorgeously simple Balinese-style dining room, a sleek mahogany bar, and an outdoor dining area overlooking a lush tropical garden; Tiki torches enhance the romantic mood after dark. The designer simplicity belies Bar Acuda's low prices. Come for an elegant family-style spread of nouveau tapas designed for sharing; highlights include grilled ahi tuna on a bed of truffled potatoes, medjool date and celery salad dressed with Parmesan Reggiano, homemade mozzarella served with sweet cherry tomatoes and fresh basil, and a foie gras torchon served with crisp Fuji apple and walnut toasts. For a decadent but delicious main, consider the slow-braised beef short ribs with date and almond *salsa seca*. This is a great choice for grown-up palates with a penchant for creative fare and casually sophisticated settings. Look for this place to shine.

See map p. 442. At Hanalei Center, 5–5161 Kuhio Hwy., Hanalei. ☎ **808-826-7081.** www.restaurantbaracuda.com. *Tapas and main courses: $6–$27. AE, MC, V. Open: Dinner Tues–Sun.*

The Beach House Restaurant
$$$$ Poipu Beach   Hawaii Regional

The open-air, on-the-ocean setting makes this place my favorite special-occasion restaurant on Kauai. The long, Japanese-inspired room is lined with shoji-like windows that make sunset a celebration every night and let in a symphony of surf after dark. The first-rate food lives up to the setting nicely; in 2006, *Honolulu* magazine once again crowned the Beach House as "Best Kauai Restaurant." Under the steady hand of chef Todd Barrett, the kitchen turns out creative island dishes that feature the best of the land and sea, from fresh-caught fish and island-raised beef to locally harvested organic greens and salt. The menu changes nightly, but count on such winners as macadamia nut–crusted mahimahi in citrus miso sauce or mint-coriander marinated rack of lamb roasted with a goat cheese–garlic crust — yum! And

Kauai's Restaurants

Bar Acuda **1**
The Beach House
   Restaurant **26**
Blossoming Lotus **11**
Bouchons Hanalei **3**
Brennecke's Beach Broiler **21**
Brick Oven Pizza **27**
Bubba's Hawaii **1, 13**
Café Hanalei **5**
Caffe Coco **14**
Casablanca **22**
Dondero's **20**
Duane's Ono-Char Burger **8**
Duke's Canoe Club Kauai **17**
Hamura's Saimin Stand **18**
Hanalei Dolphin **2**
Hanalei Gourmet **1**
Hanapepe Café and Bakery **28**
Keoki's Paradise **23**

Lighthouse Bistro **7**
Mema Thai and Chinese Cuisine **15**
Norberto's El Café **10**
Ono Family Restaurant **12**
Pau Hana Pizza & Kilauea Bakery **6**
Plantation Gardens Restaurant **24**
Polynesia Café **3, 9**
Postcards Café **4**
PukaDog **25**
Roy's Poipu Bar & Grill **23**
Waimea Brewing Company **30**
Wrangler's Steakhouse **29**

Luaus
Grand Hyatt Kauai Luau **20**
Luau Kalamaku **19**
Smith Family Garden Luau **16**

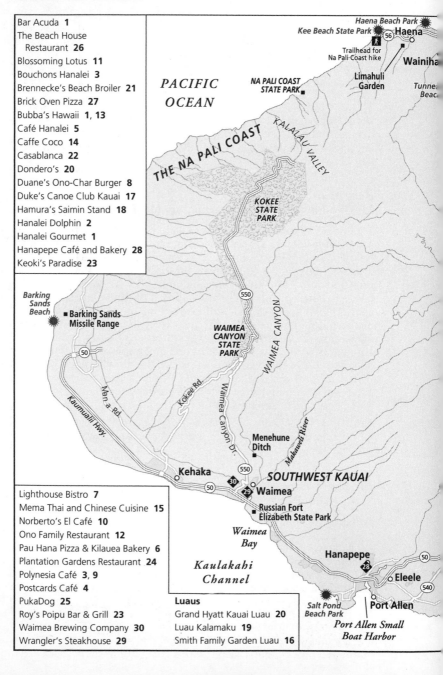

PACIFIC
OCEAN

NA PALI COAST
STATE PARK ■

Haena Beach Park ☀
Kee Beach State Park ☀ Haena
Trailhead for
Na Pali-Coast hike

Wainiha

Limahuli
Garden

Tunne
Beac

THE NA PALI COAST

KALALAU VALLEY

KOKEE
STATE
PARK

Barking
Sands
Beach
☀ ■ Barking Sands
Missile Range

550

WAIMEA
CANYON
STATE
PARK

WAIMEA CANYON

Kokee Rd.

Waimea Canyon Dr.

Kaumualii Hwy.

Mana Rd.

50

50

Menehune
Ditch ■

Makaweli River

Kehaka

550

50

30

29 Waimea

SOUTHWEST KAUAI

Russian Fort
Elizabeth State Park ■

Waimea
Bay

Kaulakahi
Channel

Salt Pond ☀
Beach Park

Hanapepe
28

50

Eleele
540

Port Allen

Port Allen Small
Boat Harbor

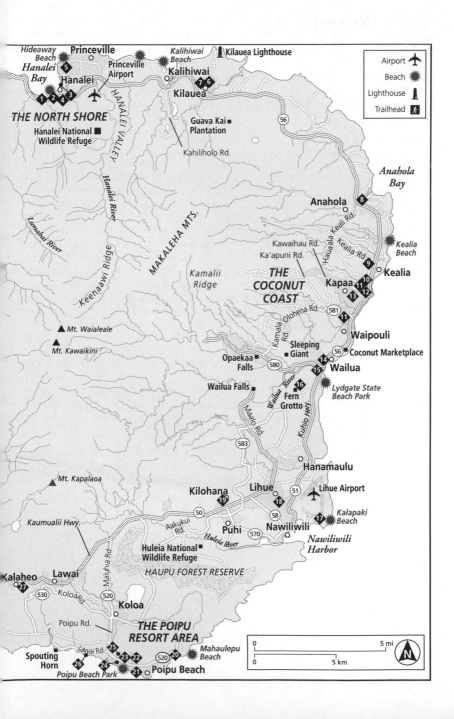

THE NORTH SHORE

Hideaway Beach
Princeville
Hanalei Bay
Princeville Airport
Hanalei
Kalihiwai Beach
Kilauea Lighthouse
Kalihiwai
Kilauea
Hanalei National Wildlife Refuge

Airport ✈
Beach ✳
Lighthouse 🗼
Trailhead 🚶

HANALEI VALLEY
Hanalei River

Guava Kai Plantation
Kahiliholo Rd.

56

Anahola Bay

Lumahai River

Keenawi Ridge

MAKALEHA MTS.

Anahola

8

Kamalii Ridge

Kawaihau Rd.
Ka'apuni Rd.

Haua'ala Keali Rd.

Kealia Rd.

Kealia Beach

9

Kealia

THE COCONUT COAST

Kapaa

581

11 10
13 12

▲ Mt. Waialeale

Kamala Rd.
Olohena Rd.

11

Waipouli

▲ Mt. Kawaikini

Sleeping Giant

56 Coconut Marketplace

Opaekaa Falls

580

14

15 Wailua

Wailua Falls

16

Fern Grotto

Wailua River

Lydgate State Beach Park

Kuhio Hwy

583

Maalo Rd.

Hanamaulu

▲ Mt. Kapalaoa

Kilohana

19

Lihue

51

Lihue Airport

50

Kaumualii Hwy.

Aakukui Rd.

Puhi

58

570

Huleia River

Nawiliwili

17 Kalapaki Beach

Nawiliwili Harbor

Huleia National Wildlife Refuge

HAUPU FOREST RESERVE

Kalaheo
Lawai

27

530

Koloa Rd.

520

Maluhia Rd.

Koloa

THE POIPU RESORT AREA

Poipu Rd.

Lawai Rd.

25

23 22

520 20

Mahaulepu Beach

Spouting Horn

26

24

21

Poipu Beach

Poipu Beach Park

0 ——————— 5 mi
0 ——————— 5 km

how can you go wrong with a dessert called "molten chocolate desire"? Strong on California labels, the wine list is pleasing but pricey. If you don't want to splurge on dinner, feel free to come strictly for the first-rate cocktails.

See map p. 442. 5022 Lawai Rd. (off Poipu Road, toward Spouting Horn), Koloa. ☎ *808-742-1424.* www.the-beach-house.com. *Reservations highly recommended. Main courses: $20–$36. AE, MC, V. Open: Dinner nightly.*

Blossoming Lotus
$$ Coconut Coast (Kapaa)   Vegan World Fusion

Let's get one thing straight — I am not a fan of vegetarian restaurants (much less vegan ones). In fact, I tend to be quite skeptical of them. It's not because I don't love good vegetable-focused dishes — I do. I just don't like being obligated to eat vegetarian, or being coerced into eating seitan or tempeh that "tastes just like chicken." Not so at this wonderful restaurant, a multiple award winner, where you just won't miss the meat — trust me. The inventive chefs find the joy in the land's natural bounty. Highlights of the endlessly creative menu include the Rockin' Moroccan spiced and seared tofu, served with gingered adzuki bean couscous, braised oyster mushrooms, and sautéed greens with a truffled lemon cream sauce; and a terrific spanakopita, a Greek classic given the Blossoming Lotus twist with marinated tofu, organic island greens, and sun-dried tomato sage sauce. Ingredients are kosher and certified organic whenever possible. Those dishes marked by a lotus on the menu are "Living Foods" selections, not heated above 116°F to preserve heat-sensitive enzymes, which raw foods aficionados consider to be highly nutritious. The high-ceilinged room is attractive with a pleasant ambience, and service is friendly and casual. Wine and beer are available, and live music or DJ adds to the mood most nights. The restaurant also serves a terrific vegan brunch on Sundays from 10 a.m. to 2 p.m.

Just a few doors down, the **Lotus Root Juice Bar and Bakery** ($), at 4-1384 Kuhio Hwy. (☎ **808-823-6658**), serves breakfast and lunch items, including bountiful wraps and organic plate lunches, daily from 7 a.m. to 6 p.m.

In the Historic Dragon Building, 4504 Kukui St. (at Kuhio Highway), in the heart of Kapaa town. ☎ *808-822-7678.* www.blossominglotus.com. *Reservations recommended. Main courses: $12–$18 at dinner; all items under $10 at Sun brunch; $2–$12 at breakfast and lunch (Lotus Root Juice Bar). Open: Dinner nightly, Sun brunch; Lotus Root Juice Bar breakfast and lunch daily.*

Bouchons Hanalei
$$$ North Shore   Japanese/Island Eclectic

Neither raw fish nor live entertainment gets any better on Kauai than what you'll find at this loftlike second-floor restaurant and sushi bar (formerly called Sushi Blues), which is one of the most satisfying and fun places to eat on the island. The first-rate sushi chef is a master with ultrafresh fish, much of it caught in island waters or flown in from Japan. There's also a big bar with a dizzying menu of martinis, tropical drinks, international beers, wine, and sake; a kitchen that prepares very good island-style seafood, chicken, and steaks for sushi-phobes; and gorgeous Bali Hai views. The restaurant hosts live music — generally jazz and blues — that creates a welcoming party atmosphere Wednesday through Sunday nights; call or check the Web site for the schedule.

See map p. 442. In Ching Young Village, 5–8420 Kuhio Hwy., Hanalei. ☎ *808-826-9701 or 808-828-1435.* www.sushiandblues.com. *Reservations recommended. Sushi: $4–$12. Combos and main courses: $18–$30. MC, V. Open: Dinner Tues–Sun.*

Brennecke's Beach Broiler
$$–$$$ **Poipu Beach   American/Seafood**

"Right on the Beach, Right on the Price." If you have kids in tow, skip the Beach House in favor of this fun, casual restaurant, which boasts ocean views galore. The fresh fish specials attract locals and visitors alike — always a good sign of consistent quality. Well-priced and well-prepared seafood and prime rib dinners (all of which include the creamy New England–style chowder or the appealing salad bar) are guaranteed to make Mom and Dad fans, and the best burgers in Poipu (plus a children's menu) will keep the kids happy. This longtime favorite is so welcoming and laid-back that you can come in straight off the beach for baby back ribs, kiawe-broiled (mesquite-broiled) seafood kebabs, or surprisingly good veggie selections. The restaurant has great sunset mai tais, too, plus a full menu of island-style munchies at happy hour (2–5 p.m.). The ground-floor Beachside Deli offers cold beer, fresh sandwiches, and shave ice for your day at Poipu Beach Park.

See map p. 442. 2100 Hoone Rd. (across the street from Poipu Beach Park), Poipu Beach. ☎ *888-384-8810 or 808-742-7588.* www.brenneckes.com. *Reservations recommended for dinner. Main courses: $6–$15 at lunch. Complete sunset dinners (including salad bar or chowder): $20–$40 (most under $28). AE, DC, DISC, MC, V. Open: Lunch and dinner daily.*

Brick Oven Pizza
$ **Kalaheo   Pizza**

Just a ten-minute drive from Poipu Beach, this full-service mom-and-pop pizza restaurant has been serving up Kauai's best pies for a quarter of a century. It's the real thing: traditional or whole-wheat crust topped with homemade sauces, high-quality cheeses, and your choice from the long toppings menu, and then baked in a real brick oven. You can choose standard-size pies to share or smaller individual ones if you and the kids just can't agree. A very good beer selection that includes Gordon Biersch and Kona brews is available to wash it all down. The setting is pleasant, with red-checked tablecloths, old license plates decorating the walls, and friendly, attentive service — but the terrific pies alone are worth the drive west from Poipu.

See map p. 442. 2–2555 Kaumualii Hwy. (Highway 50), Kalaheo (inland from Poipu Beach). ☎ *808-332-8561. Reservations not taken. Pizzas: $10–$29. MC, V. Open: Lunch and dinner Tues–Sun.*

Bubba's Hawaii
$ Coconut Coast/North Shore   American

"Bubba refuses to serve any burger costing less than a can of dog food."
"The food is hot, the service is cold, and the music's TOO DAMN LOUD."
Quick wit and commercial appeal aside, Bubba serves up one mean hamburger. It's served on a toasted bun with mustard, relish, diced onions, and lots of attitude — and is it yummy. Bubba burgers are plump and juicy, so have a pile of napkins ready and waiting. Chicken, ginger-teriyaki tempeh, and fish burgers are also available, plus variations on the standard Bubba: the Slopper (served open-faced and smothered in Budweiser chili), the three-patty Big Bubba, and the Hubba Bubba (with a scoop of rice *and* a hot dog, all smothered in chili and onions). If you need a burger fix, you can't go wrong with Bubba's.

See map p. 442. The Coconut Coast: 4–1421 Kuhio Hwy., Kapaa. ☎ *808-823-0069.* www.bubbaburger.com. *The North Shore: On Kuhio Highway (across from the Ching Young Center), Hanalei.* ☎ *808-826-7839. Everything under $8. MC, V. Open: Both locations, lunch and early dinner (to 8 p.m.) daily.*

Cafe Hanalei
$$$$–$$$$$ North Shore   Eclectic

Most people think of La Cascata, Princeville's elegant Mediterranean-Italian dining room, as the resort's premier special-occasion restaurant. But I just love Cafe Hanalei's perfect Bali Hai mood. A romantic indoor-outdoor setting makes the most of breathtaking Hanalei Bay and Na Pali views. The marvelously modern seafood-rich menu features Asian and Mediterranean accents (and includes plenty of selections to satisfy steak lovers, too). Add in first-rate service, and you've got an ideal dining experience. Book a table on the casually elegant terrace for the ultimate dinner for two. The bounteous Sunday champagne brunch boasts sushi and raw bars (all the peel-and-eat shrimp and crab legs you can put away!) as well as hot carving stations and made-to-order omelets and crepes. The food is satisfying through and through.

If you're in the mood for Italian instead, the resort's intimate and romantic **La Cascata** ($$$$) fits the bill for dinner.

See map p. 442. At the Princeville Resort, 5520 Ka Haku Rd., Princeville. ☎ *808-826-9644.* www.princevillehotelhawaii.com. *Reservations highly recommended. Main courses: $9–$30 at breakfast, $13–$25 at lunch, $29–$40 at dinner; 3-course fixed-price dinner $58 nightly; Sun brunch $53. AE, DC, DISC, MC, V. Open: Breakfast, lunch, and dinner daily.*

Caffè Coco
$$ Coconut Coast   Eclectic/International

The left-of-center alfresco cafe–cum–art gallery is an ideal spot for a low-budget romantic dinner with a bring-your-own bottle of merlot. The inventive cuisine spans the globe for ideas; everything is made from scratch and simply wonderful. You can dine casually on healthful soups, salads (including an excellent Greek), and sandwiches or opt for something more substantial. The beautifully prepared main plates include seared fresh ahi, crusted in delicate panko and served with a cilantro pesto and papaya salsa; Arista pork, slow roasted with garlic and herbs and served South American–style, with black beans, rice, and tortillas; and a couple of creative, healthful pastas. The kitchen prepares all its own breads, baked goods, juices, salsas, curries, and chutneys. Dining is in the fragrant flower-and-fruit garden, under flickering Tiki torches that set an idyllic island mood. The restaurant is an excellent choice for vegetarians, especially, but I recommend it for everyone else, too. Service is Hawaiian-style, so dine elsewhere if you're in a hurry (this is Kauai — what's your rush?). Live entertainment on Thursday, Friday, and Saturday nights adds to the already-winning ambience. A $5 corkage is charged if you bring your own beer or wine.

See map p. 442. 4–369 Kuhio Hwy., next to Bambulei (on the inland side of the street, behind the green storefront across from Kintaro Restaurant), Wailua (just south of the Coconut Marketplace). ☎ *808-822-7990.* www.restauranteur.com/caffe coco. *Reservations recommended for dinner. Main courses: $15–$21; sandwiches, salads, and lighter fare $3–$13. AE, MC, V. Open: Lunch Tues–Fri, dinner Tues–Sun.*

Casablanca
$$–$$$ Poipu Beach Mediterranean/Island

Befitting its name, this terrific all-day restaurant possesses an open-air romantic ambience with touches of the exotic; dining here is akin to being entertained post-safari on a friend's elegant outdoor patio. The setting is casually sophisticated — cool tile floors, rattan and iron chairs tucked under marble-topped tables, lazily whirling ceiling fans generating refreshing breezes. I imagine Ernest Hemingway hunched over his umpteenth drink at the bar. The exciting menu is always excellently prepared. Start the day with *Basque piperrada* (Spanish scrambled eggs) or crepes dressed with fresh island fruit. Midday brings a selection of fresh, creatively dressed sandwiches and salads, such as the *spinaci* salad, fresh spinach tossed with garlic-Dijon vinaigrette with crisp pancetta and pine nuts, or the Casa Pita plate, featuring Mediterranean-spiced chicken or lamb in a pita with minted yogurt sauce, served with a range of daring accompaniments. A menu of small tapas dishes for grazers and family-style sharing is also available midday; I adore the thick, zesty hummus served with fluffy pita. Both the island ambience and the culinary sophistication get a boost at dinner, when the beautifully presented plates shine with such flavorful dishes as *zarzuela* (Spanish seafood and saffron stew) and New Zealand rack of lamb with raisin-apricot demi-sauce. A belly dancer provides fitting entertainment on Thursday nights.

See map p. 442. At Kiahuna Swim & Tennis Club, 2290 Poipu Rd., Poipu Beach. ☎ *808-742-2929. Reservations recommended for dinner. Tapas: $4–$15. Main courses: $6–$14 at lunch, $16–$32 at dinner. DC, DISC, MC, V. Open: Lunch and dinner daily.*

Dondero's
$$$$$ **Poipu Beach** **Regional Italian**

The menu changes seasonally at this elegant Italian restaurant, but you can always count on a practiced, beautifully prepared regional menu with an emphasis on the classics. Dishes are prepared with homegrown herbs picked fresh from the kitchen garden. The setting is sublime, whether you choose to dine indoors in a beautiful marble-tiled setting reminiscent of Tuscany with exquisite Franciscan artwork or on an outdoor patio that says "Only in Hawaii." Specialties of the house include an open-faced seafood "lasagna," a pan-ocean treat of house-made black ink pasta topped with Pacific lobster, gulf shrimp, and lump blue crab meat, dressed in béchamel sauce and marinara. You might also consider the braised short rib ravioli in wild mushroom sauce (yum!) or a delectable slow-braised *osso bucco*. The tiramisu is worth saving room for. You'll pay too much, but the food, wine list, ambience, and service are top-notch, making this a winner for those evenings when you're in a celebratory mood.

See map p. 442. At the Grand Hyatt Kauai Resort & Spa, 1571 Poipu Rd., Koloa. ☎ *808-240-6456.* www.kauai.hyatt.com. *Reservations highly recommended. Main courses: $25–$42. AE, DC, DISC, MC, V. Open: Dinner nightly.*

Duane's Ono-Char Burger
$ **North Shore** **Burgers**

Bubba (see the listing earlier in this chapter) would just cringe if I called him "establishment," but compared with Duane's, Bubba is the Wal-Mart of Kauai burgers. Little more than a red-painted roadside stand with a few picnic tables and some resident wild chickens, I think Duane's sets the standard for island-style burgers, but opinions are perpetually divisive. I dream about the Local Girl, a juicy patty topped with teriyaki, Swiss cheese, pineapple, mayo, and lettuce on a bun — a perfect packet of juicy goodness. Broiled fish sandwiches and Boca burgers provide options for those who don't eat red meat. Sublime fries, shakes, and floats round out the lunchtime experience (or pop into the Whaler's General Store next door for a beer to enjoy with your burger). Stop by on the way to the North Shore or pick up a takeout beach lunch, especially if eating while chickens and stray cats hang about waiting for your scraps will bother you. (Kealia Beach in Kapaa is just a few minutes' drive to the south.)

See map p. 442. 4–4350 Kuhio Hwy. (next to Whaler's General Store, on the ocean side of the street), Anahola. ☎ *808-822-9181. Burgers: $4–$8. MC, V. Open: Lunch daily.*

Duke's Canoe Club Kauai
$$–$$$ **Lihue** **Steaks/Seafood (American/Hawaii Local in the Barefoot Bar)**

The Kauai Duke's isn't as magical as the Waikiki branch, but it's appealing nonetheless. Thanks to a wide-ranging menu and a wonderful beachfront setting, this big, bustling, tropical restaurant is pleasing to families and cuddly couples alike. The dependable menu has something for everyone, from fresh-caught fish prepared a half-dozen ways to finger-lickin'-good ribs dressed in mango barbecue sauce. Come for sunset if you can and ask for a beachfront table when you reserve; the view over Kalapaki Beach is fabulous, but some of the tables miss out. The Barefoot Bar, which spills out onto the sand and boasts its own waterfall (fake, of course), is the island's best spot for tropical noshing at reasonable prices. Live music completes the ambience.

See map p. 442. At the Kauai Marriott Resort & Beach Club, 3610 Rice St. (on Kalapaki Beach, near Nawilwili Harbor), Lihue. ☎ *808-246-9599.* www.dukeskauai.com. *Reservations recommended for dinner. Main courses: $18–$30 at dinner (salad bar included). Barefoot Bar menu (served all day): $6–$16. AE, DC, DISC, MC, V. Open: Lunch and dinner daily.*

Hamura's Saimin Stand
$Lihue   Local Hawaiian

I've eaten lots of memorable gourmet meals in Hawaii, but this nondescript lunch counter, family owned since 1951, is the place that makes me yearn for a repeat visit. Located on an industrial side street just off Lihue's main drag, Hamura's serves up Hawaii's best saimin (ramen-style noodle soup). Cozy up to one of the U-shaped counters and order off the posted menu. The saimin here comes in a variety of sizes and with a variety of extras, like veggies and a hard-boiled egg. Other offerings include succulently broiled beef and chicken skewers (a steal at $1 a stick) and Chinese pretzels, which are like hard funnel cakes. (I like to put them in my saimin — a cultural travesty, I'm sure.) Don't be put off by the brisk service; you'll feel right at home — and you'll be done eating — in no time. You can also get your saimin to go in Chinese food containers — perfect if you need a hearty bite on the way to the beach (or the airport). This cultural adventure is a culinary marvel, so outstanding that it was honored with a James Beard Award in 2006.

See map p. 442. 2956 Kress St. (1½ blocks off Rice Street; turn at the Aloha Furniture Warehouse), Lihue. ☎ *808-245-3271. Reservations not taken. Most soups and other items under $7. No credit cards. Open: Lunch and dinner daily.*

Hanalei Dolphin
$$$ North Shore   Seafood

Fresh-off-the-boat seafood and a nicely romantic tropical-garden setting on the banks of the Hanalei River make the Hanalei Dolphin a very pleasing choice for cocktails and dinner. This isn't sophisticated fare; rather, it's refreshingly simple. Choose from a wide selection of the day's catches, which come charbroiled or Cajun-style, with salad and rice, pasta, or steak fries on the side (plus hot homemade bread). Alaskan king crab is always on hand, but why bother? Go with one of the island catches, such as ruby-red ahi, moist and tender onaga (red snapper), or mackerel-like ono (wahoo). Starters include such retro classics as shrimp cocktail and stuffed mushroom caps, and sweet finishes include old-fashioned delights like strawberry cheesecake and ice-cream pie. Steaks and chicken are available for non–fish eaters.

See map p. 442. 5–5016 Kuhio Hwy., Hanalei. ☎ *808-826-6113.* www.hanalei dolphin.com. *Reservations not taken. Sandwiches and salads: $7–$14 at lunch. Complete dinners: $17–$36. MC, V. Open: Lunch and dinner daily.*

Hanalei Gourmet
$$ North Shore   American

This unpretentious restaurant in the heart of Hanalei town is a great choice for an informal bite at any time of day. Breakfast standards and lunchtime burgers, deli sandwiches, and salads give way to dinner specialties like pan-fried Asian-style crab cakes, macadamia-nut fried chicken, and charbroiled pork chops, deliciously seasoned with locally harvested salt that has its own hearty, wonderfully distinct flavor. It's easy to modulate your dinner bill by sticking with burgers and pasta. The focus is on fresh local produce, low-sodium meats, fresh-baked and whole-grain, but deliciously rather than obsessively so. Service is super-friendly and super-easygoing — but the North Shore isn't the place to be in a hurry, anyway. Choose a table on the veranda if the TV set over the bar interferes with your Hanalei reverie — or take a seat inside to catch the game. There's live music most evenings, plus pleasing tropical drinks and a good range of beers on tap. A kids' menu is available.

In the Old Hanalei School at Hanalei Center, 5-5161 Kuhio Hwy., Hanalei. ☎ *808-826-2524. Reservations not taken. Main courses: $7–$14 at lunch, $9–$27 at dinner. AE, DC, DISC, MC, V. Open: Breakfast (from 8 a.m.), lunch, and dinner daily.*

Hanapepe Cafe and Bakery
$$ Southwest Kauai (Hanapepe)   Fresh Island/Vegetarian/Italian

This bright, airy, and exceptionally friendly cafe and espresso bar has been drawing in locals and visitors alike for years for yummy, farm-fresh gourmet vegetarian cuisine. But the cafe really came into its own over the last couple of years — and now that baker Doug Jopling has arrived on the scene, Hanapepe Cafe is making a whole new name for itself as the quintessential village bakers. Start the day with multigrain pancakes, a well-stuffed frittata, or one of Jopling's celestial cinnamon buns. Stick around for a hearty, healthful salad, or sandwich on sweet challah or hearty seven-grain at lunch, or perhaps one of the restaurant's range of veggie burgers. Friday-night dinners (the only night dinner is served) are the big draw, however, now that there's fish on the previously all-vegetarian menu. The menu changes weekly, but highlights to watch for include delectable manicotti, shrimp and asparagus crepes in a creamy alfredo sauce, and anything prepared with the homemade marinara. No alcohol is served, but you're welcome to BYOB. Live music adds to the ambience, and the open-'til-late art galleries along Hanapepe Road make the entire night a memorable event. A real charmer!

3830 Hanapepe Rd., Hanapepe (turn off Highway 50 at the sign that says "Hanapepe, Kauai's Biggest Little Town"). ☎ *808-335-5011. Reservations highly recommended for Fri dinner. Main courses: $5–$9 at breakfast and lunch, $18–$24 at Fri dinner. DISC, MC, V. Open: Mon–Fri breakfast and lunch, Fri dinner.*

Keoki's Paradise
$$–$$$ Poipu Beach   Steaks/Seafood (American/Local in the Cafe)

Keoki's offers buckets of alfresco allure, with flickering Tiki torches, aloha-friendly ambience and service, and live Hawaiian music on weekends. It isn't on the oceanfront like its sister restaurant, Duke's Canoe Club (see earlier in this chapter), but it boasts a similarly lively tropical vibe and a lengthy menu highlighted by top-quality fresh fish prepared at least a half-dozen ways. Plenty of carnivore-friendly options are on hand, too, plus a decadent Hula Pie to finish. All dinners come with Keoki's surprisingly good Caesar salad, which makes meals a very good deal. The Bamboo Bar and Cafe, where there's live music on weekend nights, serves cheaper, more casual fare all day, including fish tacos, burgers, ribs, and quesadillas, plus the requisite fruity cocktails.

See map p. 442. In the Poipu Shopping Village, 2360 Kiahuna Plantation Dr. (at Poipu Road), Poipu Beach. ☎ *808-742-7534.* www.keokisparadise.com. *Reservations recommended. Cafe menu: $9–$14. Main courses: $17–$34 at dinner (with salad; most under $30). AE, DC, DISC, MC, V. Open: Lunch and dinner daily (cafe menu served all day).*

Lighthouse Bistro
$$–$$$ North Shore   Mediterranean/Eclectic

This island-style bistro keeps improving with age; it has matured into a terrific place to enjoy a casual and well-prepared North Shore dinner. The menu is a tad generic — pastas, salads, island fish — so I was pleasantly surprised with the high quality and tastiness of the burrito-like ahi wrap. My fellow diners were equally pleased with selections that ranged from a bounteous Caesar salad to a fresh grilled mahi sandwich. At dinner, the coconut shrimp in a sweet chili sauce or the chargrilled pork medallions topped with pineapple chutney are tropical delights, and the broiled sirloin steak topped with a Gorgonzola cheese and burgundy sauce will appeal to classic tastes. An extensive and pleasing wine list — with some nice affordable choices — is also on hand at dinner. There's mood-setting live entertainment four nights a week.

See map p. 442. At Kong Lung Square, 2484 Keneke St., Kilauea. ☎ *808-828-0480.* www.lighthousebistro.com. *Reservations recommended at dinner. To get there: From Kuhio Highway, turn right at the sign for Kilauea Lighthouse (at Shell gas station) and then right onto Keneke Street. Main courses: $6–$14 at lunch, $15–$30 at dinner. MC, V. Open: Lunch Mon–Sat, dinner nightly.*

Mema Thai and Chinese Cuisine
$$ Coconut Coast   Thai/Chinese

Tucked away in a nondescript minimall, Mema is worth seeking out thanks to a mammoth, culturally cross-bred menu and a dining room that's much prettier and more appealing than most at this price level. The menu leans heavily toward the Thai classics, including a satisfyingly spicy lemon-grass soup, a fresh island papaya salad, a better-than-average pad Thai, and rich coconut-milk curries that border on the sublime. Best is the house specialty: *panang* curry made with kaffir lime leaves, garlic, and other seasonings, and spiced mild, medium, or hot to suit your palate. Service is usually thoughtful, too, making Mema a winner with well-rounded appeal and an ideal place for an affordable date (made even cheaper because it's a BYOB establishment). Takeout is available.

See map p. 442. In the Kinipopo Shopping Village, 4–369 Kuhio Hwy. (just north of Haleilio Road on the mountain side of the street), Wailua. ☎ *808-823-0899.* www. restauranteur.com/mema. *Reservations accepted. Main courses: $9–$19. AE, DC, DISC, MC, V. Open: Lunch Mon–Fri, dinner daily.*

Norberto's El Cafe
$–$$ Coconut Coast   Mexican

This cool, dark Mexican restaurant marries fresh-grown island greens and fish with traditional south-of-the-border recipes, resulting in Mexican fare that's both top-quality and pleasingly authentic. Vegetarians and carnivores alike will enjoy the Hawaiian taro leaf enchiladas — corn tortillas stuffed with the spinachlike island staple, dressed in a zesty Spanish sauce, and baked to cheesy perfection. The rellenos and the fresh fish enchiladas are excellent choices, and the crisp corn chips are accompanied by a fresh-made salsa that will make your taste buds sit up and take notice. I've never been disappointed with any of Norberto's eats. Service is attentive and friendly, and Mexican beers are on hand.

See map p. 442. 4–1373 Kuhio Hwy., downtown Kapaa. ☎ *808-822-3362. Reservations accepted, recommended for larger parties. A la carte items $4–$9; complete dinners $14–$19. AE, MC, V. Open: Dinner Mon–Sat.*

Ono Family Restaurant
$ Coconut Coast   American/Local

Service isn't exactly what I'd call fast at this colorfully rustic, local-style restaurant in the heart of Kapaa, but who cares? The hearty home-style breakfasts make Ono's a fortifying place to launch a day of beachgoing or sightseeing. The coffee is strong, and the home cooking is indeed *ono* (Hawaiian for "delicious"). The menu features a full slate of fluffy omelets, pancakes (probably the highlight of the morning menu), and other breakfast standards, including several variations on eggs Benedict, all of which come topped with a perfectly puckery hollandaise. Classic burgers (including a buffalo burger) and crispy fries are midday standouts. Service has warmed up in recent years, too, making this an all-around satisfying place to dine.

See map p. 442. 4–1292 Kuhio Hwy. (on the ocean side of the street), downtown Kapaa. ☎ *808-822-1710. Most items less than $10. AE, DC, DISC, MC, V. Open: Breakfast and lunch daily.*

Pau Hana Pizza & Kilauea Bakery
$ North Shore   Pizza/Baked Goods

Some declare the pizza that issues forth from this unassuming closet to be the best in the state, and they just might be right. Fresh-from-scratch dough lays the chewy foundation for this near-perfect pie, and top-flight olive oil, whole-milk cheeses, homemade marinara, and a host of high-quality toppings serve as the culinary building blocks. You're welcome to order standard pepperoni, but even traditionalists will be tempted by such innovations as the Billie Holiday, topped with house-smoked ono (wahoo on the mainland), Swiss chard, roasted onions, and Gorgonzola-rosemary sauce, or the Provençal, a symphony of sun-dried tomatoes, garlic, roasted onions, fresh-basil pesto, and Asiago cheese. The stellar bakery also churns out a wealth of to-die-for breads, pastries, and bagels, plus coffee and espresso, making this a great place to start your North Shore day. The setting is ultra-casual, with just a few tables inside this takeout-style establishment, and a few more in the courtyard outside. If you're going to eat here for dinner, feel free to BYOB. Slices are also available for a lunch on the run (and why not throw in a macadamia-nut butter cookie or a white-chocolate scone while you're at it?).

See map p. 442. In the Kong Lung Center, Keneke Street and Kilauea Road, Kilauea.
☎ *808-828-2020. To get there: From Kuhio Highway (Highway 56), turn right at the sign for Kilauea Lighthouse and then right at Kong Lung onto Keneke Street; it's behind the Lighthouse Bistro. Baked goods: $2–$5. Whole pizzas: $12–$30. MC, V. Open: Breakfast, lunch, and dinner daily.*

Plantation Gardens Restaurant
$$$–$$$$ Poipu Beach   Hawaii Regional-Mediterranean

Housed in a former plantation house that stands on lush tropical grounds, this beautiful island-style restaurant of gleaming woods, rattan, and bamboo is just a bit too bright to be really called romantic; book a seat on the lovely garden-facing patio for maximum ambience. The top-notch gourmet island fare is prepared with a Mediterranean flair, using herbs, greens, and sweet tropical fruits grown out in the back garden, and seafood harvested from local waters. You can launch your meal with such yummy treats as pork potstickers in a sweet chili sauce, local kalua pork served Korean style, in butter lettuce cups with Asian veggies, or the sweet local pear salad served atop Kauai-grown baby arugula with toasted almonds and Gorgonzola, dressed in an orange-sesame vinaigrette. Follow with lovingly prepared entrees like house-smoked pork tenderloin with hoisin plum sauce, roast shiitake mushrooms and house-made fried rice with braised napa cabbage or the day's fresh offshore catch prepared local style as seafood laulau (wrapped in taro leaves and steamed), served with chutney made from homegrown mangoes. There's an enormous list of extravagant and beautifully prepared tropical cocktails made from fresh-squeezed fruit juices; try the cucumber mojito, made with cucumber Cruzan rum, ginger-infused simple syrup, and hand-squeezed lime juice, for a refreshing twist on the Brazilian classic; or one of the wonderful infused martinis, such as the tartly refreshing pomegranate drop, a hand-shaken blend of Meyer Lemon Fris Vodka, limoncello, and pomegranate juice. A winner through and through.

See map p. 442. In the Kiahuna Plantation, 2253 Poipu Rd. (across from Poipu Shopping Village), Poipu Beach. ☎ *808-742-2121.* www.pgrestaurant.com. *Reservations recommended. Main courses: $19–$26. AE, DC, MC, V. Open: Dinner nightly.*

Polynesia Café
$ North Shore   Pacific Rim/Mexican

At this casual, brightly colored open-air cafe, the emphasis is on serving gourmet food at paper-plate prices — and they're doing a terrific job, pleasing locals and tourists alike. The restaurant is open-air all the way, with chalkboard menus and a monkeypod bar on all sides. There's no table service; you place your order at the counter, take a seat on the rustic covered patio, and wait for your meal to be ready. Everything is made from scratch and delicious; I haven't found an exception yet. On my last visit, I tucked into the Hawaiian Variety plate, a gourmet version of the traditional local plate lunch featuring delectable pulled kalua pork and cabbage, lomilomi salmon, and sushi-grade ahi poke (marinated in soy sauce). Other menu highlights included crisp and bountiful entree-size salads, bistro-style burgers, Mexican dishes done island-style (such as ahi fajitas), macadamia-nut-crusted ahi, and plenty of vegetarian choices, such as Shanghai tofu in an orange-ginger glaze. Other perks include an espresso bar, a smoothie bar, and local favorite, Lappert's ice cream. They'll even pack you a picnic for your hike or day at the beach. BYOB. There's now a second location in Kapaa (4-1639 Kuhio Hwy.; ☎ 808-822-1945), but I recommend sticking with the Hanalei original.

See map p. 442. In Ching Young Village, 5–8420 Kuhio Hwy., Hanalei. ☎ *808-826-1999.* www.polynesiacafe.com. *Reservations not taken. Main courses: $6–$20 (most less than $14). No credit cards. Open: Breakfast, lunch, and dinner daily.*

Postcards Cafe
$$$ North Shore   Seafood

This unassuming vintage plantation house on the edge of Hanalei houses a globe-hopping seafood restaurant. Choose a seat in the schoolhouse-simple but exceedingly charming dining room or out on the wide veranda for alfresco dining. The kitchen uses no meat, poultry, refined sugar, or foods with chemical additives. But healthy doesn't mean bland. The creative kitchen pulls out the pan-cultural stops, from yummy taro fritters topped with papaya salsa to Indian-spiced potato-phyllo pockets (much like samosas) to crisp Thai summer rolls served with a spicy peanut sauce. The day's fresh-caught fish can be served grilled or blackened, with macadamia butter, peppered pineapple sage, or a honey-ginger-Dijon sauce, while wasabi-crusted ahi gets a flavorful zest from mirin soy ginger sauce. I've always loved Postcards for its innovative yet unfussy preparations and the freshness of the local ingredients; the friendly (if at times uneven) service doesn't hurt, either. No wine is served but you're welcome to BYOB for a minimal corkage fee.

See map p. 442. 5–5075A Kuhio Hwy., Hanalei. ☎ *808-826-1191.* www.postcards cafe.com. *Reservations recommended. Main courses: $18–$27. AE, DC, MC, V. Open: Dinner nightly.*

PukaDog
$ Poipu Beach   Casual American

When irreverent chef and adventure travel rogue Anthony Bourdain, of the Travel Channel's No Reservations, had the opportunity to dine anywhere he wanted in Hawaii, he headed straight for PukaDog. This simple store-front hot dog stand has Hawaiianized the hot dog for unrepentant gourmands in search of local culinary experiences.

PukaDog starts by baking a bun-size loaf of bread from their own house recipe. Once you place your order, they pierce a hole in one end (puka means "hole" in Hawaiian), toast the bun, insert a perfectly grilled Polish-style sausage, and dress it to your taste. You'll customize with your choice of secret sauce — mild garlic-lemon, spicy jalapeño, hot chili pepper, or super-hot habanero — and tropical relish (mango, coconut, banana, pineapple, papaya, or star fruit). Top it all off with the condiment of your choice; my favorite is the lilikoi (passion fruit) mustard. It's a delicious and filling tropical treat. Service is aloha friendly, and a veggie dog is available for those who don't do meat. There's now a Waikiki location, too, but this is the Puka Dog original.

See map p. 442. In the Poipu Shopping Village, 2650 Kiahuna Plantation Dr., Poipu Beach. ☎ *808-742-6044.* www.pukadog.com. *Reservations not taken. Puka Dogs: $6–$7. No credit cards. Open: Lunch Mon–Sat (to 6 p.m.).*

Roy's Poipu Bar & Grill
$$$–$$$$ Poipu Beach   Hawaii Regional

More casual than Roy's other establishments throughout Hawaii, Roy's Poipu is my favorite of the famous chain. Star chef Roy Yamaguchi's take on Hawaii Regional Cuisine has a distinctly Asian accent. Thanks to an extensive grazing menu of dim sum, appetizers, and *imu*-baked pizzas, you can easily eat inexpensively here; my husband and I got no guff at all from the waitstaff for building a meal from the starter menu (love those spinach-shiitake ravioli). Signature dishes include luscious Szechuan baby back ribs (better than dessert!) and blackened ahi with a delectable soy mustard butter. The service is friendly and easygoing, in keeping with the lively ambience, and the wines bottled under Roy's own label are affordable and surprisingly good. Roy's is a winner that continues to live up to its stellar reputation in every way.

See map p. 442. In the Poipu Shopping Village, 2360 Kiahuna Plantation Dr. (at Poipu Road), Poipu Beach. ☎ *808-742-5000.* www.roysrestaurant.com. *Reservations highly recommended. Appetizers and pizzas: $8.50–$18. Main courses: $18–$41 at dinner (most under $35). AE, DC, DISC, MC, V. Open: Dinner nightly.*

Waimea Brewing Company
$$ Waimea Island Eclectic

This casual restaurant on the sunny west side is a just-fine spot for a late lunch or early dinner after a day spent at Waimea Canyon or Kokee State Park (see Chapter 17). Housed in an attractively restored 1940s plantation house with a pleasant outdoor patio, the restaurant is easygoing and kid-friendly. The big, high-ceilinged, open-air room is barefoot casual, with shiny blond wood floors and walls decorated with Hawaii movie posters. Don't expect much from the food — straightforward bar food like Buffalo wings, burgers, nachos, and mango-stout-glazed barbecue ribs. Instead, come thirsty and order up a microbrewed Na Pali Pale Ale (the owner's favorite) or a Lilikoi Light (refreshing, with a hint of passion fruit). The IPA is the house-special beer, but it's not for the faint of heart. Service can be slow, so once you have your beer, settle in and relax. Not worth seeking out, but a reasonable stop if you're on the west side.

See map p. 442. Adjacent to the Waimea Plantation Cottages, 9400 Kaumualii Hwy. (Highway 50), Waimea. ☎ *808-338-9733. Reservations recommended for large parties. Main courses: $8–$20. MC, V. Open: Lunch and dinner daily.*

Wrangler's Steakhouse
$$$ Waimea Steaks

This popular Tex-Mex/Hawaii-style steakhouse has "cowboy" written all over it. It's a rustically charming place with good food, good service, and pleasant veranda seating. The menu leans toward hearty burritos, meaty sandwiches, and substantial salads at lunch, and good-value complete steak dinners at day's end. Your lil' pardners will love the Wild West setting and the finger-friendly food, including juicy flame-broiled burgers served with steak-cut fries. The menu also has a few fish and chicken options (like ahi with penne pasta) for non–red-meat eaters.

See map p. 442. 9852 Kaumualii Hwy. (Highway 50), Waimea. ☎ *808-338-1218. Reservations recommended for large parties. Main courses: $8–$15 at lunch, $18–$30 at dinner (soup and salad bar included). AE, MC, V. Open: Lunch Mon–Fri, dinner Mon–Sat.*

Luau!

When it comes to luau, Kauai excels in quantity rather than quality. Not one is in the ballpark with Maui's Old Lahaina Luau or Feast at Lele (see Chapter 12), or the Big Island's Kona Village Luau (Chapter 14). Still, if you want to join an island-style party on the Garden Isle, the following are your best bets; be sure to reserve in advance.

At press time, you could save up to 10 percent on the price of admission by booking the luau listed below through **Tom Barefoot's Tours** (☎ 800-621-3601 or 808-661-1246; www.tombarefoot.com).

Grand Hyatt Kauai Luau

This lively Poipu Beach luau is an expensive but generally satisfying luau choice on the south shore. It boasts a lovely tropical garden setting and a bountiful spread, which includes a full *imu* (underground pig roasting) ceremony. The lively floor show features Hawaiian and Tahitian dances as well as Samoan fire dancers in a loosely threaded narrative that tells the story of ancient Polynesian history and migration to the islands.

See map p. 442. At the Grand Hyatt Kauai Resort & Spa, 1571 Poipu Rd., Koloa. ☎ *808-240-6456 or 808-742-1234.* www.grandhyattkauailuau.com. *Reservations essential. Admission: $94 adults, $84 teens (13–20), $57 kids (6–12). Prices include open bar. Times: Sun and Thurs at 6 p.m.*

Luau Kalamaku

The old-school Gaylord's luau has been reborn as one of the most theatrical and satisfying luau productions in the islands. The party is held on the lovely grounds of a historic 1930s plantation house in the lush heart of the island, and the show is centered around telling an in-depth story of Hawaii's heritage in an artful, original showcase that the performers seem genuinely proud of. The fire-knife dancer doesn't disappoint, either. It features a traditional *imu* ceremony starring a kalua-roasted pig, plus a bountiful and delicious luau spread, a full open bar (not just mass-prepared mai tais), and traditional Hawaiian craft demonstrations and games. Expensive, but worth it — and definitely the luau to choose if you want to avoid silly audience participation.

See map p. 442. At Kilohana Plantation, 3-2087 Kaumualii Hwy. (Highway 50), 1 mile west of Lihue. ☎ *877-622-1780.* www.luaukalamaku.com. *Reservations required. Admission: $95 adults, $65 teens 12–18, $45 kids 3–11, free for kids 2 and under. Prices include open bar. Time: Tues and Fri 4:30, 5, and 5:30 p.m. check-in times available.*

Smith Family Garden Luau

This old-school luau is set among 30 tropical garden acres that are simply magical as the sun goes down. Now, if only the food lived up to the setting. Expect a traditional *imu* ceremony followed by a generous spread of decently prepared traditional dishes like kalua pig, teriyaki chicken, poi, and coconut cake alongside such familiar standards as teriyaki beef, fried rice, and Jell-O. There's a traditional *imu* ceremony, a guided tram tour around the grounds, and the "Rhythm of Aloha" show, complete with its own erupting volcano. Come expecting some good cheesy fun, and you won't be disappointed.

At Smith's Tropical Paradise and Fern Grotto, 174 Wailua Rd., just beyond Wailua Marina at the mouth of the Wailua River; turn off Kuhio Highway (Highway 56) into Wailua Marine State Park. ☎ *808-821-6895. Reservations required. Admission: $75 adults, $30 kids 7–13, $19 for kids 6 and under. Mai tai, beer, wine, and fruit punch included in admission. 10 percent online booking discount. Time: Mon, Wed, and Fri at 5 p.m. (Mon–Fri in summer months).*

Fast Facts: Kauai

American Automobile Association (AAA)

Roadside service is available to members by calling ☎ 800-AAA-HELP; however, the only Hawaii office is on Oahu (see Chapter 10).

American Express

Kauai doesn't have a branch office.

Baby Sitters and Baby Stuff

Any hotel, and most condo management offices, should be able to refer you to a reliable baby sitter with a proven track record.

Doctors

Walk-ins are accepted from 8 a.m. to 5 p.m. on weekdays, from 8 a.m. to noon on Saturdays, at the Kauai Medical Clinic, 3-3420-B Kuhio Hwy. (next to Wilcox Hospital; see "Hospitals"), Lihue (☎ 808-245-1500). There's also an Urgent Care Clinic at the same location open daily from 8 a.m. to 5 p.m.; for information, dial ☎ 808-245-1532. Or head to Kauai Medical Clinic's Kapaa Clinic at 1150 Kuhio Hwy., Kapaa (☎ 808-822-3431) on the Coconut Coast, or its Koloa Clinic, 5371 Koloa Rd., 3 miles from Poipu in Koloa town (☎ 808-742-1621). If these locations don't work for you, call the main clinic number above for advice on additional locations.

Emergencies

Dial **911** from any phone, just like on the mainland.

Hospitals

Wilcox Memorial Hospital, 3420 Kuhio Hwy., Lihue (☎ 808-245-1010; www.wilcox health.org), has a 24-hour emergency room located at the north end of Lihue next to Wal-Mart.

Information

The Kauai Visitors Bureau is located at 4334 Rice St., Ste. 101, Lihue, HI 96766 (☎ 800-262-1400 or 808-245-3971; www.kauai discovery.com). Call before you leave home to order the free *Kauai Vacation Planner* or check the Web site for lots of good information. You can stop in while you're in town, or just meander over to the information kiosks at the airport while you're waiting for your baggage and pick up a copy of *This Week Kauai, 101 Things to Do on Kauai,* and other free tourist publications; they're packed with good area maps. If you forget, don't worry — they're available from magazine racks all over the island.

Another organization worth contacting for useful islandwide information is the Kauai Chamber of Commerce, at 2970 Kele St., Ste. 112, Lihue, HI 96766 (☎ 808-245-7363; www.kauaichamber.org); its Web site is especially useful.

The Poipu Beach Resort Association (☎ 888-744-0888 or 808-742-7444; www.poipu-beach.org) can send you a Poipu area vacation planner, including a full index of lodging options, before you leave home, or answer specific questions after you arrive. Its innovative Web site lets you book accommodations online and offers an excellent interactive guide to the full range of Poipu area activities.

Newspapers

The daily island paper is *The Garden Island,* available online at www.kauaiworld.com. The *Kauai Beach Press* is a free biweekly available around town that focuses on arts, entertainment, and dining.

Pharmacies

Longs Drugs (www.longs.com), Hawaii's biggest drugstore chain, has a branch in Lihue at the Kukui Grove Shopping Center, 3–2600 Kaumualii Hwy. (☎ 808-245-7771); and on the Coconut Coast next to Safeway in the Kauai Village Shopping Center, 4–831 Kuhio Hwy., Kapaa (☎ 808-822-4915). There's also a store with limited hours on the island's west side in the Eleele Shopping Center, 4469 Waialo Rd., just off Highway 50 (☎ 808-335-0700).

Police

Kauai's main headquarters is at 3990 Kaana St., Ste. 200, in downtown Lihue (☎ 808-241-1711). If you have an emergency, dial **911** from any phone.

Post Office

The main post office is at 4441 Rice St., downtown Lihue (just off Kuhio Highway, near the Kauai Museum; ☎ 808-245-1628). Satellite post offices are all around the island; to find the branch nearest you, call ☎ 800-275-8777 or go online to www.usps.com.

Taxes

Most purchases in Hawaii are taxed at roughly 4 percent; the exact amount will vary depending on the county you're in, and may be embedded in the total purchase price or shown as an independent line item on your bill. Expect taxes of about 11.42 percent to be added to your hotel bill.

Taxis

For islandwide service, call Kauai Taxi Company (☎ 808-246-9554; www.kauaitaxico.com), which has sedans, six- and seven-passenger vans, or limos available. You can also call City Cab (☎ 808-245-3227). For service in and around Princeville and Hanalei, call North Shore Cab Company (☎ 808-639-7829; www.northshorecab.com), which will also design personalized tours for you. For Poipu area service, dial up South Shore Taxi (☎ 808-742-1525). Always arrange for pickup well in advance.

Weather and Surf Reports

For current weather, call ☎ 808-245-6001. For marine conditions, call ☎ 808-245-3564.

Chapter 17

Exploring Kauai

. . . .

In This Chapter

▶ Finding Kauai's best beaches
▶ Enjoying watersports galore
▶ Seeing Kauai's top attractions
▶ Scoping out the shopping scene
▶ Having fun on the quiet isle after sunset

. . . .

*I*f any island was made for kicking back, Kauai is it. That said, you can find plenty of wonderful things to do on Kauai, especially if you're the type of traveler who prefers communing with nature over seeking out man-made attractions and entertainment.

Check with the excellent Maui-based activity center **Tom Barefoot's Tours** (☎ 800-621-3601 or 808-661-1246; www.tombarefoot.com), which may be able to save you a few dollars on many of Kauai's activities on land and sea.

Enjoying the Sand and Surf

Kauai is the oldest of the Hawaiian Islands, geologically speaking — which means that it's had plenty of time to fashion some world-class beaches. Lined with powdery white sands and dotted with swaying palms, the island's stunning shoreline is skirted by crystal-clear waters and numerous well-developed reefs for snorkeling.

Combing the beaches

Safety takes top priority at the beach. Always check on the local surf conditions before you head into the water. At beaches without lifeguards, keep an eye out for posted signs warning of dangerous currents or conditions. If you see a red flag hoisted at any beach, don't venture into the water; the flag indicates that conditions are unsafe for swimmers. And never turn your back on the ocean; big waves can come out of nowhere in a matter of minutes.

Never leave valuables in your rental car while you're at the beach. Thieves prey on tourists, and they can get inside your car quicker than you can spread out your beach towel.

On the Coconut Coast

The following beaches are located along the Kuhio Highway (Highway 56) north of Lihue.

Lydgate State Beach Park

My favorite beach on the Coconut Coast offers the safest swimming and the best snorkeling on the eastern shore. A rock wall breaks the open ocean waves, forming a protected natural pool that's perfect for kids and first-time snorkelers. Wide, grassy lawns lead downhill to an expanse of fine-grained sand with dramatic vistas in either direction. Among the facilities are a pavilion, restrooms, outdoor showers, picnic tables, barbecues, lifeguards, and plenty of parking. Note that the waves can be rough outside the protected pool, even in summer, so beware.

See map p. 462. At the ResortQuest Aloha Beach Resort, Kuhio Highway (Highway 56), 5 miles north of Lihue (just south of Wailua River State Park). To get there: Look for the turnoff at Leho Road.

Kealia Beach

This long, wide, crescent-shaped beach is a great place to play in summer. Gorgeous golden sands fringe white-crested turquoise waters that are suitably calm, particularly at the north end — but beware winter and year-round late-day swells. This local favorite is particularly popular with casual bodysurfers. Kealia is a perfect spot for those seeking solitude because it has plenty of room for everybody to spread out, even on summer weekends; however, there are no facilities. Park in the dirt lot and don't leave any valuables in your car.

See map p. 462. On Kuhio Highway (Highway 56) just north of Kapaa town, across from the Kealia Country Store.

On the North Shore

Welcome to the finest beaches in Hawaii — but bear in mind that most of Kauai's North Shore beaches aren't safe for swimming during winter. So do yourself a favor and head to the South Shore if you want to take a dip in the winter months (Dec–Mar).

Kalihiwai Beach

This secret North Shore beach is a favorite of local families, who come to enjoy the wide and gorgeous white sands and the shallow brackish ponds that remain safe for little ones to play in even when the ocean surf kicks up. You actually get two beaches here: the main beach, which offers plenty of sand for everybody to enjoy; and the second beach — actually the shoreline of the Kalihiwai Stream (accessible via the Anini Beach Road

Kauai's Beaches and Attractions

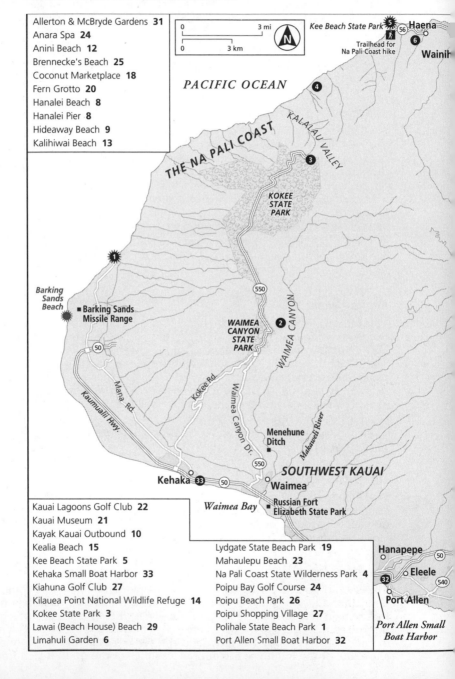

Allerton & McBryde Gardens **31**
Anara Spa **24**
Anini Beach **12**
Brennecke's Beach **25**
Coconut Marketplace **18**
Fern Grotto **20**
Hanalei Beach **8**
Hanalei Pier **8**
Hideaway Beach **9**
Kalihiwai Beach **13**

Kauai Lagoons Golf Club **22**
Kauai Museum **21**
Kayak Kauai Outbound **10**
Kealia Beach **15**
Kee Beach State Park **5**
Kehaka Small Boat Harbor **33**
Kiahuna Golf Club **27**
Kilauea Point National Wildlife Refuge **14**
Kokee State Park **3**
Lawai (Beach House) Beach **29**
Limahuli Garden **6**

Lydgate State Beach Park **19**
Mahaulepu Beach **23**
Na Pali Coast State Wilderness Park **4**
Poipu Bay Golf Course **24**
Poipu Beach Park **26**
Poipu Shopping Village **27**
Polihale State Beach Park **1**
Port Allen Small Boat Harbor **32**

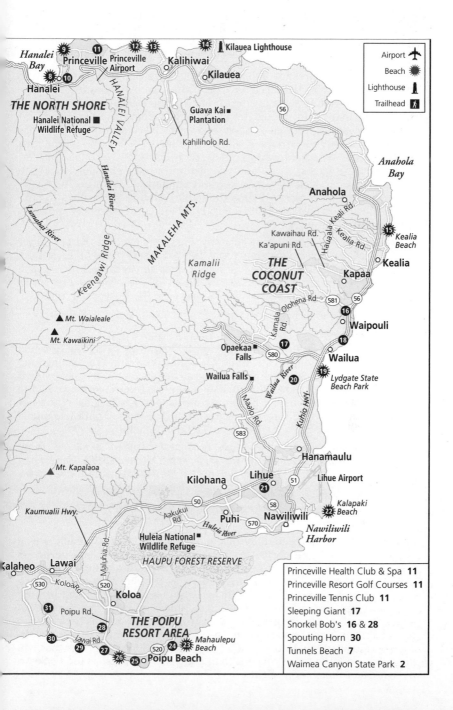

Airport ✈
Beach ☀
Lighthouse 🗼
Trailhead 🚶

Kilauea Lighthouse

Hanalei Bay
Princeville
Princeville Airport
Kalihiwai
Kilauea

Hanalei

THE NORTH SHORE

Hanalei National ■
Wildlife Refuge

HANALEI VALLEY

Hanalei River

Lumahai River

Guava Kai ■
Plantation

Kahiliholo Rd.

56

Anahola Bay

Keenaawi Ridge

MAKALEHA MTS.

Kamalii Ridge

Anahola

Kawaihau Rd.
Ka'apuni Rd.

Haalaala Keali Rd.

Kealia Rd.

15
Kealia Beach

Kealia

THE COCONUT COAST

Kapaa

Kamala Olohena Rd.

581   56

16
Waipouli

▲ Mt. Waialeale

▲ Mt. Kawaikini

Opaekaa ■
Falls

580

17

18
Wailua

Wailua Falls ■

Maalo Rd.

Wailua River

20

19
Lydgate State
Beach Park

Kuhio Hwy.

583

Hanamaulu

▲ Mt. Kapalaoa

Kilohana

Lihue

21

51

Lihue Airport

Kalapaki Beach
22

Kaumualii Hwy.

Aakukui Rd.

Puhi

570

Nawiliwili

58

Nawiliwili Harbor

Huleia National ■
Wildlife Refuge

Huleia River

HAUPU FOREST RESERVE

Kalaheo   Lawai

530

Koloa Rd.

520

31   Poipu Rd.

Koloa

Maluhia Rd.

28

30

Lawai Rd.

29   **27**   **26**

THE POIPU RESORT AREA

Mahaulepu Beach

520   **24** **23**

25 Poipu Beach

Princeville Health Club & Spa **11**
Princeville Resort Golf Courses **11**
Princeville Tennis Club **11**
Sleeping Giant **17**
Snorkel Bob's **16** & **28**
Spouting Horn **30**
Tunnels Beach **7**
Waimea Canyon State Park **2**

fork; see the upcoming directions) — from which you can wade across freshwater shallows to the wide main beach "island" in the middle. (The main beach is actually a wide sandbar separating the tranquil stream from the ocean; the ocean and river meet at one very shallow end.)

I suggest using the first set of directions that I give below so that you don't have to wade across the stream to reach the beach. (The water is waist-deep for most adults at its deepest point.) In the warm-weather seasons, the surf is usually calm enough for swimming and easy wave jumping, and the stream water is tranquil, shallow, and warm as a bathtub. Preschoolers love to toddle in the extreme shallows, and bigger kids jump off the lava rocks into the deep freshwater pool at the beach's west end (to your left as you face the waves). The shallows usually stay calm, but stay out of the surf if it begins to kick up — and stay out altogether in winter. The beach has no facilities. The crowd runs the gamut from local families to construction workers on their lunch break, but it tends to be friendly and easy-going across-the-board.

See map p. 462. Off Kuhio Highway (Highway 56) past the turnoff for Kilauea. To get there: As you head toward the North Shore, take the 1st exit called Kalihiwai Road, near mile marker 24; follow it to the parking lot. Or follow the directions for Anini Beach (see the next review); take a right at the Anini Beach Road fork (the sign says "Dead End"), and then park at the makeshift lot just before the "No Trespassing" sign.

Anini Beach

Tucked away in a million-dollar residential neighborhood, this beach is one of the most beautiful swimming beaches on Kauai. The 3-mile-long gold-sand beach is shielded from the open ocean by the longest, widest fringing reef in the islands. With shallow water less than 5 feet deep, it's the very best beach on Kauai for beginning snorkelers, and it boasts the most well-protected North Shore waters in winter. The grassy park has picnic and barbecue facilities, restrooms, and a boat-launch ramp.

See map p. 462. Off Kuhio Highway (Highway 56) past the turnoff for Kilauea. To get there: As you head toward the North Shore, ignore the 1st exit called Kalihiwai Road (the turnoff for Kalihiwai Beach) and turn right at the 2nd exit (west of mile marker 25); at the fork, follow Anini Beach Road (left) to the beach park.

Hideaway Beach

Reaching this hidden gem may take a little work, but this beach is well worth the effort. The perfectly named Hideaway Beach is a gorgeous pocket of beach in the Princeville Resort where the snorkeling is great, the sand is powder-fine, and the atmosphere is as tranquil as it gets. Even if a few other souls find their way there, everyone is happily content to keep to themselves. ***Fair warning:*** Getting to Hideaway is not for the faint of heart. From the parking lot, walk down the dirt path that runs between the two chain-link fences on the right; the path will take you to a steep staircase that leads down to the beach. It has no facilities, so bring what you need. You shouldn't visit this beach at night; the staircase is too tricky to navigate and there are no lights.

See map p. 462. In the Princeville Resort off Kuhio Highway (Highway 56), just east of Princeville Shopping Center. To get there: Go 2 miles to the entrance of the hotel; just before the gatehouse, turn into the public parking lot on your right.

Hanalei Beach

Half-moon Hanalei Bay has to be one of the loveliest beaches on earth. Gentle waves roll up the wide, golden sand; towering coco palms sway to the rhythm of the trade winds; waterfalls vein volcanic ridges in the distance. It's an excellent spot for swimming in summer; in winter, stick to the westernmost curve of the bay, where the water usually stays calm even when winter swells hit. Facilities include a pavilion, restrooms, picnic tables, and parking. This beach is very popular, but the bay is big enough for everyone to enjoy; you can usually find a spot to yourself just by strolling down the shoreline.

See map p. 462. Off Kuhio Highway (Highway 56), Hanalei. To get there: Turn right on Aku Road (just after Tahiti Nui), which leads to Weke Road and the main parking lot.

Tunnels Beach

If I had to pick one beach above all others on Kauai, it just might be Tunnels. Postcard-perfect, with swaying palms, a shelter of ironwoods, and gold sand rimming a curving shore, Tunnels is one of the most beautiful stretches of beach in all Hawaii. Go at sunset, when golden rays butter a wide-open blue sky and bounce off the green steepled ridges. The sand here is rougher and more pumice-textured than elsewhere (but somehow all the more luxurious for it). The ironwoods provide welcome shade in the heat of the tropical summer. Protected by a fringing coral reef, Tunnels is excellent for swimming and snorkeling, but beware the winter waves, of course. No facilities mar the pristine scene, so bring whatever supplies you think you may need.

You must park on the dirt access road — if you park on the shoulder of the main road, you *will* get a ticket. Heed the "No Parking Anytime" signs. If no parking is available along the access road, go ⅓ mile down, park at the Haena Beach Park, and walk back.

See map p. 462. Off Kuhio Highway (Highway 56) beyond Hanalei, 1 mile past Hanalei Colony Resort, down an unmarked drive. To get there: Turn right down the sandy access road across the street from the green house; it's just after the yellow "Narrow Bridge" sign and the 2-story light green house. Park in the alley or along the highway with everybody else, walk down the alley, and turn left at the "Beach Path" sign.

Kee Beach State Park

At the end of Kuhio Highway, Kee (kay-*eh*) is a real dandy of a beach — a small crescent of golden-brown sand nestled between soaring volcanic cliffs and an ironwood grove. This remote little spot isn't quite as lovely as Tunnels, but it comes close — and it boasts easier access and facilities. It's equally terrific for swimming and snorkeling (although a friend I recently brought here — a bona fide city girl — despised the hippie vibe).

You'll really feel as if you're at the end of the world out here. A well-developed reef keeps the water shallow and calm, making the inlet great for kids and snorkelers of all levels; nobody should venture out beyond the reef, though. Facilities include some rustic restrooms, showers, and lots of parking, but no lifeguard. Don't be surprised if you see a substantial clutch of Kauai's infamous wild chickens pecking and cock-a-doodle-doing their way around the parking lot.

Kee is where you pick up the trail head to the Na Pali Coast. It takes about three hours to hike the first 2 miles in (that's as far as I suggest you go) and back, so the heartier among you may want to plan on it; see the section "Exploring on Dry Land," later in this chapter, for further details.

See map p. 462. At the end of Kuhio Highway (Highway 56), about 7½ miles past Hanalei.

In the Poipu area

To reach these beaches, take Maluhia Road (Highway 520) from the Kaumualii Highway (Highway 50) toward Poipu Beach.

Poipu Beach Park

This big, wide beach park is the perfect beach playground: Grassy lawns with leafy shade trees skirt abundant white sand at the water's edge. It's actually a series of crescents, with the two most prominent ones divided by a sandbar: On the left, a lava-rock jetty protects a sandy-bottom pool that's perfect for small kids; on the right, the open bay is great for more advanced swimmers. The swimming is excellent, with small tide pools for exploring and great reefs for snorkeling and diving. Amenities include lots of top-notch facilities — including nice bathrooms, outdoor showers, picnic pavilions, plenty of parking, and a good restaurant and snack bar (Brennecke's Beach Broiler; see Chapter 16) just across the street. Poipu attracts a daily crowd of visitors and local residents (plus a mellow monk seal who often beaches himself here to sunbathe), but the density seldom approaches Waikiki levels, except on holidays.

See map p. 462. To get there: From Kaumualii Highway (Highway 50), turn south on Maluhia Road and follow it to Poipu Road. Go past Poipu Shopping Village and turn right on Hoowili Road, which will take you to the beach.

Lawai Beach (Beach House) Beach

This small, rocky, white-sand beach just to the west of the Beach House Restaurant isn't the most beautiful on the South Shore, but snorkelers will love it. The water is warm, shallow, clear, and delightfully populated with clouds of tropical fish. Plenty of streetside parking is available, plus some nice restrooms and showers just across the street and a grassy lawn in front of the Beach House.

See map p. 462. On Lawai Road next to the Beach House Restaurant, Poipu Beach. To get there: From Kaumualii Highway (Highway 50), turn south on Maluhia Road (Highway 520) and continue south on Poipu Road. At the "Welcome to Poipu Beach" sign, go to the right, toward Spouting Horn; it's a mile or two down, across from the Lawai Beach Resort (look for the restaurant on your left).

Mahaulepu Beach

Here is one of the finest stretches of untouched sands in Hawaii. With 2 miles of grainy, red-gold sand tucked among rocky cliffs, sand dunes, and a forest of casuarina trees, this idyllic stretch is perfect for beachcombing, sunbathing, or just watching the endless waves roll in. Swimming and snorkeling are risky, except in the reef-sheltered shallows about 200 yards west of the sandy parking lot. No facilities are on-site — just lots of pristine natural beauty. Best of all, you're likely to have it all to yourselves, except for a handful of locals who come here to kiteboard or let their dogs romp in the surf. Mahaulepu makes a wonderful place to get away from it all and discover Hawaii at its natural best.

See map p. 462. Off Poipu Road, 3 miles past the Hyatt Regency Kauai Resort and Spa and 2 miles from the end of Poipu Road (the unpaved stretch is called Weliweli Road). To get there: Turn right at the T intersection; stop and register at the security hut, drive 1 mile to the big sand dune, turn left, and drive ½ mile to the small lot under the trees.

On the western shore

If it's raining everywhere else on Kauai, just get in your car and head west. Keep going to the end of the road, and you'll find a mini-Sahara where the sun (almost) always shines.

Polihale State Beach Park

Polihale is a wonderful place to get away from it all. It holds Hawaii's biggest beach — 17 miles long and as wide as three football fields. The golden sands wrap around Kauai's northwestern shore from just beyond Waimea all the way to the edge of the Na Pali Coast. Some of the stretches of sand are accessible from the highway, but I like the remote area past the cane fields best. The safest place to swim is Queen's Pond, a small, shallow, sandy-bottomed protected inlet that's usually calm, except when the high winter surf washes over the reef — stay out of the water altogether then. Restrooms, showers, picnic tables, and pavilions are scattered throughout the park, but no lifeguards are on hand.

Be careful at Polihale year-round because this is open ocean, and swimming is dangerous. Strong swimmers can bodysurf with caution in summer, but everybody should stay out of the water in winter. *A few more tips:* Always wear flip-flops or reef shoes; the midday sand can be hotter than a griddle. Don't attempt to drive the unpaved cane road out to the beach if recent rains have left the road muddy. It's easy to get stuck, and this beach is far from civilization.

See map p. 462. At the end of Kaumualii Highway (Highway 50), a 40-minute drive west of Poipu. To get there: Drive past the Barking Sands Missile Range and follow the signs through the sugar-cane fields to Polihale. The road isn't paved, but it's flat and well graded, so just take it slow; it's about a 5-mile drive. Queen's Pond is at the

3¼-mile mark along the cane road, where the road curves near a large monkeypod tree; take the fork to the left and park almost immediately and then walk north along the beach until you come to a hollow in the rock; pass through it to the beach.

Playing in the surf

If you want to rent boogie boards, snorkel gear, kayaks, and other beach toys, Kauai has a number of reliable outlets — all of which can book organized activities for you, too.

My favorite place to rent snorkel gear is **Snorkel Bob's** on the Coconut Coast at 4–734 Kuhio Hwy. (on the ocean side of the street), Kapaa (☎ **808-823-9433**); and at Poipu Beach at 3236 Poipu Rd., just south of Old Koloa Town (☎ **808-742-2206**). The best-quality gear — the "Ultimate Truth" — rents for $8 a day, or $32 a week ($22 per week for kids) for the mask/snorkel/fins set. If you're nearsighted, you can even rent a prescription mask for $12 more, plus boogie boards, life vests, wet suits, beach chairs, umbrellas, and so on. Budget travelers can rent basic gear for just $9 per week. The people at Bob's shop can also sign you up for select activities — snorkel cruises, helicopter rides, bike tours, and luau. Both shops are open every day from 8 a.m. to 5 p.m. You don't need to reserve in advance, but advance bookings are available over the phone at ☎ **800-262-7725** or online at www.snorkelbob.com.

You can rent a set of snorkel gear from Snorkel Bob's at the start of your trip, carry it with you as you travel throughout the islands, and then return it to another Snorkel Bob's location on Oahu, Maui, or the Big Island. (All shops offer 24-hour gear return service.) I suggest renting equipment, even if you intend to go on snorkel cruises or kayak trips that provide gear. Free gear is almost always awful — and I don't want you to miss out on spotting sea turtles and other groovy critters because you're fussing with a clogged snorkel or a leaking mask.

On the North Shore, rent your gear from the friendly folks at **Kayak Kauai Outbound,** 5-5070 Kuhio Hwy., a mile past Hanalei Bridge on Highway 56 (look for them on the ocean side of the road, the third building on the right as you enter Hanalei, across from Postcards Cafe) in Hanalei (☎ **800-437-3507** or 808-826-9844; www.kayakkauai.com). Kayak Kauai rents snorkel gear, body boards and surfboards, river and ocean kayaks, and even camping and backpacking gear. (See the kayaking section later in this chapter for details on their guided kayak trips.) There's also a second location on the Coconut Coast at 4-494 Kuhio Hwy., Kapaa.

Snorkeling

Kauai does offer a number of snorkel cruises, but unless you're going to combine snorkeling with a Na Pali sightseeing trip (see the following section), I say save your money. Kauai is best known for its offshore snorkeling, which anybody can do — it only requires that you have a small amount of swimming ability and some good gear (see the preceding section for rental locations).

My absolute favorite offshore snorkeling in Hawaii is off Kauai's North Shore. **Anini, Hideaway, Tunnels,** and **Kee beaches** are all world-class, boasting crystal-clear water and a mind-boggling abundance of colorful fish.

Although placid throughout the summer months, most of Kauai's North Shore beaches become too rough for swimming during the winter. Anini Beach is well-protected enough to stay calm year-round. Kee Beach is the second-most reliable in terms of calm winter waves.

For little ones or first-time snorkelers, head to the Coconut Coast's **Lydgate State Beach Park,** where a lava-rock wall forms a natural pool that stays calm even as the waters churn around it. The calm coves at **Poipu Beach Park** make another excellent choice for beginners, whether they're 6 or 60. Of the North Shore beaches, Kee is the best protected. **Lawai Beach** isn't picture-postcard pretty, but it's my favorite place to snorkel in the Poipu area. You may even spot some little critters darting in and out of detritus left by Hurricane Iniki, such as concrete blocks and spare tires.

For details on all the beaches that I discuss here, see the section "Combing the beaches," earlier in this chapter.

Safety is key when snorkeling. See "Ocean Safety" in the Quick Concierge at the end of this book for snorkeling tips.

Cruising the Na Pali Coast and other on-deck adventures

Hawaii's most spectacular coastline is also its most isolated destination. This network of verdant valleys and cliffs on Kauai's northwest shoreline composes an unspoiled tropical paradise that few get to experience, thanks to its utter remoteness. You can see the glorious Na Pali Coast in three ways: by helicopter tour (see "Taking a flightseeing tour," later in this chapter), by hiking in (see "Sightseeing with a guide," later in this chapter), or by catching a boat ride around the bend. I like the approach from sea best; it's simply breathtaking. Most cruises combine snorkeling with sightseeing.

Kauai serves as an excellent vantage from which to see the Pacific humpback whales make their annual visit to Hawaii from Alaska between December and April. In season, most cruise operators combine whale-watching with their regular adventures.

The water can be very choppy as you cruise the North Shore. Mornings are usually calm, but the surf tends to kick up later in the day. Those of you with sensitive tummies should take Dramamine or other motion-sickness meds *well before* you set out on one of these expeditions — when you're out on the sea, it's too late for the drugs to have any benefit. Also available are nausea-prevention wristbands, which you can find at any drugstore; they seem to benefit many users.

You may be able to save a few bucks on your Na Pali Coast or other cruise by booking it through Maui-based **Tom Barefoot's Tours** (☎ 800-621-3601 or 808-661-1246; www.tombarefoot.com), which also books activities on Kauai. Tom Barefoot is a very reliable activities center that's willing to split its commissions with you so that everybody comes out ahead. You'll save 7 to 15 percent on trips with select outfitters.

Capt. Andy's Sailing Adventures

Capt. Andy runs the *Spirit of Kauai,* a late-model 55-foot, 49-passenger Gold Coast catamaran, on a number of regular trips to the glorious Na Pali Coast. The boat is sleek and comfy, excelling at both speed and stability, and the staff is friendly, extremely knowledgeable about the Na Pali Coast, and attentive. Choose from morning, afternoon, and full-day Na Pali Coast trips, which include sailing, snorkeling, dolphin-watching, and usually lunch; full-day expeditions even land on a remote beach when conditions allow. You also have the option of a sunset cruise, which includes cocktails, to either Na Pali or Poipu. Call or check the Web site for the current schedule because the Na Pali schedule is truncated in winter (but whale-watching compensates).

Capt. Andy also offers Na Pali tours for small groups in 24-foot inflatable rafts. These boats, which sit lower to the water, offer a fast, utterly thrilling ride, and are small enough to explore sea caves. Snorkeling is included, along with breakfast or lunch.

Most cruises depart from the Capt. Andy's office at Port Allen Marina Center, 4353 Waialao Rd. (at Highway 50 halfway between Poipu and Waimea), Eleele. Poipu sunset cruises depart from Kukuiula Harbor, Poipu Beach. ☎ *800-535-0830 or 808-335-6833.* www.capt-andys.com *or* www.napali.com/kauai_sailing. *Prices: Na Pali snorkel adventure $139–$159 adults, $99 kids ages 2–12; Na Pali sunset dinner $105 adults, $80 kids ages 2–12; Poipu sunset sail $69 adults, $50 kids ages 2–12; rafting trips $139–$159 adults, $99 kids ages 5–12. Note: No children under age 5 on rafting trips, no kids under age 2 on sailing trips. Discounts available for online booking.*

Captain Sundown

Captain Sundown is the only operator whose cruises depart exclusively from the North Shore, which is much closer to the Na Pali Coast. Its 40-foot sailing catamaran carries only 15 passengers, so this cruise is an excellent choice for those looking for an intimate trip. Options include year-round Na Pali sails. From April through December, you have two options: a six-hour morning tour that includes snorkeling, fishing, and a deli lunch; or a three-hour afternoon sightseeing-only sunset tour. Whale-watching is the raison d'être on the five-hour winter outing. All trips include an exciting short paddle out to the boat in a Hawaiian Outrigger canoe. This is a small family-owned and family-run business, and they're committed to making sure that you're happy, well informed, and seeing the best of Kauai. Reserve well in advance because these small-capacity trips often book up a week or more ahead of time.

Trips depart from Hanalei Beach, Hanalei. ☎ **808-826-5585.** www.captain sundown.com. *Prices: 6-hour sail with snorkeling $148–$162 adults, $128–$148 kids 7–12. No kids under age 7.*

Liko Kauai Cruises

This Hawaiian-owned and -operated company offers four-hour combination Na Pali Coast/snorkel/dolphin-watching/cave tours, with lunch. It all happens on a comfortable 49-foot twin-hulled catamaran (with padded seating, a nice plus). In addition to seeing whales in season, you'll peek into sea caves and lush valleys, glimpse waterfalls and miles of white-sand beaches, and make stops along the way for snorkeling. The narration is in-depth, culturally as well as naturally oriented, and very good. Prices include a deli-style lunch and sodas.

Cruises depart from Kehaka Small Boat Harbor, Waimea; check in at Obsessions Café, 9875 Waimea Rd. (Highway 50, adjacent to the Big Save Market), Waimea. ☎ **888-SEA-LIKO [732-5456]** *or 808-338-0333.* www.liko-kauai.com. *Prices: $140 adults, $95 kids 4–12.*

Na Pali Explorer

This terrific local, family-owned tour operator offers Na Pali Coast tours (plus whale-watching expeditions in season) aboard three of the most exciting boats to cruise the Kauai coast: the 26-foot *Explorer I,* which holds 16 passengers; the 48-foot *Explorer II,* which carries up to 35 passengers; and the 46-foot Ocean Adventurer, with a similar capacity. All are rigid inflatable boats (RIBs), the kinds of rubber inflatables made famous by Jacques Cousteau. These sleek vessels skim the surface of the water at up to 35 knots, which means that they can reach the remote, rugged Na Pali quickly, and can maneuver closer to the shore, and into hidden sea caves that other vessels simply cannot reach. The smaller boat makes up for its lack of amenities with an unparalleled thrill ride that is not for the faint of heart. The larger boat tones down the thrills a bit in exchange for comfort amenities like shaded seating, a toilet, and freshwater showers. Still, these are not fancy boats; both emphasize experience over amenities. No matter which cruise you select, count on an expert staff that's knowledgeable, friendly, and attentive. Prices include continental breakfast, a deli lunch, and/or afternoon pupus, depending on the trip you choose.

Na Pali Explorer now operates some cruises aboard its *Ocean Adventurer* out of Hanalei. If you're interested in departing from the North Shore, call for available dates.

Cruises depart from Kekiaola Harbor, Waimea. ☎ **877-335-9909** *or 808-338-9999.* www.napali-explorer.com. *Prices: $89–$135 adults, $69–$95 kids 5–12.*

Ocean and river kayaking

Kauai is an excellent place for kayaking. First-timers don't have to brave the open ocean — rather, they can paddle down the Huleia River into Huleia National Wildlife Refuge, the last stand of Kauai's endangered birds (it's the only way the nature refuge can be explored); cruise calmly along the Wailua River, freshwater playground of Kauai's ancient kings; or follow the winding Hanalei River out to beautiful Hanalei Bay. More skilled kayakers can set out for the majestic Na Pali Coast for some real excitement. Here are the best outfitters:

✔ **Kayak Kauai Outbound,** 5-5070 Kuhio Hwy., a mile past the Hanalei Bridge on Highway 56 (look for them on the ocean side of the road, across from Postcards Cafe) in Hanalei (☎ **800-437-3507** or 808-826-9844; www.kayakkauai.com), offers guided tours, or lessons and equipment rentals if you want to set off on your own. Gentle half-day river tours begin at $60 for adults, $45 for kids under age 12; extremely challenging full-day sea-kayak trips for adults run $145 to $205. The shop has its own dock if you want to explore the Hanalei River and Wildlife Refuge on your own.

Kayak Kauai Outbound also has a second location on the Coconut Coast at 4-494 Kuhio Hwy., Kapaa, just a half-mile north of the Wailua River adjacent to the Coconut Marketplace (☎ **800-437-3507**), where you can rent kayaks and gear for exploring the Wailua River Monday to Saturday. Doubles are $75 for the day (no singles available). You should reserve in advance.

✔ **Outfitters Kauai,** on the South Shore, at Poipu Plaza, 2827A Poipu Rd., just before the turnoff to Spouting Horn (☎ **888-742-9887** or 808-742-9667; www.outfitterskauai.com), has its own full slate of guided kayaking trips. It offers sea tours for skilled kayakers (including a challenging kayak trip along the Na Pali Coast in summer; $198 per person; no kids under 15), as well as a guided paddle along the Huleia and Wailua rivers for less experienced folks ($98 adults, $78 kids 5–14). Daily river kayak rentals are also available for $40 per person.

Outfitters Kauai has also expanded into kayak rentals along the lazy Wailua River; **Wailua Kayak & Canoe** (☎ **808-821-1188**) offers double and single kayaks for rental from a convenient base-yard near the mouth of the river. Call ahead and book your kayaks at least a day in advance; they're available twice daily for five-hour rentals ($75 double, $45 single) at 7 a.m. and 12:30 p.m. From Kuhio Highway, turn onto Kuamoo Road, across from Wailua Bay at the entrance to the old Coco Palms resort, to reach the base-yard, where you'll be issued equipment and a kayak on a wheeled cart, which you'll pull by hand for the five-minute walk to the river. The Wailua Kayak folks will offer you an easy-to-follow map and offer basic paddling instructions, which is all you'll need. It's really a fun and easy way to explore this tranquil paradise.

✔ **Kayak Wailua** (☎ **808-822-3388;** www.kayakwailua.com) offers well-priced rentals and guided river kayak tours from the Wailua Marina. At $40 per person (plus a 15 percent guide gratuity) for a 4½-hour guided tour, this is one of the best guided tour deals out there. First-time kayakers are welcome, and all are welcome to bring your own bag lunch (one of the ways they're able to cut back on the rate).

Ziplining through the backcountry

Multifaceted backcountry adventure tours that culminate in a thrilling zipline ride through the treetops have really taken off on the majestic Garden Isle. You have three outfitters to choose from:

✔ **Outfitters Kauai** (☎ **888-742-9887** or 808-742-9667; www.outfitterskauai. com) offers a very exciting everything-but-the-kitchen-sink kind of a trip that's a big hit among thrill-seeking visitors: the **Kipu Falls Zipline Safari**, which combines kayaking, rope swinging, ranch hay-riding, jungle trekking, cruising on a motorized canoe, and flying through the jungle treetops on a zipline into a six-hour adventure. The tour costs $175 for adults, $135 for kids 14 and under. If you want to cut right to the chase, consider the **Kipu Falls Zipline Trek** for three hours of rope swinging, hiking, and ziplining; the cost is $125 adults, $99 for kids 7 to 14. No kids under age 7.

✔ **Kauai Backcountry Adventures** (☎ **888-270-0555** or 808-245-2506; www.kauai backcountry.com) offers exclusive access to over 17,000 scenic acres, a former sugar plantation at the heart of the island, and they really make the most of it. Kauai Backcountry's 3½-hour **Zipline Adventure** is all about the zipline — no muss, no fuss. After a short four-wheel-drive transfer and a brief orientation, you'll zip down a series of seven ziplines to the valley floor below before ending your adventure with a picnic lunch and a refreshing swim in a natural swimming pool. A monumental thrill! The cost is $125 per person, and tours are offered daily at 9:30 a.m. and 2 p.m.; no kids under 12.

✔ You can also book guided jungle and Hanalei kayak adventures that include a zipline ride as part of the fun with **Princeville Ranch Adventures** (☎ **888-955-7669** or 808-826-7669; www.adventureskauai.com). Tours run $129 to $145 per person, depending on the one you choose.

Catching a wave

If you've always wanted to surf the ocean waves, now's your chance — Poipu Beach is a great place to learn. Contact **Margo Oberg Surf School** (☎ **808-332-6100** or 808-639-0708; www.surfonkauai.com), the domain of seven-time world-champion surfer Margo Oberg. Margo's accredited instructors swear that they can get anybody up and riding a wave by the end of a lesson. The price is $65 for the two-hour beginner group lesson, including equipment; book at least a day in advance. Lessons are also available for more advanced surfers.

If you already know the basics, you can rent a surfboard from the **Nukumoi Surf Co.**, across the street from Poipu Beach at Brennecke's Beach Center (☎ **888-384-8810** or 808-742-8019; www.nukumoisurf.com). A two-hour group lesson is $75 per person, and a small class size — just four students per class — means you'll get plenty of attention. Nukumoi will take students as young as 9 years old (younger if parents participate as well). Private lessons are also available. Nukumoi also rents boogie boards.

If you want to learn to windsurf, reach out to **Windsurf Kauai** (☎ 808-828-6838), which offers windsurfing lessons from Anini Beach, an excellent — and beautiful — place to learn the basics, whether you're 6 or 60. A three-hour windsurf lesson is $75. You can book windsurf lessons a couple of days in advance. Private surf lessons from the North Shore are also available but require further notice, and they depend on conditions. On the North Shore, surfboards and boogie boards are available for rent at the **Hanalei Surf Company,** in the heart of Hanalei in the Old Hanalei School Building at the Hanalei Center (directly across from Zelo's), 5–5161 Kuhio Hwy. (☎ **866-HANALEI** or 808-826-9000; www. hanaleisurf.com). To arrange for a surf lesson with Hanalei Surf's own surf champ and accredited coach Russell Lewis, call ☎ **808-346-5710.**

Hanalei Bay is the island's most popular surf spot in winter, but it's strictly for experts — so stay out of the water when the waves are up unless you *really* know what you're doing.

Hooking the big one

You simply can't find a better place in the world to sportfish than off the Big Island's Kona Coast, often called the Sportfishing Capital of the World — but if you're not going to the Big Island, you don't have to miss out. Contact **Hawaii Fishing Adventures and Charters** (☎ 877-388-1376; www.sportfishhawaii.com), which can book a first-class charter for you on the Garden Isle. Prices range from $1,225 to $1,399 for a full-day exclusive charter (your group of up to six gets the entire boat to yourselves) down to as little as $149 for a share charter (you share the boat with five other people).

I always book with Sportfish Hawaii first (☎ 877-388-1376 or 808-396-2607; www.sportfishhawaii.com; see Chapter 11 for more info), but you might also try **Lahela Ocean Adventures** (☎ 808-635-4020; www.sport-fishing-kauai.com), which takes groups as large as 14 out aboard the *Lahela,* a 34-foot Radon sport fisher, in search of marlin, ahi, mahimahi, amberjack, and other sultans of the sea. Shared charters start at $219 per angler, and the crew will filet one catch of up to 30 pounds for you.

My favorite Na Pali cruise outfitter, Na Pali Explorer, now runs **Explore Kauai Sportfishing** (☎ 877-335-9909 or 808-338-9999; www.napali-explorer.com), offering sportfishing tours out of the south shore's Port Allen Boat Harbor aboard the *Happy Times,* its 41-foot convertible Concorde Sportfisher. Prices are $135 per person for a four-hour tour, $170 for six hours of sportfishing, and $230 for a full day (eight hours). A minimum of four and a maximum of six passengers are taken out per trip.

For scuba divers (and those who want to be)

Diving on Kauai is dictated by the weather. In winter, when heavy swells and high winds hit the island, diving is generally limited to the more protected South Shore. When the winter swells disappear and the easygoing summer conditions move in, the magnificent North Shore opens up for divers; there you'll find a kaleidoscopic marine world that's one of the most diverse in Hawaiian waters. I recommend booking a two-tank dive off a dive boat. Here are the best scuba charters:

- ✔ **Bubbles Below Scuba Charters** (☎ **866-524-6268** or 808-332-7333; www.bubblesbelowkauai.com) specializes in highly personalized small-group dives, with an emphasis on marine biology. It offers up to two dives daily, plus one night dive, with most trips departing from Port Allen Small Boat Harbor on the South Shore. The daytime dives usually feature two locations, depending on conditions. The night dive is particularly awesome, often featuring octopus and other nocturnal sea creatures. Prices start at $135, with all equipment and snacks. Instruction, from beginner to refresher courses, is also offered.

- ✔ If you want to explore a wider range of dive sites — including those off the north, east, and west shores — contact **Dive Kauai Scuba Center,** 1038 Kuhio Hwy., Kapaa (☎ **800-828-3483** or 808-822-0452; www.divekauai.com). In fact, it offers so many different dives that you should call for options and prices, which range from $80 to $315 for one- and two-tank shore and boat dives. Dive Kauai also offers a "Discover Scuba" introductory program for $105 to $155, as well as a full slate of PADI (Professional Association of Diving Instructors) certification and refresher courses.

- ✔ If you've never scuba-dived before but want to learn while you're on Kauai, **Fathom Five Divers,** 3450 Poipu Rd., Koloa (☎ **800-972-3078** or 808-742-6991; www.fathomfive.com), is the company to call. In business for more than 15 years, this PADI five-star IDC facility offers charters for experienced divers and first-timers alike. It offers no-experience-necessary introductory trips — both tank boat and shore dives — for $140 to $195 per person, including class, dives, and all gear. It also offers full-on four- or five-day certification courses, as well as a range of dives — two-tank boat, night, and shore dives — for experienced divers at reasonable prices.

Exploring on Dry Land

The most enticing thing about Kauai is its natural beauty — so get in your car and explore. Take Kuhio Highway up to the North Shore — my favorite drive in all Hawaii — just surveying the beauty as you go. Stop to take in the beautiful vistas along the way, have lunch and explore laid-back Hanalei town, kick back at one of the fabulous beaches along this shore (see "Enjoying the Sand and Surf," earlier in this chapter), and watch the sunset at the end of Kilauea Lighthouse Road (23 miles north of Lihue, 7 miles east of Hanalei; turn off at the Menehune Mart). It's the best sightseeing you can do on Kauai.

Sightseeing with a guide

If you're a movie buff — or if you just want a local to show you this gorgeous island — call **Hawaii Movie Tours** (☎ 800-628-8432 or 808-822-1192; www.hawaiimovietour.com), which offers the finest guided sightseeing tour of Kauai, hands down. The $119 land tour ($109 for kids 11 and under) shows you more of Kauai in the course of a day (including private areas and estates not open to the public) than you could take in on your own if you toured the island yourself for a whole week. (The four-wheel-drive tour, priced at $131 for adults, $121 for kids, takes you to gorgeous private preserves where the company has exclusive rights.) And the movie angle serves as great context — you'll realize that you've been seeing Kauai on the silver screen for years without knowing it. Remember *Blue Hawaii, Honeymoon in Vegas, Jurassic Park,* and *Fantasy Island?* Yep — all Kauai! (Even *Lilo & Stitch* — cartoon Kauai!) Kauai's latest starring appearance was in the Ben Stiller 2008 film *Tropic Thunder,* where its verdant jungle doubles as Vietnam.

The movie tours sell out regularly, so call well in advance to book your spots and avoid disappointment. (A month in advance isn't too early in the high season.) Also, do yourself a favor and schedule a Hawaii Movie Tour for early in your trip. That way, you can go back to that hidden beach or lush garden you fell in love with for some quality time on another day. You can book tickets for specific dates right on the Web site. (Check for Internet specials, which are sometimes offered.)

If you want a more general sightseeing tour of the island, or you don't want to drive yourself to destinations like Waimea Canyon or the North Shore, contact **Polynesian Adventure Tours** (☎ 800-622-3011 or 808-246-0122; www.polyad.com), which offers a range of guided tours in minivans, big-windowed mini-coaches (good for small groups and big views), and full-size buses. The only reason to go with these folks is if you have no other way to get around; otherwise, they're not going to show you anything that you can't show yourself without the high price tag. In fact, they'll show you less, because these tours are designed only to give you an overview at each of the stops. You'll have to go back on your own if you want to really explore or take time to commune with nature — which is why I suggest that you guide yourself around in the first place. Prices run $58 to $80 for adults, $38 to $53 for kids ages 3 to 11, depending on what tour you book; reserve your Polynesian Adventure Tour online to get a 10 percent price break.

Taking a flightseeing tour

If you're going to choose one island on which to take a flightseeing tour, do it on Kauai. Kauai is the helicopter capital of Hawaii. So much of the Garden Isle's pristine natural world — hidden waterfalls, lush valleys, mist-shrouded peaks, the rugged interior of the thrilling Na Pali Coast, the spectral hues of Waimea Canyon's deepest ravines — is inaccessible by any other means. Helicopter rides are expensive, but they're worth the splurge if you want to take home memories above and beyond those of less adventuresome visitors. Most companies can even make a videotape of your ride for you to take home and relive again and again in the comfort of your living room.

There are, however, some considerations. Although all the companies I recommend feature skilled pilots and helicopters with excellent safety records, the truth of the matter is that flightseeing is risky business. Dozens of people have died in commercial helicopter crashes in Hawaii over the past decade, including accidents that occurred on Kauai. Of course, just getting into your rental car and driving to dinner — or even getting into the shower in your condo with a renegade bar of soap — is many times more dangerous than catching a 'copter ride. Still, you should make informed decisions when booking.

When reserving a helicopter tour with any company, check to make sure that safety is its first concern. The company should be an FAA-certified Part 135 operator, and the pilot should be Part 135 certified as well; the 135 license guarantees more stringent maintenance requirements and pilot-training programs than those who are only Part 91 certified. And if weather conditions look iffy, reschedule.

Be sure to book your flight in advance (at least a week before in high season). All flights depart from Lihue Airport.

✔ **Island Helicopters** (☎ **800-829-5999** or 808-245-8588; www.island helicopters.com; 55-minute island tour: $266 per person): Owner Curt Lofstedt has more than 25,000 hours of flying under his belt, and he personally selects and trains professional pilots with an eye to both their flying skills and their ability to show you Kauai. All flights are in either the four-passenger Bell Jet Ranger III or the six-passenger American Eurocopter AStar, both with extra-large windows, all forward-facing seats, and stereo headsets to hear the pilot's personal narration, which is strong on island culture and history. You'll get a free preproduced video of the tour highlights, but custom videos aren't available. You can usually snag substantial discounts by booking online via its Web site. There's a $23 fuel surcharge.

✔ **Jack Harter** (☎ **888-245-2001** or 808-245-3774; www.helicopters-kauai.com; one-hour tour: $259 per person, including $30 fuel surcharge; 90-minute tour: $385 per person, including $45 fuel surcharge): A Kauai pioneer, Jack personally started the sightseeing-via-helicopter trend — so, needless to say, he knows this island well. He flies four-passenger Bell Jet Rangers, which give everybody a great forward view and lots of leg and shoulder room, plus windows that open (great for the photographers among you), as well as six-passenger Eurocopter AStars. Jack's signature 90-minute tour hovers over the sights a bit longer than the one-hour flight so you can get a good look, but the 60-minute tour pretty much covers the island without whizzing by the big attractions in a blur. If you're a shutterbug who's counting on getting some good shots from above, though, go with the longer flight. Be sure to check the Web site for online discounts ($30 off the regular price for the hour-long tour, $40 off the 90-minute tour at press time).

✔ **Sunshine Helicopters** (☎ **866-501-7738** or 808-270-3999; www. helicopters-hawaii.com; one-hour tour: $230 to $310 per person, depending on the helicopter and flight you choose): Sunshine offers a range of birds to choose from: The six-passenger American Eurocopter AStar offers side-by-side seats (so nobody sits backward and everybody gets a window seat), while the FX-AStar offers more spacious seating with extra arm and leg room. The pricier WhisperStars offer custom bubble windows for maximum views; the first-class WhisperStar offers extra arm and leg room. At press time, online bookings made at least seven days in advance garner you a 10 percent price break.

Exploring Kauai's top attractions

For such a small, laid-back island, Kauai boasts a wealth of attractions that are worth seeking out. The Allerton and McBryde Gardens and the Kilauea Point Wildlife Refuge are my favorites of a fine bunch.

Allerton and McBryde Gardens

A former turn-of-the-twentieth-century private estate that's been transformed into a nationally chartered research facility for the study and conservation of tropical botanics, the 300-acre **Allerton Garden** is simply amazing. It's home to an extraordinary collection of tropical fruit and spice trees, rare introduced and native Hawaiian plants, hundreds of varieties of flowers, a marvelous palm collection, a series of Green Giant–size Moreton Bay fig trees that were featured in *Jurassic Park,* and some prime examples of landscape gardening featuring outdoor "rooms" and gravity-fed fountains that would have turned William Randolph Hearst green with envy. You can visit the garden only on a docent-led guided tour usually offered four times a day Monday to Saturday and occasionally on Sunday; it's a fascinating, well-spent 2½ hours for serious green thumbs and novices alike (really — I loved it, and I can't identify common houseplants), and it's well worth the price tag. The secret beach you'll visit is alone worth the trip — the view of it from above at the start of the tour was one of the most awe-inspiring views that I've ever seen.

McBryde Garden is a gorgeous research garden that focuses on the conservation and cataloging of the plants of Hawaii and the Pacific. It's home to the largest collection of native Hawaiian plants in the world (many of them rare and endangered) in a much more natural setting than what you'll see at Allerton. You can tour the well-signed McBryde Garden on a 1-mile self-guided walk daily; a tram will take you into the garden; allow about 1½ hours. You also can tour for free a gorgeous native plant garden located at the departure point.

Reservations are required for the guided tours through Allerton Garden; they are not required for the self-guided McBryde tour. Reserve your tour at least a week in advance, especially in the peak months of July, August, and September. Wear comfortable walking shoes and long pants and bring insect repellent (you'll need it). I suggest starting with the Allerton tour first and then coming back for a McBryde tour if you want more (which you very well may). You may also want to consider visiting **Limahuli Garden,** another National Tropical Botanical Garden on the North Shore (see the listing later in this chapter).

See map p. 462. On Lawai Road (across the street from Spouting Horn), Poipu Beach. ☎ *808-742-2623.* www.ntbg.org. *Allerton Garden 2½-hour guided tours: $40 adults, $20 children 10–12 (no kids under age 10). Allerton tour times: Mon–Sat at 9 a.m., 10 a.m., 1 p.m., and 2 p.m.; call for Sun tour times, which are occasionally offered. McBryde Garden 1½-hour tram ride and self-guided tour: $20 adults, $10 kids 6–12 (free for kids 5 and under). McBryde trams leave Mon–Sat at 9:30 a.m., 10:30 a.m., 11:30 a.m., 12:30 p.m., 1:30 p.m., and 2:30 p.m.*

Fern Grotto

One of Kauai's oldest ("since 1947") and most popular attractions is this tacky-touristy trip filled with Hawaiian song and hula — but it's a good bit of fun nonetheless. Flat-bottomed boats take visitors up the Wailua River to a natural amphitheater filled with ferns that's the source of many Hawaiian legends (and a popular site for weddings). Mark my words: Within ten minutes of the launch, you'll be on your feet doing the Hukilau (Hawaii's version of the Hokey Pokey) along with everybody else. The Fern Grotto is lovely; but you'll see more stunning natural beauty just by heading to the North Shore, so you have to be in the mood for the cheeky laughs as well as the ferns. Allow 1½ hours for the round-trip.

See map p. 462. Wailua Marina, at the mouth of the Wailua River. To get there: Turn off Kuhio Highway (Highway 56) into Wailua Marine State Park. **Smith's Motor Boats:** ☎ *808-821-6895.* www.smithskauai.com. *Tickets: $20 adults, $10 kids 2–12. Reservations recommended. Save 10 percent when you book online. Departures daily at 9:30 a.m., 10 a.m., 11:30 a.m., 1:30 p.m., 2 p.m., and 2:30 p.m.*

Kauai Museum

The biggest and best museum on the neighbor islands is housed in an attractive Greco-Roman–style building in downtown Lihue. If you're interested in the history of Kauai and neighboring Niihau (or if you just have a rainy day), it's definitely worth a stop. Among the holdings is a wealth of artifacts tracing the Garden Island's history from the beginning of time through contact — when Capt. James Cook "discovered" Kauai in 1778 — and the present. A short video presentation sets the context for what you'll see. The main room houses well-curated rotating exhibitions; I saw a fascinating photo exhibit documenting the reclamation of Kahoolawe, a Hawaiian island used as a U.S. military bombing target until it was returned to the Hawaiian people in the 1990s. You won't need more than an hour to see the entire museum — maybe 90 minutes if you're really interested. The gift shop is one of the island's top stops for Kauai-made crafts. Guided tours are offered Tuesday to Friday at 10:30 a.m. free with admission; reservations are required for groups.

See map p. 462. 4428 Rice St. (across from the post office), Lihue. ☎ *808-245-6931. www.kauaimuseum.org. Admission: $10 adults, $8 seniors, $3 students 13–17, $1 kids 6–12. Free admission for the whole family on the 1st Sat of the month. Open: Mon–Fri 9 a.m.–4 p.m., Sat 10 a.m.–4 p.m.*

Kilauea Point National Wildlife Refuge

I just love this place. Sitting at the northernmost tip of the Hawaiian Islands and jutting out 200 feet above the deep blue surf, this nationally protected 203-acre headland habitat is a magnet for magnificent seabirds and land birds alike. Park your car, pay your entrance fee, and walk an easy ¼ mile to the rocky headland, whose only structure is the Kilauea Lighthouse, serving as a beacon for ships arriving from Asian and South Pacific waters since 1913. Year-round you can spot red-footed boobies, Kauai's most visible seabird, which roost in the surrounding trees; the magnificent great frigate bird, with 7½-foot wings; and the endangered nene, or Hawaiian goose, the state bird of Hawaii. Depending on the time of year, you might also spot red- and white-tailed tropic birds; Laysan albatross, famous for their elaborate courtship rituals; or wedgetailed shearwaters, which like to winter at sea. Informative placards make identification easy, even for novices. Look out to sea for spectacular views; if you get lucky, you might also spot sea turtles, spinner dolphins, and Hawaiian monk seals in the waters below. Call for the schedule of interpretive programs and guided hikes. The refuge is well worth a half-hour of your North Shore time.

The wildlife refuge closes its gate at 4 p.m. daily, but don't let that stop you from parking along Kilauea Lighthouse Road to watch one of Hawaii's most magnificent sunsets. No doubt you'll have company, both locals and in-the-know visitors, as you look west to watch the sun sink into the horizon beyond Hanalei Bay, brilliantly illuminating the luxuriant Bali Hai cliffs with its warm orange rays in the process.

See map p. 462. At the end of Kilauea Lighthouse Road, 1 mile north of Kilauea. To get there: From Kuhio Highway (Highway 56), turn right at the sign for Kilauea Lighthouse (at Menehune Mart and gas station, 23 miles north of Lihue). ☎ *808-828-1413. Admission: $5. Open: Daily 10 a.m.–4 p.m.*

Kokee State Park

Keep going upland and inland through Waimea Canyon, known as the Grand Canyon of the Pacific (see the listing later in this section), all the way to the top, where you'll find a high-altitude treat: Kokee (ko-*kay*-eh) State Park. It's a whole different world up here at 4,000 feet: Kokee is a cloud forest at the edge of an upland bog known as the Alakai Swamp, where the breeze has a bite and trees look like the ones on the mainland. Days are cool, wet, and mild, with intermittent bright sunshine — sort of like the Oregon Coast on a good day. The forest is full of beautiful native plants and imports, like ohia, rare stands of koa, hibiscus, eucalyptus, and redwoods. Pigs, goats, and black-tailed deer thrive in the forest, as do a wealth of native birds.

Before you get out of the car, head 3 miles above Kokee Lodge to Kalalau Lookout, the spectacular climax of your drive through Waimea Canyon and Kokee. At the lookout, you'll enjoy a spectacular view into an otherwise-hidden Na Pali valley that's untouched by the spoils of civilization; the panoramic view is simply breathtaking. Wonderful birds reside at the lookout, which offer reason enough to come; a family of cardinals greeted me the last time I was here.

From Kalalau Lookout, head back down to the park itself. Before you explore, stop at the Kokee Natural History Museum, where a colorful clutch of chickens populates the parking lot. This small, vital museum is the place to learn about the forest and bog before you see it. If you want a bite to eat, Kokee Lodge is open for continental breakfast and lunch right next door. After your museum visit, pick up the nature trail that starts behind the building at the rare Hawaiian koa tree. (You'll see lots of expensive gifts, such as boxes and bowls, made out of this gorgeous wood in shops throughout the islands.) The easy, self-guided walk is your best introduction to this rain forest, and it's great for those who'd rather not take on a tougher trail. The less than ¼-mile walk takes about 20 minutes if you stop and look at all the plants that are identified along the way.

Here are a few tips to keep in mind when preparing for a visit to Kokee:

✔ No matter how hot and dry it is down at the beach, bring a jacket with you up to Kokee, because it gets *cold* at 4,000 feet. Average daytime temperatures range from 45°F in January to 68°F in July; on my last visit, it was 55°F up here while it was 80°F down on the coast. Also bring rain gear and an umbrella if you have it — especially if you're visiting between October and May — because the annual rainfall up here is 70 inches. You can call the museum to check current conditions.

✔ Wear good shoes, because it can be damp and muddy — hiking boots are preferable (if you don't have them, sneakers will do).

✔ The best time to visit Kokee is early in the morning. That's when you have the best chance of seeing the panoramic view of Kalalau Valley from the lookout, before clouds obscure the valley and peaks. Early morning is also the best time to spot native birds.

✔ If you're going to hike, check trail conditions (posted on a bulletin board at the museum) before you set out. Pick up a free trail map at the museum, which will allow you to pick the trail length and challenge that is right for you. Stay on established trails, because it's easy to get lost here. Get off the trail well before dark. Carry water and rain gear and wear sunscreen.

See map p. 462. At the end of Kokee Road, 16 miles north of Waimea; from Kaumualii Highway (Highway 50), turn north on Highway 550, Waimea Canyon Drive, which eventually becomes Kokee Road. ☎ *808-335-9975 or 808-335-8405.* www.kokee. org. *Admission: Free! Open: Daily 24 hours; museum daily 10 a.m.–4 p.m.*

Guided Kokee Park **Wonder Walks** are offered daily during the summer season, depending on weather conditions. Most hikes leave from the museum at 12:15 p.m. Trail choice depends on weather. Reserve ahead, as space is limited, and bring light rain gear, good walking shoes, bottled water, and sunscreen.

Limahuli Garden

If you've already visited the gorgeous Allerton Garden on the South Shore (see the listing earlier in this section) and you want more botanical experiences, head to this North Shore branch of the National Tropical Botanical Garden, where you'll find 17 lush, Eden-like acres featuring lava-rock terraces of taro and other native and introduced species. This small, almost-secret garden is ecotourism at its best. You're welcome to explore the garden on your own along a ¾-mile loop (be prepared — it's steep in some areas), which takes about 1½ hours. Or you can schedule a 2½-hour guided tour if you want botanical insight into what you're seeing. Wear comfortable walking shoes; umbrellas are available for your use in case it rains.

See map p. 462. Near the north end of Kuhio Highway (Highway 56), ¼ mile before Kee Beach (look to your left, toward the mountain), Haena. ☎ *808-826-1053.* www. ntbg.org. *Reservations required for guided tours. Admission: $15 adults, free for kids 12 and under. Guided tour: $25 adults, $15 kids 13–18, free for kids 12 and under. Open: Tues–Sat 9:30 a.m.–4 p.m.; guided tour Tues–Sat at 10 a.m.*

Na Pali Coast State Wilderness Park

Na Pali Coast State Wilderness Park is the most spectacular place in the Hawaiian Islands. This 22-mile stretch of green-velvet fluted cliffs wraps around the northwest shore of Kauai. Seven valleys crease the soaring cliffs; hidden within are waterfalls, remote beaches, and other wonders of nature that are too beautiful to be real — and more than difficult to reach. You can see it one of three ways: on a commercial cruise for a from-the-sea perspective (see "Cruising the Na Pali Coast and other on-deck adventures," earlier in this chapter); via a helicopter ride for an on-high view (see "Taking a flightseeing tour," earlier in this chapter); or by trekking in on your own two feet from the end of the road on the North Shore (park at the lot at Kee Beach; you'll see the trail head on the north side of the road, marked by a large sign). If you reach the 2-mile mark and you want to go farther, you must have a permit (permits are $10 per night and are issued in person at the **Kauai State Parks Office,** 3060 Eiwa St., Room 306, Lihue; ☎ **808-274-3444;** www.hawaiistateparks.org/parks/kauai). The total length of the trail is 11 miles, and it's a serious challenge. Visit the park's Web site for details and advice before you consider a trip longer than the 2-mile segment I describe.

Without a permit, you can also hike another 2 miles inland from the beach to Hanakapiai Falls, a 120-foot cascade. This part of the trail is more difficult, however, and it shouldn't be tackled if it's muddy. (I saw people coming out who had been literally knee-deep in mud.) Allow another three hours round-trip to the falls.

If you're planning to hike the Kalalau Trail, keep these tips in mind as you plan your adventure:

 ✔ Wear good, supportive shoes (tennis shoes or hiking boots).

 ✔ Don't attempt even the first half-mile if the trail is too muddy.

 ✔ If you're going any farther than the first half-mile, bring plenty of water, plus a hat and sunscreen; snacks and insect repellent are a good idea, too.

 ✔ Use the porta-potties at the parking lot before you hit the trail, because you'll find no facilities along it.

 ✔ If you get as far as Hanakapiai Beach, try to resist taking a dip, because currents are strong year-round and drownings occur here regularly. Don't even think about entering the water in winter.

See map p. 462. Kalalau trail head at the end of Kuhio Highway (Highway 56) at Kee Beach, about 7½ miles past Hanalei. ☎ *808-274-3444.* www.hawaiistateparks. org/parks/kauai.

Sleeping Giant

If you squint your eyes as you drive down Kuhio Highway past the 1,241-foot-high Nounou Ridge, which forms a dramatic backdrop to the Coconut Coast towns of Wailua and Waipouli, you just may see the fabled Sleeping Giant. At the 7-mile marker, look toward the mountain. It's easy to spot: The geologic giant lies on his back, with his head pointing north and slightly east, his feet south and slightly west, and he's got his great mouth open in a mammoth yawn. As island legend goes, he's a giant named Puni who fell asleep after a great feast, but he reminds me of Gulliver and the Lilliputians. You're welcome to climb the big guy if you like; the Sleeping Giant Trail offers an easy-to-moderate family hike to a fabulous panoramic view. From the parking lot, posted signs lead you over the 1¾-mile trail, which ends at a picnic table and shelter. Wear sunscreen and bring water — and a picnic, if you like.

See map p. 462. Trail head on Haleilio Road, off Kuhio Highway (Highway 56) between Wailua and Kapaa. To get there: At the Kinipopo Shopping Village traffic light (there's also a Shell Station here), turn toward the mountain off Kuhio Highway and follow Haleilio Road for just over a mile to the parking area at telephone pole no. 38; look for sign at trail head that says "NouNou Mt. Trail E."

Spouting Horn

Sort of like an ocean version of Yellowstone's Old Faithful, this *puhi* — blowhole — is quite a natural phenomenon. Big waves hit Kauai's South Shore with enough force on a constant basis to propel a spout of funneled salt water skyward like a dramatic natural fountain, 10 feet or more in the air. An additional hole blows air that makes a loud moaning sound, ascribed by

Hawaiian legend to a giant female lizard, Mo'o, who once guarded this coast-line, gobbling up any intruders that came along. Along came Liko, who wanted to fish in this area, and Mo'o rushed out to eat him. Quickly, Liko threw a spear right into the giant lizard's mouth, who then chased Liko into a lava tube. Liko escaped, but legend says Mo'o is still in the tube; the moaning sound, they say, is her cry for help (or her toothache, I'd say). You can stop by for a few minutes to admire Spouting Horn or bring a picnic and enjoy the view as you munch; the grassy little oceanfront park features picnic tables and restrooms. This spot is a popular hangout with Kauai's wild chickens, who apparently can't read the posted "No Animals Allowed" sign.

See map p. 462. On Lawai Road, Poipu Beach. To get there: From Kaumualii Highway (Highway 50), turn south on Maluhia Road (Highway 520) and continue south on Poipu Road. At the "Welcome to Poipu Beach" sign, go to the right; after you pass Prince Kuhio Park, Spouting Horn Park will be on your left (across from the entrance to the National Tropical Botanical Garden).

Waimea Canyon State Park

The great gaping gulch that Mark Twain dubbed the "Grand Canyon of the Pacific" is quite a sight — no other island offers anything like it. The nickname is apt, for the valley and its reddish lava beds remind everyone who sees it of Arizona's Grand Canyon. Kauai's version is bursting with ever-changing color, just like its namesake, but it's much smaller — only a mile wide, 3,567 feet deep, and 12 miles long. You can stop to take in the view (a great stop on your way to Kokee State Park; see earlier in this chapter), hike down, and swoop through in a helicopter. (See the section "Taking a flightseeing tour," earlier in this chapter.) As you climb north — and up in elevation — the first good vantage point that you'll reach is Waimea Canyon Lookout, located between the 10- and 11-mile markers on Waimea Canyon Road. Take a peek; you'll see why the canyon got its nickname. A few more lookout points dot the route, each offering spectacular views; Puu Hina Hina Lookout, located between the 13- and 14-mile markers at 3,336 feet in elevation, is a particular jewel.

If you want to hike in, your best bet is the Canyon Trail, which leads to the east rim for a breathtaking view into the canyon. Park your car at the top of Halemanu Valley Road, located between the 14- and 15-mile markers on Waimea Canyon Road, about a mile down from the Kokee Natural History Museum. Walk down the not-very-clearly marked trail on the 3½-mile round-trip, which takes about two to three hours and leads to Waipoo Falls and back. I suggest going in the afternoon — following your visit to Kokee is best — when the late afternoon light illuminates the canyon magnificently.

Another terrific hiking choice is the Kukui Trail, which you can follow for a steep but rewarding 2½-mile journey to the bottom of Waimea Canyon. You'll traverse about 2,300 feet in elevation each way, so make sure you're in shape to handle it. The trail head is on the right side of the road, about halfway up Highway 550; if you reach Kokee State Park, you've gone too far.

See map p. 462. About 11 miles north of Waimea; turn north from Kaumualii Highway (Highway 50) onto Waimea Canyon Drive (Highway 550) www.hawaiistate
parks.org/parks/kauai.

Outfitters Kauai (☎ **888-742-9887** or 808-742-9667; www.outfitters kauai.com) offers a guided bike ride down the slopes of Waimea Canyon for adventure-seeking travelers. It's an exciting road bike ride that traverses 12 miles from the rim of the canyon down the paved road to the shoreline. The ride takes about 4½ hours, and morning and afternoon ride are offered. The cost is $98 for adults, $78 for kids ages 12 to 14; no kids under 12, please. Call for reservations.

Hitting the links

 Always book your tee times well in advance — before you leave home, preferably — especially in high season.

 Be sure to ask about afternoon and twilight rates, which can save you a bundle. Some courses also offer discounted rates to select hotels and condos; check with your concierge or call the course directly to inquire. And for discounted tee times, check out the deals available through **Tee Times Hawaii.com** (☎ **888-675-GOLF** or 866-927-1453; www.teetimes hawaii.com).

Kauai Lagoons Golf Club

Kauai Lagoons often appears on lists of top resort courses in the United States; in 2000, *Golf Digest* awarded Kauai Lagoons its gold medal, calling the Kiele Course "one of the four finest courses in the country." The Jack Nicklaus–designed course is excellent, offering an exciting blend of tournament-quality challenge and high-traffic playability — perfect for low handicappers. The Kiele winds up with one of Hawaii's most difficult — and rewarding — holes, a 431-yard, par-4 played straightaway to an island green surrounded by water; but the signature is the par-4, 330-yard 16th, a short but demanding ocean-cliff shot whose green isn't even visible from the tee. (The trick is to hit your tee shot toward the coconut trees on the right side of the fairway.) Currently under renovation, the course will emerge even better than ever by the time you arrive. This is one of the largest practice facilities in the islands; facilities include a driving range, lockers, showers, restaurant, snack bar, pro shop, practice greens, golf clubhouse, and golf club and shoe rental. Duffers looking to work on their game can arrange for individual instruction or sign up for one of the daily clinics.

3351 Hoolaulea Way (off Rice Street), Lihue (turn at the sign for the Kauai Marriott Resort and Beach Club). ☎ *800-634-6400* or 808-241-6000. www.kauailagoons golf.com. *Greens fees: $175, twilight rates $125 after noon. Ask about discounts for guests of select hotels; also, check current greens fees, which may increase following course renovation.*

Kiahuna Golf Club

This par-70, 6,925-yard Robert Trent Jones, Jr.–designed course is a real only-in-Hawaii gem, awarded four stars by *Golf Digest*. A recent renovation has left it looking better than ever, with a fresh set of championship tees to a par 70. The challenging layout plays skillfully around four large archaeological sites, ranging from an ancient Hawaiian temple to the remains of a Portuguese home and crypt built in the early 1800s. The Scottish-style links course has rolling terrain, undulating greens, sand bunkers galore, near-constant winds, a swath of rainbow-colored vegetation, and terrific ocean and island views. A good mix of locals and visitors man the tees. Facilities include a driving range and practice greens, and a good breakfast-and-lunch restaurant, Joe's on the Green.

2545 Kiahuna Plantation Dr. (at Poipu Road), Poipu Beach. ☎ *808-742-9595.* www. kiahunagolf.com. *Greens fees: $110; $75 after 3 p.m. Check for special rates ($95 at press time, $65 after 3 p.m.).*

Poipu Bay Golf Course

Home to the PGA's Grand Slam of Golf from 1994 to 2006, this 6,959-yard, par-72 oceanfront links-style course designed by Robert Trent Jones, Jr., is already a favorite among avid golfers — including, no doubt, Tiger Woods, who has won numerous Grand Slams here. *Golf Digest* named the course one of the top ten in all of Hawaii. Fairways and greens are undulating, and water hazards are located on eight holes; the prevailing trade winds add an extra challenge. The champs play this rugged beauty, often referred to as "the Pebble Beach of the South Pacific," like a British Isles links course — smart and low. Facilities include an excellent pro shop, plus a restaurant, driving range, and putting greens, plus private lessons and daily clinics.

2250 Ainako St. (across the street from the Grand Hyatt Kauai), Poipu Beach. ☎ *800-858-6300* or 808-742-8711. www.poipubaygolf.com. *Greens fees: $200 ($140 for Grand Hyatt guests); $125 noon to 2:30 p.m., $75 after 2:30 p.m.*

Princeville Resort Golf Courses

Nestled in the glorious environs of Kauai's North Shore, these two much-heralded Robert Trent Jones, Jr., designs are the real stars of the Kauai show. One of the most breathtaking — and toughest — golf courses in all Hawaii, the Prince sits on 390 acres carefully sculpted to offer ocean views from every hole. Golfers in the know often name it the best layout in the state, and *Golf Digest* lauded it as the number-one course in Hawaii. Some holes have a waterfall backdrop to the greens, others shoot into the hillside, and the famous par-3 7th requires that you tee off over a stunning wide-mouthed gorge — dead against the wind, no less. Needless to say, accuracy is key here; if you miss the fairway, chances are good that your ball's in the drink. The Makai is more forgiving, but don't kick back just yet. It's actually three 9-hole courses in one — the Ocean, the Woods, and the Lakes — with the Lakes being the most spectacular and the Ocean being the most thrilling, thanks to a 7th hole that requires you to shoot from one ocean promontory to the other, with the blue Pacific roiling below. Facilities include a health club and spa, restaurant and bar, clubhouse, golf shop, and driving range.

Contact the resort for information about value-priced three- and seven-round packages.

In the Princeville Resort, off Kuhio Highway (Highway 56) at mile marker 27. ☎ **800-826-1105.** www.princeville.com/golf.html. *Prince course greens fees: $200 ($155 for Princeville guests); $125 after noon; $95 for 9 holes after 2 p.m. Makai course greens fees: $175 ($125 for Princeville guests); $95 after 1:30 p.m.; $50 after 4 p.m.*

Horseback riding

There's no better way to admire Kauai's remarkable natural scenery than from high in the saddle. In the Poipu area, **CJM Country Stables** (☎ 808-742-6096; www.cjmstables.com) offers a number of guided 2- to 3½-hour rides along the beach, some of which work in a break for a swim and a picnic. Prices run $98 to $125 per person, and all levels of riders are accepted.

Personally, I think that the spectacular North Shore makes even better quarter-horse stomping grounds. **Princeville Ranch Horseback Adventures** (☎ 808-826-7777; www.princevilleranch.com) can take you out on a whole host of guided rides, from a casual yet magical three- or four-hour waterfall picnic ride ($125–$135) to two- to three-hour private rides ($140–$185 per person). There's also a panoramic 90-minute ride along ocean bluffs ($80) and a chance to participate in a full-on 90-minute *paniolo* cattle drive ($135).

Always book horseback adventures with plenty of advance notice — before you leave home is best — and inquire about age, height, weight, and other restrictions.

Getting pampered at the spa

The 25,000-square-foot, state-of-the-art **Anara Spa** at the Grand Hyatt Kauai Resort & Spa, 1571 Poipu Rd., Poipu Beach (☎ 808-742-1234; www.kauai-hyatt.com), is Kauai's finest spa, and one of the best in all Hawaii. "Anara" is an acronym for "A New Age Restorative Approach," which sets the tone for Anara's touchy-feely, homeopathic-minded mission — and God bless 'em for it. This phenomenal indoor-outdoor facility — a lush paradise of fragrant gardens, open-air treatment rooms, lava-rock showers, and therapists with the magic island touch — is the perfect place to spend the day. The spa's masterminds know it, which is why they designed a full slate of spa packages that run anywhere from 1½ hours to a complete day of head-to-toe pampering. You'll spend an arm and a leg here, but it's worth every penny. Stand-alone services are available as well. This place is always booked, so reserve well ahead.

On the North Shore, **Princeville Health Club & Spa** (☎ 800-826-1105; www.princeville.com/spa.html) isn't quite so extensive, mission-oriented, or eye-catching, but its facilities are comfortable, its spa menu is appropriately lengthy, and its technicians are first-rate. (I enjoyed a sublime Aveda facial here on my last visit.) Prices are a bit lower, too.

Shopping the Local Stores

The Garden Isle isn't exactly what you'd call a shopper's destination, so don't come expecting to give your credit card an aerobic workout. That said, a few hidden gems make the Garden Isle sparkle, especially for those in search of gifts with a Hawaiian flair.

In Lihue

One of the best resources for Kauai-made crafts and gifts is the **Edith King Wilcox Museum Gift Shop** at the Kauai Museum, across from the post office at 4428 Rice St., downtown Lihue (☎ 808-245-6931; www. kauaimuseum.org). In addition to astonishing native-wood bowls that have been carved and polished to a high sheen, the shop boasts a nice collection of budget-friendly koa gifts like barrettes, bracelets, and key rings, all made from the gorgeous native wood. The little shop also has a good selection of books, lauhala bags, coconut products, and more. You can reach the shop only through the museum entrance, but the door attendant will let you in for free if you want to skip the permanent collection and head straight for the salable stuff. Hours are Monday to Friday 9 a.m. to 4 p.m., Saturday 10 a.m. to 4 p.m.

The Kauai outpost of **Hilo Hattie,** Hawaii's biggest name in aloha wear, is at 3-3252 Kuhio Hwy., at Ahukini Road (the turnoff for the airport; ☎ 808-245-3404; www.hilohattie.com). Geared to the tourist market, Hilo Hattie carries inexpensive, colorful wear that has substantially improved in quality and style in recent years. It's right by the airport, so this is a good spot to stock up on last-minute gifts before you head home.

On the Coconut Coast

My favorite shopping stop on Kauai is the **Kapa'a Stitchery,** on Kuhio Highway just north of Lihue town (☎ 808-245-2281). This friendly shop specializes in locally hand-sewn goods, from aloha shirts to tropical-print napkins to handbags to boldly patterned, beautifully made Hawaiian quilts. For do-it-yourselfers, gorgeous island- and Asian-print fabrics are sold, off the bolt, as are quilting materials and kits.

Kuhio Highway is dotted with mini-malls boasting practical stops and familiar shops, from Safeway to the Sunglass Hut. Most prominent is the **Coconut Marketplace,** 484 Kuhio Hwy., between the Wailua River and Kapaa (☎ 808-822-3641; www.coconutmarketplace.com). This open-air mall features a largely unimpressive collection of 60 or so shops, mostly of the gift variety. Highlights include **Ship Store Galleries** (www.shipstoregalleries.com), which features a compelling collection of 19th-century nautical antiques among the contemporary art; **Elephant Walk** for quality Hawaii-themed gifts; **Sole Mates** (www.sole mates808.com), specializing in such terrific comfort shoe brands as Keen, Teva, and others ideal for the outdoor island lifestyle; the **Hawaiian Music Store** (www.hawaiianmusicstore.com) for an excellent selection of island-inspired tunes; and Kauai's own **Lappert's Ice**

Cream, a must-stop for ice-cream lovers. There's a free hula show at center stage each Wednesday at 5 p.m., as well as a farmers' market every Saturday from noon to 4 p.m.

One of my favorite shopping stops in all Hawaii is **Bambulei,** 4-369D Kuhio Hwy., Wailua (☎ 808-823-8641; www.bambulei.com), which takes a little effort to find — but stick with it, especially if you're a retro buff, because you're bound to come away with a prize. It's on the inland side of Kuhio Highway just south of the Coconut Marketplace, behind the green storefront across from Kintaro Restaurant. Watch for the multicolored sign just past the Wailua intersection (where Sizzler is). Little Bambulei is home to a charmingly displayed collection of vintage Hawaii and Asian collectibles, from salt-and-pepper shakers and '50s fiberglass-shade lamps to aloha shirts and vintage bamboo furniture, plus a small but elegant selection of new aloha wear. It's a real joy to browse. Next door is Caffè Coco, an equally appealing spot for a light snack or a full meal (see Chapter 16).

Boasting an eclectic blend of old-time retailers and newer fashion boutiques, sweet old **Kapaa** town has really blossomed as a boutique row of late. All you need to do is park along Kuhio Highway and stroll the plantation-style storefronts along the few blocks, and you're sure to come away with an island treasure. **Vicky's Fabrics,** 4-1326 Kuhio Hwy. (☎ 808-822-1746; www.vickysfabrics.com), boasts Hawaii's best collection of on-the-bolt fabrics. **Jim Saylor Jewelers,** 4-1318 Kuhio Hwy. (☎ 808-822-3591), specializes in elegant custom jewelry designs and fine gems. **Hula Girl,** at 4-1340 Kuhio Hwy. (☎ 808-822-1950; www.welove hulagirl.com), specializes in the most stylish lines of aloha wear for men, women, and kids. Nearby at 4-1322 Kuhio Hwy. is **Davison Arts** (☎ 808-821-8022; www.davisonarts.com), for handcrafted island wood furniture as well as paintings and sculpture by local artists. **South China Sea Trading Company,** 4-1354 Kuhio Hwy. (☎ 808-823-8655; www.sochinasea.com), specializes in fun Asian imports.

On the North Shore

The simple town of **Kilauea** is home to the North Shore's premier shopping stop: **Kong Lung Company,** a gorgeous shopping collective housed in a historic stone building on Kilauea Road and Keneke Street, a few blocks from Kuhio Highway (☎ 808-828-1822; www.konglung.com). This airy Asian-accented gallery of design brims with beautiful home wares and gifts from Hawaii and around the world, all artfully displayed. The collections of women's wear and aloha shirts in back are the height of casual island fashion. The shop is expensive, but not overpriced; this is beautiful stuff. Out back is the **Lotus Gallery of Fine Art** (☎ 808-828-9898; www.jewelofthelotus.com), a Pan-Asian gallery (with an emphasis on works from India, Nepal, and Tibet) that's something of an oddball but nonetheless boasts some incredible gold and talismanic jewelry as well as antique artifacts and carpets. To reach Kilauea from Kuhio Highway (Highway 56), turn right at the sign for Kilauea

Lighthouse (at the gas station, 23 miles north of Lihue); a few blocks down on your right is Keneke Street and Kong Lung.

Hanalei boasts more great shopping. Two of the town's finest shops are at the entrance to Hanalei town, on the ocean side of Kuhio Highway just after the bridge and Kayak Kauai Outbound: **Ola's** (☎ 808-826-6937), a top stop for high-quality island crafts, including a gorgeous collection of jewelry and koa pieces; and **Quicksilver Kai Kane** (☎ 808-826-5594), which is great for hip aloha and surf wear. (Its groovy collection of surfboards alone is worth a peek.)

In the heart of Hanalei on the ocean side of the street, **Ching Young Village** covers the basics, from supermarket to pizza joint. Unrepentant shoppers should instead head across the street to **Hanalei Center,** which boasts a small but satisfying collection of boutiques. The standout is the **Yellowfish Trading Company** (☎ 808-826-1227), which features an eye-popping assemblage of vintage and contemporary Hawaiiana and gifts with wide-ranging appeal (read: you don't have to be a retro nut to love this place), plus vintage bark-cloth fabrics, in case you want to give your home that tropical touch. The **Hanalei Surf Company,** in the old school building at the Hanalei Center (☎ 808-826-9000; www.hanaleisurf.com), is the place to go for surf gear and beach goodies.

In the Poipu Beach area

Poipu has few notable shopping opportunities. On your way to Poipu Beach, you'll pass **Old Koloa Town,** a block-long collection of less-than-exciting storefronts. The standout exception is **Sheldon Gate Jewelry Designs,** 5330 Koloa Rd. (☎ 808-742-6591; www.sheldongate.com), for remarkable modern jewelry designs, including luminous glass bracelets.

Boutique lovers can find a good mix of sportswear, sandals, and the like at **Poipu Shopping Village,** 2360 Kiahuna Plantation Dr. (at Poipu Road). Don't miss the standout **Honolua Surf Co.** (☎ 808-742-9152; www.honoluasurf.com), a Maui-based company that makes terrific quality casual wear whose appeal reaches well beyond the surf crowd.

 My favorite stop for Hawaii-made crafts — even more so than the Kauai Museum Shop — is the visitor center at the **National Tropical Botanical Garden,** on Lawai Road across the street from Spouting Horn (☎ 808-742-2433 or 808-742-2623; www.ntbg.org), where the simply displayed collection is small but high quality. The emphasis is on affordable items such as koa accessories, lauhala hatboxes, botanical prints, and Hawaii-made paper goods, although a few excellent examples of koa calabashes and jewelry boxes are always on display.

Southwest Kauai: Hanapepe

 In a bend in the road a few minutes west of Kalaheo (turn off the highway at the sign that says "Hanapepe, Kauai's Biggest Little Town") is **Hanapepe.** This one-horse town is finally beginning to realize its years-long potential as an arts community, with an increasing number of interesting galleries popping up along its main street, Hanapepe Road. Hanapepe particularly comes alive on its weekly Friday-night art walk. But feel free to stop by any day of the week to enjoy such shopping and gallery gems as **Vintage Aloha,** 3900 Hanapepe Rd. (☎ 808-335-5797; www.vintagealoha gallery.com), for vintage-style original art reminiscent of the romantic Matson Line era by local artist Melinda Morey; **Banana Patch Studio,** 3865 Hanapepe Rd. (☎ 800-914-5944 or 808-335-5944; www.bananapatch studio.com), for affordable gifts and island-inspired original art by gallery owner Joanna Carolan and other local artists; and others. A real find for lovers of local art and off-the-beaten-path experiences.

Living It Up after Dark

Things really couldn't get much quieter than they already are on Kauai. This island is made for daytime fun — so my advice is to make sunset the highlight, enjoy a leisurely dinner, and call it a night.

If you want a bit more action, Poipu Beach is your best bet. Of course, for the most animated after-dark entertainment, head to — you guessed it — a **luau.** Kauai has some good options (and one excellent one) that increase the appeal of just-okay food with an open bar and surprisingly good island-style entertainment; for my recommendations on the island's best, see Chapter 16.

Another fine way to celebrate the end of another day in paradise is to set sail on a sunset cruise. I recommend **Capt. Andy's Sailing Adventures** — recommended earlier in this chapter, under "Cruising the Na Pali Coast and other on-deck adventures."

At the Grand Hyatt Kauai Resort & Spa, 1571 Poipu Rd. (☎ 808-742-1234; www.kauai-hyatt.com), the **Seaview Terrace** makes a lovely spot for sunset cocktails and a sunset torch lighting ceremony, followed by live Hawaiian entertainment. After sunset, head indoors to **Stevenson's Library,** a cozy library-like lounge offering live soft jazz and a noteworthy menu of after-dinner drinks, plus a sushi menu Friday through Tuesday evenings. You can even savor your drink over a game of pool, chess, or backgammon.

Even if you don't dine at the **Beach House Restaurant,** 5022 Lawai Rd., off Poipu Road, toward Spouting Horn, Poipu Beach (☎ 808-742-1424; www.the-beach-house.com), stop at the lounge for tropical cocktails and a glorious view of the sun setting over the Poipu surf.

Keoki's Paradise, at the Poipu Shopping Village, at Poipu Road and Kiahuna Plantation Drive (☎ 808-742-7534; www.keokisparadise. com), features a lengthy tropical-drinks menu in the relaxing Tiki-style Bamboo Bar, plus live music most nights.

For a similar scene in Lihue, head to Keoki's sister restaurant, **Duke's Canoe Club,** on the beach at the Kauai Marriott and Beach Club, 3610

Rice St. (near Nawilwili Harbor; ☎ 808-246-9599; www.dukeskauai.com), which also features live Hawaiian music on Friday nights.

My favorite hangout on the North Shore is **Bouchons Hanalei** (formerly called Sushi Blues), in Ching Young Village, 5–8420 Kuhio Hwy., Hanalei (☎ 808-826-9701 or 808-828-1435; www.sushiandblues.com), a cavernous and casual-chic sushi bar and restaurant that features great food and great drinks (see Chapter 16) and live jazz and blues or dance music Wednesday through Sunday nights.

Cheerful **Tahiti Nui**, 5-5134 Kuhio Hwy., Hanalei (☎ 808-826-6277; www.thenui.com), is a genuine Tiki bar that calls itself Hawaii's oldest bar and restaurant. I don't know about that, but you will find a genuinely joyful, relaxed, old-school vibe at this friendly and ultra-casual vintage Tiki hut on the fringe of Hanalei town. Come for the tropical cocktails, and call ahead for the live entertainment schedule.

Just down the road, Princeville has several nightspots. My favorite is the open-air **Happy Talk Lounge** at the **Hanalei Bay Resort,** 5380 Honoiki St. (☎ 808-826-6522; www.hanaleibayresort.com), which offers some of the finest sunset views in all of the islands. Come for cocktails at any time of day — the lounge is open from 11:30 a.m. to 10 p.m. daily for cocktails and munchies — or come to enjoy a side of live jazz with your sunset Sundays from 4 to 7 p.m., as well as live hula Tuesdays from 6:30 to 9:30 p.m.

Part VII
The Part of Tens

The 5th Wave   By Rich Tennant

"Psst — Philip! It's not too late to fly back
to a more civilized island!"

In this part . . .

This wouldn't be a *For Dummies* book without an ending
that's pure fun. In Chapter 18, you find insider tips on how
to ditch the tourist trappings and fit in like a local. And what's
more entertaining than good food? In Chapter 19, I give you the
lowdown on island dining and traditional Hawaiian eats, and
help you decipher the local culinary lingo. In Chapter 20, I'll let
lovebirds in on how to bask in the islands' romantic charms.

Chapter 18

Ten Ways to Lose the Tourist Trappings and Look Like a Local

*H*awaii may be the 50th U.S. state, but it's an ocean — and a world — apart from its mainland brethren. In fact, because it didn't join the star-spangled party until 1959, Hawaii came into the Union as an adopted adult, complete with its own unique personality, fully formed (indeed, ancient) culture, and distinct worldview.

Honolulu sits closer to Tokyo than it does to Washington, D.C. — and that makes a big difference, creating a further divide between the islands and the Eurocentric perspective that many Americans have on the world.

Even the population is dramatically different. Unlike in the rest of the United States, no one ethnic group forms a majority in Hawaii. Although Caucasian and Japanese are the two largest ethnic groups (each accounts for roughly 22 percent of the population), nearly 35 percent of islanders consider themselves of mixed ethnicity. Hawaii's residents, as a group, don't consider race a factor in marriage; they're just as likely to marry someone from a different race as not.

The fact that Hawaii is both exotic and familiar is one of its greatest appeals. It's also one of the biggest pitfalls for visitors, however: Because Hawaii is part of the good ol' US of A, many first-time visitors think that they have it all figured out. What could they possibly have to know?

You need to know a few things, it turns out. If you'd rather come across as an *akamai* (smart) traveler than advertise your status as a *Malihini* (newcomer), then this chapter is for you.

Mastering the Three Most Important Phrases in the Hawaiian Language

Everyone in Hawaii speaks English, of course. A few Hawaiian words and phrases have made their way into the common vernacular, though, and regularly pop up in everyday conversation.

You probably already know the Hawaiian word *aloha* (a-*lo*-ha), which serves as an all-purpose greeting — hello and welcome, and goodbye as well. It's a warm and wonderful word, full of grace and compassion and good feeling, so use it liberally; there's no better way to get caught up in the true spirit of Hawaii.

A second word that every visitor should learn is *mahalo* (ma-*ha*-low), which means "thank you" and is used extensively throughout Hawaii. If you want to say "Thanks very much!" or "Thank you *so* much," say *mahalo nui loa* (ma-*ha*-low *noo*-ee *low*-ah). Not only will the locals be impressed with your efforts to learn, but they'll be flattered by your graciousness, too.

Islanders don't like "goodbye" to be so permanent. So to really sound like a local, part from others warmly with *a hui hou* (ah *hoo*-ee ho), which means "until we meet again."

Discovering More Hawaiian Words

If you only know *aloha, a hui hou,* and *mahalo,* you'll do just fine. But if you consider yourself ahead of the curve and want to know a few more useful words, take a few minutes to study the following list. That way, when you're in a restaurant and the waiter offers your little ones a *keiki* menu, describes today's lunch special as particularly *ono,* or asks you if you're *pau* when he comes to clear your plate, you'll feel like a regular *kamaaina:*

- ✔ **alii** (ah-*lee*-ee): Hawaiian royalty

- ✔ **halau** (ha-*lau*): School

- ✔ **hale** (*ha*-lay): House

- ✔ **haole** (*how*-lee): Foreigner or Caucasian (literally "out of breath" — pale, or paleface); a common reference, not an insult (usually)

- ✔ **heiau** (heh-*ee*-ow): Hawaiian temple

- ✔ **hui** (*hoo*-ee): A club, collective, or assembly (for example, an artists' collective is an artists' hui)

- ✔ **hula** (*hoo*-lah): Native dance

- ✔ **imu** (*ee*-moo): Underground oven lined with hot rocks that's used for cooking the luau pig

- ✔ **kahuna** (ka-*hoo*-nah): Priest or expert

- ✔ **kamaaina** (ka-ma-*eye*-nah): Local person

- ✔ **kane** (*ka*-nay): Man (you may see this word on a restroom door)

- ✔ **kapu** (*ka*-poo): Anything that's taboo, forbidden

- ✔ **keiki** (*keh*-kee): Child

- ✔ **kupuna** (koo-*poo*-nah): An elder, leader, grandparent, or anyone who commands great respect

- ✔ **lanai** (*lah*-nigh): Porch or veranda

- ✔ **lei** (lay): Garland (usually of flowers, leaves, or shells)

- ✔ **luau** (*loo*-ow): A celebratory feast

- ✔ **malihini** (ma-li-*hee*-nee): Stranger or newcomer

- ✔ **mana** (*ma*-na): Spirit, divine power

- ✔ **muumuu** (moo-oo-*moo*-oo): A loose-fitting dress, usually in a tropical print

- ✔ **ono** (*oh*-no): Delicious

- ✔ **pau** (pow): Finished or done

- ✔ **pali** (*pah*-lee): Cliff

- ✔ **pupu** (*poo*-poo): Starter dish, appetizer

- ✔ **wahine** (wa-*wee*-nay): Woman (you may see this word on a restroom door)

Pronouncing Those Pesky Hawaiian Words and Place Names

Because the Hawaiian language has only 12 characters to work with — the five vowels (*a, e, i, o,* and *u*) plus seven consonants (*h, k, l, m, n, p,* and *w*) — Hawaiian words and names tend to be long and difficult, with lots of repetitive syllables that can really get your vocal chords into a twist. Master just a few basic rules, however, and "Honoapiilani Highway" and "Haliimaile" will be rolling off your tongue like "Main Street" and "Anytown, USA" in no time.

Half the letters in the Hawaiian language — *h, k, l, m, n,* and *p* — sound out just like they do in English. The one consonant that sounds different in Hawaiian is *w. W* usually carries the *v* sound when it follows *i* or *e;* for example, the Oahu town of Haleiwa is "ha-lay-*ee*-vah." At the beginning of words and after *a, u,* and *o,* though, it's usually your standard *w* — hence Wailea (why-*lay*-ah) and Makawao (mah-*kah*-wow), two Maui destinations.

The vowels are pronounced like this:

a	*ah* (as in father) or *uh* (as in above)
e	*eh* (as in bed) or *ay* (as in they)
i	*ee* (as in police)
o	*oh* (as in vote)
u	*oo* (as in too)

Almost all vowels are sounded separately, although some are pronounced together, as in the name of Waikiki's main thoroughfare, Kalakaua Avenue, which is pronounced "kah-lah-*cow*-ah."

Here's the most important tip to remember when trying to pronounce a Hawaiian word or name: Don't be overwhelmed by length. Get into the habit of seeing long words or names as a collection of short syllables, and you'll find them much easier to say. (Accents almost always fall on the second-to-last syllable.)

The trick is to know where to put on the breaks. That leads me to important tip number two: All syllables end with vowels, so a consonant will always indicate the start of a new syllable. One of the best examples of this is the tongue-twisting Kealakekua Bay (the famous marine preserve off the Big Island's Kona Coast), which throws nearly everyone for a loop. Break the syllables down by reading the consonants as red flags, though, and see how easy it becomes: "kay-ah-lah-keh-*koo*-ah."

The Hawaiian language actually has a 13th character: the glottal stop, which looks exactly like an apostrophe (') and is meant to indicate a pause. I've chosen not to use the glottal stop throughout this book; it's often omitted in printed Hawaiian and on things like store and street signs. Although serious Hawaiian-language students learn volumes about the glottal stop and its equal importance to its fellow consonants and vowels, you don't need to worry about it for your purposes; you can basically ignore it when you see it.

I've laid out these basics so that you can understand how the language works, but no one expects you to become an expert at pronouncing Hawaiian words. Whenever I return to Hawaii, I always feel as if it takes me a day or two to get my tongue back in working order — and I *know* this stuff. Still, practicing is fun, and with these basic tools under your belt, you'll quickly get the hang of it. Practice with the first two examples at the start of this chapter, and you'll really impress the locals when you get to Maui: Honoapiilani Highway (ho-no-ah-pee-ee-*la*-nee) and Haliimaile (ha-lee-*ee-my*-lee).

Knowing How to Give and Take Directions

Leave your compass at home — islanders have a different sense of direction than mainlanders do. Although locals do think of the islands as having north shores and south shores, west coasts and east coasts, seldom will anybody direct you by using the most common directional terms.

Instead, they'll send you either *makai* (ma-*kai*), a directional meaning toward the sea, or *mauka* (*mow*-kah), meaning toward the mountains. Because each island is basically a volcano with a single coastal road circling it, those two terms are often enough to do the trick.

When they don't suffice, locals are likely to invoke relative terms rather than "north," "south," "east," or "west." If you're standing in Kapaa on Kauai's east shore, for example, locals tell you to head toward Lihue if they want you to go south. In Honolulu, people use **Diamond Head** when they mean to the east (in the direction of the world-famous crater called Diamond Head), and **Ewa** (*ee*-va) when they mean to the west (in the direction of the town called Ewa, beyond Pearl Harbor).

So if you ask an islander for directions on Oahu, you're likely to hear something like this: "Turn left and go 2 miles Diamond Head [east], turn at the light and go 2 blocks makai [toward the sea], and then turn at the stop light. Go 2 more blocks and turn Ewa [west]; the address you want is on the mauka [mountain] side of the street."

If you're on the Big Island at a luxury Kohala Coast resort and you're heading out to catch a snorkel cruise, for example, you're more likely to hear something like this: "Go 8 miles past Kailua-Kona [south] to mile marker 109. Turn makai [toward the ocean] on King Kam Road and then left at the bottom of the hill."

Remembering That You're in the United States

If you're from the continental United States, don't say "back home in the U.S." when you're talking to folks in Hawaii. This tip seems like a real no-brainer, but that long flight across the Pacific and the one-of-a-kind Hawaiian ambience and culture can really play tricks with your mind. Islanders are, by and large, a patriotic bunch, so they don't take kindly to being left off the national map. Refer to the continental United States as the *mainland,* which is what they do.

Another very important point in the same vein: Locals are always called "islanders," never Hawaiians, unless they are of native blood, which not that many islanders are. (Hawaiian is an ethnic label.)

Wearing Sunscreen

You don't need a trained eye to spot the newest arrivals a mile away — they're the ones with the excruciating sunburns. *Way* too many newcomers fry themselves on the first day of their vacations in an overzealous quest to tan, putting a major damper on their trip — and sometimes their long-term health — in the process. The sun's rays are much stronger in Hawaii than on the mainland.

Hawaii's sun-loving population has achieved the dubious distinction of having the highest incidence of skin cancer in the United States, and as a result, it has developed quite an attachment to sunscreen. The deep-tanning Coppertone days are a thing of the past, even among the most zealous sun worshippers.

 Most locals I know use SPF 25 or 30 sunscreen on a daily basis. It's wise not to go out in the sun, even for ten minutes, wearing anything less than SPF 15; those of you with light complexions should stick with SPF 30 or 45.

I always make a special effort to apply sunscreen under bathing suit straps, on the tops of my feet, on the back of my neck, and on my ears and lips — all spots that are the easiest to forget but the most sensitive to painful burns. (In fact, I usually slather up before I get dressed in the morning.)

Sunglasses and a hat are two more important weapons for fending off the sun's rays. Throw away those $5 shades and splurge on a decent pair with UV filters to protect your corneas from sunburn and to prevent cataracts. Wear a hat with a wide brim that goes all the way around; baseball caps leave some of your most vulnerable areas — your ears and neck — exposed to the sun's harsh rays.

 Attention, Mom and Dad: Infants under 6 months should not be directly exposed to the harsh Hawaiian sun. Older babies need zinc oxide to protect their fragile skin, and kids should be slathered with high-SPF sunscreen every hour. They also need shades, hats, and other protective gear.

Dressing the Part

There's nothing more tacky-touristy than a bold tropical-patterned aloha shirt, right? Wrong!

Invented by an enterprising Honolulu tailor looking for a new way to drum up business in 1936, the aloha shirt has since spawned a whole wardrobe of bright, tropical-print wearables for men, women, and children, collectively known as aloha wear. Spirited, beautiful, easy to wear, and comfortable, aloha wear is the embodiment of the Hawaiian lifestyle — and it's acceptable just about anywhere in Hawaii, from the beach to the boardroom to the best table at a four-star restaurant. (A tiny handful of Hawaii's most expensive resort restaurants do require men to wear a jacket, but I don't recommend those places.) Of course, the key to wearing aloha wear well is understanding the line that separates the sublime from the goofy.

Look for beautiful, well-designed prints with strong colors and no bleeding. Look for quality buttons (coconut or wood are best, but not a must) and pattern matching at the seams and pockets. Top-quality brands to look for include **Kahala Sportswear, Kamehameha Garment Co.,** and the **Paradise Found** and **Diamond Head** labels, all of which have revived vintage designs; **Reyn's,** which boasts beautiful patterns in a range of flattering styles, especially for women; **Tommy Bahama's,** whose top-quality clothing lines are generically tropical but suit the Hawaii mood perfectly; and, one of my all-time favorites, **Tori Richard,** which employs some of Hawaii's finest artists to design its patterns. If you visit the Big Island, **Sig Zane's** mostly all-cotton aloha wear and accessories are the height of subdued sophistication and nature-inspired beauty, whereas on Oahu, **Mamo Howell** has elevated the muumuu to haute couture status. **Hilo Hattie** is the largest manufacturer and distributor of aloha wear, and though its stuff isn't the height of aloha fashion, it has increased substantially in quality while remaining very affordable.

 The cardinal rule of wearing aloha wear like a local rather than a tourist? *No matching.* No themed husband-and-wife shirts, no mom-and-daughter muumuu, no two garments on one person in the same pattern. Period.

Remembering Your Island-Style Manners

As in many Eastern cultures, removing your shoes when you enter a private home is common practice in Hawaii — which is one reason why flip-flops and other slip-on–style shoes are so common in the islands.

Islanders pride themselves on their laid-back manner and friendliness, and they really show it in their driving habits — so leave your need for speed at home. And don't honk your horn to chastise other drivers, which is considered the height of rudeness. If the car in front of you isn't moving quickly enough, or someone cuts you off, just let it slide. Car horns are used to greet friends in Hawaii.

Leaving Your Work Behind

Even the newly minted mainland millionaires who are buying up Hawaii real estate left and right understand the meaning of Hawaii. Don't cart your business worries halfway around the world; an island vacation is far too precious for that. Conveniently forget to give your boss your itinerary. Hawaii is the place to leave work behind and *relax.* And you can drop that rat race attitude while you're at it. I mean it: Relax!

Smiling a Lot and Saying "Aloha" to Strangers

Who knows? You may even get yourself mistaken for a local.

Chapter 19

Ten Easy Steps to Island Dining

In This Chapter

▶ Knowing what you're eating and how to eat it

▶ Maximizing your dining experiences

*E*ating well in the islands isn't a problem. Hawaii has lured some of the world's finest chefs to its kitchens and managed to cultivate some stars of its own in the process. If you love quality seafood, fresh-grown veggies, and sweet tropical fruits, you'll think that you've died and gone to heaven.

But that's far from the end of the bounty. Hawaii's melting-pot society sets a global table. Although Asian flavors and cooking styles are most prevalent, island menus travel the globe, from old-world European culinary classics to good ol' ranch-raised, fire-grilled steaks. Hawaii's cooks have even managed to put their own spin on some of the world's most revered foods — pizzas, burgers, and burritos — with rousing success.

You may, however, want to know a few things about island dining before you sit down to a meal — the first being that Hawaii has two brands of homegrown cuisine: local food (the unpretentious, hearty fare that islanders traditionally eat on an everyday basis) and Hawaii Regional, or Hawaii Island, Cuisine (the gourmet version). If you want to find out more on the culinary front, then this chapter is for you.

Fresh-Caught and Island-Raised

To say that Hawaii's seafood may be the best in the world is no stretch — in fact, some of the world's finest chefs think so. But Hawaii's bounty isn't limited to the sea. A wealth of fresh-grown vegetables, including leafy lettuces and vine-ripened tomatoes, thrives in the lava-rich soil. But fruits are Hawaii's real forte. All you need to do is head to the local supermarket to discover a whole new world of citrus and more varieties of banana than you ever knew existed.

Tropical fruit comes as no surprise, of course, but who knew that Hawaii offered so much island-raised meat? In fact, the island called Hawaii is home to the largest privately owned cattle ranch in the United States: Parker Ranch, covering 225,000 acres, including more than 50,000 cattle, and serving as the heart of Hawaii's *paniolo* (cowboy) country.

Traditional Island Eats

Local food is a casual, catchall cuisine, mirroring Hawaii's melting-pot soul. Outsider influences on the local cuisine arrived in Hawaii from all over the map, from Portugal to Japan and just about everywhere in between.

Local food is generally starch-heavy and high in calories, so don't expect it to have a positive impact on your waistline. The most quintessential element of local food is the plate lunch, which usually consists of a main dish (anything from fried fish to teriyaki beef), "two scoops rice," an ice-cream-scoop serving of macaroni salad, and brown gravy, all served on a paper plate. Plate lunches are cheap and available at casual restaurants and beachside stands throughout the islands.

A great place to try local food is at a luau. For more on luau, see the section "What to Expect at a Luau," at the end of this chapter.

The Gourmet Side of the Island Stove

About a dozen or so years ago, Hawaii's kitchens underwent a culinary revolution alongside its cultural renaissance, and — *voilà!* — Hawaii Regional Cuisine was born. Island chefs were tired of living up to a Continental standard that was unsuited to Hawaii living, so they created their own brand of gourmet fare, using fresh local ingredients in creative combinations and preparations.

This type of cuisine is often disguised under other names, such as Euro-Asian, Pacific Rim, Indo-Pacific, Pacific Edge, Euro-Pacific, and Island Fusion, but it all falls under the jurisdiction of Hawaii Regional Cuisine. Although there are variations, you can expect the following keynotes: lots of fresh island fish, many Asian flavorings and cooking styles , and fresh tropical fruit sauces.

A Translation List for Seafood Lovers

Even savvy seafood eaters can become confused when confronted with a Hawaiian menu. Although the mainland terms are sometimes included, many menus use only the Hawaiian names to tout their daily catches. What's more, some types of seafood that make regular appearances in Hawaii's kitchens simply don't show up on mainland menus at all.

You're likely to encounter many of the following types of seafood while you're in Hawaii:

- **Ahi:** This dense, ruby-red bigeye or yellowfin tuna is a Hawaiian favorite. Ahi is regularly served raw, as sushi and sashimi, or panko-crusted and seared in Hawaii Regional Cuisine. Yellowfin is the beefier of the two.

- **Aku:** This meaty, robust skipjack tuna is also known as bonito. Aku is best as raw sushi because it can get too dry if not expertly cooked.

- **Au** (ow): This firm-fleshed marlin or broadbill swordfish sometimes stands in for ahi in local dishes. Pacific blue marlin is sometimes called *kajiki,* and striped marlin often shows up as *nairagi.*

- **Hebi** (*heh*-bee): This mildly flavored, almost lemony, spearfish is sometimes the day's catch in upscale restaurants.

- **Mahimahi:** This white, sweet, moderately dense fish is Hawaii's most popular, and it shows up regularly on mainland menus.

- **Monchong** (*mon*-chong): This exotic fish boasts a flaky, tender texture and a simple flavor. It's best served broiled, sautéed, or steamed.

- **Onaga** (o-*na*-ga): This mild, moist, and tender ruby-red snapper is served in many fine restaurants; be sure to sample it if it's available.

- **Ono** (*oh*-no): *Ono* means "good to eat" in Hawaiian, and this mackerel-like fish sure It's often served grilled and in sandwiches.

- **Opah** (*oh*-pa): This rich, almost creamy moonfish is good served just about any way, from sashimi to baked.

- **Opakapaka** (oh-pa-ka-*pa*-ka): Either pink or crimson snapper, this light, flaky, elegant fish is very popular on fine-dining menus.

- **Shutome** (shuh-*toe*-me): This is what mainlanders call swordfish. It's a sweet and tender steaklike fish that's great grilled or broiled.

- **Tombo:** This is albacore tuna — but this firm, flavorful whitefish surpasses the canned stuff by miles when prepared appropriately.

- **Uku** (*oo*-koo): This gray — pale pink, really — snapper is flaky, moist, and delicate.

- **Ulua** (oo-*loo*-ah): Ulua is large jack trevally, a firm-fleshed, flavorful fish also known as *pompano.*

More Everyday Hawaiian Food Terms

All the following foods are common in plate lunches and at luau. A number of them also pop up on gourmet menus — usually with expensive ingredients and prepared with a twist, of course:

- **Bento:** A Japanese box lunch.

- **Haupia** (how-*pee*-ah): Creamy coconut pudding, usually served in squares. A favorite luau dessert.

- **Kalua pork:** Pork slow-cooked in an *imu,* or underground oven; listed on menus as "luau pig" on occasion.

- **Kiawe** (kee-*ah*-vay): An aromatic mesquite wood often used to fire the wood-burning ovens.

- **Laulau:** Pork, chicken, or fish wrapped in ti leaves and steamed.

- **Lilikoi** (lil-*ee*-koy): Passion fruit.

- **Lomilomi** (low-mee-*low*-mee) **salmon:** Salted salmon marinated, ceviche-like, with tomatoes and green onions.

- **Lumpia** (lum-*pee*-ah): The Portuguese version of a spring roll, but spicier, doughier, and deep-fried (and usually stuffed with pork and veggies).

- **Malassada** (mah-lah-*sah*-da): The Portuguese version of a doughnut, usually round, deep-fried, and generously sprinkled with powdered sugar.

- **Manapua** (man-ah-*poo*-ah): A bready, doughy bun with sweetened pork or sweet beans inside, like Chinese bao.

- **Ohelo** (oh-*hay*-low): A berry very similar to a cranberry that commonly appears in Hawaii Regional sauces.

- **Panko:** Japanese bread crumbs, most commonly used to prepare *katsu* (a deep-fried pork or chicken cutlet).

- **Poi:** The root of the taro pounded into a purple, starchy paste; a staple of the island diet, but generally tasteless to most outsiders.

- **Poke** (*po*-kay): Cubed raw fish — usually ahi or marlin — seasoned with onions, soy, and seaweed.

- **Ponzu:** A soy-and-citrus dipping sauce popular with Hawaii Regional Cuisine chefs.

- **Pupus:** Appetizers or hors d'oeuvres.

- **Saimin** (*sai*-min): A brothy soup with ramenlike noodles, topped with bits of fish, chicken, pork, and/or vegetables.

✔ **Shave ice:** The island version of a snow cone, best enjoyed with ice cream and sweet *azuki* (red) beans at the bottom.

✔ **Taro:** A green leafy vegetable grown in Hawaii; the root is used to make poi (mentioned earlier in this list), and the leafy part of the vegetable is often steamed like spinach.

Other Local Favorites

Lest all this unfamiliar food talk make you think otherwise, remember that the majority of Hawaii islanders are red-blooded, flag-waving Americans — and they love a good burger just as much as your average mainlander. Hawaii has also co-opted Mexican cuisine and made the burrito its own.

Ethnic Eats

Thanks to Hawaii's proximity to the Eastern Hemisphere and its large, multifaceted Asian population, the islands boast a wealth of fabulous Asian restaurants, including Chinese, Thai, Vietnamese, and Japanese. With the exception of Japanese, most Asian restaurants tend to be very affordable. What's more, because island palates are much more used to dining Asian-style, the dishes aren't gringo-ized for a mainland population. Dining out in Hawaii, you may just find yourself enjoying the finest ethnic food you've ever eaten.

The Joys and Sorrows of the Supermarket

Hawaii supermarkets offer a number of treats that you won't find at your average mainland supermarket. Poi, for example, comes in instant, premade, and make-your-own forms. The bounty in the seafood case is much more diverse than what you see at home; Hawaii refrigerator cases regularly contain such taste treats as sushi-grade tuna, fresh Pacific octopus, and whole squid (insert "yum!" or "yuck!" here, depending on your taste buds).

Just about any Hawaii supermarket will have multiple aisles devoted to Asian foods, from noodles to bizarre candies. The juice refrigerator case is also a treat, so don't be afraid to try something new.

Java lovers, rejoice. Every Hawaiian island except Lanai has a coffee plantation, and the local brew is available in just about any average market. All Hawaii-grown coffees are delicious, but the world-famous Kona coffee, grown on the Big Island, is the top of the heap.

The greatest bounty appears among the fresh fruits, where you'll find such fresh tropical treats as mangoes, guava, star fruit, lychee, lilikoi (passion fruit), and much more. Pineapples are another Hawaii taste treat; the small white pineapples are sweetest, and you'll usually find them clearly labeled at the market. The Big Island's lava-rich soil produces extraflavorful citrus fruits; Kau oranges, for example, are legendary for their sweetness. Even watermelon is an extraspecial treat; Molokai-grown watermelons are the best in the world — full of seeds, but fabulous.

Among Hawaii-grown vegetables, Maui onions are the ultimate treat. They're very sweet, but with a distinctive flavor all their own. Dense, purple Molokai-grown sweet potatoes are another of my favorites.

Don't shy away from tropical fruits or other foods just because you're unfamiliar with them. Islanders are friendly and talkative folks. Supermarket attendants — or even your fellow shoppers — will be happy to advise you on how to cut or clean island fruits.

Shopping in Hawaii does, however, have a downside — namely, high prices. Although you'll save quite a few bucks over three-meals-a-day restaurant dining by stocking up and cooking for yourself back at the condo, expect anything that has to wing its way across the Pacific to be more than you usually pay.

Another Island Tradition: Tropical Cocktails

In Hawaii, the mai tai is practically the official state cocktail. The classic mai tai is a magical sweet-tart concoction of Jamaican rum, fresh lime juice, and chunky ice, generally served in a tumbler and topped with a fresh sprig of mint.

Of course, mai tais may not be your thing. If that's the case, don't worry. You'll find plenty of other ways to toast your time in paradise. Personally, I'm a big fan of the piña colada. I know it's not a Hawaiian cocktail, but it never fails to put me in the tropical mood, especially when a colorful paper umbrella and a generous slice of pineapple are included.

What to Expect at a Luau

A luau is the ideal place to experience island traditions — but only to a degree, of course. Any commercial luau (read: any luau that you're likely to attend) will be tainted by its commercialism. But a few luau do a great job of bringing genuine island culture into the mix.

You can find the best luau — offering the best mix of good food, amenities, setting, and authentic culture — on Maui. The **Old Lahaina Luau** and **The Feast at Lele** are the best luau that Hawaii has to offer, hands down. If you're going to be on the Valley Isle, be sure to book your spots now; see Chapter 12.

If you're not visiting Maui, don't despair. Each island offers its own versions of the luau feast, with the Big Island garnering second-runner-up awards for its very respectable feast and top-quality entertainment at **Kona Village** or the progressive, open-air **Gathering of the Kings** luau at The Fairmont Orchid (see Chapter 14). In Waikiki, book your spot at the oceanfront **Royal Luau at the Royal Hawaiian** or the family-friendly **Sea Life Luau** at the marine playground Sea Life Park (see Chapter 10). On Kauai, your best choice is the highly satisfying **Luau Kalamaku** at the Kilohana Plantation (Chapter 16).

Upon arrival, you're likely to be greeted with a lei, made of either fresh flowers or shells, and a cocktail, often a mai tai (or fruit juice, if you're too young or a teetotaler). You'll be led to your assigned seat, usually at a communal table with chairs (although the Old Lahaina Luau now features some traditional seating, on cushions facing low-slung tables).

Cocktails are usually included in the pay-one-price admission fee to a luau. Open bars are common, but some luau limit you to a certain number or kind of drink. If it matters to you, be sure to ask when booking.

After the luau pig is unearthed from the *imu,* everyone is usually asked to take their seats. You'll be invited to fill your plate from the buffet luau spread; the best luau clearly mark the dishes so that you know what you're sampling. In addition to the kalua pork (shredded from the bone after the luau pig is unearthed), you can expect such traditional dishes as poi, the tasteless purple paste that's the staple starch of Hawaii. You're more likely to prefer such dishes as lomilomi salmon, poke, and haupia (see the section "More Everyday Hawaiian Food Terms," earlier in this chapter). If you're not an adventurous diner, don't worry — you'll find plenty of familiar dishes on hand, including chicken teriyaki, long rice, and salad. After dinner comes the evening's entertainment, usually a hula show that lasts an hour or so before the evening winds down.

Chapter 20

Ten Ways to Enjoy Island Romance

Don't cart your worries and everyday stresses halfway around the world; an island getaway with your partner is far too precious for that. In this chapter, I give you the ten best ways to find island happiness no matter how you define romance.

Luxuriating in the Lap of Luxury

Sometimes you just gotta suck it up and spend the big bucks. If staying in an oceanfront room that lets the sound of the waves lull you to sleep is important to you, or if you've found the luxury B&B of your dreams tucked away in a rain forest hideaway, don't visit Hawaii on the cheap. Spend the extra money and make memories.

If you really want to splurge on that ultra-deluxe beach resort or a zippy convertible sports car but you're worried about the cost, consider splurging for just *part* of your trip, and make more budget-friendly choices during the rest of your stay.

Discovering That You Don't Need Tons of Luxury for Hawaii to Feel Like Paradise

But maybe your budget just doesn't allow for a big splurge. Don't despair — Hawaii doesn't have to be a super-expensive destination.

Some of my happiest times in the islands have been spent sitting on the lanai of a budget condo, watching the sunrise as I sipped home-brewed Kona coffee. Room service and Frette bed linens wouldn't have improved the moment one iota.

Booking the Hot Spots Before You Leave Home

If you have your heart set on dining at a particular restaurant, catching a highly recommended snorkel cruise, or attending a certain luau, make your reservations from home.

See the "Exploring" chapters in this book for recommendations on what to do, and the "Settling In" chapters for tips on the islands' most sought-after reservations.

Setting Aside Time for Relaxation

Work plenty of do-nothing time into your plans. Keep your time loose and go with the flow; don't plan your days in the same detailed way you'd map out your itinerary on a grand tour of Europe.

A romantic getaway to Hawaii is less about seeing everything and more about leaving the conventions of regular life behind.

Enjoying a Heavenly Drive

No Hawaii road is more celebrated than the "heavenly" **Hana Highway** (Highway 36), the super-curvaceous road that winds along Maui's north-eastern shore, offering some of the most stunning natural sightseeing in the entire state.

Remember that this drive isn't so much about the destination as it is about the journey. The drive takes at least three hours — but allow all day to do it. Start out early, take it slow and easy, stop at scenic points along the way, and let the Hana Road work its magic on you. In fact, for the ultimate romantic getaway, I suggest staying overnight in Hana (see Chapter 12 for recommendations).

See Chapter 13 for full coverage of the drive.

Making Mornings Your Ocean Time

Hawaii's beaches tend to be less crowded, and the surf and winds tend to be calmer, in the morning hours — particularly in winter. Always take the day's first snorkel and dive cruise, kayak trip, or surf lesson, when conditions are calmest and clearest.

Spending a Day at Hawaii's Most Romantic Beaches

Hawaii has more than its share of beaches made for romance. Here are the finest on each island.

Oahu: Head to the misty, magical Windward Coast, where you'll find glorious **Lanikai Beach,** one of the world's most tranquil and beautiful beaches. Two petite offshore islets, called the Mokuleias, provide the perfect panoramic finish. See Chapter 11.

Maui: About 2½ miles past the town of Hana, **Hamoa Beach** is a remote, romantic spot. This half-moon-shaped beach at Maui's easternmost point is breathtakingly lovely, with surf the color of turquoise, golden-gray sand, and verdant hills providing a postcard-perfect backdrop. See Chapter 13.

Big Island: It doesn't get better than **Hapuna Beach State Park,** period. This big, gorgeous stretch has it all: glorious turquoise surf, a half-mile-long crescent of powdery-fine white sand, and delighted crowds — both locals and visitors alike — who come out to swim and play the day away. See Chapter 15.

Kauai: The perfectly named **Hideaway Beach** is a gorgeous pocket of North Shore beach in the Princeville Resort where the snorkeling is great, the sand is powder-fine, and the atmosphere is as tranquil as it gets. See Chapter 17.

Toasting the Sunset Every Evening

Sunset is pure nirvana in Hawaii — and these heavenly spots offer you and your special one a front-row seat.

Oahu: House Without a Key, at the Halekulani hotel, 2199 Kalia Rd., Waikiki (☎ 808-923-2311; www.halekulani.com), sets the Hawaii standard for the sunset cocktail hour. On an oceanfront patio shaded by a big kiawe tree, you can sip the best mai tais on Oahu, listen to masterful steel guitar music, and watch a traditional hula dancer sway with ethereal grace alongside the palms as iconic Diamond Head slopes laconically in the distance. It's romantic, nostalgic, and simply breathtaking. See chapters 10 and 11.

Maui: You can't get closer to the ocean than the alfresco tables at **I'o,** 505 Front St., Lahaina (☎ 808-661-8422; www.iomaui.com; $$$$). Overseen by the award-winning chef James McDonald, I'o is a multifaceted joy, with a winningly innovative, mostly seafood menu, first-rate service, and a top-notch wine list. See Chapter 12.

Big Island: Celebrate the daily spectacle of sunset at **Don's Mai Tai Bar at Don the Beachcomber,** at the Royal Kona Resort, 75-5852 Alii Dr.,

Kailua-Kona (☎ 808-329-3111; www.royalkona.com). The glorious colonnaded bar overlooking the surf is the height of Tiki chic, and the legendary mai tai is everything it should be. See Chapter 15.

Kauai: The **Beach House Restaurant,** 5022 Lawai Rd., Poipu Beach (☎ 808-742-1424; www.the-beach-house.com), sets the sunset standard on the glorious Garden Isle. Even if you don't dine here, stop at the lounge for a pair of sigh-worthy tropical cocktails and a breathtaking view as the sun sets over the Poipu surf. See chapters 16 and 17.

Dining in Style

Hawaii offers special-occasion diners more than enough reasons to celebrate. These are my favorite ultra-romantic dining splurges.

Oahu: Everything about **Orchids,** at the Halekulani, 2199 Kalia Rd., Waikiki (☎ 808-923-2311; www.halekulani.com), is sigh-inducing, from the gorgeous alfresco setting with its spectacular ocean and Diamond Head views to the seamless service and note-perfect surf-and-turf menu. See Chapter 10.

Maui: Despite the high prices, I just love **Mama's Fish House,** just off the Hana Highway at 799 Poho Place, Paia (☎ 808-579-8488; www.mamas fishhouse.com; $$$$$). The fresh fish is as fabulous as it can be, and the beachfront Tiki-room setting is quintessential romantic Hawaii. See Chapter 12.

Big Island: There's no finer special-occasion choice on this mammoth isle than the **Hualalai Grille by Alan Wong,** at the Four Seasons Resort Hualalai, 100 Kaupulehu Dr., Kaupulehu-Kona (☎ 808-325-8525; www.hualalairesort.com). This wonderful restaurant serves up the exquisite, inspiring cuisine of Hawaii's finest chef in a gorgeous, casually sophisticated resort setting. See Chapter 14.

Kauai: My sunset favorite, the **Beach House Restaurant,** 5022 Lawai Rd., Poipu Beach (☎ 808-742-1424; www.the-beach-house.com), is also my island dining favorite. A winning combination of creative island cuisine and one of the most romantic oceanfront settings in the islands make this Kauai's finest restaurant, hands down. See Chapter 16.

Mellowing Out Like a Local

Islanders tend to take life nice and easy. A clock doesn't rule them, and they don't like to rush. They call it "island time." While you're in the islands, do as the locals do: Take life as it comes, and leave plenty of space in your day for you and your beloved to appreciate the beauty that surrounds you.

Appendix

Quick Concierge

Fast Facts

American Automobile Association (AAA)

Although roadside service is available to members on the four major islands — Oahu, Maui, the Big Island, and Kauai — the only local AAA office is on Oahu (see the "Fast Facts: Oahu" section in Chapter 10 for contact info and hours).

For roadside assistance or information on becoming a member, call ☎ 800-AAA-HELP or point your Web browser to www.aaa.com, where you'll be linked to your regional club's home page by entering your zip code. See the sidebar "The AAA advantage" in Chapter 4 for details on the many benefits of AAA membership.

American Express

For office locations, see the "Fast Facts" sections in Chapter 10 (Oahu), Chapter 12 (Maui), and Chapter 14 (the Big Island); Kauai does not have an AmEx office. Not all services are offered at all offices, so call before you go.

Cardholders and traveler's check holders should call ☎ 800-528-4800 or 800-221-7282 for all money emergencies. To make inquiries with American Express Travel or to locate other branch offices, call ☎ 800-AXP-TRIP. For more information, visit www.americanexpress.com.

Area Code

All the Hawaiian Islands are in the **808** area code. When dialing, you can leave the area code off if you're calling someone on the same island that you're on. If you're calling someone on a different island, though, you must dial 1-808 before the seven-digit phone number.

If you're calling from one island to another island, the call will be billed as a long-distance call, which can be more expensive than calling the mainland from Hawaii. Be sure to use your long-distance calling card when calling between islands to avoid adding inflated phone charges to your hotel bill.

ATMs

All of the islands have plenty of ATMs in the major resort areas. Branches of Hawaii's most popular banks are plentiful, and all are connected to all the global ATM networks. Most supermarkets also have ATMs inside, as do many convenience stores. Do yourself a favor, though, and stock up on cash before heading off to remote areas such as the North Shore of Kauai, the Big Island's North Kohala peninsula or Volcano area, or the islands of Molokai or Lanai. These areas do have ATMs, but why waste precious vacation time tracking them down and risking that they won't be on your network?

One of Hawaii's most popular banks, with branches throughout the state, is Bank of Hawaii, which is linked with all the major worldwide networks. To find the one nearest you, call ☎ 888-643-3888 or point your Web browser to the **Bank of Hawaii**'s site www. boh.com and click on "Locations" in the upper navigational bar; if you don't find one near you, try **First Hawaiian Bank** (www. fhb.com). You can also find ATMs on the **MasterCard/Maestro/Cirrus** network by dialing ☎ 800-424-7787 or going online to www.mastercard.com; to find a **Visa Plus** ATM, call ☎ 800-843-7587 or visit www.visa.com and then click the ATM locator at the bottom of the start page.

Credit Cards

If your Visa card is lost or stolen, call ☎ 800-847-2911 or 410-581-9994. MasterCard holders should call ☎ 800-307-7309 or 800-627-8372. American Express cardholders should call ☎ 800-268-9824 or 800-528-4800 (for cardholders) or ☎ 800-221-7282 (for traveler's check holders).

Emergencies

No matter where you are in Hawaii, dial **911** from any phone, just like you do on the mainland. To locate doctors and hospital emergency rooms on the specific islands, see the "Fast Facts" sections in Chapter 10 (Oahu), Chapter 12 (Maui), Chapter 14 (the Big Island), and Chapter 16 (Kauai).

Liquor Laws

The legal drinking age in Hawaii is 21. Bars are allowed to stay open daily until 2 a.m.; places with cabaret licenses are able to keep the booze flowing until 4 a.m. Grocery and convenience stores are allowed to sell beer, wine, and liquor seven days a week.

Post Offices

To locate convenient local branches, see the "Fast Facts" sections in Chapter 10 (Oahu), Chapter 12 (Maui), Chapter 14 (the Big Island), and Chapter 16 (Kauai).

Maps

All the rental-car companies hand out very good free map booklets on each island, which are all that you need to navigate your way around. AAA members can get excellent maps of Hawaii free of charge (see listing above for AAA contact info).

If you want more complete topographic maps of each island, the best are printed by the University of Hawaii Press. They're available from just about any bookstore in the islands.

Newspapers and Magazines

The *Honolulu Advertiser* (www.honolulu advertiser.com) and the *Honolulu Star-Bulletin* (www.starbulletin. com) are the two statewide dailies; the *Advertiser*'s Friday *TGIF* section is an excellent source for researching happenings about town, particularly on Oahu. The main weekly entertainment rag is Oahu's *Honolulu Weekly* (www.honolulu weekly.com). Daily neighbor island newspapers include the *Maui News* (www.maui news.com), the Big Island's *West Hawaii Today* (www.westhawaiitoday.com), the *Hawaii Tribune Herald* (www.hilo hawaiitribune.com), and Kauai's *The Garden Island* (www.kauaiworld.com).

Hawaii magazine (www.hawaii magazine.com) is a glossy monthly that's targeted to visitors. You can usually find the current issue in the travel magazine sections at your local branch of the big chain bookstores, such as Borders and Barnes & Noble. Subscriptions are available by calling ☎ 800-333-0357 or via the Web site.

Ocean Safety

Keep these snorkel tips in mind as you don your fins and head into the water:

Always snorkel with a friend and keep an eye on each other.

Look up every few minutes to get your bearings. Check your position in relation to the shoreline and check whether there's any boat traffic.

Don't touch anything. Not only can your fingers and feet damage coral, but it can give you nasty cuts. Moreover, camouflaged fish and spiny shells may surprise you.

Before you set out, check surf conditions by calling one of the local dive or snorkel shops, which can give you the latest on local conditions and recommend alternative spots if the prime ones are too rough for snorkeling.

See chapters 11, 13, 15, and 17 for island-specific snorkel tips.

Pharmacies

Longs Drugs, Hawaii's biggest drugstore chain, has convenient locations on all the major islands. To locate the nearest branch, point your Web browser to www.longs.com and click "Store Locator" at the bottom of the home page or check the "Fast Facts" sections in Chapter 10 (Oahu), Chapter 12 (Maui), Chapter 14 (the Big Island), and Chapter 16 (Kauai).

Smoking

In Hawaii, smoking is against the law in all enclosed public spaces, period, including bars and restaurants. In addition, no smoking is allowed within 20 feet of doorways, windows, and ventilation intakes. Hotels are allowed to reserve 20 percent of their rooms for smokers, as long as they're clustered on the same floor; notable exceptions include Westin and Marriott hotels, which are now 100 percent smoke free, as are most B&Bs. Car-rental agencies also have mostly smoke-free cars; if you want a car

you can smoke in, it's best to note it when you make your reservation.

Taxes

Most purchases in Hawaii are taxed at roughly 4 percent; the exact amount will vary depending on the county you're in, and may be embedded in the total purchase price or shown as an independent line item on your bill. Expect taxes of about 11.42 percent to be added to your final hotel bill.

Time Zone

Hawaii standard time is in effect year-round. Hawaii is two hours behind Pacific standard time and five hours behind eastern standard time — so when it's noon in Hawaii, it's 2 p.m. in California and 5 p.m. in New York.

Hawaii doesn't observe daylight saving time, however, so when daylight saving time is in effect on the mainland — April through October — Hawaii is three hours behind the West Coast and six hours behind the East Coast (making it noon in Hawaii when it's 3 p.m. in California and 6 p.m. in New York).

Weather and Surf Reports

For statewide marine reports, call ☎ 808-973-4382. For statewide coastal wind reports, call ☎ 808-973-6114.

For local conditions and forecasts, see the "Fast Facts" sections in Chapter 10 (Oahu), Chapter 12 (Maui), Chapter 14 (the Big Island), and Chapter 16 (Kauai).

To check the weather forecasts online, go to www.hawaiiweathertoday.com. You can find the official National Weather Service forecast for the Hawaiian Islands online at www.prh.noaa.gov/pr/hnl.

Where to Get More Information

**Hawaii Visitors and Convention
Bureau (HVCB)**
2270 Kalakaua Ave., Ste. 801
Honolulu, HI 96815
☎ 800-GO-HAWAII (464-2924)
www.gohawaii.com

Planet Hawaii
737 Bishop St., Ste. 1900
Honolulu, HI 96813
☎ 877-91-ALOHA (912-5642) or
808-791-1000
www.planet-hawaii.com

Oahu

Oahu Visitors Bureau
733 Bishop St., Makai Tower, Ste. 1872
Honolulu, HI 96813
☎ 877-525-OAHU (525-6248) or
808-524-0722
www.visit-oahu.com

Maui, Molokai, and Lanai

**Maui Visitors Bureau (also provides
information for Molokai and Lanai)**
1727 Wili Pa Loop
Wailuku, Maui, HI 96793
☎ 800-525-6284 or 808-244-3530
www.visitmaui.com

Maui.net
www.maui.net

Kaanapali Beach Resort Association
222 Papalaua St., Ste. 208
Lahaina, Maui, Hawaii 96761
☎ 888-661-3271 or 808-661-3271
www.kaanapaliresort.com

Kapalua Resort
800 Kapalua Dr.
Kapalua, HI 96761
☎ 800-KAPALUA (527-2582)
www.kapaluamaui.com

Haleakala National Park
P.O. Box 369
Makawao, HI 96768
☎ 808-572-4400
www.nps.gov/hale

Molokai Visitors Association
The Moore Center
2 Kamoi St., Ste. 200
Kaunakakai, HI 96748
☎ 800-800-6367 or 808-553-3876
www.molokai-hawaii.com

Destination Lanai
☎ 800-947-4774
www.visitlanai.net

The Big Island

Big Island Visitors Bureau
250 Keawe St.
Hilo, HI 96720
☎ 800-648-2441 or 808-961-5797
www.bigisland.org

Hawaii Volcanoes National Park
P.O. Box 52
Hawaii National Park, HI 96718-0052
☎ 808-965-6000
www.nps.gov/havo

Kauai

Kauai Visitors Bureau
4334 Rice St., Ste. 101
Lihue, HI 96766
☎ 800-262-1400 or 808-245-3971
www.kauaidiscovery.com

Poipu Beach Resort Association
P.O. Box 730
Koloa, HI 96756
☎ 888-744-0888 or 808-742-7444
www.poipu-beach.org

Index

BUSINESS, CAREERS & PERSONAL FINANCE

Accounting For Dummies, 4th Edition*
978-0-470-24600-9

Bookkeeping Workbook For Dummies†
978-0-470-16983-4

Commodities For Dummies
978-0-470-04928-0

Doing Business in China For Dummies
978-0-470-04929-7

E-Mail Marketing For Dummies
978-0-470-19087-6

Job Interviews For Dummies, 3rd Edition*†
978-0-470-17748-8

Personal Finance Workbook For Dummies*†
978-0-470-09933-9

Real Estate License Exams For Dummies
978-0-7645-7623-2

Six Sigma For Dummies
978-0-7645-6798-8

**Small Business Kit For Dummies,
2nd Edition***†
978-0-7645-5984-6

Telephone Sales For Dummies
978-0-470-16836-3

BUSINESS PRODUCTIVITY & MICROSOFT OFFICE

Access 2007 For Dummies
978-0-470-03649-5

Excel 2007 For Dummies
978-0-470-03737-9

Office 2007 For Dummies
978-0-470-00923-9

Outlook 2007 For Dummies
978-0-470-03830-7

PowerPoint 2007 For Dummies
978-0-470-04059-1

Project 2007 For Dummies
978-0-470-03651-8

QuickBooks 2008 For Dummies
978-0-470-18470-7

Quicken 2008 For Dummies
978-0-470-17473-9

**Salesforce.com For Dummies,
2nd Edition**
978-0-470-04893-1

Word 2007 For Dummies
978-0-470-03658-7

EDUCATION, HISTORY, REFERENCE & TEST PREPARATION

African American History For Dummies
978-0-7645-5469-8

Algebra For Dummies
978-0-7645-5325-7

Algebra Workbook For Dummies
978-0-7645-8467-1

Art History For Dummies
978-0-470-09910-0

ASVAB For Dummies, 2nd Edition
978-0-470-10671-6

British Military History For Dummies
978-0-470-03213-8

Calculus For Dummies
978-0-7645-2498-1

Canadian History For Dummies, 2nd Edition
978-0-470-83656-9

Geometry Workbook For Dummies
978-0-471-79940-5

The SAT I For Dummies, 6th Edition
978-0-7645-7193-0

Series 7 Exam For Dummies
978-0-470-09932-2

World History For Dummies
978-0-7645-5242-7

FOOD, GARDEN, HOBBIES & HOME

Bridge For Dummies, 2nd Edition
978-0-471-92426-5

Coin Collecting For Dummies, 2nd Edition
978-0-470-22275-1

Cooking Basics For Dummies, 3rd Edition
978-0-7645-7206-7

Drawing For Dummies
978-0-7645-5476-6

Etiquette For Dummies, 2nd Edition
978-0-470-10672-3

Gardening Basics For Dummies*†
978-0-470-03749-2

Knitting Patterns For Dummies
978-0-470-04556-5

Living Gluten-Free For Dummies†
978-0-471-77383-2

Painting Do-It-Yourself For Dummies
978-0-470-17533-0

HEALTH, SELF HELP, PARENTING & PETS

Anger Management For Dummies
978-0-470-03715-7

**Anxiety & Depression Workbook
For Dummies**
978-0-7645-9793-0

Dieting For Dummies, 2nd Edition
978-0-7645-4149-0

Dog Training For Dummies, 2nd Edition
978-0-7645-8418-3

Horseback Riding For Dummies
978-0-470-09719-9

Infertility For Dummies†
978-0-470-11518-3

**Meditation For Dummies with CD-ROM,
2nd Edition**
978-0-471-77774-8

Post-Traumatic Stress Disorder For Dummies
978-0-470-04922-8

Puppies For Dummies, 2nd Edition
978-0-470-03717-1

Thyroid For Dummies, 2nd Edition†
978-0-471-78755-6

Type 1 Diabetes For Dummies*†
978-0-470-17811-9

* Separate Canadian edition also available
† Separate U.K. edition also available

Available wherever books are sold. For more information or to order direct: U.S. customers visit www.dummies.com or call 1-877-762-2974.
U.K. customers visit www.wileyeurope.com or call (0)1243 843291. Canadian customers visit www.wiley.ca or call 1-800-567-4797.

INTERNET & DIGITAL MEDIA

AdWords For Dummies
978-0-470-15252-2

Blogging For Dummies, 2nd Edition
978-0-470-23017-6

**Digital Photography All-in-One
Desk Reference For Dummies, 3rd Edition**
978-0-470-03743-0

Digital Photography For Dummies, 5th Edition
978-0-7645-9802-9

**Digital SLR Cameras & Photography
For Dummies, 2nd Edition**
978-0-470-14927-0

**eBay Business All-in-One Desk Reference
For Dummies**
978-0-7645-8438-1

eBay For Dummies, 5th Edition*
978-0-470-04529-9

eBay Listings That Sell For Dummies
978-0-471-78912-3

Facebook For Dummies
978-0-470-26273-3

The Internet For Dummies, 11th Edition
978-0-470-12174-0

Investing Online For Dummies, 5th Edition
978-0-7645-8456-5

iPod & iTunes For Dummies, 5th Edition
978-0-470-17474-6

MySpace For Dummies
978-0-470-09529-4

Podcasting For Dummies
978-0-471-74898-4

**Search Engine Optimization
For Dummies, 2nd Edition**
978-0-471-97998-2

Second Life For Dummies
978-0-470-18025-9

**Starting an eBay Business For Dummies,
3rd Edition†**
978-0-470-14924-9

GRAPHICS, DESIGN & WEB DEVELOPMENT

**Adobe Creative Suite 3 Design Premium
All-in-One Desk Reference For Dummies**
978-0-470-11724-8

**Adobe Web Suite CS3 All-in-One Desk
Reference For Dummies**
978-0-470-12099-6

AutoCAD 2008 For Dummies
978-0-470-11650-0

**Building a Web Site For Dummies,
3rd Edition**
978-0-470-14928-7

**Creating Web Pages All-in-One Desk
Reference For Dummies, 3rd Edition**
978-0-470-09629-1

**Creating Web Pages For Dummies,
8th Edition**
978-0-470-08030-6

Dreamweaver CS3 For Dummies
978-0-470-11490-2

Flash CS3 For Dummies
978-0-470-12100-9

Google SketchUp For Dummies
978-0-470-13744-4

InDesign CS3 For Dummies
978-0-470-11865-8

**Photoshop CS3 All-in-One
Desk Reference For Dummies**
978-0-470-11195-6

Photoshop CS3 For Dummies
978-0-470-11193-2

Photoshop Elements 5 For Dummies
978-0-470-09810-3

SolidWorks For Dummies
978-0-7645-9555-4

Visio 2007 For Dummies
978-0-470-08983-5

Web Design For Dummies, 2nd Edition
978-0-471-78117-2

Web Sites Do-It-Yourself For Dummies
978-0-470-16903-2

Web Stores Do-It-Yourself For Dummies
978-0-470-17443-2

LANGUAGES, RELIGION & SPIRITUALITY

Arabic For Dummies
978-0-471-77270-5

Chinese For Dummies, Audio Set
978-0-470-12766-7

French For Dummies
978-0-7645-5193-2

German For Dummies
978-0-7645-5195-6

Hebrew For Dummies
978-0-7645-5489-6

Ingles Para Dummies
978-0-7645-5427-8

Italian For Dummies, Audio Set
978-0-470-09586-7

Italian Verbs For Dummies
978-0-471-77389-4

Japanese For Dummies
978-0-7645-5429-2

Latin For Dummies
978-0-7645-5431-5

Portuguese For Dummies
978-0-471-78738-9

Russian For Dummies
978-0-471-78001-4

Spanish Phrases For Dummies
978-0-7645-7204-3

Spanish For Dummies
978-0-7645-5194-9

Spanish For Dummies, Audio Set
978-0-470-09585-0

The Bible For Dummies
978-0-7645-5296-0

Catholicism For Dummies
978-0-7645-5391-2

The Historical Jesus For Dummies
978-0-470-16785-4

Islam For Dummies
978-0-7645-5503-9

**Spirituality For Dummies,
2nd Edition**
978-0-470-19142-2

NETWORKING AND PROGRAMMING

ASP.NET 3.5 For Dummies
978-0-470-19592-5

C# 2008 For Dummies
978-0-470-19109-5

Hacking For Dummies, 2nd Edition
978-0-470-05235-8

Home Networking For Dummies, 4th Edition
978-0-470-11806-1

Java For Dummies, 4th Edition
978-0-470-08716-9

**Microsoft® SQL Server™ 2008 All-in-One
Desk Reference For Dummies**
978-0-470-17954-3

**Networking All-in-One Desk Reference
For Dummies, 2nd Edition**
978-0-7645-9939-2

**Networking For Dummies,
8th Edition**
978-0-470-05620-2

SharePoint 2007 For Dummies
978-0-470-09941-4

**Wireless Home Networking
For Dummies, 2nd Edition**
978-0-471-74940-0